Reason and Emotion

Review in
Ethics July
2000

Reason and Emotion

ESSAYS ON
ANCIENT MORAL PSYCHOLOGY
AND ETHICAL THEORY

JOHN M. COOPER

PRINCETON UNIVERSITY PRESS

PRINCETON, NEW JERSEY

Cooper, John M. (John Madison), 1939–
Reason and emotion : essays on ancient moral psychology and
ethical theory / John M. Cooper.
p.   cm.
Includes bibliographical references and index.
ISBN 0-691-05874-1 (alk. paper). — ISBN 0-691-05875-X (pbk. : alk. paper)
1. Ethics, Ancient.   2. Plato—Ethics.   3. Aristotle—Ethics.   I. Title.
BJ161.C66   1998
170'.938—dc21   98-11851

This book has been composed in Sabon

The paper used in this publication meets the minimum requirements
of ANSI/NISO 239.48-1992 (R 1997) (*Permanence of Paper*).

http://pup.princeton.edu

Printed in the United States of America

1 2 3 4 5 6 7 8 9 10

1 2 3 4 5 6 7 8 9 10

FOR MARCIA, STEPHANIE, AND KATHERINE

CONTENTS

SOCRATES is the earliest Greek thinker who remains a living presence in our own philosophical culture. The cosmological speculations and the physical theories of his predecessors already seemed quite archaic to Aristotle in the middle of the fourth century B.C. Socrates inaugurated a new era by abandoning cosmology and physics and making what we now call moral philosophy or ethics the first and central subject to which anyone who aspired to the name of philosopher had to turn. He had a powerful influence on later philosophers, not only through his ideas but even more through his unique way of making his life the very embodiment of his philosophy, even to the extent of allowing himself to be put to death for it. Those who succeeded him made it the governing task of the philosopher, as Socrates himself had done, to enlighten himself and others about human life—about how it should be led, given basic principles about human beings, as such, and their place, as individuals and members of a human community, in the world of god and nature. In their varying ways his successors—first Plato and Aristotle, then, in Hellenistic times beginning in the decades just after Aristotle's death, Epicurus and the Stoic philosophers—all gave precedence to questions of moral theory, while developing a wide range of additional philosophical interests. The Stoics divided philosophical discourse as a whole into three parts: "logic" (which included what we would call epistemology, philosophy of language, and the general theory of concepts and rational thought), physics, and ethics. Some of them compared the discourse of philosophy to an egg (with its shell, white, and yolk) or an animal (made up of flesh and blood on the exterior, wrapped round bones and sinews, with a soul at the center) and (according to one account) assigned ethics the position of the yolk and the soul in these analogies: the other two parts of the subject are there to subserve the needs of this central component. Epicurus predicated the study of his atomic physics, and of the grounds on which it rested, exclusively on its essential role in securing a calm, anxiety-free existence—itself, as he thought, a fundamental part of the only rationally defensible goal for human life. Even Aristotle, for whom philosophical study of theoretical matters possessed great intrinsic value, of just the sort denied it by Epicurus, had to rely on the arguments and analyses of his own moral theory to show that such studies really do deserve pride of place in the structure of a fully flourishing human life. This primacy of ethical thought for ancient philosophy is illustrated even in the case of the ancient skeptics: for Sextus Empiricus, the skeptical study of the philosophical questions of logic, physics, and ethics itself, as those were developed by "dogmatic" philosophers like Plato, Aristotle, Epicurus, and the Stoics, has its fundamental value in the way it can help one to attain a calm, undisturbed, loyal acceptance of whatever traditions of life and ethical norms hold sway in one's local community.

Ancient philosophy during the classical and Hellenistic periods produced an amazing variety of original, profound, and interesting ideas on all sorts of other philosophical topics—in logic, metaphysics, epistemology, the theory of nature, philosophical theology, and on many further issues—besides ethics and politics. Many of these were taken up and pursued further by philosophers in the Middle Ages, and some others by the philosophers of the Renaissance and early modern times—but the unifying perspective of Socrates' focus on ethics as the central task of philosophy got lost along the way. (How that happened—its causes, or at any rate its stages—would make an interesting and instructive study.) That throughout its long career the ancient philosophical tradition was able to sustain the Socratic perspective owes a great deal to the particular conception of ethics and ethical theory his philosophical successors took over from Socrates. Ethics meant more than, indeed something different from, rules of behavior. Ethics was good character and what that entailed—good judgment, sensitivity, openness, reflectiveness, a secure and correct sense of who one was and how one stood in relation to other people and to the surrounding world. Ethical theory was the philosophical study of the best way to *be,* rather than any principles for what to do in particular circumstances or in relation to recurrent temptations, or the correct philosophical basis for deriving or validating any such rules. Ancient moral philosophy—*moral* derives from the Latin word used to translate the Greek term *ēthikos* or "ethical," that is, relating to character or habits of life—investigated the human person first and foremost. It studied the specific capacities and powers, the different interests and desires, that human beings by nature develop or are born with, and how one ought to limit, arrange, and organize those for the best. This gave ancient ethical theory a deeper and potentially much larger and more interesting range of problems to investigate than a primary focus on who owed what to whom under what circumstances (and why), or what actions a good life overall demanded under what circumstances, could ever have done. Moral psychology, or the study of the psychological conditions required—the sorts of desires, the attitudes to self and others, the states of mind and feeling, the kind of knowledge and insight required—if one is to lead the best life that is humanly possible, occupied a central place for all the classical and Hellenistic philosophers. Once those psychological issues were sorted out, then the answers to questions about what to do in particular circumstances or in relation to particular personal or communal interests would follow.

This approach toward the problems of ethics yields a whole series of bold and fascinating theories. To begin with, consider Socrates' conception of virtue (and the particular virtues) as a single state of knowledge, in many ways comparable to the knowledge of trained, expert craftsmen with their responsibility for improving and maintaining the quality of human life in specific areas—and his denial that anyone could ever act in some way, judging all the while that that is not the best way to act then, but a bad one. And then there is Plato's theory in the *Republic* of three distinct kinds and internal sources of human desires, and his corresponding view that society should be organized in a hierarchical way, with philosophers on the basis of their reason-based desires ruling over other types of people dominated by other types of desires; and again, Aristotle's concept of practical wisdom as a distinct sort of understanding and knowledge, based in feeling but not driven by it, and his account of the varieties of human goods and the right way to integrate them into a well-lived, flourishing, and truly happy life. One could mention, as well, Epicurus's less well known, ingenious distinction between "groundless" or "empty"—unnecessary, excessive, obsessive—desires, and desires that treat their own satisfaction as optional, and his vision of happiness as strictly dependent upon the complete avoidance of desires of the first sort; and finally, the Stoic doctrine of morality as grounded in the knowledge of the law of nature, with its very surprising consequence that one's external conditions are irrelevant to human happiness, as are the degrees and occasions of success or failure, in achieving one's purposes—other than the purpose, if one is intelligent enough to have it in the first place, to act at all times according to the demands of true morality.

By studying the arguments through which the ancient moral philosophers attempted to ground these theories (and others), and then work out their consequences, we can expand greatly the limits of our own moral understanding and imagination, and enrich our own moral thought. At any rate, it is in that spirit that I have pursued the studies collected together in this book, and with that hope that I offer them now to a wider readership. I had no antecedent plan as I began writing these essays, more than twenty-five years ago. I followed my interests where they led—sometimes, of course, in response to requests for a paper on a more or less specific topic. As assembled here these essays do not constitute a systematic or complete survey of ancient ethical theory of the classical and Hellenistic periods. However, both in their scope and in the natural connections among the topics of the different papers, I hope they present a unified way of reading and reflecting on some of the most significant texts and issues in ancient moral philosophy from Socrates to Epicurus and the Stoic philosophers Chrysippus and Posidonius, and beyond. Fifteen of the twenty-three chapters (Chapters 4–6, 8–11, 13–16, 18–20, and 23) simply reprint with editorial alterations essays first published between 1973 and 1996. For all of these I add brief lists of Selected Further Readings, as guidance to the reader who wishes to follow the discussion of these topics, or closely related ones, in the subsequent secondary literature. These are not comprehensive lists and do not pretend even to capture the most important or the best more recent books and articles. They are intended simply to give the reader some appropriately varied avenues of entrée into what is in some cases quite a formidable mass of literature. I have tried to include in each instance at least one recent book that does contain a comprehensive bibliography; the lists should therefore enable readers fairly easily to find more extensive references than my lists themselves provide. Only in the case of Chapter 13 do I make any attempt at updating or retrospectively commenting on these essays. There, in a Postscript, I explain why a fairly common criticism of my interpretation of Aristotle's ideas about the "goods of fortune" rests in fact on a failure to understand correctly the interpretation of Aristotle's view that I present. Of the remaining eight chapters, three (Chapters 2, 12, and 17) are reworkings (in the case of Chapter 2 amounting to a completely new paper) of three previously published review-essays. Three chapters (Chapters 3, 7, and 21) contain in somewhat revised form essays prepared in the first instance for other collections that are in press as I write. The Acknowledgments give details of the place and date of publication of these and the reprinted essays listed above. Chapters 1 and 22 are published for the first time in this volume.

I owe many debts, intellectual and personal, to many people for their comments and criticisms on earlier versions of the individual essays, and for their advice and support over the years in my work on ancient moral philosophy. These are partly recorded in footnotes to the individual chapters. In addition I would like to thank Alexander Nehamas for his intellectual companionship of twenty-five years, his persistent readiness to read work in progress and advise me on it, his constant encouragement, and the enlightenment and pleasure I have drawn from his measured but firm and articulate rejection of much that appeals greatly to me in the moral theories of the ancient philosophers I deal with here. It is largely due to his suggestion repeated over several years' time that I decided to publish this book. I would like also to thank another Princeton colleague, Sarah Broadie, for her advice and encouragement, and Donald Morrison for his help in selecting the art for the book's cover. I thank Jonathan Beere and Gabriel Richardson for their careful help, under severe time pressure, in gathering citations for the lists of Selected Further Readings, and Richardson for transliterating the Greek throughout the book. The Philosophy Department at Princeton contributed financial support from its Haswell fund for this, and other research assistance. I am indebted also to the University of Pittsburgh for a sabbatical leave in 1976–77, and to Princeton University for its generous support through four research leaves since 1981; during each of these I have spent some time working on papers collected in this book. I should acknowledge also fellowship support from the National Endowment for the Humanities, the John Simon Guggenheim Foundation, the Andrew W. Mellon Foundation of New York, and the Center for Advanced Study in the Behavioral Sciences. Finally, I have Marta Steele to thank for her attentive and astute work in editing a dauntingly multiform manuscript into a more or less uniform—and finished—book.

I dedicate the book to my wife and daughters.

Princeton, October 1997

ACKNOWLEDGMENTS

CHAPTERS 3–11, 13–21, and 23 appeared in their original form, or are to appear, in the following publications. Chapters 2 and 12 are newly written essays that incorporate material previously published, as noted below. Chapters 1 and 22 have been written especially for this volume. I am grateful to the journals and publishers named below that have given permission to reprint these essays or material appearing in them.

2   "The *Gorgias* and Irwin's Socrates." *Review of Metaphysics* 35 (1982): 577–87. With permission of the publisher.

3   "The Unity of Virtue." *Social Philosophy and Policy* 15, no. 1 (Winter 1998): 233–74.

4   "Plato's Theory of Human Motivation." *History of Philosophy Quarterly* 1 (1984): 3–21.

5   "The Psychology of Justice in Plato." *American Philosophical Quarterly* 14 (1977): 151–57.

6   "Plato's Theory of Human Good in the *Philebus*." *The Journal of Philosophy* 74 (1977): 713–30.

7   "Plato's *Statesman* and Politics." *Proceedings of the Boston Area Colloquium in Ancient Philosophy* 13 (1997): 71–103.

8   "The *Magna Moralia* and Aristotle's Moral Philosophy." *American Journal of Philology* 94 (1973): 327–49.

9   "Contemplation and Happiness: A Reconsideration." *Synthese* 72 (1987): 187–216. With kind permission from Kluwer Academic Publishers.

10   "Some Remarks on Aristotle's Moral Psychology." *Southern Journal of Philosophy* 27 Supplement (1988): 25–42.

11   "Reason, Moral Virtue, and Moral Value." In *Rationality in Greek Thought,* edited by Michael Frede and Gisela Striker, 81–114. Oxford: Clarendon Press, 1996. By permission of Oxford University Press.

12   "Review of Martha Nussbaum's *The Fragility of Goodness*." *Philosophical Review* 97 (1988): 543–64. © Cornell University. Reprinted by permission of the publisher.

13   "Aristotle on the Goods of Fortune." *Philosophical Review* 94 (1985): 173–96. © Cornell University. Reprinted by permission of the publisher.

14   "Aristotle on the Forms of Friendship." *Review of Metaphysics* 30 (1977): 619–48. With permission of the publisher.

15 "Friendship and the Good in Aristotle." *Philosophical Review* 86 (1977): 290–315. © Cornell University. Reprinted by permission of the publisher.

16 "Political Animals and Civic Friendship." In *Aristoteles' "Politik,"* edited by Günther Patzig, 221–41. Göttingen: Vandenhoeck and Ruprecht, 1990.

17 "Justice and Rights in Aristotle's *Politics.*" *Review of Metaphysics* 49 (1996): 859–72. With permission of the publisher.

18 "Ethical-Political Theory in Aristotle's *Rhetoric.*" In *Aristotle's "Rhetoric": Philosophical Essays,* edited by David J. Furley and Alexander Nehamas, 193–210. Princeton: Princeton University Press, 1994.

19 "An Aristotelian Theory of the Emotions." In *Essays on Aristotle's "Rhetoric,"* edited by Amélie Oksenberg Rorty. Berkeley: University of California Press, 1996, 238–57. © 1996 The Regents of the University of California. Reprinted with permission of the University of California Press.

20 "Eudaimonism, the Appeal to Nature, and 'Moral Duty' in Stoicism." In *Aristotle, Kant, and the Stoics,* edited by Stephen Engstrom and Jennifer Whiting, 261–84. New York: Cambridge University Press, 1996. © Cambridge University Press 1996. Reprinted with permission of Cambridge University Press.

21 "Posidonius on Emotions." To appear in *The Emotions in Hellenistic Philosophy,* edited by Troels Engberg-Pedersen and Juha Sihvola, 71–111. Dordrecht/Boston/London: Kluwer Academic Publishers, 1998.

23 "Greek Philosophers on Euthanasia and Suicide." In *Suicide and Euthanasia,* edited by Baruch A. Brody, 9–38. Dordrecht/Boston/London: Kluwer Academic Publishers, 1989. With kind permission from Kluwer Academic Publishers.

IN TURNING these essays into a book, I have endeavored to impose a uniform format on materials which in most cases were originally published under widely varying editorial principles. Thus I have employed American spelling and usage throughout, avoiding Britishisms that the original editors sometimes insisted on, and the whole volume has been edited to a single standard in the use of single vs. double quotation marks, and the like. Technical considerations, however, did not permit the removal of all anomalies: certain previously published chapters do not conform, in one way or another, to the norms established for the previously unpublished chapters of the book. A Bibliography of Works Cited collects titles and publication information from throughout the volume, and this in turn permits a uniform system of citations of secondary literature in shortened form; in order, however, to free the reader from the burden of constant reference to the Bibliography in order to identify cited books and articles, I have followed the practice in each chapter of citing each item for the first time in a full enough form for those who know the literature to identify it straight off—it should then be relatively easy to fathom subsequent, more abbreviated references in the same chapter. Likewise, I have adopted a uniform system of abbreviations for ancient works; in lieu of adding a list of abbreviations to the front matter, I have spelled out the titles of primary sources at their first mention in each chapter.

In the quotation of single words and more extended passages in Greek, some of the previously published essays had Greek fonts throughout, both in text and footnotes; in others the Greek was transliterated everywhere; in yet others transliteration was practiced only in the main text—and there were intermediate cases of one sort or another, as well. We have adopted the policy of transliterating the Greek throughout the book in the main text, except when I quote whole phrases or clauses where something of potential significance for the scholarly reader would be lost if accents were omitted, as they are in transliteration—and where, in any event, the reader who knows Greek will find it much easier to comprehend what is intended if it is written in a Greek font. As to the main text, then, we have aimed at uniformity throughout the book. Technical considerations have, however, prevented perfect uniformity in the footnotes. We have left the footnotes of the previously published papers in the format that they had in their original place of publication—sometimes with Greek in Greek font throughout, sometimes in transliteration, sometimes in a mixture. In eight chapters (Chapters 1, 2, 3, 7, 12, 17, 21, 22) it was possible to edit the footnotes according to the same general principles as the main text, since these chapters were edited in computer print-out form, rather than from copies of already-published pages. Here, Greek is transliterated except where a phrase or clause required a Greek font, for the reason noted above. I should note, however, that I have attempted in the main text always either to translate single Greek words and more extended passages, or to make the meaning clear in the immediate context. In the footnotes I have followed the same policy, except where the point being pursued is of purely philological interest. Translations from the Greek and Latin, except where another translator is specifically indicated, are my own.

PART ONE

Socrates and Plato

CHAPTER ONE

Notes on Xenophon's Socrates

FOR MOST OF THE TWENTIETH CENTURY[1] Xenophon's portrait of Socrates has been thoroughly discounted by scholars as an independent source for our knowledge of Socrates' personality, philosophy, and activity as a teacher or mentor to Athenian youth. So much is this so that until very recently people with a philosophical interest in Socrates pretty well ceased altogether to pay attention to Xenophon's Socratic writings.[2] Karl Joël in his massive and influential book joined a growing chorus of his contemporaries at the end of the nineteenth century in insisting that the Socratic conversations in Xenophon's *Memorabilia* (the same goes for his *Symposium*, though Joël's principal focus was on the *Memorabilia*) were literary productions, just as much so (though different in many other ways) as Plato's dialogues were recognized then to be. They were contributions to a literary genre that grew up almost immediately after Socrates' death,[3] in which the author presented Socratic-style dialogues very much of his own construction. Not only Plato and Xenophon wrote such dialogues, but also, perhaps among others, Aeschines of Sphettos and the philosophers Antisthenes, Euclides, and Phaedo, none of whose works have survived apart from isolated quotations and short excerpts.[4] In all these cases, as with Plato, one might conclude after

---

[1] Perhaps since the publication of Karl Joël's 1700-page book, *Der echte und der xenophontische Sokrates*, 2 vols. in 3 (1893 and 1901), certainly since Heinrich Maier's *Sokrates* (1913).

[2] An exception is Donald Morrison, whose articles "Vlastos' Xenophon," "Xenophon's Socrates as Teacher," and "Xenophon's Socrates on the Just" are essential reading on their topics. See also his *Bibliography*. In *Der Historische Sokrates* Andreas Patzer has collected sixteen of the most important, representative articles (thirteen of them published in this century) by leading European scholars on the "Socratic problem." His 40-page introduction to the book is a remarkably complete, brief review of the whole history, ancient and modern, of the discussion about Socrates' philosophy, life, and character. It is an essential resource for anyone wishing to enter into the bewilderingly complex and replete literature surrounding the historical Socrates. See also the same author's *Bibliographica Socratica*, a systematically organized bibliography of 2,301 modern scholarly publications on Socrates (both editions of ancient texts and critical-interpretative writings).

[3] We have a number of ancient sources, beginning with Aristotle, for the existence of this genre: *Rhetoric* III 16, 1417a20ff., *Poetics* 1, 1447b11ff.; fr. 61 Bonitz reports Aristotle as saying (possibly in his work *On Poets*) that Alexamenus of Teos was the first to write Socratic dialogues (Diogenes Laertius III 48 confirms that in *On Poets* Aristotle stated that Alexamenus was the first to write *dialogues*—not Zeno of Elea, as others had asserted).

[4] Euclides and Phaedo figure as characters in Platonic dialogues, *Theaetetus* and *Phaedo* respectively; and at *Phdo.* 59b–c, in recounting those who were present in Socrates' prison-cell on the last day, Plato includes both Euclides and Antisthenes, and Aeschines as well (Plato was ill and Aristippus was said to be off in Aegina). Antisthenes receives no mention elsewhere in Plato, as Euclides and Phaedo never do in Xenophon, but he figures quite prominently in

investigation that such literary invention, at least sometimes, was constructed upon a recoverable basis in genuine Socratic philosophy. But, Joël argued, one certainly cannot start from the assumption in Xenophon's case or any of the others' (especially Plato's) that the author even intends to present a faithful record of some conversation Socrates actually held. Yet that assumption with respect to Xenophon was widespread in nineteenth-century writing about Socrates. Thus Friedrich Schleiermacher had defined the "Socratic problem" for scholars in 1818 by asking what more one *can* suppose Socrates to have been, beyond and compatibly with what Xenophon reports of him in his Socratic conversations—and what more he *must* have been, if Plato was to have had any right at all to present him in conversation in the way he does in his own dialogues.[5] Thus Schleiermacher began by assuming the accuracy of Xenophon's portrayal, so far as it went; the "Socratic problem" was the problem what to do, in the light of that, with Plato's account.

One thing that prevented nineteenth-century scholars from recognizing and giving full weight to the literary character of the *Memorabilia* was that, unlike Plato in presenting his dialogues, Xenophon explicitly claims historical accuracy for the conversations making up the bulk of the work. He was, after all, the author of historical writings of his own (the *Hellenica*, completing Thucydides' *History* of the Peloponnesian War, as well as the *Anabasis*), so it was easy for scholars to attribute to him a concern for historical accuracy in his reports that is more characteristic of modern historians than ancient ones. At the beginning of chapter 3 of book I, Xenophon says that he is going thenceforward to set down from his own recollection evidence of the ways that Socrates benefited those who consorted with him, both through actions revealing his own character (presumably as a model for emulation)[6] and through his conversation.[7] In this he is only

Xenophon; at *Memorabilia* III 11, 17 he is implied, along with Apollodorus (the narrator of Plato's *Symposium*), to be Socrates' most constant attendant (see what Xenophon says about Apollodorus at *Apol.* 28). Antisthenes plays a major, argumentatively aggressive role in the discussions making up Xenophon's *Symposium* (see *Symp.* 2, 9–10; 3, 4 and 6; 4, 2–5; 4, 34–44; 4, 61–64; 8, 3–6; in the *Mem.* see esp. II 5). (Xenophon mentions Plato only once, and then quite incidentally, though with a clear implication that he was someone whom Socrates cared about: *Mem.* III 6, 1.) Panaetius, the Stoic philosopher of the mid-second century B.C., is reported by Diog. L. (II 64) to have firmly rejected as nongenuine all the Socratic dialogues circulating at his time under the names of other known associates of Socrates besides these six: Plato and Xenophon, plus Aeschines, Antisthenes, Euclides, and Phaedo (and he was inclined to doubt those attributed to Euclides and Phaedo). Diogenes Laertius writes "lives" of all six of these authors; he mentions many "dialogues" (not necessarily all "Socratic" ones, of course) written by other associates of Socrates (or their "pupils"): Aristippus (25), Stilpo (9), Crito (17), Simon (33), Glaucon (9 held to be genuine, 32 others), Simmias (23), Cebes (3). Charles Kahn, *Plato and the Socratic Dialogue*, ch. 1, reviews the Socratic literature other than Plato's works, including those of Xenophon. See also Diskin Clay, "Origins of the Socratic Dialogue."

[5] Friedrich E. D. Schleiermacher, "Sokrates' Werth als Philosoph," quoted by Maier, *Sokrates*, p. 10.

[6] See *Mem.* I 2, 3.

[7] This program applies throughout the remainder of the four books, except that Xenophon

making explicit the practice he has already followed in the first two chapters of book I. There, by referring to Socrates' actions and conversations, he refutes the charges made against him at his trial and afterward in the *Accusation of Socrates* written in about 393 by the rhetorician Polycrates. From I 3 onward, he simply continues this "apologetic" discussion by expanding its scope, so as to provide evidence, with no special reference to the accusations, of the beneficial effects upon the young men of Athens of Socrates' conversations with them. Now one should note right away that, whatever one may ultimately make of Xenophon's claims to historical accuracy, he is not offering in the *Memorabilia* to give an account of Socrates as a *philosopher*—of his way of treating philosophical questions as such, of his philosophical theories or opinions, of his conception of what philosophy was and could (or could not) hope to accomplish, and the methods appropriate to philosophy's task. It is with Socrates as an educator in the broadest sense that Xenophon is explicitly concerned—as someone whose company and conversation brought out and strengthened in the young their capacities to be good and useful, god-fearing and family-respecting citizens, both informed and concerned about justice and the public good. To be sure, Xenophon knows Socrates was a philosopher and consistently so presents him. We find frequent indications in the *Memorabilia* of some of Xenophon's Socrates' philosophical views (I return to these below), but only because, as one could expect, the uplifting character of his conversation must frequently have revealed, and sometimes perhaps actually depended upon, his philosophical commitments. It cannot be overemphasized that for Xenophon's declared purposes Socrates' philosophy lies off to one side. This marks a crucial contrast with Plato, whose dialogues are relentlessly devoted to the exploration of philosophical questions, however much at the same time Plato's purpose is to portray Socrates as an outstandingly good man whose conversation was calculated to bring out the best in his hearers— even if that "best" does not coincide with Xenophon's conception. In Plato the focus is just the reverse of Xenophon's, as Xenophon explains his interests in the opening chapters of the *Memorabilia*: Socrates' philosophy is the center of attention, his moral character and moral influence lie off to one side.

Xenophon's claim to be reporting conversations from memory notwithstanding, Joël, Maier in his comprehensive work of 1913, and others had no difficulty in showing how very little basis there is for believing him.[8] Xenophon does not scruple to begin his dialogue *Oeconomicus* by saying that he is going to report a conversation he once heard Socrates hold on

---

concentrates almost exclusively upon the conversations, not the actions. It may be that books III and IV are later, independently written additions, but they carry on the program announced here near the beginning of book I. (The definitions at III 9, the anecdotes and aphorisms of III 13–14, and such occasional reportage as that in IV 4, 1–4 and IV 1, 7 and 8 admittedly do not fit perfectly under either of the two rubrics "actions" and "conversations.")

   [8] See also Léon Robin, "Les *Mémorables* de Xenophon et notre connaissance de la philosophie de Socrate," pp. 35–41.

estate- and household-management, a subject in which we have reason
to think Xenophon was himself interested and informed. But the rest of
Xenophon's own and the other ancient testimony about Socrates makes
this an extremely unlikely topic for anyone to discuss with Socrates. The
conversation that follows has indeed many of the external marks of the
Socratic conversations Xenophon presents in the *Memorabilia,* but no one
can doubt that the substance of what "Socrates" says on this topic is provided
by Xenophon himself from his own experience or sources of his own. Again,
in his *Symposium* Xenophon professes to be telling of a party at which he
was present (1,1)—but he situates it quite clearly and even elaborately at a
time (421 B.C.) when he cannot have been as much as 10 years old.[9] Can
one believe that the situation with the *Memorabilia* is essentially different?
No one can have planned to write memoirs of Socratic conversations with
the "apologetic" purpose announced in the *Memorabilia* until after Socrates'
death in 399 (when Xenophon was away in Asia on the march of the 10,000
that he wrote about in his *Anabasis*). So it does not appear that Xenophon
would have had any reason to take notes of conversations he may have
heard when he was with Socrates (between about 410 at the earliest and 401,
when Xenophon departed for Persia).[10] The evidence drawn from parallels
between different conversations within the *Memorabilia* and between the
Memorabilia and Xenophon's other writings is sufficient to cast serious
doubt upon the historical actuality of the specific conversations that he
presents. The most that could be claimed is that Xenophon is drawing upon
his general recollection of conversations he witnessed, and perhaps upon
undocumented memories of specifically memorable ones. The actual composition can only be his own creative work.

So far, I believe, one must go in rejecting nineteenth-century scholars'
assumptions of the historical veracity of Xenophon's reports. But Maier,
and especially Joël, go further, in two directions: First, they argue that a
very great deal of what Xenophon has Socrates say, and of his overall
"picture" of him and his outlook on life, is drawn in one way or another
from the Socratic writings of Antisthenes. In order to understand this, we
need to take account of views prevalent among German scholars at the turn
of the twentieth century about the history of the "Socratic movement" in
the first couple of decades after Socrates' death (that is, during the 390s
and 380s). It was thought that these decades saw a terrific battle, personal

[9] Xenophon tells us himself in the *Anabasis* (e.g., III 1, 14 and III 1, 25) that he was not
yet 30 years old at the time of the march of the 10,000 (400 B.C.); thus he was presumably
born (like Plato) early in the decade of the 420s. Diogenes Laertius's floruit of 401–400, which
would place his birth about 440, must be a mechanical application (despite the internal evidence
to the contrary given by Xenophon's own account) of the principle that a person was 40 years
old at the time of his chief known accomplishment, in this case the expedition of the 10,000.

[10] It could be, for all the evidence we have, that some associates of Socrates wrote and
circulated "memoirs" of Socrates even before his death and so may have made notes of his
conversations for that purpose. But the specifically apologetic character of Xenophon's *Memoirs*
(his *Memorabilia*) is evident throughout.

and literary, between Plato and Antisthenes, as the two principal philosophical heirs of Socrates, both teachers of philosophy at Athens and writers of Socratic dialogues.[11] They produced these dialogues to display or establish the orthodoxy of their own versions of the Socratic heritage. Allegedly Plato himself went to great lengths in his own polemics against Antisthenes, though lacking Antisthenes' writings we do not easily see this, as of course his contemporaries would have done: for example, Plato's *Euthydemus* was a sustained attack upon Antisthenean dialectic (in the guise of the logic-chopping of the characters Euthydemus and Dionysodorus); the speeches praising pederasty by Phaedrus and Pausanias in the *Symposium* are a deliciously wicked—table-turning—attack upon Antisthenes' views on love; and so on. Xenophon, who had spent most of the 390s in military activities in support first of a Persian prince and then of a Spartan king, and who had been formally exiled by the Athenians about 399, was himself no writer or teacher of philosophy. He did not have the same aims in composing his Socratic conversations as Plato and Antisthenes allegedly did in composing theirs; as we have seen, he wanted to defend his friend and teacher's memory and good reputation, while also expressing his admiration for him, explaining its grounds, and claiming Socrates' support for views of his own on important moral and social questions. But, according to Joël and Maier, who neglect these differences between Xenophon's aims in his Socratic writings and Plato's (and presumably Antisthenes'), Xenophon worked largely from the literary record in putting together his own picture of Socrates. Since Xenophon's Socrates allegedly shares a good deal with the Socrates that Antisthenes (later regarded as a forerunner of the Cynic movement that began later in the third century with Diogenes) drew inspiration from for his own philosophy, Joël and Maier think it reasonable to attribute these similarities to Xenophon's extensive borrowings from (and reactions to) Antisthenes' lost writings. In effect, according to them, Xenophon presents a politer and more gentlemanly, less rigidly ascetic Socrates, who like Antisthenes especially champions control of appetites (*enkrateia*), edification through self-denial (*ponos*), and the rejection of luxury and pleasurable self-indulgence as harmful to the soul—all or mostly derived from Xenophon's reading of Antisthenes' Socratic dialogues.

Joël and Maier draw support for this supposition from aspects of Xenophon's own personality and experience. In the first place, our evidence does not support the conclusion that he was one of Socrates' closest associates, along with both Plato and Antisthenes and many others of Socrates' more philosophically inclined "companions." As his military-political career and his non-Socratic writings show, his tastes and interests were the ones

[11] Aristippus was a third Socratic who taught and wrote philosophy; but he appears to have worked largely if not entirely outside Athens (for example in Syracuse at the court of the tyrant Dionysius I, which Plato is said to have visited about 390 B.C.) and he may not have written *Socratic* dialogues, as the other two did (Diogenes Laertius II 83–84 mentions 25 dialogues, and gives the names of 23: the titles do not betray any connection to Socrates or the Socratic circle).

conventionally approved in his aristocratic circles (and quite different from
the very unconventional, relentlessly intellectual ones of Socrates and the
more philosophical of his companions): he was a family-man devoted to
horsebackriding, hunting, sport, physical culture, and life in the country,
and at least in youth he was something of an adventurer. According to his
own report[12] of the circumstances under which he accepted the invitation
to join Cyrus the Younger at Sardis, he consulted Socrates about whether
he should go—having however apparently already made up his mind to do
it. Socrates had misgivings and advised him to consult the oracle at Delphi,
but (disregarding Socrates' misgivings) Xenophon did so only to ask which
gods should receive sacrifices in order to ensure good success on the expedition and a safe return. Socrates thereupon told him that he should certainly
follow Apollo's advice about the sacrifices! (Any irony in Socrates' last
advice was lost on Xenophon.) It is certainly quite plausible that, as Joël
and Maier suggest, a lot of what Socrates is made to say in the *Memorabilia*
expresses Xenophon's personal views (whether or not it also expresses those
of the historical Socrates), and that Xenophon's views conformed to a certain
extent with Antisthenean asceticism. As noted above, Xenophon's intent
was to show Socrates inspiring the young men to become proper gentlemen,
and for Xenophon, who counted himself one of those, that meant freedom
from subjection to one's own desires, the refusal to get money by submitting
oneself to anyone else's direction, physical and mental self-discipline, and
following one's own trained understanding where it suffices but consulting
and following oracles and divinations where it does not. It seems very likely
indeed that in much of his composition Xenophon simply draws upon his
own conception of what benefits the young in order to portray Socrates and
his conversations as beneficial—conventionally aristocratic as that conception was, but tinged with the love of self-discipline, self-denial, and independence, and a devotion to the gods and to their guidance through divination
and oracles.

In all this, Joël and Maier tend to minimize the extent of Xenophon's
personal knowledge of Socrates. The resulting picture is this: Xenophon, in
his desire to defend his friend and teacher's reputation, has drawn upon the
existing Socratic literature, especially the writings of Antisthenes, together
with his own standards of an upstanding life, to present Socrates as himself
a fine gentleman according to the unintellectual, aristocratic standards that
Xenophon himself upheld, and a teacher of young men who showed them
how, and inspired them, to live in that way. Just as his predecessors in the
genre of the Socratic dialogue had attributed to their Socrateses some of their
own philosophical views, so he too attributes *his* " 'practical' philosophy" to
the great man. One can therefore safely ignore Xenophon as an independent
source for Socrates' philosophical views. He was not interested in Socrates
as a philosopher in any event (and he was not one of his "intimates"); he

---

[12] *Anabasis* III 1, 5–7.

was not capable, really, of understanding such philosophy as he may have heard in Socrates' discourses; his portrait is essentially just an amalgam of things he read in other authors together with his own views about what it takes to be a gentleman. In any event, as Maier claims, if Xenophon's Socrates *were* genuine it would be impossible to understand how the brightest and the best of the youth of Athens came to rally about him and were so deeply affected by him as the evidence of Plato and others shows that they were. By contrast, according to Maier, provided we are careful to segregate Plato's Socratic dialogues from the later ones, we can rely on the Socrates of Plato's early dialogues to be genuine: Plato *was* one of Socrates' "intimates" and shows himself perfectly capable of appreciating the philosophical depths that we know from his influence in Athens Socrates must have had.[13] So, for Maier, Xenophon's testimony has no reliably independent value. Only Plato's counts.[14]

I believe Maier's total dismissal of Xenophon as an immediate, independent source is quite unjustified, as are his and Joël's claims that Xenophon depended upon Antisthenes' writings for his information about Socrates' conversations and his interpretation of Socrates' practical outlook and instruction of the young. Maier himself remarks that Joël (and his teacher and forerunner Dümmler) often threatened to spoil their work by exaggerated, implausible and unnecessary efforts to find traces of Antisthenes in Xenophon's works. The same remark also applies to Maier himself, however. If we possessed Antisthenes' writings, or any of them, we might of course find that Xenophon borrowed massively from him. But given only what we do possess, a sane reader will find very little reason to suspect it.[15] The fact

[13] In "Paradox of Socrates" (1971) Vlastos accepted Maier's diagnosis and based his own view about the historicity of Plato's account of Socrates in his Socratic dialogues (in part) squarely upon Maier's evidence (see pp. 1–4). He says: "Xenophon's is a Socrates without irony and without paradox. Take these away from Plato's Socrates, and there is nothing left"; and he then remarks that Xenophon's Socrates "could not have attracted men like Critias and Alcibiades," and that this account "refutes itself: had the facts been as he tells them, the indictment would never have been made in the first place." Later (1991), in *Socrates* Vlastos relented slightly from his dismissal of Xenophon (there Vlastos refers to his undoubted "firsthand testimony"), so as to appeal (pp. 99–106) to Xenophon for confirmation (despite himself) of the view of Socrates that Vlastos constructs, in both places, from the evidence of Plato. See also Vlastos's remarks in "Socratic Irony," p. 86, about the irony that Xenophon's Socrates actually does display.

[14] That is to say, only Plato's counts for the reconstruction of Socrates' philosophy. Maier's idea is essentially this: one should claim for the historical Socrates those items in the rest of the Socratic writers (Xenophon included) that can be added to the presentation of Socrates in Plato's early dialogues without disturbing anything we already "know" from Plato (pp. 149–50). Maier thinks Aristotle's well-known comments on Socrates' moral theories all derive from his reading of Plato's *Protagoras*; he thinks his report in the *Metaphysics* (A 6, 987b1–4; M 4, 1078b17–31) about Socrates and inductive arguments and definitions, with a view to syllogizing, come from his reading of Xenophon *Memorabilia* IV 6 and have no other backing. Thus Maier denies that Aristotle's reports can deserve any independent weight at all.

[15] I give below an illustrative example from both Joël and Maier, where they convince themselves that only the supposition of a borrowing from Antisthenes can begin to explain

that ancient sources attest views of Antisthenes that Xenophon attributes
in nearly identical or at any rate closely similar form to Socrates might be
due to borrowing from works of Antisthenes now lost; but we are not in a
position to know this, if and where it may be true. Our knowledge is
insufficient to rule out the possibility that Xenophon attributes these views
to Socrates on his own first-hand authority; even where ancient reports of
Antisthenes make one most strongly suspect "borrowing" by Xenophon,
the possibility is not excluded that he drew on precisely those formulations,
or illustrations, and so on, in Antisthenes because they seemed to him to
capture particularly well something he knew on his own that Socrates had
said or believed. Either way, the coincidence of Xenophon and Antisthenes
would in fact give us grounds for believing that whatever was in question
did have a strong basis in fact—whether or not it was confirmed in Plato,
and whether or not, indeed, it was actually contradicted by something
in Plato.

Here one must bear in mind what I said above, that Xenophon's Socratic
writings are decidedly different from those of Plato (and Antisthenes). He
is no philosopher, and he does not write in order to expose Socrates' (much
less his own) philosophical opinions. He writes the *Memorabilia* in order
to defend Socrates' reputation against charges that he had corrupted the
young men who had spent time with him—and, no doubt, to claim support
from Socrates for some of his own moral and social opinions. It seems to
me that, despite what I said above about the *Oeconomicus* and despite
one's frequent suspicion that Xenophon draws freely upon his own areas
of knowledge and his own ethical standards in composing his Socratic
conversations, no evidence internal or external to Xenophon justifies dismissing his claim, at least overall and in general, to be describing Socrates'
behavior, opinions, and conversation as he actually perceived them. No one
will use the *Oeconomicus* as a serious source for the real Socrates; but that
is palpably a special case that should not cast fundamental doubt on the
other Socratic writings.

In deciding how seriously to take Socrates in the *Memorabilia* and *Symposium,* careful attention should also focus on Xenophon's stated reasons
for writing his *Apology of Socrates.* He begins that work by expressing
dissatisfaction on one point with what others before him had written about
Socrates' trial. He found that the "loftiness" of Socrates' speech to the
jury (his *megalēgoria*), on which all concurred, had not yet been properly
explained, with the result—damaging to our memory of Socrates—that he
appeared to have behaved quite foolishly at his trial—inappropriately for
a supposedly wise man to whom a father might entrust his son's education.
What Xenophon means is that Socrates' discourse at his trial showed that
he did not take the charges seriously; he looked down upon the whole

---

what we find in Xenophon's text. I argue, to the contrary, that our evidence doesn't force this
conclusion on us, or even a suspicion of it.

proceeding, without in the least attempting to do what he could have done, and any sensible man would have done, to secure his acquittal.[16] If, as seems at least quite possible, one of the existing accounts that dissatisfied him was in Plato's *Apology*, Xenophon does, no doubt, show a certain shallowness in feeling the need to offer a new explanation for the way Socrates conducted

[16] See Xenophon, *Apol.* 9, 22, 32. Hansen argues, in an important recent study, "Trial of Sokrates," that in fact Plato in his *Apology* does address the issues that Xenophon raises— and Hansen concludes that therefore Xenophon must have written without knowledge of Plato's work, whether or not it had already been issued when Xenophon wrote. (In his view of the independence of Xenophon's *Apology* from Plato's, Hansen is following and accepting von Arnim's argument in "Xenophons *Memorabilien* und *Apologie des Sokrates*.") As Hansen points out (p. 32), Xenophon says in *Apology* 1 that none of the earlier writers who reported on Socrates' trial and his *megalēgoria* mentioned "Sokrates' view that, to him, death might be preferable to life"; while (Hansen says) in Plato's *Apology* at 38c and 41d we find Socrates mentioning precisely this. But this is a mistake. What Xenophon says in *Apology* 1 is that no previous writer had "shown clearly that Socrates had now come to the conclusion that death for him was more to be desired than life" (tr. O. J. Todd): ὅτι ἤδη ἑαυτῷ ἡγεῖτο αἱρετώτερον εἶναι τοῦ βίου θάνατον. This is a quite definite statement that Socrates had concluded *prior to his trial* that death was to be preferred to life, given his age and the prospect of debilitating illnesses and senility if he lived his life to a natural end. Xenophon makes it clear at the end of the work (32–33) that this is his own view as well (he says it is a "fate that the gods love" to avoid "the hardest part of life" and meet "the easiest sort of death" as Socrates did). So, according to Xenophon, having very reasonably concluded that it was time for him to die, Socrates did not waver, as a less resolute man might have done in the stressful situation of the trial, but stuck to this conviction. That is why, as Xenophon has presented him, he spoke throughout the events with high-minded disdain, not merely being willing to accept death if it came now via a condemnation but actively courting it. However, in Plato's *Apology* Socrates does not say anything nearly so definite about preferring death, and Plato does not indicate in any way that Socrates spoke as he did for that reason. Plato's Socrates says only that for all he or anyone knows, death *may* be better than life for a person (see 29a–b in his main speech, recalled at 37b in his speech after the verdict of guilty is reached); and when in his third speech, after the penalty of death is voted, he mentions that he is old and close to death anyhow (38c), it is to point out to those who voted to condemn him that they have not gained much for themselves or the other Athenians by doing so—it is not at all to suggest that for his own good he might just as well die now. As for himself, he says only that he would far rather die now, condemned after having made the sort of defense he actually made, than to have offered another sort of defense by begging for his life, placating the jurors, and so on, and to have won a reprieve thereby (38e). Nothing in Plato's *Apology* says or indicates anything like Xenophon's denial that Socrates was ill-advised to speak so loftily at his trial, because he had decided it was time to die anyhow. He had not decided that, according to what Plato has him say; he had only decided against disgraceful behavior that might prevent his death now or at any time. At 40b-c, turning now to address those who voted for his acquittal, Socrates goes a bit further. Now that the trial is concluded, he says he realizes that maybe death really is good for a man and not bad as people mostly think: all day long his *daimonion* has not opposed him at any point, yet it does often oppose him when he is about to do something bad. Notice that what Socrates had done was to intend to speak and then to speak in a way that did not ward off death as a known evil. So, he thinks, he must have been correct to act that way, and death is not an evil but even a good—or at any rate, as he puts it, "there is good hope that death is a blessing." This is a general remark about all human beings, not about himself as an old person facing senility and illness. And in any event, it cannot be taken as indicating that Socrates had concluded *before* his trial that it was time for him to die, that now death was preferable to life. It took the whole process of the trial and defense to reach

his defense. But, if so, he was presumably not alone in finding the lofty philosophizing of Plato's Socrates at his trial hard to take—and, indeed, simply out of place. To salve the legitimate concerns of such persons (the normal, solid citizens, one would think), Xenophon retails, in impressive circumstantial detail, reports he had heard from Hermogenes, one of Socrates' close associates who, says Xenophon, was present at the trial and had conversed with Socrates beforehand,[17] about Socrates' state of mind and intentions at the time. Socrates had told Hermogenes that he had been prevented by his "divine sign" from preparing a defense-speech; that he took that as an indication of divine opinion that it was now time for him to die; that, indeed, the poison administered in the prison gives an easy death without the prolonged distress to one's family and friends that a terminal illness causes, so that if he did defeat the charge, after seeking in every way to find a defense that would win his acquittal, he would only be opening himself to the distressing decline of physical and mental powers (the latter presumably particularly distressing to a philosopher) that comes with age, followed by senility and a final illness. Under these circumstances, and with the support of his divine sign, Socrates told Hermogenes, he was not going to cling to life and lower himself to persuading the jury to acquit him. Thus Xenophon explains the otherwise inappropriate "loftiness" of Socrates' defense as due to his resolve to let the conviction and condemnation come if, as he interpreted the divine sign's behavior to indicate, it was going to.

Now my point in this review of Xenophon's *Apology* is not at all to insist that Xenophon (and Hermogenes, his informant) were correct about Socrates' intent at his trial, and that therefore Plato was wrong in having Socrates give a seriously intended, though very unusual and demanding, defense (even for the reader—let alone the poor jurymen). But nothing in Xenophon's writing in the least suggests he is anything but truthful in reporting what (he had been told) Socrates said to Hermogenes. Nor have

---

its result before Socrates could conclude that, "it is clear to me that it was better for me to die now and to escape from trouble" because his *daimonion* has not interfered at any point. Furthermore, he reaches this conclusion because, as he says, a good man cannot be harmed in either life or death and his affairs are not neglected by the gods. Socrates is sure that, come what may, he is going to be well treated by the gods, so there must be some good in the death he now faces, despite his efforts to avoid it. This is not an argument for courting death, as better than continued life for such an old man as himself, but only for accepting it if and when it comes (so long as he himself remains pure and good). Socrates' last words in Plato's *Apology* are: "I go to die, you go to live. Which of us goes to the better lot is known to no one, except the god." So he continues to be noncommittal about whether death, for him, is the better thing—presumably because he does not think one should or can claim actually to know any such thing on the sort of evidence provided by the behavior of his "voice." Hansen is quite wrong to suggest that Xenophon could not have written what he did about previous writers on Socrates' trial if he had read Plato's account.

[17]Hermogenes ia a major speaker in both Plato's *Cratylus* and Xenophon's *Symposium*. He is listed by Xenophon in *Mem.* I 2, 48 among others of Socrates' nearest followers, and he is among those reported in Plato's *Phaedo* (59b) as present at the conversation on Socrates' last day.

we any reason to doubt that in writing his short account of Socrates' speeches at the trial (allegedly at second hand from Hermogenes—even if he may also, without acknowledging it, have drawn on previously published accounts), his intention was simply to bring this background information to the attention of the public, for the sake of Socrates' reputation. And in fact, I do not see why we should not suppose that Socrates *both* told Hermogenes what Xenophon says he did about its being time for him to die, *and* gave at his trial a stirring, deeply meant defense of himself and of philosophy of at least the general kind that Plato presents. Even on Plato's account, he was not arguing for his life in the latter, which according to Xenophon he told Hermogenes he was not going to do; he was willing (even aggressively so) to let the jurymen reach a guilty verdict, if they were incapable to such an extent of reasoning clearly and dispassionately about the truth of the charges. And Socrates' magnanimity in accepting the jury's verdict is of course one of the high points in Plato's portrait. In any event, real human beings rarely achieve unwavering clarity of motives and views on important personal questions, and even a Socrates, provided we attempt to take him seriously as a real person, may well have thought and spoken in somewhat different ways to different persons, or at different times about what he was doing (and what he was going to do). I return to this point below.

If one does accept Xenophon's report of Hermogenes' evidence about Socrates in the *Apology,* that is all the more reason why one should similarly believe him (not, of course, as to all the details and the occasions of the conversations he reports) when he says in the *Memorabilia* that he is drawing upon his own memory in what he writes there about Socrates. He is telling us the sort of thing he heard Socrates say in conversation with his young men that was calculated to improve them, and some of what he reports surely must represent more specific memories. Is it an obstacle that the result of trusting Xenophon to this extent will be that he heard Socrates champion the conventional virtues of the conventional "gentleman" and the attendant outlook on life? I do not think so. What one hears depends in part upon what one can hear—even when one honestly and successfully reports what was said, and without gap-filling invention or gross interpretation of one's own. It is not difficult to imagine that Socrates' talk about the virtues and their significance for a well-lived life could perfectly reasonably have been interpreted the way that Xenophon did, even if it also had philosophical depths and even revolutionary implications for morality that passed Xenophon by or did not interest him—whether those depths were of the sort that Plato found in it, or more like those found by Antisthenes. Besides, Socrates did not necessarily talk all the time with all his companions at the pitch of philosophical intensity sometimes found in Plato's early dialogues; he might have varied his subjects and his conversation to suit the occasion and the company, thus sometimes talking one way with the more philosophically gifted and another with the more ordinary boy or man, of whom Xenophon was surely not the only example in his entourage (Plato's Crito might strike one as another). What Maier and others have said may not be true, that if Socrates was as Xenophon presents him, it would be impossible to account for the attraction and reverence of Plato and others of the brilliant young men of Athens (and the irritation of the Athenians who put him to death), but it is certainly at least as difficult to imagine Xenophon and others of his kind being attracted to and held by a Socrates who wore them out with nonstop philosophical analysis. Indeed, Socrates should be regarded as all the more remarkable a person, if he was able to be both (more or less) what Xenophon shows us and (more or less) what Plato does. So I do not see any serious difficulty with accepting Xenophon's Socrates as genuine in his broad outlines.

Of course, the matter of greatest moment to me and most others interested in Socrates is what we can learn from Xenophon (or anyone else) about Socrates' philosophy: his specific philosophical opinions (if he had any); his arguments for them; the character and (so far as one can learn them) the details of his *way* of philosophizing; what someone with philosophical inclinations of his own might have learned about philosophy and how to pursue it from consorting with him—as well, of course, as how in Socrates' view and practice philosophical principles were to be lived. I have already emphasized that nowhere in his Socratic writings does Xenophon even set out to tell us about these matters. Still, as I have also said, his Socrates does have philosophical ideas (even though Xenophon makes nothing special of any link between his specifically philosophical ideas and his life), and he is sometimes seen engaging in philosophical argument. The question then is: What, if anything of substance, can we learn from Xenophon about Socrates as a philosopher? How does what we might learn from him compare with what we seem to find in the Socrates of Plato's "Socratic" dialogues? Can we rely on the genuineness of what we find in Xenophon about Socrates as a philosopher? Where Plato and Xenophon diverge, what are we to conclude about the genuine Socrates?

I have already indicated my general answer to these questions, which I hope to confirm in what follows: we have reason to believe that Xenophon's reports not only in his *Apology* but also in the *Symposium* and *Memorabilia* are based in part on his personal knowledge of Socrates, in particular on his knowledge of Socrates' moral views and Socrates' conversational practices with his young friends and others. Moreover, where they depart from that personal knowledge by showing some dependence on other Socratics' writings (Plato, or Antisthenes, for example), Xenophon's reports are controlled by his personally acquired sense of who Socrates was and what he stood for. To be sure, Xenophon is not a philosopher himself and his purpose in writing his Socratic works is not in the least to display, reflect upon, or celebrate Socrates' specifically philosophical opinions. So his testimony is inevitably of limited value for anyone whose principal interest is in Socrates the philosopher. On the other hand, the much richer account that we get in the works of Plato, precisely because Plato *is* a philosopher himself writing his own works of philosophy, is of limited value, too. I believe that the character Socrates of Plato's Socratic dialogues does represent in part Plato's own understanding of the historical Socrates' philosophical commitments, including his modes of argument and the philosophical reasons for adopting them. But Plato's own very complex engagement, as he writes these works, not only with the philosopher Socrates but also with philosophy itself, means that the issues his character Socrates faces, and even the ways he responds to them, can be expected, in ways that we cannot easily or always control, to go well beyond anything we could reasonably count as a historically accurate portrayal of Socrates' philosophical beliefs.[18] I do not suggest that the "truth" about the historical Socrates can be recovered by mechanically mapping Xenophon's Socratic writings onto Plato's, or vice versa. I do urge that an appropriately critical reading of Xenophon can teach us things about Socrates that we could not have learned from Plato alone.

Consider, to begin with, Xenophon's *Symposium.* Toward the end of this work (ch. 8) Xenophon has Socrates give a long and elaborate discourse upon *eros,* in the course of which (8, 32–35) he refers to and severely criticizes some views about boy-love that he attributes to "Pausanias, the lover of the poet Agathon." Characteristically, Xenophon introduces this discourse quite abruptly (8, 1): "Socrates now opened up another new topic for discussion"; he does not attempt any thematically unifying transition.[19] The main after-dinner talk has consisted of a serial presentation and discussion by the men at the feast of whatever knowledge or expertise, or other personal possession, they most pride themselves on, for its extraordinary value to themselves and to others with whom they are associated (chs. 3–4). There follows a playful dispute between Socrates and Crito's son Critobulus (who had prided himself most on his good looks) over which is the more handsome (ch. 5). Next the not-so-playful dancing-master intervenes to begin a rather impolite attack on Socrates, holding him responsible for the feasters' inattention to his performers; only through Socrates' tact and suavity does the company manage to preserve the tone of friendship and goodwill proper to the occasion (chs. 6–7). Despite his abruptness in introducing it, however, Socrates' discourse on *eros* is very well integrated into the work as a whole, and Xenophon has prepared the way for it quite well. The host for the evening is Socrates' very rich friend Callias,[20] who is celebrating the victory at the Panathenaic games of the young man he is in love with,

---

[18] See my introduction to *Plato: Complete Works,* and Chapter 2 below, "Socrates and Plato in Plato's *Gorgias.*"

[19] Translations from Xenophon's *Symposium* are taken from or based on Todd's Loeb translation. Xenophon's abruptness in introducing Socrates' speech appears to be part of a deliberate attempt to preserve in his *mimesis* the spontaneity and disjointedness that must have characterized conversations at such drinking parties. Whether or not those scholars are correct who have seen in this an implicit criticism of Plato's *Symposium,* the differences in this respect between Xenophon's and Plato's *Symposium*s are obvious and noteworthy.

[20] The same Callias in whose house Protagoras and the other sophists are staying in Plato's *Protagoras*; Socrates, in Plato's *Apology* (20a), says he has spent more money on sophists than anyone else in Athens.

Autolycus; Autolycus' father is among the company. In addition, Critobulus' claims for his own beauty and Socrates' playful counterclaims had naturally brought *eros* and the behavior of lovers into the earlier discussion.[21] Socrates' speech carries forward these earlier allusions to lovers' behavior, and concludes with a seriously intended and gracious compliment to his host Callias on the delicacy and propriety of his attachment to Autolycus, which according to Socrates exemplifies the highest and best form of *eros* in an older man for an adolescent boy. On this note the banquet ends, after an erotically arousing performance from the dancers, which sends the other married men home to their wives, but Socrates and Callias out to join Autolycus, whom Xenophon had discreetly sent off with his father for his evening walk, missing the sexually explicit final pantomime (ch. 9).

As I hope this brief summary has shown, *eros* in Xenophon's *Symposium* occupies as prominent, thought not formally so central, a place as in Plato's. Xenophon's work more immediately invites comparison with Plato's, however, through Socrates' detailed references in his discourse on *eros* to Pausanias's views on this subject. For, of course, Pausanias is one of the speakers on *eros* in Plato's *Symposium,* where he appears among the other guests of Agathon, his former beloved.[22] I turn below to this comparison. However, Joël and Maier firmly deny that the reference in Xenophon (8, 32) to "what Pausanias the lover of the poet Agathon has said in his defense of people who wallow in licentiousness (*huper tōn akrasia(i) enkalindoumenōn*)" can possibly be to the speech of the Pausanias of Plato's *Symposium.* They quickly infer that Xenophon can only be referring to a writing of Antisthenes.[23] In fact, they say, Antisthenes must have written a dialogue (doubtless the work we hear of under the title *Protrepticus* or "Exhortation to Philosophy") in which he himself spoke in favor of a high-minded, sex-free sort of love of a man for a boy (in fact, exactly as Xenophon's Socrates does), in opposition to the views of an allegedly effeminate Pausanias brought on the scene to speak in praise of a sexually consummated union. According to Joël and Maier, it is to Pausanias' speech in Antisthenes that Xenophon's Socrates is reacting so strongly—not to Pausanias's speech in Plato. In fact, according to them, in his *Symposium* Plato himself was deliciously parodying Antisthenes' *own* account of *eros* by putting it in the mouth of the effeminate Pausanias, while twisting it so that it *did* involve having sex off the boy. In that case, there would be no close direct association between Xenophon's and Plato's writings, and no grounds for finding in Xenophon's Socrates' remarks against Pausanias any such implied

---

[21] See 4, 11–18 and 23–26.

[22] Socrates makes overt reference to the affair between Pausanias and Agathon in Plato's *Protagoras* (315e). Delicate evidence appears in Plato's *Symposium*: Socrates' pairing of Agathon and Pausanias as among those who will surely not object to Eryximachus's proposal that the company spend their evening giving in turn encomia of *eros* (177d); evidence also appears in Aristophanes' much less delicate denial at 193b6-c2 that he means to be pairing them as perhaps halves of the same original male looking to join together again.

[23] Joël, *Der xenophontische Sokrates,* vol. II, 912ff.; Maier, *Sokrates,* 17–19n.

criticism of Plato, the author of Pausanias's speech, as one might otherwise be tempted to find.

Now for all we can *know,* it may be as Joël and Maier say. Maybe Antisthenes wrote such a work, and maybe both Plato and Xenophon, in their different ways, were drawing on and reacting to it in their *Symposium*s. However, the question for us is whether the two writings that we do possess require, or at all suggest, reference to any now lost work, whether by Antisthenes or someone else. In particular, must the reference in Xenophon to a defense by Pausanias of sexually consummated unions of men with boys be understood in that way? I think not; when the texts of Xenophon and Plato are correctly compared, it seems perfectly possible that Xenophon's reference is, after all, to Pausanias the character in Plato's *Symposium*. The main reasons of Joël and Maier for denying it are two: First, in describing what Pausanias objectionably said, Xenophon attributes to him one point that in Plato is made not by Pausanias but instead by Phaedrus (178e–179b): that the strongest army would be one made up of man-boy sexually active couples. Second, they claim, it is not even true that Pausanias in Plato *does* defend "those who wallow in licentiousness" by having sex with boys; on the contrary, he distinguishes just as Xenophon's Socrates does between a "heavenly" *eros* (love for the boy's soul) and an "earthly" one (lust for gratification from his body), condemning the latter while approving the former alone. They conclude that if we seek a writing in which Pausanias did defend sex between man and boy and in the course of that defense made the claim that the strongest army would be one made up of sexually active man-boy couples, we must look elsewhere than in Plato.

Let us take the second of these arguments first. It is crucial for understanding Plato's Pausanias' point of view to realize that he really is praising sexual relations between man and boy as a central part of the "heavenly" *eros* that he favors. His point is that it is disgraceful and abusive for a man to get a boy to gratify his sexual demands if he is motivated only by lascivious thoughts about the boy's body and not in part by an admiration for his mind, his talents, and his manly character, and if he is not offering a long-term commitment to use their relationship for the boy's manly, ethical growth and improvement.[24] So despite Pausanias's misleadingly high-

---

[24] See 180e–181a: no action as such is good or bad; it all depends on how it is done, especially in what spirit and for what purposes; hence (182a) it is disgraceful for a young man to let an older one have sex off him (*aischron charizesthai erastais*—as R. G. Bury, *Symposium*, p. 34, says, this is the *"vox propria"* referring to the converse of *diapraxasthai* at 181b5, which is "a polite euphemism for the sexual act") if all he cares about is the sex, but not if it is done "decorously" etc. Maier, but not Joël, recognizes the essentially sexual nature of the relationship Pausanias is praising under the name of the "heavenly" *eros*; but he nonetheless absolves Pausanias from attempting a "defense of those wallowing in licentiousness" on the basis of the rejection of the *eros* that is no more than lust for a boy's body. Xenophon's Socrates' point of view is different: he thinks anyone who satisfies his lust for a boy's body is behaving disgracefully and so anyone who like Pausanias glorifies relationships in which that goes on, no matter under what allegedly "ideal" educational conditions, is indeed precisely defending those who wallow in licentiousness.

minded distinction between a heavenly love directed in part to the boy's
mind and his moral improvement, and an earthly one restricted only to
enjoying his body for the sake of physical pleasure, Socrates in Xenophon
is entitled to describe Plato's Pausanias as having defended licentiousness—
if, as is in fact the case, he thinks that *any* copulation of an older man
with a younger one is licentious. And (referring now to Joël and Maier's
first argument) it is quite clear in Plato[25] that Pausanias intends his speech
as a supplement to Phaedrus's, in which he corrects what Phaedrus had
said in praise of *eros* by limiting its application to only one form of erotic
attachment between a man and a boy, the one he calls "heavenly." The
point about a lovers' army, while not actually stated by him, is therefore
clearly part of the overall case in favor of these erotic attachments that he
is making, and Xenophon does not misuse his source, if it is indeed Plato's
Symposium, by including this as part of Pausanias' "defense of licentiousness." It is true that according to Xenophon's Socrates Pausanias brought
the Thebans and Eleans in as witnesses to support his claims about lovers'
armies (8, 34), and Phaedrus does not do that in his remarks in the Plato
text on such armies (178e–179a). Pausanias himself does in fact mention
the customs in "Elis and Boeotia" (without overt reference to their armies),
but only to contrast them unfavorably with those at Athens. Athenian
customs, he says, are based implicitly on a recognition of the exclusive
value of the "heavenly" kind of *eros,* whereas the Eleans and Boeotians,
not being good at making and articulating distinctions, approve indiscrimi-
natingly of boys' gratifying the sexual demands of the men who are in love
with them, whichever type of love it may be (182b). Nonetheless, Xenophon's divergence from Plato at this point does not exclude the possibility
that he is talking about Plato's Pausanias. The practices in the Elean and
especially the Theban (Boeotian) army were well known at the time, so
that anyone reading Phaedrus's endorsement of lovers' armies would very
naturally think he had in mind these Dorian practices as tending to support
him. Furthermore, it is quite believable that Xenophon, remembering Pausanias's reference a little later to the Eleans' and Boeotians' erotic customs
in general (in which, moreover, he rejected only the lack of discrimination
in their approval of men's sexual use of boys, not the approval in itself),
ran the two passages together either from faulty memory or because he
thought it was in fact a fair summary of the import of Pausanias-
Phaedrus's speech.[26]

---

[25] The narrator Apollodorus says (180c) that several other speeches, not reported to him by
his source, intervened between Phaedrus's and Pausanias's, yet he makes Pausanias begin by
linking his own speech explicitly to Phaedrus's, which he says he is going to correct in the
way I have indicated, by distinguishing between a "heavenly" Eros who is to be praised and
an "earthly" one that is not. So Plato takes pains to draw special attention to the continuity
between these two speeches.

[26] Ivo Bruns, "Attische Liebestheorien," p. 37, had already argued the essentials of this
case, and it was quite unjustified for Maier to say his conclusion was simply "ausgeschlossen"
(p. 18n).

Xenophon's fundamental aim in this section of his *Symposium* is to express clearly and forcefully what is presumably his personal view, which he also wishes to inform his reader had been shared fully by his teacher Socrates, that a man's use of free-born boys for his sexual gratification degrades and disgraces them (8, 19) and is therefore not permissible behavior—even if, as Pausanias tries to do, one dresses it up in high-sounding "moral" and educational intentions. In his views on pederasty, Socrates in Xenophon rejects *all* sexual use by a man of the boy he is in love with, because that subjects the boy to something disgraceful (letting his body be used to give the man an orgasm, or, more generally, being made to "play the woman" to him) and damages him by getting him used to the idea of favoring and promoting pleasurable indulgence, in cases where resistance and strength of mind are called for. Anyone who subjects a boy to this treatment will be preparing him to adopt later in life a lax attitude toward his own pleasurable indulgence, and lessening his strength of mind and capacity to resist the blandishments of pleasure where that is ethically required. Thus, in Xenophon, Socrates' conception of the behavior proper for a man in relation to a young man or boy he is in love with identifies two grounds on which having sex with him is bad: it abuses him disgracefully and it damages his character.

Thus Xenophon's Socrates holds a decidedly different view of what is permissible in an erotic relationship between a man and a boy from Plato's Socrates, either in *Symposium* or *Phaedrus*: Plato's Socrates is not as outspoken in his approval of sexual indulgence within the sort of relationship he approves as Pausanias is, but no Greek could fail to see that, whatever his own personal practices may have been, Plato's Socrates was not excluding it in what he says through Diotima's voice in the *Symposium*.[27] And in the *Phaedrus,* although the most perfect divinely possessed lovers will not indulge themselves in this way (because they are fully aware of the philosophical sources and mission of their mutual infatuation), other divinely possessed pairs will—and their relationship will win for them high rewards in the afterlife (*Phdr.* 256b7-e2). It is noteworthy that nowhere in Plato is there any sense that whatever the other characteristics of the lover's attitudes and behavior to his young man may be, the lover's sexual consummation with him harms the boy, as Xenophon's Socrates maintains and many Athenians must have believed, by treating him disgracefully, as well as by encouraging in him wrong attitudes to pleasure. Plato seems to agree with his Pausanias that when the motives are sufficiently high-minded, there will be no disgrace

---

[27] It is not explicit in Diotima's speech that such behavior is part of the love that begins with attraction to one young man's body and is completed by openness to the Beautiful itself, but it is not denied either. If Diotima's theory of the hierarchy of "loves" does not imply that lower levels of love are given up as higher ones are achieved, then at any rate the active love of bodies will survive right through the whole process of ascent; absent the explicit denial, it is a short step to conclude that the sexual consummation of that love is being envisaged even in the most perfect sort of love.

(*Symp*. 182a, 183d); about the effects on the boy's attitudes to pleasure Plato is oddly silent. It would go too far to suggest that when Xenophon attacks the views of Pausanias, the latter stands in for Plato's fancy theory set out in Diotima's speech later in the *Symposium*. But it is surely true[28] that here and in Socrates' speech overall Xenophon is firmly rejecting Plato's own (as he thought essentially similar) views on permissible erotic relationships between men and boys, and firmly denying that Socrates himself ever shared them.[29]

I should add that, taken altogether, Socrates' account of good and morally acceptable *eros* in Xenophon's *Symposium* does clearly differentiate it from ordinary friendship, despite what has sometimes been maintained.[30] In his speech Socrates addresses an implicit objection that on his view of permissible *eros* it would really have nothing to do with Aphrodite (8, 15–18)—so that it would not really differ from a strong and long-lasting friendship. Admittedly, the argument Socrates gives in defence of the "Aphroditic" character of his "lovers'" behavior to one another is unhelpfully imprecise, since it might be interpreted as making any morally upright behavior of a morally good person have "Aphroditic" grace. He refers to the "lovers'" care for one another when ill, concern for one another's good, and so on, as ways they are marked by the goddess's presence, but he does not emphasize that in their case the relationship, and these behaviors, are motivated by an empassioned attachment. Socrates does, however, say that his lovers "take pleasure in looking into each other's faces," trust and are trusted, spend their time together and share a common joy and distress at one another's prosperity or ill-fortune, and are constantly solicitous of one another (8, 18). It is clear at a number of places in his discussion of these love-reactions that Socrates presupposes that, as the Greek word *eros* itself clearly implies, the senior lover is passionately attached to his young friend in a way that certainly is not characteristic of ordinary friendship, and that the junior one has responded to his attentions with a passionate response of his own. The fact that there is not supposed to be any desire at all on either side for actual sexual contact obviously does not eliminate all implicitly sexual (and so truly "erotic") basis for the relationship. If what Socrates is praising is a particularly high form of true friendship, it is not correct on that

---

[28] As Bruns argued, "Attische Liebestheorien," p. 17.

[29] On Socrates' views on love, and his "being in love" with various young men, see also *Mem.* IV 1: this seems a brief recapitulation and application of what Socrates is made to say about love in *Symp.* 8. Note also *Mem.* II 6, 28, where Socrates says that he is himself *erōtikos*, always alive with love for other men and wanting to have his love returned—so that he should be able to help Critobulus, who has asked for advice on how to draw other men to him as his friend. In Xenophon Socrates consistently separates his erotic attraction to young men from any anticipated sexual relationship.

[30] Bruns, pp. 26–27, believes Xenophon's version of Socrates' conception of love between men and boys is incoherent, inasmuch as it eliminates all the special characteristics of love (which necessarily involves sensual desires) and in effect reduces it to or replaces it by simple friendship.

ground to maintain that it eliminates from it the special characteristics of *eros*.[31]

A second topic on which Xenophon's account adds interestingly and helpfully to Plato's picture of Socrates as a philosopher concerns his views on the teachability of virtue, and on himself as a teacher.[32] Xenophon does not hesitate to describe Socrates as teaching (*didaskein*) the young men who came to him (or were sent by their fathers) how to be good men.[33] And Socrates himself in Xenophon does not hesitate to describe his work with his young men as teaching.[34] According to Xenophon Socrates did his teaching in his daily talks with his young men,[35] and not in his cross-examinations of people who thought they knew everything already, such as many of Plato's early dialogues show Socrates engaged in. On the other hand, he did this also through making them skilled in discussion (*dialektikoi*), since he held that "those who know what any given thing is can expound upon it to others";[36] Xenophon proceeds to exhibit Socrates using the question-and-answer method to take pupils step-by-step through definitions of some virtues (piety, justice, wisdom, and courage), obviously on the assumption that if they are to be virtuous they necessarily must come to know what is and is not required by that virtue, and that such instruction in dialectic is needed as a means of learning that. But Xenophon is careful to report also (*Mem.* I 2, 2–3) that Socrates never formally professed to *teach* virtue to his young men, by either of these two sorts of verbal instruction. Rather, he offered himself to them as a model for their emulation, and in that way he encouraged them in virtue and improved them. At *Symposium* 2, 5–7 the topic of the teachability of virtue, familiar to us from Plato's *Meno* and *Protagoras,* comes up briefly, before it is abandoned at Socrates' suggestion,

---

[31] Bruns also makes much, p. 28, of what he regards as an inconsistency in Xenophon's presentation of Socrates and his views on *eros*: despite what Socrates says in ch. 8 about permissible love between males, he is presented earlier as encouraging Critobulus's "coquetteries" (4, 10ff.) in connection with Critobulus's evidently physical love for Cleinias, and Socrates himself engages in coquettish byplay with Charmides over how some bare-shoulder contact with Critobulos affected himself while they were checking something together in a schoolbook (4, 27–28). But there is no inconsistency here at all. Socrates is just being shown as no moralistic prude, and someone who can enjoy and make a sexually loaded joke. Xenophon is certainly not suggesting that Socrates actually behaved any differently in love-relationships than he urged others to behave.

[32] On this topic see Morrison, "Xenophon's Socrates as Teacher."

[33] In *Symp.* 4, 24, we learn that Crito sent Critobulus to Socrates in order to cure him of his sexual infatuation with his age-mate Cleinias—and, no doubt, to improve him in more general ways as well. On Socrates as a teacher, see also *Mem.* I 2, 17; I 2, 21; II 7, 1; IV 7, 1.

[34] See *Apol.* 26 and *Mem.* I 6, 13–14, and see Socrates' conversations with Critobulus, *Mem.* II 6, 30–39, who asks to teach him lessons on how to win a man for one's friend, and with Euthydemus, *Mem.* IV 2, esp. 2, 2 and 2, 6–7, whom he tries to attach to himself as a pupil.

[35] See *Mem.* I 4, 1.

[36] See *Mem.* IV 6, 1, and also IV 5, 12. Translations from Xenophon's *Memorabilia* are taken from or based on E. C. Marchant's Loeb edition.

because it is a disputed and disputable subject, not suitable for a drinking party. And it arises again in *Memorabilia* III 9, in connection with whether courage is teachable, or instead comes by nature; Socrates' view there is the commonsensical one that some people have souls that are by their natures better able to handle fear in battle than others, but that anyone who gets appropriate instruction (*mathēsis*) and practice (*meletē*) will improve in respect of courage, whatever his natural endowments may be. He does not tell us what such practice, and especially what such instruction, would consist in.

Thus Xenophon's Socrates, like Plato's, denies that he teaches anyone virtue, but there is no hint in Xenophon of the depths and complexities of Socrates' thought on this subject such as we find in Plato. And, whatever Xenophon thought Socrates' grounds were for *not* professing to be a teacher of virtue (he does not say a word about that), it is evident that he did not suppose Socrates made a big point of not addressing his young men as their teacher; on the contrary, in Xenophon Socrates accommodates himself readily to their and their parents' expectations that they will be taught by him, and he speaks at least informally to them about his "instruction" of them. Clearly, Xenophon has no idea that Socrates had any deep reason for denying that he was a teacher of virtue, and if that term should be understood appropriately in an ordinary and undemanding sense of giving good advice and encouragement about how to live, what to prefer and what to value less, and so on, he is content to be regarded as a teacher of virtue. Perhaps, as I mentioned before, the real Socrates spoke in some contexts and to some of his young men in accordance with a more elevated and more philosophical understanding of what virtue is and therefore how one might come to acquire it, than he did in others, where he was content to speak in accordance with more usual and less demanding conceptions of these matters. Or, conceivably, it was only Plato, not the historical Socrates at all, who, reflecting upon Socrates' conversations and building on what he himself made of them, came to see so much of philosophical importance in the denial that virtue could be taught.

What, however, did Xenophon's Socrates think virtue *is*? Is it an intellectual understanding of how best to live, or (instead or in addition) some sort of affective state? When Xenophon distinguishes between Socrates' instruction of his pupils, on the one hand, and their emulation of him and the inspiration of his example, on the other, and claims that Socrates actually imparted the virtues to them by means only of the latter, one might infer that Xenophon's Socrates did not consider the virtues as purely intellectual conditions.[37] On the other hand, someone might think that virtue was in

---

[37] Alexander Nehamas (*The Art of Living*, ch. 1) argues that even Plato's Socrates—despite first appearances—has only his own life to hold up as an example and does not know its basis; his power as a philosopher consists largely in that example, much more than in any philosophical doctrines he links it to. Xenophon, in his presentation of Socrates as exemplar of the well-lived life (even if he leaves largely to one side the philosophical depth of Socrates' life), may

fact a purely intellectual condition, but not one that could be taught the ways that other, ordinary, intellectual competences can be: perhaps it requires personal insight of some sort that each one has to work up for himself, and maybe that will only come about through the emulation of a mentor such as Xenophon's Socrates.[38] Given, as I have emphasized, that Xenophon's interests are not in detailed points of philosophical theory, we should not expect to find him in the *Memorabilia* addressing these issues directly. However, two extended discussions in particular, in III 9 and IV 6, contain especially relevant information about the nature of virtue in general, according to Socrates, and about the specific virtues and their interrelationships, and related matters. It is noteworthy that Xenophon's account is congruent on these points with that of Plato's Socratic dialogues. It is quite possible that it shows some effects of Xenophon's reading of Plato, as well of course, quite possibly, of other writers whose works are lost to us (Antisthenes, for example)—though comparison of the relevant texts seems to me to show that at any rate Xenophon did not lean heavily on Plato's work. If at some points Xenophon follows Plato, his manner of doing so tends to confirm what I said above about his alleged reliance on Antisthenes: Xenophon seems to be exercising his firsthand knowledge of Socrates in selecting from other, more philosophically competent authors only what fits in appropriately with his own recollections of the man. So such resemblances of philosophical doctrine and perspective as we do see should count in favor of the historicity of the common account. In these matters then, Xenophon's reports provide valuable confirmation for Plato's much more elaborate and philosophically focused presentation of Socrates.[39] (Apart from noting some parallels, I will not go further into the question of "borrowings.")

In *Memorabilia* III 9 Xenophon reports (mostly in his own voice) Socrates' views on various points to do with courage, wisdom, *sōphrosunē* (temperance or self-control or soundness), justice, and some of their opposites. He goes on to describe Socrates' accounts of the natures of envy and leisure, then presents his ideas on kings, magistrates, and tyrants, and concludes with a presentation of Socrates' view about *eupraxia* or "acting well" as the best pursuit for a man (distinguishing that from *eutuchia* or "good fortune").[40] Xenophon tells us (9, 4) that Socrates did not separate *sophia* (wisdom) from *sōphrosunē*.[41] In confirmation, he adds that because Socrates thought that, among their options, all men choose to do (always, Xenophon

have captured more forthrightly than Plato did something crucially important about Socrates' philosophical influence.

[38] Something like this may be the attitude of Plato's Socrates, for example in *Meno* and *Protagoras,* on the teachability of virtue.

[39] Thus what follows in the next three paragraphs can be regarded as an addendum to what Vlastos says (*Socrates,* pp. 99–106) about the support Xenophon provides for his own account of the main characteristics of the philosophical views of the "early" Socrates (the historical one) as against the "middle" Socrates in Plato's works.

[40] Compare Plato, *Euthydemus* 280b, and the context, 279c–282a.

[41] Compare Plato, *Protagoras* 332a–333b.

apparently means to say) whatever they think is most for their own advantage or good (*sumphorōtata*), no one can be both wise (so that they understand that virtuous action is always best for them) and yet also not self-controlled (*akratēs*).[42] Here the context shows that "not self-controlled" means "not having *sōphrosunē*," but Xenophon's further explication of Socrates' view makes it clear that he thought Socrates actually denied, not only for the temperate or *sōphrones* and wise ones, but for all people that anyone does what he ought not to do while knowing that he ought to do the contrary. He says that when asked about people who "know what they ought to do but do the opposite," Socrates replied (in effect rejecting the questioner's assumption that such people are possible at all) that such people are *both* unwise *and* not "self-controlled" (*akrateis*), *because* all men choose to do whatever they think is most advantageous or good for them. In effect, then, Socrates is clearly denying here not only that wise people can be "uncontrolled" or vice versa, but also that *anyone* can do what is bad for them while believing that it *is* bad.[43]

Xenophon goes on to report that Socrates held that justice and every other virtue is wisdom (9, 5). Socrates argues as follows: anyone who knows *ta kala te kai agatha*, things that are fine or noble or beautiful, and good— i.e., who is wise—always chooses to do them, and no one who does *not* know them (who lacks wisdom) can even *do* them at all,[44] but just acts and all actions coming from any virtue are *kala te kai agatha,* fine and good; therefore all virtues are wisdom. He adds (9, 6) that Socrates distinguished between madness, *mania* (the opposite of wisdom), and ignorance (*anepistēmosunē*), mimicking ordinary usage. Ordinary people (though not understanding these words as Socrates himself did) distinguish between these two conditions—for them, ignorance is getting something wrong in an area outside common knowledge, whereas madness is, for example, thinking you have to stoop when going through city gates because you are so vastly tall. For Socrates ignorance of oneself (thinking you know what you do not) is *next* to sheer madness, but is not the same thing: madness, apparently,

[42] I read *akrateis* in the second sentence of 9, 4, with the principal mss and the Oxford Classical Text, in place of *enkrateis,* read by one inferior ms. and printed in the Loeb edition (perhaps by error) as it was in many eighteenth- and early-nineteenth-century editions through the editors' failure to understand the argument: Marchant, the Loeb translator, in fact translates *akrateis*—which he prints in his OCT text. (Vlastos's report of the textual situation, *Socrates* p. 101n.78, seems to be based on Dindorf's textual note, not the OCT's apparatus; assuming that the latter is accurate, it is incorrect.)

[43] Thus Vlastos's criticism (*Socrates,* p. 101–2) of Xenophon's understanding of Socrates' view on *akrasia,* i.e. of the view we associate with Socrates from our reading of Plato's dialogues, is quite unjustified.

[44] Xenophon does not explain this, but his formulation of the point is sharp and clear, sharper and clearer than anything along the same lines I can think of in Plato's Socratic dialogues. The implication is that no act that one might conventionally think was a good one, because it was what, externally speaking, the good person would do, is in fact a good one at all—because it did not originate in a virtuous character, i.e., in knowledge of what is fine or noble and good.

includes making mistakes about what sort of thing is fine and good, rather than making mere factual mistakes about what to do in pursuit of those goals. He held that a true king or magistrate (*archōn*) is not whoever by the conventional rules occupies those offices, but only whoever knows how to rule, how ruling ought to be done (9, 10–11).[45] It is agreed, he argued, that it belongs to a king or magistrate to give orders and to be obeyed, but people in fact do obey (freely, Xenophon apparently means) (only) those who know what they are giving orders about, so it can only *belong* to one who knows what they are giving orders about to give orders and to be obeyed.

In IV 6, as noted above, Socrates is presented working out in question-and-answer discussion definitions of several virtues. Piety is knowledge of what is lawful (*nomimon*) in connection with the gods (i.e., in doing honor to them): the one who knows what is lawful thinks he ought to honor them, and so he does that (since everyone does what he thinks he ought) (6, 2–4). Justice is knowledge of what is lawful in connection with men (i.e., in their dealings with one another): again, everyone does what he thinks he ought, and what is just is what is lawful, so the one who knows what is lawful, thinking that he ought to do that, does it, and so is a just person (6, 5–6).[46] The discussion of wisdom which follows (6, 7–9) seems incomplete, being run together confusingly with a discussion of courage (6, 10–11). But it looks as if the idea is as follows. The wise are wise by wisdom, but also by knowledge; so wisdom is to be identified with knowledge—not, however, with knowledge of everything (for a human being that is an impossibility), but rather with knowledge of what is good (i.e., what is useful) and what is fine or noble (*kalon*) for oneself (these are all the same things). Courage is a fine or noble thing, and it is also useful; in fact, it is useful in dealing with terrors and dangers. But since all persons always do in any situation whatever they think they ought, those and only those who know terrors and dangers (i.e., know how to deal with them, how they ought to act in relation to them) will act well and not badly toward terrors and dangers. So courage is the knowledge how to deal well with terrors and dangers, and cowardice is not knowing that.[47]

Thus we find Xenophon's Socrates maintaining that virtue is knowledge of what is good and fine or noble or beautiful, and maintaining that *akrasia* is in fact lack of wisdom, i.e., lack of knowledge of what one ought to do. And he maintains that all the (other) virtues are wisdom. These are, of course, central components of the moral theory that we associate with Socrates in Plato's Socratic dialogues. But, as my summaries make clear,

---

[45] Compare Plato, *Statesman* 259a–b.

[46] On these accounts of piety and justice, see Plato, *Euthyphro* 12c–e. On justice see also Socrates' discussion with Hippias in Xenophon, *Mem.* IV 4, in which Socrates defends pretty much the same definition of justice, in terms of what is *nomimon*. On *Mem.* IV 4, see Morrison, "Xenophon's Socrates on the Just."

[47] Compare Plato, *Protagoras* 359c–360d.

Xenophon's arguments are not precisely the same as Plato's, and at two points they go beyond anything in Plato's Socratic dialogues—in the distinction between ignorance and madness, and in Socrates' argument that a true king or magistrate is not whoever by the conventional rules occupies those offices, but only whoever *knows* how to rule.

I mentioned above, and scholars have often noticed and emphasized, that Xenophon's Socrates endorses many attitudes and practices that were later on prominently advocated by those in the tradition of Greek "cynicism." Near the beginning of the *Memorabilia* (I 3, 5–15), Xenophon gives us an extended description of Socrates' way of organizing his own life: he trained his body and his mind so that he did not have desires that he could not confidently expect to be able easily to satisfy, and to afford; he took pleasure in the very acts of eating and drinking themselves (when hungry or thirsty), and he disregarded the pleasures to be gotten from eating or drinking beyond what satisfies hunger or removes thirst, or from special and rare tastes one might get from specific food or drink. He was particularly concerned in this connection (and others) with maintaining his freedom, with not becoming a slave to his own appetites, or to anyone else's demands on him. And he advocated more than any other virtue the virtue of *enkrateia*, or self-control: the first thing Xenophon says in rejecting the charge against him of corrupting the youth is that he was *pantōn anthrōpōn enkratestatos*, the "strictest of humans" in controlling himself (I 2, 1). Xenophon devotes a whole chapter (I 5) to a discourse on *enkrateia*, where Socrates is made to say (5, 4) that this is the very foundation of virtue and the first thing one ought to establish in one's soul, since unless one is first free to disregard pleasure and pain one will never learn anything good or practice it sufficiently so as to benefit from it. The long discussion with Aristippus on pleasure (II 1), in which he blithely adopts for himself Prodicus's praise of virtue in his "Choice of Heracles," begins as another example of how Socrates exhorted his companions to train themselves to self-control in eating, drinking, and sex, and in facing cold and heat and bodily exertion and pain (*ponos*). And there is yet another chapter on *enkrateia* (IV 5), including a conversation between Socrates and Euthydemus, where Xenophon again emphasizes that Socrates was the "most practised in self-denial of all people" (*ēskēkōs hauton malista pantōn anthrōpōn*, 5, 1) and says that he presented himself as self-denying to his young men, whom he moreover exhorted more than anything else to become self-controlled themselves. Freedom depends upon it (5, 2). Indeed, those who are prey to their own pleasures are enslaved with the worst kind of slavery (5, 5). Wisdom depends upon it too, because those who are not master of their pleasures choose them instead of better things because they do not see the better ones for what they are (5, 6)—only those who have self-control can consider what is best and think through logically the various types of good thing so as to choose the ones that really are best and leave aside the ones that are bad (6, 11). In sum, *enkrateia* is the best possible possession (6, 8). In fact, self-control, which makes one able to endure hunger and thirst, resist sleep, and so on, is the best and necessary means of obtaining the types of pleasure that are actually greatest and worth any mention (6, 9). Besides that, it allows one to get pleasures of other types (knowledge of household and state affairs, e.g.) that the person prey to his immediate pleasures will never taste (6, 10).[48]

Xenophon's Socrates' thoughts about the key position among the virtues of self-control, philosophically undeveloped though Xenophon characteristically leaves them, are potentially of considerable philosophical interest. But Plato thinks he can reach deeper philosophical truths in presenting Socrates' views on how to live and what practices are most conducive to the best way of life than by dwelling on and glorifying what he must have regarded as relatively trivial—mere physical self-denial and the indifference to refined pleasures of taste and touch. His Socrates is, however, personally rather ascetic, as Xenophon's is in a much more outspoken and quasi-theoretical way. It looks as if Plato thought the ascetic side of Socrates' personal life, and (to the extent that it played a role in what he encouraged in his followers) its place in his "teaching," was not of much interest. Here is perhaps yet another case of Xenophon and Plato valuing more highly different aspects of the actual Socrates' practices and teachings.

Finally, there is the question whether virtue can be lost once it is won. Antisthenes seems to have held that it could not be, and the Stoics followed him in this.[49] In response to Polycrates' blaming Socrates for the crimes of Alcibiades and Critias (*Mem.* I 2, 12ff.), Xenophon argues that so long as they stayed with him Alcibiades and Critias were in fact good people, possessed of the *sōphrosunē* that Socrates had helped them to develop. This would of course have prevented their later hubristic and traitorous behavior. It was only later that they turned bad. But this raises the question whether in fact it is even possible to change, as Xenophon has implied these persons did, from being virtuous to being vicious. (He does not scruple to think that they actually became fully virtuous by the end of their youthful association with Socrates.)[50] With Antisthenes presumably in mind, Xenophon mentions (2, 19) that many self-proclaimed philosophers (*polloi tōn phaskontōn philosophein*) hold that a just person can never become unjust, that once one has the knowledge that virtue is, one cannot lose it. He replies that he does

---

[48] Most of these points in favor of *enkrateia* are made by Xenophon himself in the *Cyropaedia*, but that is no good reason to suppose that he is baselessly attributing the same opinions to Socrates just because they are his own. If he found Antisthenes attributing these same opinions to Socrates, perhaps in much more theoretically loaded form, that too is not a sufficient "source" from which Xenophon drew these aspects of his presentation. They may be points about Socrates' life and views with which he particularly resonated—indeed, these points might have drawn him and held him to Socrates in the first place.

[49] Diog. L. VI 105; see also VI 12–13, where Diog. L. reports (on the authority of Diocles of Magnesia, a first-century B.C. doxographer) these two sayings of Antisthenes: "virtue is a weapon that cannot be taken away" and "wisdom is a most secure fortification; it never falls down or gets betrayed."

[50] Compare Plato, *Theaetetus* 150e–151a.

not agree with this view (2, 19–23): in the case of virtue as in that of bodily attainments a person must be consistently tuned and toned by constant practice and training. Only so can one remain aware of the reasons for being just and otherwise virtuous and not lapse back into preferring other modes of action or other indulgences. Later on, in Socrates' discussion with Pericles, the son of the statesman Pericles (III 5), Xenophon attributes the same sort of view to Socrates (5, 13–14): Socrates says that the Athenians have degenerated by neglecting themselves; all they need to do is to train themselves in imitating the customs and so forth of their glorious ancestors in order to recover their lost virtue and glory. Nowhere in Plato's Socratic dialogues is the topic of losing and regaining one's virtue thus made a theme for Socrates.

My intention in the last several pages in discussing Xenophon's evidence in the *Memorabilia* about Socrates as a philosopher has not been to give a systematic or comprehensive review of this material, or a thorough evaluation of its merits. Rather, I have hoped by my summaries and comments on selected passages to demonstrate that even though Xenophon's purposes in the work relegate Socrates' specifically philosophical views to a subordinate position there is good reason to take his representation of those views seriously, and to treat it as independent testimony about the historical Socrates. I argued earlier that in Xenophon's *Apology* and *Symposium* we find important testimony independent of and partly diverging from Plato's which needs to be taken carefully into account in developing our understanding of Socrates' trial, and his views on erotic attachments to young men (and moral questions arising in connection with such relationships). We have now seen that the same is true of the *Memorabilia,* on central topics about moral virtue, its teachability and its intellectual basis, and about the impossibility of *akrasia* as it is commonly understood—as well as several other details in Socrates' moral theory. A careful reading of all three of these Socratic works of Xenophon indicates that his personal knowledge of Socrates, so different in many respects from Plato's, controls his compositions— and that, on this basis, he had formed a somewhat different view from Plato's about what was most admirable about Socrates and most important in his influence on the young men who associated with him. Every student of Plato's Socratic dialogues and of the historical Socrates will gain greatly by reading and pondering Xenophon's Socrates.[51]

[51] The first version of this chapter was written in 1993 while I was a Fellow of the Center for Advanced Study in the Behavioral Sciences. I thank the Center and the Andrew Mellon Foundation of New York for its financial support. I owe a debt of another kind to Donald Morrison, whose comments on an intermediate version helped me to make many improvements.

CHAPTER TWO

Socrates and Plato in Plato's *Gorgias*

I

Readers of Plato's dialogues cannot avoid taking some position, self-consciously or not, on Plato's relation as author to the philosophical arguments and opinions expressed by his characters. Some dialogues—for example *Sophist* and *Statesman,* or *Laws*—do not present a main speaker engaged dramatically with his interlocutors in a conflict of ideas, or social attitudes, or ways of life. Instead, we hear one person expounding to some others, and to us readers, his philosophical opinions on some topic and his reasons for holding them; the interlocutor(s) help him along by understanding and accepting what he says, by asking just the question needed to turn the exposition in the right next direction, by requesting further elucidation where we readers need it too—and the like. In such cases it seems natural—what else, it may seem, could one do?—to assume that Plato as author is straightforwardly endorsing the principal speaker's ideas and arguments: he is expounding these through the medium of this speaker's voice as his own convictions. I would insist that, nonetheless, even in such relatively straightforward cases, Plato as author of the dialogue stands back from the words of his spokesmen and withholds his full commitment; even there it is through the writing as a whole that Plato speaks to the reader, not through any single character's words.[1] Still, this may seem a rather formal point for a dialogue of such bare-boned exposition: I readily grant that no one is going to miss much about the *Sophist* or *Laws* who ignores this refinement and simply takes the words of the Visitor from Elea or from Athens as the sole repository of such philosophical communication about being or sophistry, or government and laws as Plato wishes in these works.

Much more pressing are cases where the dialogue plainly does present such a dramatic confrontation of ideas, attitudes, and ways of life. Here too, can we without loss identify the author's or the writing's communication on philosophical points with the principal speaker's theses, arguments, refutations, and rebuttals, as we can best understand those? Is the character Socrates of *Republic* and *Phaedo,* or *Crito* and *Gorgias,* or *Theaetetus* and *Phaedrus* simply and straightforwardly a spokesman for the author? Are Socrates' philosophical opinions and arguments, with all their philosophical presuppositions and commitments, ones that in writing the work Plato is representing as his own? Is what Plato wishes to communicate to his readers

[1] See my introduction to *Plato: Complete Works,* pp. xxi–xxii.

on philosophical topics through these writings contained simply in words
he attributes to Socrates, on his own or in response to his interlocutors?
Gregory Vlastos's work on Plato was from beginning to end deeply committed to a positive answer to these questions, and his student T. H. Irwin has
argued impressively in favor of his and Vlastos's "doctrinal" approach
to the dialogues, taking Socrates always to be Plato's spokesman for the
philosophical ideas he is concerned to put forward in these dialogues.[2]

There are alternative approaches, of course—and Irwin argues ably against
some of these.[3] One weakness of the Vlastos-Irwin view is that it makes
little of the fact that Plato wrote dialogues and not prose discourses of some
other sort. If their approach is correct, then in at least many cases Plato
might just as well have written expositions and developments of his own
ideas in continuous prose and in his own voice.[4] If one seriously considers

---

[2] *Plato's Ethics*, pp. 3–16.

[3] A new alternative has been proposed by Charles Kahn in *Plato and the Socratic Dialogue*:
that shortly after 390 B.C., after having already written several Socratic dialogues (*Crito, Ion,
and Lesser Hippias*) as well as the *Apology*, Plato conceived both the full-blown philosophical
view about metaphysics, morality, and politics that we find expounded by Socrates in the
Republic, and a plan for preparing his contemporary readers for its reception through a series
of Socratic dialogues of a new, "aporetic" sort devoted largely to definitions of the virtues:
Laches, Charmides, Euthyphro, Protagoras, Meno, Lysis, Euthydemus. (For Kahn, the historical Socrates had never engaged in inquiries aimed at defining moral notions, so Plato's first
Socratic works, in which actual Socratic views and practices were featured, could not have
shown Socrates engaged in any such enterprise.) But first Plato wrote the *Gorgias* (no "aporetic"
work) as a precursor, in which to lay out in a preliminary way the moral and political position
(but not the metaphysical one) he intended to espouse in quite different terms in the *Republic*:
before continuing on to write the *Republic*, he needed to prepare the way in the "aporetic"
dialogues for the introduction of a "craft" of dialectic with the task of knowing and explaining
the Forms. It counts heavily against Kahn's altogether speculative proposal that, as anyone
who has worked seriously at philosophy knows, you cannot have a full-blown philosophical
view of any sort—including, as is necessary, the well-tested arguments needed to establish it
to your own satisfaction—until you have actually worked it out in detail, either in writing or
some equivalent. This applies to recognized philosophical geniuses like Plato as much as to
others: consider the case of Kant. The claim that Plato knew what he was going to say in the
Republic long before writing it and so knew, progressively as he wrote these other dialogues,
the best way to prepare his contemporaries for its reception, leaves one simply incredulous.
Kahn cites nothing remotely resembling actual evidence for his hypothesis—only Plato's lifelong
admiration for Socrates as paradigmatic philosopher and moral exemplar, and the claim in
the *Seventh Letter* that about 390 Plato finally gave up all hope of engaging in a first-order
way, as it were, in the political advancement of Athenian society (this is the burden of the soi-
disant "speculative biography" that Kahn sets out, pp. 48–59). Kahn does, in addition, offer
a series of readings of the various dialogues that he claims belong to this preparatory group,
in support of this hypothesis. I cannot enter here into a full evaluation of these readings, but
see below on the *Gorgias*.

[4] Irwin explains (*Plato's Ethics*, p. 7) that in the case of the "Socratic" dialogues Socrates'
own claims for the special value of his systematic form of interrogation, which is directly
representable in writing only in dialogues, justify Plato's choice of this mode of composition:
since it is (only) by this means that Socrates is able to "secure his interlocutors' agreement to
moral positions that they would have firmly, often indignantly, rejected before they faced
Socrates' questions, . . . the fact that [a] conclusion is reached through this sort of interrogation

the fact that Plato's works throughout his writer's career are dialogues, one might well wonder whether his own contribution to the philosophical debates he constructs must comprise not only his character Socrates' ideas but also, in one way or another, the ideas of the other speakers and how these interplay with Socrates'. In that case we will find Plato's own ideas—what a given dialogue as a whole wants to communicate on the philosophical topics its speakers pursue—only if we pay close, positive but critical attention also to the interlocutors' views, follow up and reflect on the specific ways that Socrates does, and does not, attack them, and ask ourselves at crucial junctures in the dialectic what in dealing with Socrates' onslaughts they might have replied that they did not. Perhaps we should look for indications, in the ways that Plato presents these confrontations, of points of inadequacy or weakness not only on Socrates' opponents' side but also in Socrates' ideas, points that may need to be pursued further and perhaps along lines different from those that his character Socrates in fact has followed, if Socrates' own cherished, most basic theses about morality, politics, and happiness—ones that Plato himself surely supports—are to be sustained. These suggestions evidently open up a large topic: with such varied works as Plato's, one could expect that his role as author, even if conceived throughout in these same general terms, might vary significantly and interestingly from case to case, or among different groups of dialogues. Here, without claiming that my results can be applied in any mechanical way to other dialogues, I want to consider the single case of the *Gorgias.*

II

What is Plato's relation to Socrates in the *Gorgias?* Is Socrates there in a straightforward way Plato's spokesman? Can we surmise that at the time

---

is part of the reason Socrates offers us for believing his conclusion." But Irwin is not quite right even about the Socratic dialogues. Socrates in these dialogues cannot think that "we" (the readers) are given any reason to accept a conclusion of his in the mere fact that he has reached it by his form of interrogation applied to someone *else* (the particular other character in the dialogue)—that would mean that we were being asked to believe a conclusion true just because another person, or lots of them perhaps, had been led by Socratic questioning to accept it. But Socrates is emphatic in the *Gorgias,* to which Irwin seems to be appealing in these remarks, that he rejects any and all "witnesses" on moral questions, and speaks to the one person only, the one with whom he is carrying on a discussion (see 471e–472c). Socrates and Plato can only be asking "us" to accept the conclusion because in reading the dialogue we interrogate ourselves in the Socratic way, following along with Socrates' interrogation of the interlocutor, and find that we, too, are forced to accept the conclusion. But even if this feature of Socratic dialectic gives a plausible reason for Plato to write *Socratic* dialogues, how can it justify his writing dialogues of other types, ones in which (as in *Republic* II–X) his Socrates no longer endorses such claims for his method of interrogation, and indeed no longer interrogates his interlocutors in the way he does in the Socratic dialogues? Did Plato keep writing dialogues simply out of habit, or from inattention to his own evolving views and the form of writing that would best suit them? That is not believable.

he was writing this dialogue, Plato identified wholeheartedly with what he has this character say, not only in announcing his views but in arguing for them—and with the philosophical presuppositions of all Socrates' arguments? Is the whole of what Plato wants to say on the philosophical topics here being pursued to be found in what Socrates says, independently or in reaction and relation to what Gorgias, Polus, and Callicles, his fellow-discussants, say?

For our purposes Socrates' dispute with Callicles, in the second half of the dialogue, will prove the most revealing of the three interchanges that constitute the work. There, Callicles defends the claim (inherited from his predecessor in the debate, Polus) that the unjust life is better and happier than the just one—where "just" is understood in the conventional democratic terms of fifth-century Athens, as involving a high premium on fairness, in the sense of equality, in all civic matters. That is true, at any rate, Callicles argues, of an unjust life led by an accomplished, knowledgeable orator who is also "brave" or manly in that he does not flinch in the pursuit of whatever will gratify his appetites (for example, out of squeamishness or shame—or fear of the consequences). In the course of this defense, Callicles conspicuously employs ideas about the virtues (for example, bravery) and about the psychology of human action which depart from those Socrates himself relies on in other Socratic dialogues and indeed earlier in this one. Furthermore, these ideas line up very closely with the quite different ideas on these matters espoused by the Socrates of the *Republic*. I will argue below that a close reading of the text shows that in his counterattack, Socrates himself stands clear of these innovations in moral psychology (though he clearly notices them); he relies throughout on the understanding of these matters that he holds to in those other places. We have every reason to believe that in writing the *Republic*, Plato believed the new moral psychology presented there, and the new theory of the moral virtues based upon it, to be philosophically more defensible than the "Socratic" one. What are we to make of Callicles' foreshadowing of it in the *Gorgias*? I believe that we should see Plato in the *Gorgias* as now recognizing and drawing attention to weaknesses—doubtful points—in the "Socratic" moral psychology, ones that will have to be wrestled with (and presumably corrected in the directions that Callicles' discussion points us), if Socrates' counterdefense of justice and the just life is finally to be successfully completed—as it is certainly not in the *Gorgias*. Thus an important part of the philosophical communication conveyed by the author to his readers in this dialogue— at any rate, to those who read with the philosophical attention he is entitled to demand in writing philosophy—is that there *are* those weaknesses, those doubtful points, and that they *do* demand attention. So Socrates is not speaking simply and straightforwardly as Plato's mouthpiece in this dialogue.

III

But first I want to consider one of the passages earlier in the *Gorgias* where Socrates shows clearly his own allegiance to the "Socratic" moral psychology. This comes within Socrates' interrogation of Gorgias, the orator and teacher of oratory. Gorgias has said that his art—the one he teaches and practices himself—produces "the greatest good for humankind," a good greater than the ones that doctors, physical trainers, and financial experts control (respectively health, physical strength and beauty, and wealth): namely, "it is the source of freedom for humankind itself and at the same time it is for each person the source of rule over others in one's city."[5] Gorgias explains that he means here the power that expertise in oratory

[5] *Gorgias,* 452d2–8, translated by D. J. Zeyl, in Cooper, ed., *Plato: Complete Works* (I quote the *Gorgias* throughout in Zeyl's translation, sometimes slightly modified). W. D. Woodhead, reprinted in Hamilton and Cairns, *Dialogues of Plato,* translates similarly, and Olympiodorus in his paraphrase and commentary (5, 10) makes it plain that he understood the Greek the same way, p. 44, 2–7 Westerink. However, most translators get the bearing of the Greek wrong at d6–7. Socrates' preceding challenge on behalf of the physicians et al. requires that Gorgias mention—and the Greek in Gorgias's reply at d6–7 marks this by the repetition of τοῖς ἀνθρώποις at d6–7 (with the addition of αὐτοῖς), carrying on the similar datives at 452b1, c5, and d3–4 referring to the good for human beings that health, physical strength, and wealth constitute (see also Gorgias's boast at 451d7–8 that oratory provides τὰ μέγιστα τῶν ἀνθρωπείων πραγμάτων ... καὶ ἄριστα, "the greatest of human concerns ... and the best")—some good that oratory provides that accrues to those on whom the orator practices his art (corresponding to those on whom physicians et al. practice theirs, the patients), namely human beings gathered (as it immediately turns out, e4) at some political assemblage or other to hear an orator's speeches. But most translators, for example Irwin, misconstrue the phrase *eleutherias autois tois anthrōpois* as meaning (despite the plural, which stands in contrast with the singular *hekastōi* at the end of the sentence) "freedom for a man himself" (Irwin), viz., for the expert orator. Interestingly, Gorgias is in fact giving a double answer to Socrates' question (this is marked clearly in the Greek by the strengthened contrast ἅμα μὲν ... ἅμα δὲ at d6–7), and a double explication of Polus's initial claim (448c9) that Gorgias's is the finest—most wonderful, admirable, and enviable—of the arts (not the single one that, in effect, the other reading provides): oratory gives freedom to populations in cities and, to the orator himself, it gives the power to exercise leadership and rule over others in his city. The former of these is the "good" Gorgias puts forward as provided to those on whom the art is exercised, while the latter counts also, not unreasonably, in his eyes as a further element (perhaps the most important one) in making the art prestigious and enviable—desirable and prized by those who can acquire it, envied by everyone else. In what follows the first of these claims drops out of the discussion (unless there is a very submerged—hardly recoverable—echo of it in Socrates' denigration and dismissal at 502e2 of "oratory addressed to ... those in ... cities composed of free people," which is aimed not at all at their improvement—as if to say, of what possible good could *such* freedom be?); Gorgias does nothing to explain what he has in mind by this remark. (This perhaps explains why so many translators have failed even to notice its presence.) But presumably Gorgias's point is to claim that free self-rule by a people, as against dictatorial and enforced rule by tyrants or oligarchs, depends upon the use of argument and persuasion to make public decisions—and oratory is the art that oversees and reinforces a city's commitment to govern itself on that basis; without orators and oratory public life would degenerate into the exercise of brute force, with the loss of freedom for everyone. Much

provides for persuading political assemblages of all sorts. (Subsequently he concentrates exclusively on the benefits its possessor derives from this power—the ones that come from ruling in his city—not any that "human-kind itself" derives.)

But on what topics or areas of concern do orators offer their persuasive speeches? As Socrates says (454a1–3), all the other experts he mentioned—physicians, physical trainers, financial experts—and even experts in purely intellectual disciplines like arithmetic also offer persuasion—namely, persuasion on matters within their own special areas of expertise—when they persuade people by succeeding in teaching them any of what, as such experts, they know. What then about orators? What is their special area of expertise, in which they know how to persuade people? Gorgias replies at once (454b5–7) that orators persuade people on matters of justice and injustice: in "law courts and in those other large gatherings" he had referred to (at 452e2–3), these are the concerns at issue. In fact Gorgias had mentioned specifically meetings of the council and the assembly as well as of the law courts, and in those meetings questions of justice and injustice would not be the sole or the normal topic of discussion. So he is being a bit selective here: perhaps his reply simply reflects the fact that the primary and indispensable locale for the practice of oratory was in the law courts. More fully, as Socrates assumes later on (459d1–2), the topics of discussion in *all* the oratorical venues taken together range over "what's just and unjust, what's shameful and admirable, what's good and bad."[6] It follows at once that, according to Gorgias, justice and injustice (or that plus good and bad, shameful and admirable) constitute the area of the orator's expertise, comparable in one way or another with health (and how to achieve and maintain it) for the physician, odd and even and how many they are in a given context for the arithmetical expert, and so on.

Thus, already at this early point in his interrogation of Gorgias, and not, as most commentators have assumed, much later (at 460a3–4), Socrates obtains from Gorgias the admission that will prove in Socrates' hands so

---

of Socrates' attack on rhetoric in the remainder of the dialogue could be construed as an attack on the assertion that the sort of freedom that traditional oratory protects is worth anything at all. His description of rhetoric as a pander's art, seeking nothing further than to give pleasure to the orator's audiences, is in effect a powerful rebuttal of the value of such "political freedom." One misses a good deal of what the dialogue has to say to us by not noticing and giving some thought to Gorgias's first claim here.

[6] It seems not to have been noticed by commentators that in describing the scope of oratorical practice here Socrates anticipates Aristotle's formal division of rhetoric into three branches (political, forensic, and ceremonial), each with one of Socrates' pairs as its special subject matter (see *Rhetoric* I 3, 1358b20–28). It is noteworthy that it is Socrates, the philosopher, who is presented as giving such precise conceptual formulation to oratorical practice, whereas the rhetorician Gorgias is apparently unconcerned with such conceptual precision and clarity (Gorgias nowhere even takes explicit notice of ceremonial oratory, though he accepts readily enough Socrates' inclusion of "what's shameful and admirable"—for Aristotle the special province of ceremonial speeches—within oratory's field of expertise).

damaging to him. Already here, though without putting the point in precisely these terms, Gorgias claims (whatever exactly he thinks this comes to) that as an orator he knows justice and injustice—so that (this easy inference is, however, only drawn later, at 459e), as a teacher of oratory, as well, he ought to teach his pupils this justice and injustice that he himself knows. Taken by itself and without worrying yet about further consequences, this is a perfectly reasonable admission for Gorgias to make, and not something we should feel that Plato has tendentiously made him say: if the orator is to persuade people about the justice or injustice of particular actions under review in a law court, he must surely be well informed in *some* special way about what counts as just and unjust, so as to draw on that knowledge in constructing his case. Socrates goes on to suggest (and Gorgias agrees) that the orator differs from arithmeticians and the other experts he has mentioned in that when an orator persuades an assembled political throng about these political matters he does not actually teach them about what is just, but only persuades and convinces people who do not thereby come to know what really *is* just and unjust. By contrast, the arithmetician persuades people by teaching his science to them.[7] But that does not in any way detract from the orator's claim to know, himself, about these matters: he can use his own knowledge of them to find the best means to persuade an ignorant throng of whatever he wishes to persuade them of relevant to the particular question at hand.[8] Socrates makes this clear when he points out (and Gorgias agrees) that in the short time available to him the orator could not well "teach such a large gathering about matters so important" (455a5–6): this clearly grants (no doubt ironically on Socrates' part, though Gorgias does not hear the irony, or share it) that the orator does possess the knowledge himself—he only lacks the time. The expert orator (Socrates assumes for the sake of the argument) possesses the knowledge himself and uses it to select what to say in his speech, aiming to persuade the throng about the justice or injustice of whatever his case commits him to. Similarly, when Gorgias claims (456b) that he is better than his brother Herodicus, the physician, at persuading a patient to submit to the physician's recommended treatment, he is claiming a knowledge of good and bad—not any knowledge of health and medicine— that will enable him to get the patient to agree that it is best for him to submit.

[7] So, similarly, Socrates is thinking at this point of the physician as using his knowledge to teach and so persuade his pupils about health and illness, by getting them to know what he knows about these matters. Later, at 456b, Gorgias reminds us that physicians also use their knowledge to persuade their clients to do what they tell them (truly) is best for their health. In this second case the physician does not teach his patients what he himself knows, but only uses it to "convince" them of the truth (to use Socrates' special terminology, 454c–d). So the parallel to oratory is even closer than Socrates recognizes here. The essential difference remains, however: the physician uses his knowledge to persuade patients to do what really is healthy, whereas the orator uses his to persuade people to do what he convinces them is just, whether it really is so or not.

[8] On how this might be, compare *Phaedrus* 273e–274a, 277b–c; and see my discussion in "Plato, Isocrates and Cicero," pp. 79–85.

IV

Socrates makes it clear that he, at least, accepts the implications I have just drawn out from Gorgias's claims about the special subject matter of the orator's special persuasions. That he thinks Gorgias has now admitted or claimed that, as an expert orator, he knows about what is just and unjust is clear from his reaction when Gorgias says (rather out of the blue) that neither he nor any expert combatants of any kind should be blamed if their pupils make an unjust use of the professional skills that have been imparted to them (456c7ff.).[9] The teachers always offer their instruction with a view to its just application; so it is not the fault of any of these arts themselves if someone who has been taught them uses them to nefarious purposes. This is plausible, and is no doubt entirely correct for physical training, the case Socrates particularly focuses upon (the same would go for medicine or expertise in financial matters, even if these are not formally expertises in combat of any kind). But immediately after hearing him out on this subject Socrates announces that, in his opinion, Gorgias has now contradicted himself: "I think you're now saying things that aren't very consistent or compatible with what you were first saying about oratory" (457e1–3). As emerges later, Socrates thinks this in part because he assumes that if someone does really *know* the just and the unjust he will have to be a just person (the knowledge alone makes him so), and so he will never do *anything* unjust. But, even so, that would not provide any ground to think that Gorgias has now said something incompatible with his earlier statements unless those earlier statements included the claim that the orator *does* know the just and the unjust. So Socrates' reaction here shows very clearly that he thinks Gorgias has already admitted or claimed that the expert orator knows about justice and injustice.[10] And as we have seen, Socrates is on

---

[9] I believe Kahn ("Drama and Dialectic," pp. 80–81), is entirely correct about what prompts Gorgias to bring in this question about who is to be blamed if someone who has been taught oratory, for example by Gorgias himself, uses it to harm another unjustly. He is an alien in Athens (and in the other cities he visits and takes pupils), and as such he is in a particularly vulnerable position vis-à-vis local authority and local popular opinion (Kahn reminds us of Protagoras' similar uneasiness, *Protagoras* 316c–d). He cannot well admit that his instruction puts into the hands of his pupils what he describes as this extremely powerful tool, the power to persuade groups gathered to make political decisions, if in doing so he (and his expertise) have no regard to whether the pupils will use it justly or not. So, he claims, he teaches his pupils with the *intention* that they shall use it justly and not unjustly: the teacher of oratory "imparts it to be used justly," ἐπὶ δικαίᾳ χρείᾳ παρέδωκεν, 457b7–c1, as trainers do too in instructing theirs in boxing and similar athletic skills (παρέδοσαν ἐπὶ τῷ δικαίως χρῆσθαι τούτοις, 456e2)—so that, if any of them happen to be "rotten eggs" this is not his fault, or the fault of the expertise itself of oratory.

[10] So Kahn is wrong to say ("Drama and Dialectic," pp. 83–84n.), lamely, that Socrates' charge here is an example of Socratic irony and functions only "proleptically"—that is to say, it awaits a later admission from Gorgias (at 460a) that he knows (and will teach any pupil about) what is just and unjust, so that Socrates now takes that admission into account by anticipation when saying (ironically, from the point of view of what has in fact been said by

very good ground in so assuming: according to Gorgias, justice and injustice together provide the special subject matter on which the orator has the expertise to persuade his audience, corresponding to the subject matters of other expertises, such as medicine or arithmetic, on which they in turn have the expertise to persuade people (in their nonoratorical ways). In all these cases, oratory included, the expertise must obviously include expertise, and so knowledge, of *some* sort about that special subject matter.

Socrates next (458e3ff.) undertakes to explain to Gorgias why he thinks Gorgias has contradicted himself in denying responsibility for any unjust use of the power to persuade political decision-making groups which he imparts to pupils by instructing them in this craft. First (in his long speech at 459c6–460a2) he confirms (459c8–e1) that Gorgias does really wish to say that the orator has to know his specific subject matters—"what is just and unjust, what is shameful and admirable, what is good and bad." He does not, indeed, have to know the subject matter of physicians and other experts even if, in a political gathering or even one-on-one in private, he can persuade people to follow his advice on some medical or other technical question: he will use his knowledge of good and bad to do this, by preparing persuasive speeches to suggest (e.g.) that some course of medical treatment is a good thing (whether it is or not)—he would not do this on the same basis a physician would use to explain that it is. But he would have to know about good and bad and just and unjust and so on. Accordingly (this is the new, and, in the context, the crucial, point, 459e1–8), the teacher of oratory must impart to his pupils that knowledge of justice and injustice etc. which he himself uses in his oratorical practice, unless the pupil should already possess it. Gorgias can hardly refuse to accept this implication of his earlier admission that the orator does have some sort of expert knowledge of justice and injustice and the other special subjects on which orators exercise their

---

Gorgias up to then) that a contradiction has already come to light. No: Socrates means exactly what he says, as a careful reading of the preceding several pages of the discussion reveals. It is true that it remains for him to get Gorgias to admit that anyone who knows justice and injustice will thereby be a just person (that is Socrates' own subsequent contribution) in order to vindicate the charge of self-contradiction, but the fundamental point needed for that Socratic idea to have any bearing at all on the issues as they have taken shape so far, has indeed been asserted by Gorgias. This is confirmed by what Socrates says later, after he has completed his refutation of Gorgias, when he recalls what was in his mind when he initially made this charge: "At the beginning of our discussion," he says, you said oratorical persuasion did not concern odd and even, but what is just and unjust, and accordingly "I took it that oratory would never be an unjust thing, since it always makes its speeches about justice. But when a little later you were saying that the orator could also use oratory unjustly I was surprised" and so made the speech in which Gorgias was charged with saying something incompatible with his first statements (460e2–461a4). Here Socrates makes it plain that he has understood Gorgias all along to have committed himself "at the beginning" to the claim that expert oratory entails specialized knowledge of what is just and unjust: that is why, given his own understanding of the consequences of any *knowledge* of those matters, he saw a contradiction. He could not even have thought he saw one, if he did not think Gorgias had asserted that expert orators know these matters.

power of persuasion. Nor, as we will see in a moment, is there any particular reason from his own point of view why he shouldn't accept it. So he says, forthrightly (460a3–4): "Well, Socrates, I suppose that if he really doesn't have this knowledge, he'll learn these things from me."

It is important to see that, so far, Gorgias has not granted anything fatal to his case. His complaisant reply indicates that that is his own understanding, and I think he is correct to think so.[11] Damage is only done in Socrates' next step (460a5–c6): "Hold it there," he begins, indicating that some new consideration needs to be introduced before he can clinch his refutation. Applying his own theory that one who knows justice must be a just person, Socrates now infers (and gets Gorgias to agree) that Gorgias's previous admissions commit him to saying that no expert orator could ever use his

---

[11] Kahn thinks that the damage is already done here, in Gorgias's admission at 460a3–4, without any reference at all to special Socratic ideas about the effects on one's moral character of the knowledge of justice. He thinks Gorgias is forced here into an insincere admission "*that he trains only good men, who will not abuse their power*" ("Drama and Dialectic" p. 82, my italics) because (see n. 8 above) of his situation as an alien in the cities where he teaches: this, according to Kahn, makes it impossible for him to resist making this claim, if pressed—he can't admit the truth, which is that he teaches a perfectly amoral art, equally usable by morally good and perfectly nefarious persons, since then he would be tarred and feathered and run out on a rail. Kahn makes two palpable errors here. First, as we've seen, all in fact Gorgias is admitting here is a simple inference from his earlier claim that the orator has some sort of expert knowledge of justice and injustice (and that is not, in his own mind, at all equivalent to saying he will make his pupils into paragons of justice). There is nothing insincere in this admission. Second, it is clear that Gorgias must not here mean to be admitting (already) that he makes all his pupils good people if they are not already such when they begin their training. That would constitute a flagrant contradiction of what he has just said three pages earlier (and wants to continue to maintain—this is what Socrates is attacking) about the full possibility that a pupil of his might very well use his skills to unjust ends—for which use, however, he denies all responsibility. There his denial of responsibility was based on the reasonable idea that his teaching was imparted with a view to a just use of it, so that if some pupil did make an unjust use, it was the pupil, not Gorgias, who should be blamed; Gorgias evidently did not think that statement would get him run out on a rail; so there is no reason at all to suppose that now, three pages later, he should think that in order to avoid that misfortune he has to shift his ground and say that he actually teaches only good people, or at any rate makes them become good people in the process of teaching them oratory. Kahn makes much of the fact that in posing his question whether Gorgias teaches about justice and goodness Socrates insinuates the thought that if someone is not taught to know justice but only to seem (to his audience) to know it he will thereby be made only to seem good, without actually being good (459e6). But that only expresses, by anticipation, Socrates' own view, for which he is going to argue beginning in his next speech but one. Insinuated, as it is, as an added consequence to the main one (of the pupil's not knowing but only seeming to the audience to know about justice), it does not have to express what Gorgias recoils from, when he answers that his instruction *will* prevent situations in which the pupil does not "know justice." And, as I've explained, Gorgias cannot be recoiling here from Socrates' insinuation that perhaps his teaching only makes his pupils *seem* to their audiences to be good people, without undermining his whole position—the position he is trying to defend—about not being responsible for the misuse of his instruction. You don't defend your innocence for unjust misuse of your teaching by denying that such misuse is even possible: that is a different defense of your instruction, making much stronger claims for it.

oratorical skill unjustly. The result is that Gorgias's efforts to shield himself from blame for any pupil's immoral misuse of his teaching necessarily fail: on his own accounting, given this Socratic view about the moral effects of knowledge about justice, his responsibility as a teacher includes the responsibility to make his pupils just and fully upright people who could never do anything unjust. So if any of them use what they have learned from him unjustly, he has failed as a teacher; he *is* after all responsible for any immoral misuses of his instruction.[12]

We need to look closely at the argument Socrates uses to obtain Gorgias's agreement, or acquiescence, in this second step of his refutation. But first we should ask ourselves, What can Gorgias have been assuming, right along, was included in his own professional orator's knowledge of justice and injustice? I have suggested that he had no idea that this knowledge could entail that any expert orator would have to be a fully just and morally good person, which was why he could hold that it might be misused, to unjust ends, and why he was so complaisant in accepting Socrates' suggestion that he would pass it on to any pupil, if that were needed, as part of his instruction in oratory. No doubt he has no developed and considered view on this question; still, he must have had *something* in mind when he recognized that expert orators have expertise about justice and injustice as arithmeticians do about odd and even. What might this be?

Later, once he has disposed of Gorgias, Socrates explains his own view of what expert oratory can accomplish, given, as the discussants agree by that point, that it does not actually *know* about justice etc. He says that oratory works its persuasions by "flattering" the members of its audiences, pleasing them with what it says rather than doing them any true good: to do them good would be to get them to believe the truth about what is just

---

[12] As Alexander Nehamas has reminded me, we might note the contrast here with Socrates himself in the *Apology*. Socrates, too, denies all responsibility for the behavior of any of his associates, as Gorgias tried to do: "I cannot justly be held responsible for the good or bad conduct of any of these people, as I never promised to teach them anything and have not done so" (33b3–6)—earlier in the *Apology* (at 19d–20c) Socrates made a point of mentioning others, Sophists, who offered to teach "virtue" to young men for a fee; he explicitly denied that he was one of them. The crucial differences are two: Gorgias *did* promise to teach his pupils about what is just and unjust, and (given this argument of Socrates') anyone properly taught that must become a just person. The effect of Socrates' moves against Gorgias, as commentators often note, is to classify him as a teacher of virtue, as other Sophists claimed to be—despite Meno's declaration in *Meno* 95c that Gorgias made a point of not claiming to teach "virtue" and ridiculed the others who did make that profession. Note that in the *Gorgias* Gorgias does not himself *claim* to teach virtue (so there is no contradiction in this respect between the *Meno* and the *Gorgias*). Rather, he is forced—tendentiously—by Socrates' argument to admit that that must be what he does, given that, to the extent a pupil does not already know it, he teaches what is just and unjust. All Gorgias *claims* is to teach what is just and unjust. As I argue below, that can coherently be understood as not implying that he makes anyone a just person, and that is how Gorgias understands it. Dodds, in *Plato: Gorgias,* pp. 216–17, and the previous commentators discussed there err in supposing that Plato represents Gorgias here as actually making that much stronger claim.

and unjust, good and bad, since that would improve their souls.[13] But *how*
it pleases them Socrates does not clearly say. However, part of what he
must have in mind is clear enough: When an orator speaks before a jury,
his objective is to get them to vote for or against the justice or injustice of
some charge. As Socrates is thinking of the matter, then, the orator has to
get the jury to be *pleased* with the idea, one way or the other, depending
on the orator's particular brief, that the charge was just or was unjust: being
pleased with the one idea or the other, they vote accordingly. So what
the expert orator "knows" about justice and injustice is really only the
"knowledge" of whatever he must say about these matters to accomplish
this desired effect: how must he describe events, what spin must he put on
them, if he is to get his audience to be pleased to think of the person involved
as innocent or guilty of this or that sort of charge? (The quotes round *know*
are needed, Socrates thinks, since according to him expert oratory knows
even this much only by "routine and knack," merely preserving "the memory
of what customarily happens"; it "supplies its pleasures" by means of that
memory.[14] It has no sort of theoretical basis for deciding what is the right
and best thing actually to say on the given topic.)

V

Now Socrates' own account of rhetoric will be all the stronger if in posing
it he has succeeded in incorporating, while giving his own denigratory twist
to, the view of oratory that Gorgias has himself been working with in the
earlier part of the conversation. Indeed, if we disregard the denigratory ideas
of "flattery" (giving pleasure rather than doing any good), discovering what
it will please people to think rather than giving them good and persuasive
reasons, and having a mere "knack" rather than true expert knowledge of
anything, Socrates' account of the orator's knowledge is really quite plausible, and one that assigns arguably quite a reputable position in the life of
the city to its best orators. In fact, as one reads Gorgias's various claims
for rhetoric, one does not have to peek ahead to see what Socrates is going
to say, in order to find, lying behind his own account, this view: The expert
orator knows how to characterize persons, events, and things so that a mass
of his fellow citizens gathered to consider some political question will see
them as just or unjust, admirable or shameful, good or bad, as the case may
be, and so can reach a generally agreed decision on the matter before them.
Thus he knows and presents solid, if not necessarily conclusive reasons (or
even, perhaps, ultimately sound ones) for believing the conclusion for which
he argues.[15] This requires both a refined understanding of the grounds that

---

[13] See 462c, 463a–c, 464b–465e.

[14] 501a7–b1.

[15] On this view, though Plato does not have Gorgias pursue this line, one might argue that
expert oratory need not be immoral at all: it allows for the possibility of an "honest lawyer"

are generally taken to count in favor of one or another of these outcomes, and the oratorical ability to present those in an especially favorable light. Naturally, anyone brought up in the city should have some understanding of these general grounds—which is why Gorgias says he will teach them to a pupil only if the pupil needs this instruction—but in any event Gorgias will have to sharpen the pupil's understanding of them and teach the pupil how to formulate and present them in the most effective way. On both scores Gorgias could well think that the orator can possess a real expertise: and in particular the knowledge of the grounds that support the judgment in a particular case of "just" or "unjust," and so on, seems very plausibly taken to constitute some real expertise about justice and injustice, and the other matters upon which an orator is called to speak.[16] It is certainly the case that, armed with this expertise, an orator can "rule over" his fellow citizens even in unjust and harmful ways, but even so (as Gorgias claims initially, at 452d5–7) he contributes not a little to their capacity to rule themselves as a free people, in accordance with their considered judgments of what is just and best, without falling into inarticulate quarreling and the exercise of brute force against one another. Only with an expert orator's help and guidance can large numbers of people gathered together be mutually *persuaded* about the correctness of one outcome and so conduct their common affairs on the basis of "rational" agreement, not force majeure.

I suggest, then, that the discussion between Socrates and Gorgias as a whole, including Socrates' presentation to Polus of his own conception of what expert oratory actually does accomplish, indicates to the philosophically

---

who will refuse to take a case that he is not personally convinced is a just one. Socrates could insist, nonetheless, that expert oratory does not involve any true knowledge of justice and injustice and, in particular, that it never involves teaching a jury about justice.

[16] One might ask at this point whether Gorgias thinks that the justice or injustice of some action simply consists in whatever the relevant groups of people would decide, after consideration and under the guidance of expert orators, or whether he holds to some such debunking, sociological account of the nature of justice as one can find in Thrasymachus's outburst in *Republic* I, 338c ff. On the latter account, his idea that expert orators know what is just and teach it to any pupils who do not already know it, would amount to their knowing (in the spirit of the sociologist) how other people use the words *just* and *unjust,* what they apply it to and on what grounds, while adopting an attitude of scepticism or worse about the rational and practical bindingness on anyone of what justice demands. On this latter account, it would be especially obvious why Gorgias can think that someone who knows justice would not be motivated by that knowledge always (or even ever) to do what is just, simply because it is just—but the same holds for the other, more accommodating, view as well. Gorgias's insistence that he instructs with the intention that his teachings be used justly might seem to indicate that he is no supporter of Thrasymachean immoralism (or Calliclean immoralism, either)— so that the former view would fit better with Plato's picture of him as a decent, upstanding man. But Gorgias is no philosopher, and there is no reason at all, from the evidence provided by Plato's text, to hold that he has thought things through sufficiently even to reach these difficult questions, much less to decide one way or the other what position he wants to take on them. In these respects the views of the Gorgias of the *Gorgias* must be regarded as undetermined. His claim to have expert knowledge of justice can stand without our or his having to go into these questions.

alert reader that the foregoing is what Gorgias understands (however inarticulately and implicitly) by that "knowledge of what is just and what is unjust" which he attributes to the expert orator. In that case it is easy to see why he did not expect Socrates' inference that anyone with the knowledge of justice and injustice must be a just person, and why he certainly did not think he was committed already to the conclusion that every expert orator (anyhow, any trained by him) must be a just person. Likewise, I think, the reader should be surprised at such a suggestion, when Socrates makes it (he has already pointed in that direction, at 459e6, if not previously at 457e1–3): any careful, open-minded reader will see right away that the sort of knowledge Gorgias has in mind (assuming for now that it does deserve the name of an "expertise"—as yet, the dispute is not over that name) has nothing at all to do with any particular moral character. Moral motivation is one thing, *this* sort of knowledge is quite another. Later on, as we have seen, Socrates will claim, with a fine and quite persuasive display of his own rhetorical powers,[17] that any such "knowledge" not only does not deserve the name of an expertise, but more tellingly, it must be something trivial and disreputable—merely the ability to "flatter" a crowd by pandering to its pleasures. It is therefore nothing like the "most admirable of the crafts" that Polus initially claimed it to be (448c9), or the one that addresses the "greatest of human concerns" and produces the "greatest good for humankind" as Gorgias had added (451d7, 452d3-6). But for now, he only gives us a snappy "proof" that *any* craft that knows what is just and unjust must make its possessor a just person.

Socrates' argument (460b1-c6) turns on a verbally impressive induction—more impressive in its Greek formulation than anything modern English easily allows as a translation. In other cases—carpentry, music, and medicine—anyone who has learned those subjects (carpenter's things, musical things, and medical things—*ta tektonika* etc.) becomes thereby the corresponding kind of person, a carpenter-person (*tektonikos*), or a musical or medical person. So that is how it is in general when anyone learns a subject. So, similarly, when anyone learns "just things" (*ta dikaia*), they become a just person (*dikaios*). And, of course, a just person is one who does just things. Since Gorgias has declared that it is part of an orator's expertise to know just things, it follows that an expert orator must be a just person, who acts justly and not unjustly. It is important to notice that Socrates does not leave his argument at that but makes explicit the connection between being just and being motivated to act justly: in formulating the grand conclusion to which he has been leading he states explicitly (460c1-3) that "a just man necessarily wants (*boulesthai*) to do just things. . . . Therefore an orator

---

[17] Note that at 465e1–6 Socrates is made to draw attention to the fact that he has just spun out a long speech about the true crafts and their imitators that aim not at any good for their clients but only at pleasing them instead. He was doing what he had forbidden Polus to do (448d), but claims as excuse that when he tried to state his view in consecutive short answers to questions Polus had not understood what he meant.

will never want to do what is unjust." That is to say, Socrates does not say merely that a trained orator will never *act* unjustly in using his oratorical knowledge—this is the formal contradictory of what Gorgias had implied could happen, when he said that not the teacher or the art was to blame, but the person himself who misused it in acting unjustly. Socrates goes beyond this to point out the reason why anyone who knows just things and so has become a just person never will do anything unjust: justice involves not even wanting to do anything unjust, but always wanting to do justice.[18] By this means Plato draws special attention to the point that distinguishes being a just person from being a "carpenter person" or a musical one, namely, that the latter are not, at least not merely by means of their knowledge, motivated to use it in any particular way, whereas the just person (if justice is simply a matter of knowledge) *is* motivated in quite particular ways by possessing that knowledge. And it is a short step from there to seeing the invalidity or dubiousness of the induction itself. If knowledge of justice is like knowledge of music, all it can be legitimate to infer about the former is that possessing it puts one in a position either to do justice or to do injustice (expertly, in either case), depending upon how one is in fact motivated.

VI

It is, at long last, at this point in his discussion with Gorgias that we see Socrates committing himself to the "Socratic" moral psychology. Here (leaving aside for a moment the rather extraordinary grounds he advances for saying so) he insists that anyone who knows "just" things consistently wishes or wants (*boulesthai*) to do just actions and wishes to do no unjust ones, and in consequence always acts in those ways. Socrates is assuming that knowing "x" things implies in this case wishing or wanting (*boulesthai*) to act "x"ly, and he thinks that either no other sorts of desires exist besides these "wishes" or at any rate that one's "wishes" must always dominate any other, divergent desires one might experience. In other dialogues, when Socrates adopts similar views, we are shown something of why he holds them and are put in a position to appreciate philosophical considerations that might make them seem seriously tempting. As the contexts there make clear, Socrates thinks that more than anything else everyone wants to live well, to get what is good in life, and he believes that acting justly (and

[18] Nowhere in Gorgias and Socrates' earlier discussion of the possible unjust misuse of oratorical skill was there reference to anyone's "wanting" to act unjustly or justly; throughout, the language was simply of "doing" injustice. So when Socrates shifts here in drawing the conclusion and applying his induction to talk of what the just person as such does and does not "want," he is not simply (pro forma, as it were) picking up on something that Gorgias or Socrates himself had already introduced in stating the position that Socrates then has to refute: this is something genuinely new in the context. See 456c7–457c3, 459c8–460a2.

otherwise virtuously) is in fact an indispensable means toward this thing that everyone most wants. Accordingly, anyone who did know just things would know this fact about just action, and therefore, given this universal human want, would always want to act justly and never unjustly, and want that more than anything else.[19] Later on in the *Gorgias,* as well, Socrates turns to these issues about human desires (beginning at 466b, in his discussion with Polus, and continuing through to the end of the dialogue). But in the very brisk argument here, we find nothing at all of this kind.

What we get instead is the very abstract—purely formal—consideration, developed inductively from three examples, that anyone who knows "x" things is made by that knowledge an "x" person: a medical person, if it is medical things she knows, and so on. That principle, applied to the case of just things, yields the result Socrates needs in order to show that Gorgias has contradicted himself: that the well-trained orator always acts justly. When he adds, drawing out what is involved in being a just person, that the just person won't want ever to do anything other than just acts (with the implication that it is his knowledge of just things that provides this motivational commitment), Socrates brings in his own moral psychology, familiar from those other dialogues, but he does so entirely without any of the philosophical considerations that make it respectable. We are left with a strained analogy between knowledge of justice and knowledge of medicine, carpentry and music, decked out with an ornament of what looks, in the context, simply like an unsupported Socratic dogma about moral knowledge and moral motivation. Certainly nothing here resembles an argument for these Socratic views, nor can one see anything that could even suggest one to the reader and to Gorgias.[20] The absence of even a hint of any such

[19] See *Meno* 77b–79b, 87e–89a; *Protagoras* 356c–357e, 359c–360d; *Euthydemus* 279c–282b; *Charmides* 171d–174d.

[20] Thus I agree with Irwin, *Gorgias,* pp. 126–27, and others, that Socrates' argument here appeals to considerations he has given Gorgias no reason at all to accept. I disagree with Irwin, however, that Plato has shown us features of Gorgias's situation as a teacher and orator that would make it difficult for him not to agree with Socrates that knowing what is just entails being just yourself (see further, n. 27 below). I also disagree with Penner, "Belief-Relative Sciences," pp. 323–24, who offers a different analysis leading to the conclusion that special considerations of his own inevitably commit Gorgias to this Socratic view. Penner says we may assume either that Gorgias holds that "justice, like virtue in general, is an art of getting on in life" or else that he thinks of "virtue as the art of getting on in public life," and that either way, if one really knew what justice so construed was, one would have no motive to act contrary to justice. Gorgias certainly holds that the orator's knowledge and skill, and in particular his knowledge of what is just and what unjust, guarantees getting on well in public life, and so also in life itself. But he holds that because he regards this knowledge as sufficient to enable its possessor to get anything he wants. An orator who wants something unjust— and it is a central contention of Gorgias's that this is perfectly possible for someone having the knowledge—will get it, using his orator's knowledge (even if that knowledge is imparted for a just use). No doubt Gorgias is assuming that getting whatever you want is good for you, and perhaps he would agree with Socrates that no one with a truly useful knowledge would or could ever be motivated not to use it to obtain its benefits—but the text gives us no reason at all to suppose this. Maybe Gorgias just makes the normal assumption that people can be

explication has been felt acutely by commentators and readers of this dialogue.

Faced with this argument of Socrates, Gorgias seems nonplussed. He accepts without comment Socrates' neat analogy between the one who knows medical things (who is thereby a medical person) and the one who knows just things (who must then be a just person). He enters no objection to Socrates' added remarks about the motivational consequences of the knowledge of just things, despite the clear implications to the contrary of what were apparently his own earlier ideas about the orator's knowledge of justice. With this argument, Socrates has injected issues into the discussion that are too much for Gorgias to comprehend on the spot, or to see clearly how he ought to address them. As indeed Socrates himself says in closing the discussion with Gorgias (461a7-b2). "It will take more than a short session to go through an adequate examination of how these matters stand!" This is an indication to his readers, from Plato the author, to be added to those I have already mentioned, that important questions remain to be considered. What can this knowledge of just things be that Socrates makes an essential condition, or even the very basis, of a just moral character? Can any such knowledge be so neatly assimilated, in Socrates' way, to medical knowledge and the knowledge of carpentry, or of music? With Socrates' help, Gorgias's own conception of the orator's knowledge of just things has also assimilated it to the knowledge of such experts, but without the idea—presumably in either case—that the knowledge has the implications Socrates has drawn for action and motivation.[21] What view ought one

---

expected to act always as they think would be best, without endorsing any heavy Socratic psychological theory to establish that this is universally true. In any event, he does not think that acting justly must always be best, and he does not think that the knowledge of justice that he imparts and possesses itself dictates just action always. So even if for him such a "virtue" as the orator's knowledge always guarantees the best (self-regarding) actions by its possessor, it certainly does not guarantee conventionally virtuous actions always. Penner arbitrarily and wrongly assumes that, according to Gorgias, it does guarantee this.

Irwin and Penner, like other commentators, are far too quick to invent reasons why Gorgias might have agreed, or promptly have seen that he would have to agree, with Socrates' motivational assumptions about the knowledge of justice. They fail to pay sufficient attention to the actual argument Socrates offers in order to lead Gorgias to admit that anyone who knows what is just and unjust will be a just person, and to the fact that this argument, unlike other ones in other dialogues for related conclusions, does not allude in its premises to anything about motivation. Something about motivation appears in the conclusion simply because being just—allegedly brought about, according to the argument, through knowledge of justice—does itself have motivational implications. In *this* argument Socrates does not rely—openly, at any rate—on special motivational assumptions we could then ask whether Gorgias would or would not endorse.

[21] In the *Statesman* (259a–b), Plato makes the Visitor from Elea insist that a physician or a statesman is simply someone who knows what ought to be done, according to the principles of the science, in any given case—whether or not he is ever in the position to perform any of those functions. For the Visitor the knowledge alone entitles someone to the name "physician" or "expert statesman," and regularly recurring motivations and actions in furtherance of the goals of those expertises are left aside as nonessential.

to take of the just person's knowledge, and how should it be distinguished from other possible ways of knowing "just things"? How should we understand such a knowledge if it *is* to have the motivational implications Socrates attributes to it? These questions Plato pursues in the *Republic,* on the basis of a new psychology of moral action different from the Socratic one. Here he draws them to our attention, thereby expressing doubts or reservations about standard Socratic ideas on moral knowledge and its motivational power, but he does no more than that. These questions are further explored later in the *Gorgias* itself, in his debate with Callicles.

VII

Before leaving Socrates' discussion with Gorgias, however, one further textual point is worth noting. This gives a further indication that, far from encouraging simple acceptance of Socrates' arguments as decisive, the dialogue itself is prodding the reader to think that these issues need to be worked through first before Socrates' conclusions can be confirmed (or not). Polus reacts to the outcome of this discussion with a spluttering and indignant charge that Gorgias has fallen into a Socratic trap simply by giving in to feelings of shame,[22] strong enough to push him to concede the claim that the orator knows "what's just, what's admirable, and what's good" and to concede that if any prospective pupil came to him not knowing these things he would teach them: for "who do you think would deny that he himself knows what is just and would teach others?"[23] According to Polus, it was "from this admission" that "some inconsistency crept into his state-

---

[22] 461b3–c4: "spluttering and indignant" is Shorey's characterization of this speech, *What Plato Said,* p. 137, taking note of the grammatical irregularities in his outburst. (I owe the reference to Dodds, *Plato: Gorgias,* ad loc.)

[23] This remark casts grave suspicion on Kahn's analysis of Socrates' refutation of Gorgias. According to Kahn, not only is Polus right that shame led Gorgias to make these damaging concessions (Polus' remarks are "Plato's own signal . . . as to how this first refutation is to be understood," "Drama and Dialectic," p. 79); but it was shame that Gorgias was especially or uniquely subject to as a celebrated itinerant teacher of the elite young men of the cities he visited, someone particularly in the public eye and so vulnerable to the effects of adverse public opinion—other men, such as Polus himself, as someone not *famous* for his teaching of oratory, would be under no similar pressure of shame to concede any such thing. However, here Polus plausibly says that pretty much anyone would be ashamed to deny such a thing (see *Protagoras* 323a–c for a related statement about everyone): even Polus himself will feel the shame, but he is bold enough to say what Gorgias was not bold enough to say, namely that he does *not* teach his pupils what is just, indeed he is indifferent to that himself (on the assumption, of course, which he swallows whole from Socrates, that to know what is just is to *be* just). So on Polus's analysis, which Kahn says Plato signals is the correct one, the shame Gorgias has succumbed to has *nothing to do* with his special status as a celebrated itinerant teacher, therefore subject, as other people are not, to the intense pressure of public opinion. Kahn cannot have it both ways. Either Polus is correct on this point and Kahn's own analysis is wrong or else, if Kahn's analysis is accepted, Polus must be wrong. And if Polus is wrong about the source of Gorgias's shame, why think he is correct at all that shame led to the

ments." There are two separable components of Polus' analysis: first, that shame led Gorgias to concede something he need not and should not have conceded; and second, that the place where the "inconsistency crept in" was Gorgias's concession (at 460a) that orators know "what's just" and teach it to any of their pupils who don't already know it. It should be clear from what I have already said that I believe Polus is wrong on both counts. Moreover, a great deal in the text points to the conclusion that the author intends the alert reader to see this.

First, as to the question of Gorgias's alleged shame: One thing is very clear, that *Socrates* cannot think that Gorgias made this admission out of any feeling of shame (at any rate, out of any shame at admitting that he does not wish to make people just and good so far as he has any power or opportunity to do so). As we have seen, Socrates heard already at 457c what he took to be the contradiction in Gorgias's statements that he exposes later in 460a-e. That is, he already knew that Gorgias had said or implied that as part of their expertise orators know what is just and is unjust (so that he would have to grant, when asked, that as a teacher of oratory he would see to it that a pupil learned that); and he already saw that on his, Socrates' own, views about what knowing such a thing implied about the person who knew it, no expertly instructed orator could possibly use his oratorical skill to commit any injustice. Thus, so far as the *first* point goes— the one that Polus identifies as the concession Gorgias made out of shame— Socrates cannot think that Gorgias became committed to that out of shame. Rather (as Socrates knows very well) he became committed when he said, perfectly plausibly from his own point of view—indeed one would think almost necessarily[24]—that the topic of what's just and what's unjust is the special province of the orator, to speak about as an expert—parallel in *this* respect to the physician's knowing and speaking expertly about health.

When, at 460a, Socrates obtains from Gorgias the specific admission that he needs—not merely that expert orators know about this matter, but that those who teach the subject also teach it to their pupils—there is undoubtedly the appearance that Gorgias is conceding this out of the precise shame Polus points to. This appearance misled Polus himself, and it has led so many gullible readers of the dialogue to think Plato is signaling to his readers through Polus that Gorgias granted this point merely because he was ashamed to say openly that he would not teach justice if he had the opportunity. As I mentioned

---

concession? Why would Plato "signal" that he was correct, but then introduce something into his account of the shame about which he was crucially wrong?

[24] Polus of course misses this completely: *he* thinks that there is *no* sense or way in which expertise at oratory involves knowing about what is just and unjust, because he did not follow, or quickly lost sight of the point of, these early stages of the dialectic. He just swallows undigested Socrates' idea that anything entitled to the name "knowledge of what is just and unjust" would make anyone possessing it a just person. The result is that on his account there really is nothing about the substance or content of a speech, as opposed to the mere form or verbal dressing, that expertise in oratory enables an orator to control.

earlier, in reaching the peroration of his question to Gorgias, Socrates slips in an anticipatory reference to his own idea that someone who knows what is good will be a good person and so act in the expected way on this knowledge: in case a prospective pupil does not know what is just or admirable or good, he asks, "Will you, the oratory teacher, not teach him any of these things, when he comes to you—for that's not your job—and will you make him seem among most people to have knowledge of such things when in fact he doesn't have it, *and to seem good when in fact he isn't?*"[25] Given that subtle intrusion, it is not surprising that some readers or hearers might suppose that Gorgias was driven to concede that he would teach the pupil these things simply because of the threat here contained that if he did not say this he would shame himself by displaying an insane indifference to or cynicism about moral values. But in reality he would do no such thing, as Socrates himself as well as anyone who was carefully attending to the rest of the discussion would know, since that threat would be realized only if some further argument, not as yet so much as adumbrated, should reveal that the teaching or not of what is just etc. has anything directly to do with the furtherance or not of moral values. On Gorgias's view, as we have seen, it does not; only Socrates believes that it does.

That Gorgias sees things this way is shown, as I remarked above, by his complaisant, unruffled response: "Well, Socrates, I suppose that if he really doesn't have this knowledge, he'll learn these things from me as well." Earlier, as Gorgias knows, he has indicated that knowing about what is just etc. is part of the expertise of oratory; now he readily grants what follows from that, that he would teach these same things to any pupil of oratory who needed to learn them. That this is all he is granting is shown by his rather self-satisfied, as well as agreeable, manner: if instead Socrates' peroration had suddenly shocked him awake with a serious threat to his reputation, and he were merely fending off that threat out of shame, one would expect that to be evident in his manner of responding.[26] So on three grounds we can see that Polus is wrong about what led Gorgias to "concede" that the orator knows what is just and will teach it to his pupils: the logic of Gorgias's position about expert oratory as previously outlined demands

[25] My italics.

[26] It is worth pointing out that when Polus's time comes to make a damaging admission, leading to his downfall in the debate with Socrates, he makes it in a terse, minimal affirmation (474c8: Socrates asks him which he thinks is more shameful, doing what is unjust or suffering it; he replies "Doing it."). To be sure, that does not actually indicate embarrassment at all, but it is easily compatible with it, so that nothing in the text there (or anywhere) conflicts with Callicles' very plausible claim (482c–d) that Polus has fallen victim to the very thing that he said Gorgias had fallen victim to: the refusal, from a sense of shame, to admit openly to what he really believes. Plato's evident irony in writing this later passage is only the sharper if, as I have argued, Polus was actually *wrong* to find shame motivating Gorgias's response: he is hoist on a petard entirely of his own making—as if, by guilty anticipation, he is led by his own vulnerability to shame to find the same thing already, and culpably, present in Gorgias—where it was not actually found at all.

that he grant this; he does so in a rather elaborate, complacent as well as complaisant statement very unlike what any embarrassed person would use; and Socrates' own remarks clearly show the alert reader that he thinks, and that in fact, Gorgias is committed to this concession from the outset.[27]

What, then, about Polus's claim that the damaging admission was the concession that expert oratory includes knowing, and teaching, what is just? One could, of course, understand Polus's reference to "this admission" loosely enough to include admitting also everything that Socrates draws out from it in his subsequent analogical induction from other cases of knowing things, e.g., medical matters: it amounts to admitting that the qualified teacher of oratory teaches his pupils to be just persons, who never do anything unjust. In that sense it is perfectly true, as Polus says, that "from this admission maybe some inconsistency crept into [Gorgias's] statements." However, on the careful reading (and hearing) of the discussion between Socrates and Gorgias I have been developing, one will have to be unhappy with any such characterization of what Gorgias admitted in admitting that the orator knows and teaches to his pupils what is just. In fact, what

---

[27] As Irwin correctly points out, "Coercion and Objectivity," p. 71n. 30, Kahn is mistaken to say ("Drama and Dialectic," p. 79) that later on, at 508c1–3, Socrates "confirms" Polus's own attribution of Gorgias's downfall to shame. All Socrates confirms there is that this was *Polus's* diagnosis. Socrates' careful distancing of himself from that diagnosis is a further textual indication that the reader should not necessarily accept it. At 494c–d, when he is pressing Callicles to admit, what Callicles' own views imply, that someone who scratches away his life at whatever part of his body will live happily. Socrates admonishes Callicles not to hold back out of shame. He acquiesces when Callicles accuses him, for the second time, of just "playing the crowd" in appealing in this way to aspects of his opponents' views that most people will find shameful and thereby seeking to embarrass them; the first time (482c5), Callicles accused him of refuting Polus by shaming him into agreeing to something damaging to his position, as Polus had claimed he had previously refuted Gorgias. Yes, Socrates says (494d1–2), he's playing the crowd again, just as he did before, when he shocked Polus and Gorgias and made them ashamed (as Callicles has said)—but, after all, Callicles has promised to say with all frankness exactly what he thinks, so *he* won't hold back out of shame. This ironical and tactical remark shows neither one way or the other whether Socrates really accepted Callicles' diagnosis of his earlier effectiveness: Socrates really does think that Callicles' views have shameful consequences, and he is quite willing to admit that he is now (and earlier) "playing the crowd" and shaming his opponents if that is how Callicles chooses to describe what he is doing. Earlier, at 487a, in a long speech full of irony, Socrates has praised Callicles for having all three of the essential characteristics of the respondent needed to test properly one's own ideas in discussion—including, in particular, frankness (*parrhēsia*, saying anything one pleases however shocking), which, he says, Gorgias and Polus both lacked: they fell into self-contradiction because they were too ashamed and not bold enough to say openly what Callicles has just been saying himself, that clever people, expert at oratory, have a natural right to dominate everyone else and to use their skills to get a greater share than others of anything they want. In saying this Socrates assumes that both Gorgias and Polus also believe this sort of thing, and he implies that they came to grief because they were too ashamed and inhibited—not frank enough—to say it. But he indicates no particular statement each made out of fear of embarrassment; so he is not agreeing here with Polus's diagnosis of exactly how Gorgias was defeated, or for that matter with Callicles about Polus's downfall. Thus *nowhere* does Socrates "confirm" Polus's diagnosis of where and why Gorgias made his damaging admission.

led to the actual inconsistency—i.e., what led Gorgias to contradict the presupposition of his earlier denial of responsibility for his pupils' unjust uses of their oratorical skill, namely the assumption that someone with that skill *could* use it to commit an unjust act—is nothing in that admission itself. As we have seen, the inconsistency only results from Socrates' further argument that anyone who knows a subject must be "the sort of person the knowledge makes him," viz., in the case of the knowledge of what is just, he must be a just person.[28] Now I think it is worthwhile to insist on this. We have already seen plenty of evidence that Polus has not correctly understood the dialectic in the earlier stages of Socrates' discussion with Gorgias. This fact gives us, as readers, plenty of reason to be wary of attributing to Polus here a correct understanding of the subtleties of philosophical argument (and Socrates already emphasized at the very beginning of the dialogue that Polus is adept at spinning out speeches, but not good at question-and-answer dialectic).[29] Furthermore, as I have mentioned already, Polus is spluttering with indignation at Socrates' apparent success in refuting Gorgias when he renders this diagnosis—a sign that he may not be thinking clearly anyhow. If when we come to this statement we exercise the wariness that these hints seem to encourage, then we immediately see that by this indirection—by having the incompetent Polus tell us that X is the cause of Gorgias's downfall, when in fact it was Y—the author is forcefully drawing our attention to Y as the culpable factor. By having our attention focused in this way on Y—on Socrates' inductive argument, and his added comments on the motivational power of knowledge—we are led back to the defects that we already saw clearly signaled by the way Plato constructs Socrates' exposition of that argument, and by the adverse comparisons between it and other arguments in other dialogues for similar conclusions. And that reinforces what we have already found credible, that the outcome, for the reader, of Socrates' discussion with Gorgias is not at all a recommendation to focus on Socrates' arguments in order to discover their truth, but instead a recommendation to question deeply their presuppositions. The author is encouraging us to discover for ourselves, if we can, a better account of the moral knowledge that Socrates seems to work with, and a better account of how such knowledge necessarily motivates fine actions than Socrates seems to envision.

So it is not true, as so many have thought, that Plato is signaling us through Polus's diagnosis of Gorgias's downfall that Gorgias has in fact been shamed into admitting that as part of the expertise of oratory the orator knows what is just and will teach it to his pupils—where the shame is everyone's shame at appearing indifferent to or cynical about moral values. Indeed, exactly the opposite is true. By putting this diagnosis in Polus's mouth, Plato is showing the careful reader that this is the *wrong* diagnosis,

---

[28] Irwin correctly saw this, *Plato: Gorgias,* p. 128.
[29] 448d1–2, 8–10.

on both of the two principal counts I have distinguished. In seeing this, readers are being directed to see clearly for themselves Gorgias's true motivation in making this admission, and to think hard about what the "knowledge" of the just might actually be, and about how that might involve the sort of close tie to moral character and moral motivation for which Socrates has in fact unsuccessfully argued.[30]

VIII

Let us turn now to Socrates' debate with Callicles. By the time Callicles takes over as interlocutor (481b), the question being debated has become, Is it better from an individual's own point of view to suffer injustice than to do it, or worse? Callicles' thesis is that it is worse; Socrates fervently

---

[30] Throughout the foregoing my concern has been to determine, given the course of the discussion between Socrates and Gorgias (together with Polus's intervention at the end), what the dialogue as Plato has written it indicates to the careful reader about the philosophical issues that these speakers are contesting. Irwin, in *Plato's Ethics,* pp. 98–99, argues that Socrates' refutation of Gorgias may have more merit than, pursuing this objective, I have allowed that Plato sees in it. Irwin does not clearly address the question whether Plato, and the dialogue as he has written it, endorses this judgment of his own; he seems to base his analysis and defense of Socrates' argument simply on his own reflections on the text—what Gorgias might have replied, what the counterreplies from Socrates' side might have been, the philosophical merits of these replies, and what final outcome this extended debate ought, on these merits, to have had. However, he does conclude with the remark that we can see from his analysis that "Plato shows why the Socratic view [that possessing the knowledge of what is just entails being just] is more difficult to reject than we might at first have thought." Whatever the merits of Irwin's argument, taken on its own terms, I strongly dispute the suggestion that it represents anything we can find in Plato's own text. Irwin thinks it is a crucial claim of Gorgias that his expertise is useful to people because it helps them to get things that are good for them; he bases this on Gorgias's reference (456b) to his own skill in getting the patients of his brother, the physician, to submit to his care. He then argues that if Gorgias (disputing the "Socratic view") denies that his orator's knowledge of what is just entails that he himself is a just person, then he undermines this claim for oratory's usefulness: in that case, his audiences will be given good reason not to trust the advice he gives in his speeches, and so he cannot claim that his expertise has any "useful product"—no one will do what he advises. In fact, however, even a cursory reading of the text shows that Gorgias does not introduce the story about his brother to illustrate the usefulness of oratory, but instead its *power.* Indeed, he nowhere makes any blanket claim for oratory's usefulness to a community because it obtains what is good for them (but see my text above on how it protects the community's freedom). Furthermore, part of his claim for expert oratory's power is that it can persuade *any* political group of people to lend their votes and support to the orator's cause: so if some bunch of people in fact suspected an orator of being unjust and not seeking their good in his speech, this would make no difference to the outcome, according to what Gorgias claims for the orator's power; their distrust would not, on Gorgias's claims at any rate, lead to any diminution of oratory's effectiveness (its "product"), as Gorgias has explained that. Read carefully, then, the text lends no support at all to the idea that Gorgias will undermine his own position if he does not agree to the "Socratic view" that knowledge of justice implies a just character. So maybe *Irwin* has shown us that the "Socratic view" is more difficult to reject than we might have thought, but the text provides no evidence that Plato has done this.

holds the opposed opinion. He undertakes by questioning Callicles to get him to admit that, despite his professed immoralism, some of his own deep convictions imply the truth of Socrates' view. He does not succeed. Gorgias and Polus earlier, and Protagoras at the end of his dialogue—not to mention Euthyphro, Crito, Alcibiades, Charmides and Critias, Laches and Nicias, Lysis and Menexenus, and Hippias in their dialogues—all admit, however reluctantly and however without really believing them, that they have been argued validly into admissions that conflict logically with what they had begun by wishing to maintain. Uniquely, Callicles does not admit that Socrates has validly deduced any such conclusion from any propositions that he has seriously committed himself to[31]—and, as we shall see, there seems no reason to think Plato is presenting him as having in fact been logically forced to admit this, but refusing out of defiant and willful belligerence. By the end of the dialogue, Socrates has passionately and indeed persuasively presented his own view at length, including an eschatological myth telling of the punishments meted out in the afterlife to those who have lived lives of injustice. But he recognizes that, despite all his own arguments, Callicles continues to recommend as the best life for a human being the life led by a skilled and powerful orator—a naturally superior, intelligent, capable person—who allows his appetites to grow to their greatest extent and is not squeamish or cowardly but brave and manly in using any means necessary to fulfill whatever desire he might be feeling, without regard to the conventional morality or immorality of those means.[32] That way of life is naturally just, since, as a naturally superior person, he is entitled to rule over others and obtain the satisfactions that his enlarged appetites demand, whatever those appetites might be and whatever the consequences for others. Consequences for the weak, paltry, and cowardly human specimens who are subject to his just domination do not count to any degree against his doing what his desires make him need to do.[33]

---

[31] He does get into trouble temporarily (as he thinks) at 495e–499a, by allowing that each appetite-gratification is as good as any other, since such pleasure is the only thing good simply because of what it is; but he soon withdraws that admission as something he did not seriously intend (499b). On this see below, sect. XIII.

[32] At the end of the dialogue, Socrates fervently recommends as best the life his account has described, the one that "practice(s) justice and the rest of excellence both in life and in death," but he recognizes that Callicles' defence of the other life has not been closed off, and he can only exhort us to reject it. His last words are, "Let's not follow the one that you believe in and call on me to follow. For that one is worthless, Callicles." Note that the tense here in referring to Callicles is the present, not the past.

[33] I agree with Irwin (*Plato's Ethics*, pp. 102–3) that Callicles' conception of "natural justice" is really a conception of *justice*—of what people are entitled to, of what "natural, impartial reason" should discern as the appropriate and right way for rule and resources to be distributed within a human community. However, Callicles is far from explicit and clear about this in his initial, formal presentation of the view (483a–484c). (See especially his remarks, 483d–e, on how the more powerful animals, and indeed Xerxes the Persian king in attacking Greece, actually behave, with no reference to their being entitled to do so by some impartial principle; even in the reference to Heracles' theft of Geryon's cattle, 484b–c, any reference to an impartial

On the basis of "natural justice," then, Callicles undertakes to defend his thesis—that doing injustice is better than suffering it (and that best of all is doing injustice and not suffering any punishment as a result). The "injustice" referred to here is injustice as understood in conventional Athenian, democratic politics and civic life: it means demanding better than equal treatment under the laws and a greater than equal share of the public goods that civic life provides to the citizens.[34] It takes Callicles quite some time, until 491a-b, finally to make clear to Socrates that the "superior" people whom he has maintained have a (natural) right to rule in cities are those who are superior not in brute strength or some non-political skill, but rather in being more intelligent (*phronimoi*) "about the affairs of the city, about the way it is to be well managed" and in being "brave (*andreioi*—manly), competent to accomplish whatever they have in mind, without slackening off because of softness of spirit (*dia malakian tēs psuchēs*)" (491b1–4). Later Socrates takes care to determine that Callicles understands this intelligence and this bravery or manliness as two separate and distinct psychic conditions: as he conceives them, these are not merely two ways of describing a single condition, or two distinguishable effects in a soul of a single condition—for example, the effects of some more comprehensive knowledge. At 495c3-7, in reviewing what Callicles has said here, Socrates asks: "Weren't you also saying just now that there is such a thing as bravery with knowledge (*epistēmē*)? . . . Was it just on the assumption that bravery is distinct from knowledge that you were speaking of them as two?" Callicles says yes. Socrates hammers the point home by getting Callicles also to state that pleasure and knowledge and pleasure and bravery are equally different and distinct from one another, and he then draws together these admissions in a grand pronouncement (d2-5): "All right, let's put this on the record: Callicles from Acharnae says that pleasant and good are the same,[35] and that knowledge and bravery are different both from each other and from [pleasure, i.e.] what's good."[36]

---

principle of justice as underlying that use of brute force is implicit at best. In fact, it is far from clear that any of these behaviors would actually get counted as just under Callicles' ultimate account, since it is far from clear that Xerxes or Heracles could count as a "superior" man, i.e., brave *and* intelligent, oratorically adept and expert at the "affairs of the city.") It is Socrates himself who in interpreting Callicles uses the language of what "ought" to happen (*dei*) (488c2; 490a2, c2, d5, d7, e2, e7). Only after such instruction from Socrates on what ought to be involved in any claim as to the nature of justice does Callicles, for the first time, at 491d1 use similar language: "it's fitting" (*prosēkei*) for the naturally superior to dominate others. We should admit frankly that it requires an expansive and charitable understanding of Callicles' position to characterize it in the way, following Irwin, I am doing. As usual with Plato, it is reserved to Socrates to present a clear, philosophically well-rounded account of even his opponents' ideas. Nonphilosophers are always in need of philosophers in Plato if they are to say what they mean clearly and well.

[34] See 483b–c.

[35] I'll return shortly to this identification of the good with pleasure.

[36] In neither of the arguments he sets Callicles up for here does Socrates find it significant that, on Callicles' view, knowledge and bravery are two distinct things. We should infer that

So Callicles' view is that the superior person's political intelligence is as distinct a quality of his soul from his bravery as it also is from the pleasure he gets through his exercise of the two of them. In that case, as with Protagoras in the *Protagoras,* Callicles is diverging from the theory of the unity of virtue defended by Socrates in that other work, according to which (true) moral and political knowledge and (true) bravery are to be identified somehow with an underlying general knowledge of what is good and what is bad for human beings.[37] Accordingly, again like Protagoras, Callicles assumes that a person could have one of these virtues without the other.[38] This is already clear from the way he describes the superior person as not only intelligent but also brave, "without slackening off from softness of spirit": evidently, he considers that some people who have the requisite intelligence are disqualified from superiority by being soft-hearted and un-manly—by succumbing to the inducements of mass culture that can lead the naturally better type of person to be ashamed to make the demands that his intelligence would entitle him to, if only he would throw off such inhibitions (see 483e–484a). Perhaps he thinks this is the case of philosophers like Socrates.[39]

On Callicles' account, what the naturally superior person is entitled to, in being entitled to rule over the others—and also the greater than equal share of good things he will achieve by means of that rule—is the constant satisfaction of his enlarged appetites. His intelligence coupled with his brav-ery will see to that. Under questioning from Socrates (495a), Callicles actu-ally identifies this satisfaction—this pleasure (*to hēdu*), the pleasure of gratifying one's large and demanding appetites—with "the good." One should recall that earlier on (464b–465e) Socrates has characterized the trained orator as a flatterer of his mass audiences, one who manipulates them by giving them pleasure (*to hēdu, hēdonē*)—with no knowledge at all of or concern for their good. There, there was no suggestion that the pleasure in question would consist in the satisfaction of their appetites (for food, drink, sex, or whatever passion might replace or be added to those connatural ones). Indeed, it is pastry baking, not oratory, that Socrates says aims to give pleasures of that sort—though he uses the language of the body and its gratifications (*charites*) (465c7–d3) in place of Callicles' "appetites" (*epithumiai*) and their "fulfillment" (*apopimplanai, plērōsis,* 492a2, 8); he

---

Plato wishes here to emphasize both that this *is* Callicles' view, and that Socrates sees this clearly. On this see further below, sect. XIII.

[37] On Socrates' view in the *Protagoras,* see below, Ch. 3, sects. II–III.

[38] See *Protagoras* 329d–330a.

[39] As Alexander Nehamas suggested to me. At 485c Callicles approves of philosophical training as a young boy; he expresses warm personal regard for Socrates at 485e and elsewhere (there is no reason to take this as ironical); but at 485d he very contemptuously and impatiently accuses any adult who keeps on spending all his time, as Socrates does, doing philosophy, of being "unmanly" (*anandros*), however "naturally well favored" (*euphuēs*), and therefore in need of a beating. Taken together all this fairly strongly suggests that he does regard philosophers like Socrates as intelligent, but defective in spirit and manly bravery (and culpably so).

contrasts oratory with pastry baking, as a "knack" that panders to pleasures of the *soul* where pastry baking panders to pleasures of the body. Socrates is thinking, it seems, of the pleasure oratory gives its audiences as some sort of refined delight at finding one's own ideas approved, recommended, and manipulated by a grandiloquent speaker to yield a perhaps unexpected conclusion.[40] It would seem, then, that with his association of "pleasure" and appetites Callicles is either speaking in a limited way of only some pleasures, those that satisfy passions (whether bodily cravings or more "mental" ones that resemble them in their urgency), or else he is vaguely conceiving all pleasures on the model of these—he does not make clear which. On Callicles' account, then, the fulfillment and gratification of appetites is good, simply as such, and nothing else at all is good in that way, i.e., simply because of what it *is*.

Now Socrates has provoked Callicles into advocating hedonism as a theory of the good by pressing him to say whether in ruling over others in the city his "superior person" will "rule over" himself as well (491d): will he be (as "the many" say) "self-controlled (*sōphrōn*) and master of himself (*enkratēs autos heautou*), ruling the pleasures and appetites within himself?" It's clear that Socrates thinks he should; but Callicles contemptuously (and "frankly" or brutally) rejects any such idea. He introduces his own conception of the "correct" way to live (491e8–492a3): one should "allow his own appetites to get as large as possible and not restrain (*kolazein*) them. And when they are as large as possible, he ought to be competent to devote himself to them by virtue of his bravery and intelligence, and to fill them with whatever he may have an appetite for at the time."[41] Notice that Callicles identifies two

---

[40] Later, at 500e–501c in his discussion with Callicles, Socrates reverts to his account of expert oratory as devoted to giving pleasure to its audiences. But, oddly and perhaps illegitimately, in reviving his account he lumps together without discrimination the appetitive pleasures or pleasures of the body that the orator gets for himself and these other ones that he gives his audience—both sorts are counted as pleasures of the appetitive type, the sort of pleasure that Callicles argued actually constituted the good (503c4–6). Here he is thinking of the pleasure given to the Athenians by the long walls, the ships, the power over their allies, and the wealth that their politicians in the glory days of the early and mid-fifth century obtained for them— rather than any pleasure they got from the speeches themselves that persuaded them to vote for those projects or empower their leaders to pursue them. See 518e–519b.

[41] Commentators commonly, and perhaps understandably, speak of Callicles here and later as advocating the maximization of appetite-fulfillment or the maximum balance of appetite-pleasure over pain in a lifetime. (See Irwin, *Gorgias,* ad loc., p. 193.) But that introduces a philosophical discipline into his remarks that is not there. All Callicles is saying is that the best life involves expanding the range and extent of one's appetites and filling any appetite one has at any given moment in whatever way suits that appetite. *We* might want to raise a question immediately about appetites that work at cross purposes: what if filling one of one's appetites, at a time when one experiences it, makes it less likely that one will be able to fulfill another one arising later—or guarantees a painful appetitive condition for a time? Shouldn't one, in the interest of overall appetite-fulfillment, either think a bit about *which* appetites to allow to expand to the maximum, so as to develop a fairly harmonized set, with few or no negative aftereffects, or else develop the ability to hold off satisfying some appetites sometimes, again in the interest of overall maximal appetite-fulfillment? Callicles does not consider such

distinct stages in the preparation and pursuit of this "best" life. First, one must "unleash" the appetites in the sense that one does not train and discipline oneself *not* to hanker after some bodily experiences, *not* to dwell on food or sex or drink or power over others, but on the contrary one focuses one's attention on the pleasures one can get from all such sources and (presumably by repeated indulgence) encourages and allows one's natural interests in such things to become as strong and intense as possible, and as frequently arising. Here Callicles speaks of not "restraining" the appetites (*kolazein*): that means, as just indicated, not doing anything to prevent their growth, intensification, and frequency. But second, once that condition is achieved, one must be brave or manly and intelligent or resourceful, so that one never lacks for a means of fulfilling any appetite when it arises and never shrinks through fear or low spirits or shame from taking it. This means, at least insofar as "bravery" is needed, that one will not "restrain" an appetite in quite a different sense: one will never decide *not* to fulfill it, one will never overrule it in one's decisions—one will never, for example, give in to any contrary feeling or impulse, leading one to incline to abandon or neglect it.

Now it is quite striking that in the crucial passage just quoted Callicles uses the notion of restraint or the lack of it in connection only with the first of these two distinct stages. However, a little later in the same speech, at 492c, Callicles uses the noun *akolasia* derived from his Greek verb for "restrain"—Zeyl translates it as "lack of discipline"—to refer to the total condition vis-à-vis the appetites of the one leading this life. He says that "wantonness (*truphē*), lack of discipline, and freedom, if available in good supply, are excellence and happiness" (492c4–6). And thereafter, beginning at 493d, Socrates poses the main issue between himself and Callicles in terms of which person and life is the happier—the "orderly" one or the "undisciplined" (*akolastos*)?[42] Thus, in the later discussion Callicles' preferred "lack of discipline" and his "undisciplined" life come to cover both the "unleashing" of the appetites, so that they grow large, become intense,

---

questions of "rational prudence," at all—nor, I think, does Socrates in criticizing him (see further below, sect. XIII). Callicles is content to think that any life goes well in which one has enlarged one's appetites and is continuously able through bravery and intelligence to provide for the satisfaction of whatever *appetitive* desires one experiences at any given time. It should be plain, then, from the outset that (*contra* White, "Rational Prudence") Callicles' ideal does include consideration of the superior person's condition at more than any given single moment. It proposes as the best way of life one fulfilled at every moment with whatever one's current appetite is for (cf. 492a2–3, ἀποπιμπλάναι ὧν ἂν ἀεὶ ἡ ἐπιθυμία γίγνηται)—even if, as we but apparently not Callicles can see, this might well not be one that gave as great appetite-fulfillment overall as one might have contrived by adopting a different policy. Callicles' rejection of self-control is the rejection, precisely and only, of all and any restrictions on a) the growth of appetites and b) the satisfaction of whatever appetites one may experience at any time. So understood, Callicles' ideal is quite an attractive one—attractive in part because of its extreme simplicity. Whether on reflection it can be sustained as reasonable is a further question.

[42] I return shortly to this "orderly" life and what is involved in it.

and beset us frequently, and the refusal to deny an appetite what it wants (and the psychological strength to fulfill it). This is significant because, when one adds the second type of or element in Calliclean "indiscipline," it is obvious that the life Callicles champions, as he himself conceives it, involves overcoming a sort of weakness of will that is not allowed by Socrates' moral psychology in other Platonic dialogues of the Socratic type—and indeed earlier in this one, in Socrates' discussion with Polus.[43] Thus it is clear that Callicles recognizes the *possibility* of this sort of weakness—the sort where a person has an occurrent strong appetite for something but refuses to gratify it, because of fear or shame or low spirits generally.[44] The question arises, then, whether in opposing Callicles' claim that such an undisciplined life is the best, Socrates adopts or accepts this same view about moral psychology. When he defends instead an "orderly" life, does he mean one in which both of two conditions are realized: 1) the person restrains his appetites in the way, at his first stage, Callicles favors no restraint, and 2) he has the additional strength (the very opposite of the sort Callicles favors) to make sure that when he *does* experience an appetite that he judges inappropriate he represses it and holds it in abeyance and does not act upon it? Or does he mean simply a life in which the first condition alone is realized—because the second drops out of consideration, according to the moral psychology he holds to in other dialogues, and earlier in this one: it is not even possible to experience a desire for something, e.g., an appetite, when at that moment you really do judge it inappropriate to do what such a desire would direct you to do?

IX

It is significant, I would suggest, that in Socrates' immediate response to what Callicles has said in the long speech I have been reporting, Plato has him ignore the more inclusive meaning of "indiscipline" that we find at the end of Callicles' speech. In formulating Callicles' position, he reverts to Callicles' original formulation, distinguishing between the "restraint" (*kolazein*) of the appetites and the further determination to seek "fulfillment from some source or other" of such unrestrained, enlarged appetites (492d5–7). This opens up the possibility that in going on to champion, in opposition

[43] On Socrates' adoption of the "Socratic" moral psychology in his examination of Polus, see Irwin, *Gorgias,* notes to 468a–b, 475d. I return to this point below.

[44] It is important to notice that Callicles is not conceiving such other motives—the ones that need to be eliminated, or overruled through bravery—as additional *appetites*. His remarks on bravery and its value do not commit him to seeing any need for "rational planning" in *not* fulfilling some appetite on some occasion in order to fill up others more later on, and the like. The only "rational planning" he has in mind is whatever is involved in planning out how to fulfill any given appetite at any given moment, plus whatever may be involved in bravery's repression of such wicked and nonappetitive motives as fear of punishment, or moral revulsion, or shame and embarrassment.

to Callicles' ideal life, an "orderly" one—one given to the sort of restraint that Callicles rejects—Socrates has in mind simply a life that has not allowed appetites to grow and become pressing, one that is "restrained" in precisely the way that Callicles used that word in his own presentation of his life-ideal. The "orderly" life schedules and keeps the appetites within the bounds of reason, so that when an "appetite" arises (or begins to arise) and you judge that fulfillment is inappropriate, you simply cease altogether from that desire: there is no question of the need for a further strength of soul, opposing to it some other, more powerful impulse or desire so as to prevent it from prevailing. On this interpretation, Socrates ignores, and chooses not to confront Callicles on, the issues of moral psychology that are raised for him by the second stage of Callicles' conception of his best life. (As we will see, the objections Socrates raises against him do not require Socrates to heed them.) We saw earlier that at 495c–d Socrates is quite clear that Callicles rejects views about the unity of virtue and the necessary co-instantiation of bravery and wisdom that we see him advocating in *Protagoras* and other "Socratic" dialogues; in that case he conspicuously does not confront Callicles on that point, as he does confront Protagoras, but lets it pass, to concentrate on other issues. So in this case too, on this interpretation, Socrates does the same thing: he lets pass without comment or demur Callicles' commitment to the possibility of strong weakness of will (in which a person experiences a conflict of simultaneously occurring desires and acts on the less eligible one) and concentrates on other issues.

Is this the best interpretation of Socrates' moves in opposing to Callicles' life of indiscipline his own orderly life? I think that it clearly is. First, as I mentioned in passing above, Socrates employs the "Socratic" moral psychology, and conspicuously so, in his examination of Polus. Polus insists (466b) that expertise in oratory gives a person "the greatest power" in his city, comparable to that of a tyrant, and he regards this as an important benefit conferred by that expertise—power deserving of the name is always something good for its possessor. However, Socrates argues (467c–468e, with only some reluctance, no opposition, on Polus's part), this expertise can only be a good thing if it enables a person to get what they want—i.e., what is good for them—and oratory does not do that. One may concede that it gets the orator what he thinks best, but that is not necessarily what is in fact good for him. So, contrary to what Polus at first asserted, expertise in oratory not only does not give its practitioner the greatest power in his city, it gives no power at all. In the course of this argument Socrates asserts that it's because of what's good that we (i.e., any of us human beings) do "intermediate things" such as take a walk—or put someone to death, or banish him or confiscate his property. So, if we do any of these things, "we suppose that doing these things is better for us than not doing them" (468b6) and we don't "simply want to slaughter people" and so on, "we want to do these things if they are beneficial, but if they are harmful we do not" (c1–5). So a tyrant or orator who puts people to death does it "because he supposes that doing so is better for himself" (d3). In other words Socrates assumes here, what he asserts in the *Protagoras*, that a human being performs any and every action with the idea, and *because* she thinks (however wrongly, however ill-consideredly or unconsideredly), that it is the best thing overall for her to do just then. It follows that there is no possibility, according to Socrates' statements here, of strong incontinence—just as in the *Protagoras*.[45]

Now of course it is always possible that Socrates simply contradicts himself in the *Gorgias* on this point of moral psychology.[46] Perhaps when he comes to confront Callicles' conception of an "undisciplined life," and to argue against the value of "indiscipline" and in favor of a contrasted "order" in one's life and soul, he agrees with Callicles about the psychological conditions that support these two contrasted ways of living—large, unleashed appetites by contrast with restrained and reduced ones, on the one hand; and bravery and force in the soul, permitting one to overcome contrary impulses of all sorts that might push toward nonfulfillment of an appetite, by contrast with control by the mind and by its firm commitment to the overall good of the person, permitting one to overcome contrary impulses that push toward the fulfillment of any unapproved appetite that might arise. When we turn, just below, to examine the text of Socrates' remarks, we will see no indication that Plato is drawing attention to any such volte-face, as one certainly might expect he would do, if he does make Socrates adopt such a view of the underlying psychology of his "orderly" life. It is surely not one of the "themes" of the dialogue, as Plato writes it, that Socrates now sees the need for a different moral psychology from the one he has assumed to be correct elsewhere in Plato. But one would be surprised if Plato writes the confrontation between Callicles and Socrates in such a way that Socrates smoothly and consciously accepts and argues from psychological assumptions that flagrantly violate those that he has used earlier in refuting Polus, while shrugging his shoulders at his own self-contradiction. Plato would then be mocking Socrates' central requirement in philosophizing, a rigid adherence to logical consistency. Is he presenting Socrates, then, as so inattentive to the consequences of his own admissions or so dull-witted or flighty that he does not notice what he is doing? That would be to undermine the basis of Plato's own abiding admiration and indeed heroization of Socrates as the very model of the passionately committed philosopher leading the philosophical life with full devotion to philosophical values—even if Plato may have come to doubt the adequacy of

---

[45] It would not do Polus any good to dispute these views of Socrates in the present context, of course. It will not help his case if he says that an expert orator can kill someone, and choose to do it, even though he knows it is not for his overall good, because he is angry or smitten with a strong appetite to do it. Such an orator would still not benefit himself by such a use of his expertise, and it would still follow, on Socrates' other premises, that expert oratory could not confer any power on him.

[46] This is what Irwin thought in *Gorgias* (p. 218), and he continued to think in *Plato's Ethics* (p. 116) that this is still one viable option for interpretation.

some of his theoretical ideas and his procedures in argument. Anyone who does suppose that Socrates adopts the Calliclean moral psychology in his confrontation with Callicles will have a difficult, not to say impossible, task in constructing a coherent overall interpretation of this dialogue on that basis. The requirement of a coherent overall interpretation is a legitimate criterion in assessing the acceptability of that supposition.[47]

X

Let us turn, next, to examine the texts in which Socrates develops his objections to Callicles and explains his own conception of the "orderly" life as best. Socrates introduces this conception by reporting some things that some "wise man" has told him which imply that an undisciplined life is actually miserable, and that an orderly one is the one to choose. Saying that really we are now dead and our bodies are our tombs, this person offered an interpretation of a Sicilian or Italian myth about goings on in the underworld, using an etymologizing technique to show that in fact it describes human lives as we now live them. In the myth we are ostensibly told about what happens after their death to "uninitiated" people (people who have not had the benefit of certain religious rites): they are condemned interminably to fill up perforated and leaking jars with water carried over with sieves (presumably as an emblem of their neglected need for purification before death).[48] But according to the wise man, this myth is actually talking about conditions of life (in this "tomb" of the body): the "uninitiated" (*amuētoi*) are really the foolish ones among us (*anoētoi*) and the sieves are their souls. Foolish people make the mistake of leaving their appetites unrestrained, so that they grow to the point of insatiability; in the myth these appetites in the foolish person's soul are referred to through the guise of the "leaky jar." So, according to the wise man, this myth is telling us that foolish people condemn themselves (their souls) to continuous, desperate carrying of the various means of satisfaction—they always lose some of it on the way, out of stupid untrustworthiness and by forgetting their purpose[49]—for those insatiable and never replete appetites that they have in-

---

[47] Irwin (see n. 46 above) does not address this important requirement in either of the two books referred to in that note. I should emphasize that the question here is not, as Irwin perhaps suggests in *Plato's Ethics*, p. 216, whether we should be determined to avoid finding an inconsistency in Socrates' views in the different parts of the *Gorgias*—as if that by itself should be a constraint on an acceptable interpretation—but how, if we do find one, we are to interpret that inconsistency so that it fits together in an acceptable way with the rest of the evidence presented in the text about what Plato, the author, means to be communicating to the qualified reader about the issues that the dialogue addresses. We need a coherent account of the whole writing, not necessarily one that avoids finding an inconsistency in what Socrates says at different places.

[48] See Dodds, p. 298.

[49] This is the clear meaning, in context, of *di'apistian kai lēthēn*, 493c3—even if Dodds is right (p. 303) about the Pythagorean origin and meaning of this phrase as it may actually have

flicted upon themselves. Surely, Socrates says, we can see from this account how miserable is the life of such undisciplined fools: they have no rest, no contentment, no satisfaction even of what they have foolishly set as their goal in life, to win for the appetites what they need—that is an unrealizable task. Far better if one wisely and intelligently restricted one's appetites so that they would remain full all the time, being satisfied with whatever, according to the circumstances, was present for consumption. Having "filled up his jars" by disciplining them in this way, he "can relax over them" and "give them no further thought" (493e4–6). Such an orderly life (*kosmiōs*, 493c6) would be happier, because one's appetites would always be satisfied—such a life is always adequate to its circumstances.

I do not discuss the relative merits of Socrates' and Callicles' ideals. My only concern is to discern Socrates' underlying assumptions here, and later, in advancing his own proposal and criticizing Callicles'—and to compare those assumptions with Callicles' own. On Callicles' view appetites arise in us, so to speak, on their own; what we will do, if we are intelligent, is give them their head, first by indulging them and thus allowing them to grow, and then by fulfilling them as they arise (repressing contrary feelings of shame or fear, if necessary, in the process). Thus Callicles sees in any human soul distinct sources for the liabilities to motivations—fully formed impulses to action: at least the appetites themselves, on the one side, and fear and shame, on the other, plus the strength belonging to bravery (however this is to be conceived) that overcomes the latter whenever they arise. (It is unclear whether he thinks reason and "intelligence" are the source of a further sort of independent force toward action or serve only to provide information.)[50]

As to Socrates' own assumptions, three things are worth noting in this passage: First, Socrates says nothing about anything in either the orderly or the undisciplined life that takes up Callicles' idea that "bravery" might be needed in addition to intelligence and enlarged appetites if the best life is to result. Socrates, of course, describes Callicles' sort of person as a fool,

---

been intended by the "wise man." Dodds's own idea that for Socrates the "forgetfulness" refers to not recalling past satisfactions misses the feature of the myth which makes the jars and the sieves fail to hold the *same* thing, viz. water. Note that the leaky "souls" here are not to be identified with the already-mentioned leaky appetites—those are compared to the jars in the myth, whereas the "souls" are being compared to the sieves. Socrates' interpretation of the "wise man" is that not only do fools' appetites, being insatiable, never hold what is given to them, but their souls regarded as agents of their appetites also cannot hold on to what they are bringing to them long and securely enough to get all of it there. This latter point seems to play no role, however, in Socrates' further application of what the "wise man" said.

[50] The appetites' independence from reason, on Callicles' view, makes it possible and indeed plausible to claim, as he does, that the best life consists simply in expanding and then fulfilling the appetites. Once, in the *Republic*, Plato himself adopts Callicles' view on the independence of the appetites from reason's evaluations, he has to develop an elaborate account of the natural functions of such desires, and of those of other types, before he can feel confident that he can actually show that Callicles is wrong about which life is best. These matters are not pursued in the *Gorgias*.

not intelligent, but he simply assumes that, having large and insatiable appetites, the person will be driven always and effectively in his actions by whichever foolish appetites he is feeling at the moment. And in his own life, led by wisdom,[51] the appetites, being *ex hypothesi* always full, either motivate no action at all, with the agent acting simply from his wisdom, or else, if they do motivate action, they arise only when in his wisdom the agent judges the circumstances appropriate for consuming something. Second, Socrates' basis for calling Callicles' life "undisciplined" and his own "orderly" is simply whether it is driven by unrestrained appetites—i.e., ones so large that they have become insatiable—or by restrained appetites, i.e., ones that make no *demands* at all but always and automatically conform with the person's rational judgments about what needs to be consumed. Thus Socrates makes no place at all in his own preferred life for anything corresponding to Callicles' "bravery": he has no idea of the possible need for something in addition to wisdom in directing a good life, some further power in the soul to suppress a possibly unwise appetite. In the life he is envisaging, such an appetite could not arise: all the appetites are restrained, so to speak, in advance. So when he refers to his orderly life as led by a "self-controlled" person (*sōphrōn*, 493d7), he simply means one whose appetites are restrained and disciplined in the described way—in advance, not by applying some force to control an unruly appetite that arises even after such discipline has done its work.

Third, however, the "wise man's" interpretation of the myth of the water bearers clearly speaks of the "appetites," in the souls of both the foolish and the wise, as residing in one "part" of the soul, and it speaks of "the soul" itself, in the case of the fools, as being converted into an agent for the fulfillment of appetites grown large.[52] This seems at least to anticipate the doctrine of *Republic* IV, according to which in the case of the good and wise person it is reason that leads in the soul and makes decisions, all of which without exception are adhered to in the person's choices and actions, while appetites (and spirit too) constitute other "parts" of the soul that retain their independent motivating force but always follow along with reason's directives. Following the "wise man," Socrates is apparently conceiving of the fools' "reason" as being co-opted by the enlarged appetites

---

[51] Socrates does not mention wisdom explicitly in explaining his orderly life, but its role is clearly and immediately implied by the "wise man's" emphasis on the fact that the contrasted, undisciplined people are fools.

[52] The Greek at 493a3–4 and b1, where Zeyl reasonably translates "the part of our souls" and the "part of the souls of fools" where appetites reside, does not actually have a word for "part" but uses only a genitive with a neuter demonstrative pronoun ("that of the soul")— but the relative pronoun meaning "where" at b1 plainly invites this translation. In the *Republic*, instead of this genitive usage, we normally get a prepositional phrase meaning "in the soul," either with a pronoun ("something" or "that") or else with a noun, including on occasion *meros* (part) (442b11, c5).

and serving their bidding.[53] However, Plato has Socrates here cite and then apply for his own purposes what some other person has said. As often in Plato, this device serves clearly to distance Socrates from at least the details of what he brings into the discussion by its means—to make it clear that the reader is not to attribute too precisely to Socrates himself what he is reporting, or to think him committed to its truth. Here it serves further to allow Plato to show that Socrates has seen the implication in what Callicles has been saying, that appetites are only one type of desire, and that reason's (or, for Callicles, bravery's) forces come from somewhere else in our psychic makeup—without making Socrates confront that supposition head on, either to accept or to reject it. And in fact, as I have already remarked, Socrates leaves this aspect of the "wise man's" admonition undeveloped when he goes on later in this passage to explain in his own way its moral burden. We are entitled to infer that Socrates has seen in Callicles' statements the implication that reason (with its virtue of intelligence) and appetite with its "virtue" of being large and demanding (together with bravery and whatever force it draws on or represents) are distinct elements in a human soul, and that, taken together, they provide multiple, possibly conflicting, sources of motivation. We should also notice that Plato himself, the author, in writing Callicles' words and Socrates' report and interpretation of the myth, is drawing attention to these novel ideas. But we should recognize that Socrates does not adopt them as he constructs his own ideal of an "orderly" life, and we should not suppose he has assumed any commitment to the accuracy of any such psychological analysis simply by reporting what the wise man had to say and approving of its moral implications. Having reported the wise man's remarks, he leaves this psychological analysis entirely aside. As I pointed out, he speaks of "self-control" and the "restraint" of appetites entirely in terms of wisdom's own work in reducing the appetites to an undemanding level, and he supposes that only reason exerts any force at all in producing the orderly actions of the disciplined life.[54]

[53] Dodds, p. 300, correctly rejecting A. E. Taylor's claim (*Plato*, p. 120n.1) to find evidence here of a Pythagorean origin for the Platonic doctrine of the tripartite soul (there is no tripartition here at all), thinks that "all that need be assumed is the popular distinction between reason and impulse which is already present" in Theognis and Aeschylus. That seems to me insufficient consideration of the difference between a theoretically alert philosophical discussion, such as this one, and the philosophical innocence of such poetry.

[54] Thus when Socrates began (491d11–13) by asking whether one of Callicles' naturally superior rulers over others would "rule himself," i.e., be "self-controlled (*sōphrōn*) and master of oneself (*enkratēs heautou*), ruling the pleasures and appetites within oneself," he had in mind exactly the sort of self-control and self-mastery that he argues in the *Protagoras* is the only coherent one: control by possessing wisdom or knowledge, which makes one always know the best thing to do in any circumstances (and why) and thereby guarantees that one will do it (see *Protagoras* 357b–e). One should bear in mind that in the *Protagoras* Socrates does not so much argue against the possibility of *akrasia* as deny the ordinary understanding of the phenomenon; really it is, or is the immediate effect of, ignorance of what one ought to do and why. In this understanding of the virtue of self-control and self-mastery, he was followed

XI

But does Socrates do the same in the rest of his exposition? In what immediately follows, Socrates attempts to undermine Callicles' undisciplined life by exploring, to his disadvantage, the implications of the hedonistic understanding of the good that lies at its base. I return briefly at the end of the paper to Socrates' arguments here; for now it is enough to observe that, being focused on issues about the natures of pleasure and goodness, these arguments do not address the questions about moral psychology that interest us. Later, however, after Callicles has ceased to cooperate in the discussion, Socrates draws on an analogy with medicine and the other crafts (503d–505b, recapitulated and varied at 506c–507a), in order to explain further and defend the orderly life that he urges on Callicles, and us. We need to examine this analogy, as Socrates explains it, and its implications.

The major turning point in Socrates' debate with Callicles is reached at 499b–c, when Callicles suddenly announces his decision to withdraw an earlier admission. Previously Callicles had implied that pleasure as such was good (and the only thing good simply by being what it is); accordingly, he felt required to say that there are no bad pleasures (no matter how base and disgraceful some people's might be) (495a). Now, at 499b, he goes back on this: of course, like everyone else, he holds that some pleasures are better and others (including those disgraceful ones) are worse. He is not given an opportunity to explain how he makes such a distinction, compatibly with his hedonist conception of what is good. Socrates immediately applies his own earlier idea that a pleasure is good and worth both choosing and experiencing only when it promotes or leads to some good condition of body or soul—good in some way that has nothing to do with pleasure, but good simply because of the sort of condition that they are. The good condition of soul he identifies with the virtues, including those of "self-control" and justice that earlier Callicles had rejected for obstructing the gratification of enlarged appetites. Through all this, Callicles answers Socrates' questions, as he first says at 501c7–8, simply in order to "expedite your argument and to gratify Gorgias."[55] That is, he answers as Socrates *wants* him to answer,

---

by Xenophon, who in praising Socrates' moral character (e.g., in *Memorabilia* I 2,1), speaks first and most often of his "self-mastery" or "strength of will" (*enkrateia*, the opposite of *akrasia*), meaning not that he had strong appetites that he held in check, but rather that he did not have any of the strong appetites that undisciplined people experience. (Recall Alcibiades' story of how Socrates rebuffed his sexual advances, *Symposium* 218c–219e.) It seems that the Greeks did not find this "Socratic" usage of these terms so odd as we might; it became standard among philosophers in Hellenistic times, with its adoption by Zeno and the other Stoics.

[55] At 497b4–5 Gorgias had pressed Callicles to answer Socrates and not evade his question: there, the request that Callicles allow the discussion to be "carried through" meant that Callicles should answer the question as he really thought it should be answered. In recalling Gorgias's intervention here, Callicles gives a very different twist to what "expediting" Socrates' argument means—the Greek verb is the same as before. Callicles repeats his disclaimer, in more emphatic, even rude, terms at 505c–d. At 506b6–c3 Socrates sees that he must permit Callicles to cease

so that Socrates can explain his own view and set out his arguments. He does not answer as he himself would wish to answer, nor are his answers ones that he thinks he is logically forced to give, on the basis of earlier admissions. In effect, as I mentioned above, Callicles has now ceased to engage with Socrates at all.

Socrates soon reverts in his exposition to oratory itself, and its functions (500a). Do expert orators speak with a view to improving the citizens, to making them as good as possible through their speeches, by making their souls better (502e–503a)? That is what they would have to do if they exercised a true craft and did not merely possess a disreputable mere "knack." Already we can see that Socrates is assuming that someone *might* make someone a good and virtuous person simply by instructing them, through speeches of some sort, in how to behave—he neglects altogether any separate, independent preparation for virtue of parts of the soul other than the mind or understanding. It is in this connection that Socrates introduces the analogy with medicine and other crafts that I mentioned above. By appealing to the way such experts function, he hopes to find confirmation for his own view that self-control and justice—the bases of his "orderly" life—constitute the goodness of a soul. If so, then the test of expert oratory's claims to be a true craft will be whether or not expert orators aim at making their audiences just and well-controlled. Painters, housebuilders, shipwrights, physical trainers and doctors, he says, all work by placing into "a certain order" (*taxis tis*) the product of their craft. They do this by compelling "one thing to be suited for another and to fit to it (τὸ ἕτερον τῷ ἑτέρῳ πρέπον τε εἶναι καὶ ἁρμόττειν) until the entire object is put together in an organized and orderly way" (504a1–2). So, by analogy, an expertise that aims at improving people's souls would have to aim at introducing an order in their souls analogous to that of a beautiful painting, a commodious house, a well-made ship, or a healthy body in prime physical condition. And that, says Socrates, can only (in the first instance) be to make them self-controlled and just people (d1–3).

As one reads this, it is impossible to miss the fact that, if a self-controlled and just soul is to have "order" (*kosmos*) and "organization" (*taxis*) according to these models, then the soul must comprise distinct elements, each shaped and ordered so as to stand in some fitting relationship to the others: the strong emphasis at 504a1–2 on "the one" (τὸ ἕτερον) fitting to "the other" (τῷ ἑτέρῳ) in the model-cases (heat and cold, the wet and the dry in the body—not to mention organs like heart and lung; the keel and the cross-struts and the oars and oarlocks on a ship; the diverse colors and shapes distributed across the canvas of a painting) has this implication too plainly for any attentive reader to miss it. Of course, no analogy dictates its own application, and only selected features of the analogues are drawn

---

answering even in the disengaged way he has been doing—but he does express the hope that Callicles speak up if he thinks Socrates is saying anything wrong.

on in producing and applying an analogy. Still, in writing this passage as he has, Plato seems undoubtedly to be inviting the reader to expect that sort of application. In that case, we would expect Socrates to go on to identify or presuppose some independence of elements in a soul that need to be put into some harmonious relationship—and, in this dialogue, that would mean looking back to what Callicles said, and Socrates confirmed from him, about the independence of intelligence or knowledge and bravery or manliness from one another, and of both from the appetites. We would then have an unmissable anticipation of the theory of the human soul that Socrates works out with care and clarity in *Republic* IV—vague and imprecise and exploratory as yet, but clearly moving in the same direction of psychological analysis.

However, when we consider how Socrates actually applies the analogy, we find, just as before with the jars and the sieve, that he does not pursue these indications. As before, he avoids altogether recognizing a need for the sort of self-control that would repress (or postpone or divert) existing appetites the agent himself disapproved of, and prevent them from prevailing. Recognizing that sort of self-control, as we see from the argument of *Republic* IV (439c–d), is the clearest indication of a commitment to independent forces in a soul, working to express themselves in action, whether successfully or not. Instead, "discipline" continues to mean for Socrates the *elimination* of appetites as demanding desires—enlarged, powerful desires arising on their own and putting pressure on a person to accede to them—and it does not include "reason's" overruling or dominating objectionable appetites despite their continued demandingness. At 505a–b Socrates pursues the comparison with medicine in the following way: "Don't doctors," he says,

> generally allow a person to fill up his appetites, to eat when he's hungry, for example, or drink when he's thirsty as much as he wants to when he's in good health, but when he's sick they practically never allow him to fill himself with whatever he has an appetite for? . . . Isn't it just the same way with the soul . . . ? As long as it's corrupt, in that it's foolish, undisciplined, unjust and impious, it should be kept away from its appetites and not be permitted to do anything other than what will make it better. . . . Now isn't keeping it away from what it has an appetite for, disciplining it?

Here, as before, the "discipline" (*kolazein*) of the soul, envisaged now as being applied by a true orator or public official, is the forcible withholding of fulfillment from an appetite in order, over time, to get it to go away.[56] Once the appetites have been disciplined in this way, so that only acceptable

---

[56] See to the same effect 507d3–6. I am speaking here only of objectionable appetites—those are the only ones in need of discipline and, on Socrates' view, elimination. His theory of the wise and good person countenances what we may call appetites for food and drink, but, as noted previously, these all conform with the judgments of that person's reason about what needs to be consumed.

desires for food, drink, and so on are experienced, then the agent is to be free to fulfill such remaining desires as they arise. Thus, as before, "discipline" for Socrates means eliminating appetites—or reducing them to acceptable levels or scheduling them—and it does not include (surely because he does not even admit this as a possibility) the agent's applying some countervailing psychic force of his own to prevent unruly appetites from prevailing. One should note that Socrates mentions again the "foolishness" of the undisciplined person, as well as his lack of discipline, with the clear implication that the disciplined person—the one having desires for food and so on of the type just described—is also wise. If we look, then, for two or more distinct elements in the soul to be brought into harmonious "order" and "organization," on Socrates' understanding of the application to this case of the analogy with medicine and shipbuilding and so on, it is clear what those would be. They are the *virtues* of wisdom or intelligence and its demands, on the one side, and, on the other, the person's mind and the desires or appetites it produces. The beautiful order (*kosmos*) and organization (*taxis*) of a virtuous soul that Socrates envisions is the harmonization between the mind, together with its desires or appetites, and the principles of the virtue of wisdom itself—and, as a result of that, the harmonization of the desires with one another and their suitability for achieving the proper goals in life.[57] On the view of the orderly life and soul that Socrates continues to be developing, the soul contains no independent forces or impulses that have to be harmonized, and nothing he says tends toward psychological analysis along those lines. The flexibility demanded in applying an analogy permits this, however forcibly the reader is struck, upon first presentation, with that sort of interpretation.

XII

There is a great deal of textual evidence, then, that in opposing Callicles' ideal of an undisciplined life and in advancing his own of an orderly one, Socrates concerns himself solely with the advisability of "unleashing" the appetites and letting them grow to be large and demanding. In assessing the pros and cons of these proposals, he says nothing at all about the other aspect of Callicles' conception of the best life, in which Callicles spoke of

[57] For such an interpretation of *kosmos* and *taxis*, see also *Alcibiades* 122c4–7. In reading these passages of the *Gorgias*, one is struck with the absence of these terms from Socrates' discussion and descriptions of virtue and the virtuous life in other Socratic dialogues. Aside from this passage of *Alcibiades*, they appear to occur relevantly only in *Charmides*, in connection with Charmides' first attempt at a definition of *sōphrosunē* (temperance or self-control) as involving "orderly and quiet" actions (at 159b3 and 160c7—and in the second of these passages editors normally delete the word as a gloss). *Protagoras* 347d7 and *Meno* 90a7 hardly count as exceptions but might be mentioned for the sake of completeness.

"bravery" or manliness as also necessary, in order to overcome any remaining impulses of fear or revulsion obstructing appetite-fulfillments.[58] And he incorporates into his account of the orderly life no corresponding aspect of control needed to overcome any remaining inappropriate appetites. He seems clearly aware of these aspects of Callicles' view, and their implication that there are desires or impulses to action in a human soul beyond those belonging to the person's reasoned judgments about what to do. These aspects of Callicles' view do reoccur in the story of the jars and sieves which Socrates immediately tells in order to counter Callicles. Likewise, as we saw (p. 53 above), Socrates draws attention to the fact that Callicles considers intelligence (*phronēsis*) and bravery (*andreia*) as two totally distinct things—a second point at which Callicles' view diverges sharply from his own, as we know it from other dialogues. But Socrates chooses to leave these disagreements unexplored. The arguments he offers in order to refute Callicles attack other weaknesses (as he thinks them) in Callicles' views. He evidently thinks that these arguments are sufficient to show that the life to which Callicles urges him is no good at all. He does not address those other disagreements because he thinks he does not need to. But, from what Plato writes in preparing and presenting both sides of the dispute, the reader should infer that Plato himself does not agree. If one is to give an adequate and finally defensible account of the "orderly" life as the best one, and if one is to explain adequately how moral wisdom and knowledge can in fact direct someone's life as Socrates has always wanted to say that it must—inevitably bringing with it self-control and justice and bravery and piety[59]—then, Plato seems to be saying, one needs to consider carefully whether or not there really are additional impulses toward action in any human soul. If so, one will have to determine as accurately as one can how the perfection of the mind through wisdom relates to the perfection of the other "parts" of the soul from which those other impulses derive. Evidently, the latter would have to be somehow freestanding states of perfection—with serious implications for any conception of human virtue as some sort of unity. On such a

---

[58] He does, of course, attempt to make trouble for Callicles' hedonism by pointing out that, in addition to the good constituted by appetite-pleasure, Callicles has also recognized bravery (and intelligence) as further goods—but without showing how that can be compatible with the claim that only appetite-pleasures are good simply for what they are. See 497e–499b; I return to this passage below, but it is not relevant in the present context.

[59] At 507a–c in the *Gorgias*, Socrates argues succinctly that a self-controlled *sōphrōn* soul will also be just, pious, and brave. In this rapid exposition of his "unity of virtue" doctrine, he does not mention wisdom (as Kahn observes, *Socratic Dialogue,* p. 133), but only because throughout Socrates' discussion of the two lives wisdom (*phronēsis*) is plainly implied as the origin of *sōphrosunē* in any soul. Socrates brings this to light at the beginning of the passage, at 507a7, when he describes the soul that has the opposite to self-control as "foolish and undisciplined" (*aphrōn te kai akolastos*)—as he has done repeatedly before, beginning already in his interpretation of the myth of the waterbearers (on which see above, sect. X). Note also the etymological association of *sōphrosunē* with *phronēsis* exploited by Plato in the *Cratylus* (411e, followed by Aristotle, *Nicomachean Ethics* VI 5, 1140b12) when he has Socrates describe *sōphrosunē* as the "preservation of wisdom"; and see *Protagoras* 332a–333b.

view, what will it come to to say, say, that wisdom produces the "orderliness" of the soul—and what will such orderliness consist in? Here "orderliness" will necessarily make much more than Socrates does in the *Gorgias* of the implications of his analogy to the work of crafts like painting and medicine. And at this point the question left to the reader at the end of Socrates' refutation of Gorgias arises again: can such wisdom or knowledge of just and unjust, good and bad, admirable and disgraceful really be helpfully conceived as the same *sort* of knowledge that we find in the crafts? Plato's presentation of the debate between Socrates and Callicles raises and defines these issues for his reader—even if Socrates himself prefers to confront Callicles with his much simpler conception of the human soul and his much thinner conception of orderliness, and even if Socrates may think that he can adequately dispose of Callicles' immoral way of life without having to address these issues.

XIII

I began my discussion of Socrates' debate with Callicles by pointing out (sect. VIII above) that Socrates does not succeed, and in the end knows he has not succeeded, in bringing Callicles to admit that some of his own deep convictions imply the truth of Socrates' view that the best life is an orderly, disciplined one. Now in conclusion I return briefly to this point. Socrates develops two arguments against Callicles, before, as I mentioned (beginning of sect. XI), Callicles in effect resigns from the discussion.[60] In the first

[60] Kahn ("Drama and Dialectic," p. 106; *Socratic Dialogue,* pp. 136–37) thinks Callicles has already been "defeated" before Socrates has presented either of these arguments, namely at the point (494d–e) where Socrates mentions the pleasures of the catamite. In accordance with Kahn's overall interpretation of the dialogue, Callicles, like Gorgias and Polus before him, succumbs because of his embarrassment at admitting, what is in fact a prima facie consequence of his earlier statements, that the catamite's life will be a good and happy one. The text does not support this interpretation. Even though Callicles is discomfitted by Socrates' line of questioning—he would rather not have to say any such thing—and irritated at Socrates for pursuing it, he makes no bones about admitting, when pressed, that even a life of this sort would be good, because it allows for the gratification of enlarged appetites. (See his unequivocal response at 495b9.) When later (499b) Callicles goes back on this admission and now maintains that some pleasures (e.g., that of the catamite) are worse than others, it is definitely not out of any residual embarrassment at the unsavoriness of defending the catamite's life as good; but rather, now that Socrates has completed his two arguments (neither of which appeals to any socially embarrassing consequences of Callicles' view), Callicles sees that he must retract that admission to evade the destructive consequences of those arguments. Thus when possible embarrassment exists for apparently having to say something distasteful, something that he would prefer not to have to say, Callicles is annoyed and offended at Socrates' "playing to the crowd" by drawing attention to this feature of his view, but he forthrightly endorses it nonetheless. He only withdraws his statement that all pleasures are equally good when he sees he needs to in order to avoid a serious contradiction between this hedonist conception, on the one side, and, on the other, a) certain further ideas about the good which he does not see how to resist (these are the basis of Socrates' first argument) and b) his commitment to the value

(495e–497d), Socrates points out that (appetite-) pleasure occurs simultaneously with its opposite, the pain or distress caused by the need of fulfillment: the pain lasts all the way through the pleasure of being fulfilled; yet it seems a logical feature of anything's good state that it replaces its bad one, and vice versa, and never temporally coexists with it. It follows that having appetite-pleasure cannot be the good state for a human being (i.e., happiness)—contrary to what Callicles has apparently wished to maintain.[61] In the second argument (497e–499b), Socrates begins by obtaining from Callicles the admission that a man is good because of the presence in him of good things. Plainly, he has in mind as the relevant "good things" the virtues, or virtue; but (as we saw, sect. VIII above) Callicles insists that the *only* thing good just because of what it is, is appetite-gratification, and bravery and intelligence are *not* good in that way. For him, the only way they can be good is by leading to or supporting somehow or other the obtainment of what *is* good in that way, appetite-gratifications.[62] So on Callicles' view the only possible basis for calling someone a good man is that he is experiencing appetite-gratifications, or perhaps that over time he experiences a lot of them—more than others do. But, as Callicles has to admit, cowards, rather than brave men, experience the greater pleasure in the contexts of life where either of those qualities expresses itself; as to fools and intelligent people, there doesn't seem to be any reason to think the one sort experiences any more or fewer pleasures than the other.[63] But in that case it follows that, contrary to what Callicles was saying, brave men are *not* good men, but worse than cowards, and intelligent ones are no better than fools.

For T. H. Irwin this—really rather simple and swift—second argument is

---

of bravery or manliness in the pursuit of appetite-pleasure (for him, just as fundamental a commitment as his commitment to the value of that pleasure—and one that Socrates exploits in his second argument). (See also the correct and effective criticisms of Irwin, "Coercion and Objectivity," p. 72n.31; I would go further, however, to emphasize against Kahn that, as I have noted, in fact Callicles *does* have the boldness to say that the catamite's life is a good and happy one: he does this at 495b9, where he affirms that the good is enjoyment from any source [*pantōs*] and accepts the "many shameful things" Socrates has just hinted at as consequences of this view.)

[61] For an excellent discussion of this argument, see White, "Rational Prudence," pp. 150–51.

[62] Here is the true significance of Socrates' curious-looking emphasis (495c–d) on the fact that knowledge and bravery are each different from pleasure, i.e., from the good or what is good. The fundamental point is that, since for Callicles neither bravery nor intelligence is good in itself, he cannot think that simply by having bravery or intelligence a person can count in any way as being good.

[63] Notice that Socrates makes nothing here or elsewhere in this argument of the distinctness of intelligence from bravery—that they are two conditions, not one, in the soul. He speaks separately of the pleasures of the fools and the pleasures of the cowards, but at 498c2–3 (if we read Dodds's text, with ms F) he speaks of just two opposed groups, "the intelligent and brave men" and "the cowardly and foolish." In fact, he would get the damaging consequence he is seeking whether or not the brave and the intelligent are two distinct, not completely overlapping, classes: Callicles is left, on this argument, with no way to count bravery or intelligence (whether they are or are not distinct conditions) as bases for counting someone a good person.

a thorough refutation of Callicles' hedonism—and of any hedonism focusing upon the unrestrained fulfillment of any and all appetites. Irwin thinks it does not leave open to Callicles adjustments in his hedonist outlook, such as I explain below—ones that (at least prima facie) would allow him to combine his previously expressed high evaluation of bravery and intelligence with a commitment to the sole intrinsic value of the gratification of enlarged appetites. Irwin explains, "Socrates points out that Callicles' admiration for this well-planned and resolute way of life conflicts with the particular content he assumes it will have: the unrestrained pursuit of the satisfaction of one's appetites," since "the example of the coward shows that planning and resolution may be no better than cowardice as a strategy for maximizing pleasure."[64] Irwin concludes that Callicles is justified in refusing to make the "large sacrifice of rational agency" in forming and executing rational plans that Socrates shows would be mandatory if he stuck to the ideal of "unrestrained pursuit" and so accepted cowardice as a perfectly acceptable way of achieving it. Irwin goes on to speak of this as the "necessary preference of any rational" person—so that it is not merely Callicles that Socrates refutes; he proves on universally and fundamentally valid rational grounds that "rational order" such as Socrates has been advocating really is a virtue, one that even Callicles, being rational, must recognize—as he does in seeing and accepting the force of this argument, and resigning his brief for the sole intrinsic value of pleasure.[65]

One may object to Irwin's interpretation of this argument on three grounds. First, as I mentioned above (n. 37), Callicles' ideal was never to maximize pleasure or the gratification of appetite; it was and remains a vaguer one of living with enlarged appetites and fulfilling them as they arise. When Socrates suggests in this argument, and Callicles agrees, that a coward may have just about as much, or even more pleasure than a brave man, nothing in the text suggests that Socrates is pushing him to admit that on his own principles he ought to recommend cowardice as equal to or better than bravery, because the coward maximizes pleasure as well as or better than the brave man. Socrates' sole claim is that, with the intellectual resources available to him (given his hedonism as that has so far been explained), Callicles has to admit that the coward is as good a person as the brave man, or better (see 499a7–b1). That is damaging enough to his case. Second, Irwin's constant talk of "rational planning" and its value is very misleading. Neither Socrates nor Callicles ever uses such language. Callicles praises bravery because it enables a man not to hold back from satisfying his appetites, when pressed to hold back by nonappetitive motives, for example by fear or shame. Socrates does not say anything here or elsewhere to suggest to Callicles that in addition the brave man needs the ability to hold back from satisfying *some* appetites in order to satisfy other greater ones or avoid

---

[64] Irwin, *Plato's Ethics,* pp. 107–8.
[65] Irwin, "Coercion and Objectivity," p. 66.

greater pains, later—so as to maximize pleasure overall in his life. Yet it is that sort of planning and control that Irwin has in mind when he speaks of the value of "rational planning" that Socrates is supposedly stressing to Callicles under the guise of discussing the value of "bravery." Third, Socrates never indicates any interest in persuading Callicles of the need for "order" in the weak sense of rational planning in working to achieve one's overall goals, whatever those might be, e.g., maximizing pleasure in one's life: by "order"—what Callicles is being urged throughout to value—Socrates manifestly always means the sort of order that comes with the full virtues of self-control and justice. Socrates never speaks of any lesser kind of order or rational planning or the like, even as a halfway house, such that once he has gotten Callicles to see its value, he might hope to persuade him of the further need of these specific sorts of order and self-control, the ones that constitute the full virtues of self-control and justice. It may be that *Irwin* has shown that every rational person must agree to the need in their life for at least that halfway-house sort of order and "rational planning" or, in general, to the value of "rational agency" as such, but there is no basis in the text for saying that Plato or Socrates has shown, or even argued, anything of the kind.[66] Socrates' simple and swift second argument claims nothing so grand and portentous. He argues only that, on Callicles' thesis that appetite-satisfaction alone is good because of itself, because of its own nature, he cannot maintain that brave and intelligent people are better than cowards and fools. The latter can obtain appetite-pleasure as much or more than the former.

With the completion of this second argument (499b), Callicles withdraws his admission (495a) that all appetite-pleasures are equally good—the admission that Socrates had immediately seized upon as the basis for these two arguments. So Callicles seems to think that if he withdraws it he will be able to derail both of Socrates' arguments. He is right. He will avoid the first objection if he maintains instead that the good condition for a human being is—not: experiencing some appetite-pleasure on some occasion, but:—

---

[66] Similarly to Irwin, White ("Rational Prudence," p. 154) draws upon his own philosophical analysis to read into this argument a "concern for the future" and so a commitment to rational prudence and self-control and orderliness—at least to the extent of making sure that one's appetites do not seriously conflict and that the satisfaction of one set of appetites does not reduce the satisfaction to be gotten from another—that Callicles had not at first seen was involved in his commitment to bravery, but that Socrates is now bringing to light. To the contrary, Callicles was aware all along that his bravery meant concern for the future, but only to the extent of seeing to the fulfillment of one's presently demanding desires, and Socrates says nothing here to force or even suggest any extension of this concern to other sorts of issues; his rather simple argument to show that, on Callicles' statement so far of his hedonism, a coward is as good a person as a brave man or even better, does not say anything about any need to expand that concern to become a general "rational prudence." I think White's comments on the deficiencies of the life Callicles recommends are cogent, but I do not see any grounds in the text to suppose that his concerns were occupying Plato in presenting Callicles' views or in writing Socrates' arguments against them.

living in such a way as to get a large variety of satisfactions over one's lifetime for a large number of enlarged appetites. Not *all* appetite-gratifications are or constitute the good condition for a human being, but only the ones belonging to such a set. Such a condition might or might not exclude the catamite's life as a good one (that would depend on the facts about its pleasures), but it would certainly close off for Callicles all vulnerability to Socrates' specific objection in his actual first argument. Even if any single appetite-gratification is accompanied by and lasts only as long as its opposite, the pain of unfulfilled appetite, Callicles' position will not now entail that the good condition for a human being can coincide temporally with the bad. The good condition will now be the condition of living with enlarged appetites and regularly fulfilling them. No one can be in that condition and its opposite at the same time.

As to the second argument: if not all appetite-gratifications are equally good, but only those belonging to such a set of enlarged appetites count as good, then Callicles can argue that it is only the brave and intelligent who, precisely because of their bravery and intelligence, will in fact live a life that contains the good condition for a human being. Only they will be able to secure what is needed to satisfy those varied and enlarged appetites. In that case, Callicles can now coherently count bravery and intelligence as good— not, indeed, because of their very natures, as Socrates maintains, but because of the way they subserve our obtaining our *actual* good condition, namely, such a set of varied and enlarged appetite-gratifications.

Socrates might now (499c) have allowed Callicles an opportunity to restate his position in terms of such new ideas about goodness and pleasure; he might then have subjected those to refutation. Instead, Socrates proceeds at once to develop his own ideas about how one should distinguish good from bad pleasures: the good ones are those that lead to the good condition of the soul, i.e., virtue (including the virtues of justice, as conventionally understood, and self-control), the bad ones are those that lead to or confirm one in the vices of injustice and indiscipline. As I mentioned earlier, Callicles soon (501c) makes it plain that he is no longer answering in terms of his own views, or agreeing to things that seem so compelling that no one could deny them, or accepting implications of things he has agreed to previously. He is merely helping Socrates to go ahead with the exposition of his own ideal of life, and his arguments for it. The indications are, then, that from 499c onward Socrates is not in fact examining and refuting Callicles' views at all, but explaining and arguing directly for his own. And since, as we have seen, he has not in fact previously refuted those views in the form that Callicles reasonably comes to insist on, but only in the inadequate form that includes the premise that all appetite-gratifications are of equal value, the right conclusion for the reader to draw is that Socrates has not in fact refuted Callicles. The impassioned defense of the orderly life to which he now turns is impressive indeed, and even very persuasive. But Socrates has not done away with Callicles' quite different ideal by showing that it cannot be coherently defended. That the dialogue itself, and its author, concur in this diagnosis is clearly indicated when Callicles does withdraw his acceptance of the premise that not all appetite-pleasures are good: Socrates does not give him a chance to explain his thesis about the ideal, undisciplined life in those new terms—even though only a little thought is enough to show how he might at least have tried to do that in a plausible and coherent way. Conceivably, Socrates might have found new arguments, without departing from basic Socratic ideas about virtue and moral psychology, to overturn these new endeavors.[67] The important point is that Plato wrote the dialogue in such a way that Socrates does not even try. And, as I have already mentioned, in the last words of the work Socrates says plainly that Callicles is still holding to his position—he knows Callicles has not been silenced by any of his arguments against him, whereas in other dialogues he always ultimately finds arguments to silence the interlocutors, even if they do not really believe that Socrates' contrary conclusions constitute the truth of the matters in dispute. Whether or not he could have found Socratic arguments to silence Callicles, Plato has chosen not to. Evidently, he has come to think that Socratic views about moral psychology and virtue do not suffice to accomplish that in a philosophically satisfying way.

In the end, then, the Gorgias and its author are saying to the reader that much further philosophical work needs to be done before the Socratic defense of the moral life as best for anyone can be effectively completed. We get some clear indications where further work needs to be done—on the question whether there are human desires and impulses to action that do not derive ultimately from the person's ideas about what would be good for them to do; on the question of the unity of virtue; on the analysis of pleasure and its relation to the good; and, above all, on the content of moral knowledge, its relationship to the other human virtues, and the comparison between such knowledge and technical knowledge like that of medicine or shipbuilding. The dialogue, and Plato its author, are not communicating with the reader on philosophical subjects solely through the words of the protagonist, Socrates, but also, and independently, through those of his interlocutors and through the interplay between what is said on the two sides. We should infer that Plato is not yet ready with secure answers to these difficult questions—certainly it would be insipid to suggest that he has already worked out the theories on these points that we find in the Republic, and is teasing his readers by hinting at them here, or even that he has some idea of using such hints to prepare them for that new edifice in the later work. But the direction of his—and the reader's—further thought is clearly marked out.

What, one may ask in conclusion, has led Plato to these doubts and questions about his Socrates' ideas? Any answer must inevitably be specula-

---

[67] Perhaps the sorts of appeal to the value of "rational agency" and the need in any acceptable life—even one devoted to fulfilling deep and demanding appetites—for "rational prudence," planning and scheduling, etc., made by both Irwin and White (see n. 66 above) would be effective; perhaps other considerations might have been brought forward.

tive. Presumably Plato has a series of distinct, though related concerns. But the evidence of the *Gorgias* suggests the prominence among them of this: perhaps through reflection on the phenomenon of *akrasia* (weakness of will), Plato has come to think that even the Socratic assumption that everyone wants happiness or his overall good more than he wants anything else is not a sufficient guarantee that we will be led actually to live the best life merely through the sort of intellectual understanding of our good that would be analogous to the physician's knowledge of medicine or the mathematician's of arithmetic. If some desires—the ones that, on the ordinary account of *akrasia*, overcome our best understanding and resolve—float free from our ideas about our good, then even if we *rationally* want our overall good more than anything else, all lower-ranked desires will not always be ineffective against such rational evaluations, even when those evaluations are robustly maintained in opposition to them. In that case, we need a new account of the virtue of wisdom, and its connections to self-control, justice and bravery—of the sort that begins to emerge if we reflect on Callicles' assumptions about moral psychology. But, given only so much, it is unclear just how to proceed in working out, and arguing for, a theory of the existence of such free-floating desires, and thence to construct such a new account of the human virtues. In the *Gorgias* Plato takes only the first, essential step in that direction, by bringing to light the concerns and worries he thinks one ought to have about the adequacy of Socrates' alternative explanations of these matters—as well as the difficulties that will result for him, as we can see from Callicles' forthright and undefeated defense of the "undisciplined life," if one must opt for a moral psychology recognizing "appetite" as a separate and independent source of human motivations. How splendidly well the dialogue genre serves Plato's situation at this point in his own philosophical thinking! By adumbrating through his character Callicles the multiple-sources model of human motivation, with its possibility of open conflict between desires of different types, while continuing to present Socrates as holding to the single-source model familiar from other Socratic dialogues, Plato is able to keep the distance he needs from both alternatives while examining, exploring, and testing them, and assessing their philosophical strengths and liabilities—and inviting his readers to do the same. Plato must have learned a lot while writing this dialogue.[68]

[68] Nicholas White gave me the benefit of extensive comments on this chapter, and I would like also to thank Alexander Nehamas for his extremely helpful comments on an early draft and his help in preparing the final version.

CHAPTER THREE

The Unity of Virtue

I. Greek Philosophy and the Unity of Virtue / the Virtues

Philosophers have recently revived the study of the ancient Greek topics of virtue and the virtues—justice, honesty, temperance, friendship, courage and so on as qualities of mind and character belonging to individual people. But one issue at the center of Greek moral theory seems to have dropped out of consideration. This is the question of the unity of virtue, the unity of the virtues. Must anyone who has one of these qualities have others of them as well, indeed all of them—all the ones that really do deserve to be counted as virtues? Even further, is there really no set of distinct and separate virtuous qualities at all, but at bottom only a single one—so that the person who has this single condition of "virtue" (and only he) is entitled also to the further descriptions "honest" and "well-controlled" and "just" and "friendly" and "courageous" and "fostering" and "supportive," and so on, as distinguishable aspects or immediate effects of his unitary "virtue"?

All the major Greek philosophers[1] answered the first question in the positive: to have any one of the human virtues, where the term *virtue* is carefully and strictly applied, means that you have to have all the rest as well. And a strong tradition, exemplified especially in the moral thought of Socrates (as we learn about that thought from Plato's Socratic dialogues) and in Stoic ethical theory, insisted that really there was only a single unified condition, virtue itself, of which the particular virtues that we normally distinguish from one another are (in one way or another) actually only aspects. Why did the Greek philosophers think these things? Why, to the contrary, do so many of our contemporary moralists and moral philosophers seem not just to disagree, but not to give the question any thought—as if the basic facts of the moral life, as we experience it today, stand at such a distance from any such conception as to make it not worth serious consideration? Might we learn something useful for current moral philosophy from looking more closely at the Greek philosophers' ideas about the unity of virtue—or do we have to regard them as quaint features of an irretrievably outmoded way of thinking about the moral life?

My main interest in this essay is to investigate a bit the related ideas of Socrates and the classical Stoics on the unity of virtue, and, secondarily and

---

[1] Including Epicurus, on what seems to me the most reasonable expansion of the meager evidence we have about his views on virtue and the virtues; for discussion, see Mitsis, *Epicurus' Ethical Theory*, pp. 75–76.

by contrast as well as comparison, those of Plato and Aristotle. First, however, let me try to indicate, in an introductory way, something of why I think this topic can be live and fruitful for us today, and need not be pursued in a merely historical spirit, as an antiquated curiosity. Beginning with Socrates in Plato's Socratic dialogues, all the ancient philosophers pursued the study of moral philosophy as part of a first-order practical, moral quest— not as a theoretical inquiry into the components of morality, or the good life for a human being. And they appealed to an audience who wished to do the same, in part through reading their writings. They and their audiences wanted to make themselves better, and to improve their lives, through coming to as full an understanding as possible of what really matters in a human life, and why it matters. Now I suspect that many people nowadays (undergraduate students and general readers as well as professional philosophers) who are interested in moral theory have a motive similar to that of the ancients, but of course that is not normally announced. Current philosophical inquiry, even inquiry into ethics and the moral life, adopts the attitude not of a personal quest but of a cool and disengaged study, with the result that the study of "the moral concepts" as they function in ordinary life easily comes to occupy the forefront of philosophers' attention. If you are interested, officially anyhow, primarily just in understanding the facts of the moral life—how people actually do live when they are accounted to be living well—and the structure of the concepts that underlie that life, then very likely you will think it perfectly obvious that some people have one set of virtues, while others have others, and that no essential unity of any sort is to be looked for or found in what we take to be virtuous qualities. But if in studying moral philosophy you are investigating how best to live yourself, with the intention of then doing your best to live that way, then I think the ancients' ideas about the unity of virtue, which grew out of a similar concern, are well worth attending to. Here, of course, the notion of virtue must be understood in a somewhat special way—by now it is not a concept in very live use anyhow. It has to be understood as standing in for whatever turns out to be the basis in human psychology, once that is developed to perfection, for leading the best life; practically speaking, it is the endpoint being aimed at in the pursuit of philosophy undertaken in the spirit I just described.

To be sure, merely engaging in such a pursuit does not commit one to holding that there *is* any single, unified condition constituting this basis, or even a single interlocking set of separate, mutually supporting (or at least nonconflicting) conditions. It could be, as many philosophers nowadays profess to think, that the set of things of central value in a well-lived human life is so diverse that no such single basis for living a good human life is possible; it could be that ineliminable conflicts among these values in particular circumstances necessarily lead to the flat violation of some correct principle of living or some set of such principles, in order to satisfy others. (I suspect, in fact, that this idea is one of the principal reasons why so many of our contemporaries interested in "virtue ethics" reject out of hand all suggestion of any unity of virtue or among the virtues.) But engaging in this pursuit does at least raise the question of the unity of virtue in a sharply focused way: if one is attempting to formulate an ideal of human perfection, as a basis for doing everything possible to lead the best human life, it will certainly seem very attractive to suppose, at least as a defeasible initial position, that there is some unified condition to be defined and sought. And one will not be inclined to accept the idea, until one is really forced to do so by weighty philosophical considerations, that no fully good life is possible at all, because the fundamental values or principles that might serve to define a good life in a philosophically adequate way are fundamentally and ineradicably in conflict with one another.

II. SOCRATES AND THE UNITY OF VIRTUE

It seems to me that this is how the idea of a unity of virtue, and of the virtues, arose within Greek moral philosophy: it arose from the thought that there must be some single basis—some single state of the soul, namely "virtue"—on which to lead one's life, if one is to perfect oneself as a human being and an agent and so live a fully good life. It did not arise as a consequence of Socrates' or someone's thinking first about particular virtues (say justice or courage or piety or temperance) and then noticing that various considerations about the individual virtues seemed to urge the conclusion (1) that no one could really be a just person without also being courageous, or even, on further consideration, the conclusion (2) that really whatever it is that constitutes the justice of a just person has to be somehow the same condition as their temperance and as their courage, and then asking the question: (3) but how, exactly, is one to understand this essential unity of virtue?[2] Consider how in the *Apology* Plato represents Socrates' life as a philosopher. Almost the first thing Socrates does there, after beginning his defence at his trial against Meletus and Anytus' charges of "impiety" and corrupting the youth, is to report a conversation with Callias, the patron of the sophists, about his young sons. If they were colts or calves, he says, Callias would have no trouble finding experts who would know how to raise and train them so that they attained the specific virtue or *aretē* that suits such animals; so who has he found to train his sons in "the human and citizen's virtue"—he speaks in the grammatical singular—that correspondingly suits young humans? Callias names Evenus of Paros, presumably his current craze among the sophists. But Socrates denies to the jury that *he* ever had any idea of having the knowledge himself, which Callias attri-

---

[2] Julia Annas gives a good account of how the unity of virtue might progressively have been arrived at, or defended, in post-Platonic philosophy (Aristotle and the Hellenistic schools down to Antiochus), on the basis of such a bottom-up way of thinking; see Annas, *Morality,* pp. 73–84.

butes to Evenus, of how to train any young man in this virtue (see *Apology* 20a–c). And later in his speech, as it becomes clearer what he did profess to do, the emphasis is once more all on a single condition, whether this is called "wisdom" or perhaps "truth," or "the best possible state of one's soul"—or simply "virtue" (that is, *aretē,* being a good human being) (29e–30a). This is what he is constantly striving for himself, and what as a gadfly he is urging his fellow-citizens to recognize as the central and controlling good, the one thing that they should care about more than anything, and that they should inquire into on their own or alongside him, as the only way to show seriously that they really do care as they should for virtue, the good of their souls (36c, 38a). From the beginning, it seems, Socrates' quest was conceived as aiming for something that he recognized—and, he assumed, his contemporaries did too—as a single condition: virtue, not *the* virtues.

It is one thing to hold such a presupposition, quite another to vindicate it in practice. In the *Protagoras,* more directly than in any other of Plato's Socratic works, Socrates attempts this vindication, and, as we will see, it is to the *Protagoras* that philosophers of the following generations turned first in their own efforts to work out an account of the unity of virtue. I should add at once that I do not mean that Socrates himself sets out anywhere in *Protagoras* a clear conception of how exactly virtue is a unity, or that he argues in any positive way that it is such. Socrates makes much of the fact that he is examining Protagoras's views for consistency and plausibility, and (after his opening great speech) neither Protagoras nor Socrates is a "speaker," propounding and arguing in a direct and positive way for his own ideas on the subject of virtue. Except for an interlude when the roles are reversed, Protagoras is the "answerer" in a dialectical exchange and Socrates the "questioner." As answerer, Protagoras does, however, have a position to defend, and Socrates' role is to undermine it by obtaining Protagoras' assent to things that he can hardly see a way sensibly to deny, which Socrates can then show logically imply the negation of some part or aspect of that position. In this dialectical exchange Protagoras' position (at least initially) is that there are five distinct states of mind and character that we recognize as virtues for a human being, and that each of these is quite distinct from any of the others, both (so to speak) in its own internal constitution and in the behavior it leads to for a human being who possesses it—so that a person could possess any one of them without any of the others and could also possess any selection you like from among them.[3] But it is clear that Socrates does not just play devil's advocate in his role as questioner against Protagoras on this subject; he is quite firm in stating his own personal commitment that Protagoras is wrong—more positively, that virtue *is* a unity, a single condition of mind and character.[4] However, because his position throughout is that of questioner, he never has to say, or show, just

---

[3] See Plato, *Protagoras* 330a7–b2, 329e2–6.
[4] See ibid., 331e4–6, 359b6–7, 361a6–b3.

how he would articulate or defend his own opposed point of view. The result, as I explain more fully below, is that the *Protagoras* gives us more a challenge as to how to think through the commitment to the unity of virtue (despite the diversity of its manifestations) than a particular answer to that challenge. When, as I mentioned above, philosophers of succeeding generations, including the first Stoics, turned to the *Protagoras* for directions in pursuing this topic, they seem to have understood the dialogue in just this way.

It is worth noting that Socrates is provoked to raise the question of the unity of virtue in this dialogue because Protagoras[5] himself apparently begins by accepting the idea that there is a single condition, *aretē,* that young people should be educated to possess (in fact, that is precisely what he offers to teach them). Yet, on being questioned about this condition, he backslides (or so it seems to Socrates) into speaking of it as a plurality. Protagoras has said that if Socrates' friend Hippocrates joins him he will learn not a whole series of separate skills (astronomy, geometry, music, and poetry) but just what he came for: the subject Protagoras teaches (the *mathēma*) is excellence in deliberation (*euboulia*), both in one's private, household affairs, and in discussing and conducting a city's public business (318e5–319a2). He does not quite say that this amounts to teaching virtue, but he acquiesces when Socrates interprets it that way (first at 319e2), and indeed his own term *euboulia* is only a variant on or aspect of what Socrates means by his own preferred word, *sophia* or wisdom, for indicating the unified condition that constitutes virtue. Yet when in his "speech" Protagoras discusses how this is a teachable subject, he only once uses the word *wisdom* (*sophia: politikē sophia,* wisdom for living in a city, 321d5) in referring to it; and though he speaks equivalently of the "political" or "citizenly" skill (*politikē technē,* 322b5, 8) and again of the "virtue of the citizen" (324a1) a couple of times, he mostly speaks of his alleged subject as variously "justice" (*dikē,* 322c4, d5; *dikaiosunē,* 323a1, 6, b2, 325a1), or again "restraint" or "temperance" (*aidōs,* 322c4, d5; *sōphrosunē,* 323a2, b4, 325a1), or "piety" (*eusebeia* by implication at 323e7; *to hosion einai,* 325a1). Even in that process, in turning at 324d7–325a2 from the mythological account he has been entertaining Socrates and the others with before, to the "reasoned argument" (*logos*) he then appends, he conspicuously asserts that this thing he is claiming to be teachable is the "one thing" every person who lives in a city must possess (at least to some extent, cf. 323c1), and even that "this one thing . . . is justice and temperance [i.e., restraint] and piety" (324e3–325a1). No wonder Socrates is confused; when his turn comes to question Protagoras, he by no means drags in some artificial question to nag Protagoras when he

---

[5] That is, the character in Plato's dialogue named after him. Throughout, in referring to Protagoras and discussing his views, as also in what I say about Socrates, I am talking about Plato's characters of those names. I do not intend to be making any claims at all about the historical personages. I leave such historical questions entirely to one side.

asks what sort of unity he can possibly have in mind.[6] One should observe that nowhere in his speech has Protagoras spoken of "parts" of virtue when he has spoken of justice, temperance, and piety: he has left perfectly undetermined what he thinks about the relationship between these different words he has applied to the single thing, virtue. Nothing in what he has said has indicated or even suggested that he has been thinking all along that a plurality of perfectly distinct conditions characterize a wise and excellent citizen, sharing the name "virtue." So Socrates is only doing what is sensible in offering him the two initial options: Are justice and so on parts of virtue as a whole, or rather several names of the same unit?

I mentioned that, to judge simply from what he states and how he argues in the ensuing discussion, Socrates' own view remains in important respects undetermined. However, we do learn enough from what he says in arguing against Protagoras' view to say the following: In his initial questioning to fix Protagoras' own position in the ensuing debate, Socrates distinguishes with perfect clarity between the following two, distinct questions (329c6–e2, e2–4). First, whether (i) justice and the rest are distinguishable parts of virtue, which is a unity in the sense of a whole of parts—whether these parts are similar to one another or not, in internal constitution and in what they cause one possessing them to do—or else (ii) virtue is some other sort of unity. Second, whether a person can have any one of justice, courage, temperance, and wisdom only if they have all the others as well. Later, Socrates and Protagoras repeatedly make it clear that their principal difference is over the first issue, whether virtue is a whole of parts or some other sort of unity: if they differ, as they do, over the second issue as well— the issue of coinstantiation—it is in consequence of their difference over the first.

Furthermore, at 331b4–5, in the argument about piety and justice, to which I return below, Socrates says that in his own opinion (and he urges Protagoras to agree) justice and piety are "the same thing," or at least very similar, thus indicating (if we ignore for a moment the qualification "or at least very similar") that according to his own view virtue is some stronger sort of unity than that belonging to a whole of parts. Socrates' reason for saying that justice and piety are the same thing is that justice is both just and pious, and so is piety. (We will consider later what this might mean.) The context makes it clear that the sole reason for the reservation in "or at least very similar" is that Socrates scrupulously thinks he has so far given reasons only to accept that justice and piety share some of the same essential predicates, not all of them. The inference to draw is not that maybe after all piety and justice are not in Socrates' opinion "the same thing" but

---

[6] In preparing at 329c2–6 to raise this question, Socrates virtually quotes Protagoras's own remarks at 325a1–2: compare ὡς ἕν τι εἴη συλλήβδην, ἀρετή at 329c5–6 (justice etc. "were somehow collectively one thing: virtue") with καὶ συλλήβδην ἓν αὐτὸ προσαγορεύω εἶναι ἀνδρὸς ἀρετήν at 325a1–2 ("what I may collectively term the virtue of a man"). It is Protagoras's own formulations that provoke Socrates' confusion and his subsequent line of questioning.

different ones, merely very similar; but rather that in order to use his present line of argument to show Protagoras that they are the same thing, he would have to go through all the other virtue-adjectives and show that both piety and justice share them all—that each is not only just and pious, but also temperate and courageous and wise. A little later, because Socrates thinks that by then he *has* produced an argument—quite a different one this time—strong enough to permit elimination of the qualification, he asserts (333b4–5) that he has given good reasons to conclude that "wisdom and temperance are one thing," that is, are one and the same thing, and not merely constituents of some one thing as two of its parts. And in reaching this conclusion Socrates contrasts his own position with Protagoras's, without so much as mentioning that according to Protagoras a person can have any single virtue all by itself. He says (333a1–7):

> Then which of these propositions should we abandon, Protagoras? The proposition that for one thing there is only one opposite, or the one stating that wisdom is different from temperance and that each is a part of virtue, and that in addition to being distinct they are dissimilar, both in themselves and in their powers or functions, just like the parts of a face? . . . The two statements are dissonant.[7]

The claim of the unlikeness of the virtues to one another is connected here, as it has been already before (329d4–8, 330a4–b1), with that of their being distinct parts of virtue as a whole; the question, posed quite distinctly and separately before, of the necessary coinstantiation of the particular virtues, is something quite different, not mentioned here at all. Socrates' and Protagoras's opposition here, and indeed throughout the discussion, is over the question of the identity or nonidentity (whatever exactly that might come to) of justice and the rest with one another—not over whether anyone who has one virtue must have the others as well, that is, what has been called the question of "interentailment" or the "Biconditionality Thesis."[8] We can see this at the end of the whole discussion, when Socrates characterizes his own view, and says what he thinks his whole argument against Protagoras has shown: that not merely is courage wisdom (*sophia*)—wisdom about what is to be feared and not to be feared, 360d4–5—but "everything" (he mentions specifically justice, temperance, and courage) is knowledge (*epistēmē*), 361b1–2.

It is easy to see why Socrates states his difference from Protagoras in these terms, not in terms merely of necessary coinstantiation, even though he clearly sees that as an important additional point. If in some deep way justice, temperance, and so on are really the same condition of mind, then evidently one could not have one of them without the others—that would

---

[7] Plato, *Protagoras*, translated by S. Lombardo and K. Bell, in Cooper, ed., *Plato: Complete Works.*

[8] For the latter expression, see Vlastos, "The Unity of the Virtues in the *Protagoras.*"

seem to follow immediately. If instead they are as Protagoras wishes to say, distinct and dissimilar parts of a whole that is simply the result of their being assembled all together, then equally evidently it ought to be possible (as Protagoras says actually happens) to have any single one without all or even any of the others. If the virtues differ from one another in internal constitution and in the behavior that expresses them, what could cause any necessary coinstantiation? Thus, the difference between Socrates and Protagoras over coinstantiation follows from their difference over the unity of virtue. But suppose for a moment that, in opposing Protagoras, Socrates had intended only to assert necessary coinstantiation, and to remain uncommitted to any thesis of the unity of virtue itself—however it might be worked out and articulated in detail. Suppose he merely wanted to say that every person who is truly just, or temperate, or courageous, or pious, or wise is necessarily also all the others as well. One would immediately want to know why. What is it about justice, temperance, courage, piety, and wisdom—those conditions of mind and character[9]—that makes them necessarily coinstantiated if instantiated at all? Surely there must be something to be learned about the virtues, something about *their* natures, that is responsible for this alleged fact about their instantiations. Are they the same thing, either straightforwardly or in some complicated, deeper way? Is that why persons exhibiting one quality exhibit all the others? If not, what could possibly ground the necessity of the coinstantiation? Thus, it appears that even in his commitment to necessary coinstantiation, Socrates would naturally be seen, and see himself, as further committed to some view about the nature of virtue, and of the virtues, that would sustain that commitment. In the *Protagoras* this further commitment is in fact along the lines of the essentially unitary nature of virtue itself, and of the virtues, as against their being a merely part-whole assemblage. So it is easily understandable that Plato makes that underlying difference as to virtue itself and its relations to the particular virtues the focus of Socrates' disagreement with Protagoras.[10]

III. SOCRATES ON JUSTICE AND PIETY

So far my discussion has been unavoidably, but nonetheless regrettably, abstract. I have already mentioned that in making Socrates the questioner in this part of the discussion, Plato's text limits what we can say about

[9] Or instead, if you like, those Platonic Forms.

[10] Thus Vlastos's effort (in "Unity," pp. 234ff.) to reduce Socrates' thesis of the unity of virtue in the *Protagoras* to a misleading way simply of affirming "biconditionality"—that x is just if and only if x is temperate, and so on—fails. Some psychological and/or metaphysical truth about virtue itself, and the virtues themselves, must underlie and ground any *necessary* coinstantiation of them. It is this underlying truth that has to be explained and made out in some way, if Socrates' own position in the debate with Protagoras is to be understood.

Socrates' own views in the dialogue. However, one of his lines of questioning, though still very abstract, does give us a glimpse of how Socrates may have been thinking himself, and this will permit us to see something of moral substance. This is the notorious passage about justice and piety alluded to above (330b6–332a4). This passage occurs immediately after Socrates has established Protagoras's opinions about virtue itself and the particular virtues. It has emerged (330b3–6) that according to Protagoras no virtue other than knowledge or wisdom is "such as" (*hoion*) knowledge or wisdom, none other than justice "such as" justice, and the same holds for courage, temperance, and piety. This point Socrates wishes to challenge. So he begins his examination of Protagoras's opinions by saying that they need, then, to see what each of the virtues is really like (b6–7): in Greek, they need to learn *poion ti* (the interrogative corresponding to the relative *hoion* in the preceding) it is—"such as what" it is. He takes up first the cases of justice and piety, evidently intending to go on to the other cases as well, to show that they are all in fact "such as" each other. Now what Socrates wishes to say about justice and piety is that each is "such as" the other in that whereas, as he and Protagoras immediately agree (I will return shortly to why they agree to this, and what this agreement comes to), justice is just and piety is pious, so also piety is just and justice pious (though perhaps less immediately obviously so). In other words, each of these two is "such as" the other in being characterized identically with it, at least to this extent: justice is just *and* pious, piety is pious *and* just. (Again, I will come back shortly to these further characterizations, to see what Socrates can mean by them.) So Socrates' intention was to go on from this pair to show that each of the virtues is "such as" each of the others; in other words, that justice is just, pious, temperate, and wise, and that piety is likewise pious, just, temperate, and wise, and so on for the other cases. Each virtue is characterized in the same way as each of the others, namely by all the virtue terms— not, so to speak, only by its own. And that means that they are the same thing—no basis of distinction remains, setting any one of them off from any other. However, Socrates has to break off this line of argument before going beyond the first pair, because, though Protagoras is willing to grant him the additional points he wants (that piety is just and justice pious), he protests that this sort of commonality establishes only a slight resemblance: everything is like everything else in *some* way, he indignantly says, and such a slight similarity as this admission grants is not at all sufficient to show that justice and piety are not, overall, to be classed as "unlikes" rather than "likes" (331d1–e4)—as Protagoras had maintained in the first place. Socrates is very surprised at the idea that only a slight resemblance has been established (we will see in a moment why he may be thinking this), but rather than press the point, he yields in the face of Protagoras's annoyance and drops the line of inquiry, salvaging only Protagoras's admission that at least piety and justice are "such as" one another after all, in that each is characterized not only by its own, but also by the other's, adjective.[11] So, to that extent, Protagoras's initial assertion that no virtue is "such as" any other has been shown to be inaccurate.

But what, in any case, does all this talk of justice's being just, and further-more being "such as" piety in that it is also pious, and perhaps "such as" temperance and wisdom, too, come to? To confront this question, it is helpful to bear in mind that Protagoras agrees without hesitation when Socrates asks him whether he, too, would "vote" that justice is just (not unjust), and that piety is pious (not impious) (330c7, e2). How, asks Socrates, could anything else be pious if piety were not? Protagoras apparently takes the point, and in any event he agrees that piety is pious. So although this is an instance of self-predication in relation to a quality or other property, it must not be interpreted as relating specifically to a separated Platonic Form, considered as more "real" than what partakes in it—Protagoras is not agreeing straight off the bat to anything with any such momentous consequences. In fact, Protagoras and Socrates have just before been speak-ing of justice and so on as having or being "powers" and "capabilities," comparable to those of the eyes and ears (330a–b), and it seems clear that it is as such that they are continuing to speak of them here. What Socrates and Protagoras agree is that the "power" of justice in a person is just, and that of piety pious. But what does that mean? Here the analogy with eyes and ears may help. In one's eyes one has the power of sight; with them, one is able to see; using them one sees. What, then, is justice the power to do— what is it that a person having justice does in using it? Evidently, the obvious and basic answer is: acts justly, does justice. If we bear in mind the context here of justice as a power, something in a person that is responsible for their being able to do, and doing, certain things, as sight in the eyes is responsible for a person's being able to see and for their seeing (whenever they do see), we can perhaps understand along the following lines Protago-ras's and Socrates' ready agreement that justice is just and piety pious. They are assuming that the very nature of justice is to make what it causes, when it is active at all, be something just: as such a cause, it has within itself, so to speak, a pattern of direction in what it shapes so that the result is the justice of the product; its nature is such as to be directed at producing precisely that result. Of all powers of the human soul, justice is the very

[11] The next argument (*Protagoras,* 332a4–333b6), concerning temperance and wisdom, does not attempt to establish that these are "such as" one another, but instead that each is directly identical with the other. So it is not a continuation of the line of argument announced at 330b6–7. Having abandoned the first line of argument without completing it, Socrates now shifts to showing, pairwise, as he has now done with justice and piety, that temperance and wisdom, and then justice and temperance (333b7–334c6), and finally courage and wisdom, are related to one another by some transitive relation strong enough to undermine Protagoras's claim of distinctness and difference; when the separate arguments are put together, he will then have established that the same relation relates each one to each of the others.

one whose nature and function (however we might ultimately come to understand that) is to shape and pattern its outcomes so that they are just. I suggest that these self-predications simply record that fact: to say that justice is just is to say that by its nature justice is directed at producing, and does produce, just outcomes. If this is right, one can easily see why Socrates should think that if piety were not pious, or justice not just, then nothing else could be either of those things: if piety were not pious, it would not after all be that power that of all powers is the one directed at the production of pious outcomes—but then it would be a total mystery, or at least a mere accident, that there ever were any such outcomes, any pious actions, for example, at all.[12]

Why then does Socrates insist not only that justice is just and piety pious, but that justice is also pious and piety just? Protagoras is not certain (b8–c3) whether he should agree to these further assertions, and one can see why. If what I have just said is correct, then to agree would apparently be to agree that justice is *also* the power to produce pious actions (not merely the just ones) and that piety is the power to produce just actions (not merely the pious ones). But wouldn't that unacceptably obliterate the distinction between piety and justice? How can there be two powers that are, of all powers, *the* one directed at pious outcomes, and again *the* one directed at just ones? No, Protagoras says, there still seems to him to be some difference here that prevents a simple positive answer to the questions whether justice is pious and piety just. Nonetheless, Socrates has a point (though it is unclear to me whether Protagoras really sees it when he grants that, in a way, we do have to say that justice is pious and piety just).[13] It is surely not an attractive idea to say that justice is *im*pious, or even *not* pious, if that would mean, as it would in this context, that the nature of justice is to cause one to do impious actions or produce impious outcomes, or even to cause actions and outcomes that are other than the pious ones that might have been produced instead (and that the situation demanded). Suppose, to choose a hackneyed example, that you have promised to meet someone for lunch, and that just as the time arrives you receive news that your father has fallen seriously ill. It seems to be a duty of piety to go at once to the parent's bedside to offer assistance, and it seems to be a duty of justice to keep the promise (or at least arrange things with the promisee so that you don't have to—something, let us suppose, circumstances prevent you from doing). If your justice has the power to make you keep the promise, it also has the power to make you do something other than make the pious immediate

---

[12] In formulating this account of what "justice is just" means here, I have been helped by unpublished work by Sean Kelsey on Plato's *Phaedo*.

[13] Perhaps he is influenced by the close association (for Greek common sense) between justice and piety as regulating respectful relations, respectively, among human beings and between humans and gods—so that (see *Euthyphro* 11e–12d) one could even regard piety as nothing more than one part of justice, the part having to do with our relations with the gods. Compare what M. Frede says in his Introduction to the Hackett edition of the *Protagoras*, p. xxvi.

visit to your parent's bedside, that is, something not pious, which, in the circumstances, will also be something impious: it is impious to value keeping a promise to a friend above tending to your parent's urgent needs. Likewise, if your piety has the power to make you go at once to the parent's bedside and simply leave your friend in the lurch, then it also has the power to make you do something other than the just act of keeping the promise, which in this situation is also going to be something unjust—breaking it.[14]

Most people would think, and I agree, that there is a ready solution: the right thing is to go at once to the parent's bedside, and then, as soon as possible, to apologize to the friend—to explain what necessitated disappointing them, ask for their understanding and acceptance and do anything reasonable to reassure them of your regard and that you took very seriously the initial commitment to meet them as agreed. In that case, the claim would be that justice, in the stringencies of this unusual situation, did not, after all, require keeping the promise, or else arranging in advance to obtain leave not to; justice in these circumstances requires only explaining oneself after the fact and duly making amends. Doesn't that mean, however, that your "power" of justice, and not only that of piety, causes you to go to the parent's bedside—while also, of course, causing you further to contact the friend as soon as possible and explain the situation? If so, it seems plausible to say, not only does justice, in these circumstances, not prevent you from doing the pious act, or cause you to do the impious act of going to the meeting place instead, it also cooperates with your "power" of piety in co-causing you to do the thing piety requires, namely, to go immediately for the bedside visit. Thus, that turns out to be not only the pious action but also the just one—albeit only the first stage in a two-step course of action recommended by considerations of justice. Justice takes account of commitments coming under piety, and knows how, when they arise, to respect them—not, of course, as prominent and *standard* considerations of justice, as a promise is, but, in such special and unusual situations as the current one, considerations that have greater weight under justice than the specific terms of the promise itself do. If so, then, exactly as Socrates says, "justice is pious"—if not in the sense that it always produces pious actions and outcomes whenever it produces anything at all, then in the sense that whenever considerations of piety impinge in a situation where justice is being called upon to act, it takes account of those *as* considerations (however

---

[14] Thus, I do not think that at 331a7–b1 Socrates hoodwinks Protagoras by making him uncomfortable with the idea that justice should be accounted something impious, and contriving thereby to scare him off the true response that justice is *not* pious (because it is simply neither pious nor impious—not the sort of thing to be either of these things). Socrates does not illegitimately imply that if justice *is* not pious, then it must immediately follow that it is also impious (as if that were not a significantly different, further property). In fact, if talk of justice's being pious or not is understood correctly, that is, in accordance with what the context establishes for its interpretation, it is true, as my example shows, that if justice is not pious it must also be impious: if it causes a person to act otherwise than piously in a situation calling for pious action, it causes them also to act impiously.

irregular and unprominent) of justice itself.[15] Of course, I do not mean to say that when considerations of piety arise it will always be the judgment of justice that they should take precedence: in some emergencies it is presumably right, under justice, to go to the aid of a stranger in need, and forego attending a religious ceremony that it would have been a violation of piety simply to skip because you didn't feel like going. In that case, piety, being itself just, agrees with justice, which is pious, in seeing that that is where the priority lies (while also insisting that some appropriate amends be made to the god afterward).

Similar apparent conflicts between distinct virtues, and similar resolutions, are available in other cases as well. If Socrates had proceeded with his initial plan, he could have argued that temperance must be not only temperate but also just, because even if temperance usually requires quiet and dignified behavior, considerations of justice may nevertheless impinge that cause temperance to consider the need, as a requirement of temperance itself, to act loudly and not with great dignity—for example, in order to prevent some violation of another person from taking place. A similar argument could be made for courage and temperance, or piety and courage. All the virtues must be sensitive to considerations other than their usual and standard ones, and must be prepared, as appropriate, to treat those considerations as coming under their own aegis, when they do arise. One could argue, along the same lines as I have done above in interpreting what Socrates says about justice and piety, that justice is not only pious but also temperate, courageous, and wise, and that temperance is not only just, but pious, courageous, and wise as well—and so on for each of the remaining virtues.

What then about Protagoras's reservation that nonetheless there is some difference here between the way that piety is pious and the way that justice is pious? Can Socrates' view sustain a sufficient difference so that the two virtues do not simply collapse into one another (and into the others as well)? It seems that it can—even though, of course, Socrates is not called upon to explain how this is so. There are two considerations here. First of all, piety always causes a pious outcome whenever it is operative at all, but only causes (or co-causes) a just one when overriding considerations of justice impinge (as they do not always do) in a situation where piety is called upon to act. And contrariwise, justice always causes a just outcome whenever *it* is operative, but causes a pious one only when considerations of piety impinge and override as well. So even though (under certain circumstances) justice and piety each (co-)cause one another's outcomes, they remain distinct in that, in some circumstances, only one of them may be operative at all. Second, we can draw upon an idea of Chrysippus and other Stoics—though, as I shall argue, they put it to significantly different use. We can distinguish,

---

[15] Thus, to say that justice is pious is to say that justice is by its nature *a* power to cause pious actions, and never a power to cause impious actions. (To say that piety is pious means something connected but slightly different: it is *the* power that always causes pious actions and outcomes whenever it operates and causes anything at all.)

as I did proleptically in discussing my example above, between what is "primary" and what is "secondary" for each of the virtues. Each virtue knows everything that each of the others also knows, but they order or arrange their knowledge in different ways. Thus, justice knows all the principles of piety about what sort of respect and attention are owed to the gods, one's parents and ancestors, and one's country—it has to know these, if it is to be ready to spot circumstances in which to act on such respect becomes the just thing to do. But it primarily looks out for obligations owed as a result of promises and contracts, plus duties to individuals and groups of fellow citizens under the laws, and to others in dire need. Justice's primary and standard sensitivities are to such considerations; it has to be sensitive to the others—those of piety, for example—only in a secondary way, in case they might come into play in such a way as to alter what would otherwise be the right response, according to justice, to the situation requiring decision and action. And similarly, mutatis mutandis, for each of the other virtues. On this view, you could say that the virtues are one, and virtue itself is one, in that they and it are a single, comprehensive knowledge of all the considerations that ever present themselves for decision and action. Yet the single condition of virtue is differentiated into distinct particular virtues in that this single knowledge, if possessed at all, is organized in such a way that the different specific groups of considerations are kept jointly prominent and operative in the mind, in case evolving circumstances should call the sensitivity to them into active use. Each such sensitivity, while focused first and primarily on its own group of considerations, is also secondarily sensitive to the considerations belonging to all the others, since, again, evolving circumstances may call upon it to recognize some of them as helping to determine how in that situation to exercise its own specific power to produce outcomes. These distinct, simultaneously maintained orderings correspond to—in fact, they constitute—the full and perfect forms of the different traditionally recognized virtues of justice, courage, temperance, piety, and wisdom.

Now I freely admit—indeed, I insist—that this suggestion as to what Socrates may have in mind in this first line of argument is an extended extrapolation, not at all anything he says explicitly. I only claim for it that it takes seriously and attempts to work out as fully as possible implications for the unity of virtue deriving from clearly marked features of the context: (1) Virtues are being considered by Socrates and Protagoras as powers or capabilities to produce specific sorts of action or other outcomes; (2) Socrates' language of justice being just and, again, pious seems, on reflection, clearly intended to talk about what the power itself is like, how it is characterized, insofar as it has specific sorts of product; and (3) Socrates implies that he is prepared to argue for each of the other virtues in a way precisely similar to the way he argues with respect to justice and piety. I do not claim that this worked-out view of the unity of virtue is the view of Socrates himself in the discussion; as questioner he does not have to display a worked-out view of his own, and he does not even have to hold one in reserve—he can be weighing alternatives, seeking the most viable position to take as he poses his questions and ponders the possible answers and their consequences. The text presents him simply as wanting to hold to *some* version of a unity-of-virtue doctrine, as opposed to Protagoras's whole-of-assembled-parts view. It seems reasonable to read the dialogue as offering readers the stimulus to think through for themselves—carefully taking into account considerations and points of view arising in the discussion—the question of the nature of virtue itself and its relations to the specific, traditionally recognized virtues. I have merely been taking the dialogue up on this stimulus and challenge. It is only in that sense that I claim to find this worked-out view "in" the dialogue.

IV. Menedemus and Ariston on Virtue

In this I think I am following ancient precedent. Plutarch, near the beginning of his little essay *On Moral Virtue*,[16] provides evidence that early Stoics and their rationalist predecessors turned to the *Protagoras* in this spirit of exploration to work out their own views on these questions. As I mentioned above, it was Protagoras' reference to some "one thing" needed if there is to be a city at all—for which however he used several names: "political wisdom," "justice," "temperance" (or restraint) and "piety"—that led to the prolonged discussion with Socrates over the unity (or not) of virtue. In his effort to clarify Protagoras's intentions in this regard, Socrates poses a series of options for him to choose among. The first and (given what Protagoras has actually said at 324e–325a) the most natural question is whether he means to refer to "virtue" as a single thing that, as it happens, simply has in our language several different names—among them "political wisdom," "justice," and so on that Protagoras used for it in his speech. Partly, it seems, in order to sharpen and clarify what this question means, Socrates poses as the alternative that virtue is one in the sense of a single whole composed of the several particular virtues as its parts: accordingly, if virtue *is* a single thing with several names, these are to be understood not as names for the whole by way of naming distinct parts of it, but truly as names for the whole *as* a whole, with no further differentiation. When Protagoras answers (perhaps surprisingly) that, in his opinion, justice and so on are distinct parts of virtue as a whole—so that, despite his earlier remarks, he has to teach his pupils a whole series of things, and not really a single one, after all—Socrates poses a further pair of options. Are these parts of virtue parts of it in the same way as mouth, nose, eyes, and ears are the parts of the face, or is it rather in the way that the parts of gold[17] are parts of it—

---

[16] Plutarch, a Platonist philosopher, lived from about A.D. 50 to about 120.

[17] The Greek at *Protagoras* 329d6 is *ta tou chrusou moria*, literally, "the parts of gold"—presumably (all) the parts of the totality of gold that there is. This is, however, often or usually translated and understood as several "parts" or "pieces" of gold taken together as a single

not differing from one another and from the whole except in whatever corresponds in their case to the distinctions of size among gold's parts (329d4–8)? Here it seems that the alternative of the gold is brought in primarily as a means of clarifying the meaning of the other option; it is probably not considered by Socrates as a genuine option on its own.[18] He goes on to point out (330a4–b6) that eyes and ears differ from one another both in what they themselves "are like" or are "such as" and in what power or capability they exercise; and that kind of difference is here introduced with graphic economy by the contrast with the parts of gold, parts that do *not* differ internally (or in their natural "function") but only in such externals as relative size and shape. This time, as we have seen, Protagoras opts for the conception of parts of virtue on the analogy of the parts of the face.

Plutarch begins his Platonist discussion of moral virtue by reviewing the opinions of his opponents, having mostly in mind the Stoics. He first gives the view of Menedemus of Eretria (a contemporary of Zeno the Stoic, with philosophical affiliations to the Socratic schools of Megara and Elis, where he studied); then that of Ariston of Chios (an early associate and follower of Zeno); then that of Zeno himself; and finally that of Chrysippus.[19] Plutarch's account leaves no doubt that Menedemus opted for the first of Socrates' rejected options—that virtue is a single thing with several names. And I think that Ariston's view, as reported by Plutarch and other later ancient writers,[20] is best interpreted as inspired by the second rejected (the "gold") option—that virtue is a whole of parts like one another and like the whole in their internal constitution but differing in "externals." About Zeno and Chrysippus, Plutarch's report is less clear, but other evidence makes it seem possible that they, too, in developing their views on the unity of virtue, were working in part with an eye to offering an interpretation of Socrates' position in the *Protagoras*—quite a different one, or quite different ones, from either of these first two. I return to Chrysippus and Zeno below. Here is

---

group, making up a single pile or a single lump of gold. It is possible that the Greek does mean this, but the other alternative, which is, I think, the more natural way of construing the Greek, should be borne in mind as well; when developed as I think Ariston of Chios developed it (see below), it gives a better account of the unity and correlated plurality of the virtues than does the "pieces of gold" reading.

[18] I agree here up to a point with M. Frede in his introduction to the *Protagoras,* pp. xxiii–xxiv: only two real options are considered in the *Protagoras,* either the identity (in some sense) of all the virtues with wisdom or knowledge of good and bad, or the view that virtue is a whole of disparate parts. But (see below) I do not think the "gold" alternative is in itself vacuous; it looks to me as if Ariston of Chios was trying to make something distinctive of it. (Contrast Vlastos, "Unity," p. 225, who takes this option to represent (part of) Socrates' own preference.)

[19] Zeno of Citium, the founder of the Stoic school of philosophy, was active in Athens from the last decade of the fourth century to his death in about 262 B.C. Chrysippus was head of the school from about 232 to about 206 B.C.

[20] See also Diogenes Laertius VII 161; Galen, *On the Doctrines of Hippocrates and Plato,* VII 2. Diogenes Laertius is thought to have written in the second or third c. A.D.; Galen lived from about A.D. 129 to 199.

what Plutarch says about Menedemus and Ariston (*On Moral Virtue*, 440e–441a):

> Menedemus of Eretria did away with both the plurality and the differentiations of the virtues; he thought virtue was a single thing with many names: the same thing is called temperance and courage and justice, as with "mortal" and "human." Ariston of Chios too made virtue one thing in its essence, and called it health; but in what it is somehow related to he made the virtues differentiated and plural, just as if one wanted to call our vision in grasping light-colored things light-sight, but dark-sight in grasping dark-colored ones, and so on in other such cases. For virtue in considering things to be done and not to be done is called wisdom (*phronēsis*), but it is called temperance in bringing order to our appetites and defining what is measured and timely in pleasures, and justice in busying itself with joint enterprises and contracts with other people: just as a knife is a single thing but cuts now one thing, now another, and fire acts upon different materials with its single nature.

It is worth noting that in Menedemus' version of Socrates' "one entity, several names" alternative it would be grossly misleading to say that the different virtue-names, such as "justice" and "temperance," are claimed to be synonyms—so that the definition of "justice" would be identical with that of "temperance."[21] You can see this in the allegedly parallel case to which, in explaining his view, Menedemus assimilated the virtues. Everything that is a mortal (*brotos*—this is a Homeric and poetical noun) is also a human being (*anthrōpos*), and vice versa, but what makes them these things differs in the two cases. (So this is not a case like "pants" and "trousers" in contemporary U.S. usage: those are true synonyms.) To be a mortal (*brotos*) is to be a creature subject to death, by contrast with the gods—the *athanatoi* or deathless ones; there is a correlative poetical adjective for the gods as *ambrotoi*, a virtual synonym of *athanatoi*. To be a human being, I would suppose, is to fall into a certain natural species of living things, in contrast with other animals. Nonetheless, if we assume that the entities to which these two terms apply have a nature of their own independently of these modes of reference, then the account of the nature of the things that are mortals and humans will be a single account and presumably will give the basis for both the contrast with the gods and the contrast with other animals that "mortal" and "human" respectively convey. The different terms indicate entirely superficial differences in the point of view from which these entities are being considered—depending upon which comparison class is in view. On Menedemus's account, then, justice and temperance are a single entity with its own nature, referred to by different names indicating superficial differences in the point of view from which it can be considered.

---

[21] So if anyone thought (wrongly, as I have said) that this version of unity was the one Socrates himself favored in the *Protagoras*, it would not be a good argument against them to insist that Socrates, of all people, could not have thought that "justice" and "temperance" were *synonyms*!

It would be worthwhile to know what account Menedemus gave of these differences—however superficial and insignificant, so far as the nature of virtue itself goes, he may have thought them. Our sources do not say anything about this, however. Perhaps "justice" could be the name to use when considering virtue as binding people together into one community, "temperance" when considering virtue as beautifying the soul, and so on for the other cases. The crucial point is that for Menedemus these differences were truly superficial and insignificant, imposed by the ways *we* happen to think, without indicating any difference of nature in the underlying phenomenon, not even different real qualities it possesses—the qualities of binding people together and of beautifying the soul, say.

I suggested that Ariston, presumably dissatisfied with such a total denial of any objective difference of nature in virtue (and the virtues), opted to follow up the hint given by Socrates' analogy of the parts of virtue to the parts of gold. I mentioned above (in footnote 17) that on one reading this analogy speaks of distinct bits or pieces of gold joined to make up a whole bigger piece or quantity of gold, differing from one another and from the whole in size but not, of course, in inner nature. Since there seems to be no good reason to think that any one such "part" of the whole in question could not be possessed without also possessing the others, the analogy so interpreted would seem to support an account of virtue that did not maintain the "inter-entailing" character of the virtues, while, paradoxically, speaking of them as like one another and the whole except in externals.[22] But on the other, more natural, reading it is gold itself—the totality of the gold that there is—that is being spoken of, and its parts; and this is not something that can reasonably be thought of as having been assembled from the parts, or as being "possessed" in parts but not in the whole. Accordingly, if virtue is like gold, then when one has it one has all its parts too, and there is no question of building up to it by getting first some one part of it and then another and another; one has it first as a whole, and in having it in that way one also necessarily has all its parts.

This is how Ariston seems to have thought of it: he says that virtue is the health of the soul, a single pervasive condition—in fact, a state of comprehensive knowledge about good and bad for human beings[23]—and he says that particular virtues like justice, temperance, and practical wisdom (*phronēsis*) are that psychic health as it is directed at ("related to") its different tasks: considering what to do and what not to do, bringing order to our desires and imposing limits on pleasures, dealing with business and political affairs. These different tasks are the "externals" that correspond for virtue to the differences in relative size of the parts of gold. Ariston adds three further analogies. The whole, single power of sight is used when one

---

[22] Perhaps this is why Frede describes it as a "vacuous" option (introduction to *Protagoras*, p. xxiii).

[23] On this, see Galen, *On the Doctrines of Hippocrates and Plato* VII 2 (= von Arnim, *Stoicorum Veterum Fragmenta,* I 374 [hereafter abbreviated as *SVF*]).

looks at something light-colored and also when one looks at something dark; the whole knife and its power to cut is used whether cutting salami or fruit; the whole natural power of fire is employed whether it heats up air or water. But each of these things could be called by different names to take account of these differences in what it is standardly applied to in this precisely similar exercise of its power ("light-sight" as against "dark-sight," "salami-cutter" as against "fruit-cutter," "air-heating" as against "water-heating" fire). This is just what happens, Ariston suggests, in the case of virtue: it is a single condition of pervasive health of the soul, but it can be referred to in different ways that record real distinctions in its natural orientations. In its internal operations, it does nothing different in the different orientations; but it is an objective, not at all superficial, fact about virtue that it does have these distinct orientations to what lies outside it—it is not some mere human convention to take special notice of these via the different virtue-names. So, according to Ariston, the health of the soul (as a whole) is expressed (and in the same way) in the soul's correct thoughts about what to do and omit doing, about what levels and occasions of pleasure to have, about how to treat fellow citizens in one's political activities and associates in one's business, and in all its other directive thoughts in other areas of life. Thus, just as the world's gold and all its parts have the same constitution and natural functions, and its parts differ from one another only in externals, so virtue always functions in the same way, whether it is doing so in one relation (and so, for example, acting as justice) or another (acting as temperance).[24] Nonetheless, it is an important, objective fact about virtue that it does have these distinct orientations, just as it is such a fact about gold that it is found naturally in particular, separate places and with different concentrations.

Thus, Ariston's view moves away from Menedemus's in admitting into virtue itself real differences—constituted by the different things it is essen-

[24] In translating Plutarch, and in my explication of Ariston's view, I have allowed Ariston to be thinking of the single thing that is virtue as always and continuously entitled to all its more particular names—whether it is currently exercising itself in the specific relation appropriate to that particular virtue-name or not. After all, sight remains light-sight, whether or not it happens at the moment to be grasping light colors, simply because it retains the capacity for, and orientation toward, grasping them, just as sight itself is retained even when one's eyes are closed. And similarly for the knife as salami-cutter and fire as air-heating. However, other sources (Galen in *SVF* I 374, Clement of Alexandria in *SVF* I 376) state explicitly that according to Ariston virtue is justice (only) *when* it "assigns to each his merited share." (Clement introduces the example of a drachma-piece that gets called "the fare" when given to the shipmaster, but "rent" or "taxes" when used in other ways.) So construed, Ariston is indeed open to the objection that Long and Sedley lodge against him: his view cannot explain "why we should continue to describe a man as courageous even when he is not employing his courage." See Long and Sedley, *Hellenistic Philosophers,* I, p. 384. But this is so obvious, and so obviously valid, an objection to Ariston's view if so construed that I am very reluctant to think he meant to say that. If he did, then he blundered; what seems clearly to have been his basic idea is perfectly capable of development (as in my text) in such a way as to sidestep any such criticism.

tially related to—and not mere differences of point of view from which it may be considered. But Ariston still does not admit that the nature of virtue is such that virtue by any name can differ in itself, in its nature as virtue, from what it is under any other name. And that is troubling: surely the virtue justice is something, somehow, with its own distinct nature; and virtue itself when acting *as* justice must somehow take on or exercise a distinct aspect of its total self—a different one from occasions when it acts as temperance. Plutarch professes to think that not even Ariston's teacher Zeno took the further step of assigning to each particular virtue its own distinct nature. He reserves that honor to Chrysippus; Zeno really held essentially the same position as Ariston, expressed in different words. About Zeno he says (*On Moral Virtue,* 441a, continuing from the passage quoted above):

> It looks like Zeno of Citium, too, in one way or another went off a bit in this direction: he defines wisdom (*phronēsis*) in due distributions as justice, in correct choices as temperance, in duly enduring things as courage.[25] (In defending Zeno they consider that in these definitions knowledge [sc., of what is good and bad] is given by him the name "wisdom.")[26]

Thus, according to Plutarch, when Zeno, in defining justice, said that justice is knowledge (of what is good and bad) "in" due distributions, he meant that justice is that single knowledge *used* in a certain relation, namely in relation to questions of distribution—and the other particular virtues are similarly to be distinguished from one another and from virtue itself by appeal to other such external relationships of use. So Zeno too, like Ariston, did not recognize any distinction of essential nature between justice and courage, for example: each virtue *is* that single knowledge. However, Diogenes Laertius (VII 161) says clearly about Ariston (but without further explanation of Zeno's own view) that he "neither introduced many virtues, *as Zeno did* [my italics], nor a single virtue called by many names, as the Megarians did, but [one virtue] under the heading of being 'relatively

[25] See also Plutarch, *On Stoic Self-Contradictions,* 7, 1034c, where Plutarch repeats this claim, professing to find in these definitions a contradiction of Zeno's agreement elsewhere with the Platonic position that the virtues do differ from one another by having different natures. Indeed, these definitions would constitute such a contradiction if Zeno's view really were the same as Ariston's.

[26] This parenthetical remark reflects the fact that—as one can see already from what Ariston says above about "virtue" (that is, "knowledge of good and bad") as against "wisdom"—in Stoic theory *phronēsis* itself was only one of the particular virtues, not virtue itself: according to Ariston, it is "knowledge" in considering what is to be done and what not done. So later Stoics (perhaps beginning with Chrysippus) who wanted to hold that Zeno's view was not really different from their own insisted that in these definitions he was, nonstandardly, using "wisdom" to mean "knowledge of good and bad." Socrates in the *Protagoras* also shows a parallel unclarity in his use of the word *sophia*. Sometimes the word refers to one among the virtues, sometimes it is used to refer to the comprehensive knowledge with which (in some sense) they are all identical. Perhaps this feature of Zeno's formulations simply reflects his reliance on the *Protagoras* in formulating his own view.

disposed' toward something."[27] That is, Ariston refused to follow Zeno in
going farther beyond Menedemus and the Megarians, so as to recognize a
plurality of virtues distinct *in their natures,* not just in the externally relational way that, as we have seen, Ariston advocated.[28] Plutarch's own language in the passage quoted just above clearly suggests his lack of confidence
in his interpretation of Zeno's view, and, as I suggest below, the definitional
formulas for the particular virtues that Plutarch reports can readily be interpreted as involving the "many virtues" that Diogenes Laertius says Zeno
introduced. Given the unclarity of our information about Zeno's views, the
best way to proceed is to examine Chrysippus's theory first: I doubt that
Chrysippus's account really is, as he must have claimed, what Zeno had in
mind all along, but once we see how Chrysippus's account relates to the
view Socrates was pointing toward in the *Protagoras*—if I have been right
about that—we will also be in a position to see more clearly what Zeno
himself may have been proposing. I return to Zeno in section VI below.

V. Chrysippus on the Unity of Virtue

Plutarch limits his comments on Chrysippus's view in this part of *On Moral
Virtue* to complaining (441b) that "by invoking the genus of the 'qualified'
[that is, the category of quality] and holding a virtue to be constituted by
its own quality, he unwittingly stirred up what Plato calls a 'swarm of
virtues'—ones neither standardly recognized nor even heard of before."[29]
We can understand this complaint and see how Chrysippus was led to
adopt a theory with such consequences by turning to the account in Arius
Didymus's *Epitome* of Stoic ethics that is preserved in Book II of Stobaeus's
Selections.[30] Chrysippus held that virtue itself is a single, entrenched condi-

---

[27] That is, as we have seen, Ariston said that justice, e.g., is virtue as "relatively disposed"
to busying itself with common enterprises and contracts—that is, disposed to those things
while not changing or being differentiated internally in any way.

[28] Elsewhere Plutarch himself reports that Zeno did in fact view the particular virtues as
"differing specifically" from one another—but Plutarch claims that this is inconsistent with
Zeno's also defining the virtues in the (allegedly "relational") way he reports Zeno here (in
On Moral Virtue) to have done. See *On Stoic Self-Contradictions* 7, 1034c–d. Plutarch reasonably insists on taking the definitions to express Zeno's basic view; it is open to question,
however, whether Zeno intended them in the "relational" way that Plutarch also insists on,
in order to find a Stoic self-contradiction here.

[29] Translation after Long and Sedley. Plato uses the expression "a swarm of virtues" in *Meno*
72a, where Meno reports Gorgias's idea that there are different and distinct virtues for men
and women, children and old people, slaves and free, and for every different sort of action
and time of life.

[30] Arius Didymus wrote in the early first century A.D. (An English translation of the Stoic
part of his *Epitome of Ethics* is available in Inwood and Gerson, *Hellenistic Philosophy,* 2nd
ed., 203–32. The other part, on Peripatetic ethics, is to be published in the Clarendon Later
Ancient Philosophers series, translated with commentary by Stephen A. White; a translation

tion (*diathesis*) of the soul, "the natural perfection of a rational being qua rational" (Diogenes Laertius VII 94), its "consistent condition" or (equivalently) "the soul fashioned for the consistency of the whole of life" (VII 89). As such, it is a quality of the soul, or (equivalently) the soul itself qualified in a certain way. However, this single quality involves in one or another way (I go on to try to sort out what these ways are) a number of distinct qualities, which therefore become distinct virtues—hence Plutarch's complaint of a "swarm of virtues." Among these are not just the standardly recognized qualities of justice and temperance and so on, but all the other qualities that, as the general theory so far sketched gets amplified into details, one can come to see are involved in the presence of the one quality that is the soul's perfection. Thus, each particular virtue has its own quite particular, individual nature, alongside but in subordination to this single perfection.

The basis of the perfection of the soul, what fundamentally constitutes that condition, is the knowledge of good and bad. This knowledge tells you that (and why) virtue itself is the only human good; everything else that may be possessed or not possessed in life, that may befall or not befall a person, is only to be ranked as having the "pursuit" value of something preferred and to be worked for if it is not present, or the "rejection" value of something to be avoided so far as possible and gotten rid of if present. This same knowledge tells you that (and why) nothing possessing "pursuit" or "rejection" value is to be regretted if one's most committed efforts, respectively, to achieve and retain it, or to avoid or get rid of it, have so far failed.[31] This knowledge is necessarily a single, comprehensive theory of human nature and human life, unattainable except when a permanent, unshakable shift takes place in the state of one's mind—in one's overall grasp of the value of everything that actually is of value for a human being. With the presence of this knowledge—that is, of virtue itself—comes a whole series of subordinate virtues of two basic types. First, there are those virtues which, like virtue itself, consist in knowledge—such as justice, practical wisdom, temperance, courage, piety, and the other virtues that actually direct and shape our actions. But then, second, there are qualities that "supervene" upon this knowledge and its specific forms—things like the strength and health of the soul, and its soundness and beauty (and gracefulness, and "greatliness," etc. etc., filling out the "swarm" that so scandalized Plutarch), which result from the practical application of virtue itself (the knowledge of good and bad) and of the other virtues that consist in

---

with commentary by Julia Annas of the Stoic material is planned for the same series.) Stobaeus compiled his excerpts (*Eclogae*) in the fifth century A.D.; I refer to them with the pages and lines of the edition of Wachsmuth (as is customary, I indicate this via the "W" appended to each citation). Some relevant passages are translated in chaps. 60 and 61 of Long and Sedley; I provide references to these as appropriate (with the abbreviation *LS*).

[31] For a summary account of the Stoic theory of goods and "indifferents," see Cooper and Procopé, *Seneca*, pp. xvii–xxiii.

knowledge.[32] Since that practical use cannot fail to occur if the knowledge itself is present, these virtues cannot be absent if the others are present: so although they are only "supervenient" consequences of the presence of virtue itself, they are also so intimately involved in its presence that they can reasonably be called parts or components or aspects of that single condition of virtue or knowledge which constitutes the rational soul's perfection.

However, for the question of the unity of virtue, as that came down to the Stoic philosophers from the earlier development of the Socratic tradition, it was the relation to virtue itself of those particular virtues that actually consist in knowledge that was decisive: virtues like justice, temperance, and courage. Here Arius Didymus gives a fascinating, detailed account that is worth quoting at a little length before explaining and commenting upon it further. He begins as follows (Stobaeus II 7, 5, 63. 6W ff.):[33]

> All the virtues that are types of knowledge (that is, arts or expertises (*technai*) have a common stock of theory and, as already mentioned, the same end.[34] Hence they are also inseparable. For anyone who has one of these virtues has them all, and anyone acting on the basis of one of them acts on the basis of all.

In the last clause here we have a new, and stronger, consequence of the unity of virtue than we have yet confronted, at least explicitly. Not only (as Socrates had intimated already in the *Protagoras*) must any person who has any virtue have them all, but every action, as well, that is qualified by one (in the sense that it is done from the corresponding state of the soul) is also qualified by them all.[35] Thus, if a just person does a just act, then it is also a courageous, a pious, a temperate, and a practically wise act, etc., in that it derives not merely from his justice, but equally from all his other virtues. In working out a conception of the unity of virtue above from what Socrates says in his debate with Protagoras over whether piety is just and justice is pious, I attempted to make sense of the idea that justice, as a characteristic of a person's mind and character, required a subordinate

---

[32] Stobaeus II 7, 5, pp. 58. 9–14W (translated in *LS* 60K), 62. 15–20W. See also Diogenes Laertius VII 90 and the first sentence of 91 (where it is necessary to follow the reading of ms B as reported in the apparatus criticus of Long's text, and not retain the words καὶ περὶ φαύλους γίγνονται, if Diogenes Laertius's report is to make any acceptable sense).

[33] The passage is printed in von Arnim, *SVF*, as III 280, and translated in *LS* as 61D.

[34] At 62. 7W Arius had said: "Of all these virtues [viz., the ones that are knowledges] the end is to live following nature; but each of them makes a person achieve this through its own particular means."

[35] It seems to me unacceptable for Long and Sedley to say (*LS* I, p. 384) that, according to Chrysippus and the other Stoics, each virtuous action is done from all the virtues only to the extent that when an action is done from temperance, for example, it must avoid being done simultaneously in a cowardly, unjust, or foolish way (and that this can be avoided because the temperate man knows, in a secondary way, all the "theorems" of courage, justice, and practical wisdom). It is perfectly clear that Arius Didymus and Plutarch (see n. 36) understand the thesis in a much stronger sense than that, and if Long and Sedley's interpretation of Chrysippus can only support such a weak conclusion, that just reveals a defect in their interpretation. See further below.

sensitivity to the moral considerations clustered under the heading of piety; in other words, justice must sometimes be a co-cause of pious action as well (and must never be a cause of impious action, or of not doing a pious action when the situation called for that), but we saw no good reason to say that whenever justice produces its own special product, a just action or outcome, it also makes (or joins with piety in making) that a pious action or outcome as well. The circumstances might simply not raise at all the special considerations coming under piety. And similarly for the other virtues. Apparently Chrysippus and other Stoics saw some further entanglement of the virtues with one another than my argument so far has brought out: they thought that whenever justice is active, and produces its product, the product will not only be something just, but something pious and virtuous in every other way as well, because all the virtues have had a hand somehow in producing it.

A bit later on, Arius offers some illumination—unfortunately rather abstract—at least as to why the Stoics held this extreme view. At Stobaeus II 7, 5, 65. 12–14W he says: "[The Stoics] say that the wise [that is, fully virtuous] person does everything on the basis of all the virtues. For every action of his is perfect, so it can't lack any virtue."[36] This sounds good, thus abstractly stated. One might think, however, that since actions differ in their kinds, a perfect action of one kind (say, putting someone at their ease) might well not need or even have available to it *all* the virtues; all that its perfection requires would be all those virtues relevant to it, in its kind, and those might be fewer than all the virtues that there are—in the case cited, no courage would be involved, perhaps. Why then did the Stoics think that every action, to be virtuous at all, had to derive from the active use of *all* the virtues? In the continuation of the passage quoted in the previous paragraph, Arius gives us the information needed to answer this question, but in order to interpret it correctly we will have to look also to the briefer and less systematically organized account of the same point in Diogenes Laertius's summary of Stoic ethics. Arius goes on:

> But they differ from one another in their main concerns (*kephalaia*). Practical wisdom's main concerns are, in the first instance, to theorize about and put into action what is to be done, but on the second level to theorize also about what distributions one ought to make, <what choices one ought to make, and what one ought to endure,> for the sake of putting unerringly into action what is to be done. The special main concern of temperance is, in the first instance, to make the impulses [that produce an action] steady and to theorize about the impulses,

---

[36] Plutarch confirms this point in *On Stoic Self-Contradictions* 27, 1046e–f: "They say that the virtues imply one another not only in the sense that anyone who has one has them all but also in the sense that anyone who does anything on the basis of one of them does it on the basis of all. For they say that neither is a man who does not have all the virtues perfect, nor is any action perfect that is not done on the basis of all the virtues." Although in citing the Stoic doctrine of the mutual implication of the virtues (VII 125) Diogenes Laertius does not mention that it includes the claim that each action is done on the basis of all the virtues, his way of explicating it (VII 126) actually does imply it, as we will see below.

but on the second level to theorize about the matters that come under the other virtues, in order to conduct oneself unerringly in one's impulses. Similarly, courage theorizes in the first instance about everything one ought to endure, but at the second level about the matters that come under the others, and justice, in the first instance, investigates each person's due, but on the second level the remaining things too. For all the virtues look to the concerns of them all, and to the matters that are ranged under each other.

Plainly, the main idea here is that each of the several particular virtues "knows" everything that any of the others do: there is a common body of moral theory that they share. They differ nonetheless, in the order in which, in the different cases, the common knowledge is arranged. A. A. Long and D. N. Sedley in their translation (*LS*, 61D) speak of different "perspectives" that each virtue has on the same knowledge; more accurately, it is a matter of which items within the common body of knowledge the specific virtue attends to first, and which are attended to subsequently and because of their contribution to the specific task of the virtue in question, which is to perfect and implement the knowledge contained in the primary items. This much seems clear. To understand in greater detail what the Stoics are saying here, it is imperative not to bring to this passage, as do Long and Sedley in their commentary on it,[37] the idea that each virtue has a special area of conduct disjoint, or mostly disjoint, from those of the others—for justice, say, respect for law and the discharge of one's political responsibilities to fellow-citizens, one's duties under contracts and other mutual undertakings, and the like; for temperance, how one comports oneself in relation to the pleasures of food, drink, and sex, and in general how one behaves in relation to opportunities to spend one's time in an immediately agreeable way; for courage, how one behaves when dangers or apparent dangers arise to one's own physical well-being or immediate material interests and those of others near to one. And so on. It may well be that each of the virtues, both in popular thought and even in the completely developed Stoic theory of virtue, does have a special relation to such special areas of conduct. But, as we shall see, that is not how the Stoics are conceiving the virtues here, and not how they think the virtues are fundamentally to be characterized and distinguished from one another.

Take temperance, for example, as it is described in this passage: its main concern is with the correct formation of our impulses and with the acts of choice or selection that they constitute, in *any* and *every* action, whatever its immediate object and whatever the circumstances of its performance. Temperance is not characterized (as we saw it was in Ariston's account) *via* any special relation to the control and limitation of the pursuit of pleasure. The parallel passage in Diogenes Laertius, to which I will turn in just a moment, shows, I think, that the references under justice to "distributions" and giving each his due, and under courage to enduring things, are likewise

---

[37] *LS*, I, p. 384.

to be understood in the same broad sort of way: the thought is that in *each* action there is room for some due distribution of something to someone (if only a distribution to oneself in acting for and claiming as one's due whatever one is pursuing), and room for something to be correctly endured (if only the physical effort it takes to do the act at all). The overall thought of the Arius passage is that each virtue has one special area to address—not, in the first instance, an area of conduct, but an area in the production of any overall virtuous action; and in doing that job it has to pay due but secondary consideration to each of the other virtues' principal concerns. Thus, if one is to make one's impulses precisely correct, one must know what action is to be done and why, and what has to be endured in doing it and why, and what is being distributed to whom as their due and why—all of that must be taken into account in the particular way that one shapes and constitutes the impulse of selection and choice that is to lead to the action itself. Similarly, to know all that one needs to know about what is to be distributed to whom in any given action, one must know what action is to be done and why, and what the correct impulse is (and why) in doing it, and likewise for the endurance involved. All of that is part of what is due, of what is to be correctly distributed. And so on.

I should add that, of course, if justice, say, is the comprehensive knowledge of what is due to whom, that will mean that it "knows" not only about the minimal sorts of distributions involved when, say, on my day off and in privacy I allow myself a long hot bath, but also and even more about those much more substantial ones involved when some distribution has to be effected that really does raise issues of justice as that is normally understood. The Stoics' point will be that knowledge of those larger and more important sorts of distributional issues is just one part of an overall knowledge that includes within its scope something more elemental that is involved always in some degree in every action, even actions where these larger issues of distribution may be totally absent. Hence the Stoics can still allow that some actions will be properly called "acts of justice" as against "acts of temperance," say, even though temperance is essentially involved in the formation of the correct impulse that stands behind them: in these cases lots of specialized knowledge belonging to justice is required, but only the basic parts of what temperance knows about how to form impulses. In other cases, perhaps where lots of great immediate bodily pleasure is to be had but no larger questions of social justice are involved, very little if any of the *specialized* knowledge that belongs to justice is needed, but lots of temperance's knowledge about steady and stable impulses is, just because extra knowledge about how to form impulses is needed in order to make sure that an excited pursuit of pleasure does not ensue. And similarly there will be acts of courage where higher reaches of its knowledge are called upon than would be in just any old act requiring only the low-level endurance mentioned above. So the Stoic insistence that each virtue has work to do in the production of each and every action and therefore is partly responsible for it, does not prevent these philosophers from recognizing that, because in some actions a great amount of the specialized knowledge of some one virtue is needed but only little of others, it is natural and correct to call those in a special sense acts of *that* virtue.[38]

Clear confirmation for the interpretation I have offered comes in Diogenes Laertius's abbreviated version of the same doctrine. Diogenes says (VII 125–26) that according to what Chrysippus wrote in the first book of his work *On Virtues*, the virtues have a common stock of theory (*ta theōrēmata koina*), but that each one has its own special main concern (*kephalaion*): the concern of courage is the things to be endured; of practical wisdom, the things to be done (and not done); of temperance (he implies), the correct choices of things; and of justice, the correct distributions. But, he adds, "the things to be done are also to be chosen, to be endured, to be held to, and to be distributed":[39] so whenever practical wisdom is deliberating on what is to be done, those very same things it has to decide to do are also objects of choice, endurance, sticking with, and distributing. This means that each of the other virtues too is involved in the final, correct production of the action that it decides upon. And similarly, whenever any of the other virtues does any of its work, the others too are needed to complete the task of producing the action it is involved in co-causing: there is an element of correct enduring, and correct distribution, and correct choosing involved in *every* virtuous action; and the virtues of courage, justice, and temperance are the sources, respectively, of these elements of the action.

One should notice that according to Chrysippus's theory as Arius Didymus reports it, it is *in order for it to complete its own particular task* that each virtue "knows" the items of theory that are primary items of knowledge for the other virtues: Arius adds that practical wisdom knows the things it knows "on the second level" "for the sake of putting unerringly into action what is to be done," and that temperance knows these "in order to conduct oneself unerringly in one's impulses." (We are certainly to add the corresponding points to the less complete explanations he gives of courage and justice.) This makes good sense: one needs to attend to each of the four

---

[38] This is presumably the correct response to Plutarch's attempt in *On Stoic Self-Contradictions* 27, 1046f–1047a, to find Chrysippus contradicting his theory that each action is done on the basis of all the virtues, when he claims that the good man is not always acting courageously (*andrizesthai*) because, for that, certain particular impressions (*phantasiai*)—presumably ones of harm about to happen to one, etc.—have to have been received and appropriately responded to. It is in such a situation—where specific sorts of response are needed to specific sorts of impressions—that the "higher reaches" of courage's knowledge that I have spoken of are brought into play. For that reason, these actions, but not others where courage nonetheless does have work to do, can count as "acts of courage." (Another way to put the point is that, as Chrysippus says, every action of the virtuous person is done *kata* or "on the basis of" each and every one of the virtues; but it does not follow from the fact that an act is done "on the basis of" courage (*andreia*) that it is a case of *andrizesthai*, "acting courageously.")

[39] Diogenes Laertius, VII 126: τὰ δὲ ποιητέα καὶ αἱρετέα ἐστὶ καὶ ὑπομενητέα καὶ ἐμμενητέα καὶ ἀπονεμητέα.

areas he distinguishes in the production of an action if the result is to be a perfect action, and it is reasonable to think that each virtue, in attending exclusively to its particular area, needs to pay heed to what the others know in their own areas. But this reasonable specialization in the way that (and purpose for which) this additional knowledge is possessed by each separate virtue means that Chrysippus's theory will avoid one consequence that a similar theory with no such limitation would apparently fall victim to. A theory that assigned to each virtue without such contextual restriction all the knowledge that any other virtue possesses would seem to imply that in fact any single one of the virtues would be sufficient to guarantee that all the work of all the virtues would be completed even without the aid, or even the presence, of the others—so that really only a single special virtue would be needed in order to act always with full correctness. On Chrysippus's theory, however, justice may know everything that temperance knows about how and why to make impulses steady, but it knows this only *as* something to be duly distributed; if the impulse with which the action is done is actually to *be* steady, with all the further virtuous qualities of that steadiness, temperance is still needed in order to bring that about. Justice merely helps temperance as it makes the impulse steady by seeing the steadiness as something *due*. Each of the distinct virtues has its own work to do in helping to generate each and every completely and perfectly virtuous action. No single virtue would suffice—even though each virtue knows everything that any other virtue knows.

It is not at all clear that the same would be true for the sort of theory that Long and Sedley wrongly attribute to Chrysippus—or, for that matter, for the one I have extracted above from the *Protagoras* text on piety and justice, which I think is essentially the same. That other theory proceeds by distinguishing distinct and partly disjoint areas of life—situations where the need to stand up to threats arises, or social obligations are confronted, or temptations to have pleasures, and so on. It says that each virtue is keyed specifically to one such area, but that it also has to know all about the considerations arising in the other areas, in order not (so to speak inadvertently) to violate or unduly override them. But then the question should at once arise, why does one need more than one of the particular virtues? If each of them knows all about its own special area of conduct in a "primary" way, but also all about the special areas of all the others in a "secondary" way (that is, just in case considerations salient for those other virtues should be present in a situation in which the given virtue is called into play), why won't any *one* of them suffice as guarantee that one will do (say) not only the just, but also the temperate and the pious action, in case an action of all three types (courage, justice, and temperance) is needed? Indeed, why wouldn't any single virtue suffice to cause you to do not only "its own" actions, as required, but all the distinct actions of the several other virtues, as well? Suppose you have justice (and only justice among the particular virtues). You always do what justice requires in situations where considerations of justice arise. But you are also, through your justice, alert, though only secondarily, to all the considerations belonging to all the other virtues. Won't that mean that your justice will suffice to get you, where those other considerations do arise, to do the right thing—whether, as a result, it is both just and pious and temperate, or merely just, or even merely pious or merely temperate? Surely your alertness, through your justice, to *all* the considerations that ever do affect correct action (even if it applies only "secondarily" to some of these) should mean that your justice suffices for correct action under *any and all* circumstances: you will be aware of and properly sensitive to all considerations of all sorts that affect correct action in any circumstances whatsoever, so you can be counted on always to act correctly in every respect.

This other theory admittedly does not support the extreme Chrysippean claim that each action of a virtuous person must be co-caused in some way by each of the virtues. But that is perhaps not indisputably a weakness, as I have already suggested. However—and this plainly would be seen by any philosopher in this tradition as the basis for a serious objection—one may doubt whether this other theory really even supports the weaker claim that no person can possess any one particular virtue without possessing them all. Possibly, on further consideration, some response adequate to rebut the suggestions made in the last paragraph might be forthcoming. Perhaps one could insist that justice, say, is only sensitive to considerations relevant to the other virtues when it is already attending to considerations of justice. Again, one might suggest that you cannot learn to be, and remain, sensitive in justice's secondary way to considerations belonging to another virtue unless you are at the same time properly sensitive to them in the primary way characteristic of that other virtue. But such protestations sound like dubious special pleading—of the sort that Academic sceptics loved to pounce upon. The desire to avoid having to resort to that may have led Chrysippus to his radical rethinking about the special "areas" of each virtue's concern. If, in the first instance, each virtue controls a single aspect found in, and needed by, each and every virtuous action, and not some externally defined set of circumstances found in some actions but not others, then it is easy to see that no single virtue ever suffices for any virtuous action, and that, accordingly, if a virtue's function is to produce virtuous actions, no single virtue can occupy a person's mind without the presence also of the others. Chrysippus reached this result by following out the dialectic begun by Socrates' insistence in the *Protagoras* that we ought to say not only that piety is pious, but also that it must be just, temperate, courageous, and wise—where those predications are understood in the way I suggested earlier. Nothing short of adopting his position would give us an indisputable unity of virtue which both permits the existence of particular virtues with their own distinct natures and requires the possession of all of them if any one is possessed. If that was what Socrates was driving for in the *Protagoras,* it now seems that only Chrysippus's theory can give us everything that Socrates wanted.

VI. ZENO ON THE UNITY OF VIRTUE

Earlier I postponed discussion of Zeno, in order to consider Chrysippus. Near the end of section IV, I quoted from Plutarch's *On Moral Virtue* Zeno's thumbnail definitions of some of the virtues, and we find these same definitions in many other sources. According to these, justice is virtue or knowledge of good and bad "in" due distributions, temperance is virtue or knowledge of good and bad "in" correct choices, courage the same knowledge "in" duly enduring things. It is clear that Plutarch interprets these differentiating conditions as references to distinct and partly disjoint areas of life, as Long and Sedley wrongly did for Chrysippus, and as I did in extracting an initial account of the virtues from the *Protagoras.* (That is how Plutarch can suggest that Zeno's position was really the same as Ariston's). And this is presumably correct. After all, the fixation on different areas of life in order to differentiate the virtues is one that any reader of the *Protagoras,* and indeed other dialogues of Plato, would assume as a starting position, natural to anyone brought up with the common Greek understanding of the virtues. It would, however, still not necessarily follow that Zeno was only stating the same view as Ariston's in different words. As I pointed out earlier, Ariston was bent on denying any substantial, so to speak internal, distinctive nature to any of the virtues (even though it was a fundamental fact about virtue itself that it does have distinct areas of employment): the virtues were all straight knowledge working in precisely the same way, only on different objects, like a knife cutting salami instead of fruit. As we also saw, there is strong evidence (recorded even by Plutarch) that Zeno intended to maintain that the particular virtues do have distinct natures, that they differ specifically from one another: justice is one quality, temperance another, courage yet a third. It is not difficult, *pace* Plutarch, to see what Zeno might have had in mind. Perhaps he conceived of the knowledge of good and bad applied to circumstances of justice ("in" due distributions, as he put it) as one distinctive part of, or way of structuring, that overall knowledge, among others: perhaps justice is that overall knowledge structured in such a way that the knowledge of what is owed to others is held "primarily" in mind, with other elements of that knowledge assigned "secondary" positions in relation to that "primary" knowledge. If so, justice would have a distinct nature from the nature of the other particular virtues, with their different areas of application and therefore different orderings of the single, common knowledge that constitutes virtue itself. If that is what Zeno had in mind, then he was holding the view that I have myself developed by reflecting on what Socrates says about the distinctions among the virtues in his examination of Protagoras on the connections between piety and justice. Indeed, in my own analysis above of *Protagoras* 330b–332a, perhaps I have simply been retracing Zeno's own reasoning! In that case, Zeno reached his own position on the unity of virtue, according to which virtue itself is a single knowledge, but the particular virtues (justice, courage, temperance, and so on) are qualitatively distinct orderings of that single knowledge, by studying this part of the *Protagoras*. In any event, Chrysippus must have been wrong to claim that his own radical, and radically new, way of construing the areas of operation of the distinct virtues was already present, at least implicitly, in Zeno's definitions. He would in this case merely be doing what ancient philosophers commonly did—attributing his own original contributions to the recognized founder of the school, as what the founder had "really meant."[40]

We do not have a satisfactory basis in knowledge of Zeno's own writings to determine whether this interpretation is correct. It is very tempting, however, to see the history that Plutarch recounts for us in *On Moral Virtue,* beginning with Menedemus and going on to Ariston, Zeno, and Chrysippus, as representing successive stages in the Hellenistic philosophers' grappling with the dialectic about the unity of virtue begun in Plato's *Protagoras.* Menedemus opts for the position, mentioned by Socrates and rejected by Protagoras, that virtue is a single thing simply called by several distinct names. This was reasonably found unsatisfactory, so Ariston tries out the suggestion, again rejected by Protagoras, that virtue is a whole of parts, where the parts are conceived in the way that the parts of gold are parts of it. Zeno finds that unsatisfactory and prefers to extract from Socrates' discussion with Protagoras the position, again one that Protagoras rejects, that each virtue is "such as" each of the others, understood in the way I earlier suggested: each virtue has its own special area of conduct to control, but in doing so it also has to know everything the other virtues do about their own areas. That looks good but on close consideration turns out to have defects too—as we saw above, it is not clear that it really enables us to insist that no one can have any single virtue without having all the others as well. So, finally, Chrysippus works out a radically comprehensive account of the virtues, and the unity of virtue itself, that goes much farther than one would initially have thought necessary in order to defend the thesis of unity. Our evidence does not permit us to say definitely that these philosophers worked out their successive views on the unity of virtue from progressively deeper probing of the issues raised in Plato's *Protagoras.* But much illumination can undoubtedly be brought to the study of the question of the unity of virtue in Stoic thought by working, as I have done, on this assumption.

Both Socrates in the *Protagoras* and all the other philosophers I have been discussing are agreed that knowledge—specifically, the single, unified, comprehensive knowledge of what is good and bad for human beings, or

---

[40] In support, Chrysippus could point to the fact that, in his own formulations, essentially the same language Zeno had used recurs: of justice dealing with "distributions," temperance with "choices," courage with "endurances," and so on. It must be admitted that Zeno's quite brief formulations do not actually give any detail that clearly reveals (as Ariston's for example do) the differentiation of the virtues by way of specific, mutually disjoint areas of life as their province. So far as the language goes, they could be interpreted as referring instead to different "areas" in the constitution of a single virtuous action.

in a human life—is not only sufficient for, but actually constitutes virtue. To have that knowledge is to be a virtuous person; virtue consists of that knowledge. It is about *the* virtues that these philosophers disagree: even if they all, except Menedemus, do agree that these are in some sense parts of virtue itself, the way that they are parts differs according to the different theories. They are virtue used in this or that certain area of life (Ariston); or they are that knowledge organized in one or another different way, so as to control correctly one's attitudes and behavior in relation to issues that arise in these different areas of life (Socrates in the *Protagoras,* Zeno); or they are that knowledge organized in different ways so as to direct and affect correctly different aspects of any and every virtuous action, plus immediate and valuable psychic accompaniments of its active presence in the soul (Chrysippus and standard Stoic doctrine after him). These philosophers can be satisfied with the exclusive attention to "cognitive" aspects of mind and character that this implies because they are all agreed that—at a minimum—it is only a person's mind that affects their behavior, or that is the legitimate basis for evaluating their moral standing. Any feelings one may have that are independent of one's evaluative judgments have no direct effect on one's behavior and are irrelevant to moral evaluation.

VII. Plato and Aristotle on the Unity of the Virtues

Now, as is well known, Plato in the *Republic* and Aristotle in his ethical and political writings generally, are not parties to this latter agreement. They hold that, in general, human behavior and attitudes, including those of virtuous persons, are affected not only by an agent's evaluative judgments (that is, "cognitive" aspects of mind and character) but also, independently from those, by nonrational feelings, desires, and emotions. If being virtuous means being a perfected human being, as all the Greek philosophers assume (Plato in the *Republic* and Aristotle included), then no account of virtue can be correct that attends solely to those cognitive aspects. First of all, in principle at any rate, given the independence of nonrational motivations from the rational ones, it would even be possible for someone whose cognitive functions were perfectly in order not always to behave as a virtuous person should, through the effect of errant nonrational desires. Second, even if we waive that possibility, it cannot be enough to achieve complete perfection as a human being if those functions are in order but nonrational motivations persist that involve you to any extent in contrary attractions— attractions whose evaluative contents are not morally approvable. Plato and Aristotle would, I think, both argue that when one's cognitive functions are in perfect order, somehow that has the consequence that no immoral feelings are experienced; so if one's cognitive functioning is perfect, one is never motivated at all to act contrary to what one judges best. Nonetheless, it seems reasonable to insist that the perfect condition of a human being that constitutes our being virtuous must include, as a separate aspect or aspects, specific perfections of the nonrational feelings and desires. They, too, must be put into perfect order if virtue is to be attained. Thus, knowledge, or perfection in the rational part of the soul, is only one part of virtue; some other perfection, or perfections, are needed as well, for the nonrational parts—even if the perfection of our rational natures carries with it as some sort of consequence that those parts will be perfect too.

It is clear from this that neither Aristotle nor Plato can endorse a doctrine of the unity of virtue, in the traditional sense in which Socrates in the *Protagoras* and his successors discussed above did so. Consistently with their moral psychology Aristotle and Plato cannot, and they did not, believe that having the knowledge of what is good and bad in a human life—what Plato in the *Republic* usually calls *sophia,* and Aristotle *phronēsis—is* the same condition as having human virtue. To have human virtue, one indeed requires that knowledge, but other, separate conditions as well; having this knowledge is just one among the virtues (it is *the* virtue of the rational part for Plato, and for Aristotle it is the one among reason's virtues that affects practical decisions and practical life). Distinct other conditions are needed as additional virtues—the virtues of the nonreasoning parts of the soul, what Aristotle calls the "ethical" or "moral" virtues (*ēthikai aretai*).[41] However, Aristotle and Plato both hold that a certain primacy is to be given among the virtues to wisdom, in such a way that, as Aristotle puts it (*Nic. Eth.* VI 13, 1144b31–32, 1145a1–2), "[i]t is not possible to be a good person in the full sense without practical wisdom (*phronēsis*), nor yet practically wise without ethical virtue. . . . For together with the presence of practical wisdom—*one* virtue—all the [ethical][42] virtues will be present." So, for them, though virtue is in no sense one condition—no single state of mind and character—the complex of conditions that makes it up is a single and unified *cluster,* formed around and dominated by the single virtue of wisdom (Plato) or practical wisdom (Aristotle).

So much one can say the two philosophers share. At this point, however, it becomes necessary to mark certain distinctions between them. I turn first to Aristotle. Even in his reduced claim of unity for virtue, Aristotle is accepting that the knowledge of good and bad that is needed for each of the

---

[41] In his account of these virtues, Aristotle accepts—with a vengeance, one is tempted to say—the view that keys them each to a single area of human life and conduct: temperance for how to behave in eating, drinking, and sex; courage for how to behave in war and related dangers; "good temper" for how to react to insults and in general how to understand and relate to one's own personal dignity; and so on. Plato's account in the *Republic* is markedly different. I return to this difference below.

[42] That this qualification is intended is plain from the immediately preceding context, where the contrast between the "full" virtues and the so-called "natural" ones is a contrast within the scope of ethical virtue, only. Aristotle does not maintain here, or clearly anywhere else, that reciprocity exists between the possession of theoretical-intellectual virtue and ethical virtue. (Since Plato regards *sophia* as, in Aristotle's terms, simultaneously both theoretical and practical, for him this question hardly arises in a clear way.)

separate other virtues—courage, justice, temperance, and so forth—is one and the same: a comprehensive such knowledge, not a piecemeal and limited one specific to each. Recent discussions have explained admirably, to my mind, why Aristotle adhered to such a view of the knowledge component, if one can speak that way, of each of what he distinguishes as the "ethical" virtues—and why he was reasonable to do so.[43] Briefly put, it is that any knowledge about, say, the values involved in courage (as a way of feeling about and reacting to dangers) and in courageous action must see the place of these values in a single overall scheme of moral or ethical goods and bads, including all those involved in all the other ethical virtues; as T. H. Irwin puts it, only a "global point of view" can find the appropriate mean that constitutes any of the virtues—or, one might add, its effective expression in any particular circumstance. That there *is* a knowledge component—and, ultimately, this single one—in every ethical virtue is established for Aristotle by the reflection that, properly understood, each of these virtues is a refined, intelligent, flexible mode of response, sensitive to every sort of nuance in a situation calling for action, in a way that no simple, non-knowledge-based way of feeling could ever be. Here Aristotle introduces, to very good effect, the distinction between "natural" or purely feeling-based "virtues" and the feeling-directed-by-thought virtues that he counts as "full" ones. The former do not involve knowledge, but the latter ones do. Moreover, this knowledge, the possession of which constitutes practical wisdom, cannot really be present without the ethical virtues, because (it is assumed) wisdom must be so solid and steady an understanding of the truth that its knowledge can never be dislodged: with it, one can never even be tempted to change one's mind, not even for a second, about the right thing to do and the right way to feel. Without the ethical virtues, however, one is inevitably subject to the possibility of such wavering in one's thoughts, under the pressure of the bad or inaccurate feelings about things that the absence of those virtues would leave you prey to.[44] Finally, on this Aristotelian conception, it is not simply the case that you have to have all the ethical virtues in order to have practical wisdom, and vice versa. There is more than a mutual dependence of the two sorts of practical virtue on one another; the ethical virtues actually "cluster" around practical wisdom because *it* is the virtuous condition that gives direction to, and shapes and controls the workings of, these other virtues, the virtues of feeling. In this way, the ethical virtues are crucially dependent on practical wisdom—not the other way about.

The situation is rather different when one turns to consider Plato's view in the *Republic*. First of all, Plato anticipated Chrysippus—as, of course, the latter must have been fully aware[45]—in dividing the responsibilities of

---

[43] See T. H. Irwin, "Disunity," (esp. pp. 66–72) and Julia Annas, *Morality,* pp. 73–79.

[44] See Aristotle, *Nicomachean Ethics* VI 5, 1140b11–21.

[45] In chaps. 15–16 of *On Stoic Self-Contradictions,* Plutarch reports a whole series of passages from a work of Chrysippus, "Against Plato on Justice," that object to things Plato says in the *Republic* about justice as a virtue of individual persons.

the various virtues in the way we have seen that Chrysippus did. For Plato, rather than each virtue's controlling our relation to and behavior toward a distinct set of circumstances arising from time to time in any human life, each virtue controls instead some aspect of an overall psychological condition that is responsible for *each and every* action, whatever the particular circumstances are that call it forth. Wisdom is the knowledge (belonging, of course, to reason among the three parts of the soul that the *Republic* recognizes) of what is best for each of the other parts and for the whole soul or person constituted from these three parts. And of course, no virtuous action can occur that does not issue in an appropriate way from such knowledge. Courage is the specific virtue of the second part of the soul, "spirit" or the locus of competitiveness and personal and social ambition and the need for esteem in one's own eyes and those of others: it consists in the firm commitment of "spirit" to adhere in its operations to, and to support, the rules and decisions laid down by reason. Courage, too, must play a role in each and every virtuous action: every virtuous action expresses and follows in part from that felt commitment of the "spirit." Temperance is the condition in which each of the three parts, in whatever way is possible for each, constantly recognizes and agrees that reason is entitled to rule and give direction to the operations of the soul and consequently to provide the structure and organization of the agent's life. There is a firm place in every virtuous action for the operation of this virtue too: only if the other parts of the soul are actively expressing this recognition in the production of the virtuous action will the action be done with the full self-expression and full range of satisfaction that is an essential component of any act of virtue. Finally, justice is the condition in which each of the aspects of the soul is alert to, and actively makes its own proper contribution to the active life of the person whose soul it is, while *not* attempting to usurp the proper function of any other such aspect. Clearly, justice is also a virtue that is needed and must participate in any and every virtuous action.[46]

This difference between Plato and Aristotle over how to characterize the virtues and distinguish among them has important consequences for their respective ways of endorsing the idea that virtue, overall, is a unified complex of distinct conditions. To begin with, for Plato but not for Aristotle, justice and not (or not merely) wisdom is in a way the "anchor" for the unity of the virtues. For Plato, both justice and temperance are conditions shared among all the parts of the soul; but temperance is more an enabling condition for the virtuous employment of the parts—justice is that actual employment itself. On Plato's account, being temperate means having your soul-parts so structured that reason knows it is to decide and rule, while spirit and appetitive desire are constantly ready to follow reason's lead, without undue resistance. But justice is the positive condition in which the parts actually *do* their natural jobs, and do so fully: where justice is present, and precisely

---

[46] For this account of the different virtues, see Plato, *Republic* IV, 441c–443b.

because and insofar as it is present, reason *does* issue its orders and decisions (on the basis of its knowledge, i.e., wisdom), spirit *does* harmoniously uphold and press for their implementation (using its courage), and appetitive desire *does* contribute its force where that is needed, and stands aside where it must—each part carefully refraining from usurping or interfering with the others' functions.[47] Thus, part of reason's job *is* to become and be wise, part of spirit's is to become and be courageous, and it is, of course, part of the job of each of the three powers in the soul to agree, each in its own way, that reason is to rule.[48] Justice, then, as the condition in which each part of the soul does its own job, is the condition requiring the presence of temperance, too, in the soul. In this way, justice is the linchpin of the whole system of the virtues—it is the necessary condition for the active, cooperative, psychic activity that must lie behind each and every virtuous act. Of course, since wisdom is the condition in which reason gives its correct orders, including of course ones directing how the other powers are to express themselves in any given action, it and not justice is the directive virtue—in a way corresponding to Aristotle's practical wisdom. So the whole complex of virtues, for Plato too, can be said to "cluster" around wisdom. Nonetheless, justice, as the condition that demands that each part really does do its job, is the background, regulative condition under which wisdom comes to be present and to give its directions.

However, only a little reflection will reveal that Plato's claim, on these bases, of the necessary coinstantiation of the virtues is a little artificial. Why must all three parts be doing their jobs fully, with all their separate virtuous conditions fully in place, in order for any of the parts to be doing its job? In particular, why can't spirit and appetite do their jobs fully, and achieve their full condition of virtue, even in a soul where reason and its proprietary virtue of wisdom are as yet (and maybe permanently) absent?[49] That would

---

[47] It is easier to see what this last, negative clause means for spirit and appetite than for reason. However, one should note that a reason that does its natural job must not only work hard at knowing the truth about human values, across the board, and reach decisions on that basis, it must in doing so *not* put the pursuit of its own pleasure ahead of anything else (and thus must not take on the functions of appetite, the pleasure-seeker); likewise reason must not form such a strong impression of its own excellence and preeminence (that is, the excellence and preeminence of the person whose reason it is) that it acts with intellectual arrogance and self-promotion (thus usurping some of spirit's functions).

[48] It is not often noted that it is in such terms as these that Socrates first introduces his account of the virtues (of the individual person) in *Republic* IV. Having worked out his account of the virtues of the city (428a–433e) in the order wisdom-courage-temperance-justice, he begins his account of the individual's virtues (after brief and purely formal references to wisdom and courage, 441c9–d4) with his target, justice itself (441d5–442b10), after that defining courage (b11–c4), wisdom (c5–9), and temperance (c10–d3). And in stating what justice or each-part's-doing-its-own-job entails, he makes a point of saying that, for reason, that includes its being wise, for spirit, its being courageous (441e4–5, 442b8).

[49] It seems that Plato has good reasons for dismissing as impossible the contrary position, where reason has its full virtue of wisdom, while the other virtues of justice, courage, and temperance are nevertheless wanting because the other parts of the soul are unruly. It is implicit

mean that each was fully attuned to the commands of reason—so structured that whatever commands reason gave they would follow, in their respective ways—and that each readily ceded to reason the power to judge and decide; while, in addition, spirit's special power of supporting and aiding reason was fully and unfailingly at reason's beck and call. Why is that not possible, even in a person who lacks the full grasp of the truth about values? Why should one not have reached the position where one's other soul-powers are fully and correctly disciplined so as to do their part under reason's guidance, even if reason itself does not yet, and perhaps never will, issue unfailingly correct instructions? Since Plato insists on the independence of the three parts of the soul, it would seem this must be possible.[50] Of course, such a condition would not quite yet constitute the full possession of all the other virtues besides wisdom. *Ex hypothesi* courage would indeed be present, but justice requires that *all* the soul-parts do their jobs, and a reason lacking wisdom would not yet have done its full job; and arguably without wisdom reason would not quite be making its full contribution to the soul's temperance either. But since both of the parts of the soul other than reason *would* be doing their natural jobs fully and correctly, and would possess fully their full complement of virtuous dispositions, it seems merely arbitrary to deny that any of the other virtues can be present without wisdom. It does seem that spirit and appetite could be fully disciplined and so could possess their full virtues, whether one calls them courage and temperance or not, even in the absence of wisdom.

Plato may be able to answer this objection. It is not enough, he might say, in order for spirit and appetite to have their full virtues that they be in a condition to follow reason wherever and in whatever way it directs. There is a specific, detailed schedule (as it were) of particular responses in particular situations that reason itself demands (even if only *the* reason of the wise person actually imposes them). Hence, anyone's powers of spirit and appetitive desire remain defective, simply as the natural powers that they are, if they are not yet structured so as to exhibit that particular range of responses

---

in the whole scheme of education for the *Republic*'s guardians that people whose appetites and spirited desires are not reined in and shaped and controlled through early moral training will lack the capacity to think correctly and learn what needs to be learned about true values in order to follow the course of intellectual training needed to develop their minds to the point where they achieve this knowledge. Of course, that early training does not establish full courage, justice, and temperance, but it does establish the first stages in their full development. And one might be willing to grant Plato that anything short of that full development (whatever exactly that might consist in) would prevent the actual establishment in one's mind of the full *knowledge* of good and bad that is required for wisdom—given, as I noted above, that that means the sort of permanent and unwavering grasp that could not be guaranteed if wayward desires or impulses of spirit, of any sort, remained.

[50] This is not the only point at which a view like Chrysippus's, otherwise similar to Plato's, comes off stronger: because Chrysippus does not recognize separate soul-powers independent of reason, he is in a better position to argue that with the one perfection of reason (and only with it) comes the perfect condition also of those aspects of an action that show its courageousness, temperance, and justice.

and other expressive displays. Their nature is fulfilled by obeying reason's own demands, not the arbitrary demands of any particular person's reason. Accordingly, simply being trained to follow rigorously the individual agent's actual rational judgments about actions does not constitute the virtues of these parts of the soul. And Plato could add that, in any event, there is no sharp line to be drawn between spirit's or appetite's accepting the rule of reason and their having some specific trained feelings about values, circumstances, and actions: to be ready to follow reason wherever it directs must mean being ready with some particular set of trained sensitivities about recurring situations. This makes it seem likely that there is no condition, for spirit and appetite, of "being ready to follow reason *wherever* it directs." Any condition of readiness must be keyed in advance to the particular directions from reason that spirit and appetite are going to receive. So long as wisdom is absent, spirit and appetite, it could be said, can at best be disposed to follow the specific sort of guidance provided by a specific, somewhat defective reason—not to follow reason wherever it may lead.

I think there is something in these replies. However, it would be much easier to make them stick if one held, as the Stoics did, that the additional necessary conditions, which Plato assigns to spirit and to appetite, were actually certain special conditions attaching to knowledge itself—special further cultivations of the rational power, beyond the simple knowledge of what is good and bad. If the particular sorts of feeling that virtue requires for performing an action are themselves just identical with, or inherent consequences of, particular ways of looking rationally at the action and its circumstances, and if these are aspects or components of an overall comprehensive understanding of values, then it would make no good sense to say that *those* aspects of a comprehensive, rationally correct outlook might possibly be achieved in advance of that overall wisdom itself. But once, with Plato, you make them conditions of independent psychic powers of spirit and appetite, it seems very hard not to grant that some state of those powers that constitutes their fully perfected, virtuous condition might be achieved independently of reason's possession of its truly perfected, virtuous state. There must be some possible condition somewhere between the omnibus readiness to do whatever one's reason might command, and the full establishment in spirit and appetite of true reason's particular schedule of feelings, that would constitute the virtuous state of those powers. Perhaps we could think of this condition as a specific, though not yet fully structured, set of responses that is ready for, and in some sense demands as its final fulfillment, the direction by a fully informed reason that will only be attained once wisdom is present. In any event, it does seem to me that the only indisputably sound basis on which Plato in the *Republic* can deny this possibility, and so affirm with full conviction even the necessary coinstantiation of the other virtues with wisdom, is to abandon the tripartite analysis of the soul, in favor of the Stoic view that "spirit" and "appetite" are really just reason in particular guises.

I conclude that Plato's own theory of the virtues in the *Republic* supports a less certain commitment to the view that the virtues constitute a unified complex of conditions, clustering around wisdom, than Aristotle's theory does. Like Chrysippus after him, Plato attempts to explain the virtues in a way that involves each of them in every virtuous action, by controlling some specific aspect of the psychology of virtuous persons in all their actions. He also wishes to maintain that the virtues constitute a unified condition—that no one can have any single virtue, but only all of them at once. But, as we have seen, in order to maintain this latter position, he can be pushed toward denying the independence from reason of spirit and appetite—and ultimately to the psychological theory of the Stoics. Ironically, then, the final outcome of such a defense of the unity of *the* virtues is a position, like the Stoics', in which you are committed to something yet stronger: the unity of virtue itself, as the single perfection of reason itself. Note that this problem does not arise if one attempts to differentiate among the ethical virtues on the basis of the different and distinct circumstances of action characteristic of each virtue, as Aristotle does, rather than on the basis of each virtue's contribution to each and every virtuous action, as Plato does. Aristotle's theory, as we have seen, has no difficulty in maintaining the unity of the virtues, clustering around practical wisdom, without falling off into a Socratic- and Stoic-style unity of virtue itself. It seems, then, that a Greek theorist who wishes to maintain merely a version of the unity of *the* virtues is better advised to follow Aristotle's manner of differentiating the ethical virtues from one another than to follow Plato's (and Chrysippus's).

It seems that Plato continued to maintain the necessary coinstantiation of the virtues in dialogues later than the *Republic*, without, however, apparently addressing these difficulties. Certain passages of *Statesman* and *Laws* might suggest that he gave up thinking of the virtues as a unity, whether in view of these difficulties or not. On closer examination, however, although we do find important new nuances—closely related to the Aristotelian distinction between "natural" and "full" virtue that I alluded to above—the basic position on coinstantiation seems to be retained intact. In the last section of the *Statesman* (305e–311c), the Visitor from Elea explains the principal work that an expert statesman or king must do in directing the "weaving together" of the citizenly fabric of his city, with the assistance of his subordinate educators, judges, and other administrators—all with their own separate expertises. He notes that two "parts" of virtue—courage or manliness (*andreia*), and temperance or moderation (*sōphrosunē*)—and those who possess them are unlike and "at odds with" one another (*diapheresthai*); they "go in opposite directions" and are even, in some sort of way, "extremely hostile" to one another.[51] The one "virtue" makes people immediately resistant to any mistreatment, outspoken in defense of what they value,

---

[51] See Plato, *Statesman* 306a–b, and, for the quoted words, 308b and 310a.

unwilling to take things lying down or seek accommodation, and so on. The other has the opposite effect: moderate people are always ready to avoid a disturbance, they will grant that their opponents "have a point" and will always seek an accommodation satisfactory to both sides rather than endure a breach of psychic or physical peace. (The task of the statesman is to "weave together" into a common, cooperating fabric a population made up in large part of people with these differing and competing "virtues.")[52]

All this may suggest that Plato is now acknowledging that some people can have one set of virtues, others another. However, the Visitor is not speaking here of actual or full virtues—as if there could be a conflict among full or true manliness and quietness of character—but only of two natural orientations that different people are born with: these are people who by their natures incline or tend in one or the other of these two directions (see 308a4 *rhepontes*, 309b3 *sunteinousas*). They have to be educated before they actually come to have *any* virtue, whether courage *or* temperance. As the Visitor explains, nobility or true virtue is attained only when people with different appropriate natural orientations come to possess with steadiness a single, shared "opinion" about what is "fine, just and good" (309b–c): this shared knowledge will bring it about that they all agree about what is to be done, and agree in taking steps to achieve it, whatever their natural orientations might, if untrained and unchecked, incline them to do. That they reached that stable fineness of character, supported by knowledge, on one natural basis rather than the other—aggressiveness, say, rather than a preference for accommodation—does not mean that they have one full virtue (courage, say) without the other (temperance): they have both. The Visitor seems to be thinking just as Aristotle does in Book VI of the *Nicomachean Ethics*. Despite differing initial natural starting points, whose effects may well continue to be felt, different types of people may nonetheless acquire all the full virtues, and indeed cannot have even the full virtue for which they are most naturally suited without also having all the others as well. That is so, because in order to have the knowledge necessary for any full virtue, one has to appreciate fully and be moved by all the good reasons there are for all the possible sorts of virtuous reaction to things and events— even those reactions that are not natural and spontaneous for oneself but rather for a person of a different natural type. In the *Laws* Plato sometimes speaks similarly of "courage" and "temperance" when he has in mind only disparate and differently distributed natural tendencies, but he clearly reserves the full attribution of virtue to those who possess as a unity all four of the "full" virtues—courage, temperance, justice, and wisdom to- gether. Thus, at 963e the Athenian speaks of courage (*andreia*) as having to do with fear and as a "natural" possession, apart from reasoning, found

---

[52] The interpretation of the *Statesman* here and in this paragraph and the next is developed more fully in Chapter 7, "Plato's *Statesman* and Politics."

also in wild animals and children; but, leaving it still as a challenge how this is to be understood, he also (964a) speaks of the virtue that is the single end of all his legislation (963a) as a unity of the four cardinal virtues. Evidently in this unity courage is something different from that "natural" possession.

VIII. CONCLUSION

Beginning with a study of the commitments of the character Socrates in Plato's *Protagoras* regarding the "unity" of virtue, we have followed successive efforts of later—mostly Stoic—rationalist philosophers to work out conceptions of the moral virtues that would sustain those commitments. As we saw, first Menedemus of Eretria, then Ariston and Zeno, and finally Chrysippus accepted Socrates' idea that virtue is some single condition of a human soul or mind, and looked to the suggestions Socrates made and the issues he raised in his debate with Protagoras, as a means of developing their own (successively more satisfactory) views. Of these, Chrysippus's was the most original and interesting, as well as the most extreme—and the most successful. Like his fellow Stoics and (as it seems) Socrates in the *Protagoras,* he made virtue a matter simply of knowledge—a comprehensive, deeply embedded, lasting knowledge of what is good and bad and otherwise valuable or disvaluable for human beings. But following Plato in the *Republic,* he differentiated from one another the particular virtues of wisdom, courage, justice, and temperance by assigning to each a specific task in the formation of any and every virtuous action, as such. Though on this theory (counterintuitively, perhaps) every virtue plays a role in the generation of every virtuous action, Chrysippus is also able to maintain the commonsense idea that some virtuous actions deserve to be counted as acts of justice, others as acts of courage, and so on. In these and in other respects, the result is a coherent, powerful theory.

Plato in the *Republic* and subsequent dialogues, and Aristotle in his ethical and political writings, adopt an ethical psychology according to which human actions are determined by more than the agent's evaluative judgments: separately generated emotions and feelings have a role to play as well. Accordingly there can be no question for them of a strict unity of virtue: virtue is a complex of separate conditions, some of them conditions of the mind, others conditions of the emotions and feelings. Nonetheless, both Plato in the *Republic* and Aristotle maintain that these virtues constitute a unified condition, such that no person could have any one virtue without all the rest. In examining Plato's and Aristotle's theories of this "unity of the virtues," I argued that ultimately only Aristotle's version of this common thesis stands up well to criticism. Thus, if one is inclined to embrace the tripartite ethical psychology of Plato and Aristotle, Aristotle's theory of the virtues has more to be said for it than Plato's; but if one is attracted to the more relentlessly rationalist psychology of Socrates (in the *Protagoras*) and the Stoics, then Chrysippus's theory of the virtues is the strongest option.

I began by suggesting that there might be valuable lessons for contemporary moral philosophers in this history. Have I sustained this suggestion? I leave that to the reader to decide.[53]

[53] I thank Christopher Bobonich and Panos Dimas for their helpful and interesting written comments on an earlier version of this chapter.

CHAPTER FOUR

Plato's Theory of Human Motivation

I

Everyone knows that in the *Republic* Plato advances the theory that the soul has three independent parts (reason, spirit, and appetite, as they are usually called in English). Using this theory he constructs an account of the human virtues: each of the three parts of the soul has its own special role to play in a human being's life, and virtue, for us, consists in each of them playing its own role fully and in harmony with the others. Thus human virtue taken as a whole, according to the *Republic,* is a complex interrelationship among three separate psychological elements, each of which has its own indispensable contribution to make.

Now this theory of virtue contrasts sharply with the Socratic theory found, for example, in the *Protagoras.*[1] According to the Socratic theory, virtue is essentially a property of the intellect (and never mind what other parts of the soul there may be). That Plato in the *Republic* is self-consciously rejecting this Socratic theory is by now well accepted; and most philosophical readers no doubt agree that the *Republic*'s theory is a distinct improvement. Even if knowledge by itself does motivate action, as Socrates evidently though obscurely assumed, there are surely other motivating factors as well, and being virtuous must therefore partly consist in having these other factors, whatever they may be, in some special condition or other. After all, it will be agreed by all parties that to be virtuous is to have one's practical attitudes and dispositions—whatever it is that affects one's actions and the ways one is inclined to act—structured in some special way; the virtuous person's

---

[1] In referring in this paragraph to the conception of virtue espoused by the character Socrates in Plato's early dialogues as "Socratic," I follow the by-now conventional scholarly practice, according to which this character's central views are attributed to the historical Socrates. Conventions are dangerous things, and this one should certainly not be accepted as uncritically as it often seems to be (for a recent defense of it, see W. K. C. Guthrie, *History* III, pp. 349–55). It is worth emphasizing in this connection that, though of course he also had other evidence now lost to us to go on (the oral tradition, plus writings of Antisthenes, Aeschines, and other Socratics), Aristotle plainly attributes to the historical Socrates essentially the same views on the virtues that one finds Plato's character Socrates espousing in the early dialogues (see esp. *Magna Moralia* I 1, 1182a15–23; also, *MM* I 20, 1190b28–32; 34, 1198a10–12; *Nicomachean Ethics* VI 13, 1144b17–21, 28–30; III 8, 1116b3–5; *Eudemian Ethics* I 5, 1216b3–8); and at *Nicomachean Ethics* VII 2, 1145b22–27 and 3, 1147b14–17 verbal echoes with the *Protagoras* (compare 352b8–c2) strongly suggest that he relied directly on Plato's dialogues at least some of the time for his conception of the historical Socrates' philosophical views. So Aristotle's treatment of Socrates confirms the correctness of this convention, however antecedently dubious it might seem.

practical attitudes must be such as always to produce the (or a) virtuous and right action in the given circumstances. And if not only one's thoughts about what is good and bad, but also ways one feels about things (whether or not those are also ways one thinks about them) constitute practical attitudes affecting the ways one is inclined to act, then obviously virtue must be something more complex than the Socratic theory represents it as being. It must involve not just well-informed, correct thought about what is good and what bad for a person, but also certain specific states of feeling about these matters as well. From this perspective Plato's *Republic* theory can be seen as a stage in the progression from Socratic rationalism to the Aristotelian theory that moral virtue is an interfusion of reason and desire—reason having the truth about the ends of life and how to achieve them, and desire embodying these truths so that the person habitually wants just the things that reason says are worth pursuing.

This picture, though I believe it correct as far as it goes, does push to one side the details of Plato's theory of what motivates human action; his view that there are *three* parts of the soul is treated as an uninteresting oddity, wisely omitted by Aristotle from his account of virtue.[2] Even Platonic scholars, who as a group are not noted for their sensitivity to Platonic error, sometimes admit to being embarrassed by this part of Plato's theory;[3] and it is indeed not easy to resist every clever freshman's impression that Plato held there were precisely *three* parts of the human soul only because he needed three in order to push through the argument launched at the beginning of the *Republic's* second book. Assuming that justice in the state must be the same as justice in the individual, and having plausibly argued that

[2] Thus Aristotle (*Nic. Eth.* I 13, II 5–6) describes virtue of character simply as the proper coordination between reason on the one side and nonrational desire, in general, on the other. He says nothing in this context about any differences there may be in kinds of nonrational desire. In other parts of his ethical theory, however, Aristotle does in fact preserve the distinctions that led Plato to regard the human soul as having three parts. He regularly divides ὄρεξις (desire) into three subkinds, βούλησις, θυμός and ἐπιθυμία (see *de An.* II 3, 414b2, III 9, 432b3–7; *de Motu* 6, 700b22; *EE* II 7, 1223a26–27, 10, 1225b25–26; *MM* I 12, 1187b36–37), and he assigns the first to reason itself (*de An.* 432b5, 433a23–25; *Topics* IV 5, 126a13), making the latter two belong to the "nonrational element" (*De an.* 432b6). Thus Aristotle holds (with Plato; see below) that reason has a special kind of desire of its own and he divides non-rational desires into the same two species as Plato recognized (see below). His acceptance of the Platonic theory that there are three distinct kinds of desire has important though frequently unappreciated effects on his moral psychology, as can be seen for instance in his concept of προαίρεσις (decision, rational choice): *EE* II 10 makes clear (see 1226b2–5, 1227a3–5), as *Nic. Eth.* III 2–3 does not, that the ὄρεξις that is according to Aristotle a component of προαίρεσις is a βούλησις, i.e., a desire belonging to reason itself, and not any non-rational desire. (J. Burnet, presumably relying on these *EE* passages, attributes this view, correctly in my opinion, to Aristotle in the *Nic. Eth.* too: βούλησις, he says in commenting on *Nic. Eth.* III 3, is "the appetitive element in προαίρεσις," *The Ethics of Aristotle*, pp. 109, 131, 132.) See Chapters 10 and 11 below.

[3] See most recently Penner, "Thought and Desire in Plato," pp. 111–13; also Hardie, *A Study in Plato*, pp. 142–43, and F. M. Cornford, "Psychology and Social Structure in the *Republic*," pp. 262–64.

justice in the state requires the recognition of three separate classes of citizen making three different contributions to the social welfare, Plato is committed to there being correspondingly three separate parts of the soul performing three different functions in the organization of the just individual's life. Does he then simply force the facts of human psychology to fit theoretical preconceptions derived from these other parts of his argument? Or does he after all produce cogent independent reasons, based in unbiased reflection on facts about individual human beings, for adopting this theory?

In this essay I want to argue that when understood properly Plato's theory presents in a quite subtle and interesting way undoubted facts about the psychology of human motivation, and that this theory accounts for some central features of human beings better than other later theories are able to do. Though there is no denying that Plato's way of parceling out the different forms of human motivation seems at first rather primitive, and is at all events somewhat alien to our way of thinking, it has a powerful rationale of its own that is worth exploring. In fact, there is good reason to think that for Plato, despite the order of exposition, the view that justice requires three distinct social classes rather derived support from than gave support to the theory that the soul has three independent parts.[4] It is the psychological theory that Plato thought more firmly anchored in the facts. If this is right, then in reconstructing the argument of the *Republic* one must give the psychological theory pride of place.

II

It is evident that the question "How many distinct parts has the soul?" can only have a clear sense and receive a definite, non-arbitrary answer if it is understood against the background of some well-defined theoretical interest. Plato makes clear enough his own point of view when he first raises his question about the parts of the soul (435b–c). He asks whether there are in each of us three things corresponding to the three kinds of person the recognition and proper use of which he has argued is essential to good order in a city. Now it is by what the three kinds of person do or don't do that the city's corporate life is determined—what it does and doesn't attempt to do, what its overall aims are, what it succeeds or fails in doing, whether

---

[4] This is certainly suggested by his remark at 435e–436a that if, as the foregoing political analysis has asserted, there are three types of persons suited for three distinguishable kinds of social work, that can only be because there are in each human being three psychological elements or powers, the special strength of one or another of which in a person is what makes him belong to one or another of the three social types. Similarly, at 544d6–e5 (cf. 545d1–3), Socrates argues that what determines the character of a city as timocratic, or oligarchic, or democratic, etc., is the character of those individuals in it who are in command: where people dominated by spirit, concerned about competitive values, govern, the city will be a timocracy (547e1–4, 548c6–7), and so on for the other cases.

for good or ill. Similarly, then, the question how many parts the soul has, and whether it has three parts, as the city does, is the question how many distinct types of psychological input go to determining a person's choices and voluntary actions, that is, the pattern of his life is general. Plato's theory that there are three parts is, roughly, the theory that there are three psychological determinants of choice and voluntary action.

Now there is a familiar modern theory, going back to Hobbes,[5] that a person's actions are the joint product of his (relevant) beliefs and desires and nothing else—desire providing the original motive force and belief factual information about how to act in order to satisfy desire. On this theory there are two sorts of determinants of action, belief and desire, one of which (desire) is the exclusive source of motivation while the other (belief) contributes only factual information, but no additional impulse to action. There is a misleading superficial similarity between this theory and Plato's. For on Plato's theory (as indeed on Aristotle's) in some ways the basic division is between reason on the one side (*to logistikon,* literally the calculating part) and appetite and spirit together on the other. And since reason is assigned the job in the soul of being wise and knowing the truth (441e 4–5, 442c 5–8) it seems at first sight not unnatural to think of it as playing the same role as belief plays on this modern theory; Plato would then be admitting *one* source of information but (surprisingly) dividing motivating desires into two classes, the appetitive ones and those issuing from "spirit."

But this interpretation is incorrect. On Plato's theory all three of the parts, reason as well as appetite and spirit, are independent sources of motivation; the contrast between reason and the other two is not really akin to the modern theory's distinction between inert, purely factual belief and motivating desire. This fact does not emerge with perfect explicitness until the ninth book, where Socrates advances the claim that "as there are three parts, there are also three kinds of pleasure, one peculiar to each part, and so with desires" (580d 7–8, tr. Grube). That is to say, there are desires of reason as well as bodily appetites and impulses of a spirited nature. Strikingly, the word for "desires" here, *epithumiai,* is the word used throughout the *Republic* as the generic name for the urgent bodily appetites (thirst, hunger and sexual desire) that serve as paradigms for the third part of the soul, *to epithumētikon,* which is so named after them. The desires of reason are

---

[5] See for example *Leviathan* ch. 8: "For the thoughts are to the desires as scouts and spies, to range abroad and find the way to the things desired." Bernard Gert argues (Introduction to Hobbes, *Man and Citizen,* pp. 13–16), that Hobbes does not limit reason to this scouting and spying function, but thinks that in addition it seeks *one* end not set by passion, viz. the avoidance of one's own violent destruction. On Gert's view not Hobbes but Hume is the originator of this modern view. It seems best, however, to interpret Hobbes as holding that the avoidance of violent destruction is the object of a settled and constant passion experienced by all persons that serves as a background against which varying particular passions arise and decline. On this interpretation, Hume's conception of reason as only "the slave of the passions" (*Treatise,* ed. Selby-Bigge, p. 415) is just a reformulation of the Hobbist view; Hobbes deserves the credit or blame for originating the familiar modern view.

thus implied to be strong impulses of some kind which we experience simply and directly because we possess the power of reason, the power to figure things out (*logizesthai*) and know the truth. Socrates specifies one of these desires a little later in the ninth book when he says that "It is obvious to anyone that the part by which we learn is always wholly straining to know where the truth lies" (581b 5–6, tr. Grube). On Socrates' view, then, merely in virtue of having minds—of having the capacity to inquire into and discover the truth—we possess the *desire* to do these things. According to Socrates, the desire to know the truth cannot be wholly explained as the outcome, say, of our discovery that knowing the truth helps us to advance the goals which our appetites, or other reason-independent desires, incline us toward; nor does it result simply from the discovery that, to use Kantian terminology, our sensibility is so constituted that we happen to find knowing the truth (or thinking we know it) gratifying. One's desire to know the truth might be strengthened in these ways, but there always remains an irreducible desire for knowledge that is not dependent on an interplay between reason and other aspects of our nature. This desire is an original constituent of human nature, as much so as our appetites themselves, or our sensibility in general. Socrates admits that not every person feels it as strongly or as steadily as some people do, and that some people's actions are motivated by it more often than others' are, but it must be active to some extent in everyone's life; the consequence of supposing that someone never experienced this desire would be that that person had no mind at all, and so was not a human being after all.

But intellectual curiosity is not the only desire Socrates attributes to reason. For in the fourth book he assigns to reason a double job: to know the truth and to rule (*archein,* 441e4, 442c5) in the light of it. For reason to rule here takes the form of its deciding on its own authority what is the best thing to do, issuing injunctions (442c6, *tauta parēngelen*), and seeing to it that the required action is undertaken. And just as Socrates makes the desire for knowledge—that is, the desire which leads reason to perform one part of its natural job—the direct consequence of our rational nature, so, I believe it can be shown, he also assigns to reason an inherent desire to perform the other part of its natural job, that of ruling.[6]

That according to Socrates human reason has, so to speak, an innate taste for ruling, just as it has an innate taste for knowing, can be most convincingly brought out by considering the way in which he attempts to argue the distinctness of reason from appetite. Notoriously, he thinks that the fact that sometimes reason opposes appetite shows that they must be distinct parts of the soul: his example is an incompletely described case where a man is thirsty, that is (as he says) desires, yearns for, and has an impulse to, drink (βούλεται πιεῖν καὶ τούτου ὀρέγεται καὶ ἐπὶ τοῦτο ὁρμᾷ, 439b1),

---

[6] I have been anticipated in this interpretation by Cross and Woozley, *Plato's Republic,* pp. 118–19.

but something else, which comes from reasoning (ἐχ λογισμοῦ, d1), pulls him back (ἀνθέλχει, b3) and forbids drinking (χωλύει πιεῖν, cf. c6–7, 9). There are several unclarities about this example (and, indeed, the other cases of conflict that Socrates argues prove that there are distinct parts of the soul). The text is not explicit as to whether in saying that reason opposes appetite he means merely that the object which appetite goes for reason rejects, or rather that reason in rejecting the object also addresses and opposes the appetite itself. A moment's reflection shows that he had better have in mind the stronger thesis if he is to have any chance of ending up with precisely three parts (and not indefinitely many), and, as we shall see, it *is* quite clear that this is how he conceives the opposition of *spirit* and appetite (cf. 439e–440a).[7] So, following T. H. Irwin,[8] I shall interpret him as claiming that because reason sometimes rejects an appetite—i.e., insists that an appetite is *not* to be acted on, that it does *not* constitute a reason, say, to drink whatever liquid may be in question—reason and appetite must be distinct. Still, however that may be, the text does make it clear that Socrates is conceiving reason as a *force* which works counter to appetite, pulling the agent back from what appetite pushes him toward. He draws an analogy (439b8–11) between what goes on inside this thirsty man and what happens when an archer draws his bow: just as the archer's one hand pulls the bow to him while the other hand pushes it away, so thirst moves him toward the drink while reason pulls him back from it. This shows that already in Book IV reason is being conceived as itself a source of desires, of motivating conditions. But clearly enough, the desire of reason at work in this case is not plausibly represented as what I've been calling intellectual curiosity; so, apparently, reason has other desires than the desire to know the truth. That the rational desire at work in the thirsty man's case is a form of the desire of reason to *rule,* will emerge from consideration of an objection that might be raised against Socrates' use here of the archer analogy.

It might be claimed that this analogy is misleading, and that whatever can legitimately be meant by saying in a case like this that reason pulls one back, does not justify the attribution to reason of any motivating force of its own, on all fours with that belonging to thirst. For suppose I am thirsty but know the only available water is boobytrapped so that I'll get a painful

---

[7] And cf. 554d–e, where Socrates speaks of a conflict among appetites in the "oligarchic" man's soul; his "better" appetites (his love of money, thriftiness etc.) do battle with and win out over his "worse" ones (his occasional extravagant lusts, thirsts, hungers). This man, Socrates implies, has a kind of self-control, but one that is far from being a virtue, since the appetite that prevails keeps control not (as reason would do) by the logical and rational force of ideas, but by inducing instinctual and irrational fear—the irrational fear of what will happen if money is spent in order to gratify the base appetites. Plato shows no sign of discomfort here in recognizing conflicts within what he continues to think of as a single part of the soul. This is reasonable if he did not mean to argue in Book IV that just any conflict of desires betrays a difference of origin (i.e., a difference of type of motivation) in the desires, but hardly otherwise.

[8] *Plato's Moral Theory,* p. 327.

electric shock upon coming into contact with it. I thereupon hold back because I want to avoid this pain. Here, although it may be fair enough to say that reason restrains me, this does not imply that reason is the original source of any motivating desire not to drink; what motivates me to abstain from drinking is my aversion to pain. If one is to speak in terms of forces here at all, then, the forces that come into conflict are these two physical desires, thirst and the aversion to pain, neither of which has its origin in any capacity for reasoning. If this is an example of the sort of conflict Socrates has in mind, then he is not entitled to treat reason as a motivating force on its own, and so the question doesn't arise, what *kind* of desire of reason is working here.

I think, however, that in the case as just described, Socrates would actually agree that only the aversion to pain motivated abstention; if one takes desires simply as givens and limits oneself to working out how to satisfy them, allowing, for example, whichever is the stronger to determine one's action, or working out and following some scheme whereby the totality of one's desires may be satisfied as fully as possible, then there seems no doubt that one's calculations have not contributed anything to the already existing motives to action. In a similar case (554d9–e1) Socrates speaks of opposed appetites, not a conflict of reason and appetite. Presumably, then, he thinks that not every case of conflict is like this, even if some may be. In fact there seems no doubt that on the *Republic*'s scheme reason is taken to be capable of deciding on its own theoretical grounds which ends are worth pursuing, and does not merely (as the calculating just described does) provide the means to, or work out some balance among, appetitively or otherwise given ends.[9] When it proposes an end on its own authority, Socrates evidently

---

[9] Here I mean to attribute to Plato the stronger of two possible models one might have in mind for what it is for reason to rule in our lives. (1) According to the weaker view reason as a ruler accepts desire as the ultimate criterion of value; on this view, that a thing is, or would under certain conditions come to be, desired (whatever the nature and source of the desire in question) is reason's sole basis for assigning actual or potential value to anything and so giving it a weight in its calculations. Given this criterion of value, and the facts about what one desires or might come to desire, reason's role is to work out a best overall scheme of life, with strategies and tactics for dealing with particular problems that may arise, and to decide on appropriate action in individual circumstances. In carrying out this task, reason aims at satisfying one's desires as fully as possible, taking into account how much one wants various things, how distressed one would be without them, how getting or failing to get something one wants affects one's ability to get or enjoy other things one wants, and so on. On this model, for reason to rule is (a) for it to be free to decide, upon an impartial survey of the relevant facts about the world and about one's desires, how one should live and act, and (b) for its decisions to be effective. Once reason decides on an object of pursuit or a mode of action in some situation it may contribute a new desire of its own (the desire to pursue or do that *because* it is supported by reason), but this desire only comes in as a reinforcement of the antecedent desires whose satisfaction reason was previously deliberating about. (2) On the second, stronger model, reason's work, and the desires it gives rise to, are more fundamental. Here, instead of taking desire as the criterion of value in its object, reason presumes to be able

thinks, reason also, at least sometimes, contributes a *desire* of its own (the desire to achieve that end), and this is an additional motivating force, over and above whatever other kinds of desire may also be operating. Perhaps, therefore, the case Socrates has in mind is one where such a reason-generated desire comes into conflict with an appetite.

If so, the conflict Socrates has in mind is of the following sort. The thirsty man has worked out (or any rate holds) on grounds of reason that health is a good thing, a more important good than the momentary gratification of appetite. He also desires to preserve his health *because* it is a good thing, and this desire (a product of reason) conflicts with his thirst; in the case envisaged the desire of reason wins out, and the man abstains. Now presumably Socrates does not hold that the desire for health is part of the original constitution of human nature (as the desire for knowledge is apparently thought to be); it is instead the consequence of a higher-order desire for good, as such, together with the grounds, whatever they are, on which health is thought to be a good. So what is inherent in reason is the desire for good, as such—not the desire for any particular good. And Plato does of course in the *Republic* (e.g., 505d11–e1), as elsewhere, speak of this desire as one which all human beings have. We are now, however, in a position to say something more illuminating about the status of this desire in human life than simply that everyone has it. The desire for the good can now be seen as equivalent to the desire on the part of reason to work out the ends of life on its own and to achieve them. Reason wants to do these things *on its own,* that is, without treating the fact that one has an attachment for a thing grounded in appetite or spirit or any other source of desire there may be as a ground for pursuing it. Thus the claim that the desire for the good is inherent in reason itself amounts to the claim that anyone who possesses

---

to decide by appeal to its own principles what things are good and how good they are; that, as may happen, these are also desired, and the degree to which they are desired, have nothing to do with their value (except to the extent that having a desire may constitute recognition of some antecedent value). It would not be easy to specify what according to Plato these principles might be, but the following example may indicate the general idea. We speak of the good of living things in general (not just animals), and we consider a creature's good to consist, at least in part, in its attaining, and functioning in, its natural mature state. The satisfaction of desire obviously cannot be the basis for such a judgment where plants are concerned, and it is not implausible to exclude it even in the case of animals. We might well expect an animal to find satisfaction for its desires in the natural functioning of its mature state, but if it did not one need not conclude that its good lay elsewhere, but only that, through some perversion, it failed to enjoy its good when it had it. In the *Republic*'s theory the function of the form of the Good is to provide the knowledge of those principles of goodness that will permit reason to work out a scheme of ends for an individual to aim at achieving in his life and to make particular decisions as circumstances require (on this see Chapter 5 below). Given this knowledge one will know, for example, that and why eating or drinking is a good when it is (because health requires it, and health is a good); but from reason's point of view one's appetites for food and drink themselves provide no reason at all for thinking that these are good things. Similarly for all other nonrational desires.

the power of reason wants to think out on his own, on purely rational grounds, what goals to pursue in life, and to achieve those goals. He wants, in other words, reason to rule in his life.[10]

III

It is as independent influences on action, sometimes in conflict, sometimes in harmony with desires of reason, that appetite and spirit figure in Socrates' theory. Let us consider appetite first. Unfortunately Plato is not careful to give a systematic general description of the sorts of desires that he counts as appetitive; in the fourth book he focuses simply on what he calls the "clearest" (*enargestatas*, 437d3) instances of what he has in mind, thirst and hunger and (he adds a little later, 439d6) sexual desire, allowing his treatment of these examples to substitute for a general account. Indeed, he insists on quite a narrow construction of even these appetites: if I am thirsty for beer or hungry for chocolate these desires are not, he says, correctly classified merely as thirst or hunger (cf. 437d8–e6). They are thirst or hunger modified by some addition (e7–8). He does not indicate exactly what the relevant addition is, but presumably it is an acquired liking for the taste of beer and chocolate respectively (together perhaps, in the former case, with a liking for the way beer makes me feel). Thirst, just by itself, unmodified by these or other additions, is simply for drink, hunger simply for food.

These examples, and this treatment of them, might suggest that Plato limits the appetitive desires just to the basic recurrent biological urges, and indeed only to that part of them which is primitive and unmodified by the effects of experience. On the other hand even in this passage he refers several times to "other appetites" than these three (439d7, 436a11f., 437d2–3);[11] and he gives an interesting example of such an appetite when in telling the story of Leontius, he refers to Leontius' "appetite" (*epithumia*, 440a1) to look at some corpses piled by the road. In the same context, arguing that spirit never allies itself with appetite (440b4–7), he points out that a decent man if he thinks he has been in the wrong cannot become angry even if he is subjected, in just retaliation, to hunger and cold and other such physical deprivations (c1–5)—so that being shivering cold is or gives rise to an

---

[10] This interpretation of Plato makes it easy to see how Aristotle might have arrived at his distinction between theoretical and practical reason. Theoretical reason is simply reason used to pursue one of the two ends that according to Plato rational beings qua rational have got, viz. to know the truth; practical reason is reason pursuing its other end, the end of ruling our lives. Hence Aristotle can say that in both employments reason aims at truth (*Nic. Eth.* VI 2, 1139b12)—not truth in the one case and something else (say, good) in the other. For he, just as much as Plato, conceives of reason as having the power to rule in the stronger of the two senses distinguished above (n.9), and accordingly the desire of reason to rule is for him the desire to achieve and enforce practical truth, i.e., the correctness of ends as well as means.

[11] And notice that at 437d11–e2 "modified thirst," while Socrates insists it is not merely *thirst*, is nonetheless classed as an ἐπιθυμία.

appetite with which spirit refuses to ally itself. Later, especially in Books VIII and IX, the love of money is repeatedly treated as an appetite—indeed where we might expect the expression "appetitive part" Plato fairly often in these books writes "money-loving" (*philochrēmaton*) or "profit-loving" (*philokerdes*) part instead.[12] And the democratic man, whose principle of life is said (561b2–c3) to be to give free and equal scope to each of his appetites, is credited not merely with a large variety of particular appetites for many different kinds of food and drink and sex, but also with appetites for various athletic and political pursuits and even, on occasion, for, as he imagines it, doing a little philosophy (561c–d).[13] Thus desires that embody modifications of the basic appetites for sex, drink and food (e.g., the desire for lobster) are nonetheless still appetitive desires; likewise physical desires which would not ordinarily be called appetites, such as the desire when cold to be warmed up, or the aversion to pain, count as appetitive, as do ghoulish impulses like Leontius' for looking at dead bodies. So also the love of money and the liking for physical exercise. *Some* kind of liking for such things as political activity and dabbling at philosophy also counts. What principle of unity is Plato relying on here? Is there really one at all?

In considering this question let us begin where Plato does, with the recurrent biological urges for food, drink and sex. Socrates' first concern is to convince his interlocutors that there are *two* independent sources of motivation, reason on the one side and appetite on the other. For this purpose it is essential to choose examples that are undoubted cases of desires motivating action but where there is equally no doubt that these are desires not having reason as their source. Desires for specific kinds of food or drink or acquired likings of any kind will therefore not do: the generation of these desires obviously involves the use of *some* power to reason, at least to the

---

[12] Plato justifies these epithets at 580e5–581a1 by saying that the principal use of money is to provide the means by which the appetites can be gratified.

[13] In developing his account of the various types of unjust person (timocratic, oligarchic, democratic, tyrannical) Plato makes it clear that, just as the "timocrat" (550b5–6) has yielded the governance of his soul to his θυμός, so the "oligarch", the "democrat" and the "tyrant" are all ruled in different ways by appetite. The "oligarch" is said explicitly (553c4–7) to enthrone appetite as his ruler, which means that in his plans and decisions his ultimate aim is constantly and only to gratify appetite; being dominated by appetite, he forces the other parts of the soul to want and get satisfaction only from assisting in this effort (553d1–7). But his pursuit of appetite takes the perverted form of aiming at fulfilling first what Plato calls the "necessary" appetites and, beyond them, only the appetite for the mere accumulation of the *means* (money) whereby these and other appetites might be satisfied. The "democrat" (559d–561e) refuses to follow the oligarch in repressing his other appetites, and ends by establishing equality for all appetites: he allows himself to acquire any and every appetite that his circumstances and nature make it possible for him to acquire, and then he indulges all his appetites in turn, on an equal basis. A consequence of this account is that, as noted in the text, when, in accordance with his scheme, the democrat goes in for athletic, political and philosophical pursuits, the desires for these things that he is bent on indulging must be construed as appetites, desires belonging to the ἐπιθυμητικόν, odd as this may seem. They are not desires of spirit or reason.

extent of noticing and remembering the effects on oneself of various eaten and drunk objects or various external conditions and activities. And even if, as I believe Plato would ultimately want to argue, these rational powers ought not in such cases to be construed as belonging to the part of the soul which *he* calls "reason," to assume that at this point would certainly be confusing. Nor is it necessary for him to do so. There seems no doubt that hunger and thirst, understood as simple urges for food and drink, arise wholly from physiological causes (cf. διὰ παθημάτων τε καὶ νοσημάτων παραγίγνεται, 439d1–2), without any intervention from or detour through reason, not even through these equivocal processes of noticing and remembering. It is equally clear that these things have a direct motivating influence on action, as the fact of conflict to which Plato appeals very clearly indicates. Hence by concentrating on hunger and thirst as his "clearest cases" he can convincingly demonstrate the existence of motivating desires that work altogether independently of reasoning of whatever sort. And that is all he wishes, and needs, to show at this point in the argument.

Once it is established that there *is* such a source of motivating desires, independent of reason, it is not difficult to recognize other desires besides the recurrent biological urges as having essentially the same status. Thus there are other desires besides hunger, thirst, and sexual appetite that are based on physical and physiological causes: e.g., the desire to be warmed up when cold, or, in general, the aversion to pain. And certain other more complex desires can be treated as transformations of these and other such appetites: thus all particular likes and dislikes in food and drink. Some tastes are simply found to be pleasant, and those which are, generate, by straightforward physical causation, desires for them. These desires, in turn, give rise, provided one knows what external objects need to be manipulated in order to get the pleasure, to further desires for those objects themselves. (This is what justifies Plato in counting the desire for money as appetitive: see 580e5ff.) So, even though what we (but, as I have indicated, not Plato) would classify as rational powers may be involved in the constitution of such further desires, it is not at all events motivating reason, but only calculation undertaken in the interest of the appetitive goal of physical gratification. In this way, beginning from simple hunger and thirst, we can explain why thirst for beer or hunger for chocolate should count as desires of the same basic type: all these desires rest ultimately on brute facts about our bodily constitution and about the means by which pleasurable bodily states may be caused.

It does not seem, however, that Plato means to limit the appetitive desires to those whose origin lies in such facts about our bodily constitution. At any rate, Leontius' ghoulish desire to look at dead bodies, or the democratic man's liking for philosophical dabbling might seem poor candidates for this kind of treatment. It might give one pause, however, that when Leontius is overcome by his appetite and his spirit intervenes to chastise him for overruling his reason and gaping at the bodies, Socrates says spirit places the blame on his *eyes:* "Go ahead and look," Leontius is quoted as saying, "you wretched things; get your fill of that lovely scene" (440a2–3). This might suggest that according to Plato it is the constitution of eyes (at any rate Leontius') that makes looking at corpses so fascinating to him: in the same way as my particular tastebuds are responsible for the fact that I enjoy the taste of orange juice, Leontius' eyes give him a pleasure caused by the sight of dead bodies. It would be difficult, however, to sustain this suggestion: it seems certain (unless we are to understand Leontius' attraction as straightfor-wardly sexual) that whatever it is about dead bodies that so interests him has something to do with some way in which he is thinking of them—some thrill-inducing contrast between living, animated human beings and these limp and broken figures, say—and it seems too much to believe that anyone's eyes are naturally so constituted as to be given some pleasure by being exposed to dead bodies *when* so conceived. Leontius' imagination is at work here, and, surely it, rather than the eyes, is the most important source of the pleasure he is seeking.

Still, the workings of the imagination might be thought of as the source of pleasure in the same way as the bodily senses are. A person simply finds certain imaginings interesting or amusing or thrilling, just as he simply finds certain tastes appealing; his imagination is so constituted that these things appeal to him, and having found them so he forms the desire to witness them again. The pleasure in question may not be a bodily pleasure, and its source may not be the constitution of his body and its organs; it is nonetheless a brute fact about his way of being affected by the physical world that looking at corpses gives him pleasure, so that if imagination, and not the bodily organs, is its source, still, the desire for that pleasure is independent of reason's desires to know the truth and to rule his life. Whatever precisely the imagination may be it is on Plato's view linked essentially to the world as it appears rather than to reason, understood, as he understands it, as devoted to knowing, and governing in accordance with, the truth. This suggests the possibility of taking Leontius' castigation of his eyes as implying not that these bodily organs, but rather, more generally, that attending to the physical world independently of the discipline of reason, is the source of his pleasure. Certainly, reference to vision and its organs, the eyes, often does play this symbolic role in the *Republic.*[14]

What then about the democratic man's pleasure in dabbling at philosophy? If this is to be construed as an appetitive pleasure, then it must be sharply distinguished from the corresponding pleasure of the true philosopher, since

---

[14] The ὁρατὸς τόπος (visible place) (508c2) described in the analogy of the sun is also the realm of τὸ γιγνόμενόν τε καὶ ἀπολλύμενον (what comes to be and passes away) which if the soul attends to in working out its general conceptions of things, instead of to the νοητόν (intelligible), it will fail to reach any understanding (d6–9); and when a soul does that it is reduced to taking resemblances for reality (476c5–7) and ruling in accord with the false and inadequate conventional standards (479a3, d3–5) that have been developed over time by others who likewise relied on experience without philosophical thought to guide their lives.

that is a pleasure of reason. In enjoying philosophizing the philosopher is enjoying the pursuit of the truth; his desire for this pleasure is the expression of his reason's desire to know the truth. The democrat, then, is not led by an interest in the truth to engage in philosophical activity. What does lead him to it? Presumably, he simply finds something appealing about it: the manipulation of words, the process of deduction, the surprise of discovery, or whatever, interests and amuses him. Yet since this is unconnected with any serious pursuit of the truth, philosophy remains only a game—so it is no surprise that, on Socrates' account, the democrat only intermittently plays at it and does not acquire any deeper and more permanent attachment. *His* desire to philosophize, then, counts as an appetite because he attends only to the superficial, "visible" aspects of philosophy, features of it that he happens to find interesting. This interest is for him as much a brute fact about his interaction with the physical world as Leontius' interest in viewing corpses. Neither of these is a recurrent biological urge, nor even such an urge modified by the addition of likings for particular tastes or smells or bodily feelings. Yet they have their ultimate origin simply in facts of experience, in the fact that the person in question happens to get a certain pleasure from doing these things, and this justifies classifying them together with the bodily appetites. They are independent of reason in the same sort of way, and can be opposed by reason on the same sort of grounds.

IV

We come at last to spirit. Socrates' standard name for the source of this third type of motivation, *to thumoeides*, derives from a Greek word, *thumos*, that by Plato's time seems to have been in ordinary use mostly as a name for anger: the word is in fact etymologically the same as our word "fume"—someone in a state of *thumos* would be "fuming" about something. But in Homer, where it appears very frequently, the word has a broader usage: it names the part of themselves to which Homeric heroes speak, or which speaks to them, when they are aroused for action, and into which they, or some tutelary deity, pour might and strength when their prowess is about to be put to the test. It is thus the immediate source of action, especially vigorous action, and the seat of emotion, especially those emotions (anger, for example, but also on occasion sexual passion as well) that motivate vigorous and bold action.[15] As we shall see, Plato's theory of *thumos* is obviously much indebted to Homer; taking his account of *thumos* altogether, the developments in Books VIII and IX together with the initial argument in Book IV, *thumos* seems closely connected in Plato's eyes, as in Homer's,

[15] Claus in the latest discussion of the Homeric usage of soul-words (*Toward the Soul*) argues that in Homer θυμός like μένος, ἦτορ and κῆρ, with each of which it is in many contexts easily interchangeable, has the central meaning of "life-force," but with a special connection to personal affection (see his ch. 1, esp. pp. 37–42).

with vigorous, competitive action. But in his account in Book IV Plato appeals exclusively to various forms of anger, and not to any of the other desires and emotions that get assigned to *thumos* in Homer. His examples cover a fairly wide range: they range from the fury of screaming infants (441a7–9) and barking dogs (b2–3), to Odysseus' outrage at the sexual misbehavior of Penelope's maids with her suitors (441b4–c2), to Leontius' annoyance and disgust with himself for giving in to his ghoulish fascination for corpses and the aroused sense of justice which causes a man to insist on his rights, even though the effort may cost him such deprivation and pain as to seem hardly worth it. Later in the fourth book courage emerges as the specific virtue of this part of the soul (442b5–c3), and in Books VIII–IX it is constantly described as the honor-loving (*philotimon*) and victory-loving (*philonikon*) part, because, as Socrates says in one place (581a9–10), spirit is "always wholly striving for power and victory and good repute"—i.e., apparently, the reputation for effectiveness, single-mindedness, strength of character and other "executive" virtues. (A reputation for sensitivity and compassion, or wittiness, or brains, or even judiciousness would not count in *this* context as good repute.) So the spirited part expresses itself first of all in ordinary anger of various sorts; secondly in the moral feelings of shame, outrage and the offended sense of justice; and thirdly, in the desire to assert oneself, to be effective both in one's own private life and in the community's. What is it that in Plato's eyes links these things together—what is the principle of unity here?—and why does he think that together they constitute a third sort of motivation, coordinate with desires of reason and appetitive desires?

As before, his argument depends upon appeal to the fact of conflict. But his method of arguing from striking examples fails him in this instance. He argues first that *thumos* is distinct from appetite, by the example of Leontius, who becomes angry at himself (more specifically at his appetite for corpse-gazing)—here appetite is opposed by anger, so this anger is a desire deriving from another source than appetite. Then he argues that *thumos* is distinct from reason: first of all because babies and animals get furious but do not have the power to reason (that is, the power to figure out the truth of things and direct their lives in accordance with the truth), and secondly by the example of Odysseus, whose anger (more specifically, outrage) at the maids is opposed by his reason. Odysseus' anger impels him to punish the maids on the spot, but that would upset his rational plan to kill off the suitors, so his rational desire to do the latter opposes both the action proposed by anger and the anger itself.[16] His anger is therefore a desire deriving from another source than reason. One trouble with this two-stage argument is

[16] Notice that in the passage Plato cites from Homer (*Odyssey* XX, 17; *Republic* 441b6) Odysseus addresses and reproves his κραδίη, i.e., his anger or his heart conceived as the seat of it, bidding it to be calm and endure without making a fuss. The conflict in this case, as in that of Leontius where spirit and appetite conflict, involves a direct criticism by the "higher" faculty of the "lower," and not merely conflicting impulses to action.

that it presupposes that all the cases of anger in question are of the same type and derive from the same internal source; but it is not obvious, and certainly requires argument to show, that that is so. One cannot assume just because all these phenomena can be called "anger" that they are in relevant respects all alike. Indeed, it is clear that whatever screaming babies and attacking dogs are feeling is very different from what Leontius feels, and the fact that the latter is no appetite does not imply that the former cannot be. It is conceivable, I think, that all we have here is the opposition between reason and appetite all over again—Leontius' anger being a second desire of reason opposing that ghoulish appetite, the baby's and the animal's fury and Odysseus' outrage being nothing but appetitive desires opposed, in the latter case by reason.[17] What's required, in order to close this gap in Plato's argument, is a closer consideration of how these forms of anger are actually constituted, to see whether they, or any of them, really are a new kind of motivation coming into conflict sometimes with desires of reason and sometimes with appetites.

It will help, I think, in doing this, if we turn first to consider what Plato says about spirit in Books VIII and IX; we can apply what we learn there so as to eke out a satisfactory interpretation of the book IV examples. In Books VIII and IX Socrates develops an account of four kinds of person who lack the virtue of justice as he has defined it, because reason is not in control of their lives. We have seen already that for reason to be in control of a person's life is for him to have worked out on exclusively rational and theoretical grounds what goals are worth pursuing and to have patterned his life around the pursuit of those goals. The four bad kinds of person Socrates describes are conceived by him as people in whom another part of the soul has grown strong, displacing reason and establishing its own control over them and their lives.[18] So the person whom he calls timocratic is someone in whom *thumos* has fixed the goals around which he has patterned his life. Socrates describes the timocratic person as "somewhat self-willed and a

[17] This is the view taken by Cornford, Hardie, and Penner.

[18] Plato's highly metaphorical talk of the displacement of reason from its throne and the usurpation of power by θυμός or by appetite (550b4–6, 553c4–d7) is potentially very misleading. He does not mean either that reason ceases altogether to function (see 553d) or that the usurper actually begins to perform reason's functions of calculating out what to do, declaring where the overall good lies and deciding accordingly. What happens instead is simply that, yielding to the importunities of the usurping desires (i.e., accepting the strength or frequency of these desires as criterion of the value of their objects), the person's reason comes to adopt, as its *own* general view of what *is* good for him, the overall plan of gratifying those desires first and foremost. In doing this reason fails to perform its most essential task, namely to work out on its *own* theoretical grounds where the good actually lies; and that is why Plato says reason is no longer ruling in such a person's life, and why he says that instead those other desires rule, the ones to which reason has abdicated its own responsibility to set goals. But reason continues to be the only part of the soul in which judgments about overall good and those desires for good that follow upon them are located.

little bit on the uncultured side . . . harsh with his slaves . . . but gentle with free men and very obedient to authorities, a seeker after public office and public esteem, not thinking himself worthy of office because of his ability as a speaker or anything like that, but because of his accomplishments in battle and military affairs, and a devotee of athletics and hunting" (548e4–549a7); he will be disdainful of money and the pursuit of it, while nonetheless placing a rather high value on having it (549a9–b2, cf. 548a5–b2). In sum, the person dominated by *thumos* is "a haughty man and a seeker of public esteem" (*hupsēlophrōn te kai philotimos anēr*, 550b7). It is worth emphasizing that Socrates only claims that this kind of outlook results where *thumos*-motivations are not only particularly strong in a person but develop freely, without being trained and directed in subordination to other values: he insists that the people who will make the best warriors in his ideal republic must be by nature unusually "high-spirited" (*thumoeideis*, 375a11–12, e10), but the description just quoted will not fully apply to them because they have been educated to respect philosophical values and to seek the good of their fellow-citizens, so that though *thumos* governs them *what thumos* directs them to do will not be the same as for Socrates' timocratic man. And, of course, where *thumos* is subordinated to appetite, as in the person whom Socrates calls oligarchic, it will bring its special motivations in support of the agent's dominant appetitive values: the oligarchic man does not permit his *thumos* to "admire and esteem (*timan*) anything else but wealth and the wealthy or to seek public esteem on any other ground than the possession of money and whatever else contributes to that" (553d4–7).

The central idea suggested by these and other passages of Book VIII is that *thumos* is understood by Plato as that wherein one feels a) the competitive drive to distinguish oneself from the run-of-the-mill person, to do and be something noteworthy within the context provided by one's society and its scheme of values; b) pride in oneself and one's accomplishments, to the extent that one succeeds in this effort; c) esteem for noteworthy others and (especially) the desire to be esteemed by others and by oneself. Because competitiveness can be so variously directed, and the bases of self-esteem (and pride and esteem for others) can vary so widely, *thumos*, if this is what it is, can in different people support widely different courses of action and ways of life, and this Plato claims it does. But it does not seem to me unnatural to think that someone in whom competitiveness and the desire for esteem and self-esteem were particularly strong should tend toward the athletic, military and political pursuits, to which Plato says the *thumos*-dominated person will especially devote himself; these are obvious, as well as traditional, activities in which a man, at any rate, can hope to make himself stand out from others as esteem and self-esteem require and competitiveness implies.

I suggest, then, that the motivations that Plato classifies under the heading of spirit are to be understood as having their root in competitiveness and the desire for self-esteem and (as a normal presupposition of this) esteem by others. Can we make sense of Plato's examples of anger in Book IV along these lines? Three of the five fall immediately into place. When Odysseus in disguise comes upon Penelope's maids cavorting with her suitors his immediate impulse is to punish them on the spot: the sight of such disorder in his own household is naturally a blow to his self-esteem (self-respecting noblemen don't permit that kind of thing), and his anger is a response to this affront. It urges him to act immediately to restore order and therewith prove himself deserving of the esteem which he feels is placed in jeopardy by the continuance of this state of affairs. His anger thus represents a traditional view of things to which his continued self-esteem is tied: he will feel bad about himself unless he acts at once to vindicate his honor. Yet his reason does not support this traditional view: from reason's point of view delay does not mean indifference or weakness or cowardly acquiescence, and there is (Odysseus thinks) no *reason* for him to think less well of himself for delaying (in fact, quite the contrary, since he plans eventually *both* to punish the maids *and* to kill off the suitors). But though this is how he thinks, it is not how he feels. The reaction of his *thumos* shows that his self-esteem, the way he feels about himself, is tied up with a certain traditional view of the king's dignity, not with the view implied by his own rational planning. Hence reason and spirit in his case are in conflict over what to do. A bad upbringing, Socrates suggests (cf. 441a3), has corrupted Odysseus' spirit, causing him to feel differently about things than he thinks.

Similarly for Leontius. On a considered view of things Leontius rejects corpse-gazing as a bad thing or at any rate nothing to take any interest in. Yet he continues to have an appetite for that sort of thing. Unlike Odysseus, Leontius's *thumos* is in agreement with his reason: he feels that corpse-gazing is *sordid,* and does not want to be the kind of person who goes in for it; in fact, perhaps, he aspires to be the kind of person who makes the goals of reason his goals and has no others. Hence when he incontinently acts on this rejected desire not only does his reason disapprove of what he has done, but he also suffers a blow to his self-esteem: the anger he feels at himself (it might equally have been shame or simply exasperation) is the natural response to this failure to measure up in his own eyes. The situation is the same with the man who responds with anger to what he judges is unjust treatment: it is natural to think that the perceived injustice is taken by him as a sign that the perpetrator disregards or belittles him and his interests, and his anger is the normal and natural response to such a slight. Not to become angry would be a sign that one acquiesced in the perpetrator's estimation of one's worth or importance, and no one who feels self-esteem could do that. So here too anger expresses the competitive desire to acquire and preserve self-esteem.

The other two examples of *thumos* appealed to in the Book IV argument are less easy to accommodate. Screaming two-week old babies and ferocious dogs presumably have no self-conception (I assume the dogs are not even self-conscious) and so though their anger may express some primitive form of competitiveness, it is at any rate not a form that has anything to do with self-esteem that their anger expresses. But perhaps Plato counts these cases of anger as motivations of the same kind as Leontius' and Odysseus' because he sees them as the central primitive phenomena which get transformed, as we mature, into the full-fledged competitive desire for self-esteem that expresses itself partly in anger like Leontius' and Odysseus', as well as in the admiration and emulation of others, the disdain for anything lowly, and the aspiration for solid accomplishments which we have found attributed to *thumos* in Books VIII and IX.

If I am right that competitiveness and the desire for esteem and self-esteem lie at the center of what Plato understands by *thumos* in the *Republic,* it is not difficult to show that *thumos*-motivation is a different kind of motivation from either the desires of appetite or the desires of reason, as Plato construes them. It is different from appetite because appetites lack the self-reference which is essential to esteem and self-esteem; and it is different from the desires of reason, which may of course be self-referential, because of the way in which it is constituted. There are two aspects to this difference between *thumos* and reason. What a *thumos*-desire desires is competitive success and the esteem from others and oneself that comes with it. Like all objects of desire one can, of course, say that in desiring all this, *thumos* (or the person *qua* experiencing *thumos*) regards it as good. But that does not mean that a *thumos*-desire is a desire for good (a "good-dependent" desire) in the way that the desires of reason are. The difference has to do, so to speak, with the order of priority between the desire itself and thoughts about good. In the case of reason, thoughts about what is good come first, a desire being formed for whatever one thinks (rightly or wrongly) is good. But in the case of *thumos* the desire for competition and esteem comes first (without regard to any antecedent question whether these things really are good, or if they are why they are so), and thoughts about good then follow.

This difference connects with a second one. For although as Plato says a person's *thumos* tends by nature to support his reason's judgments about good and desires for that, it does not always do so. That is because the origins of one's *thumos*-desires do not in any event lie in rational processes of reflection, but in all kinds of contingencies in one's upbringing and subsequent life. *Thumos* develops under the influence of how other people (especially one's parents) respond to and treat one. How we feel about ourselves—under what circumstances we experience a blow to our self-esteem, what we aspire to be and do, what competitions we enter—are to a large degree determined by our experiences in childhood, even if as adults we can partly remove or refine the effects of our upbringing so as to make the way we feel about ourselves conform with our rational conceptions of how we ought to live. It is possible, even normal, to find oneself, as Odysseus did, with conflicting conceptions and attitudes, some derived from the influence of events in earlier life in forming the basis of our self-esteem, others the product of considered rational judgment. It is natural, Socrates says, for these attitudes to be in agreement, for a person to feel good and bad about himself in just the ways that conform to his rational view of how he ought to live.[19] This is the result of the inherent authority of the truth, which is ideally the possession of reason, on which both his rational view of things and the basis of his self-esteem ought to converge. But they do not always do so, and even when they do the basis of a person's self-esteem is to be accounted for not simply by appeal to any rational argumentation he went through but to his personal experience in his developing social relationships.

On Plato's tripartite theory, then, competitiveness and the desire for esteem and self-esteem are an innate form of human motivation, distinct from the appetites and reason itself and equally as basic as they are to human nature. There is certainly no denying that this kind of motivation, in its many guises, does play a very large part in the conduct of any human being. Any plausible theory of human motivation must surely pay special attention to it. It is a considerable merit of Plato's theory of the human soul in the *Republic*, whatever its other shortcomings, that it gives fuller and more explicit recognition to this fact than subsequent theories have done.[20]

---

[19] Thus Socrates says (441a2–3), understandably enough, that θυμός is by nature reason's helper (ἐπίκουρος), and he describes it as entering disputes between reason and appetite or reason and outside agents as the ally (σύμμαχος) of reason (440b2–4, c7–9). It is harder to understand why Socrates so flatly insists (440b4–7) that one *never* finds anyone's θυμός intervening in a dispute between reason and appetite on appetite's side. He himself later describes the oligarchic man as enslaving both his θυμός and his reason to his appetite for money (553d), but just as the dominance of this appetite is not sufficient to prevent spendthrift desires from arising altogether (554b7–c2), so it presumably is not sufficient to prevent reason or θυμός from occasionally rebelling and generating desires not subordinated to the pursuit of wealth. And if, after all, reason and θυμός are independent of one another, why could not a desire of reason (e.g., to spend some money for the public good) arise that conflicts with the master-appetite, only to be opposed by θυμός for that very reason? When, as with the oligarchic person, θυμός has been habituated to support appetite, this is only what one should expect: reason's desire to act generously should be felt by θυμός as disgraceful—soft-hearted, a sign of weakness or sentimentality, etc. That Socrates does not envisage this possibility in Bk. IV is presumably to be explained by supposing that he assumes there that appetitive gratification is such a simple and easy thing to arrange, or if difficult so obviously in itself nothing to be proud of, that when reason opposes it the love of competition *could* not find any scope for activity except on reason's side (i.e., on the side whose winning out might show that something worth crowing over had been achieved). This thought seems natural enough, and appropriate to the context in Book IV; but it is nonetheless quite naive, as the account of the oligarchic man in Book VIII shows.

[20] I am grateful for helpful comments on earlier versions of this chapter from a number of people, especially Annette Baier, Gail Fine (my commentator when I presented the first version at Cornell), Cynthia Freeland, John Hare (commentator on a version delivered at a New Jersey Regional Philosophy Conference), and Alexander Nehamas.

Selected Further Readings

Irwin, T. H. *Plato's Ethics,* chapter 13. New York and Oxford: Oxford University Press, 1995.

Kahn, Charles. "Plato's Theory of Desire." *Review of Metaphysics* 41 (1987): 77–103.

Klosko, George. "The Rule of Reason in Plato's Psychology." *History of Philosophy Quarterly* 5 (1988): 341–56.

Price, Anthony W. *Mental Conflict,* chapter 2. London and New York: Routledge, 1995.

Reeve, C.D.C. *Philosopher-Kings: The Argument of Plato's "Republic,"* chapter 3. Princeton: Princeton University Press, 1988.

Woods, Michael J. "Plato's Division of the Soul." *Proceedings of the British Academy* 73 (1987): 23–48.

CHAPTER FIVE

The Psychology of Justice in Plato

ONE IMPORTANT MERIT of the recent spate of articles addressing the *Republic*'s central thesis, that all and only those who are just lead flourishing, fulfilled lives, is to have directed attention anew to Plato's moral psychology—specifically to the links Plato tries to forge between the love for knowledge and understanding and the aversion to (at any rate) much of what would ordinarily be counted as unjust treatment of other people.[1] It has rightly been seen that the core of Plato's response to Thrasymachus' challenge lies in this novel—even paradoxical—thesis about the nature of what a contemporary theorist would call "moral motivation." In this essay I want to examine directly and on its own account Plato's theory of the just person's psychology, leaving aside for the most part the controversies that have loomed so large lately about his justification for using the word "just" (*dikaios*) to describe the person whose psychology this is. The state of mind Plato describes has not, I think, been adequately represented in the recent literature, and my interest is more in what kind of person this is whom Plato calls just, than in whether he is correct in calling him that. My discussion will direct attention more than has been usual in this context to the *Republic*'s metaphysics, and less to its political and moral theory, narrowly conceived. I hope thereby to illuminate somewhat the Platonic conception of human perfection and to bring out both the close links between the psychology and the metaphysics of the *Republic* and some of the often unnoticed consequences that Plato's metaphysics has for his psychological theories.

I

Plato develops his account of the psychology of the just person in two principal stages. The later stage, found in *Republic* V–VII, is the more important for present purposes, but before turning to that I must take up briefly the earlier account of book IV. Plato's argument in the later books cannot be understood properly except in conjunction with the book IV account, aspects of which it is intended to fill out, and some of the recent literature on book IV contains misconceptions about the argument there that must be cleared away before we can proceed.

From the beginning of *Republic* IV it is taken for granted that to be just is to be in a psychological state which shapes and directs one's voluntary

---

[1] See especially Richard Kraut, "Reason and Justice in Plato's *Republic*."

actions, one's choices and one's preferences over a very wide range of practical concerns. Plato, for reasons we need not go into now, takes it that such a complex state cannot be adequately understood by treating it as a disposition to exhibit any single, or even any complex set of, independently and non-question-beggingly specifiable sorts of action. Justice must be characterized instead in internal, psychological terms, as a condition of a person's action-, choice- and preference-producing apparatus, specified by reference to interrelationships among the different elements of this apparatus itself. So, having fixed these elements as three, reason, aspiration[2] and appetite, Plato concludes that justice is the condition of a person in which each of these three plays always and only a certain single role, one for which it is naturally suited. Reason, on its own and without interference from the others, determines how it is best for the person to be and act; aspiration identifies with reason's directives, regarding them as objects to strive for and making the person dissatisfied with himself if through his own fault they are not attained; and appetite, restrained and moderated by reason and aspiration, drives him on toward pleasures of eating, drinking, sex, and other bodily gratifications when and as, and only when and as, reason approves. When each of these three psychological elements performs just its assigned job, then, Plato holds, the person in that psychological condition is just; and if in any way or to any degree these elements fail to do their jobs, or attempt to do anything else, such a person is not just. It does not follow, of course, that he is *un*just. As Socrates admits (472b7–d2), it may well turn out that no one fulfills these conditions perfectly; still, the definition is no less correct and no less useful for that, since we are free, for all practical purposes, to count as just those who sufficiently nearly resemble the person so defined. If it can be shown that only a perfectly just person is truly well-off, and lives a fulfilled life, then the more nearly anyone approximates to this internal condition the closer he will come to leading the perfectly flourishing human life: we need perfect models of just and unjust persons so that "however we find them to be as regards flourishing or its reverse, we will necessarily have to agree also that whoever of ourselves is most like them will have a share [of flourishing] most like theirs," 472c7–d1.[3] Strictly, then, only the person who fully attains precisely this psychological condition is just.

Even so, it is obvious enough that Plato has presented no sufficiently determinate theory of justice until he explains more fully what the role of reason is to be and how it is to go about performing it. He explains at some length in books III and IV what functions the other two parts are to perform,

---

[2] For the idea for this rendering of the Greek θυμοειδές, I am indebted to Gosling, *Plato*, ch. III.

[3] On the same principle Plato justifies the moral and political subjection of everyone else in his ideal state to the philosophers: by being so subject they approximate as closely as is possible for them to the state of soul possessed by the philosophers, and so also to the condition of flourishing enjoyed by them. See 590c–d.

but with the simple idea, which is all I have enunciated so far, that reason is to rule—to determine what is to be done and to put these determinations into effect—one has at best a formal criterion from which no substantive choices and preferences can be derived. Plato is deliberately vague in book IV on this point, since he is not yet in a position to define the role of reason more precisely; but he is not nearly so vague even in IV as he is sometimes thought to be. For in the full statement of what the function of reason is, Plato says not merely that reason is to rule but that it is to rule *with wisdom:* "Does not it belong to the rational part to rule, being wise and exercising forethought on behalf of the entire soul, and to the principle of high spirit to be subject to this and its ally?" (441e4–6, tr. Shorey). And a little farther on he characterizes wisdom: "But [we call an individual] wise by that small part that ruled in him and handed down these commands, by its possession in turn within it of the knowledge (*epistēmē*) of what is beneficial for each and for the whole, the community composed of the three" (442c5–8, tr. Shorey). So a person's reason is not doing its job unless three conditions are met: first, it *knows* what it is best for him to do; second, it makes all its decisions in the light of this knowledge; and third, its decisions are effective.[4] The main contribution of books V–VII is indeed to work out a theory of what this knowledge consists of; but already in IV Plato is explicit that unless one's reason has this knowledge, whatever exactly it amounts to, it is not performing its work fully and adequately.

It follows from what has been said so far that on Plato's account no one is just, strictly speaking, who does not have *knowledge* of what is best to do. True belief is not sufficient for an individual's justice in the *Republic,* nor, I think, though this is a more complicated question, for any other virtue of individuals.[5] It is true that Plato conspicuously defines a *city's* courage (429a–430c) in terms of the deep-dyed belief (not knowledge) of the soldier-class in the correctness of the laws and institutions of the city they serve. But it is noteworthy that he denies that this condition of belief makes the soldiers themselves brave, except in a qualified sense: it makes their city brave, but it gives them, as Socrates cautions, only "civic bravery" (*politikē andreia,* 430c3), not bravery *tout court.* It makes them consistently do the things one expects of brave citizens—they are fearless and selfless soldiers and police officers—but they are far from having the philosopher's pervasive strength of character, that will not let one rest content until one has achieved the fullest possible understanding of what is good for oneself and why it is so.[6] Similarly the city's justice is defined as the condition in which each class

---

[4] Thus it is clear that Plato does not work even in *Rep.* IV with what Kraut calls the "non-normative" conception of reason's rule, pp. 208–11.

[5] This has been denied by Gregory Vlastos, "The Argument in the *Republic* that 'Justice Pays,' " pp. 665–674, and its revision and expansion, "Justice and Happiness in the *Republic,*" pp. 66–95; see esp. the latter, pp. 92–94.

[6] See 503b7–504d3: to give the best possible account of the virtues one must take a longer route than was taken in describing them in book IV, one which makes explicit reference to

sticks to its own social work (432d–435a), but this does not mean, nor does Plato anywhere suggest, that people who do stick to their social work thereby show themselves to *be* just. They do what is just, but whether they *are* just is obviously not settled by pointing to their behavior alone. "Doing one's own social work" is presented only as a description of just action. It is not presented as part of the definition of the condition of justice itself—except, of course, the justice of a city, which is a different matter entirely.[7] Here Plato does not even allow an analogue of "civic bravery," and for a very good reason: in defining the city's justice he has said nothing about the internal condition(s) of the citizens, which cause(s) them to act justly, so he has not provided any ground here, as he has in the case of bravery, for attributing even a reduced form of the virtue to the individuals themselves. Once these points are duly noted, one sees that Plato consistently restricts justice, as a virtue of individuals, to those who possess within themselves *knowledge* of what it is best to do and be.[8]

---

knowledge of the good. Notice especially 503e: we require as rulers those who do not shy away like cowards (ἀποδειλιάσει) in the face of difficult intellectual tasks (and, to the same effect, 535b5–9); see also the martial and gymnastic metaphors of 534b8–c3.

[7] Vlastos concedes this point in the later version of his paper ("Justice and Happiness," p. 79), but insists that according to Plato a city can be just only if its citizens are just. A moment's reflection shows this to be an extraordinary view for anyone to hold, and especially so for Plato who, as we have seen, very clearly requires wisdom and knowledge of anyone who is just: surely he cannot have slipped even temporarily into allowing *all* the citizens of his city to have this knowledge? In fact the passage Vlastos cites for this view (435e1–436a3) says nothing of the kind. It does not say that in general "moral attributes," as Vlastos has it, come to be predicated of a city only by the antecedent possession of the same attributes by its inhabitants. Plato's point is a more limited one, in accordance with his aims in the passage in which it occurs. Socrates is suggesting, as he will presently argue, that each of us contains three psychological elements corresponding to the three classes of the state. An indication of this, he thinks, is the fact that whole nations are commonly thought to have predominant characters (ἤθη, e2)—the Scythians, for example, to be high-spirited, the Athenians devoted to learning and the Phoenicians fond of money. These characters must attach to these nations by transference from their members (and given that the three characters in question seem to suggest the prominence of the ends of one or another of three distinct parts of the soul, this usage therefore implies that human beings do have the three distinct parts in question). What is true of such predominant national characters need not be true of other properties, not even all "moral attributes"; and Plato nowhere says it is (544d–545b, the only other passage where any similar point is made, applies it to the same restricted set of attributes as we find in this passage). So far as the moral virtues are concerned, as I argue in the text, Plato says different things about different ones: wisdom belongs to the city because the rulers are wise (cf. the repeated emphasis on ἐπιστήμη, 428b6, c11, d8, e8, 429a1–3), bravery because the soldiers have a qualified form, at least, of bravery; justice and moderation, however, though they belong to the city in each case because of *some* property of the citizens, do not devolve upon it from the citizens' being even in a qualified way just and moderate. This seems to me a perfectly sensible view; it is, in any event, for better or worse, what Plato thought.

[8] Hence for Plato only accomplished philosophers can be just. Things would have been different, and better, if like Aristotle he had conceived of a kind of practical knowledge substantially independent of the use of theoretical and scientific powers. He was precluded from doing this by the status of the good-itself in his theory; see below, sect. III.

II

Clearly, then, one cannot know what the just person according to Plato is like until one has some grasp, at least, of the nature and substance of this knowledge. For a person's considered conception of how it is best to be and act inevitably colors his attitudes to himself and to other people, as well as establishing or altering more particular attachments and antipathies—and especially so in the case of someone who is so structured that there is no possibility of opposition or resistance to the effective and total adoption of the recommendations of his reason. And if one wants to know what the state of mind of Plato's just person would be, one will have to know something about how he thinks and feels in these respects.

In book IV itself, as already remarked, little is said about what the just person knows. It is noteworthy, however, that the wisdom he is said to have is described merely as knowledge of what is advantageous to himself (442c5–8). Yet earlier in the book the same name, *sophia,* is given to the knowledge, possessed by the rulers of the ideal city, "which takes counsel about the city as a whole as to how it would best order its relations to itself and to other cities" (428c12–d3; cf. 429a1–3). Unless Plato is guilty here of a gross equivocation, he must suppose that it is one and the same knowledge that knows both these things.[9] No doubt part of his reason for supposing this derives from his conviction that it is only in cities that human beings realize their full nature; but there is a more general reason as well. For both of these accomplishments essentially involve knowledge of what is good (for the city, for the individual); and you cannot, Plato thinks, know any such particular good without knowing the good-itself: "Whoever cannot mark off in his discourse the form of the good, separating it from all other things . . . you will say knows neither the good-itself nor any other good" (534b8–c5). To be sure, merely knowing the good will not by itself suffice—at any rate not for knowing how best to run a city. This is why Plato insists that before coming to know the good his rulers must spend fifteen years getting experience in city management (539e2–5). Still, the only part of what either sort of person knows that counts, on a strict view, as knowledge (the sort that encompasses understanding, of why things are the way they are and how they ought to be) is knowledge of the good-itself. Without this, all the experience in the world would be useless. So what Plato describes in book IV now as knowledge of how one ought to live oneself, now as knowledge of how a city should conduct its affairs, is in the end nothing less than knowledge of the *megiston mathēma,* the good-itself.

Thus we are led directly up to the central metaphysical theories of the *Republic.* This part of the dialogue is extremely difficult to interpret, since

---

[9] Aristotle, *Nic. Eth.* V, 1141b24–25, ἔστι δὲ καὶ ἡ πολιτικὴ καὶ ἡ φρόνησις ἡ αὐτὴ μὲν ἕξις, τὸ μέντοι εἶναι οὐ ταὐτὸν αὐταῖς, κτλ, simply reformulates in his own terminology this view of Plato's about these forms of σοφία.

Socrates himself refuses to speculate about what the good-itself might be (506b2–e5) and for the most part offers only the treacherous analogies and parables of sun, line and cave to convey those aspects of it that he *is* willing to hazard an opinion on. But without claiming to offer any proof that this is what Plato means, and avoiding scholarly controversy so far as possible, I risk the following summary of what is relevant in Plato's views on the good-itself for our present inquiry.

First, pending a qualification to be entered directly, the good-itself is a good thing, over and above the good things of this world:[10] over and above, that is, both individual good things like particular persons and events, and such things as a quiet, studious life or a cool drink on a hot day which one might speak of as good things, though they are not individuals but classes of individuals.[11] Unlike these other good things, however, it is not merely a good something-or-other, or good as such and such, or good for so and so or from such and such a point of view. To use Aristotelian language, one could say its essence is to be good; it is not, like every other good thing, essentially something else (a meal, a person) that, for one reason or another, happens to be good (is accidentally good).[12] Its goodness is not, therefore, diluted and compromised by being mingled with and made dependent on other features of things, as is true of every other good. Thus its goodness is pure, as that of no other good is. Furthermore, it is the only perfect good. Every other good, being good only in some respect or relation or from some point of view, is also not so good, or even quite bad, in some other ways.[13] No other good can possibly be as good as this one: the very best imaginable human life, for example, will still not be as good as this is, and so not as good as it is possible to conceive something as being.

Given the purity of the good-itself, and the impurity of every other good, it should be apparent why Plato says that one cannot know any other good except by knowing this one. Knowledge here, as usual in Plato, is taken to entail understanding, so that to know, e.g., a good life is not just to know which life is good, and from what points of view or in what circumstances, and so on, but precisely to understand what this goodness itself is that one

---

[10] I do not follow Vlastos in interpreting Plato's claims that the *F*-itself is *F* as in most cases predicating *F*-ness only of the *F* things of this world—at any rate this move cannot be made with the good-itself. See "The Unity of the Virtues in the *Protagoras*" and "An Ambiguity in the *Sophist*."

[11] I owe a debt here to N. R. Murphy, *The Interpretation of Plato's Republic*, ch. VI, and to Gosling, "*Republic* Book V: τὰ πολλὰ καλά, etc," 116 ff., though my interpretation is not identical, I think, with any of the various ones they seem to have in mind.

[12] Hence it is misleading to say, as I just did, that it is a good *thing*. "Good" belongs to it in much the way that "man" does to me, and it would be misleading or nonsensical to call me a man thing: that would invite the inappropriate question, "Man *what*?" So the good is *a good,* but, Plato will insist (to Aristotle's exasperation, cf. *Post. An.* 83a30–35) not *a good thing.*

[13] For a defense of this interpretation of the perfection of Platonic forms, see Nehamas, "Plato on the Imperfection of the Sensible World."

attributes to it with these qualifications. To understand that, however, is to conceive a good that stands apart from all such qualifications—in short, to form one's conception of goodness on the good-itself.

Given the perfection of the good-itself, and the imperfection of every other good, it is apparent why Plato insists that adequate practical thinking requires constantly keeping this good uppermost in one's mind. Everyone wants what is best, but the only sure criterion of goodness in any other thing is the degree to which it approximates the goodness of this perfect good. Any other criterion of goodness, based, say, merely on some conception of human needs and interests, cannot fail to be inadequate, since it must represent as the ideal, as the final achievement, something that cannot be that. Clarity and truth require that all partial standards be seen and treated as such.

So much for what one might call the functional properties of the good-itself. How about its substance or nature? Here Socrates is deliberately least informative. One may, however, render this curious entity more concrete by thinking of it somehow or other as a perfect example of rational order, conceived in explicitly mathematical terms: a complex, ordered whole, whose orderliness is due to the mathematical relationships holding among its parts. This is, I think, implied by the mathematical nature of the higher education that Plato prescribes in *Republic* VII (524d ff.) as preparing the way for dialectic, which itself culminates in the knowledge of this entity, and by the role which he assigns to knowledge of the good as completing and supporting the mathematical sciences of arithmetic and geometry (511c6–d1, 533b6–d1).[14] It should be recalled that the last stage of the preliminary studies, mathematical harmonics, already encompasses the idea that certain numerical relationships are in themselves harmonious and itself provides some explanation for why they harmonize (531c3–4); notice, too, that Socrates recommends the study of music for this reason especially, saying that this makes it "useful for the investigation of the beautiful and the good" (c6–7).[15] Thus mathematics and philosophy merge at their borders, and mathematics itself is capable, on Plato's account, of handling and partially explicating evaluative notions.

III

If this account of the good-itself is right, what must be the state of mind of the person who has a firm grasp on it? First of all, Plato emphasizes in many places, he must be a lover of learning (a *philomathēs*). This is so, to begin with, because only someone who felt a natural affinity for reading and thinking and abstract discussion and had learned to value these things more

---

[14] It also accommodates those later reports of a lecture *On the Good* that, to the surprise of some of its hearers, had to do with mathematics and little else (cf. Aristoxenus, *Harm.* 2.20.16–31.3).

[15] On this see Gosling, *Plato*, ch. VII.

highly than almost anything else could ever have persevered through the rigorous course of training that must be undergone to achieve it, with the attendant restriction of bodily gratification and curtailment of other sorts of pleasant pursuit. This knowledge is obviously not easily won, and if justice requires having it, and only a studious sort of person, who cares relatively little for other pursuits in comparison with intellectual ones, can achieve it, then no one can be just who is not that kind of studious person. This argument depends, of course, on somewhat doubtful causal connections, and it is worth noting that much the same conclusion follows more directly and firmly from the very nature of what the just person according to Plato knows. He knows the good-itself and therefore whatever he values he values strictly in the light of a comparison between that thing and the good. Whatever exhibits more fully and perfectly the sort of rational order that the form of the good possesses as its essence he values more highly than other things. Naturally, it would be rash to claim to know how he would rank things in the light of this knowledge. But it does seem inevitable that he would find in intellectual work generally, and contemplation of the good-itself in particular, the most nearly adequate instances of rational order in the natural world. This is so because pure, i.e., theoretical, rational thought is to the greatest degree possible completely determined by the requirements of rational order itself: by contrast, desires, material objects and everything else that is a mixture or combination of thought and bodily things and events, even when they do exhibit rational order, must remain a joint product of reason and something else. What such good things are like is largely determined, not by the demand for orderliness, but by the nature of these things themselves. The best pure thinking, on the other hand, is almost wholly the product of rational orderliness itself. Thus the contemplation of the good, and in lesser degree all other abstract scientific thought, since in these activities the impulse for rational order confronts less in the way of alien material to work upon, must be the most perfect earthly embodiments of good; and just men and women would know this and make this knowledge effective in their own lives. Hence they would prefer this kind of thinking to everything else; in it they would be closest to the good-itself, the only perfectly good thing there is.

On the other hand, it does not follow that they would always choose to live a contemplative's life, retired among their mathematical books and constantly engaging in philosophical discussions. Perhaps one would choose this if all he cared about was *his* realizing the good so far as possible. But a just person is a devotee of *the* good, not *his own* good; and these are very different things. Knowing the good, what he wants is to advance the reign of rational order in the world as a whole, so far as by his own efforts, alone or together with others, he can do this. He recognizes a single criterion of choice: What, given the circumstances, will be most likely to maximize the total amount of rational order in the world as a whole? And here he has a wide arena for possible activity. He can not only impose rational order on his own soul, thinking rational thoughts and satisfying rationally controlled appetites of his own; he can help to bring rational order to the souls of other individuals, and to their social life. To be sure, under certain conditions (for example, perhaps, those characteristic of Plato's own time: cf. 496c5–e2) he might find it rational not to work for the improvement of anything except himself. If conditions make it impossible for his efforts to bear fruit, then his time would be wasted in interesting himself in others: the reign of rational order would not thus be advanced, or not significantly enough to compensate for the loss of pure thinking the world would have to suffer in consequence of his taking time off from his studies. On the other hand, conditions need not always be so bad as that. There may be others intelligent enough to reach the higher intellectual realms themselves and willing to learn from him how to achieve them; and society itself may be ready, if he and others who know the truth work together, to accept their recommendations for its improvement. Under such conditions it would seem that the interests of rational order would be better served by his devoting himself, some of the time, to private teaching and to cooperation with other intellectuals in bettering the condition of mankind generally—in addition, of course, to doing a substantial amount of philosophical work of his own. This combination of activities, it seems plausible to say, would under such conditions constitute his best answer to the question: How can I maximize the total amount of rational order in the world as a whole?

Hence I believe Plato is perfectly entitled to the answer his Socrates gives to Glaucon's complaint (519d8–9) that it is unjust to make those who in the ideal city have reached the goal of intellectual culture leave off intellectual work and spend some of their time putting their knowledge to practical use in the improvement of the lives of others. Socrates answers, in part, that, on the contrary, it would not be fair of them to refuse, seeing that they have themselves exploited the city's institutions for their own intellectual benefit (520a6–c1): and, Glaucon now agrees, just people, such as these men and women are, will not refuse to do what is fair (*dikaia gar dē dikaiois epitaxomen*, e1). In saying this Socrates is transparently appealing to common sense principles of justice, which he elsewhere (see 538d6–539a1, esp. the implications of e6, *ta alēthē mē heuriskēi*) rejects as not true. But there is no cause for alarm, since the purer principles Plato himself has been espousing lead to the same conclusion. That these philosophers are just means, on Plato's account, that they know the good-itself and act always with a view to advancing rational order in the whole world. And given the conditions prevailing in the ideal state it does seem very reasonable to think that they would, on their own principles, opt for the mixed political and intellectual life which Socrates insists on.

On the other hand, it is right to emphasize the other part of Socrates' reply to Glaucon as well. For, he insists, they will go down into the cave unwillingly (*hōs ep' anankaion*, as Glaucon puts it, 520e1, cf. 540b4–5), that is to say not thinking that (of all things!) the good is to be found in the activities of ruling (cf. 521a5–6, b4–5) and recognizing that there is a life better than the political one (520e4–5, 521b9). They deliberately and freely (520d6–7) choose a life for themselves that is less good than a more singlemindedly intellectual life, of which however they are individually capable. The life they renounce is better because, taken just by itself, the activities it contains exhibit, on balance, a greater amount of rational order than do the combination of activities in the alternative. Furthermore, this life can be said to be in general the ideal best for any human being. There is no activity that comes closer to perfect embodiment of the good than contemplation, with understanding, of the good-itself and the other forms; and given, as Plato makes very clear, that human beings can come into existence who can engage in this activity more or less uninterruptedly, it follows that no other human life could be so good as this one. Hence if the degree of the philosopher's *eudaimonia* is judged by comparison with this ideal, Plato's philosophers will settle for a less flourishing existence than they might have had (519e1–520a4; cf. 420b4–8, 465e4–466a6). On the other hand, as previously noted, a true philosopher never concerns himself merely with his own good. His ultimate end is to improve not just the small part of the world that is constituted by his own life, but the whole of it, this part taken together with all the rest. So if a philosopher opted, under the conditions Plato envisages, to ignore everyone else in order to make his own life realize the good more perfectly and fully, he would fail to achieve the goal he was aiming at as nearly as he might have done. And if the degree of one's *eudaimonia* is measured by how close one comes to realizing one's ultimate end, such a philosopher would be less *eudaimōn* than he would have been by living the mixed political and intellectual life Socrates and his interlocutors were urging. And if one further supposes, as Plato certainly does, that human nature is such that left to themselves most people would always lead *very* disordered lives, it seems fair to say that any philosopher who ever opts for the mixed life will actually be more *eudaimōn* than any who opts for the purely intellectual life: any philosopher would always *prefer* the mixed life, and he would recognize any situation in which it was rational for him to choose a life of pure contemplation instead as one where external conditions alone, by preventing his efforts on others' behalf from bearing fruit, forced him to settle for less than he had wished to achieve on behalf of the good-itself. So, as Socrates intimates (420b4–5), his philosophers, making the choice to spend some of the time in the cave, but most of it in the world above, would be the happiest and most flourishing men there ever in fact can be.

This shows beyond any reasonable doubt that Plato's just man is no egoist, in any acceptable sense of this term. Not only does he not do everything he does out of concern for his own good, he never does anything for this reason. Even where he acts to benefit himself, recognizing that he does so, his reason for acting is that the good-itself demands it. That *his* good demands it is strictly irrelevant. By the same token, at no time does he act to benefit others out of regard for them and concern for *their* good, just because it is theirs. Again, he confers all benefits out of regard for the good-itself, not out of regard for these more immediate human beneficiaries. As Plato makes clear, the philosopher turns to this work with regret, *hōs ep' anankaion,* and not with any independent attachment to these activities themselves or to those at whose good they are directed. For him there is no pleasure or interest in them for their own sakes. This is, I think, the direct consequence of the role played in Plato's theory by the form of the good. It is the ultimate object of pursuit, yet lies outside the world. Hence no worldly thing or activity can, because of its own properties, because of what *it* is, interest the just man; anything interests him only as a means of coming nearer to the good-itself. Certainly this must be true for most ordinary human activities and interests, involving as they do the expression of appetites and emotions. To this rule there is a single exception, the activity of rational contemplation itself. Since that is the summit of human experience anyone who takes pleasure in it and loves it for its own sake will not be in danger of compromising his pursuit of the ultimate end itself. Because the just person's decision whether to use, or continue to use, his knowledge for the benefit of others is contingent on factors outside his control, he must avoid developing sentiments of attachment to other people and to the normal round of social and political life. But there is no possibility that someone who can contemplate the forms with understanding could ever be forced by circumstances to give up this activity entirely. This worldly attachment, therefore, is firm in a way that no other can be. This means that though the just man in Plato is no egoist, and no altruist either, but a sort of high-minded fanatic; still, his fanaticism is such as to allow him permanent and deep interests in one part of his own good, whereas he cannot similarly have any permanent and deep attachment to any other person's good. This is the only concession that one must grant to the common charge that Plato's just man is a covert, or not so covert, egoist.

I said a moment ago that all this is the consequence of the role played in Plato's theory by the form of the good. Aristotle was right, I think, to insist most emphatically that there is no such thing as a good-itself and that even if there were, one ought not to direct one's practical thinking at it as ultimate end. At any rate, the consequence of this insistence is something his own moral sensitivity seems to have made him very reluctant to give up: by placing the object of ultimate pursuit *in* the world Aristotle is able to make room for a wide variety of ordinary human pursuits, interests and attachments as themselves permanent constituents of the final good.[16] He could therefore present a moral psychology that corresponds much more closely

---

[16] Cf. Cooper, *Reason and Human Good in Aristotle*, esp. ch. II, and Chapter 15 below, "Friendship and the Good in Aristotle."

than Plato's does to ordinary moral experience. No doubt Plato would not regard this as a defect in his own theory or a point in favor of Aristotle's; but the fact itself is worth reflecting on.

Selected Further Readings

Annas, Julia. *An Introduction to Plato's "Republic,"* chapters 3–6, 10. Oxford: Clarendon Press, 1981.

Gill, Christopher. "Plato and the Education of Character." *Archiv für Geschichte der Philosophie* 67 (1985): 1–26.

Irwin, T. H. *Plato's Ethics,* chapter 18. New York and Oxford: Oxford University Press, 1995.

Kraut, Richard. "The Defense of Justice in Plato's *Republic.*" In *The Cambridge Companion to Plato,* edited by Richard Kraut. Cambridge: Cambridge University Press, 1992, 311–37.

Reeve, C.D.C. *Philosopher-Kings: The Argument of Plato's "Republic,"* chapters 2 and 5. Princeton: Princeton University Press, 1988.

Santas, Gerasimos. "The Form of the Good in Plato's *Republic.*" *Philosophical Inquiry* 2 (1980): 374–403. Reprinted in *Essays in Ancient Greek Philosophy*, II, edited by J. Anton and A. Preus. Albany: State University of New York Press, 1983, 232–63.

———. "Two Theories of the Good in Plato's *Republic.*" *Archiv für Geschichte der Philosophie* 67 (1985): 223–45.

White, Nicholas P. "The Rulers' Choice." *Archiv für Geschichte der Philosophie* 68 (1986): 22–46.

CHAPTER SIX

Plato's Theory of Human Good in the *Philebus*

IN A WELL-KNOWN, if imperfectly understood, passage of the *Philebus* (23b–27c) Socrates sketches a general ontology. He divides what there is into four ultimate genera: the "indeterminates" (*apeira*), the "determinants" (*peras echonta*), the combined things generated by the union of a determinant and an indeterminate (*meikta*), and, fourthly, the causes of these combinations (*aitiai*). Though this passage has often been interpreted as an isolated "digression," it is presented in the text as making an essential contribution to the predominately ethical dispute, concerning the nature of the good and its relations to pleasure on the one side and knowledge on the other, which is the dialogue's official topic. Much of the interest of this passage therefore ought to lie in its use for these ethical purposes. In this essay my aim is to show how Socrates' fourfold ontology is applied in working out a theory of human good and resolving the dispute between himself and Protarchus as to which of the original pair, pleasure and knowledge, is more responsible for the goodness of whatever it is that does in fact constitute human good.

I

For our purposes the most important of the four genera Socrates distinguishes is the third, the genus of *peras-apeiron* combinations. For it is into this genus that he places (27d7–10) the "mixed life" combining pleasure with knowledge, which he and Protarchus have provisionally agreed (20e–22b) to identify as the human good. It is noteworthy that everything else that Socrates explicitly states belongs to this genus is likewise something that he holds to be good—health (25e8), music (26a4), the seasons (26b1), beauty and strength of body and fine qualities of character (26b6–7), and certain pleasures (most prominently the "pure" ones, for example the pleasure of learning the truth [52c4–d1]). In fact, in placing these things in the third genus Socrates seems to imply (though he does not openly state) not just that all the members of this genus are good things but that their being the good things they are is a consequence of their being constituted by a combination of *peras* and *apeiron*. That is, he seems to adopt the view that to be a good thing just *is* to be such a combination. I begin, then, by assuming without further discussion that Socrates intends his theory of *peras-apeiron* combinations to be a theory of good things, as such—that is, of what makes any thing that is good be the good thing that it is.

Socrates' theory of these combinations is expounded largely through two examples, music (26a2–4) and the seasons (a6–b3), products respectively of a human craft and the operations of natural causes. Each of these is good and beautiful (*kalon*, 26b1, 7), and is so according to Socrates in virtue of the fact that in it some *apeira* are subjected to *peras*. For music four *apeira* are mentioned: high, low, fast, and slow—the bases, in fact, of harmony and of rhythm (cf. 17c11–d1 and d4–6). These are *apeira* because they have in them "the more and less," "the strongly and weakly" (24a9, c1–3). That is to say, if something is such as to be by its nature merely high, then what it is is essentially comparative: it is high in comparison with something less high, higher than something lower (and similarly for low, fast, and slow). Thus if I sound a note and now go on to play something high, i.e., higher than it, an indeterminate range of sounds will qualify: any of them can be my high sound. My sound may or may not be in any key, relative to the first sound; it may or may not be within a musically acceptable range of it. No fixed sound is determined by the notion of *being high*; it is a matter of indifference, and so no part of the nature of a sound as high, that it should fall into any such patterns and limits. The higher, as Socrates puts it, "keeps on advancing and does not stand still" (24d4). He also says there is a struggle of opposites within it, by which I take him to mean that it is what it is, high or higher, only by standing in contrast with something lower than, and so opposite to, it (cf. 25d10–e1). Plainly, then, to make music we must put an end to this indeterminacy. Sounds must be produced whose natures are such as not to be merely high or low, and whose durations are such as not to be merely fast or slow. According to Socrates' theory, it is the function of determinants, numerical ratios or proportions (25a7–b1), to do this: a determinant "imposes number" (25e2) on whatever it gets to be in, putting a stop to the struggle of opposites in it (d11–e1) and doing away with that which is "far too much and indeterminate" (26a7). And in fact musical sound is constituted by the conformity of tones to rules that define definite and precise mathematical ratios, expressible in terms of one whole number to another. The pitches of the sounds that are permitted to follow any given sound stand in (not just any, but certain definite) precise numerical ratios to it, and similarly for their lengths. Indeterminacy is done away with by the application of ratio and proportion: what follows a given note is not a high note, but one or another of certain definite notes, determined by standing in certain precise ratios to it. Musical theory is preeminently the theory of these ratios.

It is important to observe carefully both that and how, when these indeterminates enter into music, their indeterminacy is done away with. The sounds a musician makes are what they are *because* they are produced in conformity to certain patterns. As Socrates later puts it, there is a cause (*aitia*) of their being as they are (26e2–4), and this is the musical intelligence of their progenitor (30b3–4). So their falling into the musical patterns they exemplify is essential to what they are. And musical sounds are not high or low (to be that is to be indeterminate) but precisely proportioned and measured (26a7–8): the measurement and classification of sounds by high and low or fast and slow gives way in music to measurement and classification by numerical ratios. So the sounds produced by a musician (despite the fact that a nonmusician may think of them as merely high or low) are not that at all, but measured and proportioned. By the same token, if someone not exercising musical intelligence sounds two notes in succession that happen to fall into a musical pattern, the notes themselves, given their origin, are not measured and proportioned; they only give that appearance. We can say, then, that in music certain indeterminates (the high, the low, the fast, the slow) are subjected to certain determinants (the system of musical ratios) by the action of musical intelligence, with the result that determinate sounds (and no longer indeterminate ones) get produced. Here we have clear examples of Socrates' four ontological classes—indeterminates, determinants, combined things, and causes—and of their interrelations in the world.

In a precisely similar way, Socrates argues, the seasons result from the imposition by cosmic intelligence of certain definite proportions on the wet, the dry, the hot, and the cold—those proportions, to wit, which are necessary to preserve the world as a varied and excellent arena for living things.

II

Music and the seasons, then, have indeterminates in their constitution only in the hypothetical sense that, if the determining ratios that in fact characterize the weather and musical tones were removed from them, both weather and tones would be reduced to the status of indeterminates: the weather would then be, by nature, merely hot or cold, wet or dry, and tones would have the nature of high or low, fast or slow sounds, and these are all indeterminate things to be. Indeterminates enter the constitution of musical sounds and the seasons by having determinant ratios fixed upon them, and being made to give up their indeterminacy.

How does this theory of *peras-apeiron* combinations apply to the mixed life? Unlike the seasons and music, this life is a complex, having two separate ingredients, pleasure and knowledge. When it is first introduced into the discussion, it is only very vaguely specified. It has both pleasure and knowledge in it, and both the pleasure and the knowledge are recognized to be good things in themselves (things without which life would not be satisfactory for a human being, not merely because of the further things their absence would make unavailable, but because of the very natures of the pleasure and the knowledge themselves); but no attempt is made at this point to determine which forms of knowledge and which types of pleasure it will contain. Later, having developed a theory of the kinds of pleasure and a theory of the kinds of knowledge, Socrates will argue that all forms of knowledge, but only some forms of pleasure, can be allowed as ingredients in the human good;

but, as we shall see, he reaffirms the earlier agreement that all the forms of pleasure and knowledge that do go into the mixture are good things, each of which makes its own special contribution to the goodness of the whole. But if both pleasure and knowledge, as they enter the mixed life, are good things, where is one to look for the two elements, *peras* and *apeiron*, which, since the mixed life belongs to the genus of combined things, must be found within it? Plainly, despite what Philebus apparently implies at 27e7–9, the pleasure that is an ingredient in this life (whatever may be true of the pleasures found in the hedonist existence he prefers) is no *apeiron*: as previously noted, at least some of the ingredient pleasures are distinctly denied to be *apeiroi* (52c). Nor, given that the determinants are numbers, can knowledge play the role of *peras* in the mixed life. In fact, if my hypothesis is right, and Socrates means to be saying that to be good is to be a *peras-apeiron* combination, one must look for both *peras* and *apeiron* in the constitution of each of the two ingredients: if pleasure and knowledge in the good life are good things, then each of these two must be a combination of *peras* and *apeiron,* and the life that is made up of them will itself be a combination partly in virtue of that fact.

Apparently, then, the pleasure and the knowledge which together make up the mixed life are constituted by the imposition of determining ratios of some sort on something that would otherwise be merely indeterminate, randomly variable, characterized by a conflict of opposites, and so on. How is this to be understood? Socrates does not explicitly work out his theory in the text of the *Philebus,* but I think that much of what he does say about the way pleasure and knowledge enter the mixed life betrays the fact that he is thinking of them in this way (cf. especially the implications of 52c1–d1, 65d9–11). So in what follows I begin by sketching out a theory of knowledge as a *peras-apeiron* combination; space limitations prevent a comparably complete treatment of pleasure, but I hope to show that some major distinctions Socrates draws among the kinds of pleasure derive their sense from the underlying claim that all the pleasures of the mixed life belong to the genus of combined things.

III

Let us begin with two preliminary points about knowledge. Protarchus, in agreeing that no human life can be satisfactory in which there is no knowledge (21b–d), evinces only a very circumscribed conception of what knowledge is. Clearly, he sees that it is an indispensable good thing to understand one's present, past, and future conditions of life, but no doubt he envisages in this nothing beyond some rather simple egocentric self-knowledge. Still, having recognized that human nature includes an intellectual component as well as a sensitive and that the intellect's good, knowledge, is an integral part of human good over all, it is now up to the philosophical theory of knowledge, and not to Protarchus' arbitrary conceptions, to explain what the nature of this good is and how it is articulated into kinds. Socrates undertakes this task later in the dialogue, beginning at 55c. He distinguishes three chief types of knowledge: the applied, and in a certain sense empirical, disciplines (music, the medical arts, agriculture, navigation, carpentry, and building are named here), the pure mathematical sciences, and, thirdly, dialectic (i.e., logic-cum-metaphysics—the "science" which, among other things, contains the theories of those generic units, pleasure, knowledge, and the good, partially deployed in this very dialogue). Despite their differences, all these forms of intellectual culture are assigned a place in the human good. They are all good in themselves, good because of what they are. Now to say this is to place a value on these things quite apart from any usefulness they may have for various purposes. The medical art, for example, is here being valued as a form of intellectual discipline, not merely because of the value of health, to which it may serve as a means. It is, so to say, the practice of medicine itself that is seen to be good. Similarly for the other forms of knowledge. In this argument, in short, intellectual functions are prized not as artificers of the good, in the sense of creators of some independent product, but as elements in it.

What then are the *peras* and *apeiron* which combine to generate these forms of intellectual activity? Notice, to begin with, that not all mental activity is structured and disciplined as the forms of knowledge here in question are. One can think indeterminately, as for example in fantasizing or in making loose and disconnected conjectures about how something is to be conceived or explained. Such thinking is not pinned down in its content through organization under the principles of any body of knowledge. Still, all thought, being a product of the mind, is by its very nature intelligent, at least in the minimal sense that it falls somewhere on a variable scale of intelligence. So acts of undisciplined thought are intelligent at least comparatively and relatively—more or less intelligent than other possible or actual such acts. But they are not intelligent in any more determinate sense, for it is only in disciplined thinking that appeal is made to fixed measures of adequacy. In fact, were it not for the organized crafts and sciences, all thought would have this indeterminate character: it would be groping, disconnected, essentially arbitrary—the marks of indeterminacy in the other spheres Socrates mentions. So intelligence itself, conceived apart from these disciplines, is indeterminate in the same way as we saw heat and cold are. Intelligence, then, so conceived, is a plausible candidate for the *apeiron* that is one element from which knowledge is generated on Socrates' theory.

Presumably, then, we must look to the various basic principles employed in the several crafts and sciences to find the element of *peras* or proportion. Of course, in a metaphorical sense one could say that all disciplined knowledge is proportioned—viz., proportioned to the nature of its object. So far, however, this need not involve any definite numerical relationship, as Socrates' theory requires. However, as we have seen, subjects like music and the seasons, which are among the objects of knowledge, are on Plato's view themselves structured by ratio and proportion, so that in these cases a science or craft in being proportioned to its object will have among its principles a set of ratios, namely those which are essential to the constitution of its objects. Furthermore, it seems likely that Plato thought that all genuine crafts and sciences have objects of this kind. Hence it could be said that it is by the imposition of these ratios on what would otherwise be indeterminate intelligent thought that the scientific and artistic disciplines are generated.

IV

In some such way as this, then, one can make sense of the claim that the crafts and sciences are all *peras-apeiron* combinations of a certain sort, and so things good in themselves. On the other hand, Socrates holds some of them to be of greater intrinsic value than others. Thus he ranks "empirical" disciplines like music and carpentry below the pure mathematical sciences, and both of these below dialectic. In making these evaluations Socrates carries over to knowledge two terms of comparison he originally introduces in discussing pleasure: "purity" and "truth." Some manual arts, like some pleasures, are "more impure" than others (55d6–8), and in general the manual arts are less pure than mathematics and mathematics than dialectic. The same forms of knowledge that are classed as "purer" are also twice called "truer" or "the truest" forms of knowledge (58a4–5, 61e3–4), with the implication that the others are less true or even false forms. But though the ranking according to purity coincides with the ranking according to truth, it is important to see that these terms themselves have distinct meanings. As Socrates employs them, purity and impurity are ontological notions: they indicate something about the nature and constitution of the things to which they apply. Truth and falsehood, on the other hand, are epistemological: they attach to things in virtue of the true or false beliefs and conceptions which human beings naturally form under their influence or which are in some other way naturally found bound up with them.

Consider purity and impurity first. From their first appearance (52c2), "impure" pleasures are identified as those in whose constitution there is some essential link to pain, the very opposite of pleasure. It is not just that the pleasure is normally or always accompanied by pain or as facts stand purchasable only at the price of pain; the very experience that is enjoyed is enjoyed in part precisely as being painful, or as involving pain in some way. Thus, in Socrates' conception of the bodily appetites as forms of distress, *what* is enjoyed in satisfying an appetite is something that combines pain (the appetite) with pleasure (its relief). If, for example, what one enjoys on some occasion is eating-while-hungry, then an essential part of the pleasurable experience is the pain or distress of appetite. Other similar mixed experiences include scratching an itch (46a8–9), when that is something one takes an interest in and enjoys, masochistic sexual practices (47a3–9 may suggest such a case), and malicious pleasures in the theater and else-where (48b ff.). In pure pleasures, by contrast, what is enjoyed is something by its own nature fine and attractive (*kalon*) and not, like these, interesting only because they combine distress with a contrasting state or process of release or amusement (51c6–7): for example, the discriminating sensory awareness of geometrical designs, clear musical tones, pure colors, and fine smells, in all of which the use of the senses is not linked to the satisfaction of appetites but is a direct response to the inherent fineness of the objects being enjoyed, and the pleasures of disciplined discovery and learning (51c–52b).

It follows that the pure forms of knowledge are those which do not combine knowledge with its opposite, ignorance, but present knowledge in an unadulterated form. The impure forms also provide us with knowledge, but only by mingling it with ignorance or, what amounts to the same thing, failure to know. Socrates links purity of knowledge with clarity and accuracy (*saphēneia* and *akribeia*: see 56a7, b5, c5–6, 57b6, c1–3, c7, d1) and with truth itself (*alētheia* 57d2, 58c3, e2, 59b7–8). His idea seems to be that knowledge, as such, aspires to obtain a clear grasp of the truth about some subject matter, and to represent that truth precisely and accurately—that is to say, as appears from the emphasis on mathematics in the context, to exhibit it as being fully determined, in all its details, by principles that express, as it were, the underlying nature of the objects that are known. Dialectic and pure mathematics realize this ideal to a high degree. Geometry, for example, demonstrates the whole truth about the objects it studies; everything that is true about plane figures as such it represents as following by rigorous proof from the principles of the science. And dialectic establishes determinately the whole nature of the units it studies; nothing is true of these units, as the units they are, that dialectic does not exhibit as being true of them. Here the intellect penetrates the whole of its subject matter; nothing is left obscure or accounted for only approximately. By contrast, empirical disciplines necessarily fail to achieve this ideal. Given the nature of their subject matters, they cannot determine with precision the whole truth about the objects they study. Failing in clarity and accuracy, they remain to a considerable extent ignorant of what they set out to know. Thus the rules of music, and even those of more exact crafts like carpentry, do not suffice to dictate uniquely what sound should be produced or what will count as a flat surface; the craftsman has to use his eyes and ears to select from within an acceptable range, and even then sufficiently neighboring alternatives would do just as well. Even the natural sciences, in attempting to discover the origins of the world order and how and why various things happen within it, are studying particular facts and events (59a7–8), and no account of these can bring within its scope every detail about what happens. On different occasions things happen slightly differently, and some of these differences will always remain unaccounted for by the natural scientist's principles (59a2–b9).

Purity and impurity of knowledge thus has to do with the degree to which knowledge (i.e., clear and accurate representation of the whole truth) is attained in any given subject area. It is not so evident what Socrates means by ranking some forms of knowledge as "truer" forms than others. The fact that the word here has the same sense (cf. 61e6) as it has elsewhere in the dialogue in application to pleasures gives us, however, a thread to follow in sorting out what is admittedly a confusing discussion. The contrast between truth and falsehood when first introduced (36c6–12) is used to characterize pleasures by reference to the truth or falsehood of some proposition that might be regarded as in some sense contained in the pleasure itself; a person who thinks falsely that he is going to acquire riches and now gets pleasure from picturing himself enjoying their use (40a9–12) is accused of experiencing a false pleasure. Later, however, when the pure pleasures are described as true (beginning at 44d3; see also 51b1, 52d6–8, 53c2) there is no reference to any true or false judgment contained in this way within a pleasure—it is not that impure pleasures all make factual mistakes about what is going on, or will go on, in the world. Socrates defends this application of the idea of truth by appeal to the example of white color (52d6–53b6). The truest and at the same time most attractive and, indeed, whitest (53d4–6) of white colors is the purest white, the one completely free of admixture of any other color (a6–7); any less pure white falls short precisely with respect to truth. Clearly there is here no suggestion that a color, as such, makes a factual assertion, possibly true, possibly false, about the world. What then about the pure colors, pure pleasures, and pure forms of knowledge entitles them all to be called true?

One thing seems clear. The greater truth of the pure white color is connected with the fact that it provides a perfectly adequate instance of what white is. A mixed color, being something for whose nature the color white is only partially responsible, does not do this. Hence one might expect someone who formed his conception of white color by examining mixed whites, rather than pure ones, to have only an inadequate conception of the color white. He would have difficulty in sorting out what in the mixed color derives from the white that is in it and what from its other ingredient colors. The impure, mixed colors could thus be said to have a natural tendency to mislead. In order not to be misled about what belongs to white color as such, one must avoid looking to these mixed whites, and look instead to pure white. From this it is an easy step to describing the mixed whites themselves as false. It is their nature to induce false beliefs about the color, white, that they are instances of; so they are by nature false. If this is how Socrates is thinking of the matter, then his claim will be that impure pleasures and impure forms of knowledge, mingling as they do pleasure or knowledge with its opposite, have a natural tendency to mislead us as to the nature of pleasure or knowledge, and so as to their own natures. At the same time, the reference here to false beliefs provides perhaps a sufficient link to the falseness of the factually ungrounded pleasures. On Socrates' account, all false pleasures naturally tend to mislead, and that is why they are called false; the factually ungrounded ones misrepresent the particular facts of some situation, the impure ones misrepresent instead the very nature of pleasure.

But how, exactly, do the impure pleasures do this? It is true that, since pleasure is a generic unit, each impure pleasure instantiates perfectly *a* pleasure, the particular pleasure it is. On the other hand, any pleasure is what it is by the place it occupies in the whole system of pleasures; and here is where misrepresentation can occur. Someone who forms his conception of pleasure predominately on the impure ones and who neglects or hardly experiences the pure pleasures of sense and intellect, will inevitably make the mistake of thinking that in these pleasures one finds the whole of what pleasure can contribute to one's life. So he will be led to the further mistake of trying to realize in his life the value that pleasure provides by overconcentration on them. To be sure, a careful and informed person who knows the pure pleasures, and knows they more adequately embody what is valuable in pleasure, will not be misled by the impure pleasures. Recognizing that the value pleasure contributes is better realized in the pure than in the impure pleasures, he will avoid the mistake of devoting too much attention to the impure ones. Still, since it is their nature to mislead, they deserved to be called false.

The impure forms of knowledge are false for exactly the same reason. A person whose acquaintance with intellectual discipline extended only to the more precise practical crafts and natural science carried on in an empirical spirit, and who formed his conception of intellectual work from these activities, would think that in these one finds the whole of what knowledge has to contribute to one's life. Hence, if he thought the exercise of knowledge a good thing, he would be led to devote very much of his time to them. But the truth is that what is so valuable about knowledge—accuracy and clarity in the representation of the truth—is only inadequately attained in these pursuits. Pure mathematics and dialectic are more adequate, and someone who had experience of these studies would accordingly value empirical studies and the practical crafts much less highly than these purer forms of knowledge and would devote less of his time to them. So, because, unless one knows the pure ones as well, the impure ones will be misjudged, these are by their natures misleading and false.

V

Purity and truth, then, and impurity and falsehood, are closely connected in Socrates' argument; but they are not the same thing. Why, however, does Socrates admit impure and false knowledge at all as an ingredient in the human good (62a–d)? To admit it is to admit something whose nature it is to be ignorant and obscure and which naturally misleads. It is easy to see that the pure forms of pleasure and knowledge will have to be included (provided that human beings are capable of achieving them). Socrates claims, however, that the pure forms "mixed together will [not] be sufficient (*hikana*) to produce for us the completely satisfying life . . . we will still need something not like these [i.e., impure]" (61e7–9). He recalls here the argument of 20b–23b, where in agreeing that neither knowledge nor pleasure alone was "sufficient" Socrates was claiming that each of the two is good by its own nature and a necessary part of human good over all. So, in saying now that some impure forms of pleasure and knowledge are needed, he is claiming that these are good by their natures and necessary parts of human good. Why does he say this?

Confusingly, in arguing for their inclusion he does not so much elaborate on any positive good the lesser forms contribute as concede their necessity in a weaker sense. Protarchus says it is "necessary" (*anankaion*, 62c8) to practice the applied crafts "even to find one's way home every day"— evidently including here all the disciplines that contribute directly to the maintenance of human life in a more or less biological sense. Others, however, including music, Protarchus says are necessary "if our life is to be any sort of *life* at all" (62c3–4)—presumably meaning that without them our lives would not be interesting enough. Now in both cases what Protarchus emphasizes seems to be the value of the products of these arts, rather than any value achieved directly in the practice of them: human life itself and musical tunes are good things, so the arts that are responsible for them are themselves necessary. But though these *are* grounds for thinking that human beings need to cultivate the arts and crafts, they do not show why they should be admitted as ingredients in the human good, rather than merely as necessary conditions for something else that is. Unless Socrates is simply confused at this point he must be supposing that once one grants that these crafts really are necessary for human life, in the sense Protarchus has in mind, one is in a position to see why they are a worthy object of interest and devotion, in themselves, for a human being. After all, he has emphasized that even the lesser crafts embody some firm and accurate thinking (otherwise they would not count as intellectual disciplines at all): they do contain a measure of the clarity, accuracy, and truth that are the special values contributed by the genus, knowledge. As such, they belong to the class of combined things, things good by their natures. Once one recognizes that the practice of these crafts is *necessary* to human life, and so a permanent feature of it, there is good reason to think that the range of good things that every human being should organize his life round will include these, that is, that these goods are necessary ingredients in human good over all. A human being who did not take an interest in some reasonable selection of these activities for their own sakes would lead a deficient life not just to the extent that he would be deprived of their products, but because he would miss out on the special value that attaches to the use of these forms of knowledge. For a human being, given human nature and the conditions of human life, a combination of diverse intellectual interests is appropriate. Some of these are more valuable, taken singly, than others, but they all have a unique contribution to make, as forms of intellectual discipline, to our good. There is no danger, as Protarchus remarks (62d1–3), that a person leading such a life would be misled or seduced by the impure forms; having experience of the full range of types of knowledge, he would have an accurate grasp of their nature and value, and would accord them their proper place, but only that, in his life.

In this way, then, the "necessary" but impure forms of knowledge can be seen, as Socrates claims, as indispensable components of the human good. Essentially the same rationale holds also for the "necessary" impure pleasures. Matters are complicated here, however, by the fact that, whereas Socrates counts all the impure forms of knowledge as necessary, he divides the impure pleasures into two classes and grants the necessity and goodness of only one of these two groups. The others are not necessary at all, and in fact are mostly bad. So we will have to consider carefully what his grounds are for making this discrimination and exactly where he draws the line.

Socrates does not specify which pleasures he has in mind as the necessary ones (62d8–9), but no doubt he means the pleasures of satisfying normal and healthy appetites: these are "necessary" in the sense that the activities that give rise to them are necessary for the maintenance of life—everyone has to eat and drink and have sex, and under normal conditions one cannot help enjoying doing so. The language of necessity here does not, of course, any more than it did with the forms of knowledge, imply that these pleasures are valuable only instrumentally. Indeed, Socrates in his only description in this context of these pleasures, does not even mention their necessity as means, say, to health, but treats them instead as *expressions* of a healthy state of body and mind: these are the pleasures "that go along with health and with soundness of mind (*sōphronein*) and in fact those that arise as companions of all virtue, like attendants on a goddess, and accompany it everywhere" (63e 4–6). That is to say, as a result of bodily health, soundness of mind, and virtue of character in general, Socrates claims, one will take a certain pleasure in eating, drinking, and having sex; and this pleasure, being normal, healthy, and virtuous, is itself a good thing. And, once one grants that these virtuous pleasures, however precisely they are constituted, are themselves good, the further fact that the activities in question are necessary to the maintenance of human life provides a strong reason for thinking that any human being ought to organize his life partly round the regular pursuit of them; and this is to say that these pleasures are a part of human good over all. The healthy satisfaction of normal bodily appetites yields pleasures which, though impure and false, are nonetheless good and deserve to be treated as permanent ingredients in the combination of things that makes a human life completely satisfying. Human nature and the conditions of human life being what they are, a combination of pleasures—pleasures of learning, pure sensory pleasures, and so on, but also the necessary pleasures of the appetites—is appropriate for a human being. The pure pleasures are more valuable, taken singly, than the necessary impure ones, but each of these pleasures has a unique contribution to make to our good. Nor will the falsity of these good appetitive pleasures, accompanied as they are in this mixed life by the pure ones, cause the agent leading it to overestimate the value of enjoying satisfying his appetites or to seek other types of appetitive enjoyment.

It is not yet clear, however, exactly how Socrates is conceiving of the good appetitive pleasures. What *is* the "normal" pleasure of eating, for example, and what is the special value it contributes to a good human life? This question is particularly pressing because the pleasures that Socrates is especially concerned to show are not good, those he calls "the greatest and the most intense" (63d3–4), are bodily pleasures of what one might have thought was essentially the same type. He rejects as not good or even bad the pleasures of the glutton, intense pleasures of drinking (the quenching of a prolonged and very pressing thirst) and some sexual indulgences (cf. 65c5–7, 65e9–66a3). How is Socrates conceiving these pleasures if they can seem to him pleasures of a different basic type from the "normal" and good appetitive pleasures?

In answering this question one must attend to Socrates' most common description of the rejected pleasures, as the "most intense" ones. Intensity, on Socrates' analysis, is the product of the juxtaposition of a felt deprivation, or even a bodily irritation, such as an itch, and the release from it that comes about in satisfying the need or removing the irritation. A pleasure is quite intense if the tension produced by the deprivation or irritation is very great, and the release from it is very sudden: the sudden reduction of the tension produces an exciting, exhilarating experience. The obvious applicability of the analysis to sexual orgasm is of course no accident; but Socrates extends it to cover other appetite gratifications, including the glutton's, despite the fact that some of these cases apparently involve no pronounced build-up and release of tension in a sudden discharge. Socrates' idea seems to be that in many cases of bodily pleasure what is enjoyed is only or predominately such an experience of discharge of tension, and that what is found attractive in these cases is the intensity of the experience of release. Thus the glutton may well not have a pleasure of eating that is as intense as that which an ordinary starving man might get from gobbling down a plate of eggs, but the fact that he has set out to enlarge not just his capacity but his appetite for food shows that what he is interested in is the experience of gratifying, and so releasing the tension built up in, that enlarged appetite. Though his pleasure may not be as intense as the starving man's, intensity is nonetheless essential to it. The point, then, of classifying a pleasure as one of the "most intense" ones has to do essentially with the focus of the pleasure. If the person experiencing a pleasure is, as such, concentrating on and enjoying the experience of release from tension, then this is an "intense" pleasure, whether or not the release happens on that occasion to be extremely intense in comparison with other similar pleasures.

Now it is clear that even in the normal gratification of normal appetites experiences of this intense type will have to take place. Anyone who enjoys eating a meal while hungry will experience release from the tension of appetite, and this will necessarily have some degree or other of intensity. On the theory I am attributing to Socrates, however, this will not be enough to make the pleasure in question an intense one. Whether *it* is intense will depend upon what in the experience is being enjoyed. If what is enjoyed is not, or not merely, the release from tension, then the pleasure (or one of the pleasures) taking place then will not belong to this class. With this point in mind it is possible to show how the healthy gratification of normal appetites might plausibly be conceived as not belonging to the class of intense pleasures at all. (I shall illustrate this only for the pleasures of eating and drinking, leaving aside sexual pleasure.) What a healthy and sober-minded person enjoys, it might be suggested, is not at all, or not especially, the experience of release from tension. What he enjoys, or principally enjoys, is the activity of maintaining his physical substance and preserving his bodily health. Appetites are, no doubt, the naturally unavoidable occasion for engaging in these activities, and felt deprivation is therefore essential to them, but he enjoys these activities because of their role in self-maintenance, and not (or not just) for the release of tension they involve. The healthy and sober-minded person has developed appetites that accord with his actual physical needs for food and drink: he hungers and thirsts when his organism needs replenishment in order to maintain itself in health, and wants only such food or drink as is healthy. He does not manipulate or expand his appetites, or postpone gratification, in order to get intense experiences; once his appetites have been established in accordance with his physical needs, he indulges them as they arise, but without taking any very great interest in the experience of release itself. What he enjoys is the natural human activity of self-maintenance. By contrast, the corresponding pleasures of bad and intemperate people are all of the "intense" and bad variety. Their pleasures consist in enjoyment of discharged tension. What is enjoyed in the two sets of cases differ widely, and this means that the pleasures themselves belong to different types.

In this way it is possible to make tolerable sense of the idea that, although all the so-called "bodily" pleasures are false and impure, nonetheless they fall into two quite distinct types, one of which is a type of good pleasures, whereas the other is not. It is a point in favor of my account that it coheres very well with the fact that Socrates supports his rejection of the latter pleasures by claiming that they belong to the class of indeterminate things (the *genos tou apeirou,* 52c6–d1). He claims that the intense pleasures "admit of great degrees" and "go through body and mind both less and more" (52c4–5,7), thus recalling his earlier association of indeterminacy with the admission of more and less. And on my account one can see why this is justified. What is enjoyed in these pleasures is the sudden and intense discharge of tension, and this makes the experience enjoyed in their case something essentially relative and subject to random variation in the way we saw other indeterminates, such as the high and the low in pitch, were: insofar as something is an experience of this type it is intense, but intensity is not a determinate notion. An experience that counts as intense does so only by comparison with something of the same type less intense than it, so that insofar as it is the nature of an experience to be intense it can vary very widely in degree while remaining just what it is—its nature as intense does not in any way control or limit such variation. And since the nature of a pleasure is determined by the nature of what it is the pleasure of (cf. 51d8–9), it follows that these pleasures are also indeterminate things.

By contrast, the healthy gratification of normal appetites, as I have suggested Socrates is construing it, is not an indeterminate thing. The activity enjoyed, that of maintaining one's physical substance, is by *its* nature fully determinate. What counts as maintaining one's physical substance is determined by objective facts about one's organism and about available foodstuffs. In the end scientific inquiry determines what a self-maintenance diet will require and what free choice it will permit, so that the activities of self-maintenance will be prescribed on the basis of scientific principle, which implies considerable precision and determinateness in what the agent who takes pleasure in self-maintenance must be aiming to do. And, again, since the nature of a pleasure is given by the nature of the activity, the pleasure of self-maintenance is a determinate, and not an indeterminate, pleasure.

It is possible, then, to develop a plausible rationale by which to mark off within the class of appetitive pleasures some which are by their nature intense from some others which are not. The former, along with the pleasure of scratching an itch, are declared to make no contribution to the goodness of a good life, and this judgment is supported by the theory of good things as constituted by the imposition of some *peras* on an *apeiron*: such pleasures have no *peras* in their constitution and so belong to the *genos tou apeirou,* all the members of which are bad or at best indifferent in value. Healthy gratification of the appetites is not like this, however. It is a good and necessary pleasure and so makes its own direct contribution to the goodness of a good life. The theory of good things as *peras-apeiron* combinations supports this judgment, just as it also supports the classification of all the pure pleasures as in themselves good. In both cases what is enjoyed are objectively determined, precise natures, whose attractiveness is fully inherent in them.

Selected Further Readings

Bobonich, Christopher. "Plato's Theory of Goods in the *Laws* and *Philebus*." *Proceedings of the Boston Area Colloquium in Ancient Philosophy* 11 (1994): 101–39. Lanham, Md.: University Press of America, 1995.

Frede, Dorothea. *Plato "Philebus,"* Introduction. Indianapolis and Cambridge, Mass.: Hackett, 1993.

Irwin, T. H. *Plato's Ethics,* chapter 19. New York and Oxford: Oxford University Press, 1995.

Moravcsik, Julius M. E. "Forms, Nature and the Good in the *Philebus.*" *Phronesis* 24 (1979): 81–101.

CHAPTER SEVEN

Plato's *Statesman* and Politics

AT THE OUTSET of Plato's *Statesman,* Socrates and the others present at the discussion declare its purpose to be to give an account of the person who is an expert statesman (*politikos*). So the dialogue ought to be about expert political rule (*politikē*)—what at its best it should be like. Yet a very great deal of the dialogue is taken up with general methodological questions: how to proceed systematically and correctly in setting out a sound view about the nature of any such reality as the ideal statesman—any form, anything truly existing in the nature of things as a norm whether for human aspiration or for the direction of purely physical processes in bringing natural things into being. In fact, the Visitor from Elea, who follows the invitation of the others in setting out step by step his own view of the nature of the statesman or (equivalently) of statesmanship, is explicit that explaining statesmanship is actually a subordinate purpose of the discussion. His main and much more important purpose is to teach Young Socrates (his discussion partner) and the others present how to be better dialecticians, that is, better at grasping and expressing the full truth about any such norm actually existing in reality: setting out the nature of the statesman or, in the earlier part of the same conversation reported in the *Sophist,* that of the sophist, is the second priority.[1]

In the *Statesman* the Visitor starts with expertise (or, equivalently, experts) in general and intends to work his way progressively down a path defined by divisions he makes at each stage within the form or class he has reached immediately before. This path will then constitute the nature of statesmanship, according to his understanding of what statesmanship is. Running one's mind down this path, noticing just how at each stage what is selected for further division differs from but is also like what is set aside, will constitute the state of mind of knowing the nature of statesmanship.[2] Early on he decides to describe the statesman as an expert at caring for human beings in masses, in "herds" as he puts it, differing in characteristic ways from the different expertises other people have for caring for other animals, whether in herds or in some other context. But he notices that before his task

---

[1] See *Statesman* 286d–287a.

[2] See 258c3–7. Throughout I cite the Greek text, including the line numbering (which occasionally differs from that of Burnet's OCT), of Rowe (*Plato: Statesman*); this text, which was constructed with advance knowledge of the revised OCT by D. M. Robinson, is preferable in many places to the latter. Unless otherwise noted, all translations from the *Statesman* in what follows are Rowe's, in the revised version of his translation printed in Cooper, ed., *Plato: Complete Works.*

is "finished off to complete perfection" (267d1) and this characterization can be accepted, he must find the right means of singling the statesman out under that heading. He must set the statesman apart from a whole host of other experts who may with some show of legitimacy lay claim themselves also to be "carers for the human herd": he mentions merchants, farmers, millers and bakers, gymnastic trainers and physicians too (267e–268a) and by the time he is finished he adds a significant number of additional, and interestingly different, sorts of co-claimants, whom we will have to attend to closely in due course. In fact, only well after the midpoint of the dialogue (beginning at 287b), using the model of expertise at weaving wool clothing, does the Visitor finally begin separating these other "carers" off so that the statesman and his expertise can be singled out on their own, and the others put into their proper relationships to him, as possessing sorts of expertise distinct from his. Only very late in the dialogue, at 305e, is the task of definition finished. From 305e to the end of the dialogue at 311c, the Visitor then gives us, in the light of this separation off of the other claimants, what, as I have suggested, we have awaited all along—some account of what political rule at its best should be like. Here the Visitor discusses how in carrying out his task the expert statesman as previously defined "weaves together" the citizens of his city so as to create the beautiful "fabric" under which a well-governed, happy city lives.

My interest is to consider the implications for political theory of these closing pages of the dialogue—both the final account of how the statesman does his "weaving" job, and the separation off from him of the other claimants to the title of "carers" for humans in a mass who really do turn out to have a substantial title to be exercising a statesmanly skill (since, of course, it is ultimately not allowed that even they actually possess that skill, or any part of it). On my way of reading the dialogue, it is in these two sections that the core of its political thought is to be found. It is that political thought that I would like to concentrate upon.

I

In the introductory discussions of both *Statesman* (257a1–258b3) and *Sophist* (216a1–218c1) the Visitor and his fellow-discussants all consistently speak exclusively of his target in this dialogue as the statesman (*ho politikos*, or *ho politikos anēr*).[3] Intuitively, following the derivation of the Greek

[3] M. H. Hansen has pointed out, in "The Athenian 'Politicians,'" p. 36, that the Attic orators, whose writings are our most extensive source for Athenian political and constitutional practices in the fourth century, including relevant linguistic usage, never use this designation (with a sole exception—a passage in a speech of Aeschines dating from shortly after Plato's death). It is only used much by philosophers, beginning with Plato, and most often, Hansen says, as a complimentary term to denote the true political leader (as most of the time in the *Statesman*). However, in a significant number of diverse passages Plato speaks of *politikoi*, without any

word, one immediately thinks of a *politikos* as one who governs in a *polis*, or free self-governing city. So one envisages someone who works within a framework of political institutions, engaged in *some* sort of give-and-take discussion and negotiation with at least *some* of his fellow-citizens in deciding on laws and reaching decisions—in a free, self-governing city the laws and decisions are adopted in the citizens' name, as *theirs*. However, at the very beginning of the *Statesman*'s divisions leading to a definition of the statesman, the Visitor suddenly brings kings into the discussion (258e8), and establishes the basis for a habit that persists right through his subsequent exposition: that of referring to the target of the inquiry both as the statesman (or statesmanship) and as the "king" (or "kingship" or "royal rule"). He establishes this basis by way of a notorious argument (258e8–259c5) that identifies the knowledge that constitutes anyone's entitlement to the name of statesman with the very same knowledge that alone entitles anyone to the name of king, whether or not he ever actually performs any of the functions of that office.[4] And, to boot, this argument identifies the same

overtone at all of commendation, simply as those who as a matter of fact actively concern themselves with and take part prominently in the political process—in fact, pretty much the people whom the orators would normally refer to as *hoi rhētores* or *hoi rhētores kai stratēgoi* (the "speakers" or "speakers and generals"—the ones prominently engaged in introducing motions and so forth in assembly and council and other democratic political venues). (See, above all, *Apology* 21c4, 22a8, 22c8, 24a1, but also, among other passages, *Alcibiades* 133e9; *Phaedrus* 248d5, 257c5, 257e3, 258a1; *Euthydemus* 290d2, 305c7; *Gorgias* 473e6, 484e2, 513b8, 515c3, 519b4; *Meno* 95c10, 99c1, 99d2, 100a1–2; *Laws* 693a6.) Indeed, one gets the strong impression from these passages that the term must have been commonly or standardly used at the time in that way (see in addition *Sophist* 217a)—despite its absence from the Attic orators' works. (The orators do commonly use the verb *politeuesthai* and its present participle, meaning those who engage in political processes and affairs, as one citizen among others, to indicate much the same group.) Nonetheless, it does not appear that either Plato or his readers would assume that the *politikoi* were a recognized profession or quasi-profession, into whose expertise or other credentials it might seem a matter of course to begin a discussion. From the outset (in the *Sophist*, as well as in the *Statesman* itself) the discussion is driven by a specifically philosophical insistence of Plato's own that political affairs are important enough for there to be some real knowledge that we might hope to attain about how they ought to be conducted. The "statesman" being investigated here is the one who possesses that knowledge, not (as indeed the Visitor makes quite plain later, 291a ff.) someone who functions successfully within any existing constitution, as success would normally be measured there. As Rowe rightly says (*Plato: Statesman*, p. 2), the Visitor is seeking "the proper specifications for someone charged with running, or helping to run, a city-state or *polis*." However, Rowe's emphasis on the *polis* (not something else) as what is to be run implies—and the derivative term *politeuomenos*, used by the Attic orators to cover much the same semantic territory as Plato's *politikos*, itself clearly indicates this—that a *politikos* would naturally be understood to be one citizen of the city dealing with his fellow-citizens on some basis of equality, as that common status itself demands. Thus he would be understood from the outset as a *political* leader, one whose leadership would be exercised in some sort of political context.

[4] The immediate objective of this argument, in its context, is to find some means by which to answer the question implied at 258e4–7 (and answered explicitly at 259c10–d2, immediately after the argument is concluded)—viz., whether the statesman is to be classed as an expert of the "practical" or else of the "purely theoretical" type, as those have been distinguished at 258d4–e2: the examples given to establish these two categories are arithmetic and carpentry

knowledge with the knowledge that makes someone an expert ruler over slaves and that which makes someone an expert manager of a household and estate.

I call this argument notorious because it so provoked Aristotle that he devoted the whole first book of his *Politics* to its refutation.[5] In what follows in the *Statesman,* it is in fact only the identification of king and statesman that the Visitor carries forward—the expert slave-master and expert householder drop immediately and permanently by the wayside. Obviously, the whole purpose of the argument is to establish this single identity; the other two alleged equivalents are brought in solely—if I may speak bluntly—as camouflage. To any Greek reader the supposition that what a king needs to know is precisely the same thing that a statesman does—a *politikos,* one who

---

or manufacture as a whole. In the latter the knowledge is "naturally bound up with practical actions"; the former are *psilai tōn praxeōn* ("don't involve any practical actions"). This argument concludes that kingly and statesmanly expertise are to be identified with one another (259c1–5). Given that, the answer to the initial question now follows easily. It is perfectly obvious that a *king* stands aloof from all hands-on government, leaving all that sort of thing to those who carry out his orders (so 259c6–d3): other sorts of "king" (as we now have to call them: statesmen, slave- and household-managers) may have to do "little bits" with their hands and bodies in exercising their rule (c6–7), but we can now see that, in their case too, we should count only their "understanding and force of mind" as belonging to their expertise. Without this identification of statesman with king, one could well have imagined that the sorts of work in listening to others, accommodating to their points of view, hammering out a consensus, etc., that an ordinary expert politician must engage in would count as "practical actions" with which his knowledge was essentially "bound up"—so that the statesman would count as a "practical," not a "purely theoretical" expert. However, given the identification of king and statesman that has been provided in this argument, the Visitor can immediately (259d3–4) assert that the right thing to do, then, is to "take all these things together—the statesman's knowledge and the statesman, the king's knowledge and the king—as one, and put them into the same category," i.e., into the category of "purely theoretical experts." (My translation here departs from Rowe's, which misconstrues the sense of εἰς ταὐτόν ... συνθήσομεν: for parallels for the correct understanding, see first of all 276e2, but also 260e6, 263d7–8, 266e9, 281c9–d1. Taken Rowe's way, the sentence pointlessly repeats 259c1–4; in fact it usefully collects together the *two* conclusions that have just been drawn, 259c1–4 and c10–d2.) Without this identification it would not have been so easy to establish that the statesman *is* a purely theoretical rather than a "practical" expert. (Robinson's decision in the revised OCT to transfer 259d3–6 out of its place in all the manuscripts back so as to follow 259b6 is a stunning example of editorial hubris and ignorance: these lines, as translated just above, are absolutely essential where they stand; and if there *is* a "gap" in the argument just after b6, the only reason is that as Plato wrote it, the argument truly *is,* as I show below, invalid! Furthermore, if inserted after 259b6, these lines would make the argument valid only by introducing as one of its premises precisely the principal conclusion the Visitor wants to derive from it: that kingly and statesmanly knowledge are one and the same thing!)

[5] Aristotle does recognize kingship as one just and valid form of rule in a *polis* (*Politics* III 14, 1284b36–37), and under certain circumstances the best and justest one. But he still refuses to call it a *politikos* kind of rule (see for example I 7, 1255b19–20 and the contrast at III 1287b38–39 between a *basilikon* and a *politikon* type of justice and advantage; there are many such passages spread through the *Politics*): the person who is entitled to rule as a king is so far above ordinary good people in his moral qualities and associated knowledge that he rules not as one *among* them, but as a sort of god providentially found in their company.

knows how to rule in a *polis,* a free, self-ruling community—must have been, to put it mildly, a great provocation. In the Greek world of Plato's time, kings are precisely rulers over more or less vast territories, the individual cities within which are governed not by themselves (their citizens, or any of their citizens) and freely but, ultimately at least, in subordination to and direction by the king or his personally selected officers. How could the knowledge of a statesman—involving as it inevitably would the ability to explain and argue for policies and practical decisions so that they would be adopted or freely acquiesced in by the community itself in whose name they would be put into effect—be the same as that of a king, who certainly does not have to know any such thing, since a king sets himself up as the only one who knows, and who as a result demands simply to be obeyed?[6] In fact, I think myself that the Visitor's argument here is not just invalid but so flagrantly so—hence the value of the "camouflage"—that the dialogue itself (as distinguished from its principal speaker, the Visitor from Elea) uses its invalidity (evident once you pause to examine it) to mark the thesis it alleges to establish as highly questionable—the thesis, that is, that the expertise of the ideal statesman is precisely the same expertise as the ideal king's, that statesmanly and kingly rule do not differ in principle in any way.[7] The

[6] Christian Wildberg has reminded me of the presentation in Euripides' "political" plays (*Children of Heracles* and *Suppliant Women*) of the ancient kings of Athens, Theseus and his son Demophon, as founders of the democracy. Though possessed of regal authority, they consult the people in the assembly to obtain democratic support for their actions and policies and show the kind of concern for the mass of people and their intelligent participation in government which a democratic statesman might show. Perhaps Plato's Athenian readers, familiar with this backdating of the origin of democratic politics, would be less resistant to the conception of an expert king as also a "political" ruler than I have indicated. Nonetheless, the fact remains that Plato does not rely on such associations to establish this connection but, as I have emphasized, goes to the trouble of constructing an elaborate philosophical argument to support it (for which see the next note). It is only at the end of the dialogue that (as I shall argue) Plato allows us to see in the exercise of kingly rule anything resembling the concern for the mass of people and their intelligent participation in government that one sees prefigured in Euripides' political plays (on which see Zuntz, *The Political Plays of Euripides*).

[7] By "the argument here," I mean the stretch of text running from 258e8, where the thesis to be established is announced in the form of a question to Young Socrates, down to 259c5, where Young Socrates, having "followed" the Visitor to that conclusion (see 258e11), now agrees that the right answer to give to the Visitor's initial question is yes: "it's clear that there is one sort of expert knowledge concerned with all these things; whether someone gives this the name of expertise in kingship, or statesmanship, or household management, let's not pick any quarrel with him." (For the Visitor's immediate purpose in establishing this equivalence, see n. 4 above.) First (259a1–b6) the Visitor draws on an analogy to medical expertise (including expertise at public medicine) to argue that the right criterion for whether someone possesses the king's expertise is solely whether he knows what a king should know, not whether he actually does or ever will occupy the office of a king. Next (b7–8) the Visitor and Young Socrates agree (as obvious) that household managers and slave-masters are the same thing. (Aristotle will object vehemently to this: in defense, it could be pointed out that expert management of a household and its estates at any rate includes as a central part the knowledge how to direct the work of slaves, and it could be argued that no one could truly know how to do that unless he or she also knew how to run the rest of the household, namely direct the activities

reader is invited to place and hold a question mark above this thesis, even while the Visitor goes blithely ahead on the principle that expert king and expert statesman are one and the same thing. It is only when, at the end of the dialogue, we learn enough about just how, as "king," the statesman will rule, that we can see what really does justify this thesis—and, indeed, its real implications.

For my present purposes I do not need to insist upon this admittedly disputable exercise in hermeneutics—the claim that the dialogue is placing a question mark over the Visitor's thesis by making it depend upon a flagrantly invalid piece of augmentation. Indeed, I can relegate to the footnotes (see nn. 4 and 7) the question of the argument's validity. It is enough to insist that anyone who reads this part of the dialogue and its immediate sequel must realize that, in the first instance, the assimilation of statesman with king here goes in that direction: the statesman or ruler in a *polis* is being elevated to some kingly or royal status. We are henceforward to understand the target of our inquiry as the expert king (or expertise at royal rule)—the commander from on high, the person with such a perfect knowledge of what is good for human beings that he is entitled to direct the lives of everyone else, who owe him both thanks and obedience as a result; once we establish what that knowledge is, we can call this same person by courtesy, as it were, also the expert statesman (since it is in a single *polis* that he rules).

---

of the free persons making it up, since the two must go intimately together; it need not be implied that under the envisaged single knowledge the free people would have to be treated the same way that slaves are.) Third and finally it is argued (b9–11) that ruling a large household and ruling a small city (*polis*) cannot differ (since the one does not differ in size from the other, it is implied, it can hardly differ in any other relevant way), so that expertise in ruling a city must be the same thing as expert management of a household and its estates. I take it that this third premise amounts to the claim that the rule of an expert *politikos*—the person who has expertise in ruling in a *polis*—is the same as expertise at household management. (Aristotle objects vehemently to this premise, too—this time it is indeed difficult to find anything to say in favor of the Visitor's claim.) But if these are the three premises of the argument, it flies in your face that the conclusion does not follow (and never mind whether all or any of the premises are true): the second premise only identifies slave-master with householder, and the third only adds to that cluster the statesman; but the first premise only tells us that the expert king (and so any expertise with another name that is identical with his) is whoever knows what the king should know, and since neither the second nor the third premise says anything about kingship, nothing can validly be inferred about any identity of king and statesman (or king and householder or slave-master, either). Of course, if the third premise is understood to say that *whoever* rules in a city has a knowledge that can't differ from that of an expert household manager, whether he is called a king or a statesman, then that already, as a presupposition of a *premise* of the argument, asserts the important conclusion that the Visitor is attempting to establish—that expert kingship and expert statesmanship are the same thing. So the argument fails because of petitio principii. But, as against this way of taking the third premise, note that at 259a6 a *chōra* is given as what a king rules over, something much larger than a single city, the scope of the rule being spoken of at b9, where it is and has to be given as a *polis*. It might seem not too much of a stretch to make *statesmanly* rule not differ from that of expert rule over a large household (as the third premise claims), but a king's expertise must surely include much more than rule merely over a city.

That that is how the Visitor is proceeding is made clear from the fact that his first subsequent moves lead him rapidly and inexorably to a sort of "kingship" that only a god could exercise. His first moves construe the herders among whom he looks for the king all to be responsible for the bringing into being in the first place of their animals, and not just for the subsequent management of them (261a10–b2, d3–5): the cowherd, for example, controls which of his cows his bulls will mount, and when. Only a god could be responsible for not just the management of human life, but the actual bringing or coming into being (*genesis*)[8] of human beings themselves.

The Visitor does, of course, eventually correct this error, by telling the "myth" of the two cosmic eras defined by the alternation in the direction in which the cosmos turns (268e–274e). In one of these eras, the gods, personally directing the course of nature, not only generate human beings from the earth by their own action, without any sexual intercourse by the humans, but provide a perfect climate for them and all the food and drink they need. The Visitor leaves it open how they would spend the abundant leisure time that results from this divine largesse (272b8–d5), but I take it that this too would be the effect of arrangements made by the gods for them in their god-given physical and mental constitution as they came forth from the earth: it would not be up to them, as it is now up to us, to decide for themselves how to spend their free time. Such divine rule, the Visitor says (275b9–c1), is "greater than" kingship, since a king must be a human being like those he rules over; a king, the target of our inquiry, must belong to the other era, when human beings "have to live their lives through their own resources and take care of *themselves*" (274d4–5)[9]—they must not only produce their own children by sexual reproduction, but provide somehow for themselves the shelter, clothing, food, and other necessities, as well as the social context they also need under these changed circumstances, if they are to live truly good lives. However, even once this correction is made, we are left with the clear impression that our truly human kingly ruler, like the divine kingly ruler of the other era, will take everything into his own hands, as kings traditionally claimed to do. He will decide unilaterally and on the basis of his own self-sufficient alleged knowledge the arrangements for and all the circumstances of his subjects' very restricted exercise of free choice as these communal goals are being pursued. The Visitor implies that there is a legitimate basis for the confusion that led to the identification of *our* expert king with the divine ruler in the other cosmic era. So the Visitor must be conceiving our king as exercising similarly benignly intended but dictatorial rule—not as a tyrant, of course (see 276e), but as a dictator nonetheless. Hence, even after the Visitor brings home to us that he is searching out expertise at ruling in our cosmic era, not the other one, we still feel his original identification of statesman and king as in effect an

[8] See 261b1, d3.
[9] Translation by Rowe, slightly altered.

attempt to reduce (or rather elevate) the expertise of the "political" ruler to that of the "royal" one.

I shall argue that this, despite initial appearances, is a great mistake. It is gradually brought to light as the Visitor proceeds, but made obvious only in the last stages of the dialogue, that in fact, for him, expert kingly rule actually embodies at a fundamental level many of the arrangements that we would associate rather with political (i.e., statesmanly) rule—not, of course, that it embodies them in a way that allows for the full panoply of political decisionmaking institutions of an actual Greek city.[10] Once the Visitor completes his work we can see, looking back, that the initial identification of expert statesman and king really paves the way for a reduction of kingship to statesmanship—not the other way round, as first appears. If I am right that the flagrant invalidity of the argument establishing this identification invites the reader to place and hold a question mark above it, then we can see that fact as signaling in a way the later developments. Thus the identification will turn out to be not nearly so noxious as it first appeared, and the question mark will remove itself in an unexpected way by the end of the dialogue. Leaving that hermeneutical question aside, however, as I say, I want to turn now to these later developments.

II

At 277d, shortly after he presents the "myth," the Visitor abruptly announces that we will need to draw upon a "model" if we are to succeed in delineating the functions of the king or statesman in such a way as to relate them to, but separate them from, those of the other contenders for the title of "carers for the human herd" that he has already mentioned. This model will have to be another expertise, one whose essential features we already understand, so we can work them out quite easily. If we choose our model well, we can use it to bring to light what we are looking for in the case of the statesman's expertise that will allow us to relate it to but separate it from the other contenders: a correct model is something that closely resembles what it is a model for. The model the Visitor chooses is the expertise of the weaver (279a–b). His idea is that we should first look closely at the relationships among the weaver, responsible for the final production of a woven woolen garment, and the various other—independent—expert artisans who contrib-

---

[10] One advantage to the Visitor in starting out provisionally with the statesman conceived as a dictatorial ruler is that that allows him to explode via the myth the idea that any human king even though called a "shepherd of the people," in any way resembles an actual shepherd tending to his flock. Thus he strikes a blow against one prevalent and obnoxious but oddly persuasive image which kings had always used to represent their relationship of benevolent dominance over the people they ruled. Once this is accomplished, the deflation continues, as we gradually learn about the other independent experts whom the truly expert human "king" must enlist and direct as partly independent producers of some parts of his own product.

ute in one or another essential way to his ability to complete his work and whom he directs as his subordinates.[11] We will then have the key we need so as to understand the work of the expert king or statesman. The Visitor makes a great deal of the importance to be attached to going through this model in extreme detail—indeed, for most of us nowadays, excruciating and bewildering detail. (Presumably these details would have been more familiar to a fourth-century Greek.) He introduces another of his methodological digressions (stretching from 283a9 to 287b3) specifically in order to explain why a discussion of precisely the length of his is of precisely the right length—neither too long nor too short. The appropriate length of a philosophical discussion is to be measured not in relation to other discussions—as if the right length were neither much longer nor much shorter than the average, or than other good ones—but in relation to what the principles of dialectical philosophy itself decide is right in the given case, because dictated by the requirements of the particular substantive issues.[12] Thus, the Visitor strongly emphasizes the importance not just of the general idea that the king or statesman is to be compared in his work to a weaver of woolen clothes, but of details of the model and the detailed ways in which it applies to the art of statesmanship. So we are justified—indeed obligated, if we wish to read the dialogue with the care that it itself asks for—in reading and applying this model extremely closely. To that task I devote the remainder of this chapter.[13]

In setting out the model, the Visitor goes through the making of the tools needed and the stages in the preliminary preparation of the wool, followed by its step-by-step treatment as it is turned into a woven garment. He

[11] It is noteworthy that the Visitor does not actually specify here that the other expertises—which he describes at 280b2 as "cooperative" (*sunergōn*) with that of the master-weaver—are in fact in some way under his direction, as his subordinates (*hupēretai*, a term that is used repeatedly of the "cooperative" arts associated with statesmanship, beginning at 289c4): but see 308d4–e2, where in referring to the "educators" who are one class of experts that the statesman-king will have as his subordinates the Visitor says that the statesman-king will lay down prescriptions for and direct them "in the same way that weaving follows along with the carders [et al] . . . , prescribing for and directing them, giving indications to each group to finish their products in whatever way it thinks suitable for its own interweaving."

[12] The importance of what he says here is marked externally by the fact that this "digression" occupies the very middle pages of the dialogue. Plato is a careful writer, and a survey of his dialogues suggests strongly that often (not always) he is sensitive to what he places at the center of the writing, as a position of focal importance in the composition as a whole.

[13] In fact, I go into certain points of detail more fully and explicitly than even the Visitor does. I take it that what the Visitor tells Young Socrates about the crucial need for a model if we are to learn what statesmanship is and about the importance of surveying and applying the model down to the level of details, is meant for us readers too. We have things to learn from this dialogue about statesmanship, as the Visitor and Plato are conceiving it, that go beyond what the Visitor, with his primary purpose of instructing Young Socrates in the practice of dialectical division and definition, actually states. As readers, we are being invited to think through for ourselves the model and its implications, and pursue on our own, beyond the point where the Visitor leaves them, the issues about how political rule will be administered that he only lightly touches upon.

identifies the different expert artisans responsible for performing the various tasks along the way to this goal. All of these are described as in effect the weaver's "co-workers" (*sunergoi*, cf. 280b2) but (waiving for the moment a non-essential qualification) they are also his subordinates (*hupēretai*), working under his direction. However, the Visitor distinguishes emphatically between the arts that craft the tools—spindles and shuttles and so on— needed to do the work of preparing and then weaving the wool—and those that do the work of preparation and weaving itself. The former—the tool-makers—he calls "contributory causes" (only) (*sunaitiai*) of the making of clothes (281c2–5, d11, e7–9): they count as some sort of causes because (e2–5) in the absence of their products (the tools) the arts that work the things themselves up (the clothes) to final completion could not accomplish their respective tasks. But they are only contributory and not full causes in the making of clothes, because though the work of these toolmaking arts is necessary if that other work is to be done, it is not actually part of it: in making a tool for carding or woof-twisting or weaving itself, one is not yet doing anything to the materials that will eventually constitute the final product, a piece of woolen clothing.[14] For this reason, if one were concerned, as the Visitor is in the case of statesmanship, to set aside related expertises as nonetheless distinct from the weaver's, the toolmaking arts related to weaving would pose no difficulty. They do not "lay claim to" anything more than the status of such "contributory" causation in the making of woven articles (281c2–5).

Only the remaining experts—carders, fullers, woof- and warp-spinners, and so on—will "dispute the role of looking after and producing clothes with the capacity which is the art of weaving, conceding a very large part to it, but assigning large shares to themselves, too" (281b7–10), because they are (full) "causes" (*aitiai*, 281d12, e10, 282a1) of the production of the garment, as of course the weaver himself also is. They work directly on the material, the wool, that will ultimately be fashioned into it—even if the carders and fullers only receive the wool from the shears of the sheep-farmers and clean and comb and smooth it out so that the process of combining and separating, which is the essence of weaving, can begin. These other arts are (as one could put it) full "co-causes" with the weaver's art, which itself (besides giving general overall direction to the others) is limited to doing only the final weaving of warp and woof into the woolen cloth, the finished product of the whole process.[15] They are full co-causes because

---

[14] Plato's distinction between what I am calling contributory causes (*sunaitiai* or *sunaitia*) and (full) causes (*aitiai* or *aitia*) first occurs in *Phaedo* 98b–99d, though without use of the term *sunaition*. It is explicit in *Timaeus* 46c–e and 76d. This passage of *Statesman* is essential reading for the correct understanding of the distinctions Plato draws in those other places.

[15] Strictly, the Visitor seems to reserve the name of "subordinates" (*hupēretai*) for those who belong to the second of these two groups—the full (co-)causes of the product (see 308d6ff.); whether on purpose or not, he does not actually call the "contributory causes" "subordinate" arts to the master-weaver's, even though the master-weaver does of course give general overall

they all act at some particular point within the process of actually fashioning in some way the material coming from the sheep that will constitute that product, just as the weaver himself does. For that reason they can be counted, as the Visitor does count them, as legitimate and serious claimants to the name of "producers of woolen clothing," which is the same name one would at first be inclined to use to capture the art of weaving itself. However, theirs are not the same arts as that of weaving—ordinary language makes that evident enough.[16]

Nonetheless, it is not sufficient to say merely that weaving is the "finest and greatest" of the arts that concern themselves with making woollen clothing (281c7–d1). We need to show how these relate to weaving, so as to be clear just how they are like and how they differ from it. In fact, they are subordinate to the weaver's art: it is the latter's function, because only he knows the detailed character of the final product he is in charge of producing in any instance, also to know what the products of his co-workers at each stage need to be like if those preliminary products are to be most effective in bringing to perfection the final product, the clothing he is aiming to make with their assistance. The weaver gives directions to the carders, woof-spinners, et al. as to what to produce, in addition to performing the crucial final stages of combining together in the right way the warp and the woof—the product of the warp- and the woof-spinners' arts. Thus, although legitimate, in the sense of truly serious (by comparison with any shuttle-maker's claims to this effect), the claims made by fullers and carders and woof-spinners to do the same thing that weavers do can be rebutted. They *do* do some work of their own in actually producing the woolen product—so they *are* "producers of woolen clothing." However, because they do not possess the knowledge of the final product that is needed if their expertise in working up the wool is to be applied in just the required way in bringing the particular product to completion—only the master-weaver knows that—and because they do not perform the function of finally combining warp and woof into the cloth itself, they do not do any part of the weaver's own work. Their expertise is fully distinct from his.[17] It is important to observe, however, and the Visitor never says anything to contradict this, that the

---

direction to their work. I leave this minor qualification to one side. In the *Cratylus* (390b) Socrates says that the user of a tool, e.g., the weaver in the case of a shuttle, not the maker of it, is the person whose job it is to know whether the correct form has been given to it, and to instruct the maker in what he is to produce (not, however, be it noted, in how he is to go about doing it). There is no reason to think the Visitor holds a different view. Perhaps, however, he feels it would be going too far to describe the toolmaker on that ground as the weaver's subordinate; it is more suitable to reserve that term for the others, the co-causes, who of course similarly receive instructions from the weaver but who also work in close association with him on fashioning the material itself that constitutes the garment.

[16] See the Visitor's comments 280e6–281b6.

[17] So similarly, when we come to apply the model to statesmanship, there will be legitimate, serious claimants to the statesman's functions, whom it is important to see do have strong claims to do just what the statesman does, who nonetheless can be distinguished from him

weaver is not, as such, and need not be, a master also of these other, subordinate crafts—any more than he needs to be a master of the arts devoted to producing the tools needed for weaving. He does not give instructions to the other experts in their expertise, or direct them in the steps to be taken in carrying out his general instructions about what sort of warp or woof or pulled wool he may need for the particular job of weaving he is engaged on. All of that is up to the individual artisan himself, as part of the free exercise of his own expertise, under *its* direction, not that of the weaver.

After laying out this model, the Visitor allows himself to be interrupted for the methodological discussion I mentioned above (beginning of sect. II), before turning to apply the model to the case of the king-statesman. He begins this application by reiterating the distinction between "contributory causes" and (full) "causes," thus marking its importance for all that follows:[18] he has, he says, already separated off from the king-statesman the herders of other sorts of animals than humans, so what remains is to take note of all those expert workers in the city itself (not its surrounding countryside) whose expertises are either contributory causes (*sunaitiai*) or full causes (*aitiai*), along with his, in enabling him to complete his work (287b3–7). We receive no clear, independent characterization of the king-statesman's work until the Visitor's last words at the end of the dialogue (311b–c): the king's or statesman's function is to "rule and direct" the work of these others in the city so that he "brings [the citizens'] life together in agreement and friendship and makes it common between them" and thereby makes the city itself as "happy" as a city can be. I return to this characterization below, but for now we need to pursue the Visitor's efforts to identify and distinguish from one another the expertises in the city that the king or statesman oversees in the manner of contributory causes, and those that he oversees as full (but subordinate) co-causes with him of this "product."[19]

Although the distinction between subordinate expertises that are contributory and those that are (full) causes with a master-expertise is one of the key elements of the "model" that are to be carried over in its application, the Visitor does not continue the terminology of contributory vs. full causes much beyond its first reintroduction at 287b. He makes it clear from the outset that all the crafts of toolmaking, however the tools are used within the city and its life, are only contributory causes in relation to the exercise of the king's expertise. In retrospect at 289c8 he says explicitly that he

---

and ultimately set aside as very closely associated subordinates in the division leading to the statesman.

[18] I take it that this distinction between contributory and full causes is one of the "letters" or "syllables" found in the model of weaving that are then to be applied in the appropriate way, according to the account the Visitor gives at 277d–278e of what a model is and how to use it, in the case of kingship or statesmanship. The other "letter" or "syllable" present in the model that seems to play a role in delineating the target of statesmanship is that of combination and separation (see 305e8ff.)

[19] The following account of these subordinate expertises is summarized in the Appendix to this chapter.

also classes the whole string of arts and crafts that he has unrolled in the immediately preceding passage as contributory and not co-causes—the making of vessels and conveyances and walls and houses and armaments and clothing,[20] to be sure, but also that of paintings and music, the mining of ores, and all the provision of food and the other means of care for the body (including the physician's and the trainer's arts), plus all the expertises of the animal tenders who have already been separated off from the king on a different basis (see 287b4–5). These are not all anything like makers of tools for the king's use in his own work, but they are counted nonetheless as contributory and not full causes in relation to his work. But that (289c8) is the last appearance in the dialogue of either term, *aitia* or *sunaitia*. We are left with the impression at that point that the expertises to be taken up in what immediately follows will now be the co-causes—no longer the contributory ones.[21] However, we do not get to any of the co-causing expertises until much later, in fact only with the introduction at 303e10–304a2 of the expert generals and judges and that expertise at oratory which, as the Visitor says, "in partnership with kingship persuades people of what is just and so helps in steering through the business of cities." I will have to come back to this important passage. But first I need to explain why I think that it is only these last "subordinates" and not the others that he has dealt with immediately previously (from 289d) that the Visitor is ranking as co-causes with the king or statesman in his work.

To begin with, one should note that in this last passage (303e10ff.) the Visitor describes these practitioners, by contrast with all the preceding ones, as "more akin" (*sungenes*) to the king and "closer to" or (literally) "more together" with him (*homou*, 303d5). He explains our task at this point (303d9–e10) by drawing on an analogy with the refining of gold. He says that gold-refiners need first to remove earth, stones, and lots of other quite different materials from their sample, leaving only the precious metals; only

---

[20] See 288b7: the art of weaving, in producing its product (wool clothing), is thus only a contributory cause, in relation to the king's or statesman's expertise.

[21] It is precisely at this point (289c4) that we find the Visitor for the first time speaking of the experts he is now to discuss as "subordinates" (*hupēretai*) (admittedly not always as subordinates *of the king*)—language he uses continually thereafter of these personages, including others to be added later who are explicitly claimed to be the *king*'s subordinates. See 289d6, e5; 290a5, b2, b5, c1; 291a2; 304a1; 305a8, c7; 308d5. This might suggest that the Visitor is simply shifting to new terminology, intending now by "subordinates" to capture all the various expertises that co-cause with the king or statesman, under his direction, the king's product. In fact, however, I think this impression would be mistaken. Among the "subordinates" are slaves and day-laborers (289d, 290a); these (and other "subordinates," such as heralds), or their expertises, are not clearly classified (or classifiable) as "contributory causes" of the king's product, but the Visitor is certainly not thinking of them as full co-causes of it, either. Perhaps the lessened prominence of the terminology of contributory vs. co-causes from 289c simply reflects the Visitor's sense of the inevitable complexity of the kingly expertise in relation to the truly global compass of the expertises subordinate to it. He continues to apply the distinction, as a crucially important lesson to be learned from the model, while not insisting that it cover all the terrain in the neat way that it did in the model of weaving.

then do they get to work separating off by means of fire the other precious metals that are "akin to" gold and "commingled" with it—he mentions copper, silver, adamant—so as finally to reveal the unalloyed gold itself. So we too have now already set aside all the expertises that are quite different from the kingly and statesmanly one and have left before us the much more difficult task of dealing with those that are "precious and akin to it."[22] This exclusive association of the expert generals, judges, and political orators (and others to be added later) with the expert statesman as being "akin to" him, as silver is akin to gold, and "together with" him seems to me strongly to suggest that what has preceded, even after the first list—of toolmakers, farmers, physicians, etc.—has been compiled and set aside as "contributory causes," are also not to be classed as full co-causes with the statesman in doing his work. They must be further "contributory causes" of one sort or another (even if the explanation of "contributory causes" in terms of what produces "tools" and closely related such items may not clearly apply to them).[23]

Meanwhile, we should notice that by classing expert generals, judges, and political orators as "akin to" expert kings or statesmen, the Visitor is implying a close association between the sort of work they do and the king's own work. It is this kinship that makes these experts the only true, substantial claimants actually to do that work, in displacement of him—even if, as we shall see, their claims, too, must be rejected, just as were those of carders to do the work of weaving. It will turn out that they, too, are subordinates of the king, working under his supervision, in the same sort of way that an expert carder or warp-twister works under the supervision of the master-weaver; just as the master-weaver's expertise and function are distinct from those of even these co-working subordinates, who like him work directly upon the fabric itself that is their common product, so, the Visitor will argue, generals, judges, and political orators possess co-working, independent expertises of their own, while working together with the king and under his overall supervision on a fabric of their common crafting.

Some confirmation for the view that only these "kin" expertises count as co-causes in relation to the king's work can be found in the way the Visitor begins his investigation at 289c4 of the personages who are left over after all the so-called "tool"-makers have been set aside, and in some of what he says to characterize their relationship to the expert statesman. He first describes "the class of slaves" as among the group of workers in the city that he has now to deal with (289c4, d10–e2); soon he adds hired day-laborers and merchants, money-changers, shipowners, and retailers (289e9–290a5). These are "in service to" or subordinates of, not the king, but various of the artisans already mentioned, or of other private or professional persons:

---

[22] I alter Rowe's "related to" for *sungenē* at e10 to "akin to" in order to preserve in the English the continuity of language we find in the Greek.

[23] These are the expertises grouped together under "B" in the chart in the Appendix.

farmers, manufacturers, and so on (289d4–5, see also *hēmin* at 290a8 and 290c4–6). He says it is quite out of the question to suppose that any of these experts (experts at being *slaves?*—imagine!) will claim the king's or statesman's expertise.[24] In fact, the reason they come in at just this point, and not previously, where the crafts that are overtly ranked as only "contributory causes" are set aside, is that the Visitor suggests (289c4–6) that it is within the larger class of "those people who are subordinate to others" that we will find the experts who really *do* dispute with the king for a claim to be workers of the "fabric" of social life that is his prerogative—that is, I take it, the experts who *can* legitimately claim to be co-causes with him (though subordinate ones) of that fabric. So these first additional experts are mentioned as people who do subordinate work of the *wrong kind* to be taken seriously as claimants for that rank: we set them aside in order to see better which subordinates really have to be taken seriously. So, I take it, they too are to be ranked as only "contributory causes" for the accomplishment of the king's and these others' common work.

The Visitor is on the threshold of locating these most legitimate claimants when he comes to the priests at 290c8: not because priests as such (in their praying and sacrificing) do anything that could challenge the king for his function or a share in it, but because (the Visitor says) in Egypt kings were required to come from the priestly caste and in some Greek cities one of the highest official civic magistrates (notably, at Athens, the so-called "king *archon*") had as part of his functions to offer the most important annual sacrifices to the gods on behalf of the city (290d8–e8). Clearly, the Visitor is here on the threshold of finding in the leading public servants, or magistrates, of a Greek city the experts for whom he has been looking: among these are the ones that he will eventually both rank as subordinates of the expert king or statesman in a well-ordered city, and assign a function as true co-causes with him of the product of the kingly art.

However, another delaying digression intervenes before the Visitor can cross that threshold (291a ff.): this time not another methodological excursus but a detour through a group of people whom he insists lack any serious claim at all to be co-causes with a true statesman of his work. These are the actual political leaders and chief rulers or magistrates in any of the then-existing constitutions, who accept the basis of rule on which their particular constitution is established—whether it belongs under the heading kingship, or aristocracy, or (lawful) democracy, or deserves that of any of the recognized opposites to these: tyranny, oligarchy, or (lawless) democracy. The only expertise any of the rulers under current constitutions may possess gives them no legitimate claim to the expertise needed by a well-run city. So any expertise of theirs is no basis for a legitimate claim to be co-causes with the king, much less to be possessors of the kingly or statesmanly art themselves. They are in fact only experts at all in the sense that a sophist

---

[24] See 289e1–2; 290a1, a5–6.

has been revealed in the earlier part of the discussion, that presented in the dialogue *Sophist,* to be one: they are "experts in faction; . . . as the greatest imitators and magicians, they turn out to be the greatest sophists among sophists" (303c1–5). Each of them pretends to, and convinces their fellow-citizens that they possess, the expert knowledge of how to rule in a city, but in fact, according to the Visitor, they have absolutely nothing of it. In a lengthy section (291a1–303d3) the Visitor criticizes existing constitutions and makes out his claim that rulers in them are all charlatans. There is much to learn here about the Visitor's views about how truly expert kings rule, a sort of rule that these pretenders imitate badly at best; I come back to this toward the end of the chapter. For now, my point is that this *is* a discussion off to one side, which serves not to identify any legitimate or serious claimants to be "co-causes" alongside the expert king, but to attack the claims of current constitutions and their officers to any of the actual knowledge requisite to confer any entitlement to rule at all.

III

The conclusion of this section takes us at last to the point (303d4), as I have argued, where we do finally meet with expertises that are true co-causes with the statesman of the statesman's product. What do we find? With distressingly few pages left in the dialogue (only eight Stephanus pages, 303d–311c, out of the 55), what can we learn about how the Visitor conceives the cooperative but subordinate roles of these statesmanly and royal co-workers, and the common life of the city that results from the fabric that they and the statesman-king create together within it, under the latter's direction? First, we should recall that, as I have already mentioned in passing, at 308d4–5, e5ff. the Visitor adds to his list of three co-causing expertises— those of the general, the judge, and the political orator—a fourth, that of the educators of the young (*paideutais kai tropheusin,* e5). About these he says (and by implication the same applies to the others as well) that they receive their directions from the king or statesman in just the same way that the weaver gives instructions to the co-causing crafts subordinate to him: they are independent experts, knowing things that the king or statesman does not know, about how to achieve the particular outcomes the statesman knows to ask for in the formation of the characters of the general citizenry that it is their responsibility to undertake (308d). (I return below to the nature of these instructions.) In discussing the general and the political orator earlier, he has put the same point slightly differently: there (304d3–5) he said that the statesman's function is to tell the political orator when to use his powers of persuasion, and on whom, and when not, but (perhaps) to allow the issue to be settled by force—the orator's knowledge, as such, does not include knowing that. Similarly, the general's expertise does not extend to knowing when to make war and when to withdraw on friendly terms; he will be directed in these matters by the statesman or king himself (304e9–11). As for the expert judge, he has the expertise, and the good character, to interpret well in light of the particular circumstances the laws laid down by the statesman or king on the basis of *his* expertise, and to apply them correctly and fairly without bias or taint of corruption (305b4–c3).[25]

The model of weaving makes it clear why and how these expertises count as full co-causes of the statesman's own product, whereas all those gone through earlier—expertise in clothes-making or house-building, merchantry, farming, and so on—count only as contributory causes. The expert states-man's "product" is a communal life in the city that is as good and happy for the citizens as possible—that is, a life in which to the greatest degree possible they have and exercise the virtues of character necessary for being a good person and living a good life. All the other expertises provide only external means or contexts for the development and exercise of such good moral qualities. These four expertises—that of the educator, the political orator, the judge, and the general—oversee aspects of that moral life itself, which the statesman regulates overall, by defining the ultimate goal and giving the needed directions to these, his co-workers, in pursuing their own professional objectives. Here one needs to bear in mind that war was a regular part of the life of any Greek city, and important virtues were associated with it: the general, in knowing how to marshall and train the male citizen body, as well as lead them out to war, knows how to bring them to possess, and then leads them in suitable occasions for the exercise of, developed forms of certain important qualities of character that are essential to being a good person and living a good life. Similarly the judge maintains fairness and equity in the community's business activities and thus contributes in a crucial way to a different aspect of the good life of the citizens.

Of more interest to us are the orator's and the educator's roles. A striking fact about the last pages of the *Statesman,* in contrast certainly with the *Republic,* is that the Visitor argues in effect that all the citizens of the city he envisages (or perhaps only all the male ones—I come back to this point

---

[25] Here one may note an important difference between the politics envisaged by the Visitor and that worked out in the *Republic.* These subordinate expertises are independent bodies of knowledge, though their exercise is controlled by the statesman-king. The statesman himself does not have to possess these expertises in order to exercise proper control over their use— any more than the master-weaver has to have the carder's expertise. In the *Republic* Socrates makes a point of insisting that the philosopher-kings must have previously received the whole regimen of instruction and learned all the occupations assigned to the auxiliary guardians (the judges and generals and political orators—if there are any—and, presumably, the educators of the young in the ideal city). So they possess all the expertises of their assistants—indeed only they possess these in the highest degree and the most perfect form. They do not practice them, because they have better things to do with their time; but they are fully capable of doing so. The one knowledge they do have, of the Form of the Good, makes that possible. Even though in the *Statesman* the Visitor does not speak about the education needed to produce a fully expert statesman, the force of the model of weaving indicates that here the expert educators, generals, judges, and political orators possess expertises distinct from the statesman's, which they can possess fully without any substantial share of the statesman's knowledge.

below) will be capable of, and will be trained by these educators so that they actually possess, a fairly high level of positive, fully active virtues of character. They are not restricted just to the sort of passive and simple-minded, fawning acceptance of their rulers' and guards' instructions that in the *Republic* was the best that most people could be expected to attain. The Visitor draws attention to what he claims are two types of basically good personality (he may think there are others as well—he does not say) that are naturally found among humans, but that if allowed to develop unchecked and without correct education lead to a condition where the two types of person hate, are at odds with, and violently disagree with one another—and when this hostility arises in connection with the most important communal matters, it constitutes "a disease which is the most hateful of all for cities" (307d8–9). The first group are people who "incline more towards courage" (308a4): they naturally incline toward vigorous action, toward taking a confrontational attitude when opposed or thwarted, or when they come up against something they object to, and they are little inclined to seek compromise or to yield before anyone else just because there will be unpleasantness if they do not. The others by nature tend toward the opposite extreme, "inclining towards the moderate" (309b4): they tend to dislike open disagreements, they always seek to smooth things out with others, to seek accommodations, not to allow the peace to be disrupted, and to avoid confrontation at all cost. If each type of person is allowed to grow into the extreme that his basic personality inclines him toward, these "natural virtues" (as Aristotle calls them)[26] develop into no virtues at all, but become the source of that "hateful disease" for cities that the Visitor mentions. Yet if properly educated, people of these two basic types can both become truly virtuous to quite a high degree, even while each group remains *inclined* in the direction that their nature inclines them. In consequence they can become capable of living together in harmony, and in mutual agreement about the most important matters.

This happens when the people of both types, through education, receive a "divine bond" fitted into their minds—the part of them that the Visitor says is eternal—which consists in a "true" and "firmly settled"[27] opinion (*alēthēs doxa meta bebaiōseōs,* 309c6) about "what is fine, just, and good." Receiving this divine bond means (as I argue just below) that they come to see and accept reasons—though reasons less fully explanatory than those having full knowledge would recognize—why, sometimes, they should *not* do what they are respectively inclined to do: that is, why if they are of a naturally "courageous" sort not to push for confrontation or, if they are naturally "moderate," not to shy away from standing up for their beliefs, and not to yield in order to seek accommodation and avoid unpleasantness.

---

[26] It often goes unnoticed that Plato here in the *Statesman* is addressing the same range of moral phenomena as did Aristotle in his doctrine of "natural virtue" (*Eudemian Ethics* III 7, 1234a23–34; *Nicomachean Ethics* VI 13).

[27] Here I depart from Rowe's translation, which gives "guaranteed."

This education "weaves together" these two opposite tendencies, in such a way that members of each group, while retaining their own natural and inborn tendencies, also—because of this education of their minds—exhibit the effects of the other tendency. Each comes to possess both *genuine* courage and *genuine* moderation—neither remains at the level of merely "natural" versions of these virtues—but in a different way in each case.[28] One sort of person has courage but not moderation also as a "natural" endowment, while the other sort, while likewise having both genuine moderation and genuine courage, has only moderation and not courage as a development of their natural orientation.[29] This effect is the result of the educator's expertise, exercised under the control and direction of the expert statesman, who of course oversees all the "weaving" that goes on in his city by establishing each sort of weaving's particular objectives in relation to the overall project.[30]

As I interpret it, the "true" and "firmly settled" opinion about "what is fine, just, and good" that the expert educators introduce into the minds of the citizens of the expert statesman's city involves the citizens' coming to see and accept good reasons for so regarding certain actions and dispositions—it involves a significant development of their own moral understanding. It is true that in the *Meno,* in what is presumably the first effort in Plato's works to draw a distinction between knowledge and true opinion or belief, true belief is characterized as something that could drop into a person's mind from out of the blue—perhaps through the action, occasion by occasion, of a tutelary god: the person with (mere) true moral belief would be like someone who does not know the way to Larissa but only by a series of unaccountable hunches makes the right turns along the route and so guides people correctly to that destination.[31] Such a person, as Socrates emphasizes there, would lack any grounding in reasons (*logoi*) for what he does, and would be doing no better than merely guessing the way (see *Meno* 98b1).

---

[28] See 309e5–6, where the point is made explicit that only once these opinions are properly settled in a person's mind can he count as "genuinely moderate" (*ontōs sōphrōn*). The same point about courage is made, in less explicit language, at 309d10–e3.

[29] See 310a3–5: this bonding through correct opinions unites in them "parts of virtue that are by nature unlike each other and tend in opposite directions." In other words, according to the Visitor's account, when either of these contrasted types of person receives this bond through education they unite in their characters these two "parts" of virtue, viz. courage and moderation: see 308e8–309b1.

[30] There are further merely "human" weavings and bondings that the statesman also oversees (310a7–e8): through intermarriages over time, the population comes to contain some people who have natural tendencies of both sorts, as well as others who remain, so far as original natural endowment goes, clearly of the naturally courageous or the naturally moderate sort. See 311a4–9, with its reference first to people of "both qualities" and then to those having merely the dispositions of, respectively, the naturally courageous and the naturally moderate. But the educational bonding of both tendencies in the way I have described—so as to produce a population all of whom are both genuinely courageous and moderate, whatever their initial and persisting natural tendencies may be—is clearly counted as the crucial one (310e7–11).

[31] See *Meno* 97a–b, 97e–98a, 99c–d.

However, the Visitor in the *Statesman* regards the possession of his "divine bond" *within* one's mind as constituting a ground for being counted a significantly virtuous person. This already strongly suggests that he must not be conceiving the true belief or right opinion that this bond imparts in the same way that Socrates regarded it in the *Meno*—it is not a matter of just making correct particular judgments without having any grasp of some reasons why those are correct. Not even in the *Meno* does Socrates seriously intend to say that a person whose ability is limited to regularly guessing correctly the right thing to do should count in any way as a virtuous person.

In addition, however, we should recall that in the *Theaetetus* (a dialogue marked externally, along with the *Sophist,* as preceding the *Statesman* in a common sequence) true belief (*doxa*) is introduced by Theaetetus (187b4) as a better candidate than perception for constituting knowledge precisely because *doxa* involves what Socrates has argued perception does not: a "process of reasoning" (*sullogismos,* 186d3), some "calculations" (*analogismata,* 186c2–3), one's soul being "busy by itself about the things which are" (187a5–6), the soul's reflecting on and comparing together what is perceived by the senses.[32] A little later (190a) Socrates offers his own account of opinion or belief (*doxa*). Belief or opinion occurs when the mind, whether after "carrying on a discussion in which it asks itself questions and answers them itself, affirms and denies" or in a sudden leap, arrives at something definite, addressing to itself a "statement" (*logos*) in which "without divided counsel" it makes a consistent affirmation. In the *Sophist* (263e–264a) the Visitor adopts for himself precisely this view of Socrates'. So when the Visitor speaks later in the same conversation (but now in the *Statesman*) about that true and firmly settled opinion that the educators introduce into the citizens' souls, we are entitled to assume that he means the same sort of thing by "opinion." He means something that involves engaging their power to think—to reason, to analyze, to judge.

I said above that the Visitor conceives this education as being offered to all the citizens, or at least all the male ones. My evidence for this is what the Visitor says at 308e8–309b1, that people who turn out under education to be "unable to share in a disposition that is courageous and moderate" (note the *and* here) but inevitably veer off into excess and injustice will be killed or expelled from the city, or subjugated as slaves. The rest, he says— that is, by implication, all those who are left in the city as citizens—have natures "capable of being composed and stable in the direction of nobility." On the other hand, he also says a little later, at 311a1–2, that the offices of the city will be entrusted to the various ones who have been educated in this way (apparently all of them), and in the peroration at the end of the

---

[32] Translations from the *Theaetetus* are M. J. Levett's as revised by M. F. Burnyeat, in *Plato: Complete Works,* ed. Cooper. Note that at 186c Socrates goes so far as to say that some human beings never do rise to the level of *doxa* but remain mired at that of mere perception, along with the animals. Obviously, *doxa* for him now is a fairly high intellectual accomplishment.

dialogue he speaks of the "fabric" that will have been woven through this education and through the assignment of these people to the city's offices as being spread over "all the other inhabitants . . . both slave and free" (311c3–4). Which free people are these? Presumably the women and children, plus perhaps any foreigners living in the city. So the inference to draw from all the Visitor's statements, if they are to be made consistent with one another, is that only all the *male* citizens (who remain after the completion of the educational process) will have a share (perhaps in turn) in one or another of the offices (those of educator, judge, general, and political orator, plus others not precisely specified),[33] on the basis of their overall virtue plus the acquisition of the specific expertise for that office. These male citizens, forming the "fabric" of the society, will lead their own lives at a high level of moral excellence and will direct the lives of the other citizens so that they too will live as morally well as they are capable of living.

So much for the role of the educators. How about the political orators? Now that we have seen that part of the function of the expert statesman is to produce, with the help of his subordinate experts, a male citizen body that itself consists only of persons of a high degree of human excellence, it should be clear why expert political orators are needed. Notice, first, that the very fact that the Visitor provides for such experts makes it plain that in the city ruled by an expert statesman there will be regular occasions for using political persuasion. That must mean that the people—at least all those educated to the level of moral virtue that we have seen the civic educators aiming at—will be given explanations of new policies, or of changes proposed in the laws; and the matters at issue will be argued out with them so that they are able to see and grasp, if not the full truth about why the statesman's view on them is correct, at any rate the attractive and plausible, more concrete considerations that do in fact speak adequately (and soundly) in favor of the statesman's view.[34] Citizens of this sort, the

---

[33] See 311a4–6.

[34] The orator does not instruct them, but in the Visitor's words only tells them "stories" (304c10–d1): *dia muthologias alla mē dia didachēs.* The emphasis here is on what the orator does not do rather than on what he does: he does not bring the people to understand and accept complete, decisive explanations of what needs to be done or why some change in the law is required (as it were, going back to first principles and deducing his conclusions from them plus the contingent facts). That would be beyond their capacities (see 292e, 300e4–5). The orator is engaged in persuasion (304a1), and "stories" (*muthoi*) is the Visitor's general term for his means of doing that. Given what I have said above about the development of the citizens' powers of practical reasoning through their education, it should be clear that the "stories" the political orators address to them cannot be of the same sort or have the same function as those the rulers tell the auxiliary and the working classes in the *Republic,* for example the myth of the metals told at the end of Book III: that *Phoinikikon pseusma* is an absurd tale that Socrates says it would take a lot of persuasion to get anyone actually to believe (but, then, you never know). In the *Statesman* the term has been used for the myth that the Visitor himself has told about the two eras, and that was meant as a means of making clear to Young Socrates and the others the difference between human expert rule and divine: they were meant to reason out its implications and see its point, not just take something on faith.

Visitor obviously and reasonably must think, deserve nothing less: not to persuade, but instead just to force things through willy-nilly, would be to deprive them of one important context, for which they are otherwise suited by their own knowledge and moral training, for further developing and exercising their moral qualities. So the ruler would be making them less happy than they are capable of being if he did not offer this persuasion, which would defeat his stated final objectives in all his work.

IV

In conclusion, I want to go back briefly to the Visitor's discussion of the defects of the current constitutions. As I mentioned (end of sect. II above) we can learn from this discussion something important about how the Visitor thinks the expert statesman or king will rule. It must be obvious in much that I have said already, though I have not brought this out explicitly, that on the Visitor's view knowledge in the relevant area, and the personal virtues that go along with that knowledge, are the sole valid criterion for legitimate access to political power at any level. It is because, and only because, the expert statesman *is* expert at what it takes to make a human community happy that he is entitled to rule. Except for knowledge nothing at all matters in the least—not, for example, the consent of the governed either to the regime in general or to particular measures undertaken by it. Nonetheless, as we have seen, once one thinks a bit about what the statesman's knowledge itself entails about how one ought to rule such a community, it comes readily to light that—at least on the Visitor's view—such a political expert will encourage the development in his city of independent experts of a number of different types who will work together with him, but under his guidance, to direct the rest of the life of the citizens. Furthermore, his and their common aim is to prepare all the citizens for, and maintain them in, a fairly full life of fully expressed independent virtues of their own. Accordingly, we find the provision of political oratory as one of the subordinate expertises—with the implication, or near implication, that the city will have some sort of public assembly as one of its institutions, as well as boards of independent magistrates of the sort that Greek cities commonly had.[35]

No doubt the *muthoi* the orators will tell will include any appeal, whether involving literal story-telling, such as the Visitor's myth-making, or not, to reasons in support of the desired conclusion—reasons the people will be able to understand, and which really do indicate the truth, though without actually establishing it. The point is that the orators will give the people sound reasons, ones that they can understand and approve of as a basis for the statesman's enacting or deciding whatever may be in question.

[35] I do not mean to imply by this that on the Visitor's view any assembly of the citizens will have the authority to reject, or even to force modifications in the expert statesman's decisions about new laws, or the repeal of old ones, or other measures. The functional equivalent might exist under the version of the constitution that the Visitor mentions (300e–301a) as the best "imitation" one might manage of the best one, where no true expert was available to rule in

Now in fact the Visitor has already argued vigorously and provocatively for the central thesis here, that knowledge and only knowledge (in the relevant area) gives anyone a legitimate entitlement to rule. He does this in the long section 291a1–303d3 where, as I mentioned above (sect. II), he constructs his argument to show that the people holding power in existing governments have no legitimate basis at all on which to claim the title of expert statesmen-kings. They are really charlatans—the "greatest sophists among sophists." Near the beginning of that section, the Visitor presents the three "criteria" (*horoi*) by which existing forms of government are "defined" (292a5–8). These are the criteria by which the allegedly good and just governments (true kingship, aristocracy, and law-abiding democracy) are commonly set apart from the bad and unjust ones (tyranny, oligarchy, and lawless democracy). These criteria are as follows: Does a government (1) maintain itself in power by the use of force, or by the consent of the governed? Is it (2) so constituted as to recognize special rights of the poor, or again special rights of the rich, to hold power? Does it (3) exercise rule via the institutions of law, closely adhered to—not violating established written law, but only if necessary attempting to change it, again by established legal means—or does it simply disobey a law or cancel it when it suits? It is interesting and significant, I think, that earlier the Visitor has himself apparently accepted some of these common ideas about correct rule. At 276e he offered to divide the tyrant off from the expert king who is the target of his divisions by using the distinction that the former's manner of rule is by force, the latter's "voluntary" or "by consent."[36] Here, however, he insistently denies that "any of these constitutions is correct, when it is defined by these criteria" (292a5–6) and that "the criterion in the things in question must not be" any of those criteria "but some sort of knowledge" (c6–9). But does that mean that the true king will *not* necessarily rule with the consent of his citizens, that is, over citizens who voluntarily uphold his rule? I think it does not, and that, in principle anyhow, the Visitor's earlier use of the criterion of rule by force vs. voluntary rule does not establish any inconsistency between what he said then and what he now goes on to say about kingly rule.

To see this, one must keep in mind the distinction I drew above between the simple point that it is knowledge, not consent or anything else, that establishes the correctness and justice of the knowledgeable ruler's rule, and

---

a city (see 301e2–4, cf. 300c4–6). So the existence of a group of "political orators" under the expert statesman's rule does not mean that there will be any politics of negotiation, and so forth, of the sort familiar to us and to Plato's contemporaries. Nonetheless, the provision for a process of explanation and reasoned persuasion is no small recognition of the importance in the expert statesman's city of a politics that involves the citizens actively in understanding and supporting in a spirit of independence the laws and other rules under which they live.

[36] Compare 276e7–8 τῷ βιαίῳ τε καὶ ἑκουσίῳ with 291e1 πρὸς τὸ βίαιόν που καὶ ἑκούσιον ἀποσκοποῦντες. Rowe translates the same word ἑκούσιον in the first passage as "voluntary" but as "consent" in the second.

the question how that knowledge will make him think it is best to exercise his rule. We have seen from what follows later in the dialogue that the Visitor does believe that expert knowledge itself will lead to kingly or states-manly rule that is in fact exercised on citizens who are willingly and volunta-rily governed by it. The expert ruler will make arrangements for his citizens to be brought up in virtue and to participate in government to the extent of meeting in the assembly to exercise their judgment in coming to under-stand and so to approve of governmental actions. The ruler will make these arrangements because, as he will correctly judge, the good of the people itself, which is his controlling aim, demands it. Thus the legitimacy and justice of the expert statesman's rule does not depend upon the fact that it is exercised with the consent of the people, if the requirement of consent is thought of as some principle of right imposed from outside upon the ruler's otherwise legitimate freedom of action. But because the ruler's expert knowl-edge itself establishes this as the correct and just way to rule, at least under normally achievable circumstances, that is how he *will* rule (if circum-stances permit).

However, at 296b5–c3 the Visitor provocatively compares the expert ruler to the expert steersman or physician. He insists that steersman and physician do not in any way depart from their expertise if they use force to get their clients to do what their steersman's or physician's knowledge tells them they ought to do. The only criterion for the correctness of what a physician, as such, does is that it conform to the rules of the art of medicine: if a doctor "does not persuade his patient" but "forces" him or her "to do what is better," such use of force cannot correctly be called an "unhealthy mistake contrary to the expertise in question," nor can it be said that the patient has "had unhealthy things done to him by the doctors who used force on him."[37] Correspondingly, the Visitor says, if an expert ruler "forces

---

[37] Strikingly, the Visitor neglects here to observe the distinction the Athenian draws in the *Laws* (see IV, 720aff.) between two types of what are called physicians, the true experts who know medicine in a properly systematic way and their "assistants" (*hupēretai*, 720a7)—inferior rote-workers who have no systematic knowledge. According to the *Laws* account, the true physician exercises his art mostly on free persons, and therefore with explanations and persua-sion as to what he is ordering, not by the use of force: "he gives no prescription until he has somehow gained the patient's consent, and then continually uses persuasion to gain his cooperation as he tries to complete his restoration to health" (720d6–e2). The rote-workers are suited to treat slaves, with whom force and not persuasion is the accepted way to proceed. Plainly, if the Visitor had observed this distinction, he could not have insisted so blankly as he does on the total disconnection of the physician's expertise from the use of persuasion. On the other hand, what the Visitor actually says remains true: even if for the sorts of reasons given in the *Laws* a physician ought (as a matter of professional principle) not use force on his free patients, one who unnecessarily forces a pill on a patient, when medical knowledge indicates that the patient needs to take it, does not do anything unhealthy to him—and, strictly speaking, that is all the Visitor maintains. If I am right about the overall point he wishes to make with this comparison, the Visitor is not recommending the use of force, either for physicians or for political rulers, nor is he indifferent to it. His point is that expert rulers will work to make it possible always to rule with persuasion and consent, and he presumably

through what is better without the use of persuasion" (296b1), even if what he does is a plain violation of his own previously written law, it cannot be said (sc., merely *on that ground*) that "those who have been forced have had shameful, unjust, and bad things done to them by those who did the forcing" (296d3–4). Now when this whole topic of force and disregard for law is first introduced, the Visitor remarks (296a7–9) that *people say* that "if someone recognizes laws that are better, contrary to those established by people before him, then he must introduce them by persuading his city to accept them in each case, but not otherwise." Young Socrates, as he does two other times in this part of the dialogue,[38] takes the initiative here and expresses agreement with this view of how politics should proceed: "Well then? Is that not a correct view?" It is often overlooked, but is again significant, I think, that the Visitor's answer is not "No," or even "Let us see," but "Perhaps. But first things first . . ." He then proceeds with the account I summarized just above, of what really does constitute the correct basis— namely the possession of knowledge—on which just behavior in a ruler rests: this account constitutes the "first things" that need to be considered before we can give a clear and adequate response to the question whether a person must bring in new laws by persuading his city to accept them, and not otherwise. The Visitor's careful response here is an indication on Plato's part, I am sure, that once all the proper distinctions are in place and properly applied it really does turn out that under expert rule laws will not simply be overridden and violated, but the new ones needed to replace now-defective ones will be brought before the people for their understanding and acceptance, before they are promulgated and before what they authorize is put into effect. This may not be what expert rule demands under all circumstances, but rule of this sort is what expert rule itself aims at and knows how to achieve under most circumstances.

There is more about Plato's view of politics in the *Statesman* to be culled from this section of the dialogue. In particular there is the question of what principles and practices of government are required by justice, that is, by the demand that knowledge shall so far as possible be in command, in case no expert at ruling is actually present in a city. I do not discuss those issues here. But I hope to have shown that under circumstances of ideal justice, where an expert statesman *is* present, the Visitor does not think that the expert's rule will be kingly in the traditional sense that I outlined at the beginning of the chapter—dictatorial and without allowing scope for any

---

thinks the same for physicians too (though he does not make a point of that). In either case, force will be used only when circumstances do not permit persuasion. Even on the Visitor's account of medical knowledge, use of persuasion remains the norm.

[38] See also 292a9, 293e 6–7. In these passages, as at 296a10, Young Socrates shows an independence of mind that is not prominent elsewhere in the dialogue, and each time it is to express approval of some customary Greek idea about what makes for acceptable politics that we too would think had real merit. There is a creative tension at all three places between Young Socrates and the Visitor.

independence of action among the citizens themselves, that is to say, without providing for any real politics at all. Once we reach the end of the dialogue and work out and absorb all its lessons, we see that the starting point of the whole process—the simple, invalidly argued principle that expertise at kingly and at statesmanly rule are the same thing—actually harbors a significant *downgrading* of the king, if the latter is conceived in this traditional way. The king is assimilated to the statesman, not the other way about.[39]

APPENDIX

EXPERTISES SUBORDINATE TO STATESMANSHIP

A. *"Contributory Causes" (287c–289c)*

1. Toolmaking (287d)
   (Includes all of weaving's "contributory" causes)
2. Vessel-making (287e–288a)
3. Conveyance-making (288a)
4. "Defence"-making (clothes-making, house-building, city-wall-making, etc.) (288b) (Includes weaving and all its "co-causing" subordinate expertises)
5. Provision of arts and amusements (288c)
6. Provision of natural materials to be used in the other crafts (288d–e)
7. Provision and management of food and its proper assimilation (288e–289a) (Includes physicians and gymnastic trainers, farmers, millers, and bakers: cf. 267e7ff.)

[Cowherding etc. have already been separated off in the initial division (289b–c)]

B. *Further "Contributory Causes" (289c–290d)*

8.1 Working as a slave (289d)
8.2 Merchanting, retailing, money-changing, shipping (290a)
    (Includes merchants: cf. 267e7ff.)
8.3 Working as a day laborer for hire (290a)
8.4 Working as a herald, or secretary or subofficial to state officeholders (290b)
8.5 Prophesying or divination or other interpretation of the gods' wishes etc. for human beings (290c)
8.6 Working as a priest, in making sacrifices to and begging things from the gods (290d)
    (Suggests thought of the King-*archon* at Athens, and other magistrates . . .)

---

[39] I thank Christopher Bobonich for helpful comments and suggestions on an early version of this chapter, and Phillip Mitsis and Gisela Striker for their useful questions and comments on the occasion of its presentation at the Boston Colloquium for Ancient Philosophy meeting at Harvard on October 24, 1996. I am particularly grateful to Christopher Rowe, who read the penultimate version anonymously for the *Proceedings of the Boston Area Colloquium in Ancient Philosophy* and prepared a set of extremely helpful comments and queries; I was able to improve my discussion significantly through attempting to respond.

C. "Causes" (303d–311c)

9. Political oratory (304b–e)
10. Generalship (304e–305a)
11. Expertise as a judge (305b–c)
12. Public Educators (308d4–6)
[13. Others unspecified? (311a)]

PART TWO

Aristotle

CHAPTER EIGHT

The *Magna Moralia* and Aristotle's Moral Philosophy

IT HAS BEEN NEARLY FIFTEEN years since Franz Dirlmeier published his defense of the authenticity of the *Magna Moralia*.[1] Reviews of the work were not numerous.[2] Nor can it be said that published discussions of Dirlmeier's views have provided the critical evaluation of his arguments and conclusions that the importance of the subject certainly demands.[3] For, obviously, if Dirlmeier is right, and the *Magna Moralia*, at any rate in content, is the work of Aristotle himself, composed earlier than either of the other two extant expositions of his moral philosophy, we have in this work an extremely valuable tool for tracing out Aristotle's philosophical development, as also for the interpretation and evaluation of his moral philosophy itself.

The importance of the *Magna Moralia* in this latter connection deserves emphasis, since it tends to go unmarked by most non-philosophical scholars, Dirlmeier included. First, on some issues the simpler treatment found in the *Magna Moralia* presents more adequately a basic insight which the other, more elaborate treatments tend to obscure;[4] these insights can be claimed

---

[1] See his translation with commentary, *Aristoteles: Magna Moralia* (1958).

[2] I know of only one full serious review, that by Düring in *Gnomon*. Only three other reviews seem to have appeared, by Gigon, C. Fabro, and P. Pédech, none of which is very searching. (Pédech, drawing no distinction between Dirlmeier's views in his commentary and the argument of his 1939 article, attributes to him belief in a second-century date for the *Magna Moralia*!) In addition D. J. Allan devotes part of his review of Dirlmeier's commentary on the *Eudemian Ethics* (see pp. 142–43) to a rebuttal of some of Dirlmeier's claims for the *Magna Moralia*. Gigon and Allan do not, while Düring does, accept Dirlmeier's thesis of the substantial authenticity of the work. See also Düring's *Aristoteles*, 438–44.

[3] Treatments of Dirlmeier's views on the *Magna Moralia* occur in Gigon, "Die Sokratesdoxographie bei Aristoteles" (esp. 192ff.); Merlan, *Studies in Epicurus and Aristotle*, 83–93; and Karl Bärthlein, "Ὀρθὸς λόγος". Pier Luigi Donini, in his dissertation, *L'Etica dei Magna Moralia* deals often and in detail with Dirlmeier's interpretations of particular points; he accepts somewhat mechanically the traditional view of the work's authenticity, but regards it (pp. 222–25) more as an independent work by an aristotelizing Hellenistic writer than as in any sense a commentary on or condensation of the two Aristotelian *Ethics*. This is certainly an improvement over the older version of the traditional view, but seems, as will be clear from what I say below, sect. II, an inadequate theory for many passages of the *MM*.

[4] Thus *MM* 1.16 comes closer to recognizing the importance of intention in determining responsibility than the elaborated, but negative, treatment in *Nicomachean Ethics* 3.1. Likewise the account of the "final good" in *MM* 1.2 is a necessary supplement to *Nic. Eth.*'s much less straightforward and distinct treatment. Again *MM* 2.7.1204b4–1205a6 gives a much clearer version of Aristotle's rebuttal of Speusippus' doctrine that pleasure is a γένεσις ("becoming") than *Eudemian Ethics* 6.12 (= *Nic. Eth.* 7.12) 1152b33ff. does. (Though the difficulty of the latter version is not caused by overelaboration.) The exposition of the theory of the three types

for Aristotle, if the treatise is genuine, and used to bring into clearer focus the theories of the other ethical writings. Secondly, in several instances the *Magna Moralia* includes discussions of important and difficult points never explicitly faced in the other treatises: the most noteworthy instance of this is the discussion of the question what to do in case the rules of two virtues dictate conflicting actions in a particular situation (*MM* 2.3.1199b36–1200a11).[5] Thirdly, where the *Magna Moralia* differs in doctrine from either of the other treatises the exact determination of the differences, if they can be presumed to be due to Aristotle himself, always throws interesting new light on the theories and arguments of the other version. Thus the *Magna Moralia* (1.33.1193b24–30) explains justice as a mean between getting more and getting less than one's share. If the treatise is genuine then its account of justice both serves to explain the occasional half-survival of the same view in *Eudemian Ethics* 4 (= *Nicomachean* 5) and to point up the nature and degree of Aristotle's later achievement in getting beyond such a restricted understanding of justice (on this see further below, section II). Again, the fact that the *Magna Moralia* consistently, clearly and repeatedly (1184a29–38, b33–39 with 1204a26–29, 1185a25–26, 36–39, 1208b3–6) maintains a unified conception of *eudaimonia* as consisting, without discrimination, of the exercise of both the moral and the intellectual virtues, cannot but throw important new light on the related theories of the *Nicomachean* and *Eudemian Ethics*.[6]

In all these ways then, as well perhaps as others,[7] the *Magna Moralia* is a very important document for scholars and philosophers interested in

---

of friendship in *MM* 1208b36–1209a36 has important implications for the origin of the theory (cf. esp. 1208b10ff.) which help to bring the theories of *EE* and *Nic. Eth.* into better focus.

[5] The other four problems discussed in *MM* 2.3.1199a14ff. are of varying interest. But they and the opening chapters of the treatise (1.1–3), which discuss various ways a thing can be good and to which nothing quite corresponds in the other treatises, should not be overlooked by any student of Aristotle's moral philosophy.

[6] I think something similar should be said about the *MM*'s well-known emphasis on ὁρμαὶ φυσικαί (natural impulses) and φυσικὴ ἀρετή (natural virtue) as necessary presupposition for the acquisition of moral virtue (1198a8–9). I believe careful reflection will show that the *Nic. Eth.*'s theory of virtue is incompatible with this thesis. The notion of φυσικὴ ἀρετή appears in the *Nic. Eth.* only in books 6 and 7, which are also *Eudemian* books, and even there (1144b1ff.) Aristotle does not make it, or ὁρμαὶ φυσικαί, a *necessary presupposition* of (complete) moral virtue.

[7] Dirlmeier (commentary on *EE*, pp. 366–67, 492–93, 497–98) revives the view of Spengel, *Ethischen Schriften*, 499–503) and von Arnim (*Die drei aristotelischen Ethiken*, p. 96, and "Echtheit," 114–15), that the present concluding chapters of the *EE*, 8.1–3, in fact have been misplaced in our MSS. from the end of book 6, and that therefore *EE*, like *MM*, concluded with the treatment of friendship. His and their chief argument is that the corresponding chapters of *MM* (2.7.1206a36–2.10) do precede the treatment of friendship. Dirlmeier's motive for wanting to make this adjustment is apparently to underscore the truth that *EE* 8.3 is not to be interpreted as the counterpiece to *Nic. Eth.* 10.6–8, with its intellectualist revision of the definition of εὐδαιμονία. This motive I applaud; though the truth in question is not made doubtful by reading these chapters where they stand. But so far as I can see they cannot have preceded book 7, since at 8.3.1249a17–18 Aristotle refers back to the argument of book 7.2.

understanding Aristotle's moral philosophy—*if* it is, in fact, Aristotle's work. In this paper I will try to show, mostly by considering the philosophical content of the work, that the *Magna Moralia* can only be plausibly interpreted as, in substance at any rate, the work of Aristotle, representing an earlier stage in the development of his moral philosophy than either the *Eudemian* or the *Nicomachean Ethics*. In this I agree with Dirlmeier. But as I am not persuaded by his treatment of the more narrowly philological grounds on which scholars have tended to reject the treatise, I first indicate what I take to be the main inadequacies of Dirlmeier's views on the date and method of composition of the work. But though Dirlmeier does not, in my judgment, adequately meet the philological grounds of objection to the treatise, these objections can be very largely disarmed, and I will suggest a way in which this can be done. My hope is that once it is seen clearly that the state of our text does not require, or even strongly suggest, the inference that someone other than Aristotle is the author of the *Magna Moralia*, the arguments from its content which I advance in section II will then be admitted to weigh the balance strongly in favor of its Aristotelian origin.

I

A large part of Dirlmeier's commentary (which, with its introduction, runs to three hundred and eighty-odd pages) is devoted to rebutting the charges that have been made against the *Magna Moralia*'s authenticity. The grounds of objection have chiefly fallen into four groups. (1) Matters of language and style in which the *Magna Moralia* seems to diverge sharply from the admittedly genuine works; (2) a few personal and other references allegedly pointing toward a post-Aristotelian date; (3) supposed Stoic influences in terminology and doctrine; (4) a general impression, very strong in a few relatively isolated passages, that the author of the *Magna Moralia* wrote with the *Eudemian* and *Nicomachean Ethics* open before him, excerpting, condensing and abbreviating so as to produce a kind of handbook of Aristotelian moral theory.[8] Dirlmeier, following von Arnim, shows, I think, that the passages which have been thought to betray Stoic influence do not do so.[9] What he says on the other heads, however, is open to serious objection in several ways.

1235b30ff.—an argument, indeed, found nowhere else in the Corpus. Dirlmeier's invention (*EE*, p. 497–98) of a passage for *EE* 6 in which the same thing was said is gratuitous at best.

[8] I omit mention of Jaeger's claim ("Ein Theophrastzitat" that the *MM* cites Theophrastus at 1198b9–20. This claim was always suppositious, and Dirlmeier disposes of it effectively (pp. 354–56).

[9] See, for example, pp. 439; 202–5, 257–58, 349–50; 268–69; 291 (not that everything he says is correct, or that more might not be said). Dirlmeier is also right (pp. 118–19, 423) to reject Tennemann's objections to the *MM*'s "moralistic" conception of god at 1207a6–17.

To begin with, the view he adopts about the *Magna Moralia*'s peculiarities of language and style is strained and dubious in itself and hardly consistent with his treatment of some of the personal references.[10] Dirlmeier recognizes, as he must, that the *Magna Moralia* was not written down in its present form by Aristotle. His strategy, however, is to reduce the influence of Aristotle's "editor"[11] to the minimum, viz., to "externals" of language.[12] Stylistic peculiarities he hopes to account for in another way. The treatise has always struck readers as pedantic and schoolmasterly, consisting as it does of discussions for the most part simply strung together, without much attempt at large-scale composition, and with frequent personal and quasi-dramatic touches, such as references to the author in the first person singular, use of second person singular where Aristotle more normally uses impersonal τις, introduction of objections by personifying the counterargument or by a subjectless "he says," and such practices as beginning an explanation or defense of a thesis by *dia ti*? ("And why so? Because . . ."). These, and other such, peculiarities Dirlmeier seeks to explain partly by the idea that the *Magna Moralia* is an early work, composed by the young logician Aristotle in the style of the *Topics*,[13] and partly by the unfalsifiable but rather desperate hypothesis that the *Magna Moralia*, unlike the other treatises, preserves Aristotle's actual classroom style.

By emphasizing its affinities to the *Topics* (and other early logical works) Dirlmeier commits himself to a date for the work perhaps as early as the early 350's and certainly not later than about 350.[14] But this is hardly compatible with the reference (1197b22) to Mentor, the man who betrayed Aristotle's friend Hermeias to the Persian king; this, as Dirlmeier recognizes in passing (see his comment ad loc.) could not have been written before about 342 at the earliest. And similarly the passage (1205a23) referring to Neleus, son of the exemplary Coriscus, can hardly have been written before about 340 and perhaps dates from considerably later.[15] Dirlmeier also runs into difficulties over the reference (2.15.1212b23ff.) to, and implied defense of, the doctrine of god as self-thinker. For since he accepts a late date for *Metaphysics* Λ (XII), he must, most implausibly, imagine the reference not

---

[10] Düring has also noticed this incongruence (review, pp. 552, 557).

[11] So Dirlmeier, without adequate discussion, characterizes the interloper. See below, pp. 199 ff.

[12] It should be acknowledged that Praechter (*Philosophie*, p. 370 n. 1) and Theiler, *Die Großen Ethik* anticipated Dirlmeier in arguing for the independent Aristotelian origin of the content of the *MM*, while allowing the actual writing to have been done by someone else.

[13] This he thinks accounts for the serial ordering of arguments and some of the dryness of exposition. I find his arguments from the supposed affinity of *MM* to *Topics* (itself much overstated) extremely dubious: see below, beginning of sect. II.

[14] For this dating of the *Topics* see Düring, *Aristotle's Protrepticus*, p. 287.

[15] On Mentor and Neleus see Düring, review, p. 552, as well as Dirlmeier ad loc. (Dirlmeier accepts Wilamowitz's correction of the manuscripts at 1205a23: see Wilamowitz, "Neleus von Skepsis.")

to be to Aristotle's own argument in Λ but to an otherwise entirely unknown Academic pre-cursor.[16] The *Metaphysics* reference will cause no difficulty if, as I am inclined to believe in any case, (the main body of) Λ is an early work.[17] But the other two passages pose considerable obstacles to Dirlmeier's defense of the *Magna Moralia*: at the very least, if the treatise was composed before about 350 then some special explanation must be provided for the occurrence of the references to Mentor and Neleus. But Dirlmeier seems not to have even noticed the discrepancy.

Thus Dirlmeier's treatment of the stylistic peculiarities of the treatise is both unconvincing in itself and at variance with his way of handling the references to Mentor and Neleus. He is no more convincing in what he says about the linguistic oddities of the work. As noted above, Dirlmeier maintains that the "editor" who prepared Aristotle's manuscript for publication limited himself to providing some of the "externals" of language in which to clothe Aristotle's thoughts (p. 147). At one place, indeed, Dirlmeier goes to the extreme of claiming that the "editor" betrays his presence *only* in his preference for *huper* with genitive where Aristotle would write *peri* (p. 185)! In fact, however, on Dirlmeier's own account elsewhere, un-Aristotelian language is much more prevalent than that in the treatise. Thus the use of *to holon* as adverb (meaning "in general," "on the whole") is, at least given its frequency in this work, certainly un-Aristotelian (cf. Dirlmeier's comment, p. 156). There is also the remarkable fact, noted by Dirlmeier on p. 158, that Ionic forms of *oida* (to know) are not merely frequent in the *Magna Moralia*, but the only ones used at all. And other less striking usages might be cited as well.

When the number and pervasiveness of these linguistic peculiarities is taken properly into account, I think Dirlmeier's hypothesis of an "editor" who published Aristotle's own lecture notes with a few light alterations of language is untenable. The very mention of an *editor* who not only touches and patches here and there, but regularly supplies some of the *prepositions* and *adverbs* is really quite suspect. No other work of Aristotle, all of which, one supposes, were at least lightly edited, shows any such features. How *did* it happen that the supposed original Aristotelian manuscript of the *Magna Moralia*, and it alone, underwent such treatment? Dirlmeier attempts no answer and no plausible one suggests itself.

The very least that one must infer from these facts about the language in which the treatise is written is that if it contains Aristotle's own notes put out by someone else, this man was no mere editor. He must have worked from an original text which was very incomplete, since he found it necessary to write at many places *huper* where Aristotle, if he had written up the same

---

[16] Cf. Merlan, *Studies*, and Düring, review, pp. 550–51.

[17] In fact if *MM* is authentic and an early work, the appearance of the reference to *Metaph.* Λ becomes a very strong additional argument in favor of an early date for Λ.

materials, would have written *peri*, and his own idiom shows also, as I have noted, in other ways throughout the work. But if the materials were incomplete enough to require the "editor" to compose many of the actual sentences in his own words, there must have been plenty of opportunity, and perhaps in some cases actual need, for him to fill out the argument here and there, both by adding examples and in other ways. Once you admit, as Dirlmeier reluctantly does, and as one must, that the work was actually written out in someone else's words than Aristotle's, you must expect to find *some* substantive intrusions in the text, so that Dirlmeier's insistence on the total authenticity of the work's contents would in any case have to be tempered. (So the simplest hypothesis, I should think, by which Dirlmeier could reconcile his early date for the *Magna Moralia* with references in the text to Neleus and Mentor would be to suppose that these were added later by the "editor".)[18] If, then, our text originated in a manuscript of Aristotle's own, we must reckon with the strong probability that this manuscript was very incomplete and has been considerably filled out by whoever prepared it for publication.

It is of course possible for all we are likely ever to know, that this is how our text came into being. But there is a simpler and more natural way, on the hypothesis of the substantial authenticity of the *Magna Moralia*'s contents, of accounting for all the genuinely un-Aristotelian aspects of style and language found in the treatise, without indulging in conjectures about an Aristotelian manuscript whose condition might have seemed to call for just the sort of expansion we seem to find in the *Magna Moralia*. This is by the supposition that the *Magna Moralia* is a student's published notes of a course of Aristotle's, not based on any Aristotelian manuscript but on what he actually heard Aristotle say. Editing, if any, would be of his own old notes, not Aristotle's. In setting down his notes originally he would naturally have written partly in his own idiom and style; in preparing them for publication, or for his own later use in lectures, he could easily have added the examples of Neleus and Mentor, and perhaps filled out the notes in other ways. In this way all the linguistic facts could be plausibly accounted for and such facts as the appearance of the references to Mentor and Neleus easily accommodated. I need not claim that this hypothesis *does* correctly explain the genesis of our *Magna Moralia*; it is enough to point out that, in advance of a study of the treatise's contents, this possibility stands completely open, and is in itself no less believable than the generally current hypothesis of a post-Aristotelian author who worked primarily from Aristotelian sources known to us independently of his version.

---

[18] This is a better guess than Düring's supposition (review, p. 557) that Theophrastus (or someone) added them on the occasion of his reading Aristotle's notes to a beginning ethics class in the Lyceum. Does Düring then suppose also that Theophrastus (or whoever) was identical with Dirlmeier's "editor?"

II

But is the substance of the treatise Aristotle's own work, rather than a pastiche of the other *Ethics*? Dirlmeier here does what one must do, namely read right through the work testing each section to see how it compares with the corresponding passages, if any, in the other treatises. I think there is no doubt that he proves the insufficiency of the standard view, that the *Magna Moralia* has its origin in a condensation and distillation of the *Eudemian Ethics* or of the *Eudemian* and *Nicomachean* both. There are in fact only two fairly brief passages where in organization and argument the *Magna Moralia* "follows" the *Nicomachean* in preference to the *Eudemian*.[19] Elsewhere the affinities are all to the *Eudemian*. But I agree with Dirlmeier that no one who reads the *Magna Moralia* carefully and sensitively, noticing and understanding the points of divergence in form, organization, and argument, can believe that it derives directly from the *written text* of either or both of the other *Ethics*. Dirlmeier is not, however, always careful enough to distinguish this kind of independence, which he amply establishes, from that kind of independence he wishes to prove: that of a work composed without knowledge of the others, and by the same author. For, even if the *Magna Moralia* is thus textually independent, it might still have been composed as a handbook of Aristotelian moral philosophy by someone other than Aristotle: the author might have learned his philosophy from reading (or hearing) the *Eudemian Ethics*, and then composed his handbook without consulting the texts as he went along. Dirlmeier repeatedly emphasizes that Aristotle himself wrote the *Nicomachean Ethics* without working directly from the text of the *Eudemian*: why should not a second party have done the same in the *Magna Moralia*?

To prove its Aristotelian authorship Dirlmeier relies principally on matters of form and language. In the first place, there is the alleged affinity, already mentioned, to the *Topics* and other logical works: he calls the *Magna Moralia* "Ethica logice demonstrata" (p. 175), and says it is composed *more topico* (p. 205), "with the logical interest" predominating. It seems to me highly questionable whether anything much can be made of these claims. The *Topics* consists for the most part of somewhat disjoint analyses of modes of argument, because its interest is predominantly in the *form* of valid and invalid arguments of a very wide range of types. The interest is in the study of the arguments themselves, and not so much in any large-scale *theory* of arguments; hence, the disjointedness, serial order, etc. In the *Magna Moralia*

---

[19] 1.5.1185b13–9.1187a4 (corresponding roughly to *Nic. Eth.* 2), and 2.13–14 (1212a28–b23) (on the sense in which the good man loves himself, corresponding to *Nic. Eth.* 9.8). How comes it that *MM*, the earliest ethics, deals with these matters in a way which in the end (*Nic. Eth.*) Aristotle finds on the whole satisfactory, while yet during the interim (*EE*) he sees fit to alter his treatment quite considerably? Dirlmeier doesn't even face the question squarely. See below, p. 210 f.

the predominant interest is in any case in the *content* of the arguments, such interest in form as there is being simply that of the self-respecting philosopher concerned for the validity of his reasoning.[20] So the disjointedness here certainly does not have the same causes. Nor does Dirlmeier cite any reason to expect a man in turning from work on a handbook on dialectical argumentation to lecturing, or composing a book on ethics, to treat this new and different subject matter in a somewhat similar handbook style. Hence such affinities as there may be to the *Topics* provide no strong argument in favor of Aristotelian authorship.

On the other hand, Dirlmeier also emphasizes many matters of linguistic usage, and small matters of style, of which some link the *Magna Moralia* to the logical works, some to Plato and the Academy. These observations, spread through his commentary, are varyingly impressive;[21] but my own sense is that cumulatively they are not sufficient to settle the question of authorship. The author, if not Aristotle, might himself have spent time at the Academy, perhaps while Aristotle was a member, thus picking up mannerisms, distinctions, etc., linking him to the Academy in general and to the Aristotle of the *Organon* in particular.

Thus, while one must attach some weight to considerations of language and style, further arguments are clearly needed. Such arguments can only be founded on the philosophical content of the work. Dirlmeier does on occasion take note of philosophical divergences which can plausibly be explained on the theory that the *Magna Moralia* presents less mature Aristotelian doctrine,[22] but he seems to shy away from such judgments (perhaps on the ground that they are too "subjective"). Certainly judgments of this kind are frequently inconclusive; but often, also, they are not. I think there are many passages of the *Magna Moralia* of which "immaturity" of doctrine is an extremely plausible explanation[23]—and a much more plausible one

---

[20] It is, in any case, rather the *EE* than the *MM* which betrays in its mode of exposition Aristotle the young logician: the emphasis on ὑποθέσεις and deduction which marks that work (cf. Allan, "Quasi-mathematical method in the *Eudemian Ethics*") is surely to be interpreted as the application of the *Posterior Analytics'* theory of scientific reasoning to the subject matter of ethics—as the *De Caelo* is its application to cosmology.

[21] Among the most interesting are the formulary resemblances between doctrines in *MM* (and *EE*) and the Academic *Definitions*: cf. pp. 104, 215, etc.; noteworthy, too, is the *MM*'s listing (1185b5–6) of ἀγχίνοια, εὐμάθεια and μνήμη (quick wit, cleverness, memory) as intellectual virtues: as Dirlmeier rightly observes (p. 207) these are repeatedly referred to as virtues by Plato, but are not listed in *EE* 5 (= *Nic. Eth.* 6), while again they turn up in the *Definitions*.

[22] Most notably with respect to the shifting uncertainty of the *MM* as to whether the intellectual virtues, to which however, it never refuses to grant the title of "virtue," are grounds of praise: pp. 208–9, 345–46, 352–53.

[23] I list just a few of the most important of these: 1184a8–14 (definition of τέλειον [complete], which, as the context [a3–38] shows, covers what in *Nic. Eth.* is divided between τέλειον and αὔταρκες [self-sufficient]); 1188b18–24 (what are called in *Nic. Eth.* 3.1 μικταὶ πράξεις [mixed actions]—the conception though not the name is prominent also in *EE*, cf. 1225a1–33—are, without comment, treated as ἀκούσια [involuntary]); 1193b10–18 ("legal justice" is not πρὸς ἕτερον [in relation to another], which contradicts *EE* 4 [*Nic. Eth.* 5] 1129b25–27; but the

than the alternative, that someone whose knowledge of Aristotle's teachings was drawn from the *Eudemian* and/or *Nicomachean Ethics*, wittingly or unwittingly, made alterations of the kind we find in *Magna Moralia*. Indeed, in two cases I think it can be practically demonstrated that this explanation is correct. When one adds the fact that the author himself claims to be Aristotle, by referring to the *Analytics'* doctrine of the syllogism as his own (1201b25), I think the matter is settled.

The two passages I think are decisive are 1.1.1182b6–1183b8, the critique of an abstract or universal Good, and 1.33, on justice.

All three of the ethical treatises insist that ethics, as a practical and not a merely theoretical inquiry, ought to concern itself only with concrete questions about the good of human beings, and not at all with whatever more universal or abstract goods there may be. In the *Nicomachean Ethics* (1.6) the sole object of attack and rejection is the Platonic Form of the Good, against which Aristotle argues both that there isn't any such thing and that if there were ethics should take no account of it. In the *Eudemian Ethics* (1.8) the chief focus of the discussion is again on the Platonic theory, and these same two points are again made (1217b16–23, 25–1218a32, as against 1217b23–25, 1218a33–38), but there is in addition a brief section (1218a38–b6) dealing separately with the claims for attention of something called *to koinon agathon*, "the common good." We are evidently (cf. 1218a8–15, *MM* 1182b12–14) to understand this as what all good things are supposed to have in common, regarded now *not* as something separated apart from those good things (as a Platonic Form would be) but had or possessed in common by each of them equally: in short, good regarded as a proper universal instead of as a Form. In the *Magna Moralia* interest in the "common good" (introduced as *to koinon en hapasin huparchon agathon*, 1182b11–12) expands to such an extent that it dominates the discussion (1182b10–1183a24), while the Platonic theory is relegated to a relatively brief final section (1183a24–b8); and though the main arguments are significantly different from those in the *Eudemian* and *Nicomachean Ethics*, it is only against the common good, and not against the Form, that the author makes any of the points made in the other treatises (cf. 1183a7–23 with *EE* 1217b35–41, *Nic. Eth.* 1096a29–34).

This altered main interest of the *Magna Moralia* is certainly not easily explained as the work of a post-Aristotelian. For, among other reasons, Aristotle's mature theory makes the claim that "good" is said in all the categories grounds for treating it as a word not of one but of many senses. On this view there cannot *be* anything which all good things as such have in common, so that the idea of a *koinon agathon* must be regarded as empty. On this the *Eudemian* (1217b25–35) and the *Nicomachean Ethics*

---

later version has, by deeper reflection, discovered a different and important way in which "legal justice" is πρὸς ἕτερον); 1208b36–1209a36 (the theory of the three εἴδη or forms of friendship is developed in the course of treating an ἀπορία and not simply announced as in *Nic. Eth.* 1155b18–19, and in effect, in *EE* 1236a16).

(1096a23–29) agree.[24] This is why the *Nicomachean* does not even mention a *koinon agathon* other than the Platonic Form, and why the *Eudemian* treats it only in passing and as subsidiary to the Form. Why then does a supposed post-Aristotelian writer take such a strong and independent interest in the unhypostatized *koinon agathon*? One might, of course, invent a controversy among Aristotle's successors on this point for the *Magna Moralia* to be engaged in, but for this there is no warrant. In fact close study of the texts shows that special interest in a non-Platonic *koinon agathon* marks a stage of Aristotle's *own* thinking, a stage *earlier* than that of the *Eudemian Ethics*. It follows that the *Magna Moralia*, which betrays this interest, reports Aristotle's argumentation at that earlier time.

It is well known that in his essay *On Ideas* Aristotle rebutted the Platonists' argument "from the sciences" (*Metaph.* A9, 990b12) by pointing out that even if this argument proves there are things besides particulars, it does not prove there are Forms: for "there are besides particulars the things they have in common (*ta koina*), which *we* maintain are the objects of the sciences."[25] This theory of *koina* as an alternative to Platonic hypostatization, appears also in the logical works;[26] and it is plainly about *koina* in this Aristotelian sense that the *Magna Moralia* is speaking when it says: ἕτερον γὰρ τῆς ἰδέας τοῦτο δόξειεν ἂν εἶναι. ἡ μὲν ἰδέα χωριστὸν καὶ αὐτὸ καθ' αὑτό, τὸ δὲ κοινὸν ἐν ἅπασιν ὑπάρχει: This would seem to be different from the Form; for the Form is separate and itself by itself, while the "common" belongs to them all (1182b12–14). So the suggestion that political science must in the first instance get to know *to koinon agathon* amounts to the claim both that there is a *koinon* in this Aristotelian sense in the case of "good," and that political science must study it.

In the *Nicomachean* and *Eudemian Ethics* the corresponding suggestion about the Form is disposed of in two stages: as noted above, Aristotle argues first that there is no such object of study, and secondly that even if there were it would not help the political scientist, or any other specialist, to know about it.[27] The *Magna Moralia*, however, argues only that political scientists must not concern themselves with the *koinon agathon* (nor with the Platonic

---

[24] Even if ἀγαθόν is treated as a πρὸς ἕν λεγόμενον (a term with "focal meaning") (cf. Owen, "Logic and metaphysics in some earlier works of Aristotle," esp. p. 180) it remains true that the word has many senses, with no common definition covering all its instances. So that the later reservations of the *Nic. Eth.* (1096b26–31) do not affect this point.

[25] Alexander of Aphrodisias, *in Metaph.* 79.17–19, citing the Περὶ Ἰδεῶν (cf. 79.5): ἔστι γὰρ παρὰ τὰ καθ' ἕκαστα τὰ κοινά, ὧν φαμεν καὶ τὰς ἐπιστήμας εἶναι.

[26] E.g., *Soph. Ref.* 178b36ff., as a solution to the Third Man; cf. *Metaph.* 3.6.1003a8–12, 7.13.1039a1–3.

[27] *EE* states this program explicitly (1217b19–25), and *Nic. Eth.* plainly follows it implicitly (1096a17–b31 on existence, b31–1097a14 on usefulness). At 1218a37–b1 *EE* apparently means to affirm the corresponding two points about a nonseparated κοινόν (so also Allan interprets: "Aristotle's Criticism of Platonic Doctrine concerning Goodness," 277): in any case it certainly follows from what is argued at 1217b22–35 (cf. ὥσπερ οὖν οὐδὲ τὸ ὂν ἕν τι ἐστι περὶ τὰ εἰρημένα, οὕτως οὐδὲ τὸ ἀγαθόν, b33–34) that there is no κοινὸν ἀγαθόν.

Form), without denying the existence of any *koinon agathon*, whether "separated" or not. In fact, the *Magna Moralia* has no qualms about actually stating the common definition of "good" (1182b20–21); whereas the argument of the two *Ethics* clearly implies that there is no such definition. *Magna Moralia* is content to deny to political science any need to be concerned with it, while yet affirming its existence. The principal argument of the *Eudemian* and *Nicomachean Ethics* against its existence, that because "good" is said in all the categories it must have so many different senses, is not even adumbrated anywhere in the *Magna Moralia*. It is true that the claim is made (1183a9–10) that "good" is said in all the categories, but this thesis is put to a quite different use. The argument here (1183a7–23)[28] is that even in a single category, like that of time, what is good is not the subject of a single science; rather the doctor knows when is a good time for an operation, and the pilot when is a good time to sail, and so on. If then in *each* category one finds not one but many sciences dealing with good, so much the less will one expect to find a single science dealing with what is good in all the categories at once. This is a straightforward argument *a fortiori*, and does not depend on or involve the theory that good is a *pollachōs legomenon*, or term said in many ways.

The argument of this section of the *Magna Moralia* therefore has the following features. (1) It concentrates specially on the proposition that political science should have in view in its reasonings the realization of the "common" good, an unhypostatized *universale in rebus*. (2) It does not deny, but affirms, the existence of such a "common" good. (3) It is familiar with the doctrine of categories, and holds that there are items in all of them which are good, but does not argue on this basis that "good" is ambiguous and that there is no goodness common to all good things. It would seem that we have here the record of a stage of Aristotle's thinking about "good" which antedates both that preserved in the *Eudemian* and that of the *Nicomachean Ethics*. At this time he himself accepted the existence of *koinon agathon* alongside the other *koina* whose existence he proposed as an alternative to Forms. This is why he deals more fully with the suggestion that politics must study this than with the corresponding suggestion about the Platonic Form. The former was for him a live question, while the latter was not. Later, when he came to think that because there are good things in all the categories good must be a *pollachōs legomenon*, so that there is no such *koinon*, the question ceased to be a live one. He then naturally recast his

---

[28] It corresponds to *EE* 1217b35–1218a1 (*not* to b25–35) and *Nic. Eth.* 1096a29–34 (*not* to a23–29). Dirlmeier's failure to see that two separate arguments are given in *EE* and *Nic. Eth.* leads him wildly off in his analysis of *MM* 1183a7–23: see pp. 176–77. The same failure, in the case of *EE*, has led Allan ("Aristotle's Criticism," pp. 284–86, cf. esp. his way of running together the two arguments in his summary on p. 285) to misunderstand the clear meaning of 1217b33–35, which states as the conclusion of a completed, *independent* argument that there is no unified science of goodness because there is nothing common to all good things as such. (On this Owen is right, "Logic and Metaphysics," pp. 165–66.)

treatment of the "abstract good" so as to make it a historical, anti-Platonic discussion such as we find in the *Eudemian* and *Nicomachean Ethics*. Certainly no follower of Aristotle's, whether wittingly or unwittingly, can have produced our text out of the more orthodox arguments of the other works.

These considerations show conclusively, I think, that at least the part of the first book just analyzed goes back to some Aristotelian text or discussion earlier than either *Eudemian* or *Nicomachean Ethics*. Examination of the *Magna Moralia*'s treatment of justice will show that this is no isolated case. This can be done relatively briefly, since two of the points that need to be taken account of have been mentioned already.[29]

Magna Moralia 1.33, like the *Eudemian-Nicomachean* account of justice, begins with a distinction between two senses of *to dikaion*. First, there is the sense of the word in which, because the law of the city enjoins the performance of virtuous acts of all kinds, and anything enjoined by the law can be called *dikaion*, "just" acts would include acts of virtue of whatever kind, brave, temperate, pious and the rest. (Commentators of the *Nicomachean Ethics* call this "justice" in the universal sense.) Secondly, and more narrowly, there is a sense of the word in which only fair dealing counts as just action, and it is naturally with justice in the second sense of the word that both discussions are primarily concerned. The *Magna Moralia*, however, draws the distinction in an importantly different way from the *Eudemian-Nicomachean* account. The *Magna Moralia*, noting that fairness and unfairness consist in attitudes one has to other people and their good, contrasts the narrower with the broader sense of justice as respectively relational and nonrelational: the temperate man, who will of course also be just in the broad sense, need stand in no particular relation to others in doing (at least some of) his temperate actions (1193b12–17). But the *Eudemian-Nicomachean* account makes it a principal part of its theory that in both senses justice is a relational notion:[30] insofar as a temperate man can be regarded also as just (in the universal sense) he must think of his actions as conforming to the law and therefore as contributions to the general good which it is the aim of the law to promote. The contradiction here is quite explicit. Universal justice ἀρετὴ μέν ἐστι τελεία, ἀλλ' οὐχ ἁπλῶς ἀλλὰ πρὸς ἕτερον (*Nic. Eth.* = *EE* 1129b26–27); ἀλλὰ τὸ δίκαιον τὸ πρὸς ἕτερον ἄλλο τοῦ εἰρημένου κατὰ νόμον δικαίου ἐστίν (*MM* 1193b15–16). It is surely incredible that anyone writing a compendium of Aristotelian ethics who knew the other treatment should thus boldly contradict his main source.[31]

---

[29] Above, p. 196 and note 23.

[30] It is this fact that, Aristotle implies (1130b1–2), makes the double usage of the word at once intelligible and difficult to see through (1129a26–28).

[31] The contradiction consists in the affirmation and denial that τὸ κατὰ νόμον δίκαιον or justice as following the laws is πρὸς ἕτερον, something that consists in a relation to others. It is plain that πρὸς ἕτερον bears this same sense in both statements. The fact that καθ' ἑαυτόν ("by himself," "solitary," *MM* 1193b13, 15) contrasts with πρὸς ἕτερον differently than καθ'

But on the assumption of authenticity it is not difficult to account for this divergence. It is plain that the *Magna Moralia* takes a much too simple view of the relation of universal, or legal, justice to the particular virtues enjoined by it—and that the *Eudemian-Nicomachean* account shows deeper insight and more sophistication. The author of the *Magna Moralia* simply equates acts of (universal) justice with acts of temperance, courage and so on, as the case may be, and hence, naturally enough, infers that acts of (universal) justice have no necessary relation to other persons. But this is wrong, and in the other discussion Aristotle takes some pains (1129b25–1130a8) to explain why: as already noted, an act of (say) temperance is only also an act of (universal) justice if done *as* owed to someone else (perhaps the community as a whole, or the ruler, or some fellow citizen, Aristotle suggests [1129b14–19, 1130a5]). Aristotle seems to have in mind two different ways in which a virtuous act might be regarded as a contribution to someone else's good. First, some acts of courage are undertaken in defense of the life and property, not of the agent himself, but of others, and a corresponding point might be made for temperance, good temper and other virtues.[32] Now on this ground one could only argue that a person displays justice in the universal sense when exercising some virtue to the material benefit of some other person besides himself—by bravery in battle, or leaving someone else's wife unseduced, and so on. But one could not maintain that *private* acts of bravery (defending merely oneself) or temperance (not overeating), etc., showed (universal) justice. Secondly, however, Aristotle seems also to have in mind a way in which *all* virtuous acts, whether publicly or merely privately beneficial in the way just noted, can be thought of as *pros heteron*. For in a well-organized city, according to Aristotle, the laws aim to advance the happiness of all the citizens in common (1129b14–19), so that, since happiness consists partly in morally virtuous action, the law "bids us to live according to each of the virtues and forbids us each of the vices" (1130b23–24). Hence one may regard one's virtuous disposition and its exercise, whether private or public, as a contribution to the well-being of the city just in themselves: it is in the exercise of one's own virtue, whatever the circumstances, that one makes one's fundamental contribution to the communal good.

Now in making this second point Aristotle marks an essential advance on the theory of the *Magna Moralia*. For even the *Magna Moralia*'s solitary temperate man can, from this point of view, also be acting for social ends and so be acting *pros heteron*: he need only regard his own temperance as just in itself part of the communal good. It would thus seem that the *Eudemian-Nicomachean* account shows the fruit of deeper reflection, which enabled

---

αὑτόν ("in himself," "for his own advantage," *Nic. Eth.* 1129b33), ἁπλῶς (1129b26) or πρὸς αὑτόν (1130a6, 7) do (P. Trude, *Der Begriff der Gerechtigkeit*, pp. 59–62, cited with approval by Dirlmeier, p. 313), does not imply that πρὸς ἕτερον has a different sense there. Provided the sense is the same, the contradiction remains.

[32] This seems to be the point Aristotle relies on at 1129b31–1130a8: see esp. b33–35.

Aristotle to correct the earlier, over-hasty classification of justice in the broader sense as not consisting in a relation to others. Certainly the facts can very easily be accommodated in this way, while, as noted above, they can hardly be squared at all with the hypothesis of a post-Aristotelian author familiar with the orthodox doctrine.

This theory of the origin of the *Magna Moralia*'s discussion of justice is also suggested by other facts. Thus the *Magna Moralia* gives an account of "particular" justice, justice in the sense of fair dealing, which from the point of view of the *Nicomachean Ethics*, is both restricted in scope and very poorly articulated. The restricted scope comes out already in the definition of the just man as the man who wants to have what is equal—neither getting more by acting unjustly nor getting less by being unjustly treated (1193b25–30), than his share.[33] Obviously in this conception justice and injustice only show themselves in situations where a man is actually competing with others for some good thing: the just man limits his competitiveness and desire for gain in ways in which the unjust man does not. Justice, in effect, is fairness in making or accepting distributions between oneself and others (1193b20–23); the more general case of parent or arbitrator or judge distributing goods where he is not party to the distribution is not taken account of in the definition at all.[34] In fact, justice on this definition seems perfectly to exemplify the *Magna Moralia*'s general thesis about the moral virtues (1186a33, b33–34, 1190b7, etc.), that they are *mesotētes tōn pathōn*, mean states of the passions. Justice turns out to be essentially the proper control of one's competitive instinct for gain: the just man has neither too much, nor too little, but the right amount of this *pathos*. Now not only does this view make justice the exact counterpart of the other moral virtues (without the disruptions caused in the theory of the mean by Aristotle's recognition in the *Eudemian* and *Nicomachean Ethics* of the anomalous character of justice [cf. 1133b32ff.]), but it is also a very natural first sketch for a Greek and a student of Plato's *Republic* to have produced. The general equation of *pleonexia* (graspingness) with *adikia* would certainly predispose any Greek to the sort of account the *Magna Moralia* gives, and this predisposition would certainly be reinforced for Aristotle, if he is the author of that account, by the way in which Thrasymachus in the *Republic* builds on this usage in his theory of what injustice is.

Here again, the *Eudemian-Nicomachean* treatment shows the fruits of further reflection. In their theory the circumstances of justice are generalized

---

[33] Compare *EE* 2.3. 1221a4: κέϱδος-ζημία-δίκαιον (gain-damage-justice) and the theory of *two* opposed vicious types (the κεϱδαλέος or acquisitive and the ζημιώδης or self-damaging) adumbrated at a23–24. The limitation evident here was corrected by the time the detailed treatment of book 4 was composed. Contrast *Nic. Eth.* 2.7. 1108b7–8.

[34] Hence the situation of the judge or arbitrator, which rightly occupies the center of the discussion in *EE* (*Nic. Eth.*), is only alluded to briefly in *MM*, in a kind of appendix (1196a34–b3).

to include indifferently the assignment of the right amount of goods (and evils), no matter who the persons may be to whom the assignment is made (cf. 1134a1–6). And because the case where a man is assigning goods to himself is a special case, Aristotle rightly tends to avoid it, discussing instead the actions of judges and arbitrators.[35] On this improved conception it is not essential to justice that a just act involve the renunciation of possible, but unjust, gain on one's own part. And, on the other side, the motives to injustice could, in principle, be quite varied: not merely excessive desire for gain, but also simple hatred and willful arbitrariness, can now be accommodated. The essential thing is whether or not the right assignment of goods has been made—and the motives leading someone to fail to make it are now a subsidiary question. The *Nicomachean Ethics*, by defining the virtues as means in passion *and action* (1106b16–17),[36] perhaps intends to make room for virtues like justice, which, so understood, is a virtue of action only, with no peculiar range of emotion under its control. In any case the official *Nicomachean* account of justice as a mean (1133b29ff.) mentions only actions and not passions. (It is interesting to notice, however, that even in this later treatment the appeal of the *Magna Moralia*'s more primitive scheme is not completely overcome. In one passage (1136b34–1137a4) Aristotle assimilates the judge who knowingly hands down an unjust decision to Thrasymachus' grasping man, who is motivated by excessive desire for gain: according to Aristotle, even if he does not profit materially from the transaction, the judge at least gets an excess of *some* good—gratitude, perhaps, or revenge! Here Aristotle plainly writes under the influence of the old, restricted conception of justice; on his own current theory he ought to feel no need at all to treat the judge as a *pleonektēs*, and it is certainly to be regretted that he did not take the opportunity here once and for all to break the old tie between *adikia* and *pleonexia*.)

The upshot is that although Aristotle takes the essential first step in *Eudemian Ethics* 4 (= *Nicomachean* 5) toward getting beyond the oversimple conception of justice as consisting essentially in the limitation of one's competitive instinct for gain, he never freed himself entirely of this idea. He recognizes the essential irrelevance of the identities of the parties to a distribution, but does not, apparently, have a clear grasp of the consequences. Both the success and the failure support the thesis that the *Magna Moralia*'s theory of justice is the work of a less mature Aristotle.

I think that my examination of the philosophical content of the *Magna Moralia*'s theory of justice shows beyond reasonable doubt that that theory

---

[35] This is the true source of what some commentators have found to be objectionably legalistic in Aristotle's account. The judge looms so large primarily because he represents the general case, where the facts can be observed free from the confusions introduced by considering the special case concentrated on by Plato and the earlier Aristotle.

[36] The *EE* is less explicit than *Nic. Eth.* in including actions as well as passions, but cf. e.g., 2.3.1220b21–35, esp. πράξει (b25).

was constructed by Aristotle himself at some time before the composition of the *Eudemian Ethics*.[37] I have shown the same for the *Magna Moralia*'s critique of universal Good. Many other passages could be added, but I think these are decisive.

The only significant doubts about this conclusion, so far as I can see, are prompted by the two passages where, as I said above,[38] the *Magna Moralia* "follows" the *Nicomachean Ethics* in fairly clear preference to the *Eudemian*—to which, however, on my account, it is chronologically closer. Why Aristotle should have revised, in the *Eudemian Ethics*, the treatment accorded to these matters in the *Magna Moralia*, only to revert to it in the *Nicomachean*, is certainly not easy to say. On the other hand, one must not expect to explain *everything*: Aristotle can have had motives for doing what seems unfathomable to us. I do not think the facts are entirely inconsistent with the supposition of the priority of the *Magna Moralia*'s version of these two passages;[39] but in any case, the anomaly, difficult as it is to explain, must not be allowed to outweigh the arguments for authenticity presented above.

I have defended both the substantial authenticity of the *Magna Moralia* and its importance as a source for the study of Aristotle's moral philosophy. But I have also emphasized the undoubted, though not precisely determinable, influence of an intermediary on the transmitted record of what Aristotle said. One is not infrequently tempted to find this influence at work in the exposition of the detail of Aristotle's arguments.[40] This is indeed to be expected. But I do not find any evidence that the writer has, either deliberately or through oversight or incapacity, altered any important element of Aristotle's teaching in the lectures being reported. The proof of this is the degree

---

[37] The same conclusion could be reached, I think, from a consideration of the *Magna Moralia*'s failure to distinguish distributive, corrective and "reciprocal" justice and their spheres.

[38] Beginning of sect. II and note 19.

[39] On the question of *MM* 1.5. 1185b14–1187a4 see Allan, "*Magna Moralia* and *Nicomachean Ethics*"; Dirlmeier, *Magna Moralia* pp. 145–46; Allan, review, pp. 142–43; Dirlmeier, *EE*, ed. 2, 143. As for Allan's claim that the author of *MM* here cites the (*Nicomachean*) *Ethics* by name (1185b15), and thereby shows himself not to be Aristotle: (1) Dirlmeier shows that the reading ἐκ τῶν ἠθικῶν would not *normally* mean, and so probably does not mean, "from the *Ethics*." (I do not think he succeeds in showing that it *could* not mean that.) (2) Dirlmeier's (and in effect Stock's) own favored translation, "from the phenomena (*Erscheinungen*) of moral character," "from the (observed) facts about character," which is in itself possible enough, does not fit the context: if these facts of character can be *observed* then they are not ἀφανῆ and there is no need to consider what is observed to happen in matters of bodily health as a visible indication of what happens in the formation of character. (3) I therefore agree with Spengel and others (most recently Düring, review, p. 551) that we should emend to ἐκ τῶν αἰσθητῶν (from observable facts): I take Stobaeus's ἐκ τῶν αἰσθήσεων (II 7, Wachs. p. 137, 25) to be very strong grounds for this alteration, given the well-known fact that his text is plainly based at this point ultimately on the *Magna Moralia*. If this is correct, the question of priority must be decided on internal grounds alone, if at all.

[40] Likely cases which can be briefly indicated include 1187a35-b4 (compare *EE* 1222b20–1223a8), 1188b25–26 (which seems to betray a formal structure for the argument of chapters 12–16 like that of *EE* 2.7–9, but without any other sign that this is so); also certain arguments which hardly make sense as they stand can be presumed to be faulty reports, e.g., 1205a7–15.

to which convincing and good philosophical sense can be made of at least the main drift of all the *Magna Moralia*'s discussions, together with the fact that the sense which emerges requires to be explained not as derivative from, but as the ancestor of, the mature Aristotelian doctrine. This means that the *Magna Moralia* can only be used with care in giving an account of the genesis and content of Aristotle's moral theory; but it can and must be used.

SELECTED FURTHER READINGS

Kenny, Anthony. *The Aristotelian Ethics*, chapter 9. Oxford: Clarendon Press, 1978.

Rowe, Christopher J. "A Reply to John Cooper on the *Magna Moralia*." *American Journal of Philology* 96 (1975): 160–72. Reprinted in *Schriften zur aristotelischen Ethik*, edited by C. Mueller-Goldingen. Hildesheim: Olms, 1988.

CHAPTER NINE

Contemplation and Happiness: A Reconsideration

I

When one considers Aristotle's contributions to ethical theory one might have in mind any of several different things. One might think of his contributions to the subsequent history of moral philosophy, from Hellenistic and Greek Christian times to the Middle Ages, the Renaissance, Victorian England and nineteenth-century Germany, say. Or one might consider the ways in which his views have influenced recent and current work in moral philosophy, and ways in which they might further illuminate (or, as may be, darken) current discussions.

A distinct third possibility, which I will be following in this essay, is to discuss Aristotle's contributions to ethical theory by addressing his ideas in a systematic way and in some detail on their own, looking for what is unique or specially distinctive about them, without special reference either to contemporary theory or to the ways in which his ideas were interpreted and put to use in the subsequent history of ethics. Along these lines, one could discuss his moral psychology—his theory of the nature and function of human reason, how reason when used fully controls nonrational desires and evokes its own kind of motivation ("rational wishes," *boulēseis* in the Greek). Or one might consider his theory of what a moral virtue is, and the ways in which, and reasons why, he thinks such fairly comprehensive states of character, involving judgment, perception and feeling, must take precedence in a philosophical account of the moral life over any appeal to principles of moral behavior (rules or laws). Or one might think of Aristotle's views on the methods of ethics. Or his conception of practical knowledge, of what and how the fully virtuous person can legitimately lay claim to *know* (and so to be right, as opposed both to wrong and to neither right nor wrong) about how human beings ought to live. All these are aspects of Aristotle's moral philosophy that have recently and deservedly attracted the interest of philosophers and philosophically minded scholars, and several of them are topics on which one might develop instructive comparisons or contrasts with Kurt Baier's work (see n. 19 below).

But if one is looking for what is unique, special, most distinctive in Aristotle's philosophy, then, as I have said, one will not limit oneself to topics that, for better or worse, are found specially attractive by contemporary philosophy. Accordingly, I want to concentrate on a single Aristotelian doctrine, one that I suppose no philosopher today is likely to find much use for but that is nonetheless a distinctive Aristotelian contribution to philosophical thought. This concerns the priority, in some sense or senses, that he claims for theoretical over practical activity. Though Aristotle's debt here to Plato in the *Republic* is plain, his momentous distinction and separation of the theoretical from the practical uses of the mind make the problems he faces and the theory he develops to respond to them distinctively his own, and not just one version of a common Platonic-Aristotelian idea. And Aristotle's immediate successors among the Greek philosophers, Epicurus and the old Stoics, were very far from sharing his outlook; this is especially noteworthy in the Stoics, who thought accurate philosophical knowledge, or devotion to study of any such recherché kind as Aristotle championed, was strictly not necessary for the fullest achievement of the natural human potential in which, as they in common with Aristotle held, human happiness consists. Human virtue, according to the Stoics, doesn't include that sort of thing, and beyond a certain fairly minimal acquaintance with physical theory, human happiness is attainable without it. Among the ancient Greek philosophers only Plotinus took over and adapted to his own uses something like the Aristotelian viewpoint, but of course the neo-Platonic metaphysics with which it gets mixed up makes for a theory of a very different shape, and one that has a different moral significance. The same is true of such medieval Aristotelians as Aquinas. So Aristotle's views on the special value of theoretical activity, and his identification of a contemplative life, in some sense of that term, as the best for a human being, are distinctively Aristotelian contributions to ethical theory. And since Aristotle's views on this topic are not easy to make out with any precision, and are currently the subject of scholarly controversy, it is perhaps especially worthwhile to offer a discussion of them, in gratitude and friendship, to Kurt Baier on his seventieth birthday.

II

I will limit myself in what follows to discussing Aristotle's theories in the *Nicomachean Ethics*. Remarkably, only in the *Nicomachean Ethics*, and not in the *Eudemian Ethics* or the *Magna Moralia*, nor yet in the *Politics*, does Aristotle explicitly compare the value of theoretical study as against practical activity. Only in the *Nicomachean Ethics* does he, in consequence, explicitly maintain that (however this is to be interpreted) the best human life is a contemplative one. The *Eudemian Ethics*, in its only discussion (Book II, Chap. 1) of what constitutes human happiness (*eudaimonia*), says simply that happiness is "activity of complete virtue in a complete life" (1219a38–39), and there the context is explicit that "complete virtue" means all the specifically human virtues, the moral ones taken together with the intellectual (see 1219a37; 1219b26–1220a12). So Aristotle's view in the *Eudemian Ethics* is that the best life for a human being is one devoted jointly to morally good actions and excellent theoretical study: *eudaimonia* consists in a combination of these two, and does not define a form of life that he calls, or that deserves to be called, especially contemplative.[1] It is indeed an interesting question why in the *Eudemian Ethics* Aristotle rested content with this formulation, but departed from it in the *Nicomachean*. But we can only hope to give an answer after we have seen in some detail what Aristotle's view in the *Nicomachean Ethics* actually is.

In the *Nicomachean Ethics* Aristotle develops his theory of human happiness (*eudaimonia*) in two disjoint stages. There is a preliminary account at the beginning of the treatise (Book I), and the subject is taken up again at the end (Book X, chaps. 6–8), where certain details not previously entered into are worked out. In particular, it is only in Book X that Aristotle compares the values realized in excellent theoretical study with those of good practical activity and concludes that the ideally good human life will be a contemplative one. This means that the main elements of what we think of as Aristotle's *moral* theory—his theory of the virtues and vices of character, of practical knowledge, deliberation, weakness of will, pleasure, friendship, etc., all of which are set out in the central books, II–IX—are presented within the framework of the vaguer preliminary account of happiness in Book I; they nowhere presuppose, anyhow not explicitly and officially, the concluding, more refined theory contained in Book X, chaps. 6–8. But when the later refinements are taken into account it is, to put it mildly, not clear whether one can any longer legitimately interpret Aristotle's *moral* theory as one would drawing only on material from the first nine books. Adopting the perspective of the contemplative ideal, as this is presented in Book X, threatens to alter in significant ways one's conception of the structure and content of the moral life as this was apparently analyzed in the earlier books. Some people have even questioned whether there is any way to interpret the moral theory of the *Nicomachean Ethics* so as to make it compatible with the contemplative ideal of Book X. Perhaps, in the end, one should simply admit that Aristotle works with two distinct, mutually incompatible conceptions of human happiness in the *Ethics*: a preliminary, vaguer one that supports a life of moral virtue, citizenship, and practical activity taken seriously for its own sake, into which Aristotle fits his account of moral virtue and related topics in the middle books of the treatise; and the refined, contemplative conception, which makes no room for the kind

---

[1] In the brief concluding paragraph of his discussion (Book VIII, chap. 3) of *kalokagathia*, the comprehensive virtue of "nobility" (so M. Woods, *Aristotle's EE*), Aristotle describes *kalokagathia* as "complete virtue" (1249a16), the virtue composed of all the particular virtues that have been discussed one by one in the course of the treatise, i.e., in Books III–V. At 1249b9–16, Aristotle assigns some kind of priority to theoretical study and, by implication, to its virtue of *sophia*. I have attempted to work out in detail the sort of priority here envisaged (see *Reason and Human Good in Aristotle*, pp. 136–43), arguing that it leaves intact the independence of the moral virtues as well as their separate and distinctive value. But whether or not this interpretation is accepted, this passage gives no basis for thinking Aristotle intended to take back his earlier identification of *eudaimonia* with the exercise of all the virtues and to identify it, in any sense, with the exercise of just one of them, *sophia*.

of engagement with other people (anyhow, fellow-citizens) quite generally that provides the fabric of the moral life as previously analyzed. On that reading, when in the end Aristotle argues that the contemplative conception gives the more correct account of human happiness, it will follow that his attitude towards moral virtue is strictly qualified at best, if not actually compromised altogether. For his preference for the contemplative conception will mean that he can defend the life of moral virtue only as the second best, not the best, life for a human being. (And, indeed, on one plausible interpretation, he says precisely that in a prominent place in his discussion in Book X, at the end of chapter 7 and the beginning of chapter 8, 1178a4–10.)

III

As this brief sketch has, I hope, made clear, it is extremely difficult to decide whether Aristotle has a consistent theory of the good human life, and if he does, what place in that theory he gives to theoretical study. An unusual number of valuable discussions published in the last 15 years or so, and especially some work done in the past several years, have done a great deal to advance our understanding of the relevant texts, despite the fact that their authors continue to come to divergent conclusions on the central question.[2] I think we may now be in a position, if not to construct a definitive interpretation, at any rate to elaborate and defend one particular interpretation as the most convincing of the possibilities the texts leave open. For further progress requires the candid admission that Aristotle is himself, partly for good reasons that he states, to some extent responsible for the confusion that surrounds his views on this topic. He emphasizes that both the preliminary and the final accounts of happiness are given in sketches only (1094a25; 1098a21; 1176a31; 1179a34). And he repeatedly warns against speaking on ethical topics with "exactness" (akribeia), since so much here depends on particular facts about individual agents and their situations (1094b11–27; 1098a26–1098b8; 1103b26–1104a11). Any correct statement about all human agents must be subject to exceptions, and the more detailed one makes one's account the more subject to exceptions it will be, since it is not possible to produce a satisfactory qualified generalization, listing the exceptions and the respects in which and the reasons why they count as such. Hence, Aristotle insists, if one wishes to make one's general theories as true as possible, one must be content often not to enter into details at all. Thus Aristotle himself warns us not to expect anywhere in the Ethics a fully articulated account of happiness, and so (perhaps) not to

---

[2] I may mention here Ackrill, "Aristotle on Eudaimonia"; Hardie, "The Final Good in Aristotle's Ethics"; Hardie, "Aristotle on the Best Life for a Man"; David Keyt, "Intellectualism in Aristotle"; Kraut, "A Dominant-End Reading of the Nicomachean Ethics"; Jennifer Whiting, "Human Nature and Intellectualism in Aristotle"; Timothy Roche, "Ergon and Eudaimonia in Nicomachean Ethics I."

expect one that would make it clear precisely what role moral virtue and what role theoretical study must occupy in the best human life: if one is to speak correctly of *the* best life, perhaps one must leave these matters in some respects undetermined, subject to individual variation. In any event, it is essential to recognize that because he intended to write only a sketch Aristotle has left us a text that is unavoidably open to alternative interpretations, even ones which one feels sure, and can to some extent successfully argue, were not intended by Aristotle himself.

When I first thought of writing something on Aristotle's theory of human happiness, more than fifteen years ago now, I quickly became convinced that in his final account of happiness in Book X of the *Nicomachean Ethics* Aristotle so elevates the value of intellectual activity of the highest kind that he leaves no room at all in the ideal, contemplative life for morality as ordinarily understood and as analyzed by himself in earlier books.[3] I thought commentators failed to see this, or actually denied it, because they found this view so repugnant, even outrageous, that they simply did not allow themselves to consider whether Aristotle, after all a very great philosopher, could have adopted it. In any event, the palliatives they introduced in order to avoid attributing this discredited view to Aristotle seemed to me on examination altogether without merit as interpretations of Aristotle's actual words. Aristotle certainly seems to say plainly and repeatedly in Book X that happiness, or as he sometimes says instead, "complete happiness," *is*—actually consists in—contemplative activity, carried on for a complete lifetime (1177a7–8, 17–18; 1177b24–26; 1178b7–8, 32). And if one takes seriously Aristotle's treatment of happiness from the very beginning of the *Ethics* as the (one and only) end for the sake of which we rational, adult human beings should do *everything* that we do, I did not see how to combine this apparent equation of human happiness and the activity of philosophical thinking with the kind of commitment to morally good action that on Aristotle's own, as I thought, excellent analysis is essential to having a morally virtuous character.

The morally virtuous person has a permanent and deep attachment to his family, his personal friends, and his fellow-citizens, to serving their needs and furthering their short- and long-term good. He is also attached to his own normal and natural emotional and bodily satisfactions, and to the exercise of a normally wide range of intellectual capacities and interests. It is hardly credible that he should see this complex balance of attachments as just what one should induce in oneself and regularly express in one's more particular choices and actions, in order to further one's philosophical work. Aristotle does say once in the *Nicomachean Ethics* that *phronēsis*, the intellectual virtue of practical wisdom or understanding that dictates the structure of evaluations making up the morally virtuous state of charac-

---

[3] See Cooper: *Reason and Human Good in Aristotle*, chap. III.

ter, gives instructions for the sake of philosophical wisdom (1145a9), i.e., in order to make theoretical understanding of the metaphysical first principles of reality, and its exercise, possible. And in other works of Aristotle and in the ancient Aristotelian tradition one finds moral virtue described as, in effect, a condition of quiescence in which nonrational desires and interests impinge on and distract the mind as little as possible from its own work, which is wholly philosophical.[4] In the passage just cited Aristotle does not, however, say that in shaping and supporting one's moral character in just the way it does one's practical understanding (*phronēsis*) has *solely* in view the aim of providing conditions favorable for the acquisition and exercise of philosophical wisdom. And a careful reading of his detailed descriptions of the particular moral virtues makes it clear that he thinks the morally virtuous person values the multifarious persons, things, experiences and activities that he cares fundamentally about independently of the effects that so valuing them has on his capacity and opportunity for philosophical work.[5] No doubt the full development of our theoretical capacities does depend upon a due measure in our emotional and other nonrational attachments to other people and in the satisfactions of social, political and family life; otherwise, with excessive or even in some cases deficient likings for other things, we might well not be able to take enough interest in theoretical concerns or to enjoy them sufficiently in order to come to actually experience for ourselves what (as Aristotle thinks) is so uniquely and overwhelmingly valuable in them. And knowing this will be a central item in the knowledge on the basis of which the man of practical understanding strives to maintain for himself that due measure in his other attachments.

But what makes the measure in question a due one in the case of each range of nonrational desires and satisfactions is not merely that it makes possible, for those whose native endowments tend in that direction, the development and uninhibited exercise of their theoretical powers. It also answers to the independent values for a human being of all those other objects, activities and relationships on which the nonrational desires themselves are immediately directed. It is a cardinal fact about human nature if, as Aristotle in effect claims, the morally virtuous state, in answering to the objective values of this wide range of objects of ordinary human concern, also provides a condition of quiescence in which the higher intellectual interests can be awakened, developed and satisfied. But it is important to realize that it is this already fairly optimistic application of natural teleology on which Aristotle's moral theory rests, and not the much more extreme, altogether implausible, belief that the state of desire characteristic of moral virtue is fully dictated by the pursuit of intellectual self-development alone.

[4] *Eudemian Ethics*, 1249b22–23; *Magna Moralia*, 1198b12–20; Theophrastus in a scholion found in a Vienna manuscript and published by G. Heylbut, "Zur Ethik des Theophrast von Eresos", p. 195.

[5] See Cooper, *Reason and Human Good*, pp. 105–10.

So I found myself forced to the conclusion that Aristotle's final and fully considered theory of human happiness in Book X of the *Ethics* does not build upon his analysis of moral virtue in the earlier books, but is actually inconsistent with it, in the sense that anyone who successfully led the contemplative life recommended in Book X as the ideal one for a human being would not and could not be at the same time a morally virtuous person, leading a moral life as we, and Aristotle in the earlier books, understand it.

This was not a conclusion I was happy to come to. Not because I thought this substantive moral view was without merit or was unworthy of the great Aristotle: on the contrary, I thought there was something possibly salutary in the idea that the practices of morality and the moral way of life were suitable only for most human beings under most circumstances, and not necessarily for those whose capacities and fundamental interests set them apart from the communal life that is the best most of us can aspire to. What was bothersome was rather the thought that Aristotle had composed the *Nicomachean Ethics* with so little regard for consistency that in most of the work he could write as if moral virtue and the practices of morality are an essential part of the happy life, the best life for a human being (any human being), while in one fell swoop at the end of the work he takes this back— and without properly explaining what he is doing by, for example, revisiting moral virtue briefly to draw out the consequences of his revised theory of happiness for the moral life. (The cryptic remark that the life according to moral virtue is a secondarily happy one [1178a9] can only be interpreted as, at best, a gesture in that direction.) One might rather have expected the second treatment of happiness to supplement and complete the vaguer first one, without overturning any of the substantive conclusions about the best life and its contents that are arrived at by working out the implications of that first treatment. If Aristotle had been intending eventually to present two separate life ideals—a less ideal but more widely suitable life devoted largely to moral virtue, and a more ideal contemplative life suited only for philosophers and not involving common morality at all—surely he ought to have made this clear in a preliminary way already in the first book and to have presupposed it at many places as he proceeded through the intervening discussions.

That he does not do this certainly encourages the hope that it may be possible, despite what I argued in my book, to interpret the theory of happiness in Book X so that it does cohere with the rest of the treatise. Several attempts in this direction have recently appeared, or are about to appear, in the scholarly literature, and though in my opinion none of them succeeds in disposing adequately of the formidable obstacles Aristotle's text throws up, enough real progress has been made to incline me now to think an interpretation along these general lines has rather more favorable prospects than I used to think. In what remains I will develop and defend one such interpretation.

IV

I said above that the strongest evidence in the text of Book X supporting an intellectualist ideal that leaves no room for morality is found in those passages where Aristotle says, or at least seems to say, that happiness (*eudaimonia*) is, actually consists in, the single activity of excellent theoretical thinking. Eventually I will want to suggest that this is not in fact what Aristotle intends to say in these passages. We can take a first step toward understanding what Aristotle does mean by considering the first of these passages, the very first sentence of Book X, chapter 7, with which Aristotle introduces his account of the contemplative life. In the preceding chapter he has argued that happiness does not depend essentially upon pleasant leisure-time activities (οὐκ ἐν παιδιᾷ ἄρα ἡ εὐδαιμονία, 1176b27–28), various forms of play, even although these, or some of them, are in fact both chosen and worth choosing for their own sakes. The happy life, he insists, requires seriousness; happiness depends not on bodily pleasures and such like, indulged in for fun, but rather on activities of virtue (οὐ γὰρ ἐν ταῖς τοιαύταις διαγωγαῖς ἡ εὐδαιμονία, ἀλλ᾽ ἐν ταῖς κατ᾽ ἀρετὴν ἐνεργείαις 1177a9–10). Aristotle begins chapter 7 by recasting this conclusion from chapter 6 as follows: "If happiness (*eudaimonia*) is activity of virtue, it is reasonable (that it should be) of the most superior virtue" (εἰ δ᾽ ἐστὶν ἡ εὐδαιμονία κατ᾽ ἀρετὴν ἐνέργεια, εὔλογον κατὰ τὴν κρατίστην).

Now in order to appreciate accurately the significance of what Aristotle is saying here one must notice that he is using the word *eudaimonia* in a way that is very common (in fact, overall the most common) in the *Nicomachean Ethics*, but is rather unusual for the English expressions proposed as translations for it—"happiness," "flourishing," "a good life," and so on. We expect "happiness," for example, to denote a property or condition either of a person or of his life, perhaps during some particular, relatively brief time, perhaps over major portions or even the whole of his life. We don't ordinarily use the word "happiness," as Aristotle uses *eudaimonia* here, to refer to a single, concrete activity or type of activity, and when we meet such uses, as when someone says that happiness is a full stomach and a dry diaper, our amused response is partly due to recognizing a transferred usage—roughly, calling a cause by the name of its effect. Aristotle does sometimes use the Greek word *eudaimonia* with this first sense, that of a property or condition of persons or their lives. We have an example of this in *Nicomachean Ethics* Book X, chapter 6, as just summarized: Aristotle says that the happy life (1177a2–3) and again that happiness itself (1177a10) does not depend upon the fun one has in leisure-time pursuits. But this is not for Aristotle's theory the basic usage of the term. The basic use is only reached when he goes on to specify what happiness in this first sense *does* depend upon: virtuous activity in general, activity of the most superior among the human virtues, or whatever. It is through the presence of that in a person's life, or as engaged in by him, that it becomes appropriate to describe him and his life as being happy (*eudaimōn*). In the first book of the *Ethics* Aristotle makes the search for the nature of happiness the first business of practical philosophy, saying (1095a17–20) that "happiness" is the name usually given to the highest of goods achievable in action, i.e., to that good which is rationally wished for for itself alone, every other thing that is pursued or done being done for the sake of it. Plainly, happiness here is not to be understood as a property or condition of a person or his life; it is some simple or complex specific good that human beings can attain in their lives that will, in the derivative usage of the term, make them and their lives happy. That is why he immediately goes on to mention concrete things like pleasure, wealth, honor, health, the Form of the Good, and virtue as sample candidates for what happiness really is. The question "What *is* happiness?" which Aristotle takes up in the first book and returns to in Book X is a question in the first instance about particular good things we can possess, use or do. Which one of these, or which combination of them, is of such a nature that it is appropriately regarded as the best good, in the sense of a good that is choiceworthy for itself alone while other lesser goods are all of them in one way or another choiceworthy for its sake? People who succeed in attaining this best good are the happy ones, the ones whose lives are happy, but the happiness that Aristotle's theory is supposed to clarify for us and advance us in pursuing is not the happiness that comes to characterize ourselves and our lives because we possess some such good, but rather that good itself, whatever it turns out to be.

Hence if in the first sentence of Book X, chapter 7, Aristotle says, as it certainly seems that he does, that happiness *is* excellent theoretical thinking of some sort, he will be saying that excellent theoretical thinking is the *whole* of what a person should aim ultimately at in his life, the sole thing such that having and engaging in it makes his life happy. Nothing else but this will make any independent contribution to the goodness of his life; in particular, moral virtue will not. Is this what Aristotle means? I think now that there is good reason to doubt it.

V

To see this, recall that Aristotle formulates his own theory of the nature of happiness in Book I—what I've been calling his preliminary, vaguer account—in language that closely resembles his language here in Book X. In that well-remembered passage Aristotle states his theory as a conclusion from what he has argued is the essentially rational nature of human beings and the rational character of specifically human virtue: "if that is so, the human good turns out to be virtuous activity of soul, and if there are more than one virtue, of the best and most complete virtue" (εἰ δ' οὕτω, τὸ ἀνθρώπινον ἀγαθὸν ψυχῆς ἐνέργεια γίνεται κατ' ἀρετὴν, εἰ δὲ πλείους αἱ ἀρεταί, κατὰ τὴν ἀρίστην καὶ τελειοτάτην, 1098a16–18). It is legitimate to expect that whatever relationship is intended here between happiness conceived of as virtuous activity of the soul and activity of the best and most complete virtue, the same relationship will be intended in the Book X passage, where Aristotle says that if happiness is virtuous activity it is *reasonable* that it should be of the most superior virtue. Now the Book I passage is surrounded by a rich context which offers a multitude of aids for its interpretation. If by drawing on this context, we can gain a full understanding of the sentence from Book I, we can hope to use what we learn there to help us understand the sentence of Book X. I want to suggest that the sentence of Book I does not, despite initial appearances, identify happiness with the single activity of the best virtue; likewise the sentence of Book X does not.

Two principal features of the Book I context are immediately relevant to the interpretation of this sentence. First, as I have noted, this sentence formulates the conclusion of an argument; so one would expect what it says to follow from the premises, or at any rate to be related to them in such a way that one can see how on the basis of just these premises Aristotle means to recommend just this conclusion. Second, in seeking confirmation for his theory, as expressed in this sentence, in the remaining six chapters of Book I, Aristotle has no fewer than four occasions to restate, in substantially different language, the essentials of his own position. One would expect the original statement of the theory to be interpretable so that it supports all four of these paraphrases.

Let us consider first the four paraphrases. In three of the four (1100a4–5 [cf. 1099b26]; 1101a14–16; 1102a5–6) Aristotle says clearly that according to his theory happiness is activity of *complete* virtue (in two of the three he adds: under certain conditions, viz., over a complete life and equipped with sufficient external goods).[6] He does not say explicitly in any of these passages, as he does in the *Eudemian Ethics* where he actually includes a reference to complete virtue (*teleia aretē*) in his official formulation of his theory defining happiness (1219a35–39), that by "complete virtue" he means all human virtues, but there is little doubt that that, which is at any rate the most natural meaning of the phrase, is what he intends. Several times, in describing the activities that make up happiness in these chapters, Aristotle makes it clear that he thinks of virtuous activities of all types—moral as well as intellectual—as included within happiness, that is, as all of them constituents of it.[7]

---

[6] J. L. Ackrill, "*Eudaimonia*," p. 28, draws attention to these passages (anyhow two of them, the first and third) and emphasizes their bearing on the interpretation of Aristotle's theory as earlier formulated. Ackrill, conveniently for his interpretation, omits to notice the fourth passage, on which see below.

[7] See especially 1099a17–20; 1100b19–20. Furthermore, as Grant and Gauthier have seen (see their notes to 1098b22–23), Aristotle's intention in the whole passage 1098b22–1099b8 is to argue that *his* theory makes *all* the features that different previous thinkers have identified

Now just this view—that happiness is activity of complete virtue, activity of specifically human nature perfected in all its relevant aspects—is the conclusion that the premises of Aristotle's own earlier argument in 1097b24–1098a15 themselves most strongly suggest.[8] He argues that happiness or the human good must be some sort of active exercise of our rational power, namely the employment of that power as it exists when perfected by its and our specific virtue, because the good of any living thing consists in the perfected exercise of its specific nature as the kind of thing it is. And since (see 1098a4–5)[9] our rational power is a complex thing, having several aspects and functions, the perfected exercise of our specific nature will require several activities, the activities of the virtues that perfect the several aspects and functions of our rational power. Thus Aristotle's own argument seems to require the conclusion that happiness is activity of complete virtue, i.e., activity of all the specifically human virtues, the ones belonging to our rational capacities.

But does Aristotle's conclusion, stated in the sentence at 1098a16–18, actually say this? J. L. Ackrill, with the eager acquiescence of David Keyt, has claimed that it does: when Aristotle says that happiness is "virtuous activity of soul, and if there are more than one virtue, of the best and most complete virtue", Aristotle simply means by "the best and most complete virtue" the virtue that is constituted by the sum of all the human virtues, moral and intellectual—in short, just what he means later by the simpler and most perspicuous phrase "complete virtue."[10]

However, this construction of the phrase "best and most complete virtue" is certainly a very unnatural one (no less so in Greek than in English), and

---

one by one as essential to happiness, essential to it: virtue, *phronēsis, sophia*, pleasure, external prosperity, 1098b4–7. So his theory of happiness was intended to make the exercise of *sophia*, the virtues of character, and practical wisdom (I take it that with *phronēsis* at 1098a24 Aristotle is referring to Socrates' theory, cf. 1144b17–19) all elements in the activity that, according to him, happiness is.

[8] This is asserted by Ackrill, "Eudaimonia," p. 28, and explained in detail by Keyt, "Intellectualism," pp. 365–67.

[9] Grant, followed by Ramsauer, Burnet and Gauthier, argued that these lines were not written by Aristotle, but by an early reader, who added them in the margin of his text as a gloss, drawing on what Aristotle says in Book I, Chapter 13, about the division of the soul. This *may* be so, for all we are able to tell now; but since we have no actual record of any manuscript's ever having existed that omits these words we do not possess any evidence that Aristotle did not write them. Certainly the existence of the *hapax legomenon epipeithes* at 1098a4 is no sign of other than Aristotelian origin. So we have to assume that these lines were written by Aristotle.

[10] Ackrill, "Eudaimonia," p. 28; Keyt, "Intellectualism," p. 365. Keyt writes as if this interpretation is "available" to him simply because Ackrill has offered it in print. Beyond pointing out that the conclusion so interpreted makes it follow naturally from what precedes, he does nothing to defend this construction of the sentence against the very powerful objections to it that I had already made in *Reason and Human Good*, p. 100n.; he does not even repeat Ackrill's reasons for thinking the Greek *can* mean what he says it does. On the interpretation of this phrase see further Hardie: "Aristotle on the Best Life," pp. 38–40; Hardie is right to stress the relevance of 1099a29–31 to this issue (see below).

two textual considerations show that it cannot be right. First, as Ackrill himself notices, the expression "most complete virtue" cannot fail to remind the reader of Aristotle's elaborate discussion and classification a page earlier of ends as more or less complete, and his characterization of *eudaimonia* itself as the "most complete" *end*. But Ackrill is wrong to think that the explanation of completeness given in this passage supports his construction of the phrase "most complete *virtue*" as meaning the sum of all the particular virtues. Aristotle says that happiness is the most complete end, in a semi-technical sense he specifies—it is the end that is *most* chosen for its own sake and so *least* chosen for the sake of anything other than itself (1097a25–1097b6). But Aristotle in rapid succession goes on to assign two further related characteristics to happiness. Happiness is also (1097b6–16) a self-sufficient end, as one would expect a complete end, anyhow one chosen for its sake alone and not for the sake of anything else, to be. And (1097b16–20) happiness is the best and most choiceworthy good in a special sense: the value that one has in having it cannot be increased by adding anything good to it, for the reason that it is to be conceived as a comprehensive good, somehow already containing whatever good you might think to supplement it with by adding to it. But if his mention of these further features of happiness shows that on Aristotle's view the most complete good is also a comprehensive end, including other goods somehow in it, that does not show that the most complete *virtue* must similarly be a complex construction out of particular virtues like justice, courage, practical wisdom, philosophical wisdom, and so on. Aristotle says quite plainly (1097a30–34) that the predicate "most complete" means chosen always for itself alone and never for the sake of anything else. The most complete virtue will therefore be the virtue that is chosen always for itself alone and never for the sake of anything else. And in Book X, when he returns to take up the topic of happiness again, Aristotle does precisely argue at some length (1177b1–4, 12–18) that the single virtue of philosophical wisdom *is* chosen for its own sake alone, and not, like the practical virtues, chosen also for further goods it brings us. To be sure, Aristotle does not compare philosophical wisdom and the other virtues in Book I with respect to completeness in this sense, but there seems no possibility for doubt either that it is this comparison which he is anticipating when he speaks of the activity of the best and most complete virtue, or that he expects his reader, having been told explicitly what "most complete" means, to recognize that the virtues may vary in respect of completeness in this special sense, and that if they do, then happiness requires the most complete of them.

This conclusion is confirmed by what Aristotle says in the fourth of the subsequent passages of Book I where he refers back to his own theory of happiness and paraphrases it. This time (1099a29–31) Aristotle says that on his theory as earlier stated he has identified happiness with "the best activities or with one of these, the best one." Unless by "activity of the best and most complete virtue" Aristotle meant activity of the *single* particular virtue, among all the particular human virtues, which is best and most complete, this sentence has nothing to refer back to. In particular, if by the best and most complete virtue he means the sum-total of all the virtues, as Ackrill thought, then nowhere in his account of happiness has Aristotle previously said a word about the best single activity and its role in happiness.[11]

VI

There seems, then, no way around the fact that by "activity of the best and most complete virtue" Aristotle is referring to the activity of a single virtue, whichever is most chosen for itself and least for other things—in fact, as he will only make clear in Book X, but not until then, the activity of perfected theoretical study. But what then is he saying happiness is? Is there any way for us to interpret his statement so as to make it (1) follow reasonably well from its premises, (2) amount to saying that the human good is activity of complete virtue, of the sum total of the moral and intellectual virtues, as three of the four paraphrases require, and (3) contain in its second half a special reference to some one particular virtue (in fact philosophical wisdom, as it turns out) as required by the human good?

I think there is. In the past those who have understood the reference of Aristotle's expression "best and most complete virtue" in the way I have argued is correct have supposed the purport of the sentence is this: happiness or the human good is virtuous activity in general; or rather, if it turns out that there are several virtues of distinct types, happiness is the activity of the best virtue, the one that is worth choosing for its own sake most and least for its contribution to other wished for things—in fact the activity of philosophically accomplished study. So construed, Aristotle will be offering two alternative, mutually incompatible conceptions, the choice between which will depend solely on whether there are differences among the human virtues with respect to completeness. The first, but not the second, of these alternatives follows acceptably enough from the premises of the argument. And in the four subsequent passages we have examined Aristotle will be referring first to the one view, then to the alternation of the two views, as what on his stated theory happiness is: three times saying that his view is the first (happiness is activity of *complete* virtue), once saying it is either the first or the second (happiness is either the best activities, or a single activity, the very best of all). This is surely intolerable. And, I now think, it is unnecessary.

[11] One could add, with Hardie: "Best Life," p. 39, that "activity of the *best* and most complete virtue" at 1098a17–18 can hardly mean anything other than what "the best activity" does at 1099a30.

Bearing in mind that what Aristotle professes to be offering us here is a vague and preliminary sketch, one which we know he will take up and develop further in Book X, one ought not to expect him to be offering a choice between clear and discrete, incompatible alternatives at this point. Rather, the alternatives ought to be related as vaguer and less vague versions of the same view, so that consequences developed on the basis of the vaguer conception will stand firm when the refinements brought by the less vague conception, once it is fully presented, are taken into account.

If, now, we consider just the first part of the sentence, we notice two things. First, it does follow strictly from the premises of the argument as Aristotle has formulated them. Throughout, he has spoken of *a* work and *a* virtue for human beings as such, as for eyes and hands and feet and flute-players, the other terms of the analogies he exploits in reaching his conclusion. He nowhere mentions multiple works or multiple virtues of human beings or any of these other things. So what follows and, strictly, all that follows, from the premises is that human good is activity of human virtue. But second, if there *are* multiple works and multiple virtues that human nature encompasses, then the vague formulation ("happiness is activity of human virtue") leaves it open that someone should count as having achieved happiness by exercising only one or some of these virtues over a sufficiently extended period. Anyone who exercises even *one* human virtue will satisfy this "definition": he will have engaged in "activity of human virtue" for a "complete lifetime." In particular, and particularly outrageously, if the virtues differ in value (if there is a *best* one among them), someone will count as having achieved the human good just because he has acquired and exercised the lesser virtues, without having the highest and best. That is, he will, given this vaguer conception which does follow from the premises as actually stated, have achieved the human good without having *fully* perfected his nature as a human being. Plainly, however, this does not accord with the general tenor of the argument: though the premises speak only of *a* human work and *a* human virtue, Aristotle obviously means to imply that happiness should involve *all* of a human being's natural works being done in accordance with the virtue or all the virtues appropriate to each.

So Aristotle has good reason to amplify and clarify his "definition" in order to rule out this unwanted inference, and it is reasonable, in the light of what I have just said, for his reader to understand that that is what he is doing. Read, then, as following from the preceding argument, its explicit premises together with their evident general import, this concluding sentence will be understood in the following way: happiness is virtuous human activity, and if there are more than one human virtue happiness is activity of all of them, including most particularly activity of the best among the virtues. In other words, the result of considering what to say happiness is, if it turns out that there is more than one human virtue, is not to identify happiness with a single virtuous activity, that of the best virtue, but rather to emphasize the need for them all, including in particular the best one among them.[12]

Now this is not all that needs to be said about this sentence (I have not yet taken fully into account Aristotle's description of the best virtue as also the most complete one). But let us pause to take stock. I have suggested that there is a way of understanding the conclusion of Aristotle's argument in Book I that both makes it follow well enough from the argument's stated premises, and permits sense to be made of each of Aristotle's four paraphrases of his theory in the immediately following chapters. The three places where Aristotle says his own theory has identified happiness with activity of complete virtue correctly summarize the import of the whole "definition" as earlier presented. Aristotle's conclusion that happiness is "virtuous activity of soul, and if there is more than one virtue, of the best and most complete virtue" does say that happiness is the active exercise of *all* the specifically human virtues. But it says this indirectly and by implication, as following from the insistence that happiness requires activity of the best and most complete virtue. And it is this special mention and emphasis on the activity of the best and most complete virtue, neglected in these three passages, that is taken up again in the fourth reformulation (1099a29–31), where Aristotle says his theory makes happiness "the best activities or one of these, the best one." To be sure, Aristotle omits to make it explicit here that, in its earlier context, his reference to "activity of the best and most complete virtue" was intended to make happiness consist in the best activity of all, not singly, but as completion to the activity of the other virtues. Nonetheless, it is easy to see on my interpretation of 1098a16–18 how what Aristotle says here could seem to reformulate what he said earlier on about happiness, whereas on Ackrill's interpretation it manifestly could not.

But how can Aristotle say here that, on his view as earlier stated, happiness (that is, as we have seen, the good thing that by itself makes a person and his life happy) may *be* the single activity that is the best of all activities? After all, I have argued that his intention in mentioning activity of the best virtue was to say, not that happiness might *be* that single activity, but that it might be that one taken together with all the other specifically human virtuous activities. But one must remember that Aristotle's theory of happiness throughout Book I is a preliminary sketch only. It points forward to the discussion in Book X, where it is resumed and completed, albeit still only at the level of a sketch. In fact the relationship to the Book X discussion is immediately marked for the attentive reader by the double characterization of the virtue that Aristotle says is particularly needed if there turn out to be more than one virtue, as "the best *and most complete* virtue." As I have argued, it is plain in the context why happiness requires the activity of the best virtue, along with the others: happiness requires the perfection of our nature as human, i.e., rational, beings, and that in turn requires the exercise

---

[12] In arguing for this interpretation I am in agreement with Roche, "*Ergon* and *Eudaimonia*."

of the best virtue. But why the "most complete" virtue, in the sense of the one chosen most for its own sake and least for the sake of other good things? Nothing in the premises of the argument, which set out connections among a thing's natural work, its virtue (*aretē*) and its good, offers any basis for saying that, if there are several essential human works and several human virtues, the virtue that is "most complete" will be especially needed. It is only when the topic of happiness is taken up again in Book X that the importance (as well as the identity) of the "most complete" virtue is explained; and in explaining it, as I will show in a moment, Aristotle develops his theory of happiness in such a way that he can then say (with a certain qualification) that the activity of the most complete virtue, philosophical wisdom, *is* itself happiness. In short, when at 1099a29–31 Aristotle says that on his already-stated theory happiness may *be* the single best activity, he is reformulating that theory in anticipation of the development it will undergo in Book X. Hence, in order to understand what he means by this reformulation, and to see how it might really *be* a reformulation of the theory as previously stated, we must look ahead to Book X.

VII

As I noted above, Aristotle begins his reconsideration of happiness in Book X by remarking, in language reminiscent of his preliminary account of happiness in Book I, that "If happiness is activity of virtue, it is reasonable (that it should be) of the most superior virtue." We have now seen that in the similar language of Book I Aristotle does not mean to say that happiness consists in the activity of some single virtue, but rather to emphasize the special need for the activity of the best virtue, as completion to the others, if one's life is to express the full perfection of human nature. So we ought to interpret this opening sentence of Book X, chapter 7, in the same spirit and sense: having argued in the previous chapter that happiness does not consist in amusements and games but rather in the serious side of life, in fact in "the activities of virtue" (1177a10), he now adds that, if that is so, happiness especially requires the activity of the most superior virtue. This first sentence of Book X, chapter 7, should not be taken to identify happiness with any single virtuous activity alone, as at first sight it might seem to, and as it is often taken to do.

But having said that happiness must be in accordance with the most superior virtue, Aristotle goes on at once to say that the activity of the most superior virtue, which will be an activity of contemplative study, *will* by itself constitute (not happiness, but) "*complete* happiness"—*hē teleia eudaimonia* (here the word for "complete" is the same word used in Book I to talk about "complete virtue" and the "most complete" of the virtues). What does this mean? The concept of "complete happiness" is introduced here for the first time in the *Nicomachean Ethics* (it is completely absent from the other ethical treatises), and it is not obvious at first sight what it amounts to. However, Aristotle explains it implicitly in what immediately follows (1177a19–1177b26), where he takes some pains to confirm that to say that the activity of contemplative study is "complete happiness" is in agreement with the various criteria of happiness that he has argued for previously. In order to understand this we must remind ourselves of what I emphasized above: that in seeking an account of *eudaimonia* or happiness Aristotle is looking for that single type of activity or experience, or whatever, or naturally unified set of activities or experiences, which is the best we are capable of, and that, by its presence in a person's life, makes him and his life a happy (*eudaimōn*) one.

Now in earlier discussions, and particularly in Book I, Aristotle has appealed to several "criteria" that he thinks people are antecedently agreed any candidate for happiness, in the sense specified, ought to satisfy: if happiness is an activity, then it ought to be the best activity, an immediately pleasant one, something desired as far as possible for its own sake alone, self-sufficient, and freely engaged in at leisure rather than forced on us by circumstances and our need for mere survival. Taking these criteria up one by one, Aristotle argues here that the activity of contemplative study, of all the activities human beings are capable of, best and most fully exemplifies the antecedently agreed-on criterial characteristics of happiness, and he infers from that that this activity is "complete happiness." By this expression, accordingly, he means to describe the activity of contemplative study as the one that best and most fully exemplifies the (as it were) "nominal essence" of happiness, the conception we have antecedently of engaging in philosophical theory about what constitutes happiness. The force of the "complete" in "complete happiness" is therefore, as David Keyt has argued,[13] "perfect or fully realized," but in the sense of most completely satisfying the criteria that give preliminary focus to the inquiry into the nature of happiness. Aristotle has argued in Book I, as we have seen, on independent grounds that happiness is virtuous activity carried on throughout a complete life, including morally virtuous actions as well as excellent theoretical study within the scope of this "virtuous activity". He does not take this back now, but only points out that one of the two types of virtuous activity in which happiness consists, namely excellent theoretical study, satisfies the preliminary criteria of happiness more fully than the other does, and so deserves to be singled out as, so to speak, the more perfect version of the general unified category of activity, virtuous activity, which constitutes happiness. If, after all, happiness itself (i.e., virtuous activity through a complete lifetime) satisfies the preliminary criteria, as Aristotle of course claims it does, that will be in special measure due to the presence in it of excellent contemplative study, since this activity *does* unreservedly possess the required characteristics.

[13] Keyt, "Intellectualism," pp. 377–78.

Once one sees that by "complete happiness" Aristotle means only one of the constituents of happiness and not happiness as a whole, special significance attaches to the fact that in the whole of Book X, chapters 7–8, where Aristotle develops and explains his views on the place of contemplative study in the best life, he is concerned solely to argue that contemplative study is "complete happiness" in the sense that we have seen he gives to this phrase at its first appearance, at 1177a17. He repeats this characterization of contemplation twice later on (1177b24 and 1178b7), and when near the end of his discussion he does once say (1178b32) simply that "happiness" itself (not "complete happiness") is "some sort of contemplative study," the omission of the crucial qualification is surely not significant. It comes in a passage that draws consequences from the fact, argued just before (1178b7–23), that "complete" happiness (not happiness altogether) is contemplation. (This passage announces its theme at the outset (1178b7–8) by saying: "And that complete happiness is some activity of contemplative study can be shown also from the following considerations.") So he probably means simply to repeat his earlier statement that contemplation is complete happiness, i.e., the kind of virtuous activity that most fully exemplifies the properties that we antecedently expect happiness to have. (I return to this passage in conclusion below.)

VIII

Once (by 1177b26) Aristotle has established to his own satisfaction that excellent contemplative study is "complete happiness" in this sense, he uses this conclusion to develop his notorious contrast between two lives, a "life of the intellect" and a "life of the other kind of virtue." We are now in a position to offer a natural and satisfying interpretation of the sense of this contrast. When Aristotle first refers to the "life of the intellect" at 1177b26 (*ho toioutos bios*) and 1177b30 (*ho kata touton*, i.e., *ton noun, bios*), the immediately preceding context makes it clear that he is referring to the life that someone leads who has achieved "complete happiness" in a complete life, i.e., who has engaged in excellent contemplative study regularly in his mature lifetime, with a clear and full understanding of the place and importance of this activity in the best human life.[14] And, as we have seen,

---

[14] Ibid, pp. 372–74, ignoring the evidence of 1177b26 (where *ho toioutos bios*, being the *bios* of the previous line, cannot be the activities themselves of study that constitute "complete happiness," when they occupy a "complete length of life," but must rather be the complete life in which they occur), interprets the "life of the intellect" here and later in Book X to be contemplative activities themselves that occur within the best life. I had already argued in *Reason and Human Good*, pp. 159–60, that this cannot be right, since *bios* in Greek means not a part or aspect of a life (as when we refer to a person's sex life, or his religious or intellectual life), but a whole mode of life. Keyt misinterprets Aristotle, *Politics*, I, chapter 8,

the life of such a person is one devoted not solely to the cultivation and exercise of the intellect, but rather to the exercise of *all* the human virtues, with the virtue of the theoretical intellect occupying a special place as the culminating perfection that, when added to the virtues of character and practical thought, completes the full perfection of human nature. Aristotle

---

and Plato, *Laws* V, 733d7–734e2 in a bizarre attempt to show that in Greek *bios* has a use parallel to this modern one of "life".

In fact, in the *Politics* passage Aristotle discusses the various lives, i.e., modes of life, that different peoples live, depending on how they sustain themselves: some have marauders' lives, some lives of hunting, others the farmer's life, and so on. Keyt draws special attention to 1256b2–6, where Aristotle remarks that some tribes combine more than one distinct way of gaining a sustenance: some lead "a nomadic and at the same time marauding (life), others a farming and hunting (life)". He apparently thinks that such combined lives are combinations of the one *life* (a nomad's or a farmer's) and the other *life* (a marauder's or a hunter's); the combined life has as its two constituents these distinct lives, i.e., the distinct activities of wandering in pursuit of food, or marauding, or hunting or farming. But that is neither what Aristotle says, nor any implication of it. It is just a mistake to think that because in leading a combined life a population combines two or more distinct ways of sustaining itself, which is all Aristotle says here about such lives, their life combines two or more *lives*. Significantly, he speaks of each combination as *a* life, e.g., "a nomadic and at the same time marauding *life*"; he does not say those who live this way lead a nomadic life and at the same time a marauding one, nor yet nomadic and marauding *lives* at the same time. And even if the reference of *toutōn* in *migmuntes ek toutōn* at 1256b2–3 is the five simple types of life just named, it doesn't follow that what one finds in the combined nomadic and marauder's life is the nomadic *life* and the marauding *life*, rather than the wandering and the marauding in virtue of engaging in which one group is said to live a simply nomadic and another a simply marauding life. To suppose that this does follow just begs the question at issue. An alternative understanding, which is moreover consistent with the undoubted usual sense of *bios* as "(mode of) life," is that in the "nomadic and marauding life" the tribe moves about from place to place getting its living, as nomads do, but supplements this with raids on resident populations as they pass them by. They lead one and only one *bios*, (mode of) life, which combines these two ways of sustaining themselves. Throughout this passage, then, *bios* can, and I think does, mean "mode of life"; it is nowhere used to refer to an aspect or part of any person's or any group's mode of life.

The Plato passage seems superficially more amenable to Keyt's interpretation. It comes at the end of the long general preface or preamble (V, 726a1–734e2), in which the Athenian lays down and justifies the central idea that the city's laws, as he will detail them later, should aim at making the citizens be as thoroughly virtuous and act as thoroughly virtuously as possible. Granting (733a3–4) that we all individually want a predominance of pleasure over pain in our lives, the Athenian argues that the way to achieve what we want is to live a life of physical fitness and virtue—that is, a life at once characterized by physical health, courage, temperance (or self-control), and wisdom (or prudence). Hence, by living under laws effectively designed to promote these characteristics, we will be getting the sort of life we all recognize that we want. To make this case the Athenian first considers separately the "temperate life" (*ho sōphrōn bios*), the "wise life," the "courageous life" and the "healthy life" and argues that each of these lives is superior in the balance of pleasure over pain it contains to its opposite—the self-indulgent, the foolish, the cowardly and the diseased life respectively. From this he concludes (734d2–734e2) that since each of these lives is thus superior to its opposite, then, putting them all together, the life that has the virtue of the body (health) and also the virtue of the soul (courage, wisdom and temperance) is superior to *its* opposite, and so the person who has this life lives overall and as a whole more happily than his opposite.

It is in this concluding sentence, if anywhere, that Plato uses the word *bios* in the way that

argues on three grounds (1177b26–1178a8) that this life really is the best
and happiest one for us, despite the fact that it is beyond the powers of
ordinary human beings and something that we can aspire to only insofar
as there is something divine and not merely human in us, viz., our theoretical
intellects. In interpreting his arguments we must bear carefully in mind that
it is this mode of life, devoted jointly if differentially to theoretical study
and moral action, for which he means to be arguing. So understood, his
arguments are as follows.

First, the intellect is the best thing in us, so that its excellent exercise is
better than the exercise of the other virtues (1177b28–29), and precisely
because it is something divine we will add something of superior power and
worth to our lives by doing everything we can to realize as fully as possible
the presence of this immortal element in us (1177b33–1178a2). Second, it
can plausibly be argued that each person is (1178a1–2) his intellect (or, at
any rate, is his intellect more than he is any of the other elements in his make-
up, 1178a7), because his intellect is the "controlling and better" element in

---

Keyt needs in order to support his interpretation of the *Nicomachean Ethics*, viz., to refer to
separate phases or aspects of a person's life as parts of the overall life, or way of life, that
results when they are added together. What suggests that he does mean to use it so is the word
sullēbdēn which I have translated as "putting them all together," i.e., as Keyt would have it,
putting all these four lives together. But again this *need* not be the meaning (what gets put
together may instead be the four virtues of body and soul that characterize and define in turn
the four lives previously mentioned: it is by reference to this combined virtue, *aretē kata sōma
ē kai kata psuchēn*, 734d4–5, that the Athenian goes on to characterize the "combined" life),
and reflection on Plato's theory of the unity of the virtues strongly suggests that it is not. For
Plato holds that no one can have any one virtue without having them all, so that the temperate
(mode of) life, that led by the person who possesses the virtue of temperance, will be the same
(mode of) life as that of the wise, or the just or the courageous. Accordingly, when in this
passage he speaks separately of the temperate, the wise (prudent) and the courageous life, he
is speaking throughout of the same life, the overall virtuous one, considering in turn the
pleasures and pains that it has as a direct consequence of the temperance, wisdom and courage
respectively of the person leading it. One does not produce the overall virtuous life mentioned
at the end by adding the temperate life of someone who has only that single virtue to the wise
and the courageous life led by other individuals, much less by adding together the temperate
actions of the one person (as if those, rather than the life he leads in consequence of them,
actually constituted the temperate life being referred to here!), and the courageous actions and
the wise actions of yet other persons. (It is true that since the unity of virtue doctrine does
not cover physical health, the healthy life can be a life led by a separate individual, so that
one might in Platonic terms try to make *sense* of the idea of adding this life to the other, the
virtuous one; but Plato's way of describing the overall life here in fact treats physical health
in parallel to the moral virtues.) So the life of physical health and moral virtue that Plato refers
to is a life which combines, not the four previously mentioned *lives*, but the four previously
mentioned *characteristics* used to describe those lives. It is exactly as with the passage from
Aristotle's *Politics*: *bios* means "(mode of) life" throughout, as it means elsewhere in Greek
literature, and is nowhere used to refer to distinct aspects or phases, or distinct sets of actions
or activities, found in a single mode of life.

Ironically, as I argue in the text, Keyt did not need to adopt the desperate and foredoomed
tactic of arguing that the "life of the intellect" just *is* the intellectual activities that are part of
the best human life, in order to reach the conclusion he wanted to reach, that the best life is
one devoted to the exercise of all the virtues, and not just the virtues of the theoretical intellect.

him, and a thing should be identified with that in it which controls and is better than the others.[15] So one ought to choose the life that includes and places proper emphasis on excellent theoretical study, rather than one that omits this, being devoted only to the exercise of the moral virtues: to choose the latter is to choose not one's own life, but that of a different kind of person, one not having a theoretical intellect and so not properly to be identified primarily with that (1178a3–4). Finally, as has been argued previously (see 1113a25; 1113b2; 1176b24–27), what is by nature proper to each thing is best and most pleasant for it, so that if each of us is (by nature) more than anything else his theoretical intellect, the "life of the intellect," that is, a life devoted to the exercise of all the human virtues but with special emphasis on the virtues of the theoretical intellect, will be proper to us, and so best and most pleasant, and, in consequence, happiest for us (1178a4–8).

Throughout this discussion, then, the life of the intellect that Aristotle champions is one devoted to all the human virtues but in a special degree to excellent contemplative study. It is not, as I used to think, a life led in single-minded devotion to the intellectual values realized in such contemplation.[16] Accordingly, when Aristotle contrasts with this life a "life of the other kind of virtue," and ranks this second life below the other one in happiness (it is happy "in the second degree," 1178a9), he is referring to the life someone leads who has recognized the value of the moral virtues and the practical, citizenly life they support, and has perfected himself in respect of them, but has not carried his self-perfection further to include the development and exercise of the virtues of contemplative study. It is reasonable of Aristotle to say that this life, too, is a happy one, since it contains virtuous activities, activities of the type which constitute happiness and which by their presence in a life over a sufficient duration, according to his theory throughout the *Ethics*, confer happiness on it. But since such a life is at the same time deficient with respect to that very type of activity, it is not, morally good though it be, the best life for a human being. Happy it is, but not the happiest we are by nature capable of.[17]

---

[15] I accept what Keyt says about these qualified identity-statements, pp. 379–80; even if, as the context shows, the intellect here in question is the theoretical intellect (this controls by being not what exercises control but what control is exercised on behalf of—cf. 1145a6–9), a full account of the identity of each person will identify us in part, though in lesser degree, with the practical intellect, the non-rational desires and, in fact, the living body as a whole.

[16] Accordingly I no longer have the reason I had in my book *Reason and Human Good* (pp. 163–65) for denying that the person leading the life of the intellect would be a morally virtuous person who would not just engage regularly in actions required by the virtues but would do them in the full possession of these virtues. So I would now interpret the reference to the contemplative person's acting "according to virtue" at 1178b6, 1179a5–6, 9, straightforwardly, as meaning "acting virtuously."

[17] It is perhaps worth emphasizing Aristotle's seriousness and explicitness in holding that a human life devoted to moral virtue but without special attention to philosophical and scientific inquiry and knowledge would, despite the primacy of the latter in what is in *fact* the best life for a human being, nonetheless count as a happy one. He says at 1178a9 (with *deuterōs* I understand *eudaimōn* from the previous line) that this life will be a happy one in the second

IX

At the end of his discussion of *eudaimonia* in Book X (1178b7–1179a32), Aristotle confirms these conclusions by taking up and developing the connections, only adumbrated in what precedes, between the human "life of the intellect" and the life the gods lead. I conclude my own discussion by considering the bearing of what Aristotle says here on the proper understanding of his conception of human happiness and the place of contemplative study in it.

Aristotle points out (1178b8–9) that we take it for granted that not only some human beings, but gods too, are happy (*eudaimonas*), and indeed that the gods are in the highest degree happy, happier than any human being ever is or can be. The gods' happiness cannot, however, consist even in part in morally virtuous actions since the gods are not affected by the conditions that make that kind of action either possible or appropriate. Their happiness must instead consist exclusively in (some kind of) excellent contemplative study: it is that that makes them and their lives not just happy but happy in the highest degree, happier than any human being. So the excellent contemplative study that human beings are capable of, being the human activity that is most akin to the activity of the gods that constitutes their *eudaimonia*, must be our "complete happiness" (1178b7–8), the element in our happiness that most fully realizes the characteristics that make an activity count as a happy one in the first place; it must be the *eudaimonikōtatē* (1178b23) human activity—the one most of the nature of happiness, or (perhaps) most contributory to the happiness of the happy human life.

Earlier Aristotle argued that some contemplative study is "complete happiness" by enumerating various preliminary "criteria" of *eudaimonia* and arguing that contemplative study possesses these characteristics more completely than other human activities do. Now he confirms this conclusion by adding that such study is the whole of the happiness of the gods, and the happiness of the gods must be the most perfect and most fully realized kind of happiness. But he immediately takes his argument one step further. He recalls the fact of ordinary (Greek) usage, one he has mentioned previously (Book I, chap. 9, 1099b32–1100a1), that we don't speak of any other animal than human beings as being happy or as possibly "sharing in" happiness (*eudaimonia*). Other animals can lead better or worse lives, and of course for each of them there is by nature a kind of living that realizes their good, but we do not call these lives happy, nor do we describe whatever in an animal's life makes it good as (a kind of) happiness. (We don't speak of

degree, and at 1178a21–22 he speaks of "the happiness (*hē eudaimonia*) that depends upon the moral virtues," thus referring to the morally virtuous actions that occur in the "life of moral virtue" as (a) *eudaimonia*. This is in accord with his general usage of the term *eudaimonia* as described above (sect. IV): the morally virtuous activities in the life of moral virtue are the good it contains in virtue of which it can be characterized as happy, and so they count in the primary sense of the term *eudaimonia* as the *eudaimonia* of or in this life.

canine *eudaimonia*, as it were.) Earlier Aristotle had explained this restriction by remarking that other animals do not engage in "noble actions," the actions in which, as he had explained, the virtues or excellences of reason are expressed; especially relevant in the context was, of course, the absence from animal lives of the *moral* virtues. But now (1178b24–32) he argues that this usage correctly reflects and is grounded in the narrower fact that among animals only human beings are capable of contemplative study. It is because we can, while other animals cannot, contemplate in much the way that god does, that the best human life is not just best, but *happy*, and that a certain activity, or certain activities, in that life are entitled to be called "happiness." So, he says, human life is happy to the extent that there is in it something resembling the divine activity of contemplation. "Happiness extends just so far as contemplative study does, and those who contemplate more (or in a higher degree) also have more (or a higher degree of) happiness, not incidentally but in virtue of the contemplation" (1178b28–31).[18]

Here Aristotle claims that, in the nature of things, divine and human contemplation are the only things that are entitled to be described without qualification as *eudaimonia*. And ordinary usage, he says, which recognizes *eudaimonia* as a particularly wonderful sort of good, reflects this fact when it denies to other animals any share in happiness. Nonetheless, in the case of human beings, Aristotle's own theory throughout the *Ethics* has maintained that all the human virtuous activities of all types, both the theoretical and the moral and practical ones, are entitled, when they occur as part of a complete life, to be counted as elements in our *eudaimonia*. There is no good reason to think he withdraws, or contradicts, that theory here. If human beings are capable of *eudaimonia* only because they are capable of contemplative study, that does not mean that the *eudaimonia* they achieve, when they do achieve it, consists of nothing but the contemplation they engage in. Likewise, the assertion that one human being is happier than another the more he contemplates does not imply that the human being who contemplates not at all but lives a thoroughly "practical," but morally good life, has no *eudaimonia*.

---

[18] I have translated the second part of this sentence, admittedly somewhat awkwardly, in such a way as to bring out what I take to be its double import. In the first part of the sentence Aristotle says, in effect, that *eudaimonia* extends only to gods and human beings, because only they can engage in contemplative study. In the second part I take him to convey simultaneously two connected points: (a) gods are happy in a higher degree than any humans, because they contemplate in a higher degree (more continuously, and with a higher type of contemplation); (b) among human beings, the ones who contemplate more are happier than those who contemplate less. In both cases the difference in happiness is a direct consequence of the contemplation found in the superior lives: the happiness that consists in the gods' contemplation is superior because of the superior character of that contemplation, and the happiness in the lives of human beings who contemplate more is superior to the happiness in the lives of those who contemplate less because of the character and value of the added contemplation.

Aristotle's claim seems rather to be that those very morally virtuous activities, which *do* partly constitute a human being's *eudaimonia*, only count as a (kind of) *eudaimonia* because of some connection in which they stand to the activities of contemplative study in which the happy person also engages. These latter, by contrast, get their title to the name *eudaimonia* directly, because of their intrinsic character, a character that makes them appropriately akin to the gods' contemplation. But what is this connection? Aristotle does not say, but perhaps his thought is this. We have known from the beginning (from Book I, chapter 7, onwards) that human reason, by contrast with divine reason, is complex: it encompasses practical as well as theoretical functions, and its practical functions again are divided between those consisting simply in thinking and those consisting in ways of feeling and (in general) in non-rational desirings. The good for a human being is accordingly a combination of all the activities in which these functions, when perfected, express themselves. So morally virtuous action and excellent contemplative study are linked together as perfections of human reason and so as aspects of the overall human good. But since, of these activities, only excellent contemplative study is found in the divine life, the life which consists of nothing *but* happy activity and is the paradigm for happiness wherever else it is met with, it turns out that it is the happiness of the human contemplative activities that makes morally virtuous activities also instances of happiness. Given the common character of both these types of activity as expressions of the perfection of human reason, then, Aristotle seems to be saying: if one of them because of its kinship to the divine activity counts as happiness, so does the other. On this view, the whole perfection of human reason, in each and every one of its aspects, gives us a share in that wonderful good that common usage testifies to by recognizing gods and humans as the only living beings that can have happiness. Because we *can* contemplate, the other uses of our minds, when they express virtues proper to us as human beings, also, though in lesser degree, give us a share in happiness.

Carefully interpreted, then, Aristotle's bold derivation of human happiness from our kinship with the gods grounds, and does nothing to undermine, the theory of happiness that he has presented throughout these concluding chapters of the treatise. According to this derivation, "complete happiness" is found in excellent contemplative study, but happiness is also found in morally virtuous activity, and the best and happiest life for a human being is a life successfully and effectively led in recognition of the permanent value to a human being of the use of perfected human reason in all its aspects and functions. The net effect, then, of Aristotle's return at the end of the *Nicomachean Ethics* to the topic of happiness as sketched in a vague and preliminary way in Book I, is indeed to bring out the priority in several connected respects of excellent contemplative study to the other types of excellent rational activity. But he does this in such a way as merely to refine the earlier account, while preserving intact its central claim that the human good consists in the regular and full exercise over a complete lifetime of all the human virtues. The revised theory of happiness in Book X is, after all, fully compatible with the accounts of the moral virtues, practical reasoning, friendship, and the other topics taken up in the middle books of the treatise.[19]

SELECTED FURTHER READINGS

Broadie, Sarah. *Ethics with Aristotle*, chapter 7. New York: Oxford University Press, 1991.

Crisp, Roger. "Aristotle's Inclusivism." *Oxford Studies in Ancient Philosophy* 12 (1994): 111–36.

Curzer, Howard J. "Criteria for Happiness in *Nicomachean Ethics* I.7 and X.6–8." *Classical Quarterly* 40 (1990): 421–32.

Heinaman, Robert. "Eudaimonia and Self-Sufficiency in the *Nicomachean Ethics*." *Phronesis* 33 (1988): 31–53.

———."Rationality, Eudaimonia and Kakodaimonia in Aristotle." *Phronesis* 38 (1993): 31–56.

Irwin, T.H. "The Structure of Aristotelian Happiness." *Ethics* 101 (1991): 382–91.

Kraut, Richard. *Aristotle on the Human Good*, chapters 1 and 5. Princeton: Princeton University Press, 1989.

Lawrence, Gavin. "Nonaggregatability, Inclusiveness, and the Theory of Focal Value: NE 1.7 1097b16–20." *Phronesis* 42 (1997): 32–76.

Reeve, C.D.C. *Practices of Reason*, chapter 4. Oxford: Clarendon Press, 1992.

Roche, Timothy D. "*Ergon* and *Eudaimonia* in *Nicomachean Ethics* I: Reconsidering the Intellectualist Interpretation." *Journal of the History of Philosophy* 26 (1988): 175–94.

White, Stephen A. "Is Aristotelian Happiness a Good Life or the Best Life?" *Oxford Studies in Ancient Philosophy* 8 (1990): 103–43.

[19] This chapter was first prepared for and presented at a conference on Contemporary Ethical Thought and the History of Moral Philosophy held at Marquette University, October 4–6, 1985, with support from the Franklin J. Matchette and Mellon Foundations. It was then presented in a festschrift for Kurt Baier.

CHAPTER TEN

Some Remarks on Aristotle's Moral Psychology

I

Aristotle the moral philosopher seems very much in vogue these days. Among the philosophers of the traditional pantheon he, alongside perhaps only Thomas Aquinas, has been adopted as patron of the increasingly prominent philosophical movement toward moral theory based on the virtues, rather than on moral rules or other principles of behavior. Yet Aristotle and medieval Aristotelians such as Aquinas are by no means the only important philosophers of the past who regarded the acquisition and constant employment of the virtues as the center both of morality itself and of a correct theory of what morality demands of us. Aristotle does not differ at all in this respect from the whole of the main tradition in ancient Greek moral theory, descending from Socrates and including Plato, the Stoics Zeno and Chrysippus and their followers, and the many Aristotelian and Platonist philosophers of later antiquity. And quite a few post-Renaissance moralists, both Christian and secular, shared this much of Aristotle's outlook. To mention only the most celebrated, one can think, for example, of Spinoza, of Butler and Hume, all of whom treat morality as the possession of certain personal qualities, in fact a set of virtues, rather than conformance to some set of moral rules. Presumably, then, Aristotle's position as patron owes something to special features of *his* understanding of what the virtues are and how they shape and are otherwise connected to the truly moral life—features that give his theory greater appeal than those of these other philosophers. Nor in very gross terms is it difficult to see, or to guess at, some of the special attractions of Aristotle's theory. A virtue for Aristotle is a matter of one's character, where that is understood as a certain *unified condition* of both feeling and reasoned judgment, and both reasoned judgment and trained sensitivity and perceptiveness with regard to significant features of actual situations as they arise or are anticipated. Aristotle's conception of virtues makes them properties of great psychological complexity and depth, and partly in consequence it is easy to see why, if he is right about what a virtue is, virtues might deserve to be regarded as central to morality.

On the other hand, when it comes to the detail of Aristotle's theory, where its interest and supposed philosophical strengths will either be confirmed or, perhaps, proven illusory, those who invoke Aristotle's authority often say little, and what they do say is so obviously selective as to leave one doubtful whether they have a properly balanced appreciation of all the actual complexities of Aristotle's theory. At a number of important places, in fact, I believe Aristotle's theory of the virtues is not correctly represented in the recent philosophical literature, or for that matter in the more scholarly literature, either.

In the time available I will obviously not be able to set out and argue properly for a complete interpretation of Aristotle's theory of what a virtue of character, such as justice or courage or generosity, regarded as psychological properties of individual persons, is. Instead, I will begin by listing what I take to be the seven central claims Aristotle makes in this psychological connection about the virtues of character. This will at least give a summary of what would need to be worked out in detail in order to get a complete and properly balanced understanding of his theory. (See the Appendix.) You will notice from this list that at the center of Aristotle's understanding of what it is to have a character, and what it is to have a good or virtuous character, lies a certain distinction between reason (or, more properly, practical reason), on the one hand, and nonrational or nonreasoning desires, on the other. According to Aristotle, having a character at all, and a fortiori having a good character *consists* in a settled, trained disposition of a person's capacity and tendency to experience some range of *non*rational desires, or other nonrational feelings, and, partly in consequence of those desires or feelings, to act in certain characteristic ways.

Now Aristotle's fundamental thesis in this whole area, that human beings do have nonrational desires and other feelings that need to be disciplined and controlled, and that to have a character is, precisely, to be in some particular settled condition with respect to non-rational feelings, was by no means universally accepted by philosophers in antiquity. The ancient Stoics, who correctly thought that Socrates as represented in Plato's early dialogues held, even took it for obvious, that adult human beings have *no* non-rational desires, developed an elaborate and complex theory of the virtues of character (one at least as complex as Aristotle's own) that strenuously and apparently rather persuasively maintained that these virtues are settled conditions of practical reason itself, and not of nonrational desire, for the simple reason that there were no nonrational desires (that is, none in any adult human being). Now obviously the Stoics were not denying such facts of everyday experience as that human beings sometimes feel anger or fear or sexual arousal or grief (things that Aristotle counts as nonrational desires and feelings); they held rather that these psychological phenomena are *not* nonrational feelings, in the relevant, Aristotelian sense, at all, but states of our rational minds. If we are to understand Aristotle's theory adequately, either from the historical or the philosophical point of view, it seems to me crucial that we understand as clearly as we can Aristotle's theory of the human desires, which counts anger, fear, and other such feelings as nonrational, precisely as one alternative to the account of these phenomena provided by the Stoics. If instead, as I suspect most contemporary readers of Aristotle do, we simply accept Aristotle's view of these matters, without seriously entertaining the Stoic alternative, we will certainly miss much of the force and interest of Aristotle's position.

In what follows I am going to concentrate on Aristotle's distinction, which as I have said is central to his theory of the virtues of character, between nonrational desires and reason itself in the generation of human action. I will have the contrast with the Stoic theory in mind throughout, but will only turn explicitly to the Stoics at the end of the chapter, where I will offer some brief comparative remarks that I hope will help to sharpen our understanding of both the historical and the philosophical significance of Aristotle's theory.

II

To begin with it is necessary to understand clearly how Aristotle uses the word "desire" (*orexis*) when he speaks, as he does in the contexts which will interest us, of occurrent desires, desires that are actively influencing in some way an agent's behavior on some occasion. Such a desire is taken by Aristotle (and in this the Stoics are in complete agreement) as more than merely an *inclination* to want to have or experience or do something; it is a fully fledged, completed such want—an active psychological movement toward getting in an appropriate way, or experiencing or doing, whatever it is the desire for. Aristotle says at one place in discussing weakness of will (*Nicomachean Ethics* VII–*Eudemian Ethics* VI, 1147a34–35) that *epithumiai* or appetitive desires like thirst, understood not as a set of uncomfortable bodily feelings but as a desire *for drink*, actually have the power to set the bodily limbs themselves in movement. And the same holds for all other desires: they are fully realized psychological movements that move the limbs and so initiate action, unless some other similar psychological movements outweigh them or add some weight of their own so as to diminish or deflect their influence on the relevant bodily parts. So in maintaining that human beings have *non*rational desires, Aristotle is maintaining that human beings are capable of being set in movement and action in ways that are completely independent of the use of their rational capacities—that is, as I will explain more fully below, independently of any rational, i.e., reasoned, *thoughts* they may have about what *to do,* about what is *to be done.* On Aristotle's view, to be desiring food or drink, where these are appetitive desires, or to have an angry desire to retaliate against some supposed offense, is, as such, both to be moving psychologically toward relevant action *and* to be so moving without thinking, in one's rational mind, that these things *are to be done*—in fact, one might be thinking, quite on the contrary, that they are definitely *not* to be done. When the Stoics deny that human beings have any nonrational desires at all, precisely that is what they are denying. According to them, appetitive and angry desires, whatever else they involve,

involve centrally the rational, i.e., reasoned thought that the actions they are moving the agent to do are *to be done*. These are mistaken, erroneous thoughts, the Stoics hold, but the errors are errors of reasoning, not some other kind of errors.

Now in coming to grips with Aristotle's theory, the first thing to notice is that, in common with Socrates, Plato, the Stoics and Epicurus, Aristotle held what is for us the strange-seeming view that reason is *itself* the source of a certain sort of desire, of a certain sort of psychological impulse or movement toward action. This way of thinking is strikingly evident in Plato's *Republic* IV, but equally and in a precisely parallel way in *Nic. Eth.* I 13 (to which I will turn in a moment). Socrates in the *Republic* wants to show that there are three parts of the soul. He argues from cases of *akrasia,* first that there are appetites (in addition to reason), then that there are spirited impulses (in addition to both reason and appetite). It is worthy of notice that in his arguments Socrates *assumes* as something that does not need discussion that reason is a source of motivating force of some sort. Assuming that, his question then is whether there are other sources of motivation distinct from reason. As just noted, he argues this first for appetites. He claims that sometimes when a person's reason declares that some action is not to be done he nonetheless feels an impulse (an appetite, in fact), opposed to reason, and sometimes even acts on it. Here the opposition is clearly being conceived as an opposition of impulses or psychological movements, one coming from reason and pulling the agent back from the action, the other coming from appetite and moving him for and toward the action.[1] (Hence he can conclude we have two parts of the soul at work here, not one.) Plato's way of developing Socrates' argument, by making him assume that reason has its own impulses, makes perfectly good sense if one reflects that Socrates in earlier dialogues, notably the *Meno* and *Protagoras,* was himself thoroughly convinced that reason alone was responsible for our decisions and actions: that presupposes that reason is a source of motivation, of impulses to movement and action. Plato has Socrates in the *Republic* take that for granted, and argue that reason is not the *only* source of movements in the soul toward action. The Platonic view, as introduced in *Republic* IV, begins by accepting Socrates' earlier account of reason as a source of action, and goes on to recognize two *other* sources of action (two other parts of the soul). In other words, Plato saw the need to argue that we experience appetitive and spirited desires, where these have to be construed as nonrational, but not that we have rational desires (or whatever one is to call reason-derived psychological movements toward action). That seemed to him perfectly clear and not to need argument.

Aristotle, too, just like the Socrates of the *Republic,* when introducing the division of the human soul in *Nic. Eth.* I 13, takes for granted the motive-power of reason (which is why, as with Socrates in the *Republic,* it

---

[1] See Chapter 4 above, "Plato's Theory of Human Motivation," section II.

has so often escaped people's notice). He, too, argues that there are other motive forces, as well, the nonrational ones. He appeals (1102b13–25), just as Socrates in the *Republic* does, to the phenomenon of *akrasia* (but also to that of self-control). The *hormai* or impulses, he says, of people acting akratically go in opposite directions: *epi tanantia hai hormai tōn akratōn* (the same is true of course for the self-controlled too).[2] That is, they experience a rational desire (*hormē*)—a desire coming from their reasoned view of what to do—together with a nonrational desire of some sort, and these desires are opposed to one another. One moves them toward an action that the other moves them away from. The weak agent acts on the nonrational desire, the self-controlled person on the rational one.

Aristotle has a name for this rational impulse. It is *boulēsis* (what Ross translates "rational wish"; or more simply, just "wish" as Irwin and others translate it). In many places (in *EE* and *Magna Moralia*, in *de Anima*, in *de Motu*, and in the *Rhetoric* and *Politics*),[3] but, curiously, none in the *Nic. Eth.*, Aristotle explicitly divides *orexis* (that seems to be his established word for movements of the soul toward or away from action) into three kinds: *epithumia* or appetite, *thumos* or spirited, competitive impulse, and *boulēsis*. And he repeatedly makes it clear that *epithumia* and *thumos* are the two genera of nonrational desire, while *boulēsis* is his preferred name for the movement toward action produced by the use of reason itself, on its own.

III

Now this theory that there are three forms of *orexis*, two nonrational and one rational (in the sense that one comes from what Aristotle calls the reasoning part of the soul and two from the part or parts that do not reason) has very important implications for how Aristotle is conceiving reason itself, and correlatively for how he is conceiving the non-reasoning desires.

First of all, when he says, as he does, e.g., at *Nic. Eth.* VI-*EE* V, 1139a35 and again at *de An.* III 10, 433a23 that *nous* or *dianoia* by itself does not produce movement (i.e., any psychological movement toward or away from action), one must not assume that this means that reasoning about what to

---

[2] The *Eudemian Ethics,* in a different context, agrees about this analysis of *akrasia* and self-control: 1224a31–32, ἐναντίας ὁρμὰς ἔχων αὐτὸς ἕκαστος αὑτῷ πράττει.

[3] See, e.g., *EE* II 7, 1123a26–27 and II 10, 1225b24–26; *Magna Moralia* I 12, 1187b37; *de Anima* II 3, 414b2 and III 9, 432b5–6 and 10, 433a22–26; *de Motu* 6, 700b19; *Rhetoric* I 10, 1369a1–4; *Politics* VII 15, 1334b17–25. Aristotle seems already in the *Topics* to have appropriated *boulēsis* as the name for desire coming from reason: see IV 5, 126a6–13, where he says roundly that *boulēsis* (=*orexis agathou,* 146b5–6) is *en tōi logistikōi,* by contrast with *to epithumētikon* and *to thumoeides.* The nearest Aristotle comes in *Nicomachean Ethics* to dividing all *orexis* into these three types is III 2, 1111 b10–12, where he lists *epithumia, thumos* and *boulēsis* alongside *doxa tis* as potential candidates for what *prohairesis* is, but without saying that they are candidates precisely because they are *the* forms of *orexis* (contrast *EE* II 10, 1225b21–26).

do does not lead to any movement toward acting *except* when it is coupled with some or other *non*rational desire. There is also the rational *orexis,* and Aristotle's theory of the three kinds of *orexis* shows that *one* movement toward action that such reasoning might lead to is precisely a *boulēsis.* In fact this is what he says explicitly at *de An.* 433a22–25: "*nous* plainly does not produce movement without *orexis,* for *boulēsis* is an *orexis* and whenever a person is moved by reasoning he is in fact (or: also) moved by *boulēsis.*"[4]

Secondly, one must be careful to bear in mind the sense in which a wish is a *rational* desire and, correspondingly, the sense in which the nonrational desires are *non*rational. In *Nic. Eth.* VI-EE V 2, 1139b12, Aristotle says that of both theoretical and practical reason the function (*ergon*) is (to pursue and attain) the truth. One part of what he asserts in this passage about practical reason is that its function is, not just to hold views to the effect that something or other is good for us, but to do so, whether we are self-conscious about this or not, as somehow part of or the result of a process of investigation *into* the truth about what is good. That is, a rational desire or *boulēsis* is the practical expression of a course of thought about what is good for oneself, that is aimed at working out the truth about what *is* in fact good. Of course, in speaking thus about the *function* of *logos* (reason) he is describing how it operates when fully developed. He does not mean that whenever in any person a thought occurs that derives from or expresses his *logos* or reason, or whenever in consequence he has a *boulēsis,* the person has actually done any such investigating into the truth about what is good. All it means is that a *logos*-thought and a *logos*-desire are about the good in a way that lays claim to there being a reason for thinking this, and to thinking it for that reason. (This will become clearer as I proceed, when we see how similar thoughts about the good occur differently from this in the non-reasoning desires.)

This means that the nonrational desires, as such, can be conceived simply as ones that lack these special features that their origin in reason gives to the rational desires. Accordingly, nonrational desires will be desires whose causal history never includes any process (self-conscious or not) of investigation into the truth about what is good for oneself; whatever the cause of the value-judgment such a desire may nonetheless contain this cause is never

---

[4] This has very important implications, which however I will not pursue in this paper, for what Aristotle means when he says that a *prohairesis* or decision is a union of deliberative reasoning and desire (i.e., *orexis*): the desire that is an element of a *prohairesis* need not be a nonrational desire (an appetite or any other passion), but may, given Aristotle's theory that there are three types of desire, be a form of *boulēsis.* That he intends to adopt the view that it is a *boulēsis,* and not any form of nonrational desire, is not perfectly clear in the *Nic. Eth.* (either in III or VI-EE V), but it *is* clear in *EE* II 10, 1226b2–5 and 1227a3.5. The *Nic. Eth.* texts permit this interpretation, and in view of the exceptionally clear statements in the *EE,* I have no doubt that it is what Aristotle intended in the *Nic. Eth.* as well.

any reason the agent might think there is for *making* this judgment. Non-rational desires have other causes than reason, and these are the origin of whatever value-thoughts the desires may contain. (I'll explain this further as I go on.) Accordingly, nonrational desires (say, a desire for something because it is pleasant, or an angry desire to strike back at someone) may on Aristotle's theory perfectly well be propositional and conceptual in structure (they may be or involve the thought *that* something is pleasant or that someone has acted against oneself in an intolerable manner): *that* is not a feature reserved to rational desires, given the conception Aristotle is working with of reason. But they can also even contain thoughts about what is good or bad for oneself—the thought, e.g., that pleasure, or this particular pleasure, is a good thing, or the thought that vengeance is not just sweet but entirely proper, even required if one is to be a person of any worth at all.

Aristotle is clear about this last point when he says in *Nic. Eth.* VII-*EE* VI, 1149a25ff. that *thumos* or spirit sometimes hears reason but mishears what it says. For example, deliberating about what to do in the face of an apparent insult, someone's reason declares that it was in fact an insult, and his *thumos* immediately boils up, as if, Aristotle says, inferring that someone who acts in that insolent way must be punished at once (i.e., that it is right or good *to* punish such a person). And the same thing is implied about *epithumia* or appetite by his frequent claim that its object, the pleasant, is the apparent good: to experience an appetite for something is, on Aristotle's view, to find it pleasant, i.e., to take it to be good.[5] The use here of what *we* might call reason (the power to think with concepts, even with the concepts of good and bad) does not make these desires rational desires in Aristotle's sense of the word "rational"; these desires, and so the thoughts that they contain, do not occur as parts of any process of reasoning for the purpose of figuring out what one should do, i.e., what one has the best reasons for doing; nor do those value-judgments rest upon reasons. One's appetitive desire, let us assume, is a more or less immediate response to the way the thing desired appeals to one's senses; though arousal for it partly consists in the thought that it would be a good thing to have it in whatever way one desires it, that opinion is not based on any course of thought purporting to reveal any reason for thinking it good (even if at the time one does think one has such a reason), nor is it the holding of any reason, or even the holding that there *is* any reason, for so valuing it. Likewise for the anger: although, as in Aristotle's example of the anger that mishears or half-hears, it may be aroused by a thought occurring within such a course of reasoning, viz. the thought that some person has insulted you, the further thought contained in the anger, that this kind of thing must be combatted

---

[5] Does Aristotle mean that *epithumia* in human beings is in this way for pleasure taken for good, without implying or meaning to imply the same for the other animals?

forthwith, is not based on any *reason* for thinking this (even if at the time one has, or thinks one has, some reason for thinking it). You get angry because that is how you feel about insults, whether or not that is also how you think you have reason to act in relation to them.[6]

IV

Aristotle's distinction, then, between rational and nonrational parts of the soul has nothing to do with the modern distinction between reason (regarded as *the* faculty of concept-formation and the manipulation of concepts), on the one hand, and desire (regarded on its own as a concept-free faculty of urges), on the other hand. There are both conceptual thoughts and (if you like) "urges" on both sides of Aristotle's distinction between *logos* and the *alogon*—reason and the nonrational. But it also has nothing to do with the subtler distinction between thoughts about, and desires that involve thoughts about, the good, and thoughts and desires that involve no reference to the good, that has recently been used to interpret the views argued for by the Socrates of the *Republic*.[7] All three of the types of desire Aristotle distinguishes involve (as he thinks) not just thoughts, but thoughts about what is good or bad: the difference between the two nonrational types of desire and the rational one consists solely in whether or not the source of these thoughts lies in *reasons* one thinks there are for having them.

> [6] It should be clear that the distinction I have sketched in the foregoing paragraphs, and develop further below, between rational and nonrational desires requires the rational "part" of the soul to be independent in a very strong way from all our other psychological capacities, including especially our capacities for nonrational desires. The reasons for doing things, and for valuing things, that issue from the exercise of reason in this sense must be construed as arrived at independently of one's acceptance of beliefs and other commitments in and through the exercise of other capacities (including the emotions and appetites). Reason is to be thought of as operating by stepping back completely from all such commitments and examining on grounds that it itself works out what is true or false in them. When I speak of a *boulēsis,* but not, e.g., an angry desire, as resting on and being caused by (the holding of) reasons, I mean reasons so construed. We may say, truly enough, that in feeling anger we feel as we do for a reason, viz. (as it might be) that some person has insulted us, and that this is intolerable. To that extent, our anger is caused by (the holding of) that reason. But that does not count against the claim I mean to be making in the text when I say that only rational desires (*boulēseis*) rest on reasons. I do not undertake to defend this conception of reason here (I believe it is held in common by at least Plato, Aristotle and the Stoics), or, for that matter, to do much by way of defending my attribution of it to Aristotle. For present purposes all I require is that this conception should be intuitively clear enough, and have enough intuitive initial appeal, to allow us to proceed to examine and evaluate the theory of the virtues of character that, if I am right, Aristotle constructs on this foundation.
>
> [7] See Irwin, *Plato's Moral Theory*, ch. VII. Irwin is mainly concerned with the distinction between thoughts about one's *overall* good and other thoughts, and I do not mean to say that Aristotle attributes thoughts about one's overall good to, for example, appetites. However, this should not be allowed to obscure the more important point, that for Aristotle, at any rate, even appetites essentially involve value judgments employing concepts of goodness.

This is crucially important for understanding how Aristotle thinks reason can obtain control of the non-reasoning desires, despite the independence from reason that essentially characterizes them. Aristotle holds that reason controls them not just by getting them to "follow" its directions (somehow or other), but by *persuading* them: the ideal is to persuade the nonrational desires to obey.[8] Now this persuasion is only possible because the very same terms in which reason thinks about the circumstances of action and about the relative values of things in the world in general, are also employed by each of the types of nonrational desire as well. When you are angry, for example, the anger you feel contains the thought that (e.g.) some other person has done you an injury, i.e., has not only done you some harm but has done it deliberately or anyhow without paying the heed to your desires or needs that he ought to have paid, and that such a person ought to be made to suffer in return. If your reason thinks differently at any of the places where value-terms connected with good, right, ought and so on occur in this angry thought, you are internally not just pulled in different directions; you are thinking ultimately contradictory thoughts, one through your anger the other through your reason. For reason to persuade anger (in this particular case, or in general) is for it to get its own view of what is good to prevail, in the sense that this conception comes to be adopted by the nonrational part itself, as well. To cause this to happen, even intermittently, may require practice and training, of course, but in that process reason is not just exercising brute force, as one might in training an animal. It is, among other things, addressing one's anger, trying to direct its attention to features of the situation that will show one's anger, by getting it to respond not just to some narrow, admittedly anger-arousing, range of features, but at the same time to a wider and more comprehensive view of the facts, that it would be, or was, wrong to feel in that way. If anger that springs up in you on some particular occasion obeys reason and is persuaded to obey it by being persuaded thus to feel about the situation as reason, on its own grounds, thinks best, that will mean that your rational thought about the goods and bads in that situation comes to be accepted by the nonrational part, and its own responses will then be adjusted accordingly. If you judge on rational grounds (or with the claim that there *are* rational grounds) that there was no injury at all, or that, though there was an injury, there is no good reason in this case to retaliate, and your anger is persuaded, then you simply cease to be angry (anyhow, at this person). Or it might be that you judge, on reflection, that it was not a very great injury, and/or that only a small retaliation is justified; then your anger dies down to the levels appropriate to those evaluations. The way you then feel about what has happened and about what should be done about it, is exactly also the way you think, for reasons, about it.

[8] Cf. *Nic. Eth.* I 13, 1102b31: nonrational desire is also, in a sense, rational, insofar as it is *katēkoon autou kai peitharchikon*; b33, *to alogon peithetai pōs hupo logou*.

In the general case, whereby habituation brings one's tendency to become angry under the control of one's reason, reason persuades the source of anger in the soul (that from which it boils up) to adopt in general as a fixed and settled outlook on things the system of ideas about what is and is not an injury, and about what does and does not merit retaliation, etc., that reason itself has worked out by trying to discover the correct and rationally grounded considerations that reveal the actual truth about these matters. In that case, one's tendency to respond with anger comes to be always or regularly responsive to the full range of facts about situations as they arise that (and as) reason thinks relevant.

Now because Aristotle thinks that the truth about such matters—matters of value in general—is properly settled by reasoning, he thinks that this is the direction that the resolution of such contradictions *should* take. Your anger was caused not by what you rationally thought, nor by what you would rationally think if you gave reason a chance, but by (possibly obscure) causes lying in your recent or distant past experience: maybe on the occasion in question you are in an irritable frame of mind because of events earlier in the day, and that frame of mind now causes you to find fault where there was none. And so on. In any event, your having these thoughts about injury, justified retaliation and so on is caused ultimately not by any views you may hold that were worked out by rational reflection (or that claim to have a rational justification) but simply by this history of your experiences and the development in relation to them of your innate tendencies to feel in reaction to what happens to you. So where there is a contradiction it is your anger that ought to yield, not your reason. There is no good reason to think that your anger reflects the truth about the matters about which it is making claims.

Furthermore, I take it (here I am speculating a bit), Aristotle thinks that part of what it means to be rational is to have the general tendency not just to resolve such contradictions (to be uncomfortable in the face of contradictions of attitude) but to resolve them in that direction: see *Nic. Eth.* II 1, 1103a24–26, "the virtues (viz. of character) are formed in us not by (our) nature nor contrary to it; rather, it is natural to us to receive them, when we are brought to perfection by habits of feeling (and acting)," πεφυκόσι μὲν ἡμῖν δέξασθαι αὐτάς, τελειουμένοις δὲ διὰ τοῦ ἔθους. The virtues, which of course imply a resolution in reason's favor, are here said to involve the perfection of our nature as rational, i.e., human beings.

However, it is also important to bear in mind that the resolution can go in the other direction, both in individual cases and in general orientation. Faced with a conflict between how you feel about things in some respect and how you think about them, especially if this persists for a long time despite efforts on your part to adjust the way you feel, you will, *faute de mieux,* tend to adjust it in the other direction, by adopting in your rational thoughts a view about good and bad and right and wrong that conforms to the way you habitually feel: it is as if, under pressure from your stubborn desires, you decide on reflection that the correct way to determine what is good is simply to accept as authoritative how you feel. (Perhaps you then figure out some reasons to suit.) What forces us to take one of these two alternatives is the central fact that being rational creatures we cannot very readily or contentedly let the contradiction stand. We are moved, because we are rational, to resolve it in one direction or the other.[9]

V

One last point needs to be emphasized. As I have said, the nonrational desires carry with them value-judgments framed in (at least some of) the very same terms of good and bad, right and wrong, etc., that also reappear in our rational reflections about what to do and why, and can be trained by habituation to respond to events and circumstances, actual or anticipated, on the basis of the very same normative outlook that reason works out. But the nonrational desires are according to Aristotle's view a permanent fact of human life, grounded in human nature and not eliminable, even (*especially*, one is inclined rather to say) in the perfected, fully virtuous person. When a virtuous person acts on reasons, these reasons will (typically anyhow) be reflected in two distinct forms of *hormē* or impulse toward that action. He or she will act from his or her rational desire to so act (a *boulēsis*, i.e., a *prohairesis*), which explicitly rests on, is caused by, the reasons, as represented in deliberation and its conclusions, that he or she has for so acting. But he or she will also experience, and act from, some set of nonrational desires active at the moment, which also contribute their motive force in favor of this action. These do not rest on, and are not caused by, the deliberation and the reasons he or she thinks there are for the action, as they are represented in that deliberation. They are caused by the state of his or her capacity and tendency for nonrational desire (anger, pity, appetitive desire, fear, etc.), as these have developed over time in response to his or her experience of things, including of course the experience of self-discipline and training. Reason and the nonrational aspects of human nature both survive in the virtuous person, and each is called into play independently of the other, even although, by habituation, the nonrational desires have come not to diverge significantly from the rational ones and in fact not to represent to the virtuous agent any picture significantly different from the one his reason presents, of what is valuable in life and worth exerting oneself for or against.

So, on Aristotle's view, when a virtuous person loses a child in an accident he will feel grief, even be seriously affected by grief. He will act (say) in

---

[9] Given the centrality of this fact about rational beings to much of what Aristotle says about virtues and vices of character and how they come into being, it is surprising that he nowhere in the ethical writings seems to state or draw attention explicitly to it.

comforting others and being comforted by them, in burying the child, etc., both from his grief, and from his rational wishes to alleviate others' feelings, to accept their sympathy, and to show his devotion for his child. This is, in one way, one of the most attractive aspects of Aristotle's theory of virtue of character. Intuitively it certainly does not seem right that someone should be thought virtuous who behaved in all these ways (comforted others, accepted their comfort, etc.), judging these behaviors right and having and acting on the right reasons for so judging, but without feeling the grief. Aristotle's recognition of the independence from reason, and the permanence, of our tendencies to feel nonrational desire, can seem a decisive measure of the extent to which he really does take seriously the fact that we are *human* persons, and not (even potentially) some kind of gods. Having nonrational feelings, such as anger, grief, fear, etc., appropriate to the circumstances we find ourselves in is part of our fullest perfection, on his view.

It is at this point that the Stoic theory stands in most radical opposition to Aristotle's. The Stoics agree that what they and Aristotle both call *pathē* or passions essentially consist, anyhow in part, of judgments that one affirms: in an appetitive urge or an angry feeling one affirms the judgment that a pleasant experience or an act of vengeance, is good and worth having or doing. In feeling these desires one is asserting such a judgment, not just entertaining it: that is why, on both the Stoic and the Aristotelian view, these desires are *hormai*—"impulses," actual movements in the soul toward (or away from) action. Merely entertaining such a judgment, or even being inclined to assert it, would not, on either of their views, constitute a *hormē*. Furthermore, the Stoics and Aristotle agree that we come to experience these *pathē* and in doing so to assert these judgments about what is good and bad (for ourselves and others) as a result of our experiences in life as we grow up—and, of course, in particular because in our culture (as in that of ancient Greece) it is the dominant view, which we all imbibe with our mother's milk (if not also in some way from our nature itself), that the things in question (pleasure, insults by others, etc., etc.) really are good or bad, as the case may be. Anger and appetitive urges are strong feelings, and having strong feelings about these things is just what one should expect of someone who did somehow think them really good or bad.

According to the Stoics, however, this view is false. Only one's inner state (the state of one's mind as one faces external things) is either a good or a bad thing for any human being. Accordingly, on the Stoic view, anyone who puts reason in control of his life, as of course they and Aristotle thought was the road to virtue and to human perfection, will have eventually to repudiate, and to repudiate decisively, *all* the judgments about value that get affirmed in the experience of any *pathos*—anger, grief, appetitive desires such as ordinary hungry pursuit of food, ordinary sexual arousal, and so on. And by decisively repudiating these value-judgments one ceases to feel the passion too—in the absence of the thought that anything good or bad is present or in the offing, there is nothing to feel strongly about. Accordingly, on the Stoic theory, the full development of any human being from childhood to maturity to full moral perfection will pass through a phase during which passions will be experienced, but the final goal will be to cease to experience them altogether. So the virtuous person, on the Stoic view, who loses a child, may *act* very much as the Aristotelian virtuous person would act, comforting others, accepting comfort from them, and so on, but he will not feel any grief, however tiny an amount. He will only feel, and will only act from, his rational desire (his *boulēsis,* a term the Stoics take over in this context from the Platonists and Aristotle). He will have no nonrational desires or feelings, at all.

VI

Now, as this rapid summary comparison should make you expect, the Stoics concentrated their opposition to the Aristotelian view on this question of what the nature of goodness is, and which things *are* actually good. It is easy to see why. If they could succeed in showing that only a person's internal state was either good or bad for him, that only his inner state could affect him for better or worse, then it would apparently follow directly that *pathē* would all of them disappear once virtue (which both sides agreed at least included knowledge of what truly *is* good and bad) was achieved. After all, *pathos* was agreed by Aristotle to include a judgment that certain external things or events were good or bad, and if when you *knew* the true theory of what is good or bad you could show decisively that none of these things were or could be good or bad, you could not continue to hold these false beliefs. Thus Aristotle would be hoist by his own petard, the petard of his own theory of the *pathē* as containing such judgments, once the correct theory of goodness and badness was established.

But this conclusion follows only if at the same time you also deny the permanence in human beings and the independence from reason, in the sense I have specified, of the nonrational desires. Aristotle will agree with the Stoics, though not for all the same reasons, that if their theory of goodness and badness is correct anyone who comes to *know* that theory (in the sense of having *phronēsis,* or practical knowledge, of it) will also cease affirming in his thoughts, even in the thoughts contained in his non-reasoning desires, any judgment to the effect that any external thing or event is either good or bad. Practical knowledge necessarily involves bringing the nonrational desires to that extent into conformity with reason's settled judgments about the values of things. But that does not mean at all that the *pathē* will have to disappear. If the nonrational desires really are ways in which values get represented to us that are independent in origin from reason, then the developing history of the ways one is affected in one's feelings about things will include an extra last stage that Aristotle, since of course he did not in fact accept the Stoic theory of goods, did not envisage. This will be the stage at which one's tendency to become angry or to be affected appetitively will be educated so that *in* feeling those things one no longer thinks (what our culture has brought us up so that we do think) that the things one is affected by are bad or good, strictly speaking. This (as one might describe it) "refined" anger and "refined" appetitive desire will contain the thought, not that some external thing or event is or would be good or bad, but only that it has some positive or negative value of some other, lesser kind. But nonetheless it will still be anger or appetitive desire, because of its historical development from earlier versions of the underlying tendency to feel, to be affected by, the ways things *appear* to you (and not merely by the ways you think about them in pursuit of the truth about such matters). Virtue of character would still consist, on this semi-Stoicized Aristotelian view, in *feeling* passions of grief, anger, appetitive desire, and so on, but in conformity with one's fully educated rational judgments about what things are valuable, in what ways they are valuable, and why.

And that is why the Stoics conducted their argument against Aristotle simultaneously on a second front as well. Is there, after all, really any non-rational part or aspect of the human soul, in the sense in which Aristotle held that there was, i.e., as a source of desires independent of reasoning about what ought to be done? We are now in a position to see clearly that this is the really fundamental point of contention.

This brings us full circle and I cannot pursue the argument further here. But it should by now be clear that Aristotle pays a considerable price in order to maintain the independence of the human emotions from human reason which many of us nowadays find so attractive, even perhaps compelling, an idea. As we have seen, he has to assign to the emotions and non-rational desires quite a bit of what we, and the Stoics, would regard as aspects of the capacity for reason: not just conceptualization and evaluation, but, more seriously, even something perilously akin to decision. In experiencing full-fledged anger, as Aristotle thinks and we and the Stoics would insist, a person *assents* to the idea that some act of retribution is to be done, and it is only in consequence of that that she is actually moved to do it. Can one give an acceptable account of what this assent is, without being forced to admit that *it,* at least, comes from that very rational power that Aristotle wanted to set clearly apart from the nonrational desires as a separate, competing source of impulses to action? Anyone who wants to adopt an Aristotelian theory of the moral virtues or virtues of character, and so the Aristotelian psychology of action, must face this question. It must not simply be begged as it seems nowadays mostly to be. The best way to face this question is to think closely and carefully about the Stoics' objections against the very possibility of a nonrational part of the soul conceived as Aristotle conceived it.[10]

[10] In revising this essay for publication I have benefited from comments on earlier versions by T. H. Irwin, Heda Segvic and Gisela Striker, my commentator at the Conference at Memphis State University where it was first presented.

Appendix

1. Virtues of character belong to what Aristotle calls the nonrational part of the soul (*EE* II 1, 1220a10; *Nic. Eth.* I 13, 1102b13).

2. Virtues of character and traits of character in general (i.e., *ēthē*) are qualities (*poiotētes*) (that is, relatively fixed and longlasting ways of being qualified) belonging to the nonrational part, *insofar* as that part is capable of following reason; in fact, these qualities require and depend essentially upon a *prescriptive judgment* of the reason of the person whose soul is in question (*EE* II 2, 1220b5–6; and cf. *Nic. Eth.* II 5 and *Categories* 8b25ff. on *hexeis*).[11]

3. Virtues of character are in *some* way connected essentially with decisions (*prohaireseis*), and so with actions (*praxeis* in the narrower of the two senses that Aristotle's usage gives to this word): see *Nic. Eth.* VI-*EE* V 2, 1139a31.[12]

4. Virtues of character essentially involve experiencing nonrational desires, i.e., *pathē*, in an intermediate degree, i.e., in a degree that precisely suits the circumstances (*Nic. Eth.* II 6, *EE* II 3).[13]

5. It is the practical knowledge possessed by the *phronimos* that determines what the virtuous and intermediate degree of *pathos* is (*Nic. Eth.* II 6, 1107a1–2; *EE* II 3, 1220b28 with II 5, 1222a8 and b7).

6. It is not possible to have a virtuous character without having practical knowledge, nor to have practical knowledge without having a virtuous character (*Nic. Eth.* VI-*EE* V 13, 1144b30–32).

7. A virtue of character is brought into being by repeatedly feeling and acting precisely (or as nearly so as possible) as, in the given circumstances, the person having the virtue would feel and act (*Nic. Eth.* II 1, 1103b6–25, *EE* II 1, 1220a22–24; cf. *de Anima* II 5, 417a22–b2).

---

[11] Here I give what seems to be the burden of a textually corrupt passage of *EE* II that gives a sort of definition of *ēthos*; the *Nic. Eth.* nowhere gives such a definition.

[12] Here I rely on the first part of the passage that is usually cited as Aristotle's "definition" of virtue of character in the *Nic. Eth.* at II 6, 1106b36: virtue is a *hexis prohairetikē*. Nothing exactly corresponds to this definition in the *EE*, but note 1230a27, *pasa aretē prohairetikē*.

[13] Aristotle normally distinguishes just two types of nonrational desires (i.e., *orexeis*), *epithumia* and *thumos*, appetitive and spirited or competitive desire, respectively. It is by reference to nonrational *orexis* so understood that he introduces the nonrational part of the soul in *Nic. Eth.* I 13 and *EE* II 1, 1219b16–1220a4 (cf. *to orektikon*, b23, with II 4, 1221b30–32; but note that already at 1220a1–2 he mentions not *orexis* but *orexeis kai pathēmata* as what reason controls); and in the *Nic. Eth.* contexts, at any rate, virtue of character itself is introduced as the virtue that controls nonrational desire. However, when in *Nic. Eth.* II 5–6 he defines virtue of character as a *hexis,* he explains *hexeis* as conditions on our capacity to feel *pathē* (*not* nonrational *orexeis*), and gives a list of *pathē* (at 1105b21–23) that includes the two sorts of nonrational *orexis* as only two instances of a wider class: fear, grief, pity, envy, etc., as well as *epithumia* and *orgē* (anger—I assume that *orgē* is intended here as a variant for *thumos*, as at *Rhet.* I 10, 1369a4; compare the shorter list of *pathē* in the corresponding passage of *EE* II 2, 1220b 12–13, where we get *thumos* instead of the *Nic. Eth.*'s *orgē*). It is an interesting question exactly how Aristotle intends (or indeed whether he has any worked-out intention at all in this regard) to bring together these two somewhat different characterizations of what the virtues of character control. I do not pursue these questions further here, but loosely interchange "nonrational desire" with "passion."

SELECTED FURTHER READINGS

Broadie, Sarah. *Ethics with Aristotle,* chapter 2. New York: Oxford University Press, 1991.

Hutchinson, Douglas S. "Aristotle and the Spheres of Motivation: *De Anima* III." *Dialogue* 29 (1990): 7–20.

Irwin, T.H. *Aristotle's First Principles,* chapter 15. Oxford: Clarendon Press, 1988.

Striker, Gisela. "Comments on 'Aristotle's Moral Psychology,' by John M. Cooper." *Southern Journal of Philosophy* 27 supplement (1988): 43–47.

Tuozzo, Thomas M. "Conceptualized and Unconceptualized Desire in Aristotle." *Journal of the History of Philosophy* 32 (1994): 525–49.

Reason, Moral Virtue, and Moral Value

IN MORAL PHILOSOPHY Aristotle is well known to stand for the primacy of character, judgment, and perceptiveness. For him, the virtues of character and the nuanced appreciation they bring of the multiplicity of legitimate claims there always are on one's attention are the central phenomena for ethics. For many, this is an appealing view. But Aristotle's theory of the virtues is constructed upon an elaborate and well-articulated basis in psychological theory. He approaches the question what the virtues are and what of value they contribute to a human life through the postulation and analysis of several psychological capacities that he argues human beings by their nature all possess. It is a person's use of these capacities that determines how their life goes, whether for better or for worse. In order properly to understand Aristotle's theory of the virtues one must develop it explicitly from within the context of his psychological theory. I attempt to do this in what follows. As a result I am able to offer in conclusion some thoughts about what precisely that "nobility" or "fineness" or "beauty" in action is that Aristotle makes the constant goal of morally virtuous action as such, and how its pursuit fits together with the other concerns that also motivate the morally virtuous agent.

I RATIONALITY AND THE VIRTUES

We should begin by reminding ourselves that Aristotle recognizes not one but three distinct sorts of virtues (*aretai*). He claims that our specifically human nature makes us capable of acquiring all three, anyhow in principle. Each is a perfection, in some way, of a certain single, but ramified, ability that he takes to be fundamental to and distinctive of the human species. His name for this capacity, or for the "part" of the soul it constitutes, is *to logon echon*—the rational power, the ability to reason. Two types of virtue he describes as belonging to this ability in a straightforward way: they are perfections of our capacity actually to think thoughts in the course of reasoning, and so they belong to reason "in itself."[1] These are the virtues of theoretical and practical reasoning. The third, however, belongs to our ability to reason in what is obviously an extended sense of that phrase.

This is the perfection of a capacity that Aristotle follows Plato in the

---

[1] They belong to the rational power (the λόγον ἔχον) ὡς ἔχον καὶ διανοούμενον, *Nicomachean Ethics* 1.7.1098a4–5, or to what has reason κυρίως καὶ ἐν αὑτῷ, 1.13.1103a2.

Republic in attributing to human beings—a capacity to experience desires (*orexeis*) that are not, strictly speaking, exercises of reason at all. Experiencing *these* desires does not consist in having (reasoned) thoughts, nor are they motivational states that depend simply and directly upon having any such thoughts. For example, we experience appetitive desires such as thirst, understood not as the familiar bodily discomfort caused by the physiological need for water but rather as a fully completed *desire for water* (or other liquid), or for the pleasure of drinking some, that is somehow caused by that need. These physiologically based, appetitive desires are examples of what Aristotle counts as non-reasoning or non-rational desires, *alogoi orexeis*. None the less, Aristotle calls the capacity for such desires that human beings (but not other animals) have a rational one because it is capable of being rendered obedient to the rational power in the strict sense of the word.[2] This means two things. First, it can happen, and is in an important sense natural, Aristotle thinks, that a person's tendencies to experience these desires come to reflect and be shaped by, and so to follow, his reasoned judgments about what is *worth* caring about, doing, and experiencing. Secondly, and more strongly, these reasoned judgments that a person's non-reasoned desires follow can themselves come to conform to the substantive standards and requirements of reason as correctly employed. When that double condition is realized, then the desires that a person experiences that are in themselves non-rational can, in an extended sense of the word, none the less also be correctly described as rational activities, exercises of our ability to reason. Under those conditions reason is being exercised in two distinct spheres, first of all "in itself" (*en hautōi*, 1103a2) (in so far as we judge, in accordance with reason's own standards, that something is worth wanting in this appetitive way), but additionally *in* the appetitive desire itself. The appetitive desire too gets counted as an exercise of reason, since it has the character and content that it does precisely because it does follow reason.

When the capacity to experience non-rational desires is in this way under the control of one's reason, it is what Aristotle calls practical reason that has control—reason as calculative and deliberative (*to logistikon, Nicomachean Ethics* 6.1.1139a14) or engaged in thinking about action (*tou praktikou kai dianoētikou* 1139a29–30). It is by being obedient to this part or aspect of reason (in the narrow sense) that the capacity to experience non-rational desires itself qualifies as a rational power. Aristotle holds that the virtuous condition of the non-rational desires presupposes that the practical reason that they are obedient to itself possesses its own proper virtue, practical

---

[2] It is λόγον ἔχον in the sense (an extended one) that it can, or does under ideal natural conditions, obey reason, ὡς ἐπιπειθὲς λόγῳ (*Nicomachean Ethics* 1.7.1098a4, explained at some length at 1.13.1102b25–31)—the same sense, he adds at 1102b31–1103a3, in which one hears and heeds the advice of a friend or one's father (τὸ δ' ὥσπερ τοῦ πατρὸς ἀκουστικόν τι, 1103a3).

wisdom or *phronēsis*.[3] Since on Aristotle's view the human virtues are all perfections of our nature *as rational*, it is relatively easy, given what I have said so far, to understand why he holds this. A person whose reasoned view about what is worth caring about, doing, and experiencing was fully reflected in the way she experienced non-rational desires no doubt *could* be said, in a way, to have non-rational desires controlled by and obedient to her reason, even if her reasoned view was mistaken or inadequate. But having non-rational desires under rational control in this minimal sense does not bring them to a state of perfection as *exercises of reason*, and so does not constitute the state in which they have attained the virtue appropriate to them. As a rational capacity in the extended sense I have explained, the capacity for non-rational desire would be continuously subject to further improvement, until the reason it is controlled by itself fully meets all the standards appropriate for the use of reason in this context. And since Aristotle calls the virtues of the non-rationally desiring part of our nature collectively "moral virtue" or "virtue of character" (*ēthikē aretē*, 1103a5, 14–15), this amounts to saying that moral virtue (though it is a perfectly distinct psychological state or condition) presupposes and is dependent upon the virtues of practical reason, the virtues of the mind that he calls collectively "practical wisdom" (*phronēsis*).

II NON-RATIONAL DESIRES

In what follows I want to discuss in some detail these non-rational desires, in the control over which by a practical reason possessing its own proper virtue, moral virtue according to Aristotle consists. We should begin by recalling that Aristotle recognizes other desires besides the non-rational types of desire here in question.[4] This is already clear in the passage of *Nicomachean Ethics* I where he formally introduces and argues for the existence of the non-rational ones. For there (1.13.1102b13–25) he describes strong-willed (or continent) and weak-willed (or incontinent) persons (*hoi enkrateis* and *hoi akrateis*), on the occasions when they give in to or, respectively, refuse to act upon temptation, as experiencing impulses (*hormai*) that go in opposite directions (*epi tanantia*, 1102b21).[5] One of these *hormai* is

---

[3] Moral virtue, the virtuous condition of the non-rational desires, lies in a mean ὡϱισμένη λόγῳ καὶ ᾧ ἂν ὁ φϱόνιμος ὁϱίσειεν, 2.6.1107a1; one cannot have the moral virtues without at the same time having practical wisdom, 6.13.1144b31–32.

[4] See Chapter 10 above, "Some Remarks on Aristotle's Moral Psychology," esp. sects. II–IV.

[5] Strictly speaking, Aristotle only says here that the impulses of *weak*-willed persons go ἐπὶ τὰναντία, but what he says about both the weak- and the strong-willed just before, 1102b14–18, shows that he thinks the same of the strong-willed. The fact that in this phrase Aristotle explicitly mentions only the weak-willed perhaps encouraged the erroneous interpretation of Burnet (*The Ethics of Aristotle*, 61) and other older commentators, that the impulses of the weak-willed (namely, their non-rational desires) go opposite to their reason's dictates. But

described as coming from the capacity for non-rational desire and as opposing reason and going against it (*enantioumenon kai antibainon*, 1102b24–
25). The other impulse, then, is being conceived as coming from reason
itself (this is made explicit in a parallel passage of *EE*, 1247b18–19, quoted
in n. 5). And since Aristotle's whole point here is to argue for a special nonrational part or aspect of the human soul (1102b13–14), a capacity that is
part of human nature itself and so is present in every human being, he
cannot be supposing that the impulse "coming from reason" is just some
or other non-rational desire that reason has managed to capture and use in
order to achieve its own purposes. It must be a sui generis impulse, a psychic
movement towards action that is generated by practical reasoning and judgment themselves, an impulse that goes in support of the course of action
one has decided is best.[6] In the *Ethics* and elsewhere Aristotle regularly uses
the term *boulēsis* (wish, or rational wish, as it is generally translated) as his
semi-technical name for this kind of desire.

In *Nic. Eth.* 1.13 Aristotle does not pause to delineate the non-rational
desires or distinguish different types of them from one another. He speaks
of them only vaguely, as *to epithumētikon kai holōs orektikon* and as non-

---

Gauthier is right (*Aristote: 'L'Éthique à Nicomaque'*, ii. 95–96) to reject that interpretation
as, in the context, very far-fetched, and certainly not in line with Aristotle's usual view,
according to which some of what he here calls ὁρμαί are produced by reason itself: *Eudemian
Ethics* 8.2.1247b18–19, which Gauthier cites, clearly exhibits this usual view (ἆρ᾽ οὐκ ἔνεισιν
ὁρμαί ἐν τῇ ψυχῇ αἱ μὲν ἀπὸ λογισμοῦ αἱ δὲ ἀπὸ ὀρέξεως ἀλόγου). *EE* 2.8.1224a32–33,
which Gauthier cites as a parallel to this *Nic. Eth.* phrase, is, however, not without difficulties
of its own. With the (possibly confused) MS text there, it looks at first sight as if the αὐτῷ
should be taken with ἐναντίας (the strong- and weak-willed person each acts "having impulses
opposed to himself"), and that would give essentially the sense Burnet, not Gauthier, wanted
to find in the *Nic. Eth.* passage. (That is how Woods translates it in *Aristotle's "Eudemian
Ethics"*; likewise Décarie, *Aristote: "Éthique à Eudème."*) However, Aristotle is here setting
up a difficulty (namely, that it looks as if both the strong- and the weak-willed act under
compulsion and so not voluntarily), to which he goes on to reply. In replying he points out
(b5–8) that, by his own earlier definition, compulsion requires that what causes (or prevents)
movement should come from outside the thing being subjected to compulsion, whereas in *both*
these agents what causes the action is a ὁρμή inside themselves: ἐν τῷ ἀκρατεῖ καὶ ἐγκρατεῖ
ἡ καθ᾽ αὑτὸν ὁρμὴ ἐνοῦσα ἄγει (ἄμφω γὰρ ἔχει) (b8–10). (So the continent agent, in acting
against his appetite and on his λογισμός, cf. b22–23, acts on a ὁρμή, or impulse.) This confirms
that Gauthier is right about Aristotle's usual view, but it also strongly suggests that Woods
and Décarie are wrong to take αὐτῷ with ἐναντίας at a33. For the only justification in what
precedes for saying that strong- and weak-willed agents have ἄμφω [ὁρμαί] is the reference
to ἐναντίας ὁρμάς of a32–33—thus forcing on the earlier passage Gauthier's sense (that the
strong- and weak-willed person each acts "having in himself opposite impulses"). (That is how
Solomon took it in the Oxford translation.) (In that case, one must take αὐτῷ as a dative of
interest, if it is not to be emended to αὐτῶν.) In any event, *Magna Moralia* 2.4.1200b1–4
provides a close and precise enough parallel, if any is needed, in support of Gauthier's way
of taking ἐπὶ τἀναντία in the *Nic. Eth.* text. Ross translates it in this way in his Oxford
translation (first published 1925), and nearly all more recent translators agree (not, however,
Rackham or Dirlmeier).

[6] On this *sui generis* rational kind of desire, see further below, sect. IV; Chapter 10 above,
sects. II–III.

rational but capable of being persuaded by and obedient to reason. Thus at the end of the chapter (1103a3ff.) he says simply that the (human) virtues fall into two groups, depending upon in which of two senses of the word the part or capacity of the soul to which they belong is "rational." The virtues belonging to our ability to reason in the narrow or strict sense I have distinguished above are called intellectual (*dianoētikai*) ones, while the virtues belonging to non-rational desire—a rational "part" in the extended sense of the word—are called "moral" or "of character." Nor in discussing the moral virtues in general in book 2, or in detail in books 3–5, does Aristotle go into such details. Partly this is because in that discussion (beginning from 2.5) he shifts his attention from non-rational desire as such to the broader category of *pathos* (passion or emotion), which he takes rather for granted, leaving its relations to *orexis* (desire) quite undeveloped.[7] In fact, however, as one can see from a number of passages in other works, as well as in the *Nicomachean Ethics*, Aristotle seems throughout his career to have accepted from Plato's account of the human soul in the *Republic* the division of our non-rational desires into two types, appetitive and spirited (*epithumia* and *thumos*).[8] Since I wish in what follows to argue that this division plays an important, though often somewhat submerged, role in Aristotle's theory of moral virtue in the *Ethics*, I want next to discuss in some detail Aristotle's adoption, and adaptation, of this Platonic theory, paying special attention to the main passages in the *Ethics* where he announces and applies it explicitly.[9]

Consider first his account of the various types of *akrasia* in *Nic. Eth.* 7. As we have seen, it is by appealing to the psychological conditions in which agents act continently and incontinently that Aristotle argues in *Nic. Eth.* 1.13 for the existence of (human) non-rational desires. When in book 7 (= *EE* 6) he presents his developed account of continence and incontinence

---

[7] For a discussion of these matters one must go to *Rhetoric* 2.2–11. See Chapter 19 below, "An Aristotelian Theory of the Emotions."

[8] See Chapter 10 above, "Some Remarks on Aristotle's Moral Psychology," end of sect. I and n. 3. On Plato's version of this theory, see "Plato's Theory of Human Motivation," Chapter 4 above.

[9] The *Politics*, too, gives clear evidence of Aristotle's commitment to the "tripartite" account of desires. See 7.7, where in discussing what sorts of people the citizens of his best state should optimally be, Aristotle maintains (1327b36–38) that a citizen has to have a good mix of both spirit (θυμός) and intelligence (διάνοια) in order to be led towards virtue by the laws; and he traces the important virtue of friendship to the spirited capacity of the soul. Again, in 7.15 in discussing the early training of these citizens, he speaks explicitly of both θυμός and ἐπιθυμία as present from birth and needing appropriate training, so that the mind (as "ruler") can develop properly. (He speaks here, somewhat anomalously, of βούλησις as also present from birth, while reason—λόγος—emerges only later: on his usual view, this could be at best some inchoate condition of susceptibility for reasoned desires.) Finally, in 3.16.1287a30–32 he says that if not law, i.e., reason (νοῦς), but men rule in a city, one opens the door to "bestial" abuses: appetites (ἐπιθυμία) have "bestial" force, and spirit (θυμός) corrupts even the best of men when they hold office not under the rule of law. I thank Richard Kraut for help with these passages.

we find that he now distinguishes between *two* forms of non-rational desire that the weak agent may be defeated by and that the strong agent needs to master.[10] *Akrasia* in the strict and unqualified sense, he says, is weakness with respect to the "necessary" sources of pleasure, those of eating, drinking, and sex (7.4.1147b25–28) or, more generally, touch and taste (1148a8–9). Besides this type of *akrasia* there are several others, all of which are correctly counted as types of *akrasia* because of a resemblance they have (1147b34; 1148b6, 13) to the unqualified case.[11] They resemble it in that in them, too, an agent experiences a passion (*pathos*) that overcomes him so that he acts in a way he had decided not to act, and does so without having changed his mind. Accordingly, these cases are, or should be, referred to with an additional phrase that specifies what it is that the agent is mastered by or with respect to: for example, *akrasia* with respect to victory, or with respect to honor, or money (wealth), or (financial) gain (1147b31–35). By contrast, the person (and only he) who is mastered by appetites for the necessary bodily pleasures is called simply incontinent, with no added reference to that wherein his weakness lies. Now among the qualified cases of incontinence, as we shall see at length in a moment, Aristotle singles out for special attention incontinence with respect to *thumos*, "spirited" desire. All the other qualified cases, like the unqualified one itself, are cases of weakness in the presence of *epithumiai, appetitive* desires;[12] this one is a case of weakness in the presence of non-rational desires of a different kind altogether.

[10] In what follows I simplify by omitting all reference to the parallel phenomenon of continence, which in any event receives only secondary attention in Aristotle's texts.

[11] I omit from my discussion all reference to the more far-fetched set of cases of this general description that Aristotle discusses in *Nic. Eth.* 7.5, those depending upon unmastered bestial or diseased appetites for bodily pleasure—appetites lying outside the range of anything normally human. I discuss only the first set of cases, explained in 7.4 and further commented upon in 7.6.

[12] Since 1879, when John Cook Wilson published his *Aristotelian Studies*, i, it has been recognized that 7.4 contains what appear to be two consecutive expositions of Aristotle's theory of the qualified and unqualified cases of ἀϰρασία. (Cook Wilson thought they were by two different authors, neither of them Aristotle, because he thought both expositions reflect a view of the scope of temperance at odds with Aristotle's in *Nic. Eth.* 3 and *EE* 3; Gauthier and Jolif are right (p. 618 and *ad* 1148a8) to reject these suspicions.) The "second exposition" begins by making it explicit (ἐπεὶ δὲ τῶν ἐπιθυμιῶν ϰαὶ τῶν ἡδονῶν αἱ μέν ... , 1148a22) that ἀϰρασίαι with respect to "money, gain, victory, and honor" (a25–26) rest upon unmastered appetitive desires. It makes mention of ἀϰρασία περὶ θυμοῦ only at the end, bringing it in as a further qualified form, comparable in essentials with the ones based on appetites that have already been discussed (1148b12–14). But the chapter as a whole begins (1147b22–24) with the statement, evidently intended as a general thesis controlling all the subsequent analysis, that "it is evident that both continent and incontinent persons are concerned with pleasures and pains." Read on its own, then, the "second exposition" would leave one in doubt how incontinence in spirited desires is being accommodated: it is appetite that is directed at pleasure, whether bodily pleasure or not, as indeed 1148a22 itself presupposes, so how is *this* incontinence "concerned with pleasures and pains"? The resolution must lie in Aristotle's standard doctrine that θυμός is or essentially involves a form of distress or mental upset. (He exploits this doctrine in ch. 6, where, in arguing that incontinence is a morally worse condition in appetitive than

Aristotle argues at length in 7.6 that incontinence in spirited desires is less morally bad than incontinence in appetitive ones. It appears that his thesis concerns all appetitive incontinence—both the unqualified incontinence having to do with necessary bodily pleasures, and the qualified kinds having to do with pleasures that are not necessary, such as the pleasures of victory, honor, money, and gain.[13] Thus he seems to be claiming that weakness in controlling spirited desires is less morally bad than *any* weakness in controlling appetites, whether necessary ones or not. He gives four arguments to support this conclusion. In the second of these he seems clearly to distinguish between "appetites for excess and appetites that are not necessary" (*tōn epithumiōn tōn tēs huperbolēs kai tōn mē anankaiōn*, 1149b7–8), i.e., appetites for excessive bodily pleasures of touch and taste, on the one hand, and appetites for such unnecessary pleasures as those from honor, money, etc., on the other;[14] so understood, his argument, reasonable enough

---

in spirited desires, he claims that no one executes outrages (ὕβρεις) when in a distressed state of mind (λυπούμενος), and points out that therefore outrage cannot result from θυμός, though it *can* result from the pleasurable indulgence of an ἐπιθυμία.) It is easier to grasp from the "first exposition" that this is what Aristotle has in mind. There Aristotle brings incontinence in spirited desires into the account from the beginning. He lists it alongside money, gain, and honor as things with respect to which there are different types of qualified incontinence. But these three have been mentioned as among the *sources* of pleasure (τῶν ποιούντων ἡδονήν, 1147b24)—there is no reference here, as there is in the corresponding passage of the "second exposition," to appetites—so it is not too great a stretch for the reader to recognize that θυμός is figuring in the account as a source of distress or pain. In effect, the other qualified ἀκρασίαι are concerned with pleasure because that is what the unmastered desire is for, while incontinence in spirited desires is concerned with distress or pain because the unmastered desire in its case is or involves essentially a form of mental upset. (See also 7.1150a25–27, where Aristotle explicitly recognizes the difference between incontinence where one is led to satisfy an appetitive desire in order to get the pleasure—this is the sort he has been taking for granted in his discussion—and incontinence where one satisfies a desire just in order to get rid of it.)

[13] If so, then the editor of *MM* has apparently misunderstood the view of Aristotle's he means to be presenting. At 2.6.1202b10–13, he introduces what corresponds to the material of *Nic. Eth.* 7.6 with the remark that of the qualified kinds of incontinence the one with respect to anger (ὀργή) is the most blameworthy, and so takes the arguments that follow to be ranking this kind of incontinence morally ahead only of the *un*qualified kind—the one that is concerned with necessary bodily pleasures. (He also, here and in what immediately precedes, 1202a35, incautiously speaks as if Aristotle had restricted himself to incontinence as to anger, and not spirited desires generally. On this distinction see below.) Modern commentators have followed the *MM* view to the extent of assuming that in this chapter Aristotle ranks spirited incontinence ahead only of the unqualified kind, not also the other (appetitive) varieties. Yet it seems obvious that all the arguments Aristotle actually gives for ranking spirited incontinence morally higher apply equally to appetitive incontinence of all types. I should repeat (see n. 11) that in this and the next paragraph I continue to leave out of account the second broad category of qualified incontinence, that with unmastered bestial or diseased appetites.

[14] The anonymous Greek commentator who filled in the gaps in Eustratius's commentary and Heliodorus both understood the phrase τῶν μὴ ἀναγκαίων in the natural way, as making reference to appetites for the pleasures of honor etc., which are described in 4.1147b29 as not necessary (see Eustratius p. 431, 13–16 and Heliodorus p. 146, 11–13). (Aspasius says nothing clear at this point.) Modern commentators and translators have usually fudged the issue against this natural reading by treating the καί as epexegetic, which is very hard to

in both cases, is that feeling spirited desires, even ones that lead you astray, is more natural to human beings generally than desires either for excessive amounts of bodily pleasure (e.g., pleasures of eating beyond what you need to fill your stomach) or for such optional pleasures as those of lording it over others or being famous or being rich.[15] So, just as we would excuse someone who out of normal natural extreme hunger or thirst grabs food or drink without asking permission first (1149b5–6), we ought to excuse or show understanding for people who misbehave through inability to control an excess of spirit (for example, of anger)—certainly, that is much more justifiable than to show understanding for people who misbehave from excessive and not normal and universally shared bodily appetites, or from inappropriate optional appetites like excessive love of money. People ought not to have such appetites, or certainly they ought to control them if they do, whereas the former desires are wholly natural and it is understandable if someone may occasionally misbehave when experiencing them. Hence incontinence in spirited desires shows a less defective character than any of the forms of appetitive incontinence does.

But it is Aristotle's first argument for this conclusion (1149a25–b3) that deserves the closest attention. For here he says things about *thumos* and its special relationship to reason that provide a basis for distinguishing this kind of desire sharply from the appetitive kind and show its special importance for moral action generally. Spirited desires, Aristotle points out, unlike appetites (however sophisticated), can or do directly incorporate some of the reasoned evaluative reflection that might lead (or might have led) to a decision to act as those desires themselves impel one to. Thus if you conceive that you have been subjected to some insult or slight (whether subtly, so that you have to reflect carefully on the circumstances to recognize it, or flagrantly, so that it strikes you at once as being that, so that no reasoning is called for to recognize it—ὁ μὲν γὰρ λόγος ἢ ἡ φαντασία ὅτι ὕβρις ἢ ὀλιγωρία ἐδήλωσεν,

---

justify, given the second τῶν. Ross's translation is typical: "the appetites for excess, i.e., for unnecessary objects."

[15] Aristotle adds a coda to the third of his arguments (1149b13ff.), as if a further conclusion: if "this" incontinence is more unjust and morally worse than spirited incontinence, it is also ἁπλῶς ἀκρασία καὶ κακία πως (b19–20). The anonymous commentator (p. 423, 5–11), who like me takes Aristotle to be arguing for a moral ranking of spirited incontinence above all forms of appetitive incontinence, takes the πως with the whole noun phrase, not just with κακία, and offers a fascinating but strained interpretation according to which Aristotle is not saying here more than that, in comparison with spirited incontinence, appetitive incontinence (in general) counts as unqualified (that is the effect of the πως, he thinks). I prefer to suppose that, following up on the example implied in the quotations he has just given, which is a sexual one, Aristotle means by "this" incontinence at this point not appetitive incontinence in general but incontinence with respect to necessary bodily pleasures, such as sexual ones. (Thus I would follow modern translators and commentators in taking πως with κακία alone.) That does not imply, of course, that the intention of the argument itself is not to support a higher moral ranking for spirited incontinence over all types of appetitive incontinence. It plainly does do that.

a32–33), you may at once become angry (a special case of spirited desire, one for retaliation), as if (he says) reasoning (*sullogisamenos*) that it is right to fight back against this kind of behavior (a33–34). Aristotle comments on this case (a30–31) that such a person's spirited desire "hears reason" (though it does not hear from reason a directive *to* fight back: indeed, reason explicitly declines to issue any such directive), and so (b2–3), if he then acts upon it despite his reason's being against doing so, we can say that he has been overcome in a way by reason itself—not by a *mere* non-rational desire, a mere *pathos*, as would always be the case with an appetitive desire. He compares such a spirited desire to a servant who hears, as it might be, the beginning of an instruction to bring some drinks but goes off to fetch the usual Coca-Colas without waiting to hear that this time different drinks are wanted (a26–28).

It is important to notice with some care in exactly what respect Aristotle thinks such an act of incontinence (but no act of appetitive incontinence) involves being overcome by reason itself (in a way). It is plain, anyhow on reflection, that the crucial point for Aristotle is that, as with this servant, the spirited desire simply leaps by anticipation to a conclusion to which reason might be led, but is in fact not led in this case, and does so from a premise or premises that it shares with, indeed has in some sense itself obtained from, reason. What are these premises? Plainly, the mere factual information that an insult or slight has been delivered is not among them. As we have seen, Aristotle is explicit that that might have been obtained not through reasoning but only from an immediate impression (a *phantasia*), and he is also explicit that the corresponding factual information in a case of appetitive incontinence might have been obtained by reasoning too (a35), while denying that *that* incontinence involves being overcome by reason in any way. The crucial premise is rather the presupposed evaluative proposition that insults and slights are bad and offensive things, normally to be resisted or retaliated against because they represent a disregard for the value of one's own person that no self-respecting person can share, or act as if he did by accepting slights meekly. In becoming aroused, spirited desire as it were puts this evaluative outlook, which it shares with reason, together (*hōsper sullogisamenos*) with the factual information that there has been an insult, so as to reach the conclusion that it is right to fight back against it. The result is *akrasia* none the less, because though sharing spirit's offense at the insult or slight, reason in that instance regards it as improper to react on the spot. Nothing similar happens in appetitive incontinence: the liking for pleasure, as such, that constitutes an appetite is not derived from or even shared by reason; it is as it were specifically and uniquely its own evaluative outlook that appetite puts together with the factual premise that something pleasant is to be had when it rushes forward to gratification. Hence, Aristotle argues, incontinence in spirited desires is morally less bad than appetitive incontinence: it already reflects, though perhaps still very inadequately, at least some of the same broader practical concerns that reason itself endorses.[16]

As I have noted, the example Aristotle uses to make this important point about spirited desires is one of incontinence in anger. It is very important to see that anger is indeed only one quite special instance of the kind of desire Aristotle has in mind in speaking of *thumos* in book 7 and elsewhere. On Aristotle's view, and the view that became standard in Greek philosophy, anger (*orgē*) is to be understood in what must seem to us a quite narrow way. It is an agitated, distressful desire to inflict pain in retaliation upon a person who has distressed and upset oneself by delivering an unjustified insult or belittlement to oneself or some close relation or friend. This is how he defines and discusses anger in *Rhetoric* 2.2, and he plainly presupposes this conception of it throughout his discussion of the virtue of good temper (*praotēs*) and its opposed vices in *Nic. Eth.* 4.5; he specifies good temper as the virtue controlling the passion of *orgē*, and there are sufficient references to insults and retaliation to make it clear that he is holding fast to his strict definition of this passion.[17] In effect, as the definition in the *Rhetoric* clearly suggests, anger, so understood, is a special case of spirited desire, the case in which an agitated desire of that spirited type arises as a response to what one takes to have been such insulting or belittling behavior. Like the generic desire, this specific one is a passion or emotion, but it is not the *same* passion or emotion.[18]

What then can one say about the genus of desires that Aristotle has in mind under the name *thumos*? Aristotle's close association of *thumos* with reason and his comparison of its relationship with reason to that of a possibly

[16] My interpretation of this argument differs significantly from what I understand to be Burnet's (*The Ethics of Aristotle*, 313–14), adopted by Gauthier and Jolif. He speaks (correctly) of θυμός as sharing some deliberative steps with reason, but neglects to see the crucial point, that that means that it shares with reason an evaluative outlook and not just some complex factual information about what an insult or a slight is or implies.

[17] The much shorter treatment of πραότης in *EE* 3.3 seems to define it formally in terms directly of θυμός (see the references at 1231b6–7, 11, 15 to the λύπη that is or is caused by θυμός as being the locus of this virtue and its opposed vices); but even here Aristotle makes it clear by his references to insults and belittlement (b12–13) that it is in fact ὀργή that he is talking about, not θυμός in general, and in his clearest statement of what this "mean state" involves he speaks not of θυμός but of ὀργίζεσθαι (b21–23).

[18] The *Rhetoric* defines ὀργή as an ὄρεξις μετὰ λύπης with a specific kind of occasion and object (1378a31–33). I take it that the kind of ὄρεξις intended is θυμός (not ἐπιθυμία, however much thoughts of pleasure in retaliation may be involved (b1–9), and although this may often be caused by people's posing obstacles to the satisfaction of one's pre-existing appetitive desires (1379a10–22)). Aristotle standardly speaks of θυμός itself (like ἐπιθυμία) as involving pain or distress, so he does not clearly succeed in distinguishing anger from other forms of the general kind of desire in question with the phrase μετὰ λύπης in the definition. It seems, though, that he may intend by that phrase here to convey a specially high degree of distress, something like the ταραχή or turmoil he mentions frequently in the *Rhetoric* in discussing other emotions treated there (see 1382a21, 1383b14, 1386b18–19; and cf. *Nic. Eth.* 1125b34, in the discussion of good temper, where Aristotle says that the πρᾶος tends to be ἀτάραχος). That *would* contribute to marking off this specific desire within the genus.

over-hasty servant to his master should immediately remind one of Plato's description of *thumos* in the *Republic* as the natural ally of reason (440b3, 441a2–3), an auxiliary for reason in the soul corresponding to the rulers' auxiliaries in the best city. As I have argued elsewhere,[19] the root idea lying behind Plato's introduction of this third kind of natural human desire, over and above reason's desires for knowledge and for the good and appetite's for pleasure, is that there are effectively intermediate desires having always a reference to oneself, that aim at competitive exertion—at making something of oneself, of being active and in command (of oneself, and in relation to one's fellows). In his discussion of *akrasia* in *Nic. Eth.* 7.6 Aristotle adds to this Platonic picture the important idea that the underlying value recognized and asserted in this competitive type of desire is itself a version of reason's own ideal that needs only to be properly filled in in order for reason's own scheme of values to become the immediate object of this second kind of desire as well as of desires of reason's own. I will come back to this point later.

In the *Republic* Plato gives this intermediate kind of desire its own special object of pursuit, victory, and/or esteem or honor (*timē*), corresponding to appetite's pursuit of pleasure. As we have already seen, Aristotle rejects this identification: according to him, akratic lovers of honor and victory are incontinently pursuing a pleasure and so are inappropriately subject not to spirited desire but to certain appetites, appetites for victory and honor. (I will discuss below what he does think the object of *thumos* is, parallel to pleasure in the case of appetite.) Again, Plato assigns *thumos* a virtue of its own, the virtue of courage or bravery (*andreia*): on Plato's view courage consists in that condition of a person's tendencies to feel spirited desires in which he feels these always in support of the objectives and projects that his correctly informed reason announces as worth while, in despite of the inducements and obstacles posed by pleasure and pain (442b11–c3). Aristotle pointedly does not follow Plato in this either.

Initially this is because he thinks, as would be generally agreed, that the passion that courage regulates is not spirited desire in general (nor yet specific instances of it, such as anger) but fear (and confident feelings). In particular, courage concerns fear and confident feelings when one knows one is facing death or what may very well cause it, especially in battle, and these are painful things to undergo, as well as to anticipate (see especially *Nic. Eth.* 3.9). So courage must have a direct regulative relationship to appetitive desires as well—desires for the pleasure of getting out of danger's way and aversions to the pain of injury—however much it may also regulate spirited desires. More fundamentally, however, to say, as Plato seems to do, that courageous acts, as such, issue from *thumos* (a spirit of resistance, the will to fight when threatened) leaves wholly out of account what Aristotle thinks is the crucial thing in all virtuous actions, that they issue from a decision (*prohairesis*) to act that way, and are done for the sake of or because of

---

[19] Chapter 4 above, "Plato's Theory of Human Motivation."

"the noble" (to kalon). To act from thumos, however well disciplined its desires may be, is still to act from a pathos (Nic. Eth. 1117a9; EE 1229a21), not from a decision based on reasoning about what is best, and it does not immediately carry with it that love of the noble that virtue always connotes. But although on this ground he classifies facing dangers out of a spirit of resistance as one of five types of pseudo-courage, not true courage (Nic. Eth. 3.8.1116b23–1117a9; EE 3.1.1229a20–31, b26–30; 1230a22–33), he does recognize for thumos, pathos though it is, a special role in true courage that is consonant with what we have learned from Nic. Eth. 7.6 about the close relationship between spirited desires (as distinct from appetitive ones) and reason. Aristotle says that though to be sure brave men act on account of the noble, "spirited desire helps them in their work" (ho de thumos sunergei autois, 1116b31); that "courage" based simply upon a spirit of resistance is "very close" (paraplēsion ti 1117a9) to real courage; and that it needs only decision and direction toward the end (i.e., the noble) to be real courage (προσλαβοῦσα προαίρεσιν καὶ τὸ οὗ ἕνεκα ἀνδρεία [ἔοικεν] εἶναι, 1117a4–5). In other words, true courage results when an antecedent spirited desire to stand up to danger and resist any impulse to flee has added to it a considered decision to act that way just then, and itself comes to be directed toward the noble in being directed toward such actions.

There can be no doubt, then, that in his ethical theory Aristotle takes very seriously the Platonic idea that human beings by nature experience two importantly different types of non-rational desire. Moreover, he develops in an extremely interesting way the close relationship between desires of one of these types, spirited desires, and reason that Plato too had emphasized. And, as we have just seen, he makes the close co-operation of the two the basis for assigning spirited desires a specially prominent role at least in the virtue of courage.

III THREE TYPES OF VALUE

Although in discussing virtue of character in general, and the other particular virtues besides courage, Aristotle says little explicitly about spirited desires, I want now to present and develop some evidence in the texts that makes me think he means to assign a similar role for spirited desires in all the moral virtues. I will return at the end to address the question why he does not mention this role more frequently and make it more explicit.

I want to draw attention first to an important passage of Nic. Eth. 2.3. It comes in the chapter where Aristotle argues that moral virtue and moral vice are concerned with pleasure and its opposite, lupē (a term that covers being distressed or upset about something as well as physical pain): a virtuous person, just in so far as he is morally virtuous, takes pleasure in and is distressed about the right things in the right ways; a vicious person takes pleasure in and is distressed about the wrong things and in the wrong ways. At 1104b30–1105a1 he argues for this conclusion as follows:

> There are three objects of choice[20] (*ta eis tas haireseis*) and three of avoidance: the *kalon* (the noble, fine, beautiful), the advantageous, and the pleasant, and their opposites, the *aischron* (the base, shameful, ugly), the harmful, and the painful. In relation to all these the good person gets things right, while the bad person gets things wrong, but especially in relation to pleasure. For pleasure is shared with the animals, and it is involved in all the objects of choice, since the *kalon* and the advantageous also appear pleasant.

Explicit here is the thought that the good person, the person who possesses the moral virtues, is concerned for and pursues (in a correct way) all three of the objects mentioned. Though Aristotle's main point here is to argue that the good person has a special concern for pleasures (and pains), given that the other two are found by him also to be pleasant, that of course presupposes that he does pursue the two others as well, independently of any pleasure he may get or expect from them.

This list of objects of choice and avoidance was apparently current in dialectical debates in the Academy. At any rate, Aristotle cites it twice in the *Topics*, at 1.13.105a27–28 and 3.3.118b27–28, saying that "choice-worthy" (*haireton*) has these three senses, *kalon*, pleasant (*hēdu*), and advantageous (*sumpheron*). It is clear from the second of these *Topics* passages that "advantageous" is not to be taken in this context as referring simply to what is useful for obtaining an end—for obtaining, for example, as it might be, some pleasure or something "noble" or "beautiful"—but what contributes, specifically, to one's *good*.[21] "The advantageous," in short, is

---

[20] Burnyeat ("Aristotle on Learning to be Good," p. 91n.25) complains about Ross's translation here of αἵρεσις by "choice"—correctly, since that is also Ross's English for προαίρεσις, in its technical Aristotelian sense a very different thing from what is referred to here. I agree with Irwin that "decision" is a better rendering for this technical term, indicating as it does conscious, reasoned selection; "choice" is then available for use here, and is preferable, for several reasons, to Burnyeat's "pursuit."

[21] He speaks of each of the three αἱρετά as chosen as ends (τίνων χάριν, 118b27–28), and goes on in the next line to speak of other things as chosen as χρήσιμον πρός (useful for the sake of) them. This makes it clear that the συμφέρον is not the category simply of the useful for some end or other. At b35 νόσος and αἶσχος (disease and ugliness) are given as examples of things to be avoided because "disadvantageous," although disease is overall more to be avoided because it is a greater obstacle than ugliness is to pleasure and morality. Here the "disadvantage" is being judged relatively to a conception of what is the normal good state of the person—physical health and decent good looks being among them. See also *Rhet.* 1.6 (cited in the next note), 1362a21–34, where Aristotle explains συμφέροντα, i.e., goods, as things choiceworthy for themselves, things that an intelligent mind would assign to one, and things through the presence of which one is well constituted (εὖ διάκειται) and self-sufficient. Dirlmeier (commentary on *Nic. Eth.*, 306) helpfully refers to Plato, *Laws* 2. 662e8–663b6, where the Athenian states his view that the three distinct values of pleasure, moral virtue, and our own good coincide in precisely the same overall way of life.

a stand-in here for "the good" (to agathon).[22] It seems, then, that the list presents three basic categories of value—(one's) good, pleasure, and to kalon—as constituting what is ultimately "choiceworthy" for human beings. This same conception of value as coming in three distinct types lies behind Aristotle's remarks at the beginning of the Eudemian Ethics (1214a1–8), in which he disagrees with the Delian inscription that identified three different things (justice, health, and obtaining what one loves) as respectively noblest and finest (kalliston), best (ariston) and most pleasant (hēdiston): no, he says, eudaimonia occupies the summit at once of all three basic kinds of value.[23]

Now, as we have seen, Aristotle standardly holds that there are three types of human desire, as well—boulēsis, thumos, and epithumia. Furthermore, he clearly correlates the first and third of these three types of desire, "wish" and appetite, respectively with good and pleasure, the second and third of the objects of choice on his list in Nic. Eth. 2.3. Wish is always for the good or what appears good, appetite is always desire for pleasure. About an object pursued through spirited desire, thumos, he is nowhere explicit. But I will argue that, in the specific case of the morally virtuous person, he intends to correlate it with the remaining object of choice from our list: spirited desire is the desire through which the morally virtuous person is primarily motivated to pursue to kalon, the noble or fine or beautiful. The picture that emerges, then, is this. The morally virtuous person is motivated by three types of desires, each with its own special object—respectively what is good (for him), what is noble or fine or beautiful in action (to kalon), and what is pleasant. These are three distinct values, each with its own nature, and in his respective desires for them the good person gets them altogether right. What he desires as pleasant really is pleasant, what he desires as noble or fine or beautiful in action really is noble or fine or beautiful, what he desires as being for his own good really is good for him. Once we have a better understanding of what these three distinct kinds of value, and especially that of "the noble," are supposed to be, further questions arise concerning priorities and other connections among them and their correlated types of desire.

---

[22] Presumably the reason why Aristotle and his Academic friends spoke in this context of τὸ συμφέρον and not directly of τὸ ἀγαθόν is that they thought of what is chosen as something immediately present in the chosen act, and whereas pleasure and "nobility" could be thought of as typically present in acts chosen for their sakes, one's good, if aimed at, would always be in one way or another something larger than any single act, something to which it would contribute at some distance. See Rhet. 1.6.1362a17–21, where Aristotle says first that in deliberative oratory the aim (σκοπός) of the orator is τὸ συμφέρον, on the ground that the orator deals not with ends but with ways of achieving them, but then goes on to describe this as ἀγαθόν, and to include within it both whatever is good "in itself" and what is instrumental to that.

[23] Similarly Nic. Eth. 1.8.1099a24–31.

IV GOOD AND PLEASURE AS VALUES

Let me begin by discussing briefly the values of good and pleasure, and their correlated desires, wish and appetite. A wish, according to Aristotle's explanation in *Nic. Eth.* 3.4 and elsewhere, is to be defined as a desire for something good (for oneself), *as such*—or, anyhow, something thought of as good by the one experiencing the desire. It is a desire to have a thing that is (thought to be) good, for the *reason* that it is a good thing. Similarly, an appetite is a desire for something pleasant, as such; it is a desire for the pleasure of something *because* (in the desirer's experience) it *is* pleasant in some way.[24] In making the capacities for desires of these types parts of our human nature Aristotle implies that it is a natural fact about human beings that as adults they (normally) want what they think is good for them, just for the reason that it is (they think) good; and that all human beings, of whatever age, (normally) want what they find pleasant, just because it is pleasant.[25] (This is a modest claim, implying nothing about how strong or how effective in any individual person desires of either type might be.)

By making the desire for our good, as such, part of our *rational* nature (in the narrow sense) Aristotle implies that this desire is a very special one, issuing directly from our power to reason and reflect and to hold opinions about what to do that are backed up by reasons. According to Aristotle, when we hold the view that something is good for us, unless some special defect or failure occurs in our minds, we thereupon want it; and this is so not because we have learned to take pleasure in what *is* good for us or in doing whatever we take to be good for us, or because in general our pre- or non-rational likes and dislikes have developed, or been trained, in such a way that some desire of that type is "triggered" by the holding of that opinion. Besides any such contingent desire for our good that we may have, on Aristotle's view we also want our good directly, simply because that is how rational beings are. This we cannot help. By contrast, the desire for pleasure is in no way consequent upon our opinions about what is good for us; it is a further natural fact about us that we also desire what gives us pleasure, and that desire has nothing immediately to do with what we may or may not think about our own good. This too we cannot help.

It will help us to understand better and to appreciate Aristotle's attribution to human beings of a specifically rational desire for their good if we bear in mind Aristotle's own views, argued for in a preliminary way in the first

---

[24] *Topics* 6.3, 140b27ff.; *de Anima* 2.3, 414b5–6; *Rhet.* 1.10, 1369b15–16; *Nic. Eth.* 3.2. 1111b17; and *EE* 2.7, 1223a34, 7.2, 1235b22.

[25] I draw here on Aristotle's careful distinction at *EE* 2.8.1224b29–35 between appetite as belonging naturally to human beings in the sense that it is present immediately from birth, and reason with its desire as belonging naturally because they will be present if growth continues and is not disrupted.

book of the *Nicomachean Ethics*, about what a human being's good in fact consists in. Aristotle's theory equates our good with the full exercise of those natural capacities that belong to our nature as human beings and belong to no other animal. In effect, our good is the fullest development and active use, in a normal mature life, of what is most essential to our natures as human beings, namely our rational capacities themselves, in both the straightforward or narrow and the extended senses I have delineated above. The argument that this is our natural good is parallel to similar arguments about the natural good of other living things: in general, the thought is, the good of any living thing consists in its possessing and exercising unimpededly, in a normal mature life for a member of its species, those natural capacities that are distinctive of that particular life-form among all the others.

Now we do not need to go into controversial and difficult details of this argument in order to convince ourselves that the general thought lying behind it rests upon a strong intuitive basis. It is an intuitively compelling idea that all living things as such have a good, and that the good of each member of a species consists in its living an active life functioning fully according to its nature. This idea clearly lies behind all our discourse about what is harmful or beneficial for plants and animals. Aristotle's theory of the human good simply applies this compelling idea (not necessarily in an equally compelling way, to be sure) to the case of the human species in particular. It is a noteworthy feature of this general idea that it identifies the good of any living thing, for example a tree, not with the satisfaction of any desires the thing may have (after all, most of use don't believe trees have desires or any other conscious experience at all), but with some natural functioning of its life-capacities. To the extent, therefore, that the general idea is a compelling one, we can find in it a good rationale for thinking similarly of the human good; our good, too, is not a matter of having our desires satisfied, but of functioning in some way that expresses our developed natural life-capacities. On Aristotle's own theory, the first and essential part of our good consists in how the rational aspects of our souls are structured and disposed, and what in consequence of that we desire and feel about ourselves, about other persons, and about all manner of things, and what we undertake to do as a result of desiring and feeling that way.[26] Of course, it is certainly the case that having a desire satisfied is necessarily *an* objective of anyone who has that desire. So if we are in the condition that Aristotle equates with our good we will necessarily have a lot of objectives that correspond to the desires we have because of being in it. But our good does not consist in achieving them *because* they are desired, because without

---

[26] I leave out of account here the "external goods" as additional components of the good according to Aristotle. For two discussions of these further goods, see Chapter 13 below, "Aristotle on the Goods of Fortune," and T. H. Irwin, "Permanent Happiness."

them our desires would be frustrated. It consists simply in being in the condition and functioning accordingly; in general, whether any or all of these desires get satisfied is a further, separate question. That this conception of our good is at odds with the run of contemporary philosophical thought on this subject, or even at odds with mainstream philosophical thought since the Renaissance, is very much worth noting and reflecting carefully on, but there is no doubt that it involves nothing *unintelligible*. The compelling intuitive idea guarantees that.

The rational desire for our own good that Aristotle attributes to human beings must be understood against this theoretical background. If his arguments for his theory of the human good are sound, then those who understand them ought to find themselves being persuaded. Given that we all have a natural desire for our own good, those who are persuaded of his theory of the good ought to come to desire as their good what Aristotle has argued is really good for us. But according to Aristotle's theory of the different human desires, even those who hold different views about the human good will desire what they think their good consists in with a desire whose natural function, at any rate, is to direct them toward the full development of their natural capacities as (rational) human beings and towards living a life structured by the active exercise of them. If our natural good *is* this kind of active use of our powers, then we need a natural desire that will, if developed naturally, leads us to pursue it. On Aristotle's theory, that is the function of *boulēsis*.

If, then, someone is desiring to have some pleasure (say, a bodily one), and desiring it because and in so far as (he thinks) it is a good thing to have, this desire derives from his reason. His reason is in the final analysis responsible for that judgment of value, and so for this desire, which is based upon it. This desire may (and in all but fairly bizarre cases, surely would) be accompanied by another desire, having a different psychic source, for the same pleasure—an appetitive one, aimed at the pleasure not as good (in whatever way, in his rational reflections, the agent regards it as being good for him), but simply as pleasant. This second desire is a desire for it because the agent *likes* that sort of thing—quite a different ground of motivation from his thinking it good for him. Aristotle regularly connects pleasure with the appearances of things, for example at *EE* 7.2.1235b27ff., where he says that the pleasant is a sort of *phainomenon agathon* (apparent good)— and adds that it is what *appears* good to you in such a way that you may none the less not *think* it is good at all (ϰἂν μὴ δοϰῇ). In this case, you would have an appetitive desire but no rational desire for whatever the thing was that struck you in this way. As this passage from the *Eudemian Ethics* shows, the appearance of goodness that finding something pleasant involves is a "non-epistemic" sort of appearance. What you find pleasant appears good in a way or sense that is parallel to the sun's looking approximately the size of a large button, even if you know perfectly well that it is far larger (see *de Anima* 3.3.428b2–4): the knowledge of its true size does not affect the appearance in this sense. Similarly, what appears good to you because you find it pleasant is independent of what you *think* is good. The object of *epithumia*, i.e., the pleasant, is therefore the "apparent good" in a different sense from the one in which Aristotle (*Nic. Eth.* 3.4) says the object of wish is the good or the apparent good; for he explains the "apparent good" there as what a person *thinks* is good (cf. *to dokoun*, 1113a21). The object of wish is the good or the apparent good in an "epistemic" sense of "appears"— it is what one takes or holds actually to be good.

We can understand how Aristotle means that what we find pleasant appears good to us if we recall his account of pleasure in *Nic. Eth.* 10. In chapter 4 of that book Aristotle explains the pleasure that arises from good sensory and other activities as a secondary end that supervenes upon whatever the primary end of the activity may be (seeing something, learning something, contemplating the truth, or whatever). In effect, in these cases (the ones Aristotle thinks are good pleasures), pleasure is a way in which the goodness of the activity is experienced through its effects on our subjectivity in general, or our sensibility in particular. But it is in the good instances of a genus that the true nature of things of that genus is revealed, so that even when a pleasure is a bad or a base one, we can say that the effect that the activity in question is having on the person's way of experiencing it is such that it is to him as if it was a good one. It appears good to him, in the sense that its effects on his sensibility or subjectivity in general are similar to the effects on a good person of the good activities that *he* finds pleasant. In either case, the appearance has nothing to do with what the agent *thinks* is good. Even the good person in having an appetitive desire for a pleasure is wanting this effect on her subjectivity—not the good of which the effect is a reflection and on which it supervenes. In no case is an *epithumia* a desire for any good thing, whatever it may be, that the pleasure accompanies; it is for the pleasure, i.e., for a certain effect on one's subjective experience of whatever the thing is. Pleasure, as a value, is therefore a distinct kind of value from good, even where they may be mutually implicated.

V THE SPECIFICALLY MORAL VALUE: *TO KALON*

Aristotle says repeatedly in the *Nicomachean Ethics* that *to kalon* is *the* end for which the morally virtuous person as such always acts: at 1115b13 (where the reference is particularly to courage), 1119b16 (temperance), 1120a24 (generosity), 1122b6–7 (magnificence). (And see *EE* 1229a4, 1230a26–33.) Although in some of these passages he says simply that acting *tou kalou heneka* is characteristic of virtue (*aretē*), the contexts make it clear that he is talking in particular about *moral* virtue (in general) and the various specific moral virtues. When, by contrast, he explains what the virtue of practical wisdom is, he speaks only of knowledge and pursuit of things that are *good* for oneself: 1140a26–27, b4–6, 20–21; 1141b7–8, 12–14 (and see *Rhet.* 1.9.1366b20–22).[27] Practical wisdom (or the practically wise person, *as such*), then, does not act "for the sake of the noble," but for the good. We have seen already why practical wisdom should be concerned with knowledge and pursuit of things good. That follows from the fact that it is the virtue of the practical intellect, which is the immediate source of *bouleseis*, desires for the good, as such, and among desires, only of *bouleseis*. But since the moral virtues are certain conditions on the capacity for non-rational desires, if *moral* virtues (by contrast) involve in an essential way the pursuit of *to kalon*, it is plausible to think that in some way or other the non-rational desires are responsible for that. Before pursuing this suggestion, however, we need to ask ourselves what kind of value "the noble" is in the first place. It is surprising, considering the evident importance of this value for his understanding of what moral virtue is, that Aristotle does not say much in explanation of it in any of his ethical writings. Still, there are passages of other treatises (*Topics, Rhetoric,* and *Metaphysics*) to which we can turn, as well as one extended discussion in the last chapter of the *Eudemian Ethics,* in order to draw together the materials we need to construct an Aristotelian account of what sort of value the noble or fine or beautiful in action is.

In several places Aristotle connects the noble or fine or beautiful in action with what is praised or praiseworthy. In the *Rhetoric* (1.9.1366a33–34) he proposes two alternative definitions of the noble: it is either whatever, being chosen because of itself, is praised or praiseworthy (*epaineton*), or else whatever is good, and pleasant because it is good (ὃ ἂν δι᾽ αὑτὸ αἱρετὸν ὂν ἐπαινετὸν ᾖ, ἢ ὃ ἂν ἀγαθὸν ὂν ἡδὺ ᾖ, ὅτι ἀγαθὸν). The first of these definitions, the one in terms of praise or praiseworthiness, appears to recur in the last chapter of the *Eudemian Ethics,* though the manuscript text seems pretty certain to be slightly corrupt: those good things that are ends, Aristotle says there, are noble which, existing (or, with an emendation, being chosen) for themselves, are [all of them] praised or praiseworthy (ὅσα δι᾽ αὑτὰ ὄντα πάντα[28] ἐπαινετὰ ἐστίν, 8.3.1248b19–20). So, the suggestion is, praise or

---

[27] Having defined or explained, in terms of the pursuit of what is good, what practical wisdom and the other virtues of practical thought are, Aristotle does, of course, go on in raising questions about the value of this virtue (6.12–13) to describe φρόνησις as concerned with "things just and fine-or-noble and good for a human being" (1143b22–23) or simply with "just and fine-or-noble things" (1144a12). It is the intellectual virtue responsible for the just and in general the morally virtuous person's actions, and as such it does concern itself with these matters. Furthermore, if acting and feeling morally-virtuously is good for human beings, then part of what practical wisdom will know is that fact, so that in knowing about what is good it will also concern itself with what is just and what is fine-or-noble, just as it also concerns itself with what is pleasant and directs us towards that. None the less, it is moral virtue, and not practical wisdom, that is directed at τὸ καλόν *as such* (and not at it because it is good).

[28] So the MSS, but should we read αἱρετὰ for πάντα, as Spengel suggested? That would make the definition of τὸ καλόν here coincide with the first definition given in *Rhet.* 1366a35,

praiseworthiness (where the thing that carries the praise is chosen because of itself) is somehow an essential characteristic of whatever is noble. So the desire to do something praiseworthy because it is praiseworthy must be part of what is involved in the love of the noble. But what does Aristotle think deserves praise, and why?

It has recently been suggested by T. H. Irwin that what is praiseworthy about virtuous actions, and so what the desire to do a noble or fine action is directed at in it, is its being for the common good, and not merely for the good of the agent himself and his family and friends.[29] I agree with Irwin that on Aristotle's account of the moral virtues the virtues and virtuous action are concerned for the common good; and in itself the suggestion is plausible that the community, who are of course the ones who bestow praise, make a point of praising qualities of mind and character, and actions, that are directed at the common good. However, Aristotle nowhere explicitly connects working for the common good with praiseworthiness, nor is there persuasive textual evidence that he thought an action's being directed at the common good was the essential ground of its being a noble or fine one.[30]

We can get a clue to what Aristotle did think fine and praiseworthy about virtuous actions if we attend to two further things Aristotle says elsewhere about the noble—things that seem to reflect especially the fact that the word *kalon* also means beautiful or handsome in an aesthetic sense. I have in mind first two passages where Aristotle links nobility with what is fitting (*prepon*). In *Topics* 5.5.135a13 he says the *kalon* and the fitting are the same thing, and this identification is presupposed in *EE* 8.3.1249a9, where he develops an argument having as one premise the proposition that noble

---

cited just above in my text; the πάντα is suspect anyhow, being redundant after ὅσα and not usual in such phrases in Aristotle. Perhaps we have a double error in the MSS here: πάντα added by dittography after ὄντα and αἱρετά dropped by haplography through its resemblance to ἐπαινετά. Woods keeps the MS. reading except that, following Verdenius, he brackets ὄντα. But that produces a non-Aristotelian, maybe nonsensical, idea: that the noble things are those good things that are ends that are *praised* because of themselves (see *Eth. Nic.* 1.12.1101b12–18). Dirlmeier's objections to any emendation are completely misguided (commentary to *EE*, 494–95).

[29] "Aristotle's Conception of Morality."

[30] Irwin's argument is most impressive where it concerns *Rhet.* 1.9. Aristotle in discussing the virtues in that chapter repeatedly emphasizes that virtuous action and character are principal bases for justified praise and connects their praiseworthiness with the fact that they involve acting disinterestedly for other people's and one's country's sake. But Aristotle's aim in discussing the virtues in the *Rhetoric* is to provide the intending public speaker with what he needs to know in order both to find materials to draw on in constructing an encomium and to devise the means when speaking in the assembly or lawcourts to make his hearers have a high regard for himself as a good, moral person, concerned for the public interest. It is not surprising that he should emphasize this aspect of the virtues in this context; that he does so shows no more than that in the popular Athenian mind there was a strong connection between praiseworthiness and action for the good of others. Nothing follows about what a correct philosophical theory of the nature of τὸ καλόν and the bases of the praise it merits will say about these matters. The evidence Irwin cites from Aristotle's strictly philosophical works to show that he connected the praise of the fine-or-noble with support of the common good is extremely tenuous.

things are fitting things. What, however, is fitting about them? Here the concluding paragraph of *Metaphysics* XIII 3 (1078a31–b36) gives us the help we need.[31] In this passage Aristotle disputes the claim that the mathematical sciences have nothing to tell us about goodness and nobility (fineness, beauty). He begins by distinguishing goodness from nobility, saying that goodness is found only in the sphere of action whereas nobility is found both there and among unchanging entities (and so, quite possibly, among the objects of mathematics, which are unchanging things). This explicit reference to nobility of action is a helpful reassurance that in what follows he is not speaking about some special type of nobility found in the mathematical realm but about nobility in a sense that applies to noble actions as well. The highest types of nobility or fineness or beauty, he says, are order, symmetry and determinateness (*taxis kai summetria kai to hōrismenon*)[32]— and the mathematical sciences give proofs about these matters in a specially high degree. (He means, I take it, that they prove of various mathematical objects that they have properties that are particularly telling instances of order, symmetry, and determinateness.) Moreover, he says, since order, symmetry, and determinateness provide explanations for why some mathematical objects are as they are, it is clear that in a way these sciences also instruct us about that kind of explanation—explanation invoking nobility or fineness or beauty as a final cause.

The clear implication of this discussion in the *Metaphysics* is that what *to kalon* in action involves, in addition to the praiseworthiness we are told about elsewhere, is order, symmetry, and determinateness. I will say something in a moment about how virtuous actions might be thought to exhibit these properties. But first we should notice something about how these two accounts of *to kalon* (the one in terms of praiseworthiness, the other in terms of order, symmetry, and determinateness) apparently fit together. In the *Eudemian Ethics* we are told that things that have this property of nobility (e.g., virtuous actions) are chosen for their own sakes and praised or worthy of praise for that reason. In the *Metaphysics* we are told that what has this property exhibits order, symmetry, and determinateness. The connection then is this: *kala* things *as such* exhibit order, symmetry, and determinateness, and when they are chosen for their own sakes, i.e., because they do exhibit these properties, then they are praised or worthy of praise for that reason—for the reason that they are so chosen. The idea then is that when someone does actions having order, symmetry, and determinateness (in

[31] D. J. Allan ("The Fine and the Good," pp. 67–68, 70) noticed the relevance of this passage to the understanding of Aristotle's conception of moral virtue as directed at τὸ καλόν, but could not find much illumination in it.

[32] It seems that Aristotle is developing here some ideas of Plato in the *Philebus*, 64d–e ff. Plato too connects κάλλος with συμμετρία (and τὸ μέτριον), and finds these exemplified in the way elements in a complex composition (a "mixed life") fit together with one another. For Aristotle, too, κάλλος depends upon the way in which disparate elements in a life-composition fit together, as we shall see.

a high degree), precisely out of a desire for, or love of, such actions because they do have them, she and her actions deserve praise.

The link here between praise and doing an action or indeed making something with these features of order, symmetry, and determinateness makes good sense. Such action and production require discrimination and discipline, and are therefore worth praising if what they lead to is something of value. The praise of virtuous action that Aristotle has in mind in connection with its nobility or fineness or beauty is therefore akin to the praise one gives to any accomplished artist or skilled craftsman for the discipline and discrimination shown in his work. So it does not seem that Aristotle based the praise owing to virtuous actions at all on the fact that they are directed at the common good. It may be that many, or even all, virtuous actions are aimed, among other things, at the common good. But that is not the feature of virtuous actions that Aristotle thought makes them merit praise and so constitutes their being *kalon*.

But in what does the order, symmetry, and determinateness of virtuous actions consist? Let us take order and symmetry together first. The pursuit of order and symmetry, in whatever context, implies the putting together in a fitting way of disparate parts or elements in some sort of composition. What might these be in the case of actions, and what in Aristotle's theory of virtuous action might one draw on to develop an Aristotelian conception of the order and symmetry of these actions? Two things come to mind here. First of all there is the question how any given action fits together with other actions, past and future. Is this action consistent with past actions? Does it cohere well with other actions planned or expected in the future? In general, does it fit together with the agent's other actions, past and future, in such a way as to make up a balanced, harmonious, whole series of actions constituting a well-articulated and structured whole active life? And secondly there is the question how *in* any given action the agent deals with the various concerns that are or might be affected by her action: are they all given proper attention, are they balanced correctly in relation to one another, so that in the selected action the full complexity of the situation is adequately responded to?

As for determinateness, the following suggests itself. Determinateness in general implies sharpness of definition, and this suggests something about the fit in all the respects where order and symmetry are involved in the "composition" of one's actions—in the balance and harmony *within* the action, as done, of the multiple concerns the agent has in mind, and in the fit between *this* action and the series of past and future actions of which it is intended to be a part. Determinateness of fit here would mean that the fit is a close one, that there are, so to speak, sharp edges at all the borders where the pieces of the "composition" join. In other words, the determinateness in moral action qua *kalon* consists in the fact that precisely *this* action, done in precisely *this* way, is what is required just now—given what has preceded and is intended to follow. This may seem to go against Aristotle's celebrated insistence on the lack of precision (*akribeia*) necessary in the study of ethical matters, but I think it does not. One should bear in mind that what he actually says is only that a moral philosophy adequate to the facts cannot provide statements and explanations about what is to be done that attain very great precision.[33] He does not say that the choices of the morally good person are not firm and definite in all essential respects. If "the decision lies in perception" (*Nic. Eth.* 2.9.1109b23), that does not mean that perception itself about what to do necessarily leaves anything of substance undetermined, that it always or even ever leaves open a lot of options that would be equally good solutions to any practical problem—so that looseness of fit, rather than the determinateness I have sketched, would apply instead.[34]

Such an "aesthetic" interpretation of what it is for actions to be *kala*, and this way of spelling it out, draws support from Aristotle's definition of moral virtue in terms of a tendency to feel and act in an intermediate way. An intermediate is always measured against some extremes; it is a condition of harmony and balance. When he first introduces this notion (*Nic. Eth.* 2.6.1106a26ff.) and applies it to the virtues of character, Aristotle speaks in fairly gross quantitative terms: virtue selects certain intermediate amounts of feelings and some allegedly corresponding but not satisfactorily spelled out amounts of actions. But soon (already towards the end of 2.6, at 1106b21–23; and see 2.9.1109a24–30) he links the intermediacy of virtuous feeling and action with feeling and acting at the right time, about the right things, towards the right people, for the right purpose, and in the right way, and so on. These formulas are naturally seen as reflecting a concern to respond in feeling and action in a way that answers adequately to the full complexity of the particular situation, by giving appropriate recognition in the way one feels and how and what one does to a whole range of impinging claims on one's attention, claims that have to be recognized and appropriately accommodated somehow in one's feelings as one acts, and in one's action itself. This fits particularly well, perhaps, with the second of the two considerations about the order and symmetry of actions that I have mentioned, about the need to respond at one and the same time, in both feeling and action, to a large range of impinging concerns. But it connects also with the other consideration about order and symmetry and with determinateness as I have interpreted that—with the need to fit the current

---

[33] See Nic. Eth. 1.2. 1094b11–22.

[34] On my account Aristotle's conception of the καλόν bears interesting comparison with Stoic accounts of this same value-property. In the account of Stoic ethics in Stobaeus (2.63.1–5 = SVF iii. 278) we read that κάλλος of the soul consists in a certain kind of συμμετρία, and Diog. L. (7. 99–100) makes every good also καλόν because it συμμέτρως ἔχει πρὸς τὴν ἑαυτοῦ χρείαν and connects being καλόν with being τελείως σύμμετρον; and he goes on to say that this is what renders those who possess it worthy of praise (ἐπαινετούς). Cato in Cicero's *de Finibus* 3.21 describes the last stage in moral development as that in which a person *vidit rerum agendarum ordinem et ut ita dicam concordiam* and concludes that that is the *summum ... per se laudandum et expetendum bonum*. For the Stoics, too, τὸ καλόν is a matter of συμμετρία and τάξις, and therefore a ground of praise.

action in a determinate way into a continuing pattern of past and future actions—since among the currently impinging concerns will be ones relating to past and future: all these concerns must be joined and *unified* in the feelings out of which one acts and in the action itself.

VI *THUMOS* AND *TO KALON*

Let us suppose, then, that this sort of order, symmetry, and determinateness of action is the value that Aristotle means to point to and recognize under the name of nobility or fineness or beauty in action, and that he makes *the* end of moral virtue and morally virtuous action as such.[35] I suggested above (pp. 266 and 271) that, at any rate in the case of the morally virtuous person, Aristotle holds that it is through his spirited desires (his *thumos*) that he pursues *to kalon* as such; that is to say, Aristotle makes order, symmetry, and determinateness of action the immediate and constant object of the morally virtuous person's spirited kind of desire, corresponding to (his) good and pleasure as the objects of his other two types of desire. I turn now to a defence of this suggestion.

I argued above that spirited desires in general are competitive in character; they aim at self-assertion as an agent, as a person to be taken serious practical account of, in comparison and in competition with other agents. It is for this reason that Plato in the *Republic* made victory or honor the immediate object of this kind of desire, parallel to pleasure (or money, the means of obtaining it) as object of appetitive desires, as such. But we have seen evidence (end of section II above) that Aristotle refused to follow him in this. So far as I can see, Aristotle nowhere offers a replacement for Plato's rejected specification(s) as to the object of spirited desire in general. My suggestion is not that Aristotle proposes the noble or fine or beautiful as the immediate object of spirited desires in general—for such desires of non-human animals, or children, or even all adult human beings. It is only for the morally virtuous person, and only after a certain stage is reached in the special course of moral development and self-discipline that leads a person to the possession of virtues of character, that I want to claim that this is Aristotle's view.

[35] Perhaps I should say explicitly that I do not intend here or in what precedes to be offering on Aristotle's behalf a definition of moral value that in any sense reduces it to some sort of non-moral value (for example, some sort of aesthetic value). The σπουδαῖος himself is the final standard or measure of this sort of value, as of the others, and no one with a well-developed aesthetic sense, however extraordinary, would know from that which actions and which types of character were the καλον ones. I take Aristotle's characterization of this value in aesthetic terms as intended to offer a perspicuous description of one aspect of the state of mind and feeling of the morally virtuous person. We learn something interesting and illuminating about moral virtue by learning this. But there is no suggestion that anyone could become virtuous by an independent appreciation of some values with which he was antecedently fully familiar.

In an excellent article Myles Burnyeat has given a persuasive account of the process by which, according to Aristotle, a young person "learns to be good." Burnyeat speaks of the young person coming by habituation to take pleasure in "noble and just actions" and thereby becoming suited to hear lectures on ethics and ready for reason to "take hold . . . so as to form and shape for the best the patterns of motivation and response which represent the child in us."[36] As we have seen, these childish "patterns of motivation and response"—the non-rational ones—are of two types: appetitive (aimed at pleasure) and spirited. Both sorts of motivation and response must be put into a preliminary good condition, so that reason can "take hold." Burnyeat describes how this is to happen mostly for the case of the appetites: once a young person comes to take pleasure in acts of the virtues, this pleasure, and the young person's desire for it, can then be used as a counterweight in his (or others') reason-based efforts to reshape his *other* desires for pleasure—by eliminating some, reducing others, initiating him to yet others, and so on—as well, of course, as to refine and deepen this pleasure in virtuous action itself.

A parallel process for spirited desires must, then, be involved as well. How are we to conceive that? Here one should notice that in Burnyeat's account (and the principal texts of the *Nicomachean Ethics* on which it is based)[37] Aristotle says that a young person must become habituated to take pleasure not just in the doing of just actions (and others required by the virtues) but in these *as* "noble"—to take pleasure in these actions for the order, symmetry, and determinateness that is found in them, therefore. How are they to come to do that? Evidently they must first become aware of and experience the nobility and fineness of the actions required by the virtues, before discovering a pleasure *in* that nobility (and their experience of it). Here is where I believe *thumos*-desires come in. These desires, as we have seen, aim at competitive exertion, at being active and in command, at making oneself significant. Young people must initially be brought to find satisfaction for their *thumos*-desires in the order, symmetry, and determinateness of morally virtuous actions: the self-discipline required to compose such actions (individually and in appropriately connected series) makes them a salient object for that kind of desire, and presumably an especially satisfying one. Just as with appetitive desires for pleasure, so here: once, through habituation, young people do come to experience the satisfaction of their *thumos*-desires through the nobility and fineness of actions of the virtues, this satisfaction and their desires for it can be used as a counterweight in their own (and others') reason-based efforts to reshape their *other* spirited desires— by eliminating some, reducing others, initiating them to yet others, and so on—as well, of course, as to refine and deepen the satisfaction for their spirited desires to be found in the nobility and fineness of virtuous action

[36] Burnyeat, "Aristotle on Learning to be Good," 86.
[37] See *Nic. Eth.* 1.1095a2–13, b12–13; 10.1179b4–31.

itself. Once they discover and begin fully to experience the satisfaction of their *thumos*-desires in the nobility of virtuous action, and so to be able to take *pleasure* in it, they draw into a single focus both of their two kinds of non-rational desire. At the same time, and as a result, they advance to the threshold of achieving effective control of their lives by reason.[38]

We saw earlier that for Aristotle, as for Plato, spirited desires are the "ally" of reason in this process. The spirited desire for the order, symmetry, and determinateness of actions is a desire for something that these desires (initially aimed only at self-assertion, at active and competitive agency) only gradually *discover* to be satisfying. But in doing so such desires advance the reign of reason, because reason itself recognizes this order, symmetry, and determinateness as a very good thing. In order for virtue itself to be fully achieved, as we saw in his discussion of the connection between *thumos* and courage, not only must this orientation of *thumos* to *to kalon* be present, but the actions issuing from it must also be decided upon as correct (*prohaireton*). This means that when virtuous persons decide to do a virtuous action, desires both of reason and *thumos* will motivate them (often, of course, appetitive desires would join in as well). The *thumos*-desire will be a desire for whatever is *kalon* in the action, and will be a desire to do the action for the sake of that. The reasoned desire to do it (namely, the decision itself)[39] will be a desire to do it because it is good and constitutes *eudaimonia* in those circumstances. Part of the thought contained in the reasoned desire will be the recognition that a virtuous disposition of the non-rational desires, and action on that disposition, being *kalon*, is a good thing, and a fundamental good at that. So the reasoned desire or *prohairesis* to do the action will also desire it for the sake of the *kalon* in it.[40] Indeed, Aristotle almost says as much explicitly. He makes it a requirement of morally virtuous action that one decide on (*prohairoumenos*) such actions for themselves (*di' hauta*) (2.4.1104b31–32), and it seems plausible to interpret this as meaning that

---

[38] I am unsure to what extent this account of θυμός and its connection to the specifically moral value of τὸ καλόν may go beyond Burnyeat's delineation of the stages by which a good person develops over time. As will be apparent by this point, I am in agreement with Burnyeat in seeing that *Nic. Eth.* 1104b30–35, refers to three "irreducibly distinct categories of value" that "connect each with a distinct set of desires and feelings" ("Aristotle on Learning to be Good," 86). If my account differs from his, it is, first of all, in the special emphasis I place on the spirited desires as becoming focused, through habituation, on the noble or fine in action, and on the subsequent pleasure that is taken in their satisfaction through that kind of action. Secondly, I emphasize, as Burnyeat does not, the permanence of the psychological independence from reason of both types of non-rational desires. The harmony of the desires of the fully moral person (her or his rational, spirited, and appetitive desires) is a harmony of sources of motivation that remain independent of one another—not the subsumption into reason of what previously counted as independent sources.

[39] See Chapter 10 above, "Some Remarks on Aristotle's Moral Psychology," beginning of sect. III and n. 4, and the passages cited there.

[40] This parallels the situation when a person acts out of an appetite for some pleasure, and at the same time out of a desire for his good, the pleasure itself being counted as something good. See above, end of sect. IV.

one must decide on them *as* virtuous, i.e., do them *tou kalou heneka*. This does not mean, however, that the pursuit of the specifically moral value of *to kalon* by reason renders its simultaneous pursuit by *thumos* redundant, or even takes its place—any more than a desire of reason to have some bodily pleasure substitutes in the case of a virtuous person for an appetitive desire for it, or renders such a desire redundant. Indeed, the practically wise person has learned to desire the *kalon* with his reason because earlier he desired it with his *thumos*-desires. And he relies upon the continued harmonious and supportive functioning of his non-rational desires, *thumos* as well as *epithumia*, in order to hold firmly to the correct overall view of the good, holding to which constitutes his being practically wise in the first place.[41]

The specifically moral value, then—the value with which morally virtuous persons as such are specially concerned—is constituted by the order, fittingness and harmony, and determinateness of whatever possesses it. If I am right, this kind of value is for Aristotle the eventual object of one of the two types of non-rational desire that he thinks human beings are all endowed with, *thumos*. It is through *thumos* that people are first motivated to experience this kind of value, and so first enabled to know, though haltingly, what is valuable for us in it. The morally virtuous person, in whom reason has taken control, has a reasoned understanding of this kind of value and so is motivated to pursue it simply on the basis of that understanding. But she continues to be motivated to pursue this value also by her *thumos*-desires, whose satisfaction, indeed, is necessary for her to *experience* it fully. Similarly, her desires for pleasure motivate her to pursue, and their satisfaction is necessary for her to experience, those pleasures that reason determines are good for her to have. Reason gives the needed direction to the *thumos*-desires, as it does to the *epithumiai*, but experiencing *thumos*-desires and acting constantly on them is what, according to Aristotle's theory, makes the life led according to reason a *morally* virtuous one.

VII ANTI-CLIMACTIC CONCLUSION

If spirited desire plays such a crucial role for Aristotle, both in moral development and in the virtuous action of the fully virtuous and practically wise person, why does he not make this more explicit? Why does he leave it to his reader to piece the story together in this roundabout and painstaking way? In fact, shouldn't we be wary about accepting any such story as I have told, just because it does have to be so laboriously pieced together? I do not think there can be an answer to these questions that is satisfactory to *us*. But perhaps if we found as natural and compelling as Plato and Aristotle

[41] See *Nic. Eth.* 6.5.1140b11–21; 12.1144a34–36. These passages provide the background for understanding Aristotle's thesis in 12.1144a20–22 and 13.1145a2–6, that moral virtue makes the decision straight, i.e., for the true end, while practical wisdom makes the action done be rightly directed to that.

and their contemporaries must have done the idea of spirited desires as a distinct and special *kind* of desires, aimed at active agency and competitive self-promotion, we would not be making these demands in the first place. Perhaps then we would have understood Aristotle in this way from the beginning, without having to be told explicitly at every point about the special role played by spirited desire in the constitution of moral virtue.[42]

SELECTED FURTHER READINGS

Santas, Gerasimos. "The Structure of Aristotle's Ethical Theory: Is it Teleological or a Virtue Ethics?" *Topoi* 15 (1996): 59–80.

Tuozzo, Thomas M. "Contemplation, the Noble, and the Mean: The Standard of Moral Virtue in Aristotle's Ethics." In *Aristotle, Virtue, and the Mean*, edited by Richard Bosley and others, *Apeiron* 28 no. 4 (1995). Edmonton: Academic Printing and Publishing, 1996, 129–54.

[42] I would like to thank Susan Sauvé Meyer for detailed and helpful comments on an early draft of this essay, which I read to the Philosophy Department of Cornell University. I would also like to thank the participants at the Berlin conference held in honor of Günther Patzig on 25 July 1991 for their patience, and especially Michael Frede for his advice on how to reorganize and otherwise improve my presentation of the material.

CHAPTER TWELVE

Aristotle on the Authority of "Appearances"

EVERYONE has always known that every human life is significantly affected by the consequences of good and bad luck. Things happen frequently to people by luck—things out of the ordinary and unintended by them or anyone else—which they nonetheless wish, and with good reason, would or would not happen, or which, with good reason, they are pleased or regret have happened to them. People are born with special talents or disabilities, for example; things they have cared a lot about and worked hard to achieve fail, through no fault of their own or anybody else; and so on. Disputes arise, however, over whether and, if so, in precisely what ways, luck is ever responsible for our being morally good or bad persons; for whether in some situation we do or do not act badly, or do some neutral-seeming thing well or badly; or for whether, everything taken into consideration, our lives are good ones or not.[1] In her book *The Fragility of Goodness* Martha Nussbaum presents a view on these matters which is highly accommodating to the role which luck can play, especially in undermining a human life, in knocking it off its moral keel. She claims to be following an "Aristotelian" method in ethical theory in defending her conclusions, and she closely associates Aristotle with her own outlook on the importance of moral luck.[2] I believe, however, that Nussbaum misunderstands and seriously misrepresents Aristotle's actual procedures in moral philosophy. Furthermore, when correctly understood Aristotle's own views assign luck a much less substantial part in the fabric of a well-lived life than she herself wishes it to have. Nussbaum's account gives us a valuable opportunity to improve our understanding of Aristotle's outlook in ethical theory by comparing her Aristotle closely with the Aristotle who emerges from a careful reading of his own texts.

Aristotle, as is well known, makes the appeal to the beliefs of "the many and the wise," and thus to the ways things "appear," fundamental as the starting point for and, in some sense, a basic control on, philosophical inquiry in any area.[3] In explicating this aspect of Aristotelian philosophizing, Nussbaum emphasizes especially the beliefs of "the many"—ordinary, unsophisticated people. In this connection she interprets Aristotle in terms of Hilary Putnam's distinction between "metaphysical" and "internal" realism[4] and maintains that Aristotle was, like Putnam, an "internal realist" in his metaphysics and in his philosophy overall. According to her, what "the

---

[1] See the papers entitled "Moral Luck" by Bernard Williams and Thomas Nagel.

[2] See Nussbaum, *Fragility*, pp. 10–12.

[3] See the seminal paper by G.E.L. Owen, "*Tithenai ta phainomena.*"

[4] See Putnam's *Reason, Truth and History.*

many" think is what "we" think in our ordinary moments, and in making philosophy beholden to these appearances Aristotle is restricting it to telling the truth as it is "for *us*"—"our" truth, the truth about "our" world. It is when she turns to his ethical theory that we see most clearly the momentous consequences of this assimilation, and I turn shortly to those implications. But first we need to ask whether it can be correct to interpret Aristotle or any other ancient thinker in such terms—terms that, one would think, must owe their intelligibility to developments in the late-twentieth-century philosophy of language that gave rise to such distinctions among "realisms."

Slogans aside, it is not clear to me what an internal realist is supposed to believe that other people do not. When one considers carefully what Nussbaum says in expounding Aristotle's views, it turns out to be quite complicated to figure out what Aristotle is supposed to believe that makes him an "internal realist." She does indeed speak, applying Putnam's termi-nologies, of Aristotle's understanding of the truth, or the necessity, or the reality or existence, of anything as always that of the truth, necessity, reality, or existence of it "relative to" our human language, our "discourse and thought," our "conceptual scheme" and "conceptualization." She even makes Aristotle hold that our ability to *refer* to anything is relative to these things.[5] Her appeal to these ideas from contemporary philosophy of language is provoked by what Aristotle says about the role for philosophy played by *ta phainomena, ta legomena, ta endoxa*—those variously described starting-points (the "appearances," the "things that are said," the "reputable opin-ions") for any dialectical investigation, to which, in some way and degree (on this, see further below), the results of philosophical inquiry must according to him be held answerable. The burden of Nussbaum's description of Aristotle as an "internal realist" consists in her interpretation of his views on how these dialectical starting-points ought to control and limit philosophical theory. However, it is obvious, or should be, that these starting-points are a special set of *beliefs*, expressed (of course—how else would they be?) within our conceptual scheme and in our language, to which other beliefs equally expressed within our conceptual scheme, and arguably equally well or better supported by it, might be opposed. In whatever sense Aristotle holds that philosophical conclusions must be confined, as Nussbaum puts it, within "the circle of the appearances"[6]—the circle formed by the opinions of "the many"—this is plainly a much narrower, and quite different, restric-tion than the Putnamian idea that any truth we discover (or think we discover) is conditioned by and relative to our conceptual scheme, something that *we* create, and not some absolute truth, some truth about things as they are in themselves apart from conceptualization. The opinions of "the many" are just one set of opinions expressed in our concepts, and there are lots of other, conflicting ones similarly so expressed.

---

[5] See Nussbaum, *Fragility*, pp. 253–57.
[6] Ibid., p. 257.

To see this, consider Parmenides and Plato, the predecessors of Aristotle whom Nussbaum principally holds out for castigation because they fail to follow Aristotle's strictures and do not confine themselves in their theorizing "within the circle of the appearances." Suppose we attempt to approach their philosophies with the apparatus in hand of conceptual schemes, conditions for reference, and so forth, and the contrast between metaphysical and internal realism. Then it seems to me there is just as much ground for describing these opponents of Aristotle's as internal realists, in Putnam's sense, as there is for so describing Aristotle himself. After all, Parmenides' goddess (frg. B7 DK) famously insisted that one judge her account of the truth—the objective truth, a truth that flies in the face of ordinary assumptions about reality—by reason or thought (*logos*); she contrasted this with the unthinking acceptance of conventional beliefs. Likewise, Plato's Socrates, following in her footsteps, strenuously maintained in the *Republic* (508e–509b) that the (objectively existing) ultimate principle of things, the Good-itself, was immediately and equally responsible both for the being and truth of everything else there is and for its being known by us. Thus truth and reality as understood by Parmenides and Plato were (automatically, by their very natures) thoroughly "relative to" our thought and to our capacity for knowledge, and Parmenides and Plato could claim to be following principles embedded in our "conceptual scheme" in insisting on the authority of thought as a basis for determining what reality is like—even though the "reality" they were arguing for was something very, very unlike what ordinary conventional opinions assume is reality. Parmenides and Plato, just as much as Aristotle, develop their philosophical views by appealing to our thoughts and their consequences as conditioned by our conceptual scheme. When Parmenides calls being One, he claims to mean what we all mean by "one," and the arguments he gives to establish this thesis start from ideas he thinks must demand acceptance by us, with *our* ways of thinking, *our* concepts, and so forth. And similarly for Plato and the Good.

Where Aristotle differs from these predecessors is over the question whether the beliefs that ordinary people hold about what reality is actually like are true or not, and whether the fact that ordinary people hold these beliefs is any reason for thinking there is any truth in them. Aristotle respects these beliefs and insists that philosophical theory must ultimately be answerable to them (in some way or other). Parmenides and Plato do not. All parties to this dispute share a commitment to our "conceptual scheme" and to its capacity to lead us to the truth; what they disagree about is how to weigh, argue for and against, and ultimately decide between, differing beliefs all of which are expressed within it, and can plausibly be claimed to be supported by it. So it must be a mistake to try to promote Aristotle's cause and to denigrate his more rationalist predecessors by tarring the latter with the brush of (supposedly) nonsensical metaphysical realism and decking Aristotle out in the lurid but comforting colors of (supposedly) sensible internal realism. This contemporary distinction is completely irrelevant to the actual issues that separated the ancient philosophers—issues about how to proceed in working out a reliable account of how things in truth are. One could, so far as I can see, argue equally well that all three thinkers (and the ancient philosophers in general) were committed either to an "internal" or to a "metaphysical realist" view of the truth. However, to argue the latter would have the advantage of giving contemporary internal realists some worthy opponents. It also makes more satisfactory history: metaphysical realism is the more naive view, and so the one we would expect people back at the beginning of philosophy, including Aristotle, to have held—unself-consciously, of course. However that may be, questions about Aristotelian dialectic and its relation to philosophy cannot usefully be discussed by invoking this contemporary distinction.

Hence one cannot accept Nussbaum's claim that by insisting on the authority for philosophy of the "appearances," Aristotle maintains that philosophy—and ethical philosophy, in particular—is limited to finding "the order that is *in* our language and in the world around us as we see and experience it"; that any philosophical view must "commend itself to our attention by showing its relationship to our lived experience of the world and giving evidence of its ability to organize and articulate features of that experience," because "we can have truth only *inside* the circle of the appearances, because only there can we communicate, even refer, at all."[7] Nor can it be right to attribute to Aristotle the view that some god might be able to say something more, or different, about how things are in themselves, while what *we* can do, and all we can do, is say how our "deepest" attachments, and so forth, make them appear, and so how they really are *for us*.

What, then, is actually involved in Aristotle's method of appealing to the appearances? Aristotle's respect for ordinary people's views, among the other starting-points for philosophical theory about moral matters, marks a crucial division between him and Plato (and Parmenides). But what, in general, are the "appearances," and in what ways, and why, does Aristotle assign authority to them—and, among them, to the ordinary person's view of things? In a well-known passage in the introduction to his treatment of weakness of will (*Nicomachean Ethics* VII 1–2), much exploited in discussions of Aristotelian dialectic in the past quarter-century, Aristotle offers what looks like a general account and defense of his procedures. On Nussbaum's view, as we have just been seeing, Aristotle, as philosopher of and for the human truth—"our" truth—should be interpreted when speaking on philosophical subjects as a self-consciously engaged thinker, one engaged with the world as *we* experience it and speaking to others likewise, and self-consciously, so engaged. So in referring to and translating this passage Nussbaum makes Aristotle quite explicit in adopting just this attitude of attachment and solidarity. In fact, however, the original Greek marks Aristotle as detached and neutral. Here (1145b2–7), in explaining the procedures

---

[7] For the quotations in this sentence, see in order ibid., pp. 262, 258, and 257.

he will follow in investigating the nature of weakness of will, Aristotle says we must set down the appearances (*phainomena*), work through the puzzles, and thus show the truth of all, or most and the most authoritative, of the *endoxa* on the subject at hand. Nussbaum translates *ta endoxa* as "the beliefs we hold" (and she follows this up by translating *ta legomena* at 1145b20 as "the things we say"). But neither Greek expression has any explicit reference to *us* in it. Moreover, among his list of "things said" (that is the literal, neutral translation for *ta legomena*), Aristotle reports two (1145b14–17, 17–19) in which there is a difference of opinion ("some say" one thing, "others" the contradictory), and in neither case does he say "some" and "others" *of us*: he uses the third, not the first, person plural both times. So the "things said" are things *people* say, either people generally or some people otherwise unspecified, and in reporting them Aristotle describes these people in the third person, and stands neutrally apart, without in any way saying or implying that he speaks as one of a "we."

As for the *endoxa* two points should be noted. First, Aristotle elsewhere in discussing *endoxa* and the method of arguing from them divides them in two—the opinions of the many and those of the wise. So the first point to observe is that if the *endoxa* are "the beliefs we hold" this has to be taken to refer, not exclusively to the beliefs we ordinarily hold, but to those together with whatever the wise may have to say: in other words, the "we" means the whole lot of us, ordinary people with their opinions, and the "wise," or the relevant experts, with their sometimes, to the ordinary person, surprising or even outlandish opinions. But are the *endoxa* correctly translated as "the beliefs we hold" even in this more encompassing sense? There is no doubt what this Greek adjective (*endoxos*) means in contexts (even in Aristotle) other than that of the Aristotelian theory of dialectic: it means "held in esteem or honor; of high repute." And Jonathan Barnes has given excellent reasons why we should think that that is what it means in the context of Aristotelian dialectic as well.[8] The *endoxa* are the "reputable opinions" on a given subject, the ones that have some credibility because of their standing antecedent to any philosophical inquiry one may be undertaking. Thus, as with the "things said," there is no slightest hint in this Greek expression of any "we" as those who hold these opinions.

What then can one say about Aristotle's conception of the appearances, and of philosophy's commitment to them? Nussbaum, relying on the character of the items in the "things said" that Aristotle immediately sets out (1145b8–20), takes the appearances (*phainomena*) he refers to in the statement of his method to be "our most common beliefs and sayings about *akrasia*" (and that does seem to be how Aristotle intends the expression in this passage, even if the scope of the appearances elsewhere may be wider).

---

[8] J. Barnes, "Aristotle and the Methods of Ethics," pp. 498–502. My own account in this and the following seven paragraphs follows Barnes in all major points but one, concerning the degree of originality permitted in the philosophical theories defended by this method: see n. 9 and p. 287 below.

Having set down in chapter 1 the appearances, that is, the common conceptions and beliefs on the subject, Aristotle proceeds at once in chapter 2 to state the puzzles that in the rest of the book he tries to solve. This chapter begins: "Someone might raise a puzzle about . . ." and concludes, "Such then are the puzzles that arise. . . ." Now it is noteworthy that the first puzzle Aristotle mentions arises not, as others mentioned do, because the appearances themselves are, on first presentation anyhow, in conflict with one another in some respect. This is a puzzle (1145b21–22) about *how*, in acting in weakness, a person holds the correct view (viz., that he is acting badly). Among the appearances listed in chapter 1, we find it said (at 1145b12–14) that "the weak-willed person acts as a result of passion, knowing that he acts badly," but nothing else listed among the appearances conflicts with this at all. So the puzzle does not arise because there is a conflict within the appearances. However, we are now told in chapter 2, some people deny that it is possible to act knowing (*epistamenon*) that one is acting badly, and in particular, we are told, Socrates denied this (b22–24). So this first puzzle arises because Socrates (and perhaps others) denied one of the appearances as presented in chapter 1; because of what Socrates held, a puzzle arises over *how* the weak agent holds the view, as the common opinion reported among the appearances says he does, that he acts badly. Is it really with knowledge, as the common conception (but perhaps unguardedly and without conviction) seemed to say, but Socrates firmly and with arguments denied, or with something else?

Now these details from chapter 2 are crucial if one wishes to understand Aristotle's attitude to the appearances (*phainomena*) in this passage. For they show that when he goes on immediately to say that the Socratic theory is (in Nussbaum's translation) "obviously at variance with the *phainomena*" he cannot mean therein to be brusquely rejecting the Socratic account, simply because it is at variance with the common conception—as if that had sacrosanct authority. On the contrary, it is precisely because Socrates's views conflict with the *phainomena* that Aristotle says we even have this first puzzle to work through: simply to reject the Socratic account out of hand would be to rob us of any ground for puzzlement here at all. So it is evident that, according to his method, Aristotle attaches some weight to the Socratic theory, at least to something fundamental in it, as well as attaching weight to the appearance with which it conflicts. Otherwise he could not think, as he does, that there is anything here to puzzle over. Indeed, it is clear from the way he works through this puzzle (in chapter 3) and from the solution he offers to it there that he is more concerned to preserve Socrates' central contention than he is to save the ordinary person's appearances. At any rate he explicitly insists (1147b13–17) that on his solution, in the sense of knowledge in which Socrates held that it was inadmissible "that while knowledge is present anything else should master it and drag it about like a slave" (1145b23–24), it is not the case that the weak agent acts while knowing that he is acting badly. The main effect of Aristotle's discussion in working through the puzzle is to draw distinctions among types of knowledge and items known, sufficient to allow him to restrict and qualify the ordinary opinion that the weak agent knows he is acting badly, in such a way as to avoid saying that he knows this in the way Socrates said he could not. So far from Socrates' view being simply rejected because it conflicts with the appearances, the appearances are actually reworked to be made compatible with this central Socratic contention.[9]

Now Aristotle had told us that the right method is to work through a puzzle in such a way as to show the truth of the "reputable opinions," or most and the most authoritative of them. Evidently, then, he is treating this Socratic contention as one of these opinions relevant to the discussion of *akrasia*, and indeed as one of the most authoritative of them. The view he has argued for on *akrasia*, having been shown, as he thinks, to be true, itself shows the truth of the *endoxa* on which it rests, this Socratic one among them. Accordingly, in this passage Aristotle does not (*pace* Nussbaum, who in this follows recent orthodoxy) treat *phainomena* and *endoxa* as coextensive: Aristotle says that Socrates' view, which he reports as an *endoxon*, was "at variance with the *phainomena*." Moreover, as we have just seen, the method of philosophizing that Aristotle is both recommending and practicing here manifestly does not require us to stay within the circle of the ordinary appearances, within the circle of ordinary experience: he follows Socrates a considerable distance outside that circle. Indeed, he obviously thinks the great strength of his position on *akrasia* consists in its ability to claim the support of *both* the appearances (the unreconstructed view of "the many") *and* the insights of Socrates (the view on this matter of "the wise"): when the distinctions and clarifications he has introduced are applied both to the common conception and to the Socratic theory, one is supposed to see that the most basic part of each of these conflicting views survives, receiving its clearest and most persuasive articulation in the Aristotelian theory itself. On the other hand, this theory is regarded by Aristotle as a genuinely new theory, neither a restatement nor minor variant of Socrates' theory, nor just an articulation of some order that is already in our language and in the world around us as we see and experience it in ordinary life.

When one looks carefully at what Aristotle says in the opening three chapters of *Nicomachean Ethics* VII, then, one finds an Aristotle very different from Nussbaum's. Aristotle describes the *phainomena* from which he begins in a neutral, uncommitted way, as he also does the view of Socrates

---

[9] The clarifications introduced through these distinctions enable Aristotle to offer as his solution to the puzzle an account of the role of knowledge and ignorance in *akrasia* that is no simple restatement of the Socratic theory. Unlike Socrates, Aristotle can and does say that it is not ignorance that he is acting badly that causes the akratic's action, but passion (in this he agrees with the common conception); and he preserves the common opinion that the akratic does know (but only in a way) that his action is a bad one. But on the point that he himself regards as central to the Socratic view he stands firmly with Socrates and against what appears to the common person (at any rate as this first presents itself to him).

that conflicts with some of these *phainomena*. There is no hint that the *phainomena* are to be regarded as "our" view, Aristotle's and the common person's, or that the Socratic view, because it conflicts with the *phainomena*, is to be rejected in favor of "an account . . . that will remain faithful to the 'appearances' in a way the rejected" account does not.[10] Aristotle's own conclusion—his solution to this first puzzle—is not in the least confined within the limits of these "appearances," since it claims equal or greater support from the Socratic view that lies outside this circle. Nor would it be right even to say that in reaching his conclusion Aristotle confines himself within the wider limits imposed by the appearances taken together with the other relevant *endoxa*—within the circle marked out by the opinions of the many and of the wise taken together. His account of *akrasia* is a genuinely new one that is not found already stated or even adumbrated within this circle. What Aristotle claims is only that his new theory shows at least "most and the most authoritative" of the relevant items defining this wider circle to be true, and so can claim their support. Nothing in these chapters provides any platform at all for the idea that Aristotle limits himself, or thinks he ought to limit himself, to articulating the order already present in the totality of the *endoxa*, much less the order present in the ordinary way of thinking about things (what he here calls the *phainomena*).

In fact, the *endoxa* as Aristotle conceives them play quite a different and more limited, but nonetheless substantial, role. To judge from these chapters, the philosopher is not, according to Aristotle, limited to articulating views that lie already implicit in the *endoxa*, or to picking and choosing from among them (after suitable dialectical shifting and reformulation) so as to select as his own theses and theories accounts of things that are already explicitly there in the stock of reputable opinions. Sometimes this is what he will do, sometimes not: that depends on the case. But what he must always do—and the authority of the reputable opinions comes to this—is to show that the conclusions he reaches, no matter how novel and apparently unprepared by the *endoxa* themselves, nonetheless show the truth of quite a few, and those antecedently the most credible, of the *endoxa* (whether these are common opinions or theses enunciated by recognized wise people with a reputation for having studied and thought hard about the matters in question).

Why, however, does Aristotle make philosophy answerable even in this limited way to the *endoxa*? In his extant works Aristotle never addresses this question squarely, but the obvious answer (and its obviousness may explain his failure clearly to articulate it) is that there is antecedent good reason to expect that some or all of what is reputably believed is true— whether it is reputable because someone with a reputation for wisdom believes it, or because it is embedded in our language itself, or is a common- place of everyday life. The structures of our language and the commonplaces

---

[10] Nussbaum, *Fragility*, p. 240.

of everyday life are cultural artifacts that were originated, shaped and re-shaped by generations of human beings who, with their native intelligences, confronted and dealt with reality. Beliefs arrived at in that way will, to a considerable extent, at least after interpretation, contain the truth, because, as Aristotle thinks, human nature, being the nature of an intelligent animal, orients us toward finding out how things objectively are.[11] Other things being equal, intelligence when applied to a problem gets things right, or at any rate nearly so.[12] All the more does it stand to reason that those who seem to possess especially acute intelligences, if they study closely some field or question, will come away with the truth, or something near to it (see *Nic. Eth.* I 8, 1098b27–29). In this way one can see that the authority Aristotle assigns to the *endoxa* is part of a general strategy for coming to understand reality itself. One is not likely to have the truth if one simply flies in the face of all the *endoxa*, given their origin: if one has the truth, one ought at least to be able to show how, given that, other intelligent people should have thought about it as they did think.[13] This authority has nothing to do with any supposed commitment to working out how the world is *for* human experience, to the neglect of how it is in itself. How it

[11] See *Rhetoric* I 1, 1355a14–18: "For it belongs to the same capacity to discern both what is true and what is similar to it [that is, what is plausible—the stock in trade of the orator]; at the same time, human beings are by nature sufficiently oriented toward the truth and mostly they do happen upon the truth, so that a person who is good at hitting upon the truth will also be good at hitting upon the reputable opinions (*ta endoxa*) [sc., which is what an orator *ex professo* must be able to do, since these are the plausible things to put forward in mounting an oratorical argument]."

[12] Nussbaum (*Fragility*, p. 248) quotes part of Aristotle's counterargument against Speusippus's attack on Eudoxus's hedonistic thesis that what everything pursues, viz. pleasure, must be good: "For that which seems so to everyone, this we say is." She takes this to indicate that Aristotle thinks philosophy must be committed to tell the truth about our special human reality. But consider the whole context from which this quotation is taken (1172b35–1173a4): "Those who object that it's not the case that what everything pursues is good are talking nonsense. For that which seems so to everyone, this we say is, and one who attacks this belief will hardly have anything more worthy of belief to say instead. For if it is creatures without intelligence that pursue the things in question, there would be something in what they say, but if it is even intelligent ones that pursue them, how could there be anything to it?"

[13] Cf. *Eudemian Ethics* VII 2, 1235b15–17, where in discussing the method he proposes to follow in developing his own theory of friendship Aristotle says that we will get a resolution of the puzzles if our account (*logos*) allows us to show that the conflicting opinions we start from are reasonably held—for such an account will be most in agreement with the *phainomena*. See also *EE* I 6, 1216b28–31, where Aristotle says it is important to show that everyone agrees with our own philosophical conclusions (at least "in a certain fashion," that is, after their opinions have been reformulated in the light of our analysis) because everyone has a "natural aptitude" for the truth (on this passage see Barnes, "Methods of Ethics," pp. 507–9). Finally, see *Nic. Eth.* I 8, 1098b9–12, which (accepting Rassow's surely correct excision of *talēthes* at b12, and endorsing Barnes's attractive suspicion that τὰ ὑπάρχειν δοκοῦντα should be read for τὰ ὑπάρχοντα) will run as follows: "But we must investigate it (viz., *eudaimonia*) not only on the basis of the conclusion and the premises of our argument, but also on the basis of the things that are said about it: for with the true view all the properties it is thought to have harmonize (sc., in some way), while they quickly clash with a false one."

is in itself, Aristotle thinks, ought to bear a close relation to how it is for and in our experience; but he always thinks of reality as giving the lead, and it never occurs to him to entertain the idea that our experience, or our conceptual scheme, or our language, is criterial for how reality is.

In the preceding I have emphasized Aristotle's respect for Socrates' views on the strength of knowledge. But we must not forget that in developing his own account of weakness of will Aristotle is also very much concerned to preserve and vindicate the ordinary opinion that sometimes people do act, as a result of passion, knowing (in some sense) that what they do is wrong. The ordinary view is one *endoxon*, and an authoritative one at that; and Aristotle implies a severe criticism of Socrates (and Plato and Parmenides) for simply dismissing ordinary views as mistaken—as things of no account at all, making no contribution at all to the truth. And this favorable assessment of the ordinary view of things, as I have defended it in the last paragraph, undoubtedly explains many of those aspects of Aristotle's moral philosophy that Nussbaum finds so appealing. But what of moral luck? Does evidence from Aristotle support Nussbaum's enthusiastic affirmation that luck has a significant role to play in the morality of our lives, in whether or not we are able to live successful lives at all, where success is judged at least in large part in moral terms?

In one passage of *Nicomachean Ethics* I, Aristotle argues that *eudaimonia*, or what establishes a flourishing, truly successful life is achieved by some kind of learning or training and practice in the virtues, and not by luck (which would make it a direct gift from the gods to their favorites) (1099b9–25). Aristotle first gives some reasons for thinking that happiness is a better thing if it is achieved in the first way than in the second and then argues that if so, that fact is a good reason to think it does come in the first way and not in the second.[14] Here is why Aristotle says he thinks it would be an error to hold that "what is greatest and best" is governed by luck: in other realms where we find good things produced, instead of bad or worse things, it is not luck, but something else—the goal-directed processes of nature, or of skill—that produces the good ones (1099b21–23). If happiness really is the best human good, then if happiness were produced not by such

---

[14] Nussbaum, dangerously quoting only the first and last lines of this argument, comments as follows (*Fragility*, p. 320):

> If it is better that this view of *eudaimonia*, rather than the luck view, should be true, "then it is reasonable that things should be so." For "to turn what is greatest and best over to luck would strike too false a note" (1099b20–25). In other words, the rejection of the luck-supremacy view is the outcome not of a neutral empirical survey, but of a deliberation in which what we desire to find, what we feel we can live with, enters heavily into practical wisdom's weighing of the alternatives. . . . The luck view is rejected . . . because it strikes a false note, i.e., is too much at odds with our other beliefs, and specifically with our evaluative beliefs about what sort of life would be worth the living.

She leaves out of account here the reasons Aristotle himself gives for rejecting the "luck view" (for these, see below in my text) and attributes to him ideas of her own.

definite causes as learning, and so forth, in the virtues, but by luck, we would have a clash with the fact that in other realms—for example, that of nature and art—the good results are produced not by luck but by these other definite causes. So Aristotle's argument relies on something like a neutral empirical survey of how, in fact, the best things in various areas of nature and life are actually produced; he argues that, as a result of this survey, we can conclude that because *eudaimonia* is the best thing attainable in a human life it cannot be conferred by luck.

Even so, Aristotle does leave a place for luck within the constitution of the best life—though he firmly gives luck a secondary place. Moral virtue itself occupies the leading, and controlling, position. Aristotle holds that "external goods" such as good looks, wealth, a good family background, appropriate sorts of friends, children you can be proud of, and so on, are necessary if a person's virtues are to have the fullest and most desirable context for their active use in life.[15] I discuss these matters in Chapter 13. But Aristotle does not go as far as Nussbaum herself goes in allowing that luck can affect whether or not one does right or wrong in some circumstances or is a virtuous person in the first place. If ordinary people's views say that this is possible (and I doubt whether ordinary views are well articulated enough to do that) Aristotle's own commitments to the authority of the "appearances" do not commit him to agree that it is.

SELECTED FURTHER READINGS

Cleary, John J. "Phainomena in Aristotle's Methodology." *International Journal of Philosophical Studies* 2 (1994): 61–97.

Kenny, Anthony. "Aristotle on Moral Luck." In *Human Agency: Language, Duty, and Value*, edited by Jonathan Dancy and others. Stanford: Stanford University Press, 1988, 105–19.

Klein, S. "The Value of *Endoxa* in Ethical Argument." *History of Philosophy Quarterly* 9 (1992): 141–57.

Pritzl, Kurt. "Opinions as Appearances: *Endoxa* in Aristotle." *Ancient Philosophy* 14 (1994): 41–50.

Reeve, C.D.C. *Practices of Reason*, chapter 1. Oxford: Clarendon Press, 1992.

———. "Dialectic and Philosophy in Aristotle." In *Method in Ancient Philosophy*, edited by Jyl Gentzler. Oxford: Clarendon Press, 1998, 227–52.

Smith, Robin. "Aristotle on the Uses of Dialectic." *Synthese* 96 (1993): 335–58.

Wians, William. "Saving Aristotle from Nussbaum's *Phainomena*." In *Essays on Greek Philosophy V: Aristotle's Ancient Ontology*, edited by A. Preus and J. P. Anton, 133–49. Albany: State University of New York Press, 1992.

[15] See *Nic. Eth.* I 8, 1099a31–b8.

CHAPTER THIRTEEN

Aristotle on the Goods of Fortune

IN THIS CHAPTER I discuss one aspect of Aristotle's theory in the *Nicomachean Ethics* of *eudaimonia* ("happiness," or, more illuminatingly, "a humanly flourishing life" or simply "a good life"). The question I want to raise concerns the relation Aristotle establishes in the *Nicomachean Ethics* between *eudaimonia* and those goods that he describes as external (*ta ektos agatha*).

Though this is little remarked on by commentators, Aristotle's theory of *eudaimonia* in the *Nicomachean Ethics* differs importantly from what one finds in the corresponding passages of the *Eudemian Ethics* and the *Magna Moralia*. All three accounts agree in making *eudaimonia* consist in completely virtuous living (*MM*) or (what comes to the same) in completely virtuous activity (*EE, Nic. Eth.*) over a complete lifetime.[1] This is what is sometimes referred to as the "definition" that Aristotle reaches in the *Nic. Eth.* as the conclusion of his famous argument starting from the idea that human beings, as such, have an *ergon* or essential work (*Nic. Eth.* I 7, 1098a16–18). But only in the *Nic. Eth.* does he go on to say (in the next chapter, Chapter 8) that *eudaimonia* requires in addition[2] being sufficiently equipped with "external goods" (1099a31 ff; cf. 1098b26). And it appears that Aristotle's intention in the *Nic. Eth.* is actually to imbed this further requirement in a revised statement of what human happiness or flourishing essentially is. For in *Nic. Eth.* I 10, he concludes his defense of the account of *eudaimonia* developed in Chapters 7 and 8 against a certain objection

---

[1] See *Magna Moralia* I 4, 1184b28–1185a 1 (completeness of life is added at a4–9); *Eudemian Ethics* II 1, 1219a35–39; *Nicomachean Ethics* I 7, 1098a16–18. *MM* does not make a point of saying explicitly that the virtuous living or activity in question is living or activity in accordance with *all* the virtues (what *EE* calls "complete virtue"), but this is implicit in its repeated references here simply to living in accordance with *the* virtues (1184b30, 34, 36, 38), I ignore for present purposes the complications caused by the *Nic. Eth.*'s introduction at 1098a17–18 of a ranking of the virtues on some scale of goodness and completeness (on this see Cooper, *Reason and Human Good in Aristotle*, pp. 99–100 with n. 10). I take it we can speak loosely but fairly enough of the "definition" in *Nic. Eth.* I 7 as amounting to the same as the *EE* and *MM* definitions, since it is not until book X, i.e., retrospectively, that the potentialities of the *Nic. Eth.*'s formulation for a more restrictive interpretation are ever exploited (and see 1100a4 and 1101a14 where in repeating and expanding on his "definition" Aristotle speaks of "complete virtue," obviously in the *EE*'s sense of "all the virtues").

[2] That this is an *additional* requirement, and not just another way of saying, or a direct implication of, completely virtuous activity over a complete lifetime, is made clear by the language of 1101a14–16, discussed just below. But this is already implied at 1099a31ff., where the natural supplementation of the *pros-* ("(needs) in addition") at a31 and b6 is: in addition to completely virtuous activity over a complete lifetime.

by asking rhetorically, "What then prevents one from saying that that person is *eudaimōn* (flourishes, is happy) who is active in accordance with complete virtue and sufficiently equipped with the external goods not for just any old period of time but for a complete life?" (1101a14–16). Here he reaffirms his theory of what *eudaimonia* is, and this time the requirement of equipment with sufficient external goods is given an explicit place in the "definition" itself. The final and considered *Nicomachean* theory of what it is for a human being to flourish is, therefore, (a) to live a complete life (b) in the active exercise of the human virtues, of both mind and character, (c) equipped with sufficient external goods. My main purpose is to consider carefully exactly why Aristotle thinks having external goods *is* necessary for a flourishing life, the effects of their inclusion as actual constituents of *eudaimonia* on the character of his ethical theory, and the position that in consequence his theory occupies in the Greek philosophical tradition.

The fact that it is only in the *Nicomachean Ethics* that Aristotle explicitly includes the possession of external goods in his "definition" of *eudaimonia* has important implications about the history of Aristotle's writings. For already in the first century B.C., which is as far back as our more or less first-hand knowledge of the state of Aristotle-interpretation in antiquity goes, there is clear evidence that it was accepted as uncontroversial that Aristotle had advanced precisely this *Nicomachean* theory of what human flourishing consists in. Cicero in *de Finibus* II 19 says that in his account of the final good *Aristoteles virtutis usum cum vitae perfectae prosperitate coniunxit* ("Aristotle combined the exercise of virtue with prosperity over a complete lifetime"): here we find the same three conditions as in the *Nic. Eth.*, since *prosperitas*, though no simple translation of the Greek for "external goods" or "goods of fortune," is obviously intended to cover the same ground. And Arius Didymus, who became court philosopher to the emperor Augustus, in a survey of philosophical theories of the final end assigns to Aristotle what is (despite some un-Aristotelian terminology) plainly the same three-part theory,[3] and he repeats and elaborates it later on in his epitome of Peripatetic ethical theory.[4] Such formulaic statements are pretty certain to derive ultimately, either by these authors' own inspection or by that of previous authors whose word they take for it, from explicit formulations in appropriate places in Aristotle's own texts. And although in both *MM* and *EE* one *can* find statements about the necessity of external goods for the happy life, there are not many such statements and they occur only in contexts far removed from the official discussions of the nature of *eudaimonia*.[5] In the official discussions in *MM* and *EE*, the external goods

---

[3] *Apud* Stobaeus, *Eclogae* II, p. 51. 12 Wachsmuth; cf. below pp. 301–2.

[4] Stob. p. 126. 18–20 Wachs.

[5] See *MM* II 8, 1206b33–34 (in the chapter on *eutuchia*). The divisions of goods set out in I 2–3 list the external goods under two headings (as *dunameis*, 1183b27–35; as bodily and— in the narrow sense—external goods, 1184b1–6), and in between these two passages, where Aristotle spends some little time (1184a15–38) discussing the sense in which *eudaimonia* is

are omitted altogether. So the formulas in Cicero and Arius almost certainly derive from *Nicomachean Ethics* I, and not from the *Eudemian Ethics* or *Magna Moralia*. If so, then contrary to what Anthony Kenny has recently argued,[6] the *Nicomachean Ethics* was not only read during Hellenistic times, but was even uncontroversially treated as the authoritative text for Aristotle's answer to what the ancients regarded as the crucial question of ethical theory, what human flourishing actually consists in.[7] Plainly, our practice of assigning priority on the central questions of philosophical theory to the *Nicomachean Ethics* over the other treatises was standard among philosophers already by the beginning of the first century B.C. at the latest.

Let us turn then to the *Nicomachean* definition, and Aristotle's reasons for including external goods as a component of *eudaimonia*. First we need to see more closely what class of goods is in question. Aristotle uses the phrase "external goods" (*ta ektos agatha*) in two different but easily distinguishable ways, depending on which of two understandings he intends of what the

---

the best good and a complete good, it is said that *eudaimonia* is a complex composed of many goods (1184a18–19, 26–27, 30–31), but there is no distinct indication of what these are, and no explicit mention of external goods (the whole discussion is highly abstract, focusing on questions about the structure of *eudaimonia,* not about its content). References to the external goods in the *EE* are even more meagre: apart from IV–VI, which are of course also *Nicomachean* books, there are only two passing references (1218b32, 1249a15), and in neither of these is there any basis for concluding that Aristotle thinks *eudaimonia* requires possession of such goods. This implication *is* found in *EE* VI = *Nic. Eth.* VII, 1153b17–19 (on which see below, p. 297), but again this is very remote from the book II official discussion of what *eudaimonia* is and requires. (It is also found in *Politics* VII 1, 1323b40–1324a2, but that cannot be Cicero's or Arius' principal source.)

[6] See A. Kenny, *The Aristotelian Ethics.* The evidence I cite in this paragraph against Kenny's view should be added to that already assembled in my critical review of his book, pp. 388–90.

[7] The fifth book of Cicero's *de Finibus* offers valuable evidence on this point, too. For, as is well known (cf. *de Fin.* V 6–8, 75), Cicero claims to reproduce there the views of Antiochus of Ascalon, who wrote and lectured on ethics at Athens in the first quarter of the 1st c. B.C. The account of Peripatetic ethics Cicero gives in *de Fin.* V is, not surprisingly, not very faithful to the Aristotle we know from the three ethical treatises. Since Antiochus' intention was to prove that, where sound, Stoic ethical theory repeats in other and less intelligible words the views of Plato and Aristotle and their immediate successors, it is inevitable that his account of Aristotle should show a significant overlay of Stoic doctrine and Stoicising interpretation. According to Antiochus the Stoics wrongly departed from these "ancients" in holding that virtue is the only good and, in consequence, that virtue by itself (without the addition of Aristotle's "external goods") is not just sufficient for happiness but the only thing that has any effect whatsoever on the goodness of a person's life (see V 20–21). Much of the latter half of *de Fin.* V is occupied with an attack on the Stoics on this point and a defense of the Peripatetic view. It is very hard not to believe that the solution Antiochus finally gives (V 79–95) to the problem of the relation of external and bodily goods to *eudaimonia* rests partly on an interpretation of *Nic. Eth.* I 10–11, taking Aristotle (cf. 1101a6–8) to have drawn a distinction between (mere) happiness (*vita beata*), something that virtue is by itself sufficient to guarantee, and blessedness (*vita beatissima*), a higher degree of happiness that requires, besides virtue, the external goods. Certainly Antiochus could have found nothing to suggest this idea anywhere else in the Aristotelian corpus as we know it than these *Nic. Eth.* chapters. Cicero's evidence suggests, therefore, that Antiochus used *Nic. Eth.* I, and not *EE* or *MM,* as his source for Aristotle's theory of *eudaimonia*.

goods in question are external to. There is a narrower usage according to which what they are external to is the person, that is (for Aristotle) an embodied soul (cf. *Rhet.* I 5, 1360b25–26); and in fact the first mention of "external goods" in *Nic. Eth.* I, at 1098b12–14, contrasts them with *two* other kinds of goods, goods of the soul (such as the virtues and pleasure) and goods of the body.[8] But when Aristotle, shortly thereafter, mentions and then adopts the view that *eudaimonia* requires what he again calls external goods (1099a31; cf. 1098b26) he has a broader usage in mind, according to which what these goods are external to is the *soul* (cf. *EE* II 1, 1218b32, *Pol.* VII 1, 1323b24–26); he mentions good looks (*kallos*, standardly listed as a good of the body where those are distinguished from external goods, e.g., 1360b22, 1184b4) as well as external goods according to the *narrow* usage (things like good birth, wealth, political power and friends) in listing the external goods that *eudaimonia* requires in sufficient supply.[9] So it is according to the more inclusive usage that Aristotle means in this passage, and others like it, to say that *eudaimonia* requires external goods: he means that *eudaimonia* requires goods of the body together with external goods according to the narrower usage, i.e., good things one can possess that lie outside one's own mind, character, and physical make-up and constitution.

Aristotle's examples, here and elsewhere, of external goods in the more inclusive usage are limited to a somewhat conventional illustrative list: wealth, political position, friends, good birth, (good) children, good looks (often health, absent here, gets added, and sometimes also honor), so it is important to emphasize what I have just said, that the external goods we are talking about are *all* the good things a person can acquire or enjoy that lie outside his own mind and character (his soul). In fact the only goods that are *not* external are the virtues of intellect and character themselves, innate endowments of mind and personality such as cheerfulness or a good memory, pleasure, and knowledge. Now anything one aims at producing or getting through one's action will, if the decision to aim at it is a correct one, be something good in one way or another for oneself. Any *correct* object of pursuit, therefore, that one achieves by one's action and that is other than one's own virtue, pleasure or knowledge will be an external good. If for example I decide, and am correct to decide, to try to further another person's moral development, then, if my action is successful, his

---

[8] So also *MM* I 3, 1184b1–4, in the (more or less) corresponding passage. Curiously, *EE* II 1, 1218b31–35, the passage that corresponds precisely to the *MM* passage just cited and more loosely to *Nic. Eth.* 1098b12–14, gives a two-fold division of goods into those in the soul and those outside, thus using the phrase "external goods" with the broader reference I distinguish just below.

[9] Similarly the two passages of *Nic. Eth.* X where *ektos chorēgia* recurs, 1178a23–b7, b33–1179a13; in the second of these bodily health is counted as part of *ektos chorēgia*. *Nic. Eth.* VII 13, 1153b17–19 uses the threefold division, saying that what the *eudaimōn* needs is *ta en sōmati agatha kai ta ektos*.

improved soul will be a good, external to me, that I aimed at and got. Likewise if I correctly decide that a certain diet is best for me, then the items of food on that diet, being objects of pursuit in my actions, are goods at which I aim, and being external to me they are external goods. Thus it is clear that Aristotle is talking here about a very wide range of potential and actual good things. It is important to bear this in mind as we consider the reasons he gives for thinking that external goods are needed if one is to lead a flourishing life. He is talking about a wider range of potential goods than his conventional list might suggest.

At the end of our passage Aristotle remarks that the fact that a flourishing life requires external goods, as well as the goods of mind and character, leads some people actually to identify *eudaimonia* with good fortune (*eutuchia*) (1099b7–8, cf. also 1153b21–23). That is presumably because, as he remarks at *Politics* 1323b27–9, "the goods external to the soul come of themselves and by luck (*tuchē*), whereas no one is just or temperate from or on account of luck." Hence Aristotle himself sometimes describes external goods also as goods of fortune.

But why does Aristotle think that *eudaimonia* requires a sufficient supply of external goods? He gives two different reasons, one for each of two groups of external goods. First, some external goods serve as necessary or especially effective instruments in and for the doing of some virtuous actions (1099a32–33). For example, he says, in order to do *some* virtuous actions one needs a good deal of money. Presumably this money would have to be inherited, and so would come to the virtuous man by luck—to have to work long and hard to accumulate it will itself already preclude one from being fully virtuous and living in the exercise of complete virtue, since to devote oneself to making lots of money betrays a false evaluation of its actual importance, in comparison with other things one might devote oneself to instead. One can perhaps most easily understand why such money is needed by reflecting that, as Aristotle conceives him, the person who possesses the human excellences in fully developed form ought to occupy a position of visible leadership. He must be active in advancing the moral and intellectual culture of his community and one important way of doing this is to possess and use financial resources for public and private philanthropy. He should sponsor public performances of artistically and morally significant works, support other people who show promise of intellectual and moral excellence but who unluckily are not well enough off to devote themselves adequately to the pursuits necessary to their full development, and in other ways contribute to the general awareness and prestige among his fellow-citizens of the right scheme of values. In much the same way, I take it, we can understand political position and *philoi* (translated "friends"—but Aristotle means more generally, as we say, one's personal and family connections) as instruments used by the virtuous and flourishing person in his moral projects. Unlike inherited wealth it is presumably not totally a matter of luck whether one has these or not; still, luck plays an important part even here, and it seems reasonable to think, as Aristotle apparently does, that political office and good social connections can and will be used by the virtuous person in the same sort of way that wealth can be. Through all these means—wealth, political office and good connections—the virtuous person is able to influence in significant ways the tastes and the practices of his society, and further the careers of like-minded people, thereby contributing importantly to the spread and flowering within his society of the right scheme of values, the scheme of values he himself holds to, with its special emphasis on things of the mind, respect for every kind of significant human accomplishment, and good will towards other people generally.

The second reason Aristotle gives for thinking that *eudaimonia* requires external goods is not so easy to construe. What he says is this: "lacking certain things people find their blessedness disfigured—e.g., good birth, good children, good looks. For someone who is utterly repulsive in appearance or low-born or solitary and childless is certainly not a very good candidate for happiness; and presumably even less so is one whose children or friends are totally bad or were good but died" (1099b2–6). It is not at first sight clear what Aristotle means by finding one's blessedness disfigured. One might suppose that the way having bad children, or good children who died young, would disfigure even the virtuous man's happiness would be by frustrating efforts that, as a virtuous man, he would have made to produce, educate and protect his offspring. A virtuous man knows the value to himself of having good children, who grow to maturity and live fine lives in close mutual dependence with his own, and will, just because he *is* virtuous, devote considerable effort to procreating and raising such a family. If, by blows of bad fortune he is deprived of the fruits of these labors he would certainly lack some important good things, and good things, moreover, he had wanted and worked to achieve. The failure to have children would be a bad thing for him, and as such must be counted as detracting from the overall value of his life. In addition, one might expect the virtuous person, in reflecting on these facts, to *feel* frustrated and disappointed, and that psychological response might be counted as a second debit against his happiness. Somewhat similarly, being low-born or ugly might be thought to disfigure his blessedness because good birth and good looks are things that he, like any reasonable person, prizes, although in these cases the failure to have them could not even partly be regarded as the result of failures of his own efforts to secure them.[10] So one might conjecture that the disfigurement of one's blessedness in all these cases might be a matter of simply lacking or being deprived of something one very much prized and wanted to have, together perhaps with a consequent sense of frustration and disappointment.

In fact, however, I believe this is not what Aristotle has in mind. To see this one needs to consider a passage of book VII that may refer back to this

---

[10] Good birth and good looks belong to the goods John Rawls describes as assigned by the "natural lottery." See *A Theory of Justice*, p. 74.

discussion and in any event seems intended as repeating the same doctrine.[11] Here Aristotle lumps together *all* the external goods as making, at least generically, the *same* kind of contribution to the happy life. He is discussing the way that pleasure is necessarily involved in the happy life: on the view of pleasure he has argued for, a pleasure is an unimpeded activity of a natural capacity, and of course the happy life is a life of unimpeded activity of natural capacities, including prominently the capacity to know and choose various objects of pursuit in accordance with their true value. He adds (1153b17–19): "That is why the happy person needs in addition the goods of the body and external goods or goods of fortune, so that these activities will not be impeded." So the happy man needs external goods, both the ones Aristotle earlier classified as like instruments and those whose lack he said disfigured our blessedness, in order that his virtuous activities not be impeded.

It is certainly easy to see how the lack of necessary instruments impedes an activity. Think of a carpenter faced with the task of making a table from unsawn wood with hammer and nails but no saw: he may decide the thing cannot be done at all, and if he does undertake it his work will certainly be more difficult and less in any standard way carpenterlike, and also more risky (since it will be to some degree uncertain whether a satisfactory table *can* be made under these conditions). Similarly, Aristotle reasonably implies, the happy man's virtuous activities, in engaging in which his happiness actually consists, will be impeded—perhaps by being actually blocked altogether, perhaps only by being much harder to do or more uncertain of their outcome—if he lacks an ample supply of money, or political influence or social connections. But Aristotle suggests here that something similar may hold for the other external goods he mentions in the book I passage (good birth, good looks, good children). So apparently the disfiguring of the virtuous man's happiness that the lack of these goods causes is traceable to some way in which his virtuous activities are impeded if he lives without them. How is this to be understood?

Aristotle's thought, I believe, is this. Some external conditions (being good-looking, having good children, coming from a good family), while not

---

[11] The similarity of language at 1153b17–18, 21–23, to that at 1099a31–32, b6–8, makes this passage rather seem to be implicitly referring back to that one; certainly, if read as part of the *Nic. Eth.* that is how an attentive reader would take it. If read as part of the *EE* it might, by contrast, seem to introduce a rather surprising change of view (at least an important supplementation of what was said in bk. II that one might think ought therefore to have been argued there, not slipped thus offhand into a discussion of pleasure). One must bear in mind that even if, as seems likely, the common books were originally composed as part of the *EE* they may have been somewhat revised later on for inclusion into the *Nic. Eth.* (on this see my review of Kenny, pp. 387–88); it seems that 1153b14–25 may be one such passage. If so, the original *EE* may well not have contained *any* clear statement of the good and flourishing person's need for external goods. (We have no way of knowing how this part of the *EE* read in the version available to Antiochus, Cicero and others in the first century B.C.: did it have the revised versions of the common books?)

used by the virtuous person as means to achieve his purposes (as e.g., his money or personal influence might be), put him in the position where the options for action that are presented to him by his circumstances allow him to exercise his virtues fully and in ways that one might describe as normal for the virtues. Thus if one is physically quite unattractive not only will one's sex life, and so one's opportunities for exercising the virtue of temperance, be limited in undesirable ways (you may still have sex, given the circumstances, with whom you ought, and when, and to the right extent, and so retain and exercise the virtue of temperance, but the effects of this kind of control will not be as grand as they would be if you really had a normally full range of options);[12] something similar will happen all across the board. People will tend to avoid you, so that you will not be able to enter into the normally wide range of relationships that pose for the virtuous person the particular challenges that his virtue responds to with its correct assessments and right decisions. Such a person, let us assume,[13] may in fact develop all the virtues in their fully perfected form and actually exercise them in ways that respond appropriately and correctly to his circumstances; but the circumstances themselves are restricted by his ugliness and the effects this has on others, so that his virtue is not called upon to regulate his responses and choices in all the sorts of circumstances that the more normally attractive person would face, and so its exercise is not as full and fine a thing as that more normally attractive person's would be. Something similar could be said (though its limiting effects would seem more obvious to a Greek of Aristotle's time than to us) for coming from a bad family (the second century A.D. commentator, Aspasius, mentions as an example having a male prostitute for a father). Having good children, Aristotle's third example, can easily be seen to contribute to the exercise of the virtues in the same way.[14] A childless person

---

[12] This is how I would interpret Aristotle's reference to the temperate person's need for *exousiai* (opportunities), *Nic. Eth.* X 8, 1178a33.

[13] This assumption is unrealistic, of course. As Aristotle himself elsewhere insists, the development of the virtues requires practice, and someone whose circumstances prevented him from facing a normally wide range of opportunities in the course of his preliminary practice of virtuous behavior would presumably not be expected to develop the virtues, at least not in their fully perfected forms. *Perfect* (or complete) virtue must fit a person to deal correctly and sensitively with *all* the types of problems and opportunities a normally equipped normal human being might meet. But it is important to make this assumption here, in order to set firmly aside one possible misunderstanding of what Aristotle is saying. He is *not* saying that the external goods are needed by anyone if he is to *develop* (fully) the virtues; his point is rather that no one can *exercise* fully the (full) virtues he already possesses, if he lacks these further goods.

[14] One might suppose that the way that being childless or without good children would disfigure one's blessedness would be by making one disappointed and embittered with life, and so be impeded in one's virtuous activities by losing one's zest and commitment for them. But this cannot be what Aristotle has in mind: such a disappointed person is someone who allows the way things have gone for him actually to affect his character for the worse, but Aristotle clearly has it in mind that the disfigurement should be something that happens although one's character remains intact and unaffected. In the next chapters after the mention of the external goods in Bk. I (I 9–10) Aristotle discusses the person who falls into disaster, as King

or one whose children are bad people will find his virtuous activities impeded, even though he retains a firm grasp on those qualities of character that constitute the virtues, because, again, he is forced to put them into effect in circumstances that do not give his virtues their normal scope. One central context for the exercise of the virtues is in the raising of children and the subsequent common life one spends with them, once adult, in the morally productive common pursuit of morally significant ends. If this context is not realized in one's life then, Aristotle would be saying, one's virtuous activities are diminished and restricted.

Aristotle distinguishes, then, between those external goods that provide the normal and expected contexts for the exercise of the virtues, and external goods that are used instrumentally as means to the ends aimed at in virtuous activities. Even without goods of either of these types, a person might, we may assume, possess all the virtues in their fully perfected forms, but without them he would not be able to engage *fully* in virtuous action. When Aristotle says that without the sorts of goods that provide the appropriate contexts for the normal exercise of the virtues the virtuous person will find his happiness disfigured, he does not mean simply that he will fail, even if non-culpably, to achieve goals at which, being virtuous, he aimed, or will lack conditions (e.g., good birth or good looks) that he simply wanted for their own sakes (whether or not it was at all up to him to secure them). When he considers these goods, as also the more strictly instrumental goods, as making a contribution to our happiness he abstracts from the fact that in some cases the virtuous agent's own choices and actions have been aimed in the first instance at achieving and preserving them, and from the fact that they may be wished for by him for their own sakes. The contribution of the external goods to happiness which Aristotle has in mind only begins once, to whatever extent the virtuous person may himself have aimed at getting and preserving these goods, he actually *has* them. It is the virtuous actions that he is able to go on to do that constitute this contribution. So we can continue to speak of all these goods as goods of fortune—goods one either has or doesn't have by luck—since in every case, even those where the virtuous person himself is concerned in his actions to obtain or preserve them, the contribution they make to happiness, on Aristotle's theory, is not made immediately by the success of these efforts, but instead by the effects that they have on the good person's *further* action and activity. And their presence, as context for or instruments to be used in these further actions, is not something the agent controls in the way that, according to Aristotle's

---

Priam in the story of Troy did in old age (his fine children are all killed off, or driven mad, his city is razed to the ground, and so on), and insists that such a person is not a happy man—*not,* however, because his character is affected for the worse, by embitterment, loss of enthusiasm, etc., but because *though* he remains a noble and fine person, and takes what happens to him gracefully and acts nobly and virtuously in the circumstances, his activities, or many of them, are (he repeats) "impeded" (1100b29).

theory, he controls the virtuous state itself—the other salient source of the actions.

In working out this suggestion, I have been following the interpretation that one finds in three very old and authoritative accounts of Aristotle's theory that have not been given proper notice in modern discussions. It will help to bring out the significance of the theory I am attributing to Aristotle if I indicate briefly what these three sources have to say. They are, first, Arius Didymus's epitome of Peripatetic ethics (end of the 1st century B.C. or beginning of the 1st A.D.); second, our oldest surviving Greek commentator on the *Nicomachean Ethics* (or, for that matter, on any other work), Aspasius (2nd century A.D.); and, third, his successor the great commentator Alexander of Aphrodisias (end of the 2nd century A.D.). It seems clear that these authors all rely partly on a living tradition of Aristotle-interpretation that must go back to Aristotle himself, and that is good reason to take seriously what they say. I mentioned earlier that Arius Didymus includes external goods as components of *eudaimonia* according to Aristotle. But that this is so has to be inferred, since in stating Aristotle's view he does not use the expression "external goods" or any close relative familiar to us from Aristotle's own writings. His language in the crucial place is in fact unparalleled anywhere in Aristotle, and for that reason the editor of the standard modern edition has emended the text to bring it more closely into line with Aristotle's own usage.[15] But that the text is correct as the manuscripts have it is shown by the fact that both Aspasius in presenting Aristotle's view and Alexander in discussion use precisely the same language; and, moreover, both these later authors give the evidence needed to interpret its meaning, confirming that it *amounts* to Aristotle's own requirement of external goods as one element in *eudaimonia*.

The definition in Arius Didymus runs (Stob. 51.12 Wachsmuth): "the *proēgoumenē* use of complete virtue in a complete life." *Proēgoumenē* is a participle meaning literally "taking the lead" or "coming first"; there is an adverb *proēgoumenōs* that appears in later Greek that often means "by preference," and this may give a hint as to what Arius means here by a use of virtue that "comes first." But literally what Arius says is that happiness according to Aristotle is *that* use of complete virtue in a complete life that "comes first." Aspasius's phraseology is that happiness is activity according

---

[15] Wachsmuth emends *proēgoumenē* (etc.) at 51.12 and elsewhere in the Arius part of Stobaeus to *chorēgoumenē* (etc.), relying e.g., on *Politics* IV 2, 1289a33, VII 1, 1323b41f. (Cf. *Nic. Eth.* 1098b33, 1101a15). On the correctness of the manuscripts and the significance of the passages I cite from Aspasius and Alexander, see Paul Moraux, *Der Aristotelismus bei d. Griechen*, p. 353n; see also the full discussion of F. Dirlmeier, *Die Oikeiosis-Lehre Theophrasts*, pp. 15–19. Dirlmeier's attempt to link this usage of *proēgoumenos* specifically to Theophrastus, so that the definitions containing it can be claimed as his, is quite arbitrary. We do not know at what point in the tradition this word began to be used in this connection. In sense, even if not in terminology, the definitions Arius cites certainly express Aristotle's own view in the *Nic. Eth.* and that is the crucial point.

to complete virtue in a complete life in conditions that "come first" (or, possibly, in actions that "come first").[16] Now the use of this participle elsewhere in Aspasius shows that this "coming first" is coming first in the estimation and choice of the virtuous man himself—in effect, happiness is virtuous activity in *preferred* circumstances, or what comes to the same, the *preferred* virtuous activities falling under each of the virtues. For in discussing the virtue of liberality Aspasius says (52.32–35) that the liberal person has to do with both giving and taking money, "but more with giving; the primary activity (the *proēgoumenē* one—the one that "comes first") of the liberal person is in connection with that, whereas taking money is characteristic of him on a hypothesis, namely *if* he is in great need."

Alexander confirms and sharpens this interpretation in a passage in book II of his *De Anima* where he is arguing, from the Peripatetic point of view, against the Stoic doctrine that virtue all by itself suffices for happiness. One argument he gives against the Stoic view is the following (160.31–161.3): "further, activity in accordance with a craft (*technē*) covers in each case two things. On the one hand there is activity in primary circumstances (*en proēgoumenois*, lit., circumstances that "come first"), as for the flute-player if he is healthy in body and has flutes of the kind he wishes for and nothing external troubles him; on the other hand there is activity in circumstances he does not wish for (*en aboulētois*), that is, in circumstances the opposite of those just mentioned. So, just as the ends of the other crafts lie in activities with wished for things and in primary circumstances,[17] so also for virtue, supposing it too is a craft [as the Stoics do]." Alexander's implication is that for virtue to achieve its end, namely *eudaimonia*, it must be exercised in primary circumstances, the ones the virtuous agent himself, qua virtuous, wishes for.[18] And since, as Alexander's comments make clear, the primary circumstances and activities are the ones where appropriate external goods are present, one is justified in understanding him, together with Aspasius and Arius Didymus in their formal accounts of the Aristotelian theory of happiness, as representing the Peripatetics as making the possession of external goods a part of *eudaimonia*—as indeed we have seen Aristotle does in the *Nicomachean Ethics*.

---

[16] I cite here Aspasius 19.10–11, as supplemented in accordance with his remark at 22.34–35 that we must everywhere supply in thought *en proēgoumenois* when dealing with Aristotle's theory of *eudaimonia*. See also 22.25–26.

[17] Reading *proēgoumenois* for -*ais* of the manuscript at 161.2.

[18] Alexander confirms that this is his view in a passage of the *Quaestiones ethicae* (p. 148, 23–33) where he explains the Aristotelian theory of *eudaimonia*. The nub of his account makes *eudaimonia* "activity in accordance with the virtue of the rational soul, there being added, of course, 'in a complete life' . . . and furthermore 'in primary (*proēgoumenois*) circumstances'— for the primary (*proēgoumenas*) and wished-for activities require instruments" (148.30–33). (I retain the manuscript reading *boulētas* in the next-to-last line, and reject Spengel's emendation, kept by Bruns, to *bouleutas*. Comparison with Alex. *de Anima*, II 160.34, cited above, suffices to defend the manuscript tradition: if *aboulēta* can at *de An.* II 160.34 be set in contrast with *proēgoumena*, then the latter can be glossed, as here, by *boulēta*.)

The important point for my present argument is the way in which these authors introduce the requirement of external goods. They do this via the requirement that in order to be happy a person must not just have and exercise the virtues through a complete life, but exercise them in the primary and preferred circumstances for each virtue. For this puts into a perspective that would not be very easy to capture from reading Aristotle's text alone a consequence of the fact that for Aristotle the virtues (anyhow the virtues of character and practical reason) are broadly based:[19] each of them equips a person to deal effectively, correctly, and with discrimination and moral sensitivity, with a very wide variety of circumstances and conditions of life. The temperate person knows the proper value to place on food, drink, and sex and the associated pleasures, in comparison with other values. This means that whatever circumstances he finds himself in (whether in conditions of plenty or of deprivation, whether by spending time eating and drinking he will or won't affect significantly other things he values) he will act temperately so far as the use of food and drink go. And likewise for courage, and justice, and good temper, and liberality, and most of the rest (it is true that certain virtues on Aristotle's list, most notably the virtue of magnificence, are less broadly based—but the essential point is little affected by such partial exceptions). Aristotle maintains that the virtuous person even in adversity will use his virtues, and will act nobly and well. If a person has many great strokes of ill-fortune, as Priam did, "they pinch and tend to spoil his blessedness; for they inflict pains on him and impede many of his activities. And yet even in these circumstances fine character shines through, when someone bears many great misfortunes with a good temper, not because he does not feel distress but because he is noble and great in soul. . . . For we think a truly good person, a person of sound understanding, will bear strokes of fortune gracefully, and, whatever his resources at any time, do the finest actions he can, just as we think a good general, too, will use the forces he has in the best way for war . . ." (1100b28–1101a4). But plainly, in each virtue there is a more or less clearly marked out range of circumstances within which, for that virtue, the *preferred* exercises of the virtue come. The thought is this: one needs to be *basically* healthy physically and mentally, *reasonably* well-off financially, *reasonably* well-liked by others, and to have available to one a *reasonably* good supply of other things one needs by way of food, drink, and so on, *most* of the time in one's life; for the human virtues consist essentially and in the first place in the proper use of this normally expected (or anyhow reasonably hoped-for) array of goods. Clearly, of course, this does not mean that the preferred exercise of the virtues should presuppose perfect good health, or a constant supply of everything one needs—that would itself be abnormal, and would actually deprive the virtues of one normal context for their employment, namely in temporary deprivation and distress. On Aristotle's view, in some

---

[19] Compare Rawls, *Theory of Justice*, pp. 435ff.

vaguely marked out middle ground lies the active life of the virtuous person that deserves to be counted, for a human being, the happy and flourishing one; get very far outside it, on either side, and, even though the virtues and their constant exercise remain central to the life someone might lead, such a life is nonetheless not a happy one.

Now on this interpretation, in integrating the external goods into *eudaimonia* Aristotle is treating them all as if their only value lies in the contribution they make to virtuous actions in which *they* are not the, or a, goal of action. It is true that, as we have seen, he distinguishes between those, like money, that are used only as instruments in the virtuous man's projects, and others like health and good looks, but even these latter, according to Aristotle's account, are needed as antecedently existing conditions that make possible the full exercise of the happy man's virtuous qualities of mind and character. In each case the value to the happy man consists in what the external goods make it possible for him, as a result of having them, to do. Any value goods other than virtuous action itself might have just for their own sakes is denied, or at least left out of account, on this theory. The seriousness of this omission comes out clearly in examples like the following. The virtuous man will in a certain situation, if he has money available, give some of it to a promising young friend so that he can study philosophy. Here money makes possible a certain exercise of the virtue of liberality, namely giving the right amount of money to the right person for the right purpose. And that is something Aristotle's theory takes account of. But notice that the virtuous man's purpose in this case is to enable the young man to become a philosopher. Suppose he suddenly takes sick and dies not long afterward, with the result that the money is lost without this goal being achieved. Suppose also (as might well be the case) that this does not cast doubt on the correctness of the decision. After all, a decision has to be made in the light of the best information available, and it may well be that neither the formation of the liberal man's information base, nor his deliberation leading from it to the decision, can be faulted. On Aristotle's account *this* way that external goods might be thought to contribute to someone's life— by being objects of pursuit aimed at in his virtuous actions *and* achieved partly as a result of them—gets left out of account. Similarly, as I mentioned above, Aristotle does not count the failure of the virtuous man to have good children who grow to maturity as disfiguring his happiness because it frustrates plans he conceived and acted on previously *as* a virtuous man. The failure to have good children only affects his happiness insofar as it prevents the subsequent activities he might have engaged in together with them; it does not affect it by rendering his earlier actions aimed at producing and educating his children ineffective.

Why does Aristotle apparently neglect this further way goods other than virtue itself contribute to a happy life? Why, when he speaks of the contribution that goods other than the virtues make to happiness, does he not count the good the virtuous man achieves for himself by obtaining the outcomes that qua virtuous he aims at from time to time, as a second way that these goods contribute to his happiness? I think there are two separate considerations that help to explain his failure to mention this further contribution in this context. The first is a historical point.

It seems clear that in his remarks on the external goods Aristotle is strongly influenced by views about these goods that Socrates in early dialogues of Plato prominently flaunts. Socrates argues in two related passages of the *Euthydemus* (278e–282d) and the *Meno* (87d–89a) that virtue, which he identifies with a certain kind of knowledge, is the *only* thing that deserves, strictly speaking, to be called good. Socrates relies on the basic axiom that there is an essential connection between something's being good and its benefitting (and not harming) the person for whom it is good. But, he argues, any other so-called good besides virtue, construed as knowledge, *will* sometimes harm a person; its harming or, instead, benefitting him, depends on the circumstances. Socrates' discussion in these passages seems to be the origin of Aristotle's and later Greek philosophy's tripartition of (so-called) goods into external goods, bodily goods, and goods of soul: Socrates' claim is that external goods in Aristotle's broad sense, and goods of the soul other than virtue-knowledge, are not *really* goods at all, because whether they benefit or not, which is what a good must do, does not depend on them, but on something else—the circumstances. If they benefit, it is not because of *their* nature, and that shows that they are not good to begin with. What makes the difference, Socrates claims, is virtue or knowledge: the virtuous person knows how to use external goods and the other goods of his soul, and the benefit he gets from them is always ultimately due to his knowledge—his knowledge how, when, for what purpose to use them. It is the nature of knowledge or virtue, and, among supposed goods, *only* of knowledge or virtue, to benefit; only it always and necessarily benefits its possessor; so only knowledge or virtue is, strictly speaking, a good at all.[20]

These passages of *Euthydemus* and *Meno* are crucial texts for the whole later development of Greek moral philosophy, and not merely for the Aristotelian theory of the external goods and their place in *eudaimonia*. They are plainly the source, or prominent among the sources, for the Stoic theory that only virtue is good and that, in consequence, *eudaimonia* consists simply in the possession of virtue and does not require as well the Aristotelian external goods. The Stoics accepted Socrates' reasons for saying that only virtue is good, and devoted themselves to elaborating the distinctions necessary to defend successfully the Socratic theory. Now unlike the Stoics, Aristotle rejected the idea, fundamental to Socrates' argument, that what is really good must by its very nature, and so necessarily and always, benefit whoever has it.[21] This idea rests on the Eleatic confusions that Aristotle

---

[20] See especially *Meno* 87e1–2 (a good must benefit); *Euthydemus* 281d2–e5 (the external goods are not in themselves good at all; in fact only wisdom is a good, since it is needed to guide us to use the external goods to our benefit).

[21] See for example *Nic. Eth.* I 3, 1094b16–19.

found at the core of Plato's theory of Forms and that caused him to reject Platonic metaphysics altogether. But he was, as were the Stoics too, deeply influenced by Socrates' treatment of the external goods, and indeed all goods other than virtue, as having only a use-value in relation to virtue. His response to Socrates consists in emphasizing (surely correctly) the distinction between *possessing* a virtue and exercising it. The benefit that, according to Socrates, virtue does one consists in its exercise. But that puts us in a position to see, and I have discussed how Aristotle developed this point, that the exercise in question, in which the benefit that virtue entails is actually and fully realized, itself depends upon the presence of external goods, either as part of the context of action or as instruments to be used in it. Even if their value is not independent of the value of virtuous action, that does not mean that the good that virtue does is available without them. Socrates, then, was wrong to say or imply that happiness is possible without these goods.

When one takes into account the Socratic background of Aristotle's discussion, it is easy enough to see how it happens that in his account of *eudaimonia* it is only as contributing to the virtuous person's subsequent activities that the external goods figure. He is in effect taking over the Socratic view of the central and determinative role of virtue as a constituent of happiness, but insisting that, even so, external goods, since they are essential for the exercise of the virtues that constitutes happiness, must be counted in as constituents of *eudaimonia* as well.[22]

Yet in other places in his ethical writings it is clear that Aristotle did take notice of the fact that for the virtuous person these goods also play the other role I specified, as objects of pursuit or goals of action in virtuous activity. We can see this by considering the chapter on *eutuchia* (good fortune) in the *Eudemian Ethics* (VIII 2). By "good fortune" here and the "person of good fortune" (*ho eutuchēs*), Aristotle does not mean occasional good luck, such as affects all of us, virtuous as well as vicious, and the person who occasionally benefits from such good luck. He means good fortune as a settled and permanent feature of someone's way of life. He contrasts such a person with the person who acts as he does from *phronēsis* (sound understanding, actual knowledge how to act) (1246b37–1247a2). Aristotle entertains the thought that perhaps a person might mimic the same

---

[22] In a well-known passage of *EE* (I 2), Aristotle distinguishes between what amounts to necessary conditions of happiness and its actual parts and says that it is a grave mistake to treat what is merely a necessary condition (of happiness, or whatever else) as actually a constituent part of it. Of course, it is not easy to know how to apply this distinction, which is clear enough in the abstract, to particular cases. Nonetheless, it seems clear that Aristotle is not guilty, in counting external goods as parts of *eudaimonia*, of violating it. For, as we have seen, in his view the external goods are not conditions necessary either for (the exercise of) complete virtue or for a complete span of life (the other two constituents of *eudaimonia* that Aristotle recognizes); they are necessary for a *certain* exercise of the virtues, and the necessity in question is not an externally causal one. The external goods are circumstances and conditions reference to which is actually part of the essential characterization of the virtuous activities that constitute *eudaimonia*, on Aristotle's theory.

sort of life as the virtuous person, on the basis of his understanding and his trained character, leads. He would live that way by some kind of sheer luck, not as the result of his own understanding and not as the result of a fixed view of what is proper to do being imbedded in his habitual ways of feeling about and reacting to things.

In what, then, does the fortunate person, by sheer luck, mimic the virtuous man? No doubt he has all the requisite external goods that the virtuous man has and uses in his activities; but Aristotle implies that whoever has external goods, even the virtuous person himself, has them by good luck (see 1099b7–8, 1153b18, 21–22). So that is not a kind of good luck that the fortunate man has that distinguishes him from the virtuous. Perhaps Aristotle thinks that, in addition, the fortunate person acts in the context of, or uses, these external goods in just the ways the virtuous person would in the same circumstances—not, of course, that he acts for the same reasons and from the same deliberated desires as the virtuous person does, but at any rate (whatever in him produces them) he does the same actions. That would mean that his actions are the result of luck, not of his own forethought and character. But, however that may be, it is clear that Aristotle thinks of the fortunate man as mimicking the virtuous and practically wise man in yet a further way. His actions, whatever they are (and whether they are the same the virtuous man would have done), succeed in achieving the results the virtuous man, in the various situations he finds himself in, would have tried to achieve.

That this is the crucial kind of good luck that distinguishes the fortunate man from the virtuous becomes clear when near the beginning of the chapter Aristotle insists that such a kind of person really exists: "though foolish," he says (1247a4–23),

> many people are successful in matters in which luck is decisive, others also in matters where skill is involved, but there is a large element of luck, for example in generalship and navigation. . . . [T]hat it is not by practical wisdom that they succeed, is evident. For practical wisdom is not irrational but has a principle on account of which it acts thus and so, but these people would not be able to say why they succeed; for [if they could], it would be skill. For it is clear . . . that they are foolish even about those matters in which they enjoy good fortune. For in navigation, it is not the most skillful who are fortunate, but, as in dice-throwing, one man scores nothing, another throws a naturally fortunate man's throw.[23]

The good fortune of the fortunate person, then, consists primarily in his regularly achieving by his actions the more particular goals that the virtuous man too would aim at were he in the same situations—whatever corresponds for the virtuous man to the navigator's goal of arriving in port.

Now this implies that in Aristotle's view the corresponding successes will also be achieved by the virtuous man. For the governing assumption has

---

[23] Text and translation as in Woods, *Aristotle's "Eudemian Ethics."*

been that the fortunate man's life mimics that of the virtuous. The virtuous man's successes are not, however, the result of good luck. Why not? Precisely because when he achieves them, that is due to the knowledge that he possesses, but the fortunate man does not, *how* to act in those situations. No doubt this knowledge does not guarantee success (the one who has it can *fail* in his projects, by *bad* luck), but plainly Aristotle thinks that it would not count as knowledge at all, unless it made it likely that he would succeed. It is, among other things, knowledge how the world runs, and so if it is regularly applied correctly, as of course the virtuous man does apply it, the looked-for results can be expected, anyhow a large percentage of the time.

The contrast Aristotle draws in *EE* VIII 2 between the morally virtuous person and the man of good fortune thus brings out two aspects of moral virtue as he conceives it that are not much emphasized elsewhere. The practical knowledge that is the leading component of the virtuous state of mind and character does not involve merely a correct assessment of the relative values of the various things that are good for human beings and knowledge of the (morally) right thing to do in whatever conditions one finds oneself.[24] The virtuous person's knowledge how to act includes knowing how, if things go as they normally and usually do, actually to bring about the results that he aims at in his actions. And since it is usually the acquisition or maintenance of external goods (goods lying outside his own mind and character) that the virtuous man aims at in his actions, it follows that the regular success of the virtuous man's efforts to acquire, or to maintain, external goods is itself already implied by his having that knowledge how to act that his virtue involves. It should come as no surprise, therefore, that Aristotle does not mention the attainment of external goods, insofar as they are objects of pursuit in virtuous action, as something the virtuous person needs in *addition* to virtue in order to be happy. The virtuous person will generally and regularly get these goods as an immediate consequence of his being virtuous, so that they should not be counted as goods that he needs as *supplements* to virtue if he is to be happy.

Of course, Aristotle recognizes that bad luck can cause even the virtuous person to fail occasionally to attain such goods despite his efforts to do so. And sometimes (as when his children turn out bad or die young) such bad luck can be no trivial matter, something to be made good later by trying again. Aristotle's view, if I am right, is that such occasional failures (even these most serious ones) will not be such as to detract from his happiness insofar as the missing goods were wished-for outcomes of prior action, but only insofar as their absence deprives him of conditions he needs if he is to go on living in the full exercise of his virtues. Is this a reasonable view? It ought to seem so to anyone who shares (as presumably not everyone will) Aristotle's central conviction that what determines the character of a person's

---

[24] Cf. *Nic. Eth.* 1140a25–29, b4–6, and Cooper, *Reason and Human Good,* pp. 120–33.

life is what *he does*. On the one hand, a virtuous person who suffers such reverses acted knowing both that his choice of action was the, or one of the, best available in the circumstances, and that human beings never do completely control the outcomes of their actions, since nature is such that unpredictable irregularities and accidental results are simply always possible. Since he has done the best he or anyone in the circumstances could do, he should not count his own actions as in any way defective just because they did not lead to the wished-for outcomes. Insofar as happiness consists in deciding and doing what is best, his happiness has not been diminished by such failures. And on the other hand Aristotle pictures the happy person's life as a forward-looking progress from virtuous activity to virtuous activity, so that it is natural that he should regard the contribution to the virtuous man's happiness of external goods not in this backward-looking way, as crowning earlier activities with success, but as making possible continued virtuous activity in the future.

When, therefore, one takes into account Aristotle's conception of the virtuous man's practical knowledge, one sees readily enough why he integrates the external goods into *eudaimonia* in the way we saw he does. Though he recognizes that external goods are very often objects of pursuit in the virtuous man's activities, and things therefore that he values for themselves, Aristotle has good reasons for thinking that external goods are a *second* component of *eudaimonia*, alongside virtuous activity, only because of the effect they have in enabling the virtuous person to live, and go on living, a fully virtuous life.[25]

POSTSCRIPT, 1997

In this chapter I have considered Aristotle's views about how "external" goods can legitimately be counted as constituents of the happy person's happiness. The textual evidence, I have argued, shows that for Aristotle external goods are constituents of happiness in that they provide, in one way or another, the context that virtuous persons as such prefer for the exercise of their virtues. External goods are constituents of happiness in that they are bound up in this tight way with those virtuous activities themselves that Aristotle thinks constitute the very essence of the best human life. In limiting myself to the value of the external goods as constituents in this sense of the best life, I have not discussed, except incidentally, the full extent of the ways in which on Aristotle's theory these goods, or some of

[25] I wish to thank Cynthia Freeland and Nicholas White for commentaries on this chapter presented at colloquia at Boston University and the University of Michigan, respectively. David Sachs read a version of it and gave me detailed and very valuable criticisms. Written comments of T. H. Irwin enabled me to make a number of improvements in preparing the final version. I thank also the National Endowment for the Humanities for fellowship support during the period I was working on this chapter.

them, might have value—or all the ways in which a person living a fully virtuous, happy life, would in fact care about them. I mentioned that in this connection Aristotle classifies friends as an external good of the instrumental sort, while he counts a person's children as external goods of the sort whose absence implies a "disfiguring" of one's happiness. Of course, these classifications need not be intended as exclusive. Friends might also count as external goods of the latter sort. Without good personal friends, we may suppose, Aristotle thought one's life would be disfigured in a way similar to what it would be if one had bad children, or good ones who died young. So he does not imply that friends are of value to virtuous and happy people only as instruments to virtuous activities of their own that lie outside the friendship (political or artistic activities of their own, for example, which influence for the better the cultural life of the community). Aristotle's language of instrumentality here, and, more generally, his valuing goods like friends and children because they keep the virtuous person's activities "unimpeded," do not imply reducing friendship or parenthood to a morally objectionable exploitation of one's friends (if one could still call them that!) or of one's children. He is not recommending that we regard our friends and children merely as useful in enabling our own "preferred" acts of virtue.

On the contrary: for Aristotle, friendship and parenthood are moral relationships that provide central contexts for the exercise of the moral virtues, and that means that for him virtuous people will love their friends and their children for themselves. They will care for and concern themselves about their friends' and children's welfare and success simply because they love them. In doing so, a virtuous person values friends and offspring—their good qualities and their good lives—as important goods in his or her own life, too. In valuing the enhanced virtuous actions in a life lived in common with friends and good children, the happy person is necessarily responding to these other goods and caring about them in ways appropriate to the goods that they are. The enhanced virtuous activities are, in part, activities expressing such concerns. In sum: Aristotle does not count having a good friend, simply as such, or a friend's good life, as direct constituents of a person's happiness—as constituents apart from their involvement in one's own virtuous actions. But that does not mean that Aristotle does not regard friends as intrinsic goods for oneself at all, much less that he denies them their own distinct kind of intrinsic value. The intrinsic value to the virtuous person of his friends' or his children's flourishing lives is to be counted among those values that I discuss at the end of this chapter—values, as I argue there, that are to be regarded not as supplementing the value of virtuous activity itself (in the way that having friends and good children supplements it by enabling the actively virtuous, happy life in the first place), but simply as goods one can expect to arise normally and naturally from the progress of the virtuous relationship itself. Aristotle's theory of the external goods as constituents of happiness does not explicitly address these further ways that external goods can have value for a virtuous, happy person. But, as I have explained it, Aristotle's theory of the external goods as constituents of the virtuous person's happiness does nothing to deny or undermine these further ways that they have value for such a person, and for human beings generally.

SELECTED FURTHER READINGS

Irwin, T. H. "Permanent Happiness: Aristotle and Solon." *Oxford Studies in Ancient Philosophy* 3 (1985): 89–124.

Johnson, Kent. "Luck and Good Fortune in the *Eudemian Ethics*." *Ancient Philosophy* 17 (1997): 85–102.

Kenny, Anthony. *Aristotle on the Perfect Life,* chapters 5 and 6. Oxford: Clarendon Press, 1992.

Reeve, C.D.C. *Practices of Reason,* chapter 4. Oxford: Clarendon Press, 1992.

White, Stephen A. *Sovereign Virtue,* part II, chapters 3–5. Stanford: Stanford University Press, 1992.

CHAPTER FOURTEEN

Aristotle on the Forms of Friendship

I

Neither in the scholarly nor in the philosophical literature on Aristotle does his account of friendship (*philia*) occupy a very prominent place. I suppose this is partly, though certainly not wholly, to be explained by the fact that the modern ethical theories with which Aristotle's might demand comparison hardly make room for the discussion of any parallel phenomenon.[1] Whatever else friendship is, it is, at least typically, a personal relationship freely, even spontaneously, entered into, and ethics, as modern theorists tend to conceive it, deals rather with the ways in which people are required to regard, and behave toward, one another, than with the organization of their private affairs. To the extent, then, that one shares this modern outlook, one will tend to neglect, or treat merely as a historical curiosity, Aristotle's efforts to define friendship and to place it within the framework of human *eudaimonia* (flourishing), the theory of which is central to moral philosophy as he understands it. Yet in the *Nicomachean Ethics* the two books on *philia* make up nearly a fifth of the whole,[2] and this seems to me a fair measure of the importance of this subject to the complete understanding both of Aristotle's overall moral theory and even of many of the more circumscribed topics (moral virtue and pleasure, for example) to which so much scholarly and philosophical attention has been devoted. If, as I suggest, the failure of commentators to appreciate its importance is partly the effect of distortions produced by the moral outlook that has predominated in modern moral philosophy, the careful study of these books may help to free us from constricting prejudices and perhaps even make it possible to discover in Aristotle a plausible and suggestive alternative to the theories constructed on the narrower base characteristic of recent times.

All the standard treatments of Aristotle on *philia* point out that the Greek concept expressed by this word is much wider than our "friendship" (or the equivalents in other modern languages). Its field covers not just the (more or less) intimate relationships between persons not bound together by near family ties, to which the words used in the modern languages to translate it are ordinarily restricted, but all sorts of family relationships

---

[1] Kant's discussion in the *Lectures on Ethics*, pp. 200–209, is only a partial exception: he follows Baumgarten's textbook somewhat mechanically at this point, and does not integrate the phenomenon into his overall theory.

[2] Approximately the same proportion is taken up in *Eudemian Ethics* by its discussion of friendship (Book VII).

(especially those of parents to children, children to parents, siblings to one another, and the marriage relationship itself);[3] the word also has a natural and ordinary use to characterize what goes in English under the somewhat quaint-sounding name of "civic friendship." Certain business relationships also come in here, as does common membership in religious and social clubs and political parties. It is not enough, however, just to list the fairly diverse sorts of relationship that form the field of Aristotle's investigation; one wants to know, if possible, what it was about them that inclined the Greeks to group them together under this common name. W. D. Ross suggests that the word "can stand for any mutual attraction between two human beings,"[4] but, to judge from Aristotle's discussion itself, this is not true: aside from the fact that "mutual attraction" might seem to have erotic, or at any rate passionate, overtones that make it unsuitable as a characterization of, e.g., business and citizenly ties, this account clearly lets in too much. People can be "mutually attracted" to one another without in any way developing active ties—without doing anything together, or for one another—and such mere attraction would not be counted as *philia*. Aristotle is himself always careful to emphasize the practical and active element in the relationships he investigates under this name, as e.g., in the *Rhetoric* (whose discussion of friendship and hatred, II 4, is essential reading on this topic), where he defines liking (*to philein*)[5] as "wanting for someone what one thinks good,[6] for his sake and not for one's own, and being inclined, so far as one can, to do such things for him," and then characterizes a friend (*philos*) as someone who likes and is liked by another person (1380b35–1381a2). This account suggests, in fact, that the central idea contained in *philia* is that of doing well by someone for his own sake, out of concern for *him* (and not, or not merely, out of concern for oneself). If this is right, then the different forms of *philia* listed above could be viewed just as different contexts and circumstances in which this kind of mutual well-doing can arise; within the family, in the state at large, and among business partners and political cronies, well-doing out of concern for other persons can arise, and where it does so, there exists a "friendship." I suggest that if we want some

[3] Such family relationships are in fact the original and, in some ways, the central cases of φιλία. It should be noted, as the Greeks were themselves quick to see (cf. Euripides, *Phoenissae* 1446: φίλος γὰρ ἐχθρὸς ἐγένετ', ἀλλ' ὅμως φίλος), that, unlike the other types of case, family-φιλία existed even despite the absence of good-will, unself-interested well-doing, and the other practical attitudes and actions that in Aristotle's account serve to define φιλία. This is because it was assumed, as a norm, that where family ties were of a certain sort these modes of feeling and action ought to be forthcoming; their absence did not destroy the φιλία itself (as the quotation from Euripides just given illustrates).

[4] *Aristotle*, p. 223.

[5] Much harm is caused by translators who render this verb by "love," since then there is bound to be confusion when one comes to translate στέργειν and ἐρᾶν. I render φιλεῖν by "like," στέργειν by "love," and ἐρᾶν by "be in love." Ἔρως I translate "sexual attachment," reserving both "love" (noun) and "friendship" for φιλία itself.

[6] Or: "what he thinks good." The Greek is ambiguous.

indication of what is common to all the personal relationships which the Greeks counted as *philiai*, we cannot do better than follow Aristotle's lead here. At any rate, I shall argue that this definition from the *Rhetoric* does state the core of Aristotle's own analysis of *philia*. According to him, *philia*, taken most generally, is any relationship characterized by mutual liking, as this is defined in the *Rhetoric*, that is, by mutual well-wishing and well-doing out of concern for one another.[7]

If this characterization is correct, it should be clear why Aristotle's theory of friendship must be considered a cardinal element in his ethical theory as a whole. For it is only here that he directly expresses himself on the nature, and importance to a flourishing human life, of taking an interest in other persons, merely as such and for their own sake. In fact, Aristotle holds not only that active friendships of a close and intimate kind are a necessary constituent of the flourishing human life, but also that "civic friendship" itself is an essential human good. That is to say, he holds not only that every person needs to have close personal friendships in which common and shared activities are the core of the relationship, but also that fellow-citizens, who are not otherwise personally connected, ought nonetheless to be predisposed to like one another and to wish and do each other well. In holding this he is in effect declaring that the good man will conduct himself toward other persons in a spirit, not merely of rectitude (mere justice) but

---

[7] Aristotle consistently expresses this altruistic side of friendship by the use of a single Greek phrase (or its variants): the friend does well to his friend ἐκείνου ἕνεκα (1155b31). It is important to be clear from the outset what is and what is not implied by this phrase, taken by itself. (1) In Aristotle's usage, to say that one acts "for someone else's sake" means, at least, that the fact that the other person needs or wants, or would be benefited by, something is taken by the agent as by itself *a* reason for doing or procuring that something, and that he acts for that reason. (2) It seems also implied that this reason is by itself sufficient to determine the agent to action. (3) But it is not implied that this is the agent's *only* reason for acting as he does, nor, in particular, that he does not also have a self-interested reason for acting. (4) Nothing is implied about the relative strengths of the reason founded on the other person's good and such other reasons as may be at work at the same time; it isn't, for instance, implied that the agent's concern, in the given action, for the other person's good is stronger than his concern for his own. (5) Nothing specific is implied about the psychological source or nature of the agent's concern for the other person; it might be a deep emotional attachment, like the love of parent for child, or whatever passions are involved in the attachment of lovers to one another, or, as we say, the concern for the welfare of persons "just as such," or any of various other motives might be at work in a given case. As we shall see, Aristotle does have special views about the strength and the psychological source of a person's concern for his friend's good, but these are further questions the answers to which are not determined in any way by saying merely that a friend acts to secure his friend's good for his friend's own sake. In what follows, I frequently express Aristotle's point here by saying that friends act out of concern for one another, and refer to "unself-interested," or "disinterested" good-will as characteristic of friends. All these expressions should be interpreted in the light of the qualifications just noted. In particular, "disinterested" is not intended to indicate the absence of passion or special attachment. The point is just that if one is someone's friend one wants that person to prosper, achieve his goals, be happy, and so on, in the same sort of way in which he wishes these things for himself, whatever else one may want as well, and whatever explains one's having this desire.

actually of friendship. Hence it is clear that Aristotle's discussion of friendship contains a very significant amplification of the theory of moral virtue expounded in the middle books of the *Nicomachean Ethics*, and that his theory of virtue cannot be completely understood unless read in the light of it.

But does Aristotle really make well-wishing and well-doing out of concern for the other person's good a condition of friendship of all these diverse types? He seems to be widely interpreted as holding this to be a condition of only one form of friendship, while the others involve exclusively self-centered motivations. To settle this question requires a complete examination of Aristotle's theory of the forms of friendship and his views on what is essential to each. This task I undertake in what follows. I leave for treatment elsewhere the further question why Aristotle thinks no human being can flourish in whose life the activities of friendship are not an important ingredient.[8]

II

At the center of Aristotle's analysis of *philia* in the *Nicomachean Ethics* stands his theory that there are three basic kinds or species (*eidē*, 1156a7, 1157b1) of friendship, depending on what it is that attracts and binds the one person to the other. In some cases what cements the association is the pleasure, in others some advantage, that the one gets from the other; in a third set of cases it is the recognition of the other person's moral goodness. Aristotle distinguishes among the resulting friendships according to the different types of bond between the associated parties. Furthermore, Aristotle thinks that the central case, by comparison with which the others are to be understood, is friendship based on the recognition of moral goodness. This much is clear.[9] On many important details, however, Aristotle is notably obscure. I begin by mentioning two of these.

[8] See Chapter 15 below, "Friendship and the Good in Aristotle."

[9] It is not necessary for my purposes to enter more specifically into the question how Aristotle thinks the derivative kinds of friendship are related to the central case. But it should be noted that whereas in the *Eudemian Ethics* Aristotle claims that φιλία is a πρὸς ἓν λεγόμενον (1236a16–18), an instance of what G. E. L. Owen calls "focal meaning" ("Logic and Metaphysics in Some Earlier Works of Aristotle"; see pp. 169–70 on φιλία in the *EE*), he does not make the same claim in the *Nicomachean Ethics*. Instead, he relies on a looser connection by resemblance (ὁμοίωμα, 1157a1; καθ᾽ ὁμοιότητα, a31–32, 1158b6; τῷ ὡμοιῶσθαι, 1157b5), holding that the derivative relationships count as friendships by reason of resembling the central case. Owen (pp. 187–89) notes that Aristotle consistently denied that (sensible) resemblance is by itself a sufficient basis for claiming focal connection, so that repeated reference in *Nic. Eth.* to resemblance, and the total absence of the terminology used elsewhere to express focal meaning, ought surely to be taken to mark a different implied pattern of analysis from that of the *EE* (commentators from Aspasius to Gauthier to the contrary notwithstanding). On this see now the cogent arguments of Fortenbaugh, "Aristotle's Analysis of Friendship."

First, when exactly does Aristotle recognize a friendship as one involving mutual recognition of moral goodness? He usually refers to this kind of friendship by such phrases as "the friendship of people who are good and alike in virtue" (1156b7–8) or "the friendship of good persons" (1157a20, b25; similarly 1158a1, b7). He also calls this friendship "perfect" (*teleia*, 1156b7, 34), since it exhibits fully and perfectly all the characteristics that one reasonably expects a friendship to have. By calling the parties to such a relationship "good men" (*agathoi*) and describing their friendship as "perfect," Aristotle seems to imply that only to fully virtuous persons—heroes of intellect and character—is it open to form a friendship of this basic kind. So, it would follow, ordinary people, with the normal mixture of some good and some bad qualities of character, are not eligible partners for friendships of the basic type; they would be doomed, along with thoroughly bad people (1157a16–19, 1157b1–3; *Eudemian Ethics* 1236b10–12, 1238a32–33), to having friendships of the other two types, at best. Does Aristotle mean to imply that one who is not completely virtuous can only be befriended for the sake of some pleasure or advantage he brings, that no one can associate with him (unless under deception: cf. 1165b8–15) for the sake of his good qualities of character?

The second point that calls for comment concerns the two deficient types. In the course of laying the ground in *Nicomachean Ethics*, VIII 2 for his distinction between the three types of friendship, Aristotle remarks that not every case of liking (*philein*) something occurs within the context of a friendship: one can like wine, for example, but this is not evidence of a friendship between oneself and wine, because (1) the wine does not like you back, and (2) you don't wish well to the wine. Thus, he goes on, a friendship exists only where you wish to the other party what is good for him, for his own sake, and this well-wishing is reciprocated: "people say that one ought to wish to a friend what is good, for his own sake; but those who wish what is good [to someone else] in this way people call 'well-disposed' (*eunous*) [and not 'friends'], if the other person does not return the wish: for friendship is good will (*eunoia*) when reciprocated" (1155b31–34). Here Aristotle seems to endorse the central idea contained in the *Rhetoric*'s definition of friendship, that friendship is mutual well-wishing out of concern for one another; he makes it characteristic of friendships, of whatever type, that a friend wishes well to his friend for his friend's own sake.[10] That he means to make this sort of well-wishing a component of all friendship, and not just

---

[10] Strictly, of course, Aristotle only reports here what "people say," but he must be endorsing these views, since by the end of the chapter (1156a3–5) he is drawing inferences on his own behalf partly from them: friends, he says, "must wish well to (εὐνοεῖν) and want what is good for one another. . . ." That both "people" and Aristotle himself define εὔνοια as *disinterested* well-wishing (and not well-wishing *tout court*) has traditionally been taken as the burden of these lines: both Aspasius in his commentary (163.9–11, 27–29) and Bonitz in his *Index Aristotelicus* (298a45) so take them. This reading is undoubtedly correct, especially in view of Aristotle's usage elsewhere (see *Nic. Eth.* 1167a13–17 and *EE* 1241a7–8 and my discussion below, sect. IV), and I adopt it in what follows.

of some special type, is clear from the context; he has not yet distinguished the three species of friendship (he only does this in the following chapter) and is at this point merely marking off, in order to set it aside, the wine-drinker's sort of liking. The cases of liking that he retains for study, he says, are all ones in which one finds reciprocal well-wishing of the parties for one another's sake. The implication is that not only in "perfect" friendship, but also in pleasure- and advantage-friendship, a friend wishes his friend well for the friend's own sake. On the other hand, Aristotle repeatedly contrasts the two derivative types of friendship with the basic type by emphasizing the self-centeredness of pleasure- and advantage-friends; thus he says that in erotic relationships (one class of pleasure-friendships) people "love not one another but their incidental features" (1164a10–12), i.e., what gives pleasure to themselves. Similarly for advantage-friendships: "Those who are friends on account of advantage cease to be such at the same time as the advantage ceases; for they were not friends of one another but of the benefit to themselves" (1157a14–16; similarly 1165b3–4). This seems to suggest that in pleasure- and advantage-friendships each party is concerned *solely* with his own good, and this would mean that they could not have the sort of concern for one another that Aristotle seems in VIII 2 to attribute to friends. Other evidence, to which we shall turn in section IV below, seems to indicate the same thing. Which is Aristotle's considered view? Or is he simply inconsistent on this point?

It should be observed that if Aristotle holds both that pleasure- and advantage-friends are wholly self-centered, and that only perfectly virtuous persons are capable of having friendships of any other type, he will be adopting an extremely harsh view of the psychological capabilities of almost everyone. For, clearly enough, there are few or no paragons of virtue in the world, and if only such paragons can have friendships of the basic kind, then most people, including virtually all of Aristotle's readers, will be declared incapable of anything but thoroughly self-centered associations. This would be a depressing result, and one which, given Aristotle's generally accommodating attitude toward the common sense of the ordinary man, should occasion surprise, at least in the absence of compelling general reasons on the other side. In what follows I shall argue that, despite initial appearances, Aristotle does not make friendship of the central kind the exclusive preserve of moral heroes, and that he does not maintain that friendships of the derivative kinds are wholly self-centered: pleasure- and advantage-friendships are instead a complex and subtle mixture of self-seeking and unself-interested well-wishing and well-doing.

III

As already remarked, Aristotle distinguishes the three types of friendship from one another by reference to what it is that causes the parties to like one another: *triōn ontōn di' ha philousin* (1155b27)—*dia to chrēsimon, dia to hēdu*, and *di'aretēn*. Strictly, of course, it is not the actual properties of a person, but those that someone else conceives him as possessing, that are responsible for the existence of a friendship: in the case of pleasure, perhaps, there is hardly room for mistakes, but, plainly, one can be mistaken about whether someone is advantageous to know, or morally good. Though Aristotle in describing friendships usually neglects this distinction, and speaks of friends of the various types as *actually* pleasant or advantageous to one another, or morally good, he does on occasion take explicit note of the decisive role of appearances here. Thus in *Nicomachean Ethics*, IX 3 he discusses what becomes of the friendship you have made with someone, taking him to be a good person (*ean d'apodechētai hōs agathon*, 1165b13), when you find out otherwise. While such a friendship lasts, the deceived party will like his friend "for his virtue" (*di'aretēn*), even though he may in fact have none; so the friendship, from his side at least, will be a "friendship of the good." What gives a friendship its character as a friendship of a particular kind is the state of mind of the partners—their intentions toward and their conceptions of one another. Now, clearly enough, in the case of pleasure- and advantage-friends it is *some* (conceived) pleasure or advantage that their friends give them that makes them like them; the friend need not be thought to be pleasant or advantageous in every way or every context, but only in *some*, in order for the friendship to exist. One may well be friends with someone because he is a pleasant drinking-companion, even while recognizing his unsuitability as a companion in other pleasant pursuits. Up to a certain point, perhaps, a pleasure-friendship is more complete and perfect of its kind the greater the variety and scope of the pleasures the friends may share; but this is a difference in scope and perfection within a class of friendships which all belong to the same basic type. The type is determined by what it is about the other person that forms the bond, and this may perfectly well—indeed, typically will—involve a very limited and partial view of him as a pleasant companion.

It would be natural to suppose that within the class of virtue-friendships there could be a similar variation. Some virtue-friendships might involve the recognition of complete and perfect virtue, virtue of every type and in every respect, in the associates; other friendships of the same type might be based, not on the recognition by each of perfect virtue in the other, but just of some morally good qualities that he possesses (or is thought to possess). Thus, one might be attached to someone because of his generous and open spirit, while recognizing that he is in some ways obtuse, or not very industrious, or somewhat self-indulgent. Such a friendship would belong to the type, *virtue-friendship*, because it would be based on the conception of the other person as morally good (in some respect, in some degree), even though the person does not have, and is not thought to have, a perfectly virtuous character—just as a pleasure-friend need not be, or be thought to be, perfectly pleasant or pleasant in every way. Here again, the question of what type of friendship a given relationship belongs to would be settled by examining the conception of the person under which one is bound to him; if it is good qualities of the person's character, and not pleasure or advantage to oneself, that causes one to like him, it will be a virtue-friendship, even though these qualities may be, and be known to be, limited in their goodness and/or conjoined with other not so good, or even positively bad, personal characteristics.

Now it is clear, I think, that this must be how Aristotle understands virtue-friendship, considered as one of the three basic types of friendship, despite the prominence in his exposition of that most perfect instance, the association of two perfectly good men. This comes out most clearly from his discussion of friendship between unequals. Ideally, he recognizes (1158b30–33), friendship demands absolute equality—equality of status between the partners and equality of pleasure or advantage, given and received, or moral goodness, as the case may be. But in each of the three basic types (1162a34-b4) there occur also unequal friendships. Sometimes one party gives more pleasure than he gets, or benefits less from the association than his friend does, and similarly friendships exist, Aristotle claims, where one party is recognized to be morally better than the other. One class of unequal virtue-friendships is that between husband and wife (1158b13–19). Here Aristotle's idea seems to be that men as such are morally superior to women, so that a friendship between the absolutely best man and the absolutely best woman, each recognized as such, would be an unequal friendship. In such a friendship the disparity in goodness does not imply any deficiency on the side of the lesser person with respect to her own appropriate excellences; she will be perfect of her kind, but the kind in question is inherently lower. But Aristotle also recognizes unequal virtue-friendships between those whose natural status is equal (1162b6–13), and in that case the inequality must consist in one of the partners being not only less morally good than the other, but deficient with respect to his own appropriate excellences. So in this case we will have a virtue-friendship where the superior person likes the inferior for such virtues as he has (or some of them), while recognizing that his character is not perfectly good. Even more significant for our purposes is Aristotle's discussion in IX 3, 1165b23ff., of a virtue-friendship which starts out equal but is threatened with dissolution as one party improves in character and accomplishments and eventually outstrips the other. In this case it is clear that Aristotle is willing to countenance a virtue-friendship where *both* parties are quite deficient with respect to their appropriate excellences.

There can be no doubt, then, that on Aristotle's theory what makes a friendship a virtue-friendship is the binding force within it of *some*—perhaps, for all that, partial and incomplete—excellence of the character, and the perfect friendship of the perfectly virtuous is only an especially significant special case of this. For this reason, it seems preferable to refer to friendship of the central kind not, as Aristotle most often tends to do, as "friendship of the good," but, as he sometimes calls it, "friendship of character" (ἡ τῶν

ἠθῶν φιλία, 1164a12, διὰ τὸ ἦθος φιλεῖν, 1165b8–9, ἡ ἠθικὴ φιλία, *EE*
1241a10, 1242b36, 1243a8, 32, 35; cf. ἐκ τῆς συνηθείας τὰ ἤθη στέρξωσιν,
Nic. Eth. 1157a11, and ἔοικε . . . τῆς κατὰ τὸ χρήσιμον φιλίας ἡ μὲν ἠθικὴ
ἡ δὲ νομικὴ εἶναι, 1162b21–23). The expression "character-friendship"
brings out accurately that the basis for the relationship is the recognition
of good qualities of character, without in any way implying that the parties
are moral heroes. I will hereafter adopt this alternative terminology. One
should not, however, overlook the significance of the fact that Aristotle
himself prefers to characterize the central type of friendship by concentrating
almost exclusively on the friendship of perfectly good men. For it is an
aspect of the pervasive teleological bias of his thinking, which causes him
always to search out the best and most fully realized instance when attempting to define a kind of thing. Aristotle does not himself mistake the perfect
instance for the only member of the class, and there is no necessity for us
to do so. But because, in this case, I believe his readers have often been
misled, it seems best in expounding Aristotle's views to depart from his own
preferred terminology.

IV

The central and basic kind of friendship, then, is friendship of character.
Such friendships exist when two persons, having spent enough time together
to know one another's character and to trust one another (1156b25–29),
come to love one another because of their good human qualities: Aristotle's
word for "love" here is *stergein*, a word which is used most often to apply
to a mother's love for her children and other such close family attachments.[11]
Each, loving the other for his good qualities of character, wishes for him
whatever is good, for his own sake, precisely in recognition of his goodness
of character, and it is mutually known to them that well-wishing of this
kind is reciprocated (1156a3–5). They enjoy one another's company and are

---

[11] The centrality of this emotional bond in Aristotle's analysis is sometimes overlooked, but
it is there, nonetheless. In *Nic. Eth.* IV 6, 1126b16–28, in characterizing the nameless minor
social virtue which shows itself in the right sort of behavior in ordinary social intercourse—
the person who has it will openly assert his own views and preferences, as appropriate, while
also heeding and yielding to those of others when this is right—Aristotle says that this kind
of person behaves toward others in the sort of way that a friend does: "for the person in this
intermediate condition is very like what, with love (τὸ στέργειν) added, we call a good friend.
But his condition differs from friendship because he lacks passion (πάθος) and love (τὸ στέργειν)
towards those with whom he associates." Aristotle does not in *Nic. Eth.* VIII-IX (or *EE* VII)
list στέρξις formally as a condition or component of friendship, but this seems to be only
because he presupposes it as obvious. At any rate he refers frequently enough in *Nic. Eth.*
VIII-IX to friends as loving (στέργειν) one another, one another's characters, etc. Since Bywater's
index omits all of these passages, I add the following (I think complete) list of places where
the word appears in these books: 1156a15, 1157a11, 28, 1161b18, 25, 1162a12, b30, 1164a10,
1167a3, 1168a2, 7, 22.

benefited by it (1156b12–17) and in consequence spend their time together or even live with one another (*sunēmereuein kai suzēn*, 1156b4–5). Provided that no contingency physically separates them for any considerable period (1157b11–13), such a friendship, once formed, will tend to be continuous and permanent, since it is grounded in knowledge of and love for one another's good qualities of character, and such traits, once formed, tend to be permanent (1156b11–12).

Pleasure- and advantage-friendships are, according to Aristotle, counted as friendships only by reason of their resemblance to this central case.[12] Thus character-friends are both pleasant and beneficial to one another, and pleasure-friends, though not necessarily beneficial, are of course pleasant to one another, while advantage-friends derive benefits, though perhaps not pleasure, from their association (1156b35–1157a3, 1156a27–28).[13] But are there further, direct resemblances, based on properties that all three types of friendship have in common? If, as I suggested above, Aristotle means to adopt in *Nicomachean Ethics*, VIII 2 the *Rhetoric*'s definition of friendship as always involving well-wishing to one's friend for his own sake, then the types will have much in common: in every friendship, of whichever of the three types, the friend will wish his friend whatever is good, for his own sake, and it will be mutually known to them that this well-wishing is reciprocated.[14] As I have said, I believe that Aristotle does hold this view, but there are complications that must now be entered into.

The chief complication is caused by the qualifications which Aristotle immediately imposes on his statement in VIII 2 that mutually known, reciprocated *eunoia* is essential to friendship. He says that friends must "wish well to (*eunoein*) and want what is good for one another, and be known to one another as doing this, on one of the aforesaid grounds" (1156a3–5), i.e., because they find their friend pleasant, or beneficial, or possessed of admirable qualities of character. But what does Aristotle mean by this "because"? What kind of ground does he have in mind here? Perhaps he means that in a pleasure-friendship the one person wants the other to prosper *in order that* his own (the well-wisher's) pleasure may be continued or increased. Similarly, an advantage friend would want and be willing to try to secure what his friend needed, in

---

[12] The resemblance is partial at best: neither of the derivative friendships tends to be permanent (1156a19–20); neither requires an extended preparatory period of testing and getting to know one another (1156a34–35, 1158a14–18); advantage-friends do not even tend to spend their time together (1156a27–28). One can have many friends of these kinds, but only very few of the other (1158a10ff.).

[13] Thus character-friendship, by resembling in these different ways these other two types of relationship, links them to one another, despite the fact that in this crucial respect (motive) they diverge fairly widely from one another. On this see Fortenbaugh, "Aristotle's Analysis," pp. 56–57.

[14] It should be noticed also that Aristotle does on occasion say that friends of the derivative types love (στέργειν) one another (1156a14–15, 1157a28, 1162a12), thus implying at least a relatively close emotional attachment. He sometimes seems to deny this, however: see, e.g., 1164a10–11, and my discussion below, sect. IV.

order that his friend might continue to be in a position, or be better able, to see to *his* needs in due course. That is, well-wishing on the ground of pleasure or advantage would mean well-wishing in order to get pleasure or advantage for oneself. But this interpretation runs into an immediate objection. For although it is certainly possible to wish someone well both for one's own sake (because his success will bring advantages or enjoyments to oneself) and for his, it does seem incoherent to suggest that someone might wish well to someone else for that other person's sake *in order to* secure his own interests or enjoyments. To wish for someone else's good for his sake entails (perhaps means) wishing for his good *not* as a means to one's own (or anyone else's) good. But on this interpretation Aristotle would be guilty of this incoherent thought: he does not say merely that a pleasure-friend wishes for his friend's prosperity because the friend is pleasant to him, but that he has *eunoia* for his friend for this reason, and *eunoia* is defined in this very context (1155b32, where οὕτω is to be explicated by ἐκείνου ἕνεκα, b31) as wishing someone well *for his own sake*, and does not mean wishing him well *tout court*.

It might be suggested that Aristotle, despite the apparent definition of *eunoia* at 1155b32, intends the word to be understood in the reduced sense of "wishing well (*period*)" when, a few lines later, he says that friends of all types wish each other well (*eunoein*). Such a reduction in sense is in itself unlikely within the context of a single argument, however, and the evidence about Aristotle's usage of the word elsewhere seems to show that he always understands by it "well-wishing for the other person's sake." There is no doubt that this is how *eunoia* is understood in his official account of it in the *Nicomachean Ethics*, IX 5, and in the corresponding passage of the *Eudemian Ethics*, VII 7 (1241a1–14) Aristotle actually denies that *eunoia* exists in pleasure- and advantage-friendships at all, precisely on the ground that "if one wishes for someone what is good because he is useful to oneself, one would not wish this for his sake but for one's own, while *eunoia* is for the sake not of the well-wisher himself but for that of the person to whom one wishes well" (1241a5–8).[15] We shall have to return to this passage of the *Eudemian Ethics* later; for the moment it is enough to point out how decisive and explicit Aristotle is here that *eunoia* requires not just well-wishing, but even well-wishing for the other person's sake. The apparent definition of *eunoia* in *Nicomachean Ethics* VIII 2 is therefore not something put forward in passing, easily subject to immediate unannounced dilution; it is a statement of Aristotle's fully considered understanding of what *eunoia* is.

It should be recalled that the necessity for taking *eunoein* in a reduced sense in 1156a4 was caused by interpreting the claim that a pleasure- or an advantage-friend wishes his friend well *because* his friend is pleasant or advantageous to him (*dia to hēdu, dia to chrēsimon*) as meaning *in order*

---

[15] The text here, as often in *EE* VII, is obviously corrupt, though I believe the sense, as I have given it, is beyond doubt. I accept Jackson's ἕνεκα for εὔνοια of the MSS at a8, and ignore in my translation the lacuna at a7.

to secure his own pleasure or advantage. If *dia* is taken in this prospective way, as expressing merely what the well-wisher hopes to produce or achieve by his friend's prosperity, then it is impossible to interpret Aristotle coherently. But there is another, in itself more plausible, interpretation of the force of *dia* here. Notice first that if *dia* does mean "for the sake of," it ought to mean the same thing in the parallel remark about character-friendships: a character-friend wishes well to his friend *di'aretēn*, i.e., on this interpretation, for the sake of excellence of character. One might, of course, make some sense of this: a person wants his friend to prosper so that he (the friend, presumably) can wax more virtuous or continue to do virtuous deeds. But it is not the only, nor even the most natural, way of understanding the claim that character-friends wish each other well because of excellence of character. In this case, the "because" (*dia tēn aretēn*) seems more likely to mean "in recognition of their friend's having a good character," so that it expresses a consequence or result of the friend's being morally good rather than some purpose that the well-wisher has in wanting him to prosper.[16] Thus, a character-friend wishes his friend to prosper, because he recognizes his good character and thinks that it is fitting for those who are morally good to prosper. Understanding the "because" in this causal way makes it at least as much retrospective as prospective; the well-wishing and well-doing are responses to what the person is and has done rather than merely the expression of a hope as to what he will be and may do in the future. Now, if one interprets the "because" in this causal way in all three cases, as one must if one is to take it so in any of them, there is no special difficulty in understanding Aristotle's attribution of *eunoia* to all types of friends. For the pleasure-friend will now be said to wish well to his friend for his friend's own sake, in consequence of recognizing him as someone who is and has been an enjoyable companion, and the advantage-friend wishes his friend well for his friend's own sake, in consequence of recognizing him as someone who regularly benefits him and has done so in the past. Aristotle will here be making, in effect, the psychological claim that those who have enjoyed one another's company or have been mutually benefited through their common association, will, as a result of the benefits or pleasures they receive, tend to wish for and be willing to act in the interest of the other person's good, independently of consideration of their *own* welfare or pleasure. A full-fledged friendship will exist, then, when such intentions are recognized by both parties as existing reciprocally.[17]

---

[16] This interpretation is more in conformity with the predominant usage of διά, which, though it can sometimes express a purpose (cf. Liddell-Scott-Jones, s.v. B III 3), normally expresses an antecedent causal condition. Had Aristotle wanted to refer here to the well-wisher's purpose, he would presumably have written τοῦ χρησίμου (etc.) ἕνεκα.

[17] It is, obviously, compatible with these intentions (see below) that a friend should also expect his friendship to bring pleasure and/or advantage to himself: indeed Aristotle makes it very clear, as at 1156a22–24, that pleasure and advantage are both cause (δι' ὅ) and defining purpose (πρὸς ὅ) in the case of these lesser friendships. The point is that even though a person

Before this interpretation can be accepted, however, we must see how it fits with what Aristotle says in VIII 3–4, where he marks off character-friends, as "friends without qualification" (*haplōs*, 1157b4), from the other types, whom he counts as friends only "incidentally" (*kata sumbebēkos*, 1156a17, b11, 1157b4). Friends wish each other well, he says, "in that respect in which they are friends" (ταύτῃ ᾗ φιλοῦσιν, 1156a9–10): so, he explains, an advantage-friend or a pleasure-friend wishes his friend well "*qua* beneficial or pleasant" (ᾗ χρήσιμος ἢ ἡδύς, a16). Hence, he implies, advantage- and pleasure-friends are only incidentally one another's friends, while character-friends are friends in an unqualified way. In interpreting this passage I want to take up two points. First, what does Aristotle mean by saying that a friend of one of the lesser types wishes his friend well (merely) *qua* pleasant or *qua* advantageous to himself? Does this amount to saying that these types of friends regard each other exclusively as means to their own satisfaction or advancement? And second, how is it that to wish someone well "*qua* pleasant" or "*qua* advantageous" is a ground for saying that someone who does this is only "incidentally" a friend? I will take up the second point first.

Clearly enough, whether one person is beneficial or pleasant to another is an incidental characteristic of him: his being so results from the purely external and contingent fact that properties or abilities he possesses happen to answer to needs or wants, equally contingent, that characterize the other person. If, then, the conception of the other person under which one is his friend—as beneficial, or as pleasant to oneself—is something that is only incidentally true of him, the same thing must also be said of that property which one acquires as a result of so regarding him: that one is a friend of the other person must be something that holds true only incidentally. By contrast, Aristotle claims, character-friends are friends of one another essentially (*kath' hautous*, 1156a11, *di' hautous*, 1156b10, 1157b3) or without qualification (*haplōs*). Admittedly, it is not a necessary truth about any individual that he has those good qualities of character for which he is loved (just as it is not a necessary truth about the pleasant or advantageous friend that he has those properties that yield pleasure or advantage). But on Aristotle's theory of moral virtue, the virtues are essential properties of human*kind*: a person realizes more or less fully his human nature according as he possesses more or less fully those properties of character which count as moral excellences. And since individual persons are what they essentially are by being human beings, it can be said that a person (any person) realizes his own essential nature more fully the more completely and adequately he possesses the moral excellences. So if one is the friend of another person,

---

looks for pleasure or advantage from a relationship and would withdraw from it if he thought this end no longer attainable through it, he can still, on the assumption that the pleasure or advantage does remain firm, wish his friend well for his own sake. Here pleasure or advantage, assumed to be a stable property of the relationship, serves as cause, not as goal, of the well-wishing.

and wishes him well, because of good moral qualities he possesses, one will be his friend because he is something that he is essentially and not incidentally (cf. 1156b8–9: οὗτοι [sc., character-friends] γὰρ τἀγαθὰ ὁμοίως βούλονται ἀλλήλοις ᾗ ἀγαθοί, ἀγαθοὶ δ' εἰσὶ καθ' αὑτούς). And, in consequence, the property that one acquires as a result of so regarding him, that of being his friend, can be said to relate one to him essentially and not incidentally. It is because his friend is just what he essentially is, a human being, that a character-friend wishes him well; pleasure-friends and advantage-friends wish their friends well not, or not merely, as what they essentially are.

In this train of thought, the operative consideration is the conception of the other person under which one wishes him well, and since the argument here is developed directly out of the passage in VIII 2, in which Aristotle declares that friends wish each other well on account of pleasure, advantage, or moral goodness, we can find support in it for the interpretation proposed above of that earlier passage. Properly understood, neither passage denies that friends of the derivative types wish their friends well for the friend's own sake; instead, they specify what it is about the other person that supports this response. In this respect all three types of friendship run parallel. There is, however, an important difference between the well-wishing that forms part of a character-friendship and the well-wishing in the other two cases. This follows from the fact, developed in VIII 3–4, that only character-friends are friends essentially and without adventitious qualification. For given the close connection that Aristotle asserts between moral excellence and what a human being essentially is, a character-friend's well-wishing is more unrestricted, less hedged about by special assumptions and special expectations, than the well-wishing of the other types of friend. A character-friend wishes for his friend's well-being as, and because he is, a good man. But good qualities of character are, once fully acquired, permanent or nearly so (1156b12), since these properties belong to one's essential nature as a human being, and one's essential nature, once fully realized, is a permanent part of what one is. By contrast, pleasantness and advantageousness, just because they are incidental properties of a person (and depend upon the special circumstances, interests, etc., of other persons as well) are subject to change (1156a21–22, 1156b1). So character-friendships are much more permanent attachments than pleasure- and advantage-friendships are.

But these temporal limitations carry with them another limitation: in wishing well to one's friend because of his pleasantness or advantageousness to oneself, one is implicitly imposing limits of a special and narrow kind upon one's well-wishing. One's concern for the other person's good extends only so far as and so long as he remains a particular sort of person, pleasant or advantageous as the case may be: one likes and wishes well to someone conceived of as pleasant or advantageous to oneself, and the good one wishes him to have, for his own sake, is therefore restricted to what he can acquire without, thereby or in consequence, ceasing to be pleasant or advantageous. One wants him to prosper, for his own sake, and not merely as a means to one's own good; nevertheless, one does not want him to prosper in such a way or to such an extent that one no longer gets the pleasure or benefits one has received from associating with him. In short, in wishing someone well, for his own sake, because he is pleasant or advantageous, one's first commitment is to his retention of the property of pleasantness or advantageousness, and any good one wishes him to have, for his own sake, must be compatible with the retention of that special property under which, as his friend, one wishes him well in the first place.[18]

This, at any rate, I take to be the burden of Aristotle's claim that friends want good things for their friends "in that respect in which they are friends" (ταύτῃ ᾗ φιλοῦσιν, 1156a10), viz., *qua* persons pleasant or advantageous to themselves (a16) or *qua* persons of good character (ᾗ ἀγαθοί, b8–9). He does not say explicitly that the conception of the other person under which one is his pleasure- or advantage-friend implies these limitations to one's well-wishing, but he does draw the parallel inference about character-friends. Thus, Aristotle says, friends do not wish that their friends should become gods (although being a god is a very good thing) because to become a god is to cease to be a human being, and it is of a human being that one is the friend and, therefore, as a human being that one wishes for his prosperity: εἰ δὴ καλῶς εἴρηται ὅτι ὁ φίλος τῷ φίλῳ βούλεται τἀγαθὰ ἐκείνου ἕνεκα, μένειν ἂν δέοι οἷός ποτ᾽ ἐστὶν ἐκεῖνος· ἀνθρώπῳ δὴ ὄντι βουλήσεται τὰ μέγιστα ἀγαθά (1159a8–11).[19] If, then, the well-wishing of a character-

---

[18] This consequence of Aristotle's theory of pleasure- and advantage-friends is, from our point of view, perhaps not a very palatable one. One might, for example, rather think that people involved in a sexual liaison which is also a pleasure-friendship would, just to the extent that they regard one another as friends, be committed to sacrificing the liaison itself, if it came to that, if the welfare or prosperity (or some other important good) of one of them made this seem desirable. On Aristotle's account of pleasure-friendship, however, as I have interpreted it, there would be no such commitment. (If there were, that would show that the friendship was not purely a pleasure-friendship, but was verging toward being a character-friendship: cf. 1157a8–12.) Pleasure- and advantage-friendships, on Aristotle's conception, are, despite his denial that they are wholly self-centered, much more self-centered than perhaps we would be inclined to think them. It should also, perhaps, be noted here that Aristotle, on my interpretation, does not have to deny that one might (out of simple gratitude, for example) wish to do well to someone who had ceased to be pleasant or advantageous to oneself. His point is that well-wishing *as an ingredient in friendship* is limited by the other person's continuing to (be thought to) be pleasant or advantageous. Nor is this an arbitrary restriction: if those who have once been close companions cease to take pleasure in one another's company, then their friendship is dead, no matter how much they do for one another thereafter out of gratitude for past favors or pleasures. The same thing holds of business friendships. Friendship, of whatever sort, requires a continuing lively interest of one person in another, and *mere* gratitude for past pleasures or past services is not enough to provide this.

[19] I follow here the traditional interpretation, found, e.g., in Ross's translation. J. Burnet, *The Ethics of Aristotle*, p. 363, followed by Gauthier (*Aristote: L'Ethique à Nicomaque*, p. 693), takes the text to say instead that one does not wish his friend to become a god because to do so would be to wish to deprive *him* of a good, namely one's friendship. This is textually more awkward, but just possible. Burnet and Gauthier apparently opt for it because they think it attributes a more seemly (because purely altruistic) intention to this well-wisher, who is

friend is tacitly restricted to such goods as the friend can acquire while still remaining what he essentially is (a human being), pleasure- and advantage-friends, in accordance with their more restricted conceptions of other persons as their friends, will want their friends' prosperity only within the limits imposed by the existence and continuance of those special properties of pleasantness and advantageousness to themselves that ground their friendships.

Friends of all three types, then, on Aristotle's theory in the *Nicomachean Ethics*, wish for their friend's well-being out of concern for the friend himself. This is as true of a businessman who, through frequent profitable association, becomes friends with a regular customer, as it is of a husband and wife or two intimate companions who love one another for their characters. Such a businessman looks first and foremost for mutual profit from his friendship, but that does not mean that he always calculates his services to his customer by the standard of profit. Finding the relationship on the whole profitable, he likes this customer and is willing to do him services otherwise than as a means to his own ultimate profit. So long as the general context of profitability remains, the well-wishing can proceed unchecked; the profitability to the well-wisher that is assumed in the well-wishing is not that of the *particular* service rendered (the particular action done in the other person's interest) but that of the overall fabric of the relationship.[20] Here, then, one has a

---

presumed to be morally virtuous. But this is an illusion. After all, becoming a god might well entail a sufficient improvement in one's condition so that the loss of a human friendship would be more than compensated for, and in that case one's friend could hardly claim to be acting altruistically in refusing to want one to achieve this status. There is no incompatibility at all (*pace* Gauthier) in wishing for one's friend's good and wishing that he should be deified (or in some other way improve his condition at the cost of the friendship). Hence the passage only makes a coherent point if interpreted in the traditional way. Friendship, even the purest, essentially involves the desire for one's own good (as well as the desire for that of one's friend), and there is no reason to interpret away signs of Aristotle's recognition of this fact. Notice also that at the end of the passage Aristotle emphasizes (1159a11–12) that a person's first concern is (properly) with his own good, a remark that is perfectly in place on the traditional interpretation, but hardly so on Burnet's and Gauthier's.

[20] It is instructive in interpreting advantage-friendship to notice that Aristotle distinguishes two kinds (*Nic. Eth.* VIII 13, 1162b21–1163a9): one which is νομική and ἐπὶ ῥητοῖς (1162b23, 25–26: i.e., governed by explicitly agreed upon exchanges of services) while the other is ἠθική (1162b23, 31: i.e., it rests on the parties' characters, as decent people who do not need to buy one another's attentions). It is interesting to observe that in the latter sort of friendship, Aristotle says the parties give to one another ὡς φίλῳ, i.e., in the spirit in which true friends do, without looking for or soliciting any particular, exact return. In fact, as this comment betrays, it is only what Aristotle calls ἠθικὴ φιλία κατὰ τὸ χρήσιμον that counts at all as a φιλία on his own announced criteria: the other types don't really have εὔνοια for one another, so that their association is a *purely* commercial affair and hence no friendship, not even an advantage-friendship. That Aristotle is not clearer on this point here shows, I think, a certain unwillingness on his part to embrace unreservedly the idea that no association can count as a friendship that does not involve disinterested well-wishing. A comparison of this passage with the corresponding argument in the *EE* (1242b31–1243b14) will serve to place Aristotle's inconsistency on this point into proper focus. The *EE* begins by marking off the same two types of advantage-friendship (1242b31–32), νομική and ἠθική. But as the argument proceeds it becomes apparent

complex and subtle mixture of self-seeking and unself-interested well-wishing and well-doing. The overriding concern of the advantage-friend is for his own profit. But this does not mean that every action and wish of his is ultimately aimed at the realization of something profitable to himself. He genuinely likes his friend and has a genuine and unself-interested concern for his good, and he will do him services that are not motivated, at least not entirely, by self-interest. Of course, some services he will refuse, because they will cost him too much, thus endangering the general profitability to himself of the association that is the basic presupposition of the friendship and therefore of any friendly service falling within it. Other services, however, no doubt small ones for the most part, he will freely perform. The same pattern of unself-interested well-wishing and self-seeking will be found in pleasure-friendships, with mutual pleasantness taking the place of mutual advantageousness.

The admixture of self-seeking in character-friendships is significantly less than in pleasure- and advantage-friendships. A character-friend loves his friend because of properties that belong to the friend essentially, and not merely incidentally. This means that he loves him for what he himself is, and not for merely external properties, or relations in which he stands to other persons. Hence the well-wishing characteristic of such a friendship does not take place within so restricted a context as that imposed by the self-centered desires for pleasure and profit that operate in the other types of friendship. The assumption in the case of character-friends that corresponds to the assumption of the pleasantness or advantageousness of the other person in the derivative friendships, is just that the other person is a good human being. So the character-friend wishes his friend well in any way that is not inconsistent with his being the good human being he is assumed to be. He wants and expects both pleasure and advantage from his association with his friend, but aiming at these is not an essential condition of the friendship itself. He associates with a good person because of his goodness; pleasure and advantage may follow in due course, but his intention in maintaining the friendship is fixed on the goodness of the other person,

---

(b38–1243a2) that this division is provisional only; the latter type is really a confused relationship, in which the parties cannot decide whether to treat one another as *real* friends (that is, character-friends, in which case they ought not to demand repayment for their services at all) or as advantage-friends (that is, friends of the type which has just been described as *one kind* of advantage-friend, the νομική, in which case commercial practice is the accepted model for their relationship). Thus, in this passage Aristotle actually implies that it is only where an association *is* purely commercial that it can count as an advantage-friendship, as his denial in the *EE* of εὔνοια to advantage-friends (1241a3–5) also implies. The *Nic. Eth.* discussion, in insisting that the ἠθικὴ φιλία κατὰ τὸ χρήσιμον is a legitimate type of advantage-friendship, is therefore a distinct improvement; as often, however, Aristotle, in reworking this passage to bring it into line with his later views, refuses to abandon completely the earlier ideas which are causing the trouble. What results is a half-way house in which both the νομική and the ἠθική count as legitimate advantage-friendships, even though his mature view would seem to imply that the νομική is not in reality a friendship at all.

not on his pleasantness or profitability. So, although there is unself-interested well-wishing in all three types of friendship, it is both broader and deeper in a character-friendship than in the other two. For it is only in this case that the conception of the other person under which one is his friend and wishes him well for his own sake is a conception that corresponds to what he himself essentially is.

Bearing in mind these important differences between character-friends and the other two types, one might say, with some justice, that only character-friends really love *one another*, that only they really wish one another well for *one another's* sake. By this, one would mean that only character-friends concern themselves with the actual persons, themselves, that their friends are. It is in this light that I think those few remarks of Aristotle's are to be interpreted which at first sight seem to deny that unself-interested well-wishing occurs at all in the derivative friendships. Thus he says at 1156b7–11 that "the friendship of good persons who are alike in moral virtue is perfect friendship. For these alike wish good things for one another *qua* good, and they are good in virtue of being themselves (*kath' hautous*). But those who wish good things to their friends for the friends' sake are most truly friends; for they are friends by being themselves (*di' hautous*) and not incidentally." Here Aristotle appears to deny, by implication, that other sorts of friends do wish good things for one another for their friends' own sake, but in reality, as the context shows, his point would be better put by saying that although in the other friendships there *is* well-wishing for the friend's own sake, and not merely as a means to the well-wisher's good, the friend himself is conceived in an external and incidental way (he is not loved and cared for as being what he himself essentially is), so that it is not for the sake of himself as he *essentially* is that the well-wishing takes place. It is only in character-friendships that the well-wishing is for the sake of the person conceived as being what he himself essentially is; so one can hint, as Aristotle does here, though with some risk of misleading his readers, that only a character-friend acts for his friend's own sake. It is in the same way that I believe other apparently aberrant passages ought to be interpreted (thus 1157a15–16, οὐ γὰρ ἀλλήλων ἦσαν φίλοι ἀλλὰ τοῦ λυσιτελοῦς; 1164a10–11, οὐ γὰρ αὐτοὺς ἔστεργον ἀλλὰ τὰ ὑπάρχοντα; 1165b3, ἐκείνων (sc. τοῦ χρησίμου καὶ τοῦ ἡδοῦς) γὰρ ἦσαν φίλοι).

It is interesting to observe that this subtle and acute analysis of the derivative friendships, allowing for unself-interested well-wishing (*eunoia*) within the confines of an association primarily motivated by self-seeking, was not firmly worked out until late in Aristotle's career. At any rate, the *Eudemian Ethics* seems to lack it. It is a striking fact that well-wishing, which is prominent from the very beginning of the *Nicomachean Ethics'* discussion (VIII 2) as one essential component of friendship, is mentioned only twice (1236b30, 1238b5), and both times in passing, in the long chapter, *Eudemian Ethics*, VII 2, in which the theory of the three types of friendship is developed and explained. At one place (1241a1–14, mentioned above) in the *Eudemian Ethics*, Aristotle considers that the self-centeredness of the derivative friendships precludes all possibility of well-wishing out of regard for the other person; yet later on (1244a20–26) he appears to say that wanting what is good for a friend is a characteristic of all three types of friendship.[21] If this is shorthand, as it would be in the *Nicomachean Ethics*, for wanting a friend's good for his sake, then the *Eudemian Ethics* has no clear and consistent theory on this point. It should be carefully noted that in the *Nicomachean Ethics* chapter (IX 5) on *eunoia* (which corresponds to *EE* 1241a1–14) Aristotle does not repeat the *Eudemian Ethics*' blanket denial of *eunoia* to pleasure- and advantage-friends. He makes instead the more interesting, and reduced, claim that those who adopt an attitude of unself-interested well-wishing towards someone although they do not know him personally or associate with him in any way can, by prolonged and habitual association, convert their good will into actual friendship, but that the resulting friendship will always be a character-, and never a pleasure- or advantage-friendship (1167a10–14). Spontaneous good will of the kind here under discussion can only be based on admiration for goodness of character; one can feel good will toward someone whom one thinks is a good person even though one has no deep personal knowledge of his character and has not personally been affected by any noble action of his, but no one feels good will for someone else on the mere ground that he *might* be a pleasant companion or useful business partner. These sorts of good will only arise after the pleasure or the profit has begun to be actualized, and exist always as a response to profit or pleasure one has actually found in associating with someone else (cf. 1167a14–15). It is the expectation of pleasure or profit that brings one to develop such friendships as these, and there is no such thing as unself-interested well-wishing for the sake of one's own pleasure or profit (*oude gar eunoia epi toutois ginetai*, 1167a13–14). So what Aristotle denies here is that *eunoia* precedes, and possibly turns into, a friendship of one of the derivative sorts;[22] he does not deny that once such a relationship has begun, *eunoia* develops within it. The positive point

---

[21] So at any rate it seems to read if we accept Jackson's conjecture at a23. The text here is very corrupt.

[22] It is true that in VIII 2, 1155b34–1156a1, Aristotle says that it is possible to feel εὔνοια for someone whom one does not know, but takes to be χρήσιμος (to oneself), and there seems nothing to prevent such εὔνοια from growing into an advantage-friendship, under appropriate further conditions. This remark need not, however, be taken to be inconsistent with the doctrine of IX 5 as I have interpreted it. For, as Aristotle emphasizes in IX 5 (1167a14–15), εὔνοια is a normal response to having been well treated, and probably the εὔνοια envisaged in the VIII 2 passage is a response to what the well-wisher takes to have been benefits accruing to himself from the other person's activities: he is grateful, say, to his distant and not personally known superior for his efforts on behalf of their common business, and so wishes him well for his own sake. What Aristotle denies in IX 5 is only that εὔνοια can be formed merely on the expectation of future profit (or pleasure); εὔνοια formed wholly in advance of any interchange among the parties can only be based on the belief that the person is morally good, and hence can only, if at all, turn into character-friendship.

Aristotle makes here seems to me very acutely observed; in any event, it does not count against the thesis I have argued for in this section, namely, that friends even of the derivative types pursue one another's good out of unself-interested good will.

V

If I am right, then, Aristotle's views on what is essential to friendship do not, as prevailing interpretations imply, commit him to holding that almost everyone has nothing but selfish motivations. On his theory ordinary decent people are capable even of character-friendship, with all that that implies in the way of unselfish interest in others, and in any event, pleasure- and advantage-friendship themselves already involve a considerable degree of unselfish concern for the good of other persons. In concluding this discussion, I want to make three further comments about Aristotle's theory, so understood.

First of all, Aristotle does not make the mistake, which a superficial reading would seem to convict him of, of counting as *philiai*, even of a diluted sort, just any established relationship in which two or more persons to their mutual knowledge receive pleasure or profit from associating together. That it would be a mistake to call in English all such relationships friendships (in no matter how relaxed a sense) I take to be obvious; a businessman is no friend of *all* his regular customers, and when a personal relationship is more or less purely exploitative it would be taken for irony to describe the persons in question as friends. Friendship requires, at a minimum, *some* effective concern for the other person's good (including his profit and his pleasure) out of regard for him. Aristotle seems to feel, as we do, that the expectation, at least, of interest in the other person's good for his own sake was part of what the word itself conveyed. In conceding (as, e.g., at 1157a25–36) that because general usage counts as friends those bound together merely by advantage or pleasure, philosophical theory must allow that such people are friends (though of a derivative type), Aristotle is not reluctantly being forced to recognize as *philiai* certain classes of wholly self-centered relationships. His reluctance is fully explained by the facts, which he argues for at length, that these relationships are less permanent, based less on knowledge of and interest in the other person and his character, and involve to a much lesser degree the merging of one's interests and the sharing of one's life with another person, all of which are contained as ideals and, in that sense, as norms within the very idea of *philia*.

An objection might, however, be raised against this interpretation. For, it might be said, whereas Aristotle explicitly argues that the derivative types of friendship only get that name by certain different resemblances they bear to character-friendship, on my view there is one property that all friendships share: friends always have *eunoia* for one another. Why then does Aristotle not assign this property the central and unifying place in his account of the three types of friendship which on this interpretation it would seem to have? The answer seems to be that, as Aristotle understands the matter, if one is to speak strictly, having *eunoia* for one another is not, as we loosely take it and I have described it above (sect. IV), a single property possessed in common by friends of whatever type. For as he puts it (1156a3–5), δεῖ ἄρα εὐνοεῖν ἀλλήλοις καὶ βούλεσθαι τἀγαθὰ μὴ λανθάνοντας δι' ἕν τι τῶν εἰρημένων (we must wish well to our friends "on one of the aforesaid grounds") and, as we have seen, the differences in the ground of this well-wishing bring with them differences in its scope and nature. So, Aristotle seems to hold, it would be wrong to say that there is *an* attitude of unself-interested concern for the other person's good that is common to all friend-ships. Instead, there are three different, though resembling, attitudes, one characteristic of each of the three types. So also, although he remarks that in every type of friendship there is mutual and reciprocated liking (ἀντιφίλησις οὐ λανθάνουσα, 1156a8–9), he does not count this as a single property that all friendships exhibit in common, and presumably for the same reason: the basis of this liking and so its nature varies too widely from case to case.

Finally, I should emphasize that Aristotle's theory is a theory of what a friendship is, i.e., what is true of those who are friends; it does not, except incidentally, have anything to say about how friendships are formed in the first place. In some sense, no doubt, it is on Aristotle's view the desire for pleasure or profit, or the interest in moral excellence, that brings together those who then become friends. But, clearly enough, in the actual course of events, the first meeting may well be quite accidental and subsequent stages in the development of the relationship quite unmotivated by any explicit form of these interests. The casual, even unexpected, discovery of pleasure, profit, or moral qualities, may elicit the responses that lead to the establishment of a friendship, without there being any premeditation or planning on either side. It may well be only in the clear light of hindsight that one could say that the desire for pleasure or profit, or the interest in moral excellence, was working to bring these people together; Aristotle's theory does not imply any stronger connection than this between these motives and the formation of the corresponding types of friendship.

VI

This, then, is Aristotle's account of the three forms of personal friendship. There is one further form of friendship to which Aristotle devotes some attention and which, for that reason as well as for its importance to his moral theory generally, we ought explicitly to notice. This is that diluted and reduced form that I have called "civic friendship."[23]

[23] My interest in this subject and some of my ideas on it were stimulated by a conversation with John Rawls.

Aristotle does not state as explicitly as one might wish what the nature of this kind of friendship is and how it is related to the three forms of personal friendship, but it seems clear enough on examination that he regards it as a special case of advantage-friendship.[24] At any rate, he emphasizes in his account of civic friendship that the civic community is formed and survives for the sake of the common advantage derived by its members from it (1160a11–12), so that it is essential to such a community that it aims at securing what is needed by its members to support their lives (a21–23). Civic friendship, then, as the special form of friendship characteristic of this kind of community, is founded on the experience and continued expectation, on the part of each citizen, of profit and advantage to himself, in common with the others, from membership in the civic association. This is to say that civic friendship is a kind of advantage-friendship. Given the account of advantage-friendship presented above, one can say, then, that civic friendship exists where the fellow-citizens, to one another's mutual knowledge, like (*philein*) one another, that is, where each citizen wishes well (and is known to wish well) to the others, and is willing to undertake to confer benefits on them, for their own sake, in consequence of recognizing that he himself is regularly benefited by the actions of the others. In a community animated by civic friendship, each citizen assumes that all the others, even those hardly or not at all known to him, are willing supporters of their common institutions and willing contributors to the common social product, from which he, together with all the other citizens, benefits. So they will approach one another for business or other purposes in a spirit of mutual good will and with willingness to sacrifice their own immediate interests to those of one another, as friendship demands. They are accommodating rather than suspicious, anxious to yield a point rather than insisting on the full letter of their rights whenever some dispute arises.

If this is what civic friendship is, it is not surprising that Aristotle should remark that lawgivers are more concerned to foster friendship among their citizens than they are to put their relations on a footing of justice (1155a23–24). For justice can exist perfectly well among those who care nothing for one another and who would not lift a finger to help anyone else, except insofar as rules of justice might require. The sense of justice, understood as respect for fairness and legality, is compatible with a suspicious, narrow, hard, and unsympathetic character. Hence, as Aristotle says (1155a26–27), those who are merely just in their mutual relations have need also of friendship, whereas those who are friends do not need to become just in addition: since, as friends, they already feel a lively concern for one another's welfare, they already acknowledge reasons not to harm or work to disadvantage and can be expected to reach an accommodation without having to invoke strict rules of justice. Those who are truly friends will not wrong one

---

[24] So Gauthier, *Aristote*, pp. 696–97. And see *EE* 1242b22–23, ἡ δὲ πολιτική (sc., φιλία) ἐστι μὲν κατὰ τὸ χρήσιμον.

another—not, however, out of love of justice and legality, but from love of one another. Aristotle adds (a28) that it is within the context of friendship that the claims of justice are both most extensive and most insistent:[25] one owes more to one's friends than to strangers, and the closer the friendship, the more extensive are one's obligations; a breach of justice is more serious when it is a friend whom one wrongs. The more complete the sentiment of friendship is among the members of a community, the greater the extent of the requirements of justice among them and the more stringent its demands. Hence lawgivers, in being specially concerned to make their citizens friends, are at the same time advancing the cause of justice and extending its scope— justice, however, founded on mutual liking and mutual good will, rather than mere rectitude.

Beyond this, Aristotle has little explicit to say about civic friendship. It is, however, an extremely important component both of his political theory and of his theory of human character. For, given his account of what friendship is, it is not difficult to see how, in decently arranged cities, people should naturally come to have friendly feelings toward one another. In such a city the benefits of civic life will be both substantial and obvious to everyone, and anyone with even ordinary intelligence will be able to see that the benefits to him are the direct consequence of his fellow-citizens' cooperative efforts. Recognizing this, he will come to wish them well and want to reciprocate by doing his part to uphold and further the community's interests. The sentiment of civic friendship is thus seen as the natural outcome of experience and understanding of the regular operation of a decently structured civic community.

Furthermore, as we have seen, Aristotle holds that fellow-citizens who are friends will behave justly to one another, so that the process, just sketched, by which a person comes to acquire friendly feelings towards his fellow-citizens is at the same time the development of a disposition to act justly towards them. Now, although Aristotle does not say so here, those who are friends are disposed also to act courageously, generously, good-temperedly, and so on for all the moral virtues, towards one another. To have friendly feelings towards someone is thus to have the disposition to treat that person virtuously in all respects, because one loves and values him as a person. So the process by which one comes to acquire friendly feelings towards one's fellow-citizens is the acquisition of a disposition to act in all respects morally toward them, and not merely a disposition to act justly. The sentiment of civic friendship, in short, transforms what might otherwise be hard and narrow forms of all the virtues. By grounding the disposition to act virtuously on love and disinterested good will towards others as persons with whom

---

[25] Καὶ τῶν δικαίων τὸ μάλιστα φιλικὸν εἶναι δοκεῖ. Some commentators take this to mean that equity (τὸ ἐπιεικές—which Aristotle defines, in effect, at *Nic. Eth.* 1139b11–27 as being guided by the spirit rather than the letter of the law) is especially characteristic of friendship (see Grant and Stewart *ad loc.*; Ernst Hoffman takes this view for granted in "Aristoteles' Philosophie der Freundschaft"). The interpretation I have offered seems to me more natural, however. The main point is in any event an Aristotelian one: see *Nic. Eth.* VIII 9, 1160a3–8.

one shares social life to one's own and their mutual benefit, civic friendship is a necessary supplement to the virtues themselves, since only through it does a person come to have the warmth and the sympathetic attachment to other persons which one rightly demands of a perfectly and fully moral person.

Connected with this, there is a more general reason why Aristotle's conception of civic friendship is important. For although he does not argue the point explicitly for civic friendship, as he does (*Nic. Eth.* IX 9) for personal friendship,[26] it is clear from what I have just said that, on Aristotle's view, civic, and not just personal, friendship is an essential component in the flourishing human life. In order to flourish a person needs the more fully realized forms of the moral virtues that only civic friendship brings. Hence, for Aristotle, to achieve the best possible human life, one must develop sentiments of attachment to others with whom one is joined in a common social life.[27] Equally, of course, as just indicated, Aristotle thinks that no human life is really satisfactory that is not partly structured around close personal relationships founded on mutual knowledge and love. Taken altogether, then, the topic of friendship is of decisive significance for an understanding of Aristotle's moral theory.[28]

SELECTED FURTHER READINGS

Alpern, Kenneth D. "Aristotle on the Friendships of Utility and Pleasure." *Journal of the History of Philosophy* 21 (1983): 303–15.

Annas, Julia. "Plato and Aristotle on Friendship and Altruism." *Mind* 86 (1977): 532–54.

Hadreas, Peter. "Goodwill: Aristotle on the Beginning of Friendship." *Ancient Philosophy* 15 (1995): 393–402.

Kahn, Charles H. "Aristotle and Altruism." *Mind* 90 (1981): 20–40.

Konstan, David. "Greek Friendship." *American Journal of Philology* 117 (1996): 71–94.

Kraut, Richard. *Aristotle on the Human Good*, chapter 2. Princeton: Princeton University Press, 1989.

Price, A.W. *Love and Friendship in Plato and Aristotle*. Oxford: Clarendon Press, 1989.

(See also the Selected Further Readings for Chapter 15.)

[26] See Chapter 15 below, "Friendship and the Good in Aristotle," for a discussion of these arguments.

[27] It is essential to bear this in mind when reading and assessing Aristotle's theory of what a moral virtue is and how it is acquired in book II of the *Nic. Eth.* His account of the moral virtues as dispositions to feel and act in certain ways, and his theory of moral training through repeated practice, are developed largely in abstraction from their connection with these aspects of friendship. One can only form a full conception of Aristotle's theory of the virtues and of moral development by supplementing the book II account with the relevant portions of his theory of friendship.

[28] I wish to thank Richard Kraut, G. J. Massey, Alexander Nehamas, Mae Smethurst, and Charles M. Young for their comments on earlier versions of this chapter.

CHAPTER FIFTEEN

Friendship and the Good in Aristotle

IF THE NUMBER of published discussions is a fair measure, the two books of the *Nicomachean Ethics* devoted to friendship (*philia*) have not much engaged the attention of philosophers and philosophical scholars. Yet such neglect is not easily justifiable. For both in his account of what friendship is and in the various considerations he brings to bear to show what is good about friendship, Aristotle displays psychological subtlety and analytical ingenuity of an unusually high order, even for him. In this chapter I hope to show this for Aristotle's views on the value of friendship, by discussing his principal arguments in the *Nicomachean Ethics* and elsewhere bearing on this topic.[1]

I

In the *Nicomachean Ethics* Aristotle faces the question of the value of friendship in IX 9; but before we consider his answer, it is important to be clear exactly what question he means to be asking. On Aristotle's theory of the good, there is a distinction to be drawn between what is good absolutely and without qualification (good "by nature" he sometimes calls it) and what is good for a particular person or class of persons. A thing is good absolutely if it is good for human beings as such, taken in abstraction from special and contingent peculiarities of particular persons: these peculiarities may provide additional interests, needs, and wants, and on the basis of them one can speak of additional, possibly divergent, things as good for this or that particular person. Hence in asking whether friendship is a good thing, and what the good of it is, Aristotle neglects the question whether, and how, it may be good for special classes of person (bad or weak or mediocre people, for example, of one kind or another). He wants to know instead whether it is a good for human beings, as such. Now the morally good, flourishing person is a perfect human being, leading the perfect human life; so anything that is good for human beings as such (that is, good without qualification) will necessarily be good for him. So Aristotle's inquiry into the value of friendship takes the form of seeking an answer to the question whether or not a flourishing person, the perfect human being, will have any need of friends (ἀμφισβητεῖται δὲ καὶ περὶ τὸν εὐδαίμονα εἰ δεήσεται φίλων ἢ μή, *Nic. Eth.* IX 9, 1169b23–24).

---

[1] For a treatment of Aristotle's theory of what friendship is, see Chapter 14 above, "Aristotle on the Forms of Friendship."

This question itself is open to two sorts of misunderstanding. One of these Aristotle himself points out. To speak of someone's need for friends might be taken to imply some deficiency or defect in him and his mode of living—as if some essential element of his own good would be lacking to him unless he had friends to acquire or provide this for him. And of course to flourish is to be already leading a perfect, completely fulfilled life, so that, understood in this way, a flourishing person can have no *need* for friends. Since his life is already, *ex hypothesi*, perfectly complete he cannot, as Aristotle puts it, need any adventitious (*epeisakton*) pleasure (or other good) as a means of improving his condition (1169b23–28). When Aristotle asks, then, whether a flourishing person needs friends, he is inquiring whether the having of friends is a necessary constituent of a flourishing life—not whether friends are needed as a means of improving a life that was already flourishing.

In the second place, it is important to emphasize that the question to be pressed concerns the value to a person of his *having* friends. That is, one wants to be given reasons for believing that, so to say, anyone who sets out to design for himself a life that shall be a flourishing one, ought to arrange things so that he forms friendships—so that he becomes attached to certain people in ways that are characteristic of friendship, spends time with them, does them services out of unself-interested good will, and so on.[2] It seems clear that this is the question that Aristotle means to be asking in *Nic. Eth.* IX 9 (and in the corresponding passage of the *Eudemian Ethics*, VII 12, 1244b1–1245b19). At any rate it is possible, as I shall argue below, to discern in this chapter two quite profound, mutually independent attempts to answer this question, so understood.

Unfortunately, however, the largest part of Aristotle's response in the *Nic. Eth.* (the long argument beginning at 1170a13, honorifically described as the way people who consider the question "more scientifically"—*phusikōteron*—will answer it) is hard to follow unless it is construed as answering a different question. The question seems to have become this: what need has a flourishing person for *his* friends?[3] That is, on the assumption that he will form friendships in the first place, the question Aristotle discusses is why he will need or want to do things for them or with them, what use he will have for them, and why. Why will he not simply pay them no special heed? Obviously this is not a very interesting question, nor particularly difficult to answer. Given what being someone's friend means, if one assumes that a person has made friends with someone else, it follows that he has

---

[2] For these (and other) essential conditions of friendship, see Chapter 14, sect. I.

[3] The same contrast is found in the *Eudemian Ethics*. The topic is introduced (1244b2–3) as follows: ἀπορήσειε γὰρ ἄν τις πότερον, εἴ τις εἴη κατὰ πάντα αὐτάρκης, ἔσται τούτῳ φίλος. Plainly, this question addresses itself to the need of the flourishing man to have friends in the first place. Yet here too, when he comes round to answering his question (b21ff.) Aristotle apparently shifts his ground, and discusses instead why the man who has friends will spend time with them, etc.

come to have certain psychological propensities: he likes the other person, wishes him well, wants to help him when he is in need, wants to spend time with him; and so on. So of course he will have many uses for his friend: the friend will be needed in order for all these various desires to be fulfilled. Having these desires, his life will be defective unless he is able to satisfy them by engaging in the activities characteristic of friends; naturally, then, such a person will need his friends.

I take it, then, that a flourishing person's need for friends, understood as his need for *his* friends, is very easy to establish. Of course, it is easy to establish this only because in taking the question in this way one begs the more important question why one should suppose a flourishing person would make any friends in the first place. Yet, as I have just indicated, the most promising interpretation of the supposedly more profound argument with which *Nic. Eth.* IX 9 concludes makes Aristotle guilty of taking this easy path to his conclusion. When one cuts through all the complications of a very convoluted argument (Ross sets it out in a series of eleven syllogisms),[4] Aristotle's final and grandest effort, on this interpretation, comes to the following:

> (1) For a good person, life itself is a good and pleasant thing; it is always pleasant to be aware of oneself as possessing good things; therefore, the good person's awareness of himself as being alive is very pleasant and highly desirable to him (1170b1–5).
>
> (2) A man's friend is to him a "second self," so that whatever is good for him as belonging to himself will also be good for him when possessed by his friend (1170b5–8).
>
> (3) Since the good man's life and his awareness of it are pleasant and desirable to him, he will find the life of his "second self" and his awareness of it also pleasant and desirable (1170b8–10).
>
> (4) But he cannot satisfy this desire to be aware of his friend's existence except by living in company with him, so he will need his friend "to live with and share in discussion and thought with—for this is what living together would seem to mean for human beings, and not feeding in the same place, as with cattle" (1170b10–14).[5]

[4] See the footnote to 1170b19 in his translation.

[5] Alternatively, the argument might be interpreted as follows (I state just the main points): Everything that is good by nature is choiceworthy in itself, and everything choiceworthy in itself is worthy of the good man's choice. Furthermore, the good and happy man must possess everything that is worthy of his choice, since without even one of these things his life will be lacking in something it ought to have (cf. 1170b14–19). But association with people who are one's friends is by nature a good thing: this is so because in being aware of a friend and his activities one is, given that friends are "other selves," aware of oneself, and being aware of oneself is admittedly good by nature. Hence it will be worthy of a good man's choice to have a friend, and therefore he must have a friend if his life is to be completely fulfilled and lacking in nothing.

This argument is unsound. First, it is not true that the good person's life will be defective if he lacks any of the things that are good by nature and in themselves. No one can have all

Now it is quite plain that in step (2) of this argument Aristotle simply assumes, altogether without explicit warrant, that a good man will have friends. It is only if one assumes that he *will* have friends that one can apply to him, as Aristotle does in the remainder of the argument, the consequences that flow, or are alleged to flow, from the fact that a friend is to his friend as a second self. If the good man *has* friends, then of course, granted the "second self" thesis, he will take pleasure in being aware of his friend's life, as he also does in being aware of his own, and will want to be near him in order to have this pleasure. This I think is obvious and unobjectionable.[6] But until we are given some independent reason for thinking that the good man will need or want to form friendships in the first place, we are not entitled to assume that he will have the sort of attitude toward any other person which will enable him to get this pleasure and, in consequence, desire this close association. But there is not the slightest hint in this argument, so interpreted, of any reason for thinking *this*.[7]

It might be suggested that Aristotle has in mind (though certainly he does not say this here) that the pleasant self-awareness on which this argument turns is only satisfactorily obtainable through the awareness of a friend and his activities. On that basis one might be able to construct a more plausible-looking argument for Aristotle's conclusion. Thus Stewart:[8]

> In seeing, hearing, walking, etc., a man is conscious of himself—of his own existence. . . . This perception of self, however, would hardly be possible to man if his only objects of experience were his own sensations. . . . [H]is experience of his own actions would be accompanied by only a dim consciousness of a self distinguished from them. But man is not confined to his own actions. He has a "sympathetic consciousness" of the actions of his friend—of actions which are still in a sense "his own" (for his friend is a *heteros autos*), and yet are not in such a way "his own" as to make it difficult to distinguish "himself" from them. . . .

---

the things that are good in themselves; there are too many such things, and of too many distinct types (cf. Cooper, *Reason and Human Good in Aristotle*, pp. 129–30). Card games are good in themselves, but it does not follow that a person who never learns to play cards leads a less than flourishing life for that reason. If having friends truly is necessary to the flourishing life it must, then, be because friends are more than merely good in themselves to have. Secondly, even if it was granted, as perhaps it ought to be, that self-awareness is a sufficiently important good-in-itself to be a compulsory component of the flourishing life, it would still not follow that friends are a compulsory component of this life. To show that, one would have to show that self-awareness is only or best obtainable through the observation of one's friends, and (see below, next paragraph but one) this does not seem true.

[6] Despite the remarks of Hardie, *Aristotle's Ethical Theory*, pp. 331f. It is doubtless true, as Hardie points out, that Aristotle pays no attention in this argument to the fact that, however closely one may be attached to another person, one can never experience his thoughts and actions in just the way one experiences one's own. But it is not clear how this is supposed to matter to Aristotle's argument. It remains true that friends do take interest in and derive pleasure from one another's thoughts and actions, and that the interest they take in them is akin to the interest they take in their own.

[7] Nor is there a hint in this direction in the *EE* argument, 1234b23–1245b9.

[8] *Notes on the Nicomachean Ethics*, p. 392.

In other words—it is in the consciousness of the existence of another that a man becomes truly conscious of himself.

Why, however, should one believe this? No reason is given, and offhand it does not seem true that merely in order to be distinctly conscious of oneself one needs to be aware of other persons first. But even granted that one cannot attain self-consciousness except through consciousness of another person and his actions, it would still not follow that one needs friends for this purpose. Why wouldn't a casual acquaintance do just as well? Stewart describes a psychological process whereby a person, having noted the fairly gross distinction between himself and the actions of another person, is able to make the same distinction, or make it more sharply, in the case of his own actions. I do not see how the step from others' actions to one's own is made any the easier by the fact that the other person in question is a friend; the purely verbal point that, on the "other self" thesis, one can call the actions of a friend "one's own" does not seem to me to add anything to whatever psychological plausibility the process as described without it might seem to have.

In any event, as already noted, Aristotle does not here (or, so far as I can discover, elsewhere) claim the priority of other-awareness to self-awareness. He argues instead from the assumption of robust, pleasant self-consciousness in the good man to the pleasantness of his consciousness of his friend—this latter consciousness is represented, as it were, as an overflow from the good man's self-consciousness, not as something needed to create it in the first place. Interestingly, however, in the chapter of the *Magna Moralia* corresponding to *Nic. Eth.* IX 9 one does find the related point argued for, that *self-knowledge* depends upon knowledge of others:

> Now supposing a man looks upon his friend and marks what he is and what is his character and quality (τί ἐστι καὶ ὁποῖός τις ὁ φίλος); the friend—if we figure a friend of the most intimate sort—will seem to be a kind of second self, as in the common saying "This is my second Heracles." Since, then, it is both a most difficult thing, as some of the sages have said, to attain a knowledge of oneself (τὸ γνῶναι αὑτόν), and also a most pleasant (for to know oneself is pleasant)— now we are not able to see what we are from ourselves (αὑτοὺς ἐξ αὑτῶν . . . θεάσασθαι) (and that we cannot do so is plain from the way in which we blame others without being aware that we do the same things ourselves; and this is the effect of favor or passion, and there are many of us who are blinded by these things so that we judge not aright); as then when we wish to see our own face, we do so by looking into the mirror, in the same way when we wish to know ourselves we can obtain that knowledge by looking at our friend. For the friend is, as we assert, a second self. If, then, it is pleasant to know oneself, and it is not possible to know this without having someone else for a friend, the self-sufficing man will require friendship in order to know himself (1213a10–26).[9]

[9] Translated by Stock, except for the first sentence, which is taken from Armstrong's translation.

It should strike one immediately that the focal point of this argument is self-knowledge and not, as in our *Nic. Eth.* passage, self-consciousness. Thus in the *Nic. Eth.* we find *to aisthanesthai hautou*, 1170b9, with repeated use of *aisthanesthai* and its derivatives throughout the argument, whereas in the *MM aisthanesthai* and its derivatives are wholly lacking, and we find instead *to hauton gnōnai*, 1213a15, 23, *eidenai* a16, 25, *gnōrizein* a23, 16. Nor are these mere stylistic variants: one can be conscious of one's self as an entity active in one's affairs even without knowing very fully or explicitly what kind of person one is, whereas self-knowledge as presented in the *MM* argument is precisely knowledge of one's character and qualities, motives, and abilities. No doubt this kind of self-knowledge presupposes self-consciousness, but it is plainly not the same thing. The *MM* is arguing not that friendship is a necessary prerequisite to mere self-consciousness, but that it is necessary for self-knowledge.

One seems forced, then, to regard the "more scientific" argument of the *Nic. Eth.* as abortive.[10] The argument from the *MM*, however, seems more promising. Self-knowledge is certainly a more complex matter than mere self-consciousness, and the idea that it depends upon knowledge of others might strike one as plausible and important. But this argument, too, has its difficulties. First, how, exactly, is knowledge of others supposed to make possible self-knowledge? And, even more, why does self-knowledge (at any rate for the good and flourishing person) depend upon knowledge of one's friends—why wouldn't enemies or casual acquaintances do as well? Finally, it is not enough merely to say, as this text does, that self-knowledge is pleasant; for the argument to be sound, self-knowledge must be actually indispensable to the good and flourishing person. But is it?

To take the last point first: It is certainly plausible to hold, and Aristotle presupposes throughout, that a person's life could not be called flourishing unless, in addition to leading the sort of life that is as a matter of fact the best (doing acts of kindness and courage and so on) he knew what sort of life he was leading and chose it partly for that reason. Human flourishing, in short, does not consist merely in conformity to natural principles, but requires self-knowledge and conscious self-affirmation. Self-knowledge is thus an essential part of what it is to flourish.[11] As such it is an extremely

---

[10] Thus I concur with Gauthier in his judgment that "all this argumentation, which claims to be more profound but is only more tortuous, stops short," p. 693. Our reasons for this conclusion are, however, not the same.

[11] It should be borne in mind here and in what follows that having a good character, on Aristotle's theory, requires not merely correct practical *judgments* (having a certain reasoned conception of how one ought to live) but also, and even more, having this conception embedded in one's desires and thereby making it effective in one's actions. Thus to know one is virtuous requires knowing (1) what the desires are that in fact motivate one's actions, and (2) that these desires depend upon the same scheme of ends as one's reasoned conception defines for one's life. And while it may not be hard to know what one's considered view of how to live is, and even that this view is the correct one, it is quite another, and much more difficult, thing to know what conception of how to live is embodied in the desires that actually motivate one's

pleasant thing, and this is perhaps why in our text so much emphasis is laid on its pleasantness. But however that may be, there is no difficulty in granting on general Aristotelian grounds the indispensability of self-knowledge that the *MM* argument needs.

But how is self-knowledge to be attained? Notoriously, people tend to notice faults in others that they overlook in themselves; and they are equally inclined to attribute to themselves nonexistent virtues. Thus there is a double tendency to deny the presence in oneself of what one recognizes in others as faults, and to claim for oneself virtues that one does not really have at all. These threats to one's objectivity must be reckoned with by everyone, the person who in fact possesses all the good qualities of character and intellect and no bad ones no less than other people. To be sure, the qualities in himself he thinks virtuous are so, and he has no faults; but how is he to be sure that he is not deceiving himself in thinking these things, as he must be if he is to *know* what he is like? It is plausible to suggest, as our text does, that mistakes of this kind are not so apt to occur where one is observing another person and his life; here the facts, both about what are faults and what are virtues, are more likely, at least, to speak for themselves. But that just points to the problem: how attain the same objectivity about oneself that is so comparatively less difficult about others?

This is where friendship is supposed to come in. At least in friendships of the best sort, where the parties love one another for their characters, and not merely because they enjoy or profit from one another's company, intimacy (it is alleged) bespeaks affinity: my friend is, in the *MM*'s striking phrase, a second me (*toioutos hoios heteros einai egō*, 1213a12), myself all over again. Now no doubt the sense of kinship among friends, even among character-friends, can be exaggerated. Some people are certainly drawn together partly by the presence of character-traits in the one that the other lacks. Even in such cases, however, it seems reasonable to think that there must be a strong underlying similarity of character and views, and that this similarity, intuitively felt by each in the other, forms an important part of the bond between them. In any event, on Aristotle's theory (compare 1156b7–8) the perfect friendship is one where the parties are fully good persons who are alike in character. If one supposes that in this perfect character-friendship, as in other lesser ones, the friends may feel a sense of their own kinship without necessarily knowing antecedently, on both sides, in what their similarity consists, then such a friendship could well serve as the needed bridge by which to convert objectivity about others into objectivity about oneself. For knowing intuitively that he and his friend are alike in character, such a person could, by studying his friend's character, come to know his own. Here the presumption is that even an intimate friend

---

actions. In any event, it is essential to keep in mind that the self-knowledge required for flourishing is knowledge of what actually motivates one's actions, not just of what intellectualized theory of living one is prepared to defend.

remains distinct enough to be studied objectively; yet, because one intuitively knows oneself to be fundamentally the same in character as he is, one obtains through him an objective view of oneself. In the *MM*'s image, one recognizes the quality of one's own character and one's own life by seeing it reflected, as in a mirror, in one's friend.[12]

This is the nub of the argument. It is certainly ingenious, but is it cogent? The principal weaknesses would seem to be two. First, one might doubt whether, if, as seems true, people tend to be biased in favor of themselves and blind to their own faults, they are any less so where those with whom they are intimate are concerned. And secondly one might feel uneasy about the weight apparently being laid on the effectiveness and reliability of one's intuitive sense of kinship with another person. Plainly the argument only works if one can justifiably have more initial confidence in these feelings than in one's own unaided attempts to judge the quality of one's life and character. But however difficult the latter may be, is one any less open to deception through the former?

Although these are genuine doubts, not easily allayed, I think the argument nonetheless contains considerable force. For it must be admitted that self-knowledge is, under any conditions, an extremely precarious accomplishment. Neither this nor any other argument is likely to show the way to an absolutely assured knowledge of what one is really like, proof against all possible doubt. The question is just whether character-friendship provides the best means available to a human being for arriving at as secure a knowledge of his own life and character as such a creature can manage. Considered in this light I think this argument has a certain weight. For it does seem fair to believe that objectivity about our friends is *more* securely attained than objectivity directly about ourselves. And the reliance we are being invited to place on our intuitive feelings of kinship with others is not, after all, either unchecked or unlimited. For it is the sense of kinship as it grows up, deepens, and sustains itself within close and prolonged association that the argument relies on. And it does seem right to trust such tried and tested

---

[12] For the theme of self-knowledge through examination of a reflection of the self in the mirror of another self, see Plato, *Alcibiades*, 132c–133c. This passage may be the source of the *Magna Moralia*'s analogy. In explicating the *MM*'s use of the analogy, I have built especially on two features emphasized in the text. First, the good man is represented as looking at another person and his life in order to see a reflection of himself. And second, by observing this person's life he sees clearly what his own life is actually like: one cannot see what one is from oneself (1213a16), but one can see this, i.e., one can overcome this bias, by looking to another who is one's friend. The author plainly is not saying that one evades the effects of bias by trying to find out by observing from someone's behavior towards oneself what his opinion of one is. It is by observing *his* personal qualities, not by guessing his judgment of one's own, that one receives the sort of confirmation that is at issue here. And it is impossible to see how this can be supposed to happen unless, as in my expansion, one takes the knowledge acquired in looking at the "mirror" and refers it back to oneself: knowing that this other person has the same or very similar qualities to oneself (this follows from his being a true friend, one's "other self), and having observed that his character is virtuous, one now knows that one's own personal qualities are virtuous as well.

feelings. They are not "*mere* feelings" but are developed through long experience both of the other person and of oneself. This is, indeed, one reason why knowledge of one's friends might make self-knowledge possible where knowledge of a mere acquaintance, however detailed, would not: the sense of affinity, if it existed at all, could not be relied upon in this latter case, since it would not be based on prolonged and deep familiarity with him.

On the other hand, while granting some weight to the considerations advanced here, one may well feel that this argument hardly exhausts the sources of self-knowledge, or even the most important ways in which friendship might help to advance it. Still, the recognition, which lies at the center of this argument, of the social bases of a secure self-concept and of the role intimacy plays in providing the means to this, is a notable achievement.

In any event, it deserves emphasis that this argument from the *Magna Moralia*, unlike the professedly more profound argument from *Nic. Eth.* IX 9 examined above, does give reasons, however strong or weak, why one ought in designing one's life to make explicit provision for friendships. It would be wrong, of course, to conclude that in the *Nicomachean Ethics* Aristotle argues only ineffectively for this conclusion. For there are other arguments in *Nic. Eth.* IX 9 and one of them (1169b28–1170a4), though certainly not without obscurities of its own, has pronounced affinities to the *MM* argument just examined:

> For at the outset it was said that flourishing is an activity, and an activity clearly exists as something continuous and is not possessed like a piece of property. If flourishing consists in living and being active, and the activity of a good person is good and pleasant in itself, as was said at the outset, and what is peculiarly one's own is pleasant, and we can study (*theōrein*) our neighbors better than ourselves and their actions better than those that are peculiarly our own, and the actions of good persons who are their friends are pleasant to good people (for they are characterized by both the natural marks of pleasantness)—if so, then the fully flourishing person will need friends of this kind, given that he chooses (*prohaireitai*) to study (*theōrein*) actions that are good and peculiarly his own, and the actions of the good person who is his friend are of this kind.

Here, as in the *MM* passage, we find two principal claims: that the good and flourishing man wants to study (*theōrein*, 1169b33, 1170a2; *theasasthai*, 1213a16) good actions, and that one cannot, or cannot so easily, study one's own actions as those of another.[13] But why does the good person have

---

[13] I translate θεωρεῖν here as "study" (instead of "see" or "observe" or "contemplate") in order to make it clear that Aristotle is saying something much stronger here than merely that the good man wants to be aware of good actions and takes pleasure in that. In this context θεωρεῖν is no mere equivalent of αἰσθάνεσθαι; as often in Aristotle, even where it implies the use of the senses, the word carries overtones of concentrated study, of the sort involved in theoretical knowledge (its other principal meaning in Aristotle). So neither of the two central claims of this argument is found in the later argument at 1170a13–b19; nor, for the same reason, is the further claim made here, that the good man enjoys (i.e., enjoys studying) the

reason to want to study good actions? Here the *Nic. Eth.* is silent. This gap in the argument can, however, naturally be filled in from the *MM*: it is because, for reasons we have already noted, the self-knowledge that is a prerequisite of flourishing can hardly be attained by other means. And, at the same time, it is clear, as it would not otherwise be, why the other person whose actions these are must be an intimate and not merely a casual acquaintance. If I am right, then, this passage of the *Nicomachean Ethics* is intended to convey essentially the same argument in favor of friendship as we find set out in full in the *Magna Moralia*. The claim, here again, seems to be that it is only or best in character-friendship that one can come to know oneself—to know the objective quality of one's own actions, character and life.

II

A second argument, independent of this one, follows in the *Nic. Eth.* immediately after the passage just quoted. At 1170a4–11 we read:

> Further, people think a flourishing person should live pleasantly. Now life is hard for a solitary person: for it is not easy to be continuously active apart by oneself, but this is easier together with others and towards them. So, [in living with others] his activity, which is pleasant in itself, will be more continuous, as it ought to be for a fully flourishing person (for the good man, *qua* good, takes pleasure in morally virtuous actions and dislikes vicious ones, just as a musician enjoys beautiful melodies and is pained by bad ones).[14]

Aristotle's central claim here is that living in isolation causes one to be less continuously active at the things one cares most about than is consistent with leading a flourishing life. By contrast, he claims, one can be more continuously active at these pursuits if one engages in them together with others, by which he clearly means not just living in their company—sitting by the side of others, as it were, but absorbed in one's own private pursuits[15]—but making one's fundamental life activities themselves activities

---

good actions of his friend, equivalent to the later claim that he enjoys (i.e., enjoys perceiving) them. If *MM* 1213a10–26 corresponds to anything in *Nic. Eth.* IX 9 it must be to 1169b28–1170a4; certainly not to 1170a13ff.

[14] I take it that the clause in parentheses (ὁ γὰρ σπουδαῖος . . . λυπεῖται) is meant to explain why one should expect the morally good person to be continuously active. A morally good person enjoys virtuous action and (cf. 1175a30–36, b13–16) what one enjoys doing one tends to keep on doing; hence a virtuous person should tend to be continuously active when engaged in virtuous pursuits. But, as Aristotle has just pointed out, a solitary person cannot manage to be continuously active at anything. It follows that a solitary person does not really enjoy anything very much. Hence the principle that virtuous action is pleasant for the virtuous person must be understood as carrying with it the tacit assumption that such persons live their lives in social union with others.

[15] Cf. 1170b10–14: "[The flourishing person] needs, therefore, to be conscious of his friend's existence, and this would come about in their living together and sharing in discussion and thought: for this would seem to be what living together means for human beings, and not, as

shared in common with others: μεθ' ἑτέρων δὲ καὶ πρὸς ἄλλους, ῥᾷον (1170a6). Why should there be this difference in continuity of activity between a life made up of shared and a life made up of purely private activities? Aristotle does not say. Several things might be in his mind. Perhaps in a solitary life, where one has to see to all one's needs by oneself and cannot rely on others, or the products of others' work, one is simply forced to be too busy too much of the time at menial and uninteresting things for one to be free to concentrate uninterruptedly on one's most cherished pursuits. But, though this might well be true, it is hard then to see the point of Aristotle's proposed remedy: one does not have to *share* one's activities with anyone in order to have the benefits of others' assistance. Again, it might be suggested that if one tries to complete one's favorite projects all on one's own it may simply require physical exertions of such magnitude that one has to take many pauses for rest, thus rendering one's activities intermittent and discontinuous.[16] But again this cannot be all that Aristotle has in mind, since the natural remedy here would be to induce someone else to cooperate by making his skills, interests, and so on, available for one's private purposes, perhaps in return for occasional assistance from oneself: sharing one's projects with anyone else would surely not be necessary. In order to give Aristotle a reasonably plausible case for the preferability of a life of shared activities one must, then, at least supplement these points. A natural suggestion is this: Aristotle may be thinking that living in isolation causes one to lose the capacity to be actively interested in things. Even if the activity that delights one most is something that can be enjoyed by a solitary person (as is true of most intellectual pursuits), it tends not to be pursued with freshness and interest by someone living cut off from others. One tends to become apathetic and inactive without the stimulation and support which others, especially those whom one likes and esteems, provide by sharing one's goals and interests. If so, then one can see why Aristotle claims a special and essential place in any truly satisfactory human life for the sort of shared activities that only friendship makes possible: it will only, or especially, be through such activities that a human being finds his life continuously interesting and pleasurable.

Now whether or not this is what Aristotle has in mind, it is at any rate an interesting idea, and one that merits quite extensive consideration. I shall not attempt such a full-scale treatment here; still, the following points should be noted.[17]

First, by "shared activities" here I mean (and understand Aristotle to have in mind) activities that are performed by two or more persons together, and not just activities that are common to more than one person, or mutually

---

for cattle, feeding in the same place." Evidently the solitariness Aristotle finds so debilitating is at least as much a matter of psychological as of physical isolation.

[16] I owe this suggestion to Richard Kraut.

[17] Throughout the discussion which follows I am indebted to Annette C. Baier's "Intention, Practical Knowledge and Representation," and to conversations with her.

known to several persons to be common to them all. Thus two persons might be solitaire-devotees, and so have a common interest, and each might know of the other's attachment to the game, so that one could speak of their mutual interest in solitaire; but neither of these conditions is sufficient to make their attachment to the game count as a shared interest (nor of course would their solitaire games count as shared activities), for the reason that solitaire is not a game that they play together. The playing of the game is not something in which they jointly share. Now some activities are shared activities, in this sense, by one sort of necessity or another. Thus perhaps games like baseball and tennis are so defined by their rules that they cannot be played at all unless some specific number of persons, greater than one, is actively involved. In other cases, such as playing a string quartet, or doing many industrial and agricultural jobs, the work will normally have to be done together by more than one person, simply because of the physical limitations of the human body. Many activities, however, that can perfectly well be performed by single individuals in private (so far, at any rate, as the definition of what is being done, and physical capabilities, go) can also be shared. One can worship in private, or together with others; solve a mathematical problem, or write a book, alone or jointly; bathe by oneself or in company. Artistic and cultural activities are an especially interesting case. Here many activities that, narrowly considered, might seem to be personal and private are nonetheless engaged in by those who do them in such a way as to make them shared. Thus even although a single author may be solely responsible for a scholarly article, he presumably wrote it as a contribution to an ongoing subject of study to which he thinks of himself as attached jointly with others. His attitudes to his own work may be construed on the model of a game in which there are various positions, occupied from time to time by different persons, linked together by a common set of rules and shared purposes. The individual player's move, looked at in isolation, may well seem quite private to himself, but given the system of positions, rules, purposes, and so on, it is thought of by him as a contribution to the game in all the moves of which all the players share. Thus the individual author's acts of writing can be seen as part of a shared activity, namely the shared activity of advancing the discovery of the truth in the subject in question. In general, where an activity is shared one finds the following features: (1) there is a shared, and mutually known, commitment to some goal (whether something to be produced or something constitutive of the activity itself), (2) there is a mutual understanding of the particular role to be played by different persons in the pursuit of this common goal, and (3), within the framework of mutual knowledge and commitment, each agrees to do, and in general does do, his share in the common effort.

What then is there about shared activities that might make Aristotle think them in general more continuously interesting and enjoyable, in comparison with strictly private pursuits? Two things come to mind. First, if others, especially people one likes or admires, share with one in a commitment to the goal which gives the activity its sense, one's own perception of the worth or value of the activity will be enhanced and thereby one will engage in it with more interest and pleasure; if others, too, find a thing worth doing, they will provide at least a welcome confirmation of one's own attitudes. Of course, it is possible to know that others agree in finding a thing worth doing even although each engages in it in a completely private way, so that if it is a good thing to know one's own views confirmed by the experiences of others, this good is available even if one does not share one's activities with anyone. On the other hand, what is in question here is not a person's mere abstract knowledge that something is valuable and worthwhile but his actual direct experience of it *as* worthwhile. And it must not be over-looked that it is possible to know on sufficient grounds that something is good, but be unable to actually experience it as such; and it is the latter that is crucial to the enjoyment of one's own life. In a shared activity one knows of the commitment of others to the goodness of the activity in no mere abstract theoretical way. It is concrete and immediate. Hence it is only through participation in such activities that the confirmatory knowledge of others' evaluations is likely to be both constantly and directly present to one's consciousness. It seems not unreasonable to suggest, then, that the sort of confirmation of the worth of one's endeavors and pursuits that is so valuable, perhaps necessary, to a human being if he is to sustain his interests is hardly available outside of the context of a shared activity.

Secondly, where an activity is shared each of the participants finds himself engaged in a number of different ways and at a number of different points: to be sure, he participates directly only in the parts of the enterprise to which it falls to himself to contribute, but indirectly he is, in principle, involved in every stage of the process, whoever the direct agent may be. What others do as their share of the joint activity he experiences as his doing as well, insofar as he is a member of the group, and it is the group that is the agent primarily at work in it. Admittedly, in not all shared activities does every participant retain a very full sense of his own involvement in all the varied operations that go to make it up; but it follows from my characterization above of shared activities that in some degree this sense of extended participation must be present in any person who conceives of himself as engaging with others in a joint activity. One's involvement in what one is doing is thus much broader in a shared activity than it is in the case of a completely private one: there are, so to speak, many more places and types of contact with a shared activity than there can be for a private one. In a shared activity one's enjoyment, and so one's interest in what one is doing, is not limited just to what one directly does oneself. This fact has two consequences that support Aristotle's claims for shared activities. First, insofar as the agent sees his own personal activity as a contribution to a larger whole, to which he is attached and in which he is interested also through the contributions of others, the sources of his continued interest in what he directly does are much expanded. His multiple involvements in the whole activity naturally enhance the interest which he can take in the activities that he personally undertakes as a participant in the larger group activity. He is thus much more likely to sustain his interest in his own personal doings and to get pleasure continuously from them. Imagine, for example, someone who enjoys mathematics as a purely private exercise. Numerical relationships fascinate him, and he wants to spend a lot of time exploring them. Such a person is likely to neglect this pursuit after a time, and be only intermittently active at it; but if he comes to regard his activity as part of a larger group activity—so that he takes an interest not just in his own but also in others' research—he will be much more capable of sustaining his active interest in his own work because of its connection with the group activity of which he now sees it as part and in which he also has an interest. The tendency of anything long continued to become boring is thus avoided, to some extent, by finding in it additional things to be interested in. Secondly, insofar as he participates at second hand in the doings of others engaged with him in the shared activity he can be said to be active—indirectly— whenever and wherever any of the group is at work. In this sense one could say that a participant of a group activity is active even when he is not himself directly making any contribution. So, if one takes into account the activities that a participant is indirectly sharing in, one can say that those who engage in shared activities will continue to be active even when they are not directly active at all—that is, not active at all in the only way in which one can be active in a purely private pursuit.

Now I do not claim that these considerations were actually in Aristotle's mind when he said that to be continuously active is easier with others and towards others than in isolation. His failure to explain why he held this view makes it impossible to say with certainty what his reasons were. On the other hand, it is hard to imagine what he could have meant if he did not have in mind at least some of these points. In any event I think the account I have just given does show that Aristotle's view, whatever exactly he may have rested it on, is sound. Shared activities are especially valuable for any human being since they, more than purely private activities, enable one to be continuously and happily engaged in things. This is so, in sum, for three reasons: (1) they provide one with an immediate and continuing sense that what one finds interesting and worthwhile is really so, since the experience of others is seen to agree with one's own in this respect; (2) they enhance one's attachment to and interest in one's own personal, direct activities by putting them within the context of a broader group activity which is itself a source of pleasure and interest; and (3) they expand the scope of one's activity by enabling one to participate, through membership in a group of jointly active persons, in the actions of others. It is reasonable, I think, to assume that human nature is inherently such that no human being can provide entirely from within himself the sources of his interest and pleasure in his life and the activities that make it up. Nothing can be made, as it were, automatically and continuously interesting for any human being, just because of what *it* is like. A human being has to invest things with his interest, by responding in appropriate ways to them; but these responses, though no doubt subjective, are not for that reason under one's own control. They depend in part upon the firm and continued sense of the value of what one is doing and, as Aristotle's argument plausibly suggests, this can hardly be secured except through the sense that others agree with one in this. If this is so, then I think one is entitled to infer, with Aristotle, that no life can be satisfactory for a human being that does not make explicit provision for a considerable range of activities shared with others. Only by merging one's activities and interests with those of others can the inherent fragility of any human being's interests be overcome.

Now this is obviously an extremely important conclusion to reach. But Aristotle must go even further, and hold, not just that shared activities, but that activities shared with friends, are a necessary ingredient in the flourishing human life, if he is to derive from his emphasis on the greater continuousness of shared activity a defense of friendship. For even if, as I have implied, the benefits to be derived from shared activities are in many cases dependent on one's esteeming or respecting the judgment of one's fellow participants, this does not mean they must be one's friends. At any rate one does not need to have character-friendship, which is the fundamental kind and the kind which Aristotle wishes to defend, with those with whom one enjoys playing games, or performing music, or, notoriously, having sex. On the other hand, it is clear enough that the satisfactions that derive from shared activity are especially needed in connection with those activities, whatever they may be, that are most central to a person's life and which contribute most decisively to his flourishing, as he himself conceives it. For here the flagging of one's commitments and interests will be particularly debilitating; here more than anywhere else one needs the confirmatory sense that others too share one's convictions about which activities are worthwhile, and the other benefits of sharing pointed out above. Now on Aristotle's theory of *eudaimonia*, the flourishing human life consists essentially of morally and intellectually excellent activities. So the flourishing person will have a special need to share *these* activities, if his own interests in life are to be securely and deeply anchored. But according to the account of shared activities that I have given, it is an essential condition of a shared activity that the parties to it should not just be committed to the goal or goals that give the activity its sense, but should know about each other that they share this commitment. This requirement of mutual knowledge has substantial consequences where the activities to be shared include morally virtuous ones. For in order to know that someone is genuinely committed to moral values, one must know him and his character pretty closely, since commitment here just is a matter of moral character or its absence. Superficial acquaintance is for this purpose quite insufficient, as it is not where there is question of someone's interest in music or baseball, because genuinely good moral character is what is required and this is not easily distinguished from feigned or half-hearted attachment. So before one can share activities where the common pursuit of moral values is essential to what is to be done, one must come to know, and be known by, the other party or parties quite intimately. But this sort of mutual knowledge is hardly available outside of character-friendship. Hence, a human being cannot have a flourishing life except by having intimate friends to whom he is attached precisely on account of their good qualities of character, and who are similarly attached to him: it is only with such persons that he can share the moral activities that are most central to his life.

It is possible, then, to defend both Aristotle's claim that shared activities are essential to any satisfactory human life, and his implied conviction that true friendship is a necessary context within which at least some of these essential shared activities should take place.

III

I conclude that there are to be found in the Aristotelian Corpus—and, if I am right about the purport of 1169b28ff., in the *Nicomachean Ethics* itself— two interesting and telling arguments to show that true friendship is an essential constituent of a flourishing human life. If my interpretations are correct, Aristotle argues, first, that to know the goodness of one's life, which he reasonably assumes to be a necessary condition of flourishing, one needs to have intimate friends whose lives are similarly good, since one is better able to reach a sound and secure estimate of the quality of a life when it is not one's own. Secondly, he argues that the fundamental moral and intellectual activities that go to make up a flourishing life cannot be continuously engaged in with pleasure and interest, as they must be if the life is to be a flourishing one, unless they are engaged in as parts of shared activities, rather than pursued merely in private; and given the nature of the activities that are in question, this sharing is possible only with intimate friends who are themselves morally good persons.

Three points about these arguments should be noted. First, in a certain way they both emphasize human vulnerability and weakness. If human nature were differently constituted, we might very well be immune to the uncertainties and doubts about ourselves that, according to Aristotle, make friendship such an important thing for a human being. As it is, we cannot, if left each to his own devices, reach a secure estimate of our own moral character; nor by ourselves can we find our lives continuously interesting and enjoyable, because the sense of the value of the activities which make them up is not within the individual's power to bestow. The sense of one's own worth is, for human beings, a group accomplishment. Hence we need each other because as individuals we are not sufficient—psychologically sufficient—to sustain our own lives. For a god things are different; the goodness of the divine activity of contemplation is continuously evident to a god, and he needs no other person or thing to enable him to see this or reassure him that it is so: as Aristotle says in the *Eudemian Ethics*, god is his own good activity, but human good consists in relationship to others (ἡμῖν μὲν τὸ εὖ καθ' ἕτερον, ἐκείνῳ δὲ αὐτὸς αὑτοῦ τὸ εὖ ἐστίν, 1245b18–19). To argue thus the need of human beings for friendship from deficiencies in our psychological makeup both illuminates the nature of friendship and gives what I think is an entirely accurate account of its status in human affairs. Properly understood, nothing in this should be construed as undermining or detracting from the intrinsic goodness, for human beings, of friendly relations with others. For Aristotle's point is that the deficiencies which make friendship such a necessary and valuable thing are inherent in human nature itself. There is no basis in his argument for one to accept one's friendships in a regretful, still less a provisional, spirit—pining away, as it were, for the day when one's deficiencies might be made up and one could live entirely out of one's own resources without having to depend upon others at all. Since the deficiencies in question are essential to being a human being—that is, essential to being what one is, to being oneself—it is irrational to form one's attitudes in the hope of adjustments in these respects. The only reasonable attitude is to accept one's nature as it is and to live accordingly. The arguments we have considered profess to show how and why someone who adopts this attitude will be led to form friendships and to value friendly relations as fundamental and intrinsically good ingredients of the life that is best for himself.[18]

It is worth emphasizing that although in these arguments Aristotle defends the value of friendship only by showing that, for human beings, it is a necessary means to attaining certain broadly valuable psychological benefits, nothing in them commits him to denying that friendship is or involves anything intrinsically valuable. Indeed, in a few passages (1167b31–33 with 1168a5–9, and 1159a25–33), though they are not backed by much in the way of argument, Aristotle insists on the worthwhileness-in-itself of the active expression of love and on the direct pleasure that human beings take in the experience of being loved by others. These remarks are plainly not

---

[18] Of the arguments of *Nicomachean Ethics* IX 9 I have omitted to discuss the three found in 1169b8–22, since these, although they are put forward as supporting the view, which Aristotle himself favors, that a flourishing person needs friends, belong to the setting up of the dialectical problem and are not part of the solution to it. Strictly speaking, Aristotle's defense of his view is to be looked for not in these preparatory remarks, but in the official response which follows. (As usual, some aspects of the preliminary arguments are preserved in the solution.) I have omitted to discuss also the brief argument, which does form part of the solution Aristotle proposes, that by living together as friends good persons sharpen and train their moral sensibility (1170a11–13): this ought to hold only, as indeed its source (Theognis) makes clear, for the association between a young and not fully formed person and someone older and morally more mature. It does not apply to all friendships, nor, apparently, to those that Aristotle wants most especially to defend, the friendships between equally good, fully developed persons.

inconsistent with the arguments we have been examining, since there is no reason why something that is itself intrinsically good should not also be valued for other reasons. In fact, however, I think it is a mistake to see these two trains of thought even as separable, much less as competing, defenses of the place of friendship in a satisfactory human life. For, clearly, it does not follow from the mere fact that the active expression of love is found intrinsically good by human beings that a person who did not form friendships would be lacking something essential to his own good: there are lots of intrinsically good activities and no human life can, in any event, contain them all (see note 5 above). To show that the active expression of love is necessary in any satisfactory human life requires further argument establishing the fundamental importance of *this* intrinsically good activity vis-à-vis others with which it might compete for a place in a person's life. Again, and for the same reason, it does not follow from the fact that people delight in being loved that one who had all the other goods in life would still want and need the love of others. This claim could only be made good by further argument showing why, for human beings constituted as they actually are, *this* experience in particular is indispensable.[19] The arguments we have examined (and, in the *Nic. Eth.*, only these) attempt this essential task—which is why I have focused principally on them. What they do is to characterize friendship from several points of view in such a way as to make it clear why human beings should find friendship and the activities and experiences that constitute it so interesting and valuable, in themselves, as they do. According to Aristotle, we value, and are right to value, friendship so highly because it is only in and through intimate friendship that we can come to know ourselves and to regard our lives constantly as worth living. It must be granted, of course, that someone who was so constituted that he could achieve these results without forming friendships, as Aristotle plausibly thinks no actual human being could, would have been given no strong reason to form them; he would at most have been told that the active expression of love is something intrinsically good and, as we have seen, this is no more than a prima facie, defeasible reason to form friendships. Hence anyone who thinks that, nonetheless, such a friendless person would be leading a less than fully satisfactory life will not find in Aristotle anything to support his view. It may be that such a view cannot be defended; but even if it can, I think it must be granted that Aristotle's arguments capture an important part of what there is in love and friendship that is so valuable for human beings.

Finally, this emphasis on the psychological benefits of friendship is not at all incompatible with the claim that, necessarily, a friend cares for and

---

[19] Richard Kraut, in "The Importance of Love in Aristotle's Ethics," goes seriously astray in supposing that from these isolated remarks taken by themselves one can construct an adequate defense of the value of friendship (see sect. III of his paper, esp. p. 13, and further remarks at pp. 14, 16, 24). For the reasons noted in the text, they are quite inconclusive.

about another person's good in the same way in which that other person himself does so. If Aristotle is right, the psychological benefits he appeals to are not available to human beings unless one takes up the altruistic attitudes towards others which on his theory are essential to friendship. This is obviously true for the argument that only within the context of a friendship can one establish and maintain active interests that are sufficiently secure and constant so that a continuously active life can be constructed round them. This argument professes to show why one should want to become the sort of person who shares with others, on a basis of equality, his chief interests in life: the life of such a person, Aristotle argues, is more continuously active and interesting to him than anyone's life can be who lives in the sort of psychological isolation that the absence of friendship implies. But I think it is equally, though perhaps less obviously, true for his other argument, from the need for self-knowledge, as well. Admittedly, on this argument the benefit which accrues to a person from being someone else's friend is the firm sense that his own preferred activities are morally good. On the other hand, Aristotle's point is that this sense is only achievable insofar as one first and more distinctly recognizes the moral goodness of the similar life and similar activities of another person. This means that one must regard the association with one's friend, through which one first comes to know him and in which one constantly renews one's knowledge thereafter, as an association with someone who is objectively good and whose life is worthwhile in precisely the same sense as one's own. The motif of the friend as a mirror, which is indeed at best implicit in the *Nicomachean* argument, is not to be interpreted as meaning that on Aristotle's view a flourishing person treats his friend as a mere instrument by which to enhance his own self-esteem. On the contrary, this image implies that his self-esteem only gets the support he seeks insofar as he first has precisely the same esteem for the other person and his life, taken by itself, as he will come to have for himself and his own life. Aristotle's argument, in short, is that *in* loving and valuing the other person for his own sake one becomes able to love and value oneself, and this he offers in explanation and illumination of the fact that a friend loves and values his friend for his own sake, and places a high value on doing so. There is no reduction here of friendship to narrow self-love, nor, properly understood, does the need for self-knowledge empha-sized in Aristotle's argument in any way undermine or render doubtful the recognition of the worth of the other person and his life which we think (and Aristotle emphasizes in his opening account of what friendship is) is essential to any relationship deserving of that name.[20]

[20] I am grateful to Michael Bratman for forcing me to clarify the argument of the last two paragraphs.

I wish to thank Robert H. Bolton, G. J. Massey, Alexander Nehamas, Mae Smethurst, and Charles M. Young for helpful comments on an early draft of this chapter, and Richard Kraut for his forthright criticisms of a version of it read at a University of Minnesota conference on Aristotle's ethics held in March 1976.

SELECTED FURTHER READINGS

Millgram, Elijah. "Aristotle on Making Other Selves." *Canadian Journal of Philosophy* 17 (1987): 361–76.

O'Connor, D. K. "Two Ideals of Friendship." *History of Philosophy Quarterly* 7 (1990): 109–22.

Schoeman, Ferdinand D. "Aristotle on the Good of Friendship." *Australasian Journal of Philosophy* 63 (1985): 269–82.

Schollmeier, Paul. "An Aristotelian Motivation for Good Friendship." *Revue de Métaphysique et de Morale* 91 (1986): 379–88.

Sherman, Nancy. "Aristotle on Friendship and the Shared Life." *Philosophy and Phenomenological Research* 47 (1987): 589–613.

Schroeder, D. N. "Aristotle on the Good of Virtue-Friendship." *History of Political Thought* 13 (1992): 203–18.

(See also the Selected Further Readings for Chapter 14.)

CHAPTER SIXTEEN

Political Animals and Civic Friendship

ONE OF THE MOST fundamental propositions of both Aristotle's ethical and his political theory is his claim that by its *nature* the human being is a *politikon zōion*—to use the conventional translation, a "political animal," or, perhaps a bit less misleadingly, an animal that lives in cities. This proposition plays an important role in the argument of *Nicomachean Ethics* I. It is cited at I 7, 1097b11 as the ground for holding that whatever a human being's happiness or flourishing ultimately turns out to consist in, it must be something that suffices not just for his own individual good but also somehow includes the good of his family, his friends and his fellow-citizens.[1] In the second chapter of the *Politics* Aristotle cites it again (at I 2, 1253a2–3), this time as a conclusion drawn from his quasi-genetic account of the constitution of city-states from the union of households into villages and villages into the larger social units called *poleis*.[2] Because households and villages, his argument goes, are indisputably natural forms of organized life for human beings—they make it possible for creatures with the natural limitations of human beings to survive relatively easily and comfortably in their natural environment—so also must cities be, since (whatever else cities do) they certainly make more secure and comfortable the means of livelihood already, but less securely, provided by households and villages. Aristotle recognizes that this does not show that everything that *polis* civilization brings can be justified as answering to needs of human beings that result from natural and unavoidable facts about their physical make-up and the natural circumstances of human life. But, if true, it does show that the sort of life characteristic of human beings in cities is not governed *simply* by arbitrary and optional

[1] Construed literally, what Aristotle says is that the final good (τὸ τέλειον ἀγαθόν) for any individual must be *sufficient* both for his own and for his family's, friends' and fellow-citizens' good. I take it, however, that the weaker connection to these others' goods indicated in my summary is what he intends; the datives in γονεῦσι etc. 1097b9–10 are to be taken only loosely with αὔταρκες (or ἀρκοῦν, understood from αὔταρκες). Significantly, these same key expressions (τέλειον and αὔταρκες) figure prominently in Aristotle's argument for the naturalness of the *polis* in *Politics* I 2: at 1252b28–29 he says the *polis* is the κοινωνία τέλειος, . . . πάσης ἔχουσα πέρας τῆς αὐταρκείας. The two applications of these key-words are connected: the normal human being's final, and in itself sufficient, good depends essentially upon his willing and active participation in a common life together with others in a city, i.e., in a fully realized, complete human community, which is by itself sufficient to support the *whole* of what human life at its best requires. How this can be so is the main subject of this paper.

[2] I translate πόλις throughout by "city." But it is important to bear in mind that by πόλεις a Greek intended not merely what we call cities, but these taken together with their agricultural hinterland.

conventions originating from nothing more than historical happenstance. To this extent cities can demand the abiding respect of independent-minded persons, as they might not be able to do if they were (and were known to be) merely conventional and not in any way natural habitats for human beings. For, on this view, *some* form of city life is something human beings need if they are to live secure and comfortable lives.

Aristotle goes further, however. In reaching his view that city-life is natural for human beings, he says, in a famous phrase (1252b29–30), that though cities come *into* being for the sake of life (i.e., in order to make possible the secure and comfortable life I just referred to)—*tou zēn heneken*—they *are* (they exist) for the sake of "living well," of a good life (*tou eu zēn heneken*). Whatever exactly Aristotle means by a *good life*, it is clear that he thinks it is not normally available at all, not even in a less secure or less complete form, to human beings except in cities. Later on I say something further about this good life and about how Aristotle intends to link the need for that sort of life to fundamentals of human nature and the natural circumstances of human life. For the moment I simply note that when at the beginning of the *Politics* Aristotle concludes that the city is a natural thing and that the human being is by its *nature* a political animal (1253a1–3), he is thinking not just of the ways in which city-life secures the means of livelihood already provided to a human population by household and village life, but of further supposed goods (whichever ones are included in "living well") that (normally) only life in a city makes possible. That the human being is by nature a political animal means that these further goods as well are ones whose status as goods is supposed to be grounded in human nature.

Now in these two passages of *Nic. Eth.* I and *Pol.* I the context makes quite clear what Aristotle means by "political," when he says that human beings are political animals. With one significant exception the same holds good with all the other passages in the ethical and political treatises where Aristotle mentions the political nature of human beings (*Pol.* I 2, 1253a7–18; III 6, 1278b15–30; *Eudemian Ethics* VII 10, 1242a19–28; *Nic. Eth.* VIII 12, 1162a16–19; IX 9, 1169b16–22). He means that human nature demands that, in general and as a normal thing, human beings live in *cities* of some sort: cities (*poleis*) themselves or citizens (*politai*) are explicitly mentioned in both of our passages and in all but one of the others,[3] and the etymological connection between *politikon* and *polis* is plainly in the forefront of Aristotle's mind in all of them. To be a *politikon* animal is, he plainly means, to be one suited to live in *poleis*. So Ross's rather picturesque overtranslation of *phusei politikon ho anthrōpos* at *Nic. Eth.* I 7, 1097b1 as "man is born for citizenship" does not seriously distort Aristotle's meaning.

But cities are many-faceted social phenomena; moreover, as Aristotle was

---

[3] *Nicomachean Ethics* IX 9, 1169b16–22: but even here ὀθνεῖοι may be foreigners and not just strangers, so that the connection with cities and fellow-citizens will be clear enough by implication.

acutely aware, they can exhibit a variety of social structures and political organizations. Given this complexity and these variations, one wants to know as exactly as possible what it is in and about cities and life in them that Aristotle thinks human beings because of their natures need. What, so to speak, does Aristotle think is essential to city-life as such, that all cities, perhaps with differing degrees of success, give their human inhabitants and that family-life and village-life necessarily do not suffice for? Nothing in the two passages discussed so far addresses this question, particularly when one takes into account "living well," as well as mere "living," as something the city is for. But there are two further passages (one in the *Politics*, the other, perhaps surprisingly, in the *History of Animals*) where Aristotle talks about the political nature of human beings that do offer the beginnings of an answer to our question.

Significantly, in these passages, unlike those from which we began, Aristotle introduces a biological perspective. Speaking from the biological point of view, he is able to say something appropriately concrete about human nature and so to suggest what it is about city-life that humans most fundamentally need. The two passages in question are, first, *Pol.* I 2, 1253a7–18 (the continuation of the passage from *Pol.* I 2 I summarized above). Here Aristotle compares human beings with other (as he calls them) "herding" animals (*agelaia*), such as bees (this is *his* example). Secondly, there is a surprisingly neglected passage near the beginning of the *History of Animals* (I 1) which makes it possible to interpret this *Politics* passage correctly.[4] The *History of Animals* passage runs as follows.[5]

---

[4] If this *History of Animals* passage is less neglected than it formerly was, that is no doubt due to two good recent articles that devote special attention to it: R. G. Mulgan, "Aristotle's Doctrine that Man is a Political Animal"; and W. Kullmann, "Der Mensch als Politisches Lebewesen bei Aristoteles." I have profited from both these discussions, especially Kullmann's. Richard Bodéüs drew my attention to his article "L'Animal politique et l'animal économique," after I had written this part of my paper.

[5] At I 1, 488a2 there seems no doubt that one must bracket καὶ τῶν μοναδικῶν, with Schneider and Peck (I translate Peck's text). If one keeps the manuscript reading, then Aristotle will be saying that some animals that live in large groups *and some animals that live alone* are political, while others in each classification are scattered or dispersed. One might, of course, attempt on Aristotle's behalf to make sense of the idea that some of the μοναδικά animals are nonetheless political. Perhaps some of them live apart most of the year but come together briefly to do some common work; perhaps although the adults of some species live separately from one another the young continue to live with a parent even after they have become able to feed and defend themselves, so that these species satisfy the condition for living "more politically" that Aristotle refers to at VIII 1, 589a1ff.; and other ways of achieving the same result might also occur to one. Aristotle himself, however, offers no encouragement for such speculation. Aside from this passage (i.e., I 1, 488a1–14) the term μοναδικόν apparently occurs only once in the biological works. That is in IX 40, 623b10, where Aristotle introduces a long discussion (chs. 40–43) of bees and other (as he says, 623b7) insects that make a honeycomb. He distinguishes nine γένη of such creatures, six of them ἀγελαῖα and three μοναδικά. The three μοναδικά are two types of σειρήν (not subsequently, nor apparently elsewhere, further described by him) and the βομβύλιος or bumble-bee. To the bumble-bee he devotes a total of one sentence, in ch. 43 (629a30ff.): the bumble-bee gives birth under rocks, right on the ground

There are also the following differences among animals, that depend upon their ways of life and their actions. Of both footed, winged, and swimming animals, some herd together and others live solitarily, while others "dualize." And some of the herding ones are political while others live scattered. Now herding animals

---

(i.e., without having a hive the way the other wax-producers he has described do), and makes an inferior kind of honey. The bumble-bee is manifestly not by Aristotle's criteria a political animal, and there seems no reason to suspect the σειρῆνες differed in this respect. So far, therefore, as anything Aristotle actually says about any particular ones of the μοναδικά animals goes, we have no basis for thinking that *Aristotle* recognized any μοναδικά political species at all.

It seems better, therefore, to suppose that at I 1, 488a2, having distinguished the ἀγελαῖα (the ones that live in large groups, the "herding" ones) from the μοναδικά (those that live alone, the "solitary" ones), Aristotle in fact went on to subdivide the ἀγελαῖα into political and scattered: what he wrote was καὶ τῶν ἀγελαίων τὰ μὲν πολιτικὰ τὰ δὲ σποραδικά ἐστιν. This is confirmed below, 488a8–9, where Aristotle gives his criterion for being political and adds, appropriately if the political are intended as a subgroup of the ἀγελαῖα, that not all ἀγελαῖα satisfy it. Moreover, all the examples he gives of πολιτικά animals are also ἀγελαῖα.

But if this is right, what explains the manuscript corruption? Aristotle has just mentioned that some animals of each of the largest classes he recognizes (the footed, the winged, and the swimming animals) live together in large groups (τὰ μὲν ἀγελαῖα) while others live alone (τὰ δὲ μοναδικά), while yet others "dualize," i.e., (I take it) are sometimes found in herds and sometimes found living alone. After introducing the sub-division here between the political and the scattered or dispersed animals (τὰ μὲν πολιτικὰ τὰ δὲ σποραδικά ἐστιν) he returns to the first division, giving examples of both winged and swimming animals that live in herds (he omits to give examples of footed animals, such as sheep and cattle, presumably because herding footed animals are well known to everyone), and having done that mentions that human beings dualize (488a7). In context, coming immediately after these lists of ἀγελαῖα, it seems most natural to take this as saying that human beings dualize between living in large groups and living alone, i.e., dualize between belonging alongside these others among the herding animals, and not doing so but instead being solitary in life-style. (The alternative is to understand humans as dualizing between being political and being scattered or dispersed, but the intervention of ἀγελαῖα μὲν οὖν . . . ἁμίαι makes this difficult, if not quite impossible. Kullmann's suggestion, p. 432, that humans dualize between being herding and being *scattered* animals can't be right, since it draws one term of the opposition from the pair herding-solitary and the other from the pair political-scattered: it was perhaps awareness of this anomaly that led him to put it forward only with a query.) So Aristotle belatedly gives humankind as an instance of the dualizers mentioned at 488a1–2, the ones that cannot neatly be classed as either herding or solitary animals. Yet in the next sentence but one he classifies human beings as political animals: for animals to be political is, he says, to have as their function (ἔργον) some single common work, which not all herding animals, but only some—human beings, bees, wasps, ants, and cranes—do. Here human beings are counted among the herding animals. And that might seem to contradict their classification as dualizers. In fact, as I argue below, there is no contradiction. But if one thought there was, it is easy to see how the text must be corrected to get rid of it: at 488a2 read καὶ τῶν ἀγελαίων καὶ τῶν μοναδικῶν, thus making the division between political and scattered animals cut through the prior division between herding and solitary animals, so that human beings, all of whom Aristotle implies (488a7) either live in herds or solitarily, are after all included as a group in the larger class (which now becomes the union of the herding and the solitary animals) being divided into the two subgroups, the political and the scattered. In that case, when human beings are classified as political just below, no contradiction results. The human beings, though as a group political in character, can nonetheless dualize between being herding and being solitary animals, because as Aristotle will now have said, some of each of these larger groups are political in character.

are for instance (among the winged animals) the pigeon family, the crane, and the swan (no crook-taloned bird is a herder), and among the swimmers many kinds of fish, for instance those called migrants, the tunny, the pelamys, and the bonito. The human being "dualizes." Political animals are those that have as their function (*ergon*) some single thing that they all do together, and not all the herding animals have that. The human being, the bee, the wasp, the ant, and the crane are political animals. Some of these are under leaders and others are rulerless, for instance the crane and the bee family are under leaders while ants and thousands of others are rulerless. And some of both the herding and the solitary animals have a fixed home while others move from place to place" (I 1, 487b33–488a14).

The gist of the *Politics* passage is that human beings are political animals in a higher degree (*mallon*) than, e.g., bees or cranes or other similarly herding animals because they possess language.[6] Human beings alone have

---

But to make this "correction" betrays a misunderstanding of the way Aristotle employs the notion of "dualizing." He can say that an animal dualizes in some respect (as he says the seal does between being a land-animal and a water-animal because though it has a lung and sleeps and breeds on land it feeds in the sea and spends most of its time there) while nonetheless classifying it as *basically* belonging on one side or the other of the fence in question (as he classifies the seal as basically a water-animal, VI 12, 566b31). A revealing passage for our purposes is *Generation of Animals* IV 4, 772b1–6, where Aristotle says both that human beings dualize between having a single offspring and having several or many and that it is most natural for them to have one only; multiple births, being rare, are caused by excess fluidity and heat in the parents' bodies. So in our passage of *History of Animals* I 1, human beings dualize between living in large groups and solitarily, but the latter arrangement is exceptional and a departure from the norm, so that basically the human being can be classed, as by implication Aristotle goes on to class it, when at 488a10 he says it is a political animal, among the ἀγελαῖα.

Our manuscripts thus result from a misunderstanding of the implications of Aristotle's saying at 488a7 that human beings dualize (between living in herds and living solitarily). That does not in fact count against their being classified as *basically* herding animals, and so does not conflict with the apparent implication of 488a9–10 that, being political animals, human beings live in herds. Hence there was no good reason to alter the text at 488a2, as someone apparently did, to make the political animals something other than a subgroup of the herding ones.

[6] I disagree with Bodéüs, who insists that by calling the human being μᾶλλον πολιτικόν at I 2, 1253a7–8 Aristotle means that human beings have a better claim to the description πολιτικόν than other animals do (so that by implication he would be counting only the human being and not the bee, etc., as a πολιτικὸν ζῷον at all), and not that human beings are more πολιτικόν, πολιτικόν in a higher degree. On Bodéüs's interpretation Aristotle would be taking away from the non-human "political" animals this description that he had given them in the *History of Animals,* in order to avoid the supposed untoward consequence of "masking" under that generic description what is specific to human beings among animals. But the linkage between this *Politics* passage and that from *History of Animals* I 1 is not just close but positive: here again it is with other ἀγελαῖα, including bees, that Aristotle compares human beings, precisely the ones he counted as πολιτικά in *History of Animals*—not with all other animals in general, as would suit Bodéüs's interpretation better. So one cannot reasonably avoid taking Aristotle here to assert that some other herding animals are indeed πολιτικά, but that human beings are πολιτικά in a special and distinctive, more complete way. Given the implicit reference to the classification in *History of Animals* I 1, therefore, μᾶλλον πολιτικόν must be comparative. Compare VIII 1, 589a1. Had Aristotle wanted here to correct what he says in the *History of*

the capacity to conceive of their own and others' long-term and short-term advantage or good, and so to conceive of justice and injustice as well, since (though Aristotle does not say this explicitly here)[7] in general what is just is what is to the *common* advantage or good of some relevant group. Accordingly, they also have language, which is necessary in order for them to communicate these conceptions to one another: nature gives other animals, which are aware only of what is more or less immediately pleasant and painful, as refined a means of communication as they can use, by giving them the ability to call out to one another by barking, chirping, mooing, etc. As a consequence of having language, the kind of work that human beings can do together, in which their being political animals will show itself, is of a much higher order of complexity than that which bees or cranes can manage. Because they can conceive of and communicate their thoughts about their own and others' long-term and future good, and the common good which constitutes justice, human beings can form and maintain households and cities, whereas bees can only have hives and cranes only form elaborate and differentiated migration-schemes.[8] Human beings, then, like bees or cranes, are political animals in what is from the point of view of zoology (though not of course etymology) the fundamental sense of having a work or function that the members of a human group all do together; but because in this case the common work involves maintaining the structure and organization of a *city,* they are political in the further, more literal, sense of being naturally suited to life in cities, to the life of citizens.[9]

Animals, he could easily have written: διότι δὲ πολιτικὸν ὁ ἄνθρωπος μόνον τῶν ἀγελαίων ζῴων, δῆλον.

[7] But see *Nic. Eth.* VIII 9, 1160a13–14; *Pol.* III 6, 1279a17–19; III 12, 1282b16–18; III 13, 1283b35–42.

[8] On bees, see *Hist. An.* V 21–22 and IX 40. Aristotle does not repeat his classification of bees as political, and does not make a point of mentioning any single special work that bees undertake in common. (They cooperate in many different tasks in the hive and outside it that Aristotle does mention, e.g., at IX 40, 627a20ff.) But presumably it is the hive and the differentiated life in it that he has in mind. For cranes see *Hist. An.* IX 10 (again no repetition of the classification as political, and no focus on a single activity undertaken by all in common). Aristotle's distinction toward the end of the *History of Animals* passage quoted in the text between political animals that are "under leaders" and those that are "rulerless" makes it clear that in speaking of "some single thing" the members of a species do together he does not mean something *all* the members of a species cooperate together in doing. He means rather that the political species are naturally found in groups that are defined by the fact that all the members of each group (those, say, which are all under a given "leader") cooperate together in such an activity.

[9] *Hist. An.* VIII 1, 588b30–589a4 (which should be read together with *Gen. An.* III 2, 753a7–17) links the "political" character of a species with its members' intelligence (φρόνησις), on the one hand, and, on the other hand, their tendency to live with and see to the upbringing of their offspring. The *Generation of Animals* passage, while not referring explicitly to any kind of animal as political in nature, does say that the more intelligent animals, which also have better memories, and which concern themselves for a longer period with their offspring's upbringing, come to have συνήθεια καὶ φιλία ("intimacy and attachment," tr. Peck) for them even when fully grown. The suggestion is that greater intelligence in animals naturally shows

There is much of interest in these passages. First of all, as just noted, and surprisingly, when in the *History of Animals* Aristotle classifies the human being together with the bee and the crane, etc., as political animals he does not mean, despite the literal meaning of the word, that all these kinds of animals live in cities (*poleis*). There is no reference anywhere in the passage to cities or to citizenship, as there is in all the other passages from the *Politics* and *Ethics* where the political nature of human beings is alluded to. On the contrary, as he himself explains, the criterion being invoked is whether or not an animal species (only herding animals are in question, naturally) is such that it has an essential work that its members all engage in together (with the differentiation of function that goes along with that). If it does, it counts as "political," if not not, and in that case it gets classified as "scattered." (So by this classification oxen, sheep, and cattle are not political but scattered animals: obviously, being scattered is not a matter of how close to or far apart animals of a species typically stand from one another as they go about their daily business of feeding and so on, but whether what they spend their time doing is something that they have to be together to do, because it is something they do in common, as a community.)

So the fundamental point about the nature of human beings that grounds the biological classification is that humans have the capacity for, and are

---

itself in a more intensive and prolonged relationship between parents (or at least mothers) and offspring; this in turn generates ties of affection and friendship (in effect, what in the human case Aristotle calls family friendship, συγγενικὴ φιλία, *Nic. Eth.* VIII 12, 1161b16ff.); and "political" ties, both for human beings and for other animals are in some way natural extensions of these family ties. (On the connection between family friendship and political friendship, see n.15.)

Although in these passages he makes no mention of a single common work that members of political species, as such, engage in, I assume Aristotle is presupposing, as he says explicitly in *Hist. An.* I 1, that such a common work is the essential mark of a political species. Certainly the emphasis on intelligence fits in very well with this assumption, since the cooperation and differentiation of function involved in such a single work evidently requires a relatively high degree of intelligence. And while rearing broods of offspring to maturity need not involve any work engaged in within a community wider than an immediate family, Aristotle's point seems to be that that kind of cooperative concern is the natural training ground for some more extensive cooperation in which an animal's political nature is more properly exhibited. (This explains why in both passages he seems to take it for granted that the more intelligent, more family-oriented species are all of them herding animals, and not solitary ones: only such could be political in any active sense.)

It is true that Aristotle says at *Gen. An.* III 2, 753a14–15 that birds are less family-oriented than "human beings and certain quadrupeds," and that they don't develop "intimacy and attachment" toward their offspring when grown up. Birds are, accordingly, "less political"— because, I take it, the common work they nonetheless do engage in together, not being grounded in a communal family work, is less extensive. There is no reason to interpret Aristotle in either the *Hist. An.* VIII 1, or the *Gen. An.* III 2 passage as implying that animals like the crane, which engage in a common work but do not show the extended family concern of such *more* political animals as human beings, are not political at all. (In thinking about the implications of these passages about animal intelligence for Aristotle's classification of some animals as political in nature, I have profited from discussions with Jean-Louis Labarrière and from reading his paper on "La phronesis animale.")

regularly found, taking part in cooperative activities involving differentiation of function. This important point is something that the passages of the ethical treatises and the *Politics* that I first cited, where the political nature of human beings is linked simply to their fitness for life in cities, do not bring clearly to light. What we learn from the *History of Animals* theory and its extension in *Pol.* I 2, 1253a7–18 is that active participation in a city's life is that single function (*ergon*) which all the human beings belonging to that city perform together, and in the performance of which their character as political animals consists. This counts as a *single* function because, as Aristotle's account of the structure and constitution of a city makes clear, a city is a complex entity having as its ultimate elements not individual human beings as such, but human beings *in* families, households, villages, and other associations, *koinōniai*: the part of a person's active life that is carried out as a family-member or as a farmer in a particular locality, say, is seen as part of the larger complex of activities making up the life of the city of which this family and this locality are parts.[10] Once one brings the biological perspective provided by our *History of Animals* passage to bear on the interpretation of the proposition that human beings are political animals, one can see that the fundamental aspect of city life that in Aristotle's eyes marks it as natural for human beings is its involving the cooperative working together of all those who take part in it in an interlocking, differentiated, mutually supporting, single set of activities. What's essential to cities, however they may vary in other respects, is that they involve their citizens in this kind of common activity. In effect, it is by doing that that cities can provide a more secure and comfortable life than households and villages not integrated into a city can do (as we saw earlier Aristotle claims), and we may begin to anticipate that whatever exactly Aristotle means by saying that cities exist for the sake of a good life, and not just for the sake of life, this will turn out to be a life led in some more or less specific version of this kind of cooperative activity.

So far I have left Aristotle's notion of the political activity as an essentially cooperative one rather abstract. In order to begin to flesh it out somewhat, it will be useful to turn to Aristotle's distinction (drawn first in *Pol. III* 6, 1279a17–21) between the "correct" (*orthai*) constitutions and the "erroneous" (*hēmartēmenai*) ones or deviation-forms (*parekbaseis*). Since Aristotle says the deviation-forms are contrary to nature (III 17, 1287b41), we can examine life in the correct kinds of city to discover what he expects city life to be like if things do go according to nature. That should show us what he includes among the cooperative activities in which the human being's political nature shows itself.

Aristotle's criterion for a "correct" constitution is deceptively simple. A "correct" constitution is one in which the government aims at the common advantage (*to koinēi sumpheron*, III 6, 1279a17; *to koinon sumpheron*, III

---

[10] Cf. III 9, 1280b40–41: πόλις δὲ ἡ γενῶν καὶ κωμῶν κοινωνία ζωῆς τελείας καὶ αὐτάρκους.

7, 1279a28–29); in the deviation-forms the government aims instead at the advantage of the office-holders themselves (and their families) as a group. But to whom is the advantage sought in correct constitutions common, and in what sense is it common?

To the first question the natural answer would seem to be: common to all the citizens, i.e., all the free, native-born residents. In fact, I think this is what Aristotle does intend: it is at least suggested by III 13, 1283b40–41, where Aristotle speaks of "correct" rule as being "for the advantage of the whole city and for the common advantage of the citizens." But if we put Aristotle's view in this way, we must recognize that we are using the word *citizen* in a way that departs from his own explicit theory in III 1–2 of who the citizens of a city are. According to this theory, the citizens of a city are just those who have the right to take part in the judicial and/or the deliberative functions.[11] But if we were to use the term *citizen* in Aristotle's official, narrow sense in saying that correct forms of political organization aim at the citizens' common advantage, the result would be that certain correct forms would collapse into their corresponding deviation-forms. Thus, under the rule of a king, one of the types of constitution Aristotle counts as "correct," the monarch reserves to himself and his personal appointees both the deliberative and the judicial function—so that, if the aim of a king was the common advantage of what Aristotle *officially* counts as citizens, there would in fact be no distinction between rule by a king and a tyranny, its deviation-form. For in such a monarchy the unique ruler would also be the sole citizen, and so he would rule simultaneously in the sole interest of himself (as ruler) and in that of the citizen body (himself as citizen). Hence such a monarchy would also be a tyranny: rule by the ruler solely in his personal interest. Likewise there would be no distinction between aristocracy and oligarchy, either. (Aristotle's criterion would still separate "polity" from democracy.) So the citizens, whose common advantage is consulted in the correct constitutions, must include the office-holders, jurymen and assembly-members, but at least in aristocracy and monarchy others besides. How is this larger class of citizens to be determined? Aristotle speaks in this context (at III 7, 1279a35–36) of those whose common possession and common activity the city is (*hoi koinōnountes autēs*) as the ones whose advantage the correct governments seek, and by implication he describes a city when correctly constituted as an association in common of its *free* inhabitants

[11] As Newman notes, *The Politics of Aristotle,* vol. 1, 229 (and cf. 324 and 569–70), Aristotle himself occasionally uses the word πολίτης more widely than his official account permits. Newman refers to VII 13, 1332a32–35, and he might have added III 7, 1279a31–32 and III 14, 1285a25–29. These passages make it clear enough that Aristotle occasionally employs the word πολίτης in very much the same broad sense that, as I argue in what follows, he needs in order to make clear what he means by aiming "at the common advantage of the citizens." I would maintain, therefore, that even though the interpretation I offer of what this means employs the word *citizen* in a sense different from Aristotle's official one, it is a sense that Aristotle himself not only needs but actually employs on occasion, as well.

(*koinōnia tōn eleutherōn*, III 6, 1279a21). This suggests that the citizens in the broad sense include all the free-born native residents, with the presumed exclusion of the non-slave laborers, both urban and agricultural (cf. III 5, 1278a6–13). These it is, whether the form of government is a kingdom, an aristocracy, or the government in which all the (male) free-born natives participate that Aristotle calls a "polity," whose common advantage is sought in correctly organized cities.

But now we must ask, in what sense is the advantage sought an advantage that belongs to the citizens (i.e., the free-born native residents) *in common*? One way in which this might be conceived is on the model of a joint-stock company. If I own 10% of a company's stock and you own 20%, then anything that improves the competitiveness of the company or increases its earnings or profits, and so on, is for our common advantage. Here the common advantage can be broken down into the sum of the individual advantages of each of us, and these individual advantages are themselves definable and measurable independently of reference to our jointly owned company and its advantage. If, for example, the company's profits increase a certain amount because of some change in tax rate or tax policy, and my dividend goes from $100 to $200 and yours from $200 to $400, then this act of the government has been to my and your advantage by those amounts, and this advantage, being measurable in such financial terms, is definable without reference to the company and its advantage. The company's advantage is only the causal condition of my and your separate advantages. In a case like this, if you and I combine to work for our common advantage, we can, and presumably will, each be working for his own single advantage, aiming at this by means of the advantage of the company, which includes our separate advantages as constituent parts. Likewise, if some third party should take an interest in the success of our company, this person would be taking an interest in our and the other stockholders' common advantage in this purely additive sense.

In an interesting chapter of *Politics* book III, Aristotle clearly and explicitly rejects this commercial model for the kind of community a city constitutes, and implies a different account of what the common advantage of its participants consists in. Partisans of an oligarchic constitution, he says (III 9, 1280a25–31), think that a city is an association (or common enterprise— *koinōnia*) that came into and continues in existence merely for the sake of possessions (*ktēmata*), i.e., for the sake of preserving, exchanging, and increasing possessions for their economic value. And their standard of political justice, which specifies unequal shares in political power, corresponding to the unequal quantity of possessions brought into the common stock by the participating citizens, would be perfectly reasonable if their conception of what a city essentially is were correct. However, on the oligarchic conception a constitution is like a commercial treaty between two separate countries, establishing an agreement as to how trade and other business is to be conducted between their respective citizens, with guarantees for the citizens of each against various forms of cheating by the citizens of the other. And it is plain, Aristotle says, that the kind of common enterprise a city is, is badly misrepresented by any such conception of a civic constitution. For, surely, a single city with commercial relations carried on inside it is quite a different thing from two separate cities bound by commercial treaties and carrying on a similarly active and varied trade with one another. One difference Aristotle mentions is important but relatively superficial—the absence in the two-city case of a single, common system of courts and magistracies governing the commercial relations in question (1280a40–b1). But a second difference goes deeper: the people in the two cities carrying on mutual trade and commerce "do not concern themselves about what kind of persons the ones in the other city ought to be, nor are they concerned that no one covered by the agreements *be* unjust (or be vicious in any way at all). They are only concerned that they *do* nothing unjust to one another" (1280b1–5). By contrast, within a single city, people do have this further concern: of course they want not to be cheated or otherwise treated unjustly, in business or anywhere else, but they also care what kind of people their fellow-citizens are. They want them to be decent, fair-minded, respectable, moral people (anyhow, by their own lights).

One should note carefully just how strong a claim Aristotle is making here. He says those in one city who exercise their rights under treaties for mutual commerce have no general concern about the moral characters of those in another city with whom they do business: they do not concern themselves that "no one covered by the agreements *be* unjust (or be vicious in any way at all)." And he implies that civic relations among citizens of a single city, since they are not merely commercial, do involve just these concerns. That is, he holds that in cities we find a *general* concern on the part of those living under the constitution of a city and participating in its civic life for the moral characters of all those similarly engaged—a concern that *no one* taking part in civic life *be* unjust or indeed vicious in any way. This is a concern of each citizen for each other citizen, whether or not they know each other personally, and indeed whether or not they have had any direct and personal dealings with one another whatsoever. The open-ended scope here envisaged for this mutual concern of fellow-citizens for one another's good character is, as we shall see more fully below, a crucially important feature of common life in a city as Aristotle conceives it.

But is it really true that fellow-citizens do have such a concern for one another's good character? No doubt they would in any of the types of state Aristotle himself most favors, since such cities would be governed under a constitution, fully accepted by the citizens themselves, taking as its first aim to make the citizens good.[12] But would they, for example, under the very

---

[12] And it is noteworthy (see Newman *ad loc*) that Aristotle goes on only to say that (not people in general, but only) those who care about εὐνομία do think about how to make people politically good, and that *cities that deserve the name* have to concern themselves about virtue (III 9, 1280b5–12). He does not go on to say explicitly, what 1280b1–5 implies, that the

oligarchic constitution that Aristotle in this passage is trying to show is misguided? Why think that where the constitution was just an elaborate commercial treaty, eschewing all reference to people's characters and any concern for what they are *like* personally, people would differ in this respect from the citizens of two distinct cities linked by extensive trade relations? On reflection, it turns out to be very plausible that they would, and that Aristotle is right to make this fact a central objection against the oligarchic and in general commercial view of the kind of community a city is.

Even in twentieth-century liberal states, some of which (anyhow in their official ideology) fit the commercial conception rather well, Aristotle's observation seems to hold good (and in Greek city-states the features that make it do so were even more pronounced). There seems no denying that ordinary Americans, for example, are characteristically quite a bit concerned about the moral standards of people prominent in government, business, and industry and concerned in quite a different way from the concern they presumably also feel about the morality of people in similar positions in foreign countries, even ones with which the United States has extensive trading and business relationships. The typical American when she hears, say, about the attitudes Wall-Street brokers and commercial bankers have apparently quite routinely been holding about privileged information that comes their way in their professional work, or about sleaziness in government circles, feels injured in ways she certainly does not feel in hearing similar things said about people in high places abroad. Independently of any way one may expect to suffer financial losses or other direct injuries to one's interests from these people's behavior, one feels injured and diminished simply by there being such people in positions like that. Something is wrong with *us*, one feels, that among us that sort of person is found in that sort of place. That the same and worse happens in some other country may be reason to introduce special safeguards to protect our financial interests there, or, out of sympathy for the people of that country, to express our moral condemnation of that behavior, or even to join organizations directed toward removing those evils by concerted international financial pressure, etc. But it's nothing to us *personally*. Apart from a legitimate general concern we may feel about immorality wherever it occurs, it's nothing to us *Americans* what, say, French or German or Italian businesspeople are like: that's the exclusive concern of the French or the Germans or the Italians, in the sense that *they* are the ones personally injured and diminished by it.

These effects of national feeling are felt more widely, too. Americans take pride in the self-discipline and hard work of the American working force, the inventiveness, entrepreneurial spirit, and skill of American industrialists, the imaginativeness and vigor of American writers, and so on.[13] (That these

---

citizens in general, under whatever constitution, do (normally) concern themselves about what their fellow-citizens are like as persons.

[13] Leaving aside, of course, those who may for one reason or another feel excluded from full participation in American life, or, again, those who may think the potential good effects

characteristics may largely be mythical does not matter for the point I am making.) This is pride not just in accomplishments, but even more in the qualities of mind and character that (are presumed to have) made them possible. Furthermore, it seems that, typically, citizens even of a modern mass democracy feel tied to one another in such a way and to such an extent that they can and do take an interest in what their fellow-citizens quite generally are like as persons; they want to think of them as good, upstanding people, and definitely do not want them to be small-minded, self-absorbed, sleazy. What their fellow-citizens are like matters to them personally, it seems, in ways that the personal qualities of the citizens of a foreign country do not, because they feel some connection to, some involvement with— almost some responsibility for—the former that they do not have for the latter, and this makes them feel that what their fellow-citizens are like, for better or for worse, somehow reflects on themselves.[14]

In this chapter of *Pol.* III, then, Aristotle decisively rejects the commercial model for the kind of community a city is. What kind of community is a city, then, if it is not to be conceived on the commercial model? Aristotle indicates his own view a little later in the same chapter, when he goes on (III 9, 1280b23–1281a2) to explain the nature and source of the special bond between fellow-citizens that grounds their concern for one another's personal qualities. Aristotle says quite explicitly that it is friendship (*philia*, 1280b38) that does this. Friendship, he says, being the deliberate decision to share one's life with another (*hē gar tou suzēn prohairesis philia*, 1280b38–39), is responsible for such practices in cities as "connections by marriage, brotherhoods, religious festivals, and the pursuits in which people share their lives" (1280b36–38). And these, in turn, he evidently means to say, provide the specific sort of connectedness that, in Greek cities, grounds the interest in and concern by each citizen for the qualities of mind and character of his fellow-citizens generally that he has been insisting distinguishes citizenly ties from those provided by contractual agreements for mutual economic advantage.[15] For his purpose in mentioning these more

---

of these qualities are seriously compromised by injustices in the social and economic setting in which they operate, or by other contextual factors. On the importance of considerations of justice in this connection, see below 372ff.

[14] Aristotle's point, then, against oligarchic constitutions is that the official view taken in oligarchic cities of the nature of the civic bond—that it is, or is essentially like, a contract or treaty or other agreement voluntarily entered into for mutual gain—misrepresents the *actual* nature of the citizenly ties that the citizens of the oligarchic city, like all other cities, evince. The constitutions that Aristotle ranks more highly simply take explicit notice of this fact about all cities, the oligarchic ones among the others, and give it the weight in the constitution itself that it deserves to have.

[15] One should recall here Aristotle's criticisms (*Pol.* II 2–4) of the plan proposed in Plato's *Republic* (V 457c–464b) for unifying the ideal city by making each of the rulers speak, think, and feel about each other ruler in the way in which members of a close-knit, harmonious family speak, think, and feel about one another. In effect, Socrates in the *Republic* proposes doing away with separate families and separate family ties (among the rulers), replacing them with ties of exactly the same kind and strength linking each ruler to each other. He thinks of

limited contexts for common activity and the role they play in the city is to explain how it comes about that cities differ from commercial partnerships in the way he said earlier in the chapter that they do. Since that involved a concern of each citizen for each other citizen's character, he must mean that these less extensive types of common undertaking give rise to and reinforce the common activity of civic life itself, and the friendship that is specific to that life. In general, even in a Greek city-state, no citizen is bound to each of his fellow-citizens through marriage, or membership of some brotherhood, or one or another other personal relationship of friendship. Hence whatever special concern the members of these associations may come to have for one another's characters will obviously be inadequate for Aristotle's purpose here. So, although Aristotle does not say it here explicitly, the kind of friendship he has in mind is what in the *Eudemian Ethics* he discusses at some length under the name "civic friendship," *hē politikē philia* and refers to as such four times in the *Nicomachean Ethics*.[16] According to

---

the civic friendship needed in order to unify and stabilize the city as impossible so long as loyalty to the city can come into conflict with loyalty to one's family. The only effective civic friendship, he thinks, will be one resulting from the extension to the whole ruling group of just those family ties which in other, historical, cities serve to compromise it. This kind of all-inclusive family relationship is impossible in principle, Aristotle thinks (*Pol.* II 4, 1262a31)— when you call all of the children of a certain age "my son" or "my daughter," knowing that a large group of your fellow-rulers do the same, you don't and can't think and feel about them in the ways a true parent does. The misguided attempt to achieve this *both* does away with true family ties *and* makes impossible true civic friendship. All you get is a watered-down family friendship. This means that people will neither concern themselves about selected others as their sons, daughters, husbands, cousins, nor about their fellow-citizens in general. Once the family is gone, the use of the words that originally connoted family-relationships to refer instead to fellow-citizens generally, will not carry with it the thoughts and feelings that bind family members to one another (II 4, 1262b15–24), and nothing will have been done to encourage the different thoughts and feelings appropriate to fellow-citizens. On Aristotle's view civic friendship must rest upon an understanding of the *special* ways that fellow-citizens are related to one another in a common work, and these do not necessarily compete with, but supplement, the links between family-members. Civic friendship, Aristotle insists, is a specific type of friendship, distinct (e.g.) from family friendship; furthermore, it does not exist at all except where there also exist families, brotherhoods, etc., with their own specific forms of friendship, to which it is added as a natural completion: see *Nic. Eth.* VIII 9, 1160a9–10; 1160a21–30; *EE* VII 9, 1241b24–26.

[16] Oddly, this expression, or a close relative, seems to occur at most only once in the *Politics*. (The φιλία τῇ πολιτείᾳ referred to at V 9, 1309b9 (cf. 1309a34) and II 8, 1268a24 is a different thing.) This is at IV 11, 1295b23–24, where the run of the argument seems to go best if πολιτικῆς is taken with both φιλίας and κοινωνίας. Aristotle's point is that it is important to avoid the enmity that exists when a contemptuous rich class rule over an envious mass of poor people. Aristotle is clearly conceiving of this contempt and envy as being felt by the individual rich and poor persons for the members of the other group *en masse*: he has in mind a class phenomenon. So, therefore, the φιλία that Aristotle says such feelings preclude, but implies would be achievable if the middle class had power (see 1295b29–32), can only be πολιτικὴ φιλία—a friendship felt by each citizen for the other citizens *en masse*, and the only kind of friendship Aristotle recognizes that can be felt quasi-anonymously for a whole group of people. Newman (*ad loc*) says, but without explanation, that "πολιτικῆς goes only with κοινωνίας, not with φιλίας." That, however, is quite unsatisfactory: it is true enough that people who

Aristotle, then, a city is a kind of community that depends upon the friendly interest that the citizens take in one another's qualities of mind and character, as well, of course, as upon their common economic interests. In such a community the way or ways in which the government seeks to promote the citizens' good as a *common* good will depend upon the specific character of the friendship that forms the political bond within it, and the ways in which "civic friends" have and do things in common.

In order to see what this is, we must first be clear about the fact that, although Aristotle in the two *Ethics* treats civic friendship as a form of advantage-friendship, a friendship based upon the experience or expectation of mutual benefit from the activities in which it is expressed, civic friendship, like other forms of advantage friendship, is really a *friendship*. Aristotle emphasizes in *Pol.* III 9 that whereas mere mutual commerce does not involve any interest in one another as persons, any concern for what kind of people these are that one is dealing with, in civic friendship, even though it is based upon the expectation of mutual benefit just as much as such commercial relationships are, this additional interest is present. That is easy enough to understand if, like all relationships deserving the name "friendship," civic friendship involves mutual good will, trust, and well-wishing, and the mutual interest that fellow-citizens have in one another's characters is part of that good will and well-wishing. Thus what Aristotle says in *Pol.* III 9 confirms what I have argued elsewhere about civic friendship in the *Nicomachean Ethics*:[17] where civic friendship characterizes a population there exists, as a recognized and accepted norm, a certain measure of

---

respectively have contempt and envy for one another are not good candidates for friendship of whatever sort, but Aristotle is not talking about contempt and envy in general, but about these feelings as experienced by whole classes for one another, and what that undermines is not friendship in general but civic friendship in particular. So it does seem greatly preferable to take πολιτικῆς here with φιλίας as well as with κοινωνίας.

"Civic friendship" is discussed at length in *EE* VII 9–10 (see also VII 7, 1241a32), where it is classified as a special form of "advantage friendship," friendship κατὰ τὸ χρήσιμον (VII 10, 1242b22–23; 1243b4). The references in *Nic. Eth.* are at VIII 12, 1161b13; IX 1, 1163b34; IX 6, 1167b2; and IX 10, 1171a17. IX 6, 1167b2–4 makes it clear that in the *Nic. Eth.* too Aristotle classifies πολιτικὴ φιλία as an advantage friendship, although he nowhere does so explicitly. The same thing is implied by VIII 9, where in discussing civic friendship, though not under that name, he emphasizes that the *civic* community, the kind of community to which this kind of friendship is proper, is formed and survives for the sake of the common advantage of those belonging to it. Aristotle's very lengthy discussions of civic friendship in *Nic. Eth.* VIII 9–12 and *EE* VII 9–10 show clearly that he regarded this kind of friendship, though it is only a form of advantage friendship, as a very important one; he by no means treats it as a minor variation of no fundamental, independent interest. The prominence of civic friendship in the *Nicomachean Ethics* and the importance Aristotle attributes to it there is specially significant, since it seems clear that *Nic. Eth.* VIII 9–12 is intended as summarizing central aspects of the political theory developed in the *Politics*. Accordingly, we can claim Aristotle's own testimony that in the *Politics*, too, civic friendship plays a crucial, though as I have noted a somewhat inexplicit, role.

[17] See Chapter 14 above, "Aristotle on the Forms of Friendship," especially sect. VI on civic friendship.

mutual good will, and also mutual trust, among the people making up the population. Each expects his fellow-citizens in their dealings with him (political, economic, and social) to be motivated not merely by self-interest (or other private particular interests) but also by concern for his good for his own sake (for his qualities of mind and character, as Aristotle emphasizes in *Pol.* III 9, but also for other elements in his good). And in return each is ready to be so motivated in his dealings with them. This means that in a city animated by civic friendship each citizen has a certain measure of interest in and concern for the well-being of each other citizen just because the other *is* a fellow-citizen. Civic friendship makes fellow-citizens' well-being matter to one another, simply as such.[18]

Here, and not coincidentally, the comparison with a family is instructive. In a family (perhaps a somewhat idealized one—but this idealization is obviously important to Aristotle), the good fortune or success or good character of one member is *experienced* by the others as somehow part of their good as well, and in fact we do think it constitutes a contribution to

[18] Civic friendship is therefore a very special kind of friendship, different in important ways from personal friendships (whether of pleasure or advantage, or ones based on character). At *EE* VII 9, 1241b13–17, Aristotle introduces his account of civic friendship by speaking explicitly of kinds (εἴδη) of φιλία, differing among themselves in accordance with the differences in the κοινωνίαι (common enterprises) regulating the specific activities of which the φιλία in question consists: πολιτικὴ φιλία is one of these εἴδη, the one that regulates precisely those activities of which the πολιτικὴ κοινωνία itself consists, making them be carried out in the spirit of friendship appropriate to them. In the *Nicomachean Ethics* Aristotle does not use the terminology of εἴδη φιλίας in this connection, but his doctrine is exactly the same: see VIII 9, 1159b26–31. There is no cause for surprise that this friendship, unlike the personal friendships from which Aristotle naturally begins his consideration of φιλία, does not require any degree of intimacy nor even any personal knowledge of one another on the part of the "friends." Since the κοινωνία in question does not require intimacy and personal knowledge, neither, obviously, could the φιλία specific to it. One should bear in mind that in describing in very general terms the conditions that hold good for friendships, of whatever type, in VIII 2 Aristotle says only (1155b34–1156a5) that friends must both wish their friends well for the friends' own sake, and know this fact about one another—not that they must be intimate with one another, or even know each other in person. Intimacy and personal knowledge are not the only ways of knowing (or anyhow reasonably coming to believe) that such mutual good will exists, and they are not even the normal way such mutual good will gets communicated in every context where it exists. In the political context, knowledge of the nature of the constitution, of the general level of support for it among the different elements of the population, and of what's generally expected of people in that society is the normal way of knowing about these things, and it is sufficient, sometimes, to establish a reasonable presumption of good will on the part of one's fellow-citizens generally.

Taken together, these considerations show, I think, that Julia Annas was wrong in "Plato and Aristotle on Friendship and Altruism" to think that in seeking to accommodate such "objective" kinds of φιλία as civic friendship, into a common framework with the personal ones, Aristotle grossly failed to square his views on the objective with his account of the personal friendships. Annas' bias in favor of the personal friendships (understandable given *our* concept of friendship) prevents her from seeing that Aristotle from the outset of his discussions holds together in his mind—as the Greek concept of φιλία itself did—the phenomena of both the personal and the objective types of φιλία, and sets out to give a comprehensive, systematic account of them all.

the good of the other family-members. Think of how parents respond to their children's successes, and of how we refer to the character of the children's lives when we intend to be saying how things are for the parents. The members of my family are *my* people, and any good enjoyed by any of them is shared in also by me, because as members of a family what affects them affects the family, and I too am a member of that. Civic friendship is just an extension to a whole city of the kinds of psychological bonds that tie together a family and make possible this immediate participation by each family-member in the good of the others. Civic friendship makes the citizens in some important respects like a large extended family (though they are also, obviously, quite unlike a family in other respects).

Plainly, the common advantage of a civic community conceived as Aristotle conceives it, like that of a family, does not consist wholly (though of course it might well consist partly) of something that can be broken down into a sum of separate advantages belonging individually to the citizens one by one. To the extent that each citizen participates in the good of the others, a good that may belong in the first instance to a single individual (whether a material possession or a good quality of mind or character) becomes a communal good shared in by all who are members in good standing of the community. Insofar as part of the common good of the citizens is thus a set of communal goods, it is not divisible into separate shares at all, but remains indissolubly an "advantage" of the common enterprise itself in which the members of the community are associated. The citizens share equally in the whole of this part of their common good, just because they are associated in the civic enterprise and care about it.

At the beginning of *Nic. Eth.* VIII Aristotle says, obviously approvingly, that "friendship seems to hold cities together, and lawgivers seem to be more concerned about it than about justice. For . . . when people are friends they have no need of justice, but those who are just [to one another] need friendship in addition, and the strictest form of justice is found in friendship" (VIII 1, 1155a22–28). Indeed, Aristotle says that every community (and he explicitly includes here the family as well as the city) carries with it both a specific kind of friendship and a specific set of standards of justice (VIII 9, 1159b26–27; 1159b35–1160a3). But justice plays a distinctive role in the constitution of civic friendship that so far as I can see it does not play in families.[19] Even if the specific standards of justice appropriate to a family are seriously violated in various ways—if, say, the children are cold and neglectful of the parents, perhaps because earlier on the parents themselves were arbitrary, dictatorial, and selfish—the bonds which tie family members together and make each participate in the good of the others are not entirely destroyed. The parents, however neglected and wronged they may feel and

---

[19] I do not say that Aristotle was aware of this difference. At VIII 11, 1161a30–32 he takes note of the fact that in the deviant forms of constitution there is necessarily less civic friendship between rulers and ruled, because of the injustice of the constitutions. Tyranny, being the most unjust constitution, is also the least characterized by civic friendship.

be, are nonetheless affected for better or worse by the successes and good fortune and the good characters of the children (and vice versa). Injustice seems not, of itself, to destroy the relationship (the "friendship") and so it does not do away with the participation by each in the others' good. But this is not so for civic friendship.

Consider, for example, an aristocracy, one conceived according to Aristotle's lights as governed by the morally best people among the citizens. If the virtue of the rulers and their opportunity to exercise it in those most favorable of conditions for the exercise of virtue, the public affairs of a city, is bought at the price of limiting the moral development of the other citizens, or denying them appropriate opportunities to give effective exercise to good moral qualities they possess, then this would not only be an injustice (one recognized even by the aristocratic conception of justice officially countenanced under that form of constitution),[20] it would for that very reason also destroy the friendship existing among the citizens. If those excluded from active participation in the political life of the city recognized their exclusion as an injustice, they would see themselves as being exploited by the rulers for the rulers' own benefit. Their trust would thus have been violated, and a natural consequence of an uncorrected violation of trust is its destruction. Since civic friendship consists in part of the mutual trust of the citizens that they are all effectively concerned for one another's good, the destruction of this trust destroys the friendship too.

Civic friendship, then, requires that those bound together by it (seem to one another to) be behaving justly in their mutual relations (anyhow basically so). Being clear about the role of justice in making civic friendship possible is especially important because it helps one to understand just what it means to say a city is a community (a *koinōnia*) and what would be involved in the "common advantage" of the citizens who make up such a community. In a city animated by civic friendship, the citizens are engaged in a common enterprise, an enterprise aimed at a common good, in two different senses. First of all, each regards the others as wishing for and implementing through their actions his individual good (as he also intends in his actions their individual good), as and to the extent justice requires. The good in question certainly includes material interests, but is not limited to that: moral and intellectual good, regarded as individual accomplishments, are included as well. So the common good of the community will consist first of the ways in which, by the organization of civic life, the individuals making it up each severally benefit from it, that is, benefit in ways that are assignable to them each separately *as* individuals. In an Aristotelian aristocracy, for example, the well-born "better" people benefit by the education they receive that helps them to develop good moral and intellectual qualities, and by the

---

[20] See *Pol.* III 17, 1287b37–39 for a clear recognition by Aristotle of the ways in which conceptions of justice vary with political constitutions. See also *Nic. Eth.* VIII 11, where Aristotle again marks off the conceptions of justice at work in different kinds of constitution, but this time links these differences to differences in the bases of the respective civic friendships.

opportunity they later enjoy to exercise these qualities in the direction of the community's affairs. The common people benefit, too, because such a group of aristocrats are actively concerned for the good of their fellow-citizens, as justice demands, and make a principle of seeing to the economic well-being of their less well-endowed fellow-citizens and to such moral and intellectual development as they are capable of, so far as providing for that does not unfairly limit the full development of the excellences of the better-endowed.

To this extent, the common advantage of a city is the sum of the advantages of its citizens, separately considered. But where, as in this kind of aristocracy (but also in monarchies and under the more popular governments Aristotle calls "polities"), civic life involves civic friendship, it includes more than this. For where each aims in her cooperative activity at the good of the others, and not just at her own good, the good attained in the first instance by the others becomes, and is conceived of by herself as being, also a part of her own good. In this way the aristocrat participates in the good that comes to the ordinary citizens in their common life, because that is a conscious objective of many of those morally fine activities in which his principal citizenly function is carried out, and of course the attainment of one's conscious objectives (if, anyhow, one is right, as *ex hypothesi* this man is, to adopt them in the first place) makes a direct contribution to one's own good. And the ordinary citizen likewise participates in the moral and intellectual goods achieved directly by the aristocrat. That is because these are good things achieved in the course of a common life the organizing principles of which he endorses and to which he willingly contributes his part. These are, so to speak, *his* aristocrats, so that their intrinsically good qualities and intrinsically good activities are part of the enlarged good that he comes to experience by not just living in this city but being a willing, active part of it.

This account of the common good or common advantage aimed at by the government of a "correctly" constituted city brings into view something important that is easily missed. When Aristotle says that cities exist for the sake of *to eu zēn* (living well)—not just for living, or even for living together, the sharing of life (*to suzēn*)—his official view is that the "living well" in question is that of the households and village-communities that logically pre-exist the city and from which it is constituted. Sometimes, as in a remarkable passage of *Pol.* III 9, Aristotle is explicit about this: a city is "the common participation in living well by households and families, for the sake of a complete and self-sufficient life" (ἡ τοῦ εὖ ζῆν κοινωνία καὶ ταῖς οἰκίαις καὶ τοῖς γένεσι, ζωῆς τελείας χάριν καὶ αὐτάρκους, 1280b33–34). The "living well" aimed at in cities is not, anyhow not immediately, the "living well" of the individual citizens residing in it. What is aimed at is rather the living well of the constituent households and village-communities. Individual citizens' lives are affected just insofar as, in one way or another, the good living of the communities to which they individually belong carries with it the individual citizens' living well too.

But to what extent does the living well of a community imply the living well of its individual members? Plainly, in well-constituted cities of all types, and especially in monarchies and aristocracies as Aristotle conceives them, the city aims through its political and social institutions at providing both for the material well-being and for the fullest possible development and exercise of the highest and best qualities of mind and character of the citizens.[21] The city and its constituent sub-communities cannot live well otherwise than on this condition. But of course in any city, however successful, many, perhaps most, of the citizens will not attain the highest degree of civilized perfection, because of congenital limitations in their natural capacities (if not for other reasons as well). The city itself, however, will live well if those who are naturally capable of a very high degree of mental and moral perfection attain and sustain it through life in the city, and the others attain as high a degree of perfection as they are naturally capable of. So, at a minimum, one could say that in the best, most successful cities an excellent life is provided for those individuals (presumably a small number) capable of leading it, while the others get as nearly excellent a life as they are severally able to manage, given their natural limitations.

But relying on the preceding analysis, we can go further. For according to Aristotle, when civic friendship animates the life of a community, as of course one would expect it to do in any correctly constituted city, each citizen participates in *all* aspects of the good achieved through the common activity that constitutes civic life. This means that even those who are less well endowed for the excellences of mind and character share in the exercise of the excellences of the better-endowed citizens. In this way all the citizens of a successful city achieve, either directly through their own individual activities, or at second remove through participation in the city's good of which these activities are a prime element, an active, perfected, self-sufficient life.[22]

---

[21] Aristotle does not say much in detail, either in the *Politics* or in the *Ethics,* about how life in a well run, well constituted city does encourage the moral improvement of the citizens. One may, perhaps, think first of laws explicitly framed so as to require of the citizens the doing of certain actions (and omissions of others) that, if engaged in regularly and in the right spirit, will, Aristotle thinks, lead eventually to the acquisition of the moral virtues. (In *Nic. Eth.* V, as is well known, Aristotle emphasizes that "the law" requires the citizens to do acts of courage, temperance, good temper, and all the other moral virtues: see 1, 1129b19–25.) Equally important, however, is the fact that in such a city, animated by civic friendship, the mature citizens care very much about one another's characters and encourage one another and the young in the virtues by showing what the proper spirit is in which the acts of the virtues are to be done, and by making it clear that in their view acting in that spirit is the central and indispensable part of any human being's own personal good. Life in such a city is a moral education, quite apart from what the laws do or do not *require* the citizens to *do* (or refrain from doing).

[22] Aristotle's introduction in *Pol.* VII 1–3 to his discussion, beginning in ch. 4, of the ideal best city—i.e., the best constitution for a city that enjoys ideal conditions with respect to size and character of population, natural resources, etc.—gives evidence that the analysis just presented spells out implications of Aristotle's theory of friendship that he himself accepted.

    With this account of civic friendship before us, we can now see the full
implications of Aristotle's thesis that the human being is by nature a political
animal. This means, first, that like certain other herding animals, human
beings have a natural capacity and tendency to live together in cooperative
communities in which each benefits from the work of the others as well as
from his own. But secondly, because human beings can develop conceptions
of, and communicate to one another their ideas about, the long-term good
both of themselves and others and the common good of a whole group of
people living and working together, human beings have the natural capacity
and tendency to form communities (and, in particular, cities)[23] in which the

---

He begins (VII 1, 1323a17-19) by saying that in general one should expect a constitution
which is best (for any population) to be such that those living under it lead the best life available
to them in the given external circumstances. Later, again, he says (VII 2, 1324a23-25) that,
necessarily, the best constitution will be that arrangement under which anyone (of the relevant
group, i.e., of those having a part in the political life of the city) could act in the best way
and live happily—the best constitution must not discriminate against any group among the
citizens, but must provide the conditions under which (modulo the natural wealth of the land,
native talents of the population, etc.—the ὑπάρχοντα of VII 1, 1323a18) this life is available
to them, if only they do their part. When, accordingly, he raises the question (VII 2, 1324a5-7)
whether happiness is the same for each individual person and for a city, he is not concerned
merely for the question of meaning—whether what it is for a city, as such, to be happy and
successful is the same, mutatis mutandis, as what it is for a single person. (Indeed he settles
this question of meaning almost immediately, by VII 2, 1324a13.) A major concern in the
subsequent discussion is to see that there really is the coincidence he has declared there must
be between happiness for the city and happiness for the participant citizens. (Another major
concern is to deal with the threat that cities in pursuit of their own happiness will always seek
hegemony or even despotic power over neighboring cities: on this see Carnes Lord, Education
and Culture, ch. 5.) Against this background I think it is right to attach significance to some
of Aristotle's language as he formulates and discusses the relationship between happiness for
the city and happiness for the individual. When he first raises this question, he asks whether
the same life is the most worth choosing for everyone taken in common and taken separately
(κοινῇ καὶ χωρίς, VII 1, 1323a21). In answering that it is the same (1323b40-41; VII 2,
1324a5-8; VII 3, 1325b30-32), viz., the life devoted to the exercise of the virtues both moral
and intellectual, he glosses the judgment that it is "best for everyone taken in common" with
its being "best for a city" (VII 2, 1324a6) or "best for cities taken in common" (VII 1, 1323b41)
or again "best for cities and human beings taken in common" (VII 3, 1325b32). The emphasis
in these glosses on the happiness of a city being the common happiness of its people suggests
strongly that the virtuous life that a city leads when it is organized into and governed as a
true aristocracy is being thought of as a life led by its citizens, in the broad sense of "citizens"
that I have distinguished—the (free) ἄνθρωποι (1325b32) whose common possession or activity
it is. If under such a constitution "everyone in common" leads the best life, then even someone
who is not himself a virtuous person and so not constantly exercising virtues in his daily life
is nonetheless in a secondary way leading a virtuous life, by having his life merged in the life
of the whole city which itself is a virtuous one, by reason (primarily) of the virtues possessed,
and exercised in its political and otherwise communal life, by its ruling class.

[23] The reason why Aristotle thinks cities in particular, and not merely various more limited
associations for a common life, are needed and naturally pursued by human beings, is that
only cities are complete and self-sufficient associations, associations capable of developing to
their fullest extent, and giving appropriate scope for the exercise of, the virtues of mind and
character which are the core of the natural good for a human being. See above nn. 1, 15, and
T. H. Irwin, "The Good of Political Activity," esp. 74ff., 84ff.

life of all is organized in pursuit of a *common good*—a good that is common not just in the sense that each severally gets some part of a sum-total of distributable benefit, but in the strong sense that it is achieved in or belongs to the common activity that is the single life they all jointly live by merging their lives with one another's. But this common good is not available to them except on the basis of their all being, and feeling themselves to be, bound together by the bonds of civic friendship. And in the most successful cities, thanks to civic friendship, there is an important sense in which *all* the citizens, even those who individually lack the highest attainments of mind and character, can be said to be living a good and excellent life.[24]

SELECTED FURTHER READINGS

Annas, Julia. "Comments on J. Cooper." In *Aristoteles' "Politik,"* edited by G. Patzig. Göttingen: Vandenhoeck und Ruprecht, 1990, 243–49.

Depew, David J. "Humans and Other Political Animals in Aristotle's *History of Animals.*" *Phronesis* 40 (1995): 156–81.

Irwin, T. H. "The Good of Political Activity." In *Aristoteles' "Politik,"* edited by G. Patzig, Göttingen: Vandenhoeck und Ruprecht, 1990, 73–99.

Kullmann, Wolfgang. "Man as a Political Animal in Aristotle." Translation of "Der Mensch als Politisches Lebewesen bei Aristoteles." In *A Companion to Aristotle's "Politics,"* edited by David Keyt and Fred D. Miller, Jr. Oxford and Cambridge, Mass.: Blackwell, 1991, 94–117.

Schollmeier, Paul. *Other Selves: Aristotle on Personal and Political Friendship.* Albany: State University of New York Press, 1994.

Schwartzenbach, Sybil. "On Civic Friendship." *Ethics* 107 (1996): 97–128.

---

[24] I made extensive revisions after the Symposium, Aristotelicum XI, August 1987, where this essay was presented, in response to the criticisms contained in Julia Annas' excellent official commentary (especially excellent where she was more firmly in disagreement with my own views), and to written and oral comments of several of the other symposiasts. I made especially substantial additions and changes in reply to questions and criticisms of D. J. Furley and T. H. Irwin. I am indebted also to M. M. McCabe for perceptive and, for me, fruitful comments on the original embryo of the paper, presented to a Princeton Classical Philosophy Conference in December 1983; to John R. Wallach, and to Richard Kraut for discussion and written comments on an intermediate version of the paper.

Justice and Rights in Aristotle's *Politics*

IN THE NINETEENTH CENTURY, and even as late as the 1940s, when Barker's translation (or rather, paraphrase) appeared, most translators and commentators on Aristotle's *Politics* did not hesitate, in some contexts, to employ the language of "rights" in presenting Aristotle's political theory. Here I mean the use of the word *right* as a noun, to denote something possessed by a person or persons, in a political context—not the use of the adjective *right,* with its opposite *wrong,* for example, to formulate various claims about what is just or fair; the use of that by an ancient Greek writer, we can assume, would be quite uncontroversial. For example, Barker makes Aristotle speak of the judicial system as deciding the "rights of litigants," and of a constitution as establishing who shall have the "right of election" of candidates for the various magistracies.[1] Furthermore, in translating Aristotle's final, general account of what constitutes citizenship, he gives, "he who enjoys the right of sharing in the deliberative or judicial office attains thereby the status of a citizen of his state."[2] Now what is at issue in these three passages are legal rights, rights established by the laws of a given community or determined under them through the exercise of their legally established functions by constitutionally authorized bodies or officials (juries or magistrates, for example). Barker also, however, very occasionally employs the same language of "rights" where Aristotle is discussing not what some set of laws establishes or does not establish as someone's rights (legal rights), but questions about what justice itself demands or forbids in the very establishment of such systems of legal rights. Thus in *Politics* III 16 Aristotle presents an argument that "some people" make against rule by kings, namely that it is unfair and indeed unnatural where the citizens are "similar" in political ability and merit for any one of them to rule permanently over the rest. Barker translates: "On this view those who are *naturally* equal must naturally have the same *rights* and worth. . . . The conclusion drawn is that justice for equals means their being ruled as well as their ruling."[3] Here we find Aristotle, in Barker's translation, presenting an appeal by these people to "natural rights"—the rights that equals "must naturally have"—not "legal" or constitutional ones. Moreover, this claim about what justice demands is one that Aristotle accepts: it forms the basis of his own concept of the best sort of political society, one where a body of more or

[1] See *Politics* IV 4, 1291a40; IV 15, 1299a11; Barker, *Politics,* 166, 194.
[2] See *Pol.* III 1, 1275b18–20; Barker, *Politics,* 95.
[3] Barker, *Politics,* 145 (emphasis added).

less equally virtuous citizens rule in turn, as naturally and justly befits equals. Thus, for Barker, Aristotle speaks of both legal and natural rights in his own political theory, as well as in discussing the views of other theorists and the practices of different types of constitutional arrangement.

If now we turn to the recent translation of the *Politics* by Carnes Lord, we see that the language of "rights" is completely avoided. Lord prefers to speak sometimes in terms of what a person or group of persons is "entitled to" under the laws, or of what is "open" or "permitted" to them; and he usually or always sticks to "justice" or a related term to translate *dikaion* and its derivatives—whether this is justice as established by the laws of a given community or type of community, or the true or correct account (according to Aristotle) of what justice is and demands. It is doubtful, though, whether Lord avoids rights-talk as a matter of interpretative principle. He aims to translate key terms of the Greek with a single English translation throughout. Since Aristotle uses no single Greek term where we might be tempted to speak of rights, it may have seemed to him that avoiding the language of rights was required simply by his conception of "literal" translation. In his glossary under the heading "Justice (*to dikaion*)," he explicates *to dikaion* in part as "a right or rightful claim" and adds that this sense is generally rendered in his translation by "[claim to] justice."[4] So, if we take this glossary entry as his full view, Lord would not object to the interpretation that at least in these passages Aristotle is speaking of rights or rightful claims. However, as a follower of Leo Strauss, and in his avoidance of the noun *right* to render anything Aristotle says Lord may also (and despite the informal comment in his glossary) be reflecting Strauss's own considered view, which was that any attribution of a notion of "rights" to Aristotle or any other ancient thinker is so grossly anachronistic that it must be strictly avoided.[5] In the past forty years or so, I think it is fair to say that this view of Strauss's has been shared widely, and increasingly so (not always on precisely Strauss's grounds, of course) by important writers on ancient politics and political thought.[6] Perhaps this tendency is all the more prevalent today, with the onset of self-described "postmodernist" thought and the historicism in all interpretation of the past that it so often connotes. Is there anything to this objection of vicious anachronism? Were Barker and other older interpreters erring seriously in attributing to Aristotle the view that various ancient constitutions grant political and other legal rights to (some of the) people living under them, and also theories of his own about human rights under justice that specify what these political and legal rights can legitimately be? In his book *Nature, Justice, and Rights in Aristotle's*

---

[4] Lord, "*Politics*" 276.

[5] See, for example, L. Strauss, *Natural Right and History*, 182–83. Fred D. Miller cites and discusses Strauss's views in *Nature, Justice, and Rights in Aristotle's "Politics,"* 92–93 and 114–15.

[6] Miller, *Nature, Justice and Rights*, sections 4.1, 4.2, and 4.4, surveys selected prominent authors' views on this topic.

"*Politics,*" Fred Miller argues at length, with appeal to a wealth of relevant Aristotelian texts, that they were making no mistake—at least none once certain distinctions are carefully drawn, and one is careful to state what is and what is not implied by the "rights" talk these authors were so readily finding in Aristotle's texts.

Miller's discussion of the question of "rights" in Aristotle seems to me quite illuminating and, on the main issue, quite persuasive: yes, Aristotle does recognize in the constitutions and legal systems of his own time, and provides theoretical underpinnings for, features that we have every reason to render in the language of our own political thought as *rights*. (But important qualifications are needed: see below). Likewise, his own proposals about the ideal best, and the acceptable, constitutions are grounded in a conception of justice that itself establishes what can fairly be called (leaving aside again certain qualifications) not only rights of justice, but even natural rights, of at least some persons, in relation to the constitutions they do and ought to live under. It is true, of course, that Aristotle uses no single Greek term to refer either to all those legal or to these natural rights; Greek had none. But Miller is right to point to the noun *exousia* (with its verb *exeinai*)—whose basic meaning is that something is open to one, or available or permitted: one has access to it. In the context of the provisions of a constitution, both in Aristotle and other writers, this Greek term regularly records the assignment of Hohfeldian liberty or privilege rights, for example the right to vote on certain matters, or the right of eligibility for certain offices, and so on—even the right to own private property.[7] When hearing people say, as one so often does, that Greek has no word for "rights," I have always been amazed that the speakers apparently do not know about this usage; how could they say that, I have wondered, in the face of the multitude of places, both in Aristotle and in other Greek writers, where this word occurs with that meaning?

However, *exousia* rights are of course only one type of the legal rights we recognize, and, besides that, there remains the larger and (from the philosophical point of view) more basic question of rights of justice, or, specifically, of natural rights. Also, even in the case of the political *exousiai,* the liberties and privileges that, as I say, seem so clearly to be rights of the persons or groups having them, there is a line of thought that seems to me a not at all implausible warning against precipitately employing our term *rights* to render in English the provisions of any Greek constitution, or the views of any Greek writer on such matters.[8] Until this line of thought is faced squarely and taken properly into account, I fear that many will continue to

---

[7] See Hohfeld, *Fundamental Legal Conceptions.* Miller argues convincingly (*Nature, Justice, and Rights,* 101–4) that Aristotle employs *exousia* and *exeinai* to refer to what Hohfeld defines as "liberties" or "privileges."

[8] Miller seems to me not to have grasped this line of thought; at any rate he has not responded sufficiently to it. See *Nature, Justice, and Rights,* 112–15.

balk at finding the language of rights at all appropriate for rendering Aristotle's political theory into English.

The line of thought I have in mind goes back to the eighteenth-century Enlightenment, but I believe it is Hegel's version of it that has proved influential in establishing the persistent sense among scholars that talk of rights is inappropriate in discussing ancient philosophy and politics. Central to Hegel's social and political thought is the theme that antiquity differs from modernity in that ancient societies, and ancient thinkers, did not recognize any value or validity simply in the expression of an arbitrary, purely subjective, individual will, as such, whereas modern society and modern social and political thought do and must recognize that value and validity. On Hegel's view, an ancient thinker like Aristotle can perfectly well find important value in individual persons, as such, voluntarily, and on their own understandings and choice, engaging in the good activities that make the life of a community a good one; and he can locate the preeminent political value in individuals as such achieving, through cooperation in the public life of the society, their individual goods so conceived.[9] But he does not and cannot envisage as an important good the exercise of one's individual will simply in working out for oneself, in one's own subjectivity, what things one will find good, and then doing or enjoying them, as so selected. This thing that Aristotle according to Hegel cannot envisage is what Hegel calls the "principle of subjective freedom"—the idea that in possessing this power of arbitrary self-determination we have something of infinite worth in each of us individually, that must be honored and respected in any acceptable political regime. Hegel very plausibly says that this principle "dawned in an inward form in the Christian religion . . . [and] is historically subsequent to the Greek world."[10] Hence he can say that Aristotle's conception of the state and its relations to its members is "antagonistic to the modern principle in which the particular will of the individual, as absolute, is made the starting point"[11]—Aristotle's conception of the state does not recognize this infinite worth nor make it the starting point for a conception, or theory, of political justice.

Now when people refuse to associate rights with ancient societies and ancient political theories, I think that implicitly they trace the ultimate origin of the concept of rights, both historically and philosophically, to Hegel's

[9] Since these good activities are actions of the virtues, they can also be thought of as acts of duty or service to the community. This thought is one expression of the traditional idea that Aristotle, like other ancient thinkers, placed priority on "duty," instead of "right": his very conception of the good of the individual persons making up the community is of such (personally fulfilling, excellent) community service. Miller responds to Strauss's version of this idea (*Nature, Justice, and Rights,* 115), but without seeing its roots in this part of Aristotle's theory. His response is therefore inconclusive.

[10] *Hegel's Philosophy of Right,* trans. Knox, ¶185, Addition.

[11] *Hegel's Lectures on the History of Philosophy,* ed. and trans. Haldane and Simpson, vol. II, 208.

"principle of subjective freedom":[12] "rights" of justice, or natural rights in particular, are whatever persons conceived under Hegel's "principle of subjective freedom" are (allegedly) entitled to as possessors of this infinite worth. One should note that taking the particular will, as absolute, for the starting point—and so having available a notion of individual "rights" to appeal to—does not necessarily require the thought that individuals enter political society fully formed from the outside (from a state of nature, or from behind a veil of ignorance), as already formed personalities justly imposing demands and conditions on this entrance—even if, historically, this was a favored way of expressing it. So this "Hegelian" objection to finding "rights" talk in Aristotle does not amount to saying that Aristotle neither shares nor could share any conception of persons in a state of nature, and to inferring therefore that he cannot believe in rights. One could recognize that individual personalities are necessarily formed within a political society, and still take the particular will, as absolute, for the starting point. This unsettles at least temporarily one of Miller's best points against his no-rights-in-Aristotle opponents. In arguing against Strauss, Miller insists (correctly enough, so far) that it does not follow from the fact that "Aristotle would have rejected a Hobbesian theory of prepolitical natural rights" that he "did not acknowledge individual rights based on nature in some other sense" than the prepolitical "state of nature."[13] However, when he then argues that Aristotle's theory of distributive justice, applied to the specific context of the arrangement of a political regime, yields the idea that natural justice dictates some specific such arrangements, it still does not follow that the entitlements, and so forth, embedded in a constitution that satisfies the demands of distributive justice are rights (legal ones) deriving from "natural rights." This certainly does not follow, if we accept the plausible historical and philosophical story, based on Hegel, that all talk of natural rights presupposes the "principle of subjective freedom." To describe those entitlements, and so on, that way, as deriving from "natural rights," would mean that Aristotle believed that they enable the exercise of "subjective freedom" in particular ways, and that their value would at least in part be due to the value of "subjective freedom" itself. Since Aristotle did not (and, if Hegel is right about the historical situation, could not) recognize any such value, it would be, as Strauss and others have said, a gross and vicious anachronism to present his theories in these terms—in the language of natural rights.

Can we argue that this is not so—that it *is* legitimate to describe Aristotle as talking of rights of justice, or natural rights in particular, and so of legal rights too, while not thereby attributing to him the acceptance of Hegel's principle of subjectivity? I would like to think so. Perhaps the following

[12] This certainly applies to Strauss; it may not apply to Alasdair MacIntyre, but it applies also to many if not all the others whose positions Miller reviews in *Nature, Justice, and Rights,* 87–93, 111–17.

[13] Ibid., 114.

represents at least a start toward an argument that it is legitimate to interpret Aristotle in these terms. One can grant that the first full-fledged theories of rights were introduced on the basis that Hegel's story suggests; and one can grant that the centrality of theories of rights within our contemporary theory of political justice, and our contemporary politics itself, is due to our acceptance of the "principle of subjectivity" and the importance we assign to it. Furthermore, one can grant that, as a result, there is a tendency, even a strong one, when there is talk of rights at all, to feel the pressure of the history retailed in Hegel's story—and so to feel some discomfort at attributions of thoughts about rights to thinkers who had not yet heard of the "principle of subjectivity." Still, one is not obligated to make that history part of the very concept itself of a right. No doubt it is through the work of modern thinkers, with their focus on the value of "subjective freedom," that we now have available to us the single term *rights* to apply to the various entitlements, liberties, just claims on the positive action of others, positive powers, and immunities that political arrangements, under justice, provide. But why, having this useful single term, as we now do, are we not free to use it even in discussing theories of these items that are not based on the recognition of any such value? Insisting on our freedom to use it in that way gives us the advantage of being able to draw together under that single term, and present in an illuminating and systematic way, the thoughts on these topics that even an ancient thinker like Aristotle could conceive. Surely, I would argue, the history of the term's introduction into modern political discourse gives no good reason to avoid, and—given the illumination brought by thus unifying those aspects of his theory—every reason to use, the language of rights in reporting and analyzing Aristotle's theories—provided, of course, that one makes it clear that here the term *right* is being used without implying that Aristotle accepted or even had any inkling of the value of "subjective freedom." By adding the language of "rights" to the otherwise dispersed talk in Aristotle's texts of what is "just," what a certain person or group of persons has "open to it" or "is eligible for," what a given official or the people as a whole has the "authority" to do, and what someone is by justice and law "immune" from,[14] we gain by making perspicuous a central element in his theories—the ways in which individual citizens and officials are assigned their functions or their areas of freedom, and protected in their actions within them. On this basis, then, we can claim not only to be entitled, but also justified, in using the language of rights in translating and interpreting Aristotle. It is not merely neo-Aristotelian updates of Aristotle, but even scholars engaged in philosophical reconstruction of his views, who can justifiably speak of "rights" and "natural rights" in Aristotle's *Politics*.

---

[14] Miller collects and analyzes clearly and usefully (*Nature, Justice, and Rights,* section 4.3) the different linguistic means that, lacking any unifying term for "rights," Aristotle employs for these four distinct types of rights recognized in Hohfeld's analysis; he is persuasive in

To this extent, then, it is reasonable and appropriate to present Aristotle as possessing a "theory of rights"; as Miller says, "he advances a set of recognizable rights claims which have a firm basis in his theory of justice and which explain other significant features of his political theory."[15] However, it is also important, at any rate if one is doing philosophical reconstruction, not to present Aristotle's theories as if he was as centrally occupied with questions about rights as modern and contemporary theorists are, precisely because they are committed to the pre-eminent value of "subjective freedom" in politics as in the rest of our lives. This is an ever-present danger for libertarian and liberal thinkers wishing to claim Aristotle's theory of rights as an ancient precursor to their own views. As a result, their use of rights-talk in reporting and discussing Aristotle can often convey, perhaps unconsciously, the false implication that Aristotle's interest in rights derived, like theirs, from the value of "subjective freedom." Here it is worth emphasizing that when Aristotle says that something or other is "just" in a political context—for example, that it is just for the more virtuous to hold the civic offices and do the community's deliberating about the common good—this almost always can, and often plainly does, contain two sides. In this example, when Aristotle says this distribution of functions is just, he is claiming that the more virtuous have a "right" of justice to rule, but he is also claiming that this is something that, under justice, they owe to one another and to other (full) members of the community, the other free and native-born persons, if there are any, belonging to it—as of course there always will be except perhaps in some "wish-state" such as that, maybe, of Aristotle's ideal community of books VII and VIII.[16] So here Aristotle's "it is just for them

---

arguing that Aristotle does clearly recognize rights of all Hohfeld's four sorts and has a good grasp of what they each involve.

[15] Miller, *Nature, Justice, and Rights,* 90.

[16] Aristotle's ideal state, serving only as a regulative ideal, is not bound by historically or other "practically" determined limitations—so it is at least conceivable that Aristotle thinks of that ideal state as one where the citizens who take turns ruling are also all the native-born free males living within it (see Miller, *Nature, Justice, and Rights,* section 6.9). About this, the text is indecisive. In *Pol.* VII 10, 1330a25–31 Aristotle does say that ideally the farmers in the ideal state should all be slaves or barbarian subjects, working the lands for the owners (individual citizens or the state), and conceivably he intends that all the nonslaves engaged, even at the highest levels, in trade, manufacture, and the crafts will be resident aliens (but he does not distinctly say so). But he can hardly have seriously intended that somehow or other *all* the native-born free persons even in some specially favored Greek population should attain through the educational and other institutions of his city the extremely high levels of moral and intellectual accomplishment that he requires for the exercise of the rights of citizenship: that would be more than we could wish for even in our "prayers," and Aristotle's Greek readers could not be expected to grasp such an intention on his part if it is not distinctly expressed. (Perhaps Aristotle is thinking of a new city founded, like the Magnesia of Plato's *Laws,* by specially selected colonists, but the standards of virtue to be maintained at Magnesia by the successive generations of ordinary citizens are quite low, compared with Aristotle's.) So, without being explicit about it one way or the other, he may be making the normal assumption that there will be some free native-born residents of his best city, recognized by the virtuous elite as fellow-citizens, but not participating in the rights of citizenship beyond

to rule" would be very misleadingly, because badly one-sidedly, construed as meaning "they have a right to." Of course, it would be wrong to say that for Aristotle those who have the right to rule only do so because it is also their duty—as if Aristotle shared Plato's anxious wish in the *Republic* to insist that those who are qualified to rule in his ideal city would only do so as a necessity and not as something they welcomed.[17] For him, the virtuous persons will see that the exercise of their virtues in this specific, complex context, that of deliberating about and managing the affairs of a self-sufficient community, is itself an optimal exercise of their virtues, and so they would gladly undertake the task simply out of recognition that their own highest good included it. Still, they would do it, in principal part, as an exercise of justice. That means that what they would be gladly undertaking is something required by justice in relation to their fellow-citizens, and they would do it *as* so required. Rights are not nearly so central to Aristotelian politics as is the case for modern and contemporary thinkers who formulate their own political philosophies around rights.

For this and related reasons, I think that many of the places in the *Ethics* and *Politics,* if not quite all of them, where Miller thinks he is entitled to translate *to dikaion* (literally, "the just") as "a (or 'the') right" are actually not correctly so translated—these are all passages where Miller thinks Aristotle is referring to a Hohfeldian "claim right," a right with correlative positive duties of some others to do something to satisfy it.[18] Instead, I think one ought to preserve in translation the more literal term *just* or some derivative, not necessarily because no claim right is being indicated in these passages by the term, but because that is not all that it is, or may be, expressing as used there. Thus, when in *Politics* IV 4 Aristotle is enumerating the "parts" of which a city is composed and comes round to the judicial function, he specifies it as *to bouleuomenon kai krinon peri tōn dikaiōn tois amphisbētousin;*[19] Miller would have us translate or interpret this as meaning that the judge's function is to determine that to which each party has a just claim (i.e., a right).[20] However, the concerns of justice that arise in a dispute do not always concern claim rights. Think of Socrates' dispute with Anytus and Meletus over Socrates' dealings with the young men of Athens: the dispute was over whether Socrates had behaved unjustly and illegally, but the accusers did not assert any "claim right," for example to

---

being regarded as parts of the community at whose mutual advantage the laws and the rulers aim—the slaves, barbarian subjects, and resident aliens would not be part of the community even in this minimal sense, of course. (If so, Aristotle's general idea that in a "correct" constitution those holding political power rule for the common, not for their own personal, advantage would apply quite straightforwardly to this special case, as of course it ought to.) This was my own assumption in Chapter 16 above, "Political Animals and Civic Friendship," 364.

[17] See *Republic* 345e, 519c–521b.

[18] Miller, *Nature, Justice, and Rights,* 97–101.

[19] Lit., "what deliberates and decides about the things that are just for disputants." Here and in the discussion that follows, the Greek text cited is that of Ross.

[20] Miller, *Nature, Justice, and Rights,* 98.

property, against Socrates, nor did he assert any "claim right" against them or indeed anyone else. Even when the dispute is over claim rights, the resolution could involve appeals to wider aspects of justice than merely satisfying the respective claim rights of the disputants: significantly, in discussing his ideal state, Aristotle says that in order to judge well about issues of justice (*peri tōn dikaiōn*) (including claim rights, no doubt) his citizens need to know one another's characters.[21]

Again, in discussing what a citizen is and which of the residents of a polis should be counted as its citizens, Aristotle says, "Nor are those persons citizens who partake of *tōn dikaiōn* [lit., 'just things'] to the extent of undergoing and bringing ('private') lawsuits"[22] (he has in mind that sometimes treaties reciprocally open the court system of a city to citizens of other places). Clearly, I should think, *tōn dikaiōn* here simply means in effect "the court system": the people who partake of *tōn dikaiōn* not only have the right to bring (private) suits but can also be sued themselves in the city's courts. So Miller's translation, "persons who partake of just-claim rights" to the extent specified is not correct: one does not partake of a just-claim right in that one can be *sued* (any claim-right involved there will be someone else's, not one's own).[23] In defense of this rendering, Miller might point out

---

[21] See *Pol.* VII 4, 1326b14–15. Perhaps Aristotle only means that in order to determine what justice requires the judges have to know whether the people testifying are to be trusted in their evidence, but more seems intended than that—a person's just assessment or punishment and so on should at least sometimes reflect in some way their moral standing, not just the other facts of the case. In any case, in this and other passages also not mentioned by Miller where Aristotle refers to deciding about *ta dikaia* (VII 8, 1328b14, and 9, 1329a4), he is plainly to be taken as referring to decisions in court about questions of justice in general, not especially or necessarily merely ones related to "just-claim" rights. On the other hand, the reference at VI 8, 1322a5–6 to *dikas peri tōn dikaiōn* appears, from the context, to concern disputes specifically over money and property, so there (though strictly the language speaks again simply of "suits over questions of justice") Barker's translation "suits for the determination of rights" would certainly not be wrong. (Miller omits to mention this passage, too.)

[22] *Pol.* III 1, 1275a8–10.

[23] Miller, *Nature, Justice, and Rights,* 98. Miller misconstrues the Greek of the continuation, introducing a further reference to rights into his translation: "for this also belongs to those who have a community as a result of treaties (for these [rights] also belong to these persons)." ("This" plainly refers back to partaking of "just things.") He says (99 n.) that in 1275a11 (where he follows Dreizehnter in retaining the phrase bracketed by Ross) he is taking ταῦτα (these [rights]) to refer back to τῶν δικαίων (lit., "just things") and τούτοις (these persons) to οἱ . . . μετέχοντες (those who partake of "just things"). Then, however, the parenthetical clause says emptily and pointlessly that these rights (also!?) belong to those who participate in these rights. Miller could avoid making this clause empty and pointless by taking "these persons" to refer to τοῖς . . . κοινωνοῦσιν (those who have a community as a result of treaties). But in fact, given that τοῦτο (this) refers to the partaking of just things, the order of the Greek demonstratives pretty clearly makes ταῦτα refer to undergoing and bringing lawsuits (as well as τούτοις refer to "those who have a community as a result of treaties"). Furthermore, only so are satisfactory inferential relationships asserted by the two occurrences of γάρ (for). In sum, Aristotle is giving reasons to accept his claim that it is not a satisfactory criterion of citizenship that someone partakes of "just things" in a city: he says, sensibly, that (in addition to the native-born people who have access to the city's courts) noncitizens also bring and

that the ability to defend oneself in court could be highly valued, preferable to joining the ranks of women, and, in some Greek cities, foreign business-men, who had to rely on the goodwill and competence of others having access to the courts in representing them. Though that is true, however, it remains a forced (and noxiously theory-driven) reading to find talk of "rights" here. *Ta dikaia* is a very natural way of saying in Greek "the procedures of justice," that is, the court system. That that is what it means here is borne out in the language Aristotle uses to explain what the *dikaia* are that the people referred to partake of (note the double occurrence of the root *dik-*): they can *dikēn hupechein kai dikazesthai*, i.e., bring and answer private suits—the bringing and answering of suits, themselves, and not some supposed rights to do these things, are the *dikaia* that they partake of. (They cannot, of course, bring suits on public matters, for example suits claiming that someone has moved something illegal in the assembly or has corrupted the young citizens by teaching them to philosophize obnoxiously; so they do not partake of these other *dikaia*—these other matters of justice.)[24]

In finding concern for rights central to Aristotle's political theory, Miller appears to place most emphasis on a passage of *Politics* III 12 where he thinks Aristotle speaks directly of "political rights" (*politika dikaia*). His interpretation of this passage, too, can reasonably be disputed.[25] The main point of the chapter is to argue, in large part from analogy with other arts and sciences (Aristotle's example is flute-playing), that not every difference in good qualities among the citizens can support an excess assignment of political functions (*archai*),[26] but (as a first approximation) only those that make a difference in the "work" of the city, such as free status, or wealth, or high birth—and also justice and the rest of political excellence itself.[27] Just as more and better flutes (the instruments for flute-playing) ought to go to the players who are better at playing the flute, so the instruments for politics, the political offices and functions, ought to be distributed on the basis of some superior contribution (such as the ones mentioned) to the work of the city. Here Aristotle speaks, as often, of the "claims" of different groups and persons to political rule, but of course the real issue is, what justice requires of, as much as what it allows to, differently qualified people.[28] Toward the beginning of the chapter, Aristotle heaps scorn on the more open-ended idea that any excess of a good quality, of whatever kind and whether or not it makes any contribution to the work of the city, would in

---

undergo suits in the courts because of treaties with other cities, so that they too partake in the city's "just things." He is not talking merely about having claim-rights, nor indeed especially about rights at all.

[24] For the distinction between "public" and "private" suits in the courts of Athens, see for example MacDowell, *The Law in Classical Athens.*

[25] See Miller, *Nature, Justice, and Rights,* 100.

[26] See *Pol.* III 12, 1282b24–25, 1283a11: lit., "offices for ruling."

[27] See *Pol.* III 12, 1283a16–20.

[28] Note especially δεῖν, "ought" or "must," 1282b24.

itself justify a greater distribution of these functions.[29] The principle here would be that τοῖς διαφέρουσιν ἕτερον εἶναι τὸ δίκαιον καὶ τὸ κατ' ἀξίαν:[30] a satisfactory and untendentious translation of this Greek would be "for those who differ [with respect to *any* good] what is just and what is merited is different." (Miller, however, translates: "those who differ have a different just-claim right and merit-based claim.")[31] The absurdity would result that people who excel in their complexion or height or any other good quality would get *pleonexia tis tōn politikōn dikaiōn,* lit., "an excess holding of the just things of politics."[32] However we translate this unusual Greek, the context proves that the "just things of politics" referred to are political offices or functions; a satisfactory and untendentious translation might be "the functions of political justice." Miller translates the whole phrase as "an excess possession of political rights." That is surely tendentious and unjustified; it shifts Aristotle's focus away from the two aspects of justice— rights plus duties—to rights alone.[33]

In these passages I think Miller goes too far in promoting in Aristotle the sort of fixated interest in the rights of citizens that one accepting the value of "subjective freedom" characteristically has.[34] Miller makes an excellent case that Aristotle both has a concept of rights and develops interesting theories about which rights, in justice, people have, and on what basis. If we qualify this so as to make it clear that, in attributing to Aristotle concerns about and theories of legal and even natural rights, we are not implying any commitment on his part to, or even understanding of, the idea of "subjective freedom" as a value, I have argued myself that it is reasonable, appropriate, and in fact very helpful to use talk of rights in translating and interpreting him. We ought also, however, to keep firmly in mind that questions about rights are not so central in Aristotle's politics as they are in our own, precisely because he did not have any such commitment or

[29] See 1282b23–30.

[30] 1282b26–27.

[31] At *Pol.* III 13, 1283b17–18 and 21–23, he similarly translates κατὰ τὸ αὐτὸ δίκαιον as "based on the same just-claim right," where I would say it is clear that the meaning is rather "based on the same conception of justice." The context is a dispute between the champions of oligarchy, rule by the most ancient families, and rule by the free-born natives—each with their own theory of what qualities the just assignment of offices is based on. Likewise, κατὰ τὸ ὀλιγαρχικὸν δίκαιον at VI 3, 1318a24 surely means "according to the oligarchic conception of justice," not, as Miller has it (*Nature, Justice, and Rights,* 100), "based on the oligarchic just-claim right."

[32] 1282b29–30.

[33] Similarly, I would say that the phrase *archein dikaios* at *Pol.* III 16, 1287b12–13 and VI 3, 1318a24 does not mean merely "has a right to rule" or a "just-claim right to rule" (so Miller, *Nature, Justice, and Rights,* 101), but that it is "just" that he do so: the term *dikaios* may carry the nuance of a requirement as well as that of an entitlement here, and the translation ought not to obscure that.

[34] Since I have disputed his handling of so many of the passages he cites for the translation of *to dikaion* as "just-claim right," I should report that in one of these passages (*Pol.* III 9, 1280b11) the context does seem to me to support that translation.

understanding. By exploiting every conceivable passage where Aristotle may possibly be appealing to rights, libertarian and liberal writers risk blurring this crucial difference between Aristotle's political philosophy and their own.

SELECTED FURTHER READINGS

Miller, Fred D., Jr. "Aristotle and the Origins of Natural Rights." *Review of Metaphysics* 49 (1996): 873–907.
Review of Metaphysics 49 no. 4, June 1996, is a special issue devoted to articles dealing with topics raised by Miller's book, *Nature, Justice, and Rights in Aristotle's "Politics."*

CHAPTER EIGHTEEN

Ethical-Political Theory in Aristotle's *Rhetoric*

ARISTOTLE'S *Rhetoric* treats of a certain mental attainment, the developed capacity (*hexis,* 1.1.2, 1354a7) that enables a person to speak persuasively in certain contexts and on certain sorts of questions. Strictly speaking, it is the ability to speak persuasively when addressing citizens of a Greek city gathered either in the assembly to pass laws and resolutions of the people, or in law-courts as jurors to decide the rights and wrongs of disputed cases, or else on occasions of political ceremony to hear patriotic speeches. The sorts of questions on which the person with this *hexis* can speak are those that are taken up at such citizens' gatherings, namely (using the term broadly) political questions. In Aristotle's usage *hē rhētorikē* ("rhetoric") is simply a name for this capacity[1]—however much we, and he, might see broader uses for what is essentially the same capacity of persuasion that the public speaker needs to have. Aristotle holds that rhetoric, so understood, is, or is capable of being, an art—something acquired by systematic study and, once acquired, consisting in the possession of certain formulable principles through the use of which an orator can then prepare and deliver his speeches.[2]

The principal purpose of Aristotle's treatise is to develop and expound

---

[1] *Rhet.* 1.2.1, 1355b26–27; cf. 1.1.13, 1355b3–4, τῇ τοιαύτῃ δυνάμει τῶν λόγων.

[2] Aristotle argues that rhetoric is an art in the first paragraph of the treatise, at 1354a6–11. Since αὐτά at line 8 should have the same reference as ταῦτα at line 7, viz. (see πάντες . . . ἐγχειροῦσιν, 4–6), the activities of subjecting views to criticism, withstanding criticism oneself, defending oneself in court, and prosecuting a case, Aristotle's argument here seems best understood as follows. Ordinary people (οἱ πολλοί, viz., people who cannot be said to possess an *art* of speaking) do these things either at random (saying whatever comes into their heads) or by being familiar with those sorts of activity and practiced at them. (The latter group can at least be said to have some sort of settled capacity in these regards, a ἕξις). But whether they speak at random or from a practiced state, it is clearly possible to work out the causes for their success at these tasks when they do succeed—and everyone would grant that knowing causes is the function of an art. Accordingly, once one has examined these causes systematically, one will be in a position no longer to engage in these activities (ποιεῖν αὐτά) either at random or from an ability born solely of familiarity and practice, but on the basis of an *art,* i.e. in a systematic and orderly way (ὁδῷ), by following clearly formulated principles.

Cope and (presumably following him) Freese and Roberts (also as revised by Barnes) do not see that αὐτά and ταῦτα have the same reference and so they do not get Aristotle's argument exactly right. But the argument is tendentious in any case: some one could well dispute whether there must be determinate causes here, capturable in Aristotelian principles, and argue that the ability born of familiarity and practice already *was* an art, and as much of an art as is ever available to human beings in this context. Aristotle characteristically ignores this possible view, here and throughout the *Rhetoric,* presupposing his own preferred account of what constitutes an art and refusing, like Socrates in the *Gorgias,* to count the ἐμπειρία born of familiarity and practice as an art at all.

these principles in a systematic way, and so to establish rhetoric firmly as an art. He thinks all his predecessors who claimed to write a *technē tōn logōn* ("an art of speaking") had failed pretty completely even to understand what it would *take* to make rhetoric an art, and so he thinks his own *technē rhētorikē* is the very first treatment of rhetoric there has ever been that makes a serious, well-informed claim to develop it as an art. In what follows I want to discuss the status of the principles for rhetoric that Aristotle provides. In particular I want to investigate their relationship to the truths about the political matters on which the orator speaks that Aristotle himself thinks belong to what he calls *hē politikē*—"political philosophy" or "knowledge," or the "political art," the capacity that provides knowledge of the correct answers to the broadly political questions on which the trained orator is called to speak.

Aristotle belittles earlier writers of *technai logōn* because, in effect, they did not understand that if oratory is to be an art it must consist essentially of efforts to persuade by argument, that is, by advancing considerations calculated to be accepted as reasons supporting the conclusions the orator is arguing for (1.1.3–4, 1354a11–18). According to Aristotle these writers limited themselves to working up ideas on how to arouse in the hearers emotions (pity, indignation, anger . . .) that would influence their judgment in a way favorable to the orator's case. It is not that a principled ability to arouse emotions is no part of the art of rhetoric, in either Aristotle's considered view later in the treatise or his introductory discussion of his predecessors' failures. Aristotle immediately grants that this *is* a part, though only a small part, *oligon morion* (1.1.3, 1354a12–13), of the art, and in the next chapter he confirms this in articulating his own account of the most basic components of the art of rhetoric, the three *entechnoi pisteis* or means of persuasion fashioned directly by the art itself (1.2.2–6, 1355b38ff). His objection is, rather, to the manner in which this legitimate subject was treated by his predecessors. Because, according to him, they devoted *no* attention to how the orator ought to construct and present an argument for his conclusion—to organize and put forward some reasons for believing it—the appeals to emotion they theorized about and recommended must have been conceived of as entirely separate from the presentation of the case, not an integral accompaniment of it. Therefore they were doing nothing but giving instruction on how to speak off the subject, to speak about irrelevancies; and that obviously cannot be a true part of the art of oratory.

This simple point gives what is surely the correct resolution to the over-contested question whether these preliminary objections of Aristotle's to his predecessors are consistent with his own theory and practice of rhetoric as that is displayed in the remainder of the treatise, where, of course, arousing the audience's emotions is an essential rhetorical technique. It is another and entirely separate question whether 1.1, where he airs these objections, was written earlier than 1.2, where he explains his views on the three *entechnoi pisteis* and includes emotional appeal as one among them. The other differences of outlook one may see between Aristotle's views in 1.1 and his views in the rest of the first and second books, in particular his rather severe remarks at 1354a26–b16 about what a good system of laws would and would not permit those arguing cases in court to talk about, do not imply, and need not suggest, an absolute ban on emotional appeals in arguing cases in court. There may be room for appropriately "emotional" language even in simply establishing the facts of a case; and the ban on *diastrephein ton dikastēn* ("corrupting the juror/judge") by making him angry, etc., that Aristotle wants to impose at 1354a24–26 is, in its context, perfectly consistent with banning only freestanding and so argumentatively irrelevant appeals to emotion.[3]

Since, as I have noted, Aristotle has just granted that the arousing of emotions that was studied and practiced by his predecessors *was* a part, though only a small one, of the art, when he goes on to say that they mostly attended to τὰ ἔξω τοῦ πράγματος at 1.1.3, 1354a15–16 (or in the summation at 1.1.11, 1355a18–19, or at 1.1.9, 1354b17), he certainly ought not to mean "things lying outside the art's concerns."[4] This phrase must mean what it plainly does just below at 1.1.5, 1354a22–23, and again at 1.1.10, 1354b27 and 1355a2, namely "off the subject." At 1.1.3, 1354a14–16, he says that his predecessors dealt not with means of persuasion properly belonging to the art (*pisteis*) but only with "accessories" (*prosthēkai*) and with parts of a speech that are strictly off the subject, which therefore a good system of laws would simply forbid, thus leaving orators of the type of his predecessors simply with nothing to say. Here, again, therefore, he does not imply that a good system of laws would forbid appeals to the judges' emotions. He means only that good laws would forbid appeals to emotion that detracted from and were no part of the orderly presentation of the case itself being argued. So it is *irrelevant* appeals to emotion made by the orator in and through his speech (e.g., by describing shocking or uplifting events and circumstances having no bearing on the matters in dispute or on the questions of right and wrong before the court), not appeals to emotion altogether, that Aristotle here objects to.[5] Likewise, when he says (1.1.9, 1354b16–22) that in their rules about what the "introduction" and "narration" etc., of a speech should contain the previous writers made no contribution to the art itself, this should be understood carefully against the background he himself provides while saying this: *their* rules were rules about how to speak off the subject (*exō tou pragmatos*, 1354b17) in such

---

[3] These simple considerations are sufficient to undermine a good part of Solmsen's influential discussion, pp. 208–29, of alleged differences between Aristotle's "1.1 program" for rhetoric and the program from 1.2 onward.

[4] So Cope, *Introduction* p. 4, who paraphrases ἔξω τοῦ πράγματος here by "*extra artem*— outside the limits of a genuine 'Art of Rhetoric.'"

[5] Cope comes close to getting Aristotle's point here but spoils it by linking together (*Introduction*, p. 5) *all* direct appeals to emotion through "exaggerated" language with the production in court of widow, orphans, etc., as both equally objectionable in Aristotle's eyes here.

a way as to put the judges into a favorable emotional state (1354b20). He does not imply that *no* concern with the divisions of a speech and what they should contain can be part of the art of rhetoric, or that the sort of concern he himself shows in *Rhetoric* III cannot be. So Aristotle's criticisms of his predecessors in 1.1 are not at all inconsistent with his own theory and practice of the art of rhetoric later in the treatise.

As I mentioned above, Aristotle himself recognizes *three* means of persuasion that skill at speaking can enable an orator to exercise, not singly the manipulation of the addressee's emotions to which he says his predecessors in rhetorical instruction limited the art (1.2.3, 1356a1–4). First there is the argument itself (*autos ho logos,* 1356a4), the presentation of the reasons, drawn from the facts about the matter to hand, that the orator is putting forward as grounds for believing the conclusions for which he is arguing. Next, there is the speaker's representation of himself as a believable and trustworthy spokesman (*ēthos*). Finally, the speaker can put his audience in an emotional frame of mind that will encourage receptivity to his conclusions (*pathos*).[6] In fact, however, though he does not put the matter explicitly so, the first of these three "technical" means of persuasion, in the order I have just presented them—the one he calls "the argument itself"—takes a certain precedence over the other two.[7] For Aristotle, appeals to emotion are indeed a legitimate means of persuasion in oratory, but only provided they are made an integral part of the orderly exposition of and argument for the orator's case: ὅταν εἰς πάθος ὑπὸ τοῦ λόγου [οἱ ἀκροαταί] προαχθῶσιν, 1.2.5, 1356a14–15.

The same condition applies for the third of the three *entechnoi pisteis,* the speaker's representation of his own character as that of a perceptive and intelligent, morally good and well-meaning person (2.1.5, 1378a6–9): this must be done *through the argument,* δεῖ δὲ καὶ τοῦτο συμβαίνειν διὰ τοῦ λόγου, 1.2.4, 1356a8–9. Here, as the context shows,[8] *dia tou logou*

---

[6] Aristotle himself sets out the three *pisteis* in the order *ēthos-pathos-logos,* presumably because (1.2.4, 1356a13) he thinks the speaker's character as represented in his speech (and its delivery) is the most decisive means of persuasion he controls. In my paraphrase, I follow instead the order of the speech's composition—on the assumption that one begins with the plotting out of the argument, adding the other *pisteis* as one fleshes this out.

[7] At 1.1.3, 1354a15 he does call enthymemes the σῶμα τῆς πίστεως, the "substance of (the means of) persuasion." Perhaps he speaks loosely there, meaning enthymemes to stand for the whole of rhetorical proof, παραδείγματα (inductions from examples) included, as he seems also to do at e.g., 1.1.11, 1355a6–7 (see also 1.2.19, 1358a1–2, where πίστεις ἀποδεικτικαί include παραδείγματα as well as ἐνθυμήματα, and 2.25.8, 1402b12–14, where παράδειγμα is listed as one of the sources of ἐνθύμημα); in that case he will be saying that rhetorical proof as a whole (i.e., *autos ho logos*) is the "substance of (the means of) persuasion." As such, it is only natural that it should take precedence over the other two kinds of *pistis.*

[8] Notice that through this preliminary exposition of the three *pisteis* (1.2.3–6, 1356a1–20) the word *logos* wavers between meaning simply the speech (the ordering of the words spoken) and, more exactly, the speech regarded as an argument to support the case. It clearly means primarily the former at a1, where the contrast is simply with the *atechnoi pisteis* (witnesses, testimony by torture, contracts, etc.) that are provided otherwise than by the orator's exercise

does indeed mean "through the argument" and not merely "by what he says." On the latter interpretation, Aristotle would permit the orator to devote a special part of his speech to citing testimonials about his character, and another one, perhaps, to simply stirring up in his listeners the emotions he needs them to be feeling as they subsequently consider the argument. But it is precisely because his predecessors attempted to treat appeals to the hearers' emotions without seeing them in their essential connection to the construction and presentation of the argument that, according to Aristotle, what they provided was advice only about something at best ancillary and nonessential (and not even permissible under ideal rules for the exercise of the art).[9]

Though Aristotle does not point this out, his own philosophical investigations in the *Ethics* and *Politics* provide valuable support for the idea that the orator must rely on both the representation of his own *ēthos* and the arousing of various *pathē* in his hearers as means of persuasion. When in defense of the representation of *ēthos* Aristotle says (1.2.4, 1356a6–9) that we are inclined implicitly to accept the judgment of someone whom we take to be a good person, in matters that are not cut and dried and where ordinary, normally reasonable people can honestly differ in their opinions (ἐν οἷς δὲ τὸ ἀκριβὲς μή ἐστιν ἀλλὰ τὸ ἀμφιδοξεῖν), he relies (although silently) on his own careful elaboration in the *Ethics* of the claim that what I have called (in a broad sense of the term) the "political" questions on which orators speak *are* matters of this kind. And in support (again unstated)

---

of his art in speaking his own words, but it plainly means the latter at a4 (ἐν αὐτῷ τῷ λόγῳ: see the explanation of this *pistis* that he goes on to give, a19–20). After that, where he is explaining how the other two *pisteis* must be conveyed διὰ or ὑπὸ τοῦ λόγου (a5, 9, 14, 19), it means both. See also 1.8.6, 1366a8–11, where Aristotle's thought plainly is that the *same* *logos* ought to be both ἀποδεικτικός and at the same time ἠθικός: the enthymemes and other proofs offered are to be presented in language and with a manner that conveys to the hearers the impression that the speaker is an intelligent, good, and well-meaning person (or, more specifically, has qualities of character that the given audience will take as showing these characteristics). And see 3.2.2, 1404b15–18: if you know *how* to say what you ought to say, that makes the λόγος ποιός τις—that is, makes it have an appropriate ethical character. In both these passages the *logos* is both speech and argument, and it is essential to Aristotle's point that *logos* should be so interpreted. He is rejecting the idea that one's ethical character should be conveyed in a separate part of the speech, and not simply in the way in which one couches the presentation of the argument.

[9] In expounding his views on the connection of the other two means of persuasion to the first, Aristotle makes it explicit that he is departing also from some of his sophistic predecessors' views on how the speaker can make use of his own character in speaking. He points out (1.2.4, 1356a9–10) that the orator's reliance on his *prior* reputation in order to effect persuasion has nothing to do with the art, because it is not something created on the spot by the orator's skill at speaking: having and using an established good reputation (a δόξα ἐπιεικής) was an allegedly artistic device recommended by Anaximenes (assuming he is the author of the *Rhetoric to Alexander*) and perhaps also by Isocrates in his Τέχνη ῥητορική (if indeed he ever wrote one). See *Rhet. ad Alex.* ch. 38, 1445b32–34, and Isocrates *Antidosis* 278–80, with the discussion of Süss, pp. 125–31. (Other sophistical predecessors seem to have denied that the speaker's character was in any event a means of proof; see 1.2.4, 1356a10–13.)

of his defense of appeals to emotion (1.2.5, 1356a15–16; 2.1.4, 1377b31–1378a6), on the ground that (in these "political" contexts) people's judgments of things and persons are altered by their emotional states, stands his very impressive account in the *Ethics* of the nonrational types of desire, which lie at the root of the emotions, and their effects on people's reasoned views and reasoned attitudes to things.[10] When one adds that according to Aristotle's philosophical theory of ethics-politics it is fully appropriate to feel emotions as well as to have reasoned judgments concerning the sorts of value-laden topics discoursed on by orators, one sees that the philosophical grounding for his defense in the *Rhetoric* of *pathos* as a legitimate, "technical" means of oratorical persuasion is deep and extensive. Admittedly, Aristotle's emphasis on the priority of *logos*—the orator's *argument* for his conclusions—to these other *pisteis* would require significant reforms in ancient oratorical practice. But his defense of the legitimacy of *ēthos* and *pathos* as means of oratorical persuasion should be welcomed by orators not only for adding to the prestige of their craft but also for giving them a deeply considered justification for their confidence in its practice.[11]

From Aristotle's theory of the three *pisteis,* it follows at once that the principles of the art, drawing on which the accomplished, "artistic" orator will select and compose the contents of his discourse, will be just those that will allow him to do each of three things. They will allow him (1) to find and present to his listeners as persuasive considerations as the facts and circumstances permit in favor of the conclusions he is attempting to bring them to accept. And they will enable him while arguing his case (2) to represent himself to his hearers, so far as possible, as a person of intelligence, good character, and good will; and (3) to do as much as the circumstances permit to put his hearers into an emotional frame of mind conducive to accepting his conclusions and acting appropriately on them.[12]

---

[10] On this see Chapter 10 above, esp. sect. IV, and Chapter 11.

[11] For ἀκρίβεια and ethics-politics, see *Nic. Eth.* 1.3. 1094b11–27; 1.7, 1098a26–33; 2.2, 1103b31–1104a11; 8.7, 1159a3–5; 9.2, 1164b27–1165a14; also 2.9. 1109b12–26 and 4.5, 1126a31–b4. For the nonrational desires and their effects on rational judgment, see 1.13, 1102b13–25 and 1103a3–10, together with 6.5, 1140b11–20; 6.12, 1144a29–36; 6.13, 1145a2–6. On the appropriateness of feeling emotions, see in general the theory of moral virtue as lying in a mean, according to which it is *right* to feel joy, gratitude, anger, fear, pity, hatred, etc., about some of the matters that come before a jury for adjudication, an assembly for resolution, or the audience of a commemorative address for appreciation.

[12] In preparing this summary, I have taken it that when Aristotle says at 1.1.14, 1355b10–11 and 26–27 (and in the *Topics* at 6.12, 149b25–26 and 1.3, 101b8–10) that the art of rhetoric consists in the ability systematically to see in each matter τὸ ἐνδεχόμενον πιθανόν (the available means of persuasion), and not necessarily actually to persuade his hearers, he means to include under this term everything belonging to all three of the *entechnoi pisteis,* and not just the available persuasive *arguments* one could present (as one might conclude from his usage of the term πιθανόν in such places as *Rhet.* 1.2.7, 1356a19–20). Anything is πιθανόν that contributes to *pistis,* and on Aristotle's view *ēthos* and *pathos,* as well as the argument itself, do that. Note that at 1.2.4, 1356a12 Aristotle explicitly uses the term τὸ πιθανόν to cover what the speaker's good character contributes to (see also 1.8.6, 1366a13).

In order (1) to construct the actual arguments, one would expect that two sorts of principles would be involved: first, what one might call formal principles, to do with types and structures of argumentation; and then substantive ones, providing materials or strategies for selecting the specific, substantive points to weave into those structures in the case at hand. And given that the questions orators give speeches about are ethical-political in character, one would expect these substantive principles to be in some way principles of politics (in a broad sense of that term)—the principles constitutive of *politikē epistēmē,* the philosophical knowledge of political affairs. It seems plain that the principles needed to do (2) and (3) should likewise be in some way substantive, ethical-political ones, at any rate according to the treatment of *ēthos* and *pathos* that Aristotle provides in his own philosophical treatises. He describes the philosophical enquiry engaged in in the *Nicomachean Ethics* as *politikē* (*Nic. Eth.* 1.2, 1094b10–11), and that enquiry encompasses both his most thoroughgoing and fundamental philosophical treatment of the role of the *pathē* in human life and decision, and his account, from philosophical first principles, of *phronēsis* ("practical wisdom"), the moral *aretai,* and *eunoia* ("good will"), the three characteristics that he holds the speaker must attempt to represent himself as possessing if he is to exercise the means of persuasion that he calls *ēthos* (see *Rhet.* 2.1.5–6, 1378a8–15).[13] So, one might think, the orator needs to know, anyhow up to a point, the logic needed to construct valid arguments, and enough ethical and political theory, first, to find the premises needed to establish the various ethical-political conclusions that from time to time it may be his task to defend, and second to teach him what the various emotions and virtues are, so that he could know how to give a good picture of his own character and bring about the appropriate and desired emotional states in his hearers.

So it is no surprise that, in a famous phrase, Aristotle concludes from his analysis of the three *pisteis* (1.2.7, 1356a25–27) that the art of rhetoric is something like an offshoot of (or, 1.4.5, 1359b9–10, a construction from) two other arts or studies or branches of knowledge (*epistēmai*): a "formal" one, dialectic (tellingly equated with analytic, *hē analutikē epistēmē,* at 1359b10), which knows all about proofs that are deductive or apparently so (1.1.11, 1355a6–10, 1.1.14, 1355b16–17) but also about other sorts of proof ("inductive" ones, proofs by example: 1.2.8–9, 1356a35–b17), plus a substantive one, ethics, that is to say (in my broad sense of the term), politics. What *might* cause surprise in these passages (1.2.7 and 1.4.5) is that, officially, it is through rhetoric's relation to dialectic that Aristotle

---

[13] On the πάθη see *Nicomachean Ethics* 2.5 and numerous passages distributed through the discussion of the ethical virtues, too many to list. On φρόνησις see esp. 6.5, 6.7–9, but also many important remarks in books 1, 2, 7, and 10, again too numerous to list here. On the ἀρεταί see esp. 2.4–6 and the detailed analyses of 3.6–12 and books 4 and 5. And on εὔνοια see 9.5, but also the whole theory of friendship as involving εὔνοια in which this is embedded (books 8–9; see esp. 8.2); cf. Chapter 14 above.

seems to account wholly for the first rhetorical *pistis,* the *logos* itself; he seems to make rhetoric an offshoot of "politics" solely because of the orator's need to know how to represent his own character as a good one and to put his hearers into the emotional states suitable to the objectives of his speech. These are, of course, things for which the correct philosophical theory of ethics-politics does contain foundational information that might be thought to be just what the orator needs. What is surprising is that Aristotle does not mention that rhetoric is connected to ethics-politics also because the specific, substantive points the orator needs to select in constructing his arguments on the "political" subjects on which he is called to speak are matters about which the correct ethical-political philosophy will (in some sense) provide the foundations.

Nonetheless, when in 1.4–14 he expounds the specific topics that an orator must draw on for the materials of his arguments in speeches in the three branches of oratory, it is easy to see that these all do fall squarely within the area of political philosophy as this is defined and treated in Aristotle's own philosophical works: happiness and its constituents; general criteria for the goodness of anything (with analytical list of the important kinds of good things); what makes one good thing a better good than another one; the different political constitutions and their characteristic differences in conceptions of what and who is good; moral virtues and vices; injustice and unjust action (with its causes); pleasure and pleasant things, as causes of wrongdoing; what sorts of persons do wrong, and under what circumstances; acts just and unjust, and their varieties; how to compute the comparative badness of different unjust acts. In fact, at 1.4.7, 1359b16–18, in the continuation of the second of the two passages where he describes rhetoric as an "offshoot" of two other kinds of knowledge, he introduces his account of the *protaseis* (premises) for deliberative oratory by saying that he will discuss these not κατὰ τὴν ἀλήθειαν (in reliance on the truth), but only up to a lower standard, leaving the more accurate treatment to ethics-politics— which clearly implies that he is thinking of the premises needed by the orator as belonging in some sense to ethical-political theory.

Furthermore, at two places in the subsequent detailed discussion, Aristotle explicitly recognizes that this is so (1.4.13, 1360a37–38; 1.8.7, 1366a20– 22); and in several other places he either notes that some topic there being treated is useful also for one of the other means of persuasion, *ēthos* or *pathos,* which he has already said make rhetoric an offshoot of ethics-politics, or else defers treatment of it to the later discussion (in book 2) of the other two *pisteis* (1.9.1, 1366a25–28; 1.10.5, 1368b24–26; 1.10.17, 1369b14–15; 1.13.8, 1373b36–37). And there are corresponding references back in book 2 to subjects treated in book 1 as providing the material needed for finding means of representing oneself as a good person (2.1.6, 1378a16–19; 2.12.2, 1388b34–35; 2.18.1, 1391b20–21). In his introductory descriptions in 1.2.7 and 1.4.5 of the relation of rhetoric to dialectic and ethics-politics, then, Aristotle does not express clearly and fully all the grounds he actually recognizes for saying that rhetoric is in part an offshoot of or construction out of ethics-politics. As for dialectic, regarded as the study or knowledge of forms of argument, I shall leave that to one side in what follows. But the relation of rhetoric to ethics-politics that Aristotle asserts here requires closer examination.

It is obvious, and has long been recognized, that there is some connection between Aristotle's views on the relation between rhetoric and ethical-political science and those for which the character Socrates argues in the second half of Plato's *Phaedrus* (257b ff.). Socrates argues that in order to speak well on any subject a person must have a systematic, fully grounded knowledge of the truth about two sorts of things. First, he must know the full truth about the matters on which he speaks (259a4–6)—so that if there is an art of oratory at all it must include knowing all about virtue and vice, happiness and misery, good and bad (advantage and disadvantage), justice and injustice, and all the other stock topics on which orators are called to speak. To be sure, the orator's is not an art of giving instruction on these subjects, but only of speaking persuasively on them to a crowd of ordinary folk. But to do that he must appeal to considerations in favor of his conclusions that will strike his listeners as plausible (*pithana*) or likely (*eikota*), and therefore acceptable to them as grounds for believing those conclusions. And even so much as that cannot be done *well* (artistically) by someone who does not know the full truth about these subjects. The reason is, as Socrates argues (273d), that the likely thing to say is always something that resembles the actual truth, and you cannot know what will or will not resemble the truth, if you say it, except by knowing what the truth is. If, for example, you wish really to *know how* to persuade a jury that someone has done a serious injustice, you must have a thorough knowledge of what injustice *is*, so that you can reliably tell which properties of any given act and its circumstances that you might draw to the jury's attention are ones that sufficiently resemble the *real* nature of injustice so that, by dwelling on these you will convince the jury that the act was seriously unjust. Second, the orator must have a full, philosophically grounded knowledge of the nature of the human soul and all its varieties, so as to be able to tell which kind of speech (emotional, and/or richly embellished, or plain and simple, etc.) is the right (i.e., most persuasive) one to use on any given hearer or group of hearers (271b–272b). For the way of being spoken to that will be most persuasive to them will depend on the particular natures of their souls, since various features of people's souls determine the effectiveness or ineffectiveness of any of the various types of speech on them.[14]

Now this Platonic view makes rhetoric an offshoot of philosophy (specifically, the philosophical knowledge of ethical-political matters) in an extremely strong sense. For according to the Socrates of the *Phaedrus,* the knowledge of the nature of justice and injustice and of other ethical-political

---

[14] See Cooper, "Plato, Isocrates, and Cicero," pp. 79–85.

concerns that the orator must possess in order to construct his discourses artistically is obtainable only through the comprehensive ability, called by him dialectic (266b–c), to collect and divide and so come to know whole systems of eternal forms—the forms of justice and good (with their opposites), and so on. The art of rhetoric thus becomes simply one sort of applied philosophy. It is the ability a philosopher may acquire to apply his knowledge of eternal truths about the natures of things in manipulating the way these natures appear in the minds of the unphilosophical masses, so as to make them believe the ethical-political conclusions for which he argues. (At the same time, he uses his philosopher's knowledge of the human soul to beguile them through his choice of words and his manner of addressing them.)

How does Aristotle's view in the *Rhetoric* compare with this Platonic one? In one striking (and puzzling) passage of 1.1, Aristotle signals his agreement with the basic idea underpinning Socrates' argument in the *Phaedrus,* the claim that the capacity to tell what resembles the truth goes hand in hand with the ability to discern the truth itself. But he applies it to quite different effect (1.1.11, 1355a14–18):

> For it belongs to the same ability to see both the truth and what resembles the truth (*to homoion tōi alēthei*); at the same time, human beings are by nature pretty well oriented toward the truth and more often than not succeed in reaching it. Hence that person will be able to hit upon (*stochastikōs echein pros*)[15] things [to say] that are held in good repute (*ta endoxa*) who is also able to hit upon the truth.

Though the argument here, and its connection to what precedes, is admittedly not perfectly clear, the mention of *endoxa,* taken together with the parenthetical reference to dialectic itself earlier in the context (1.1.11, 1355a9), are highly significant. For in fact, as we shall see, Aristotle's appeal to the identity between the ability to see the truth and the ability to see what resembles it (viz., the *endoxa*) goes in the opposite direction from Socrates'. Aristotle does not mean that only someone who has a deep, philosophical knowledge of the truth about the nature of justice, etc. (in Aristotelian terms, someone possessing *politikē epistēmē,* i.e., *phronēsis*) can reliably know all about the *endoxa* needed to argue effectively as an orator. On the contrary, he is here in the process of identifying the artistic orator as a special sort of, or something very like, a dialectician (in his, not Plato's, sense of the term)—and dialecticians, according to

---

[15] Roberts (also as revised by Barnes) translates "makes a good guess at," but in context this is clearly wrong. Aristotle's point concerns oratory as engaged in through the ἔντεχνος μέθοδος (1355a4) and that μέθοδος does not consist in guessing what is an ἔνδοξον or what is the corresponding truth. For στοχαστικός in Aristotle meaning "aiming at and hitting" with no suggestion of guesswork (indeed with the contrary), see *Nic. Eth.* 1106b15, 28; 1109a22; 1141b13. I understand Aristotle's phrase πρὸς τὰ ἔνδοξα [or: τὴν ἀλήθειαν] στοχαστικῶς ἔχειν, literally construed, to mean, "to be so related to reputable things [or: the truth] that one is capable of hitting them [it]" (as a skilled archer is capable of hitting his targets).

his understanding, do not have to, indeed qua dialecticians they cannot, be possessed of this knowledge (see 1.2.1, 1355b27–35; 1.2.20–21, 1358a2–26; 1.4.4–7, 1359b2–18). So whatever the true significance is of Aristotle's saying that the dialectician-orator, who is able to determine what the *endoxa* are on ethical-political questions, is also such as to see the truth on these matters, his point is definitely not Socrates', that only an accomplished philosopher of politics can be an "artistic" orator.

A less significant difference between Aristotle and the Socrates of the *Phaedrus* concerns the second of Socrates' requirements for the orator— that he should possess the true theory of the human soul, in all its varieties. It is sometimes said that this aspect of the *Phaedrus* is the source of Aristotle's second and third *pisteis,* the character of the speaker and the emotional state of the hearer. For both of these have to do with states or affections of the human soul that make a difference to an orator's prospects of successful persuasion. It is noteworthy, however, that only the latter of these two *pisteis* falls within the scope of Socrates' view of the usefulness to the orator of the knowledge of the human soul. Socrates shows no awareness of the need to know the true theory of the types of soul for the sake of the orator's self-representation. Moreover, when Aristotle does overtly take up the question of the orator's need to tailor his discourse to the *particular* character of his hearers' souls—the central question for Socrates in his innovations about oratorical knowledge of psychology—he never makes this concern the subject of a special *pistis* all on its own, as in effect Socrates does. This matter is first mentioned at 1.2.11–13, 1356b26–1357a22, as an aside in the discussion of the *forms* of argument that are suitable for rhetoric, that is, in connection with the first of the three *pisteis,* the logic of the argument. There the principal point is that the addressees of oratory are pretty simple types, who do not take well to long, drawn-out stretches of argument or overly precise attention to the niceties of logical completeness and soundness. Thereafter it surfaces at several places, but only in connection with the special need to tailor an epideictic speech to suit the political constitution of the addressees, and the corresponding need (in all the genera of oratory) to tailor the speaker's self-representation to conform with the audience's politically influenced conception of what makes for a good character or with the differences in moral outlook that go along with different times of life (1.8.12, 1365b22–26; 1.8.6, 1366a8–14; 2.13.16, 1390a24–28). Aristotle decidedly does not attach the same theoretical importance as Socrates does to the knowledge of (or even dialectical inquiries about) the *varieties* of human soul as a separate, special requirement for rhetoric, enabling the orator to tailor his addresses to the specific emotional predilections of his audience; with him it is a side issue occurring sparingly at one place or another in the treatment of the three official *pisteis.* What he does attach theoretical importance to in this connection is something quite different: universal knowledge of what the various emotions are and how to bring them about.

What then does Aristotle have in mind at 1355a14–18, in saying that it "belongs to the same ability to see both the truth and what resembles the truth"? In order to answer this question, we need to consider more closely what it could mean to say that rhetoric is in part an "offshoot" of dialectic, or put together partly from it. In the passages where Aristotle says this (1.2.7, 1356a25–27; 1.4.5, 1359b9–10), summarized above, he seems to refer exclusively to the orator's need to speak using enthymemes (or, more generally, to speak giving his hearers reasons for believing the conclusions he wants them to accept and act on). For dialectic, as he implies there,[16] is the art that knows all about enthymemes and other syllogisms: what validly follows from what, what (if true) would provide a reason for believing something else. The emphasis is on the validity of the reasoning, not also on the truth or acceptability of the premises. But this is misleading. For at other places in these introductory chapters where he associates rhetoric with dialectic, he has in mind a dialectic that knows much more than merely what constitutes an apparently or a really valid argument. Thus in the first two sentences of the work (1.1.1, 1354a1–6) and at 1.2.7, 1356a30–34 and 1.2.11, 1356b32–1357a1, he clearly attributes to dialectic and to rhetoric, just insofar as it is like or derived from dialectic, a kind of knowledge of, or ability to produce, the *premises* needed to argue validly (or apparently so) in the relevant contexts. Dialectic and rhetoric are, he says, "abilities of a certain sort to provide arguments" (δυνάμεις τινὲς τοῦ πορίσαι λόγους 1.2.7, 1356a33–34), and that obviously includes both knowing about questions of validity and having command over the relevant *endoxa,* as we have seen Aristotle also implies at 1.1.11, 1355a14–18.[17]

But if by being an "offshoot" of dialectic it already follows that rhetoric is provided with a stock of *endoxa* on the subjects on which the orator is called upon to speak, what is there left for rhetoric to inherit from its other parent, being also an "offshoot" of ethical-political science? I have already referred to two extended passages (1.2.20–21, 1358a1–26 and 1.4.4–6,

[16] 1.2.7, 1356a22; cf. 1.1.11, 1355a8–10; 1.1.14, 1355b16–17, and note the implications of his identification of dialectic in this context with "analytic" (1.4.5, 1359b10).

[17] At 1354a1–6 Aristotle says that rhetorical and dialectical skills concern things that all people in some way or other know how to do—subjecting others' views to scrutiny and explaining and defending their own, attacking others' and defending their own behavior. This obviously includes knowing to some extent what particular things to say in attack or defense— things that will prove at least somewhat persuasive. At 1356a30–34 Aristotle refers back to these opening sentences of the treatise (καθάπερ καὶ ἀρχόμενοι εἴπομεν), glossing them, reasonably enough, as saying that rhetoric and dialectic are δυνάμεις τοῦ πορίσαι λόγους, again with the clear implication that they involve knowing what will be *plausible* to say (and not just how to argue logically, from however absurd or irrelevant premises). Curiously, this passage is a continuation of the passage about rhetoric as an "offshoot" of dialectic (1.2.7, 1356a20–27), which as I have said, seems to restrict rhetoric's inheritance from its dialectical parent to its formal ability to produce logically valid inferences. This suggests either that Aristotle's intention in *that* passage, despite what he actually seems to say, was to make the relation of rhetoric to dialectic the source also of its ability to produce suitable *premises* to argue from, or else (what seems more likely) that he was simply writing rather carelessly there.

1359b2–16)[18] in which Aristotle strongly insists that dialectic and rhetoric cannot pursue their investigations about ethical-political matters so far that they begin to speak basing themselves on philosophical first principles of that subject-matter. To do that is to eradicate their own natures without knowing it (1.4.6, 1359b14), and become political science itself (ἂν γὰρ ἐντύχῃ ἀρχαῖς, οὐκέτι διαλεκτικὴ οὐδὲ ῥητορικὴ ἀλλ᾽ ἐκείνη ἔσται ἧς ἔχει τὰς ἀρχάς, 1.2.21, 1358a25–26). So it is not that by being an offshoot of ethics-politics rhetoric acquires a capacity for selecting ethical-political premises that goes beyond what could have been provided already by its dialectical parent. On the contrary, these passages make it clear that rhetoric, like dialectic, is limited to knowing about and speaking from *endoxa,* regarded strictly as such (or, at any rate, not as conclusions of ethical-political reasoning of any specialized sort). The answer to our question must lie, instead, in Aristotle's conception of the very relationship between dialectic and ethical-political science, or, put equivalently, in the role of *endoxa,* regarded simply as such, in the constitution of ethical-political science, according to Aristotle's understanding of the latter. This is the true significance of his "*Phaedran*" remark at 1.1.11, 1355a14–18, where he identifies the ability to know *endoxa* (i.e., things that resemble the truth) with the ability to see the truth itself.

This is not the place for a systematic investigation of the role(s) of argument from *endoxa* in ethical and political science as conceived by Aristotle. For present purposes it may suffice to draw out briefly some implications of a single passage near the beginning of the *Nicomachean Ethics* (1.4, 1095a30–b4). Here Aristotle emphasizes the importance of the distinction between arguments from established first principles of some subject matter and arguments intended to lead toward their establishment. In setting out, as he is there doing, to develop and present a theory of the foundations of ethical (and political) theory, we are, he implies, in the position of one arguing toward first principles, and that means that we must begin from what is somehow known *to us;* obviously we cannot begin from ethical first principles, even though for questions arising about ethical and political matters those are admittedly the fundamental objects of knowledge (*ta haplōs gnōrima*), the things that must be known first if anything else is, strictly speaking, to be known at all.

In context, Aristotle develops this point by referring to the necessity that anyone beginning the study of ethics-politics have good moral habits (1095b4–13), but it has implications also for the place of dialectical argument from *endoxa* in ethics-politics. *Endoxa* about good and bad, about happiness, about justice and injustice, about virtue and vice, and so on, are what folk who, strictly speaking, do not know anything about ethics-politics nevertheless find believable on questions belonging to its subject-matter. But if they are to be suitable starting points from which reflection leading ultimately to the establishment of first principles and then of the truths that

---

[18] To these add the briefer remarks at 1.1.12, 1355a24–29 and 1.2.1, 1355b27–35.

follow from first principles can even so much as begin, *endoxa* must not only be believable for us; they must be true, or approximately true, or anyhow somehow revelatory of what really is the truth: otherwise they could not correctly be described as *gnōrima hēmin,* things (somehow) *known* to us.

It is well understood that Aristotle does treat *endoxa* in the *Ethics* as such a point of departure, and our *"Phaedran"* passage from the *Rhetoric* is an essential element in the defense he provides for so doing.[19] Let me quote it again (1.1.11, 1355a14–18):

> For it belongs to the same ability to see both the truth and what resembles the truth; at the same time, human beings are by nature pretty well oriented toward the truth and more often than not succeed in reaching it. Hence that person will be able to hit upon things [to say] that are held in good repute (*ta endoxa*) who is also able to hit upon the truth.

If human beings are by nature well oriented toward the truth, what is found believable by them has some legitimate claim to be, or anyhow to reflect, the truth. But what is believable for them as a group are the *endoxa.* So the *endoxa* are likely to be true, or (equivalently) are like the truth, and starting an investigation from them is after all starting from things "known to us"— and not merely *believed* by us.

But notice now, finally, the consequences of this line of thought for dialectic/rhetoric. The expert dialectician (and, in the area of ethical-political questions, the rhetorician) is the person above all others who knows and has command over the *endoxa* on political matters (in my broad sense of this term). He acquires this, not by studying the truth—by learning from Aristotle or some other philosopher of ethics-politics the true system of ethics and political science—but by doing two other things.[20] First, he attends in a relatively systematic way to the relevant common beliefs, and their grounds, insofar as they have any, in other common beliefs or concepts. But second, he collects and reflects informally upon the opinions of those with a reputation for high intelligence who have thought hard about and investigated these matters closely. Notice that this second task does not require being able to explain or defend the "opinions of the wise" in the same terms as the wise themselves could presumably do, or understanding the philosophical or other "technical" grounds there might be for believing them, or yet for doubting them. Nonetheless, as we have seen, Aristotle says that the dialectician/rhetorician has, as such, the ability to discern the truth itself. That is true because the dialectician's reflective ability to work with *endoxa,* being the necessary point of departure for anyone intending to acquire ethical-political knowledge, is at least the necessary springboard for the acquisition of ethical-political first principles. No doubt not all expert dialecticians or rhetoricians have the further capacities needed actually to arrive at a full understanding of the final truth in ethics and politics, but

---

[19] See further Chapter 12 above, pp. 288–90.
[20] *Top.* 1.1, 100b21–23.

they do have good control over the place, intellectually speaking, from which this process must begin. In that limited sense they have the capacity to see not only what is *like* the truth, but the truth itself, too.

This is why I said earlier that Aristotle's use of the alleged identity of the ability to see what resembles the truth with the ability to see the truth itself goes in the opposite direction from Socrates' use of it in the *Phaedrus*. Because according to Aristotle the systematic pursuit of the truth in ethical-political matters begins in a dialectical study of *endoxa* that can be conducted without knowing relevant philosophical first principles at all, dialectic (and with it rhetoric) counts as a capacity to discern the truth, but one that retains the independence from philosophy that Socrates vehemently aimed in the *Phaedrus* to deny to it. Dialectic can discern the truth in the sense that it is the capacity from which the knowledge of the truth is ultimately developed. That is why for Aristotle rhetoric is very far from being simply applied philosophy but is instead a genuinely independent art. It is an "offshoot" of ethical-political philosophy only in the sense that it has the dialectician's grasp of and control over the subjects dealt with in ethical-political science from which that science itself takes its origin.

I have been discussing Aristotle's account in the first four chapters of *Rhetoric* 1 of the relationships among rhetoric, dialectic, and ethical-political science. In most of the remaining chapters of books 1 and 2, Aristotle presents the results of a rhetorical/dialectical study of certain ethical-political subjects. His aim is to give would-be orators the information they must stock their minds with if they are to satisfy the demands of the oratorical art and speak on "political" topics as persuasively as the individual circumstances allow. For much of the way, his focus is on how to exploit the audience's tendency to accept and act upon the implications of opinions about these matters that have an authority based on their "reputability" as either widely shared, standard views in their culture or opinions held by persons known for their special insight or expertise. This is so both for his discussion of the specific "topics" to be employed in obtaining premises for argument in each of the three divisions of oratory (deliberative, epideictic, and judicial), and for what he says about how the orator should speak in order to make his hearers regard him as a knowledgeable person of good character. Here, knowledge of the *endoxa* is primarily knowledge of what is plausible, without special regard to whether or not what is plausible (to the audience) is true.[21] But in discussing the arousing of emotions in 2.2–11,

---

[21] Too often, not taking seriously Aristotle's insistence that rhetoric's treatment of the substance of rhetorical arguments is dialectical only, people refer without due reserve to these chapters in order to work out or confirm interpretations of views of Aristotle's as political or moral philosopher, on various topics. This is a dangerous error. Even if, as I have said, ethical-political theory for Aristotle begins from the *endoxa,* it does not end there, and there is no valid general presumption that his own considered philosophical conclusions will be found even well reflected in a dialectical discussion of the relevant topics. This caution applies especially clearly to the discussion of pleasure in *Rhet.* 1.11.

again by appeal to relevant *endoxa,* Aristotle is obviously relying on the at least approximate *truth* of the common views about anger, fear, and so on, and the means by which they may be aroused or stilled.[22] The account I have provided of the dialectical character of rhetoric and its consequent relationship to ethical-political science justifies both of these uses of dialectically derived premises and shows the close connection between them. I hope my remarks will be found an appropriate and useful prolegomenon to the detailed study of Aristotle's applications of dialectic in *Rhetoric* 1.4–14 and 2.1–17.[23]

Selected Further Readings

Barnes, Jonathan. "Rhetoric and Poetics." In *The Cambridge Companion to Aristotle,* edited by Jonathan Barnes. Cambridge: Cambridge University Press, 1995, 259–85.

Engberg-Pedersen, Troels. "Is There an Ethical Dimension to Aristotelian Rhetoric?" In *Essays on Aristotle's "Rhetoric,"* edited by A. Rorty. Berkeley: University of California Press, 1996, 116–41.

Garver, Eugene. *Aristotle's "Rhetoric": An Art of Character.* Chicago: University of Chicago Press, 1994.

———. "The Political Irrelevance of Aristotle's Rhetoric." *Philosophy and Rhetoric* 2 (1996): 179–99.

Irwin, T. H. "Ethics in the *Rhetoric* and in the Ethics." In *Essays on Aristotle's "Rhetoric,"* edited by A. Rorty. Berkeley: University of California Press, 1996, 142–74.

[22] On Aristotle's treatment of the emotions, and the role of dialectic there, see Chapter 19 below, "An Aristotelian Theory of the Emotions."

[23] I would like to thank Geoffrey Lloyd, my commentator at the Symposium Aristotelicum XII, August 1990, where this chapter was presented, and other members of the Symposium, especially Michael Frede, André Laks, M. M. McCabe, Mario Mignucci, and Gisela Striker for discussion and advice that was helpful to me in revising the chapter for publication.

CHAPTER NINETEEN

An Aristotelian Theory of the Emotions

I

Aristotle's ethics and political theory are constructed round a closely knit family of psychological concepts: those of happiness (*eudaimonia*), virtue (*aretē*), practical wisdom (*phronēsis*), action (*praxis*), state or habit (*hexis*), desire (*orexis*), pleasure and pain (*hēdonē* and *lupē*), choice or decision (*prohairesis*)—and the emotions or passions (the *pathē*). In his ethical treatises Aristotle elaborates theoretical accounts of all the members of this family but two: desire and emotion—and since two of the three types of desire that he recognizes (appetites and spirited desires) are cross-classified by him as emotional states, the emotions are even more isolated in that anomalous position than that may make it sound. The most we get in any of the ethical treatises is an illustrative list, the longest of which (in *Nicomachean Ethics* 2.5) reads as follows: appetite, anger, fear, confidence, envy, joy, feelings of friendliness, hatred, yearning (that is, for an absent or lost person that one is attached to), eagerness to match another's accomplishments, and pity. Aristotle provides no general, analytical account of the emotions anywhere in any of the ethical writings. And we are in for disappointment if we look for this in his supposedly scientific account of psychological matters in the *De Anima*.

As is well known, Aristotle does however develop fairly detailed accounts of some eleven or twelve emotions—on a generous count, perhaps fifteen—in an unexpected place, the second book of the *Rhetoric*, his work on the art of public speaking. Can we turn there to find Aristotle's full theory of

This essay is a lightly edited version of my 1992–93 S. V. Keeling Memorial Lecture, delivered at University College, London, in May 1993. The lecture, in turn, was based on my paper "Rhetoric, Dialectic, and the Passions." The first version of that paper was prepared for delivery at an international Symposium on Philosophical Issues in Aristotle's *Rhetoric* sponsored by the Philosophical Society of Finland, Helsinki, August 1991. Subsequently I read revised versions at departmental colloquia at Dartmouth and Pomona colleges. I would like to thank the organizers of the Helsinki symposium, and especially Juha Sihvola, for their hospitality, and the other participants, both local and from abroad, for stimulating and helpful discussion of many interesting issues in the *Rhetoric*, including the ones treated in this essay. The essay as published owes a great deal to criticisms and suggestions made in discussion on all three of these occasions, but I am especially grateful to Alexander Nehamas for his detailed and perceptive written comments on the penultimate version. It was while I was a Fellow of the Center for Advanced Study in the Behavioral Sciences that I prepared the Keeling Lecture, and I am grateful to the Center and to the Andrew W. Mellon Foundation, which provided financial support for my fellowship, for their assistance.

the emotions? Regrettably, an adequate answer must take account of a number of complexities—I will be elaborating some of these as I go along, and attempting to assess their significance. But, by way of preliminary orientation, let me give the short answer that I will be attempting to justify in the course of the essay. The discussion of the *Rhetoric*'s specifically limited set of emotions cannot be regarded as based upon or providing us with Aristotle's final, "scientific" theory (as we would be entitled to regard any comparable theory in the ethical works or the *De Anima*). Rather, what we find there is, from the point of view of Aristotle's mature ethical and psychological theory, a preliminary, purely dialectical investigation that clarifies the phenomena in question and prepares the way for a philosophically more ambitious overall theory, but does no more than that. However, as we go through the particular emotions that he discusses, we can see certain patterns emerging that, although not found in his discussion of each emotion, plainly could be made the basis for a comprehensive general theory, and one that is of considerable interest, both philosophically and historically. Having done the work on the selected emotions dealt with in the *Rhetoric,* Aristotle had achieved certain systematic insights that he could have used as the basis for a positive philosophical theory of the nature of emotions. But he never got around to doing that; at least as far as we know, he did not.

Before turning to Aristotle's accounts of the emotions in Book 2 of the *Rhetoric,* I need to say something about how the emotions fit into his overall project in that work.

At the beginning of *Rhetoric* Book 1, Aristotle argues that there are precisely three "technical" or artful ways that public speakers have of persuading their audiences. In the body of the work, including his discussion of the emotions, he aims to provide the information aspiring orators need in order to train themselves to wield these three instruments on the basis of real knowledge, and so lay claim to the possession of a true art of oratory. First, Aristotle says, public speakers need to appear to their hearers to be intelligent, good, and well-intentioned persons (that is, ones who have good character). Second, they need to induce in their audiences appropriately directed states of emotion that will influence their audiences' judgment on the matter under discussion in a way favorable to the orators and their cases. Third, they need to present reasons that the audience will find plausible and will cause them to judge as true whatever conclusions the orators are trying to promote (they need to *argue* well). It is mostly in connection with the first and especially the second of these objectives that Aristotle provides information about the emotions in Book 2. The orator needs to know how to represent himself to the audience as being moved by such emotions as will help to establish him as a good person in general, and well-intentioned toward the audience in particular; and he needs to know how to engender in them the emotions that will cause them to judge the matter as he wishes them to.

Throughout the *Rhetoric* Aristotle limits himself, in preparing and presenting his material on how to wield the three instruments of persuasion, to a dialectical survey of the relevant data from common sense and "reputable opinion" (in Greek, the *endoxa*) that bear on the matters he takes up. He does indeed say that rhetoric is something like an offshoot of both dialectic *and* ethics (or politics), but it is clear that by referring to ethics as one parent of rhetoric he does not intend to say that rhetoric borrows opinions from an accomplished philosophical theory of ethical matters. He says quite plainly, so far as the premises of an oratorical argument go, that opinions must be drawn from what is reputable and plausible, and not from the results of a special science, not even from the philosophical theory of politics or ethics (1.4.1359b2–18, with 1.2.1358a21–26)—what here he actually calls political or ethical science (*epistēmē*). If rhetoric did that it would no longer be mere rhetoric, but would turn itself into the science or theory in question, actually establishing its conclusions, rather than merely getting people to believe them on grounds persuasive to them. And it seems that this restriction to *endoxa* applies across the board: in selecting the materials from which to represent his own character in a favorable light and in engendering in the audience helpful emotions, as well, the orator will depend upon a dialectical knowledge of reputable opinions about the emotions, and not a "scientific" knowledge derived from a fully justified philosophical theory of them. Accordingly, when Aristotle in Book 2 offers to the orator information about the emotions that he is to use in engendering or preventing emotions in his hearers, this is an exercise in dialectic. He is collecting and sorting through, for the aspiring orator's benefit, the established and reputable opinions about what the various relevant emotions are, and about various relevant points about them.

Where the instilling of emotions is concerned, it is easy to see, however, that the dialectical appeal to such opinions will be different from what it is in the case of the other two instruments of persuasion. A systematic, dialectical study of the various *endoxa*—the recognized and highly reputed opinions—about what is good and bad for communities, right and wrong, legal and illegal, worthy of praise and the reverse, is obviously a very good way of preparing oneself to construct arguments on these matters before a classical Greek audience, whether in a deliberative, judicial, or ceremonial context. These are precisely the opinions that the audience can be expected to regard highly themselves, and so to be swayed by, if the opinions can be marshaled in such a way as to support logically the point of view for which the orator is speaking, or at any rate to seem to the audience to do so (see 1356a35–36). Likewise, in attempting to represent himself to the judges as intelligent and perceptive about practical matters, and as a serious person of good general character, he needs to be guided by the recognized and reputed indicators of these characteristics. For, again, it is likely that his audience will be disposed to regard a person as having good character if he displays just those indicators in his speech, and avoids displaying the contrary ones. Here what matters is to know what one's hearers will think favors a certain conclusion that one desires them to reach.[1]

When one comes to the orator's wielding of the remaining "way of persuading," by inducing the appropriate emotional state of mind in his audience, the story must necessarily be more complicated. For here it is evidently not enough to know what the audience will think people are like who are prone to become angry or afraid, or to feel pity, or to have vindictive or friendly feelings, and so on. Nor is it enough to know toward what sorts of persons the audience thinks that people typically feel these feelings, or under what circumstances and occasions.[2] (These are the three subtopics into which Aristotle divides his treatments of the emotions in Book 2 [see 2.1.1378a23–28].) The orator's purpose is actually to make his hearers feel in some of these ways, and prevent them from feeling in other ways, toward specific persons on given occasions and circumstances (toward his client in a judicial case, for example), and to use these feelings to direct or influence their judgment. Plainly, whatever the grounds are for proceeding dialectically here, it ought not to be simply because doing so gives one the ability to influence the audience's opinions about who is or isn't in a given state of feeling toward a given other person! If what he needs to do is actually to make them angry, it hardly matters whether they also think they are.

It seems clear that Aristotle's restriction of the orator to dialectical knowledge of the emotions rests upon his general view that qualification for expertise in oratory must rest only upon that kind of knowledge. But from his own philosophical point of view what makes it acceptable to him to restrict the orator in this way is that he himself believes that ethical theory (what he calls here ethical or political science, which does aim at establishing the facts about what the emotions really are, and so on), itself starts from,

[1] Here and throughout this discussion of *endoxa* I restrict my attention to the aims and practices of the individual Aristotelian artistic orator. His function is to do the best the circumstances permit to find things to say that his hearers will take as bases for believing whatever it is he is arguing for; his art does not consist in discovering the truth and attempting to persuade them of that. Two considerations should be borne in mind, however, lest my discussion give the impression that for Aristotle the art of rhetoric is completely value- and truth-neutral. First, as we will see more fully below, Aristotle thinks that the *endoxa* the orator appeals to in marshaling his argument and representing his character bear a strong positive relation to the truth—they somehow reflect, and so indicate, the truth. Second, his remarks at 1.1 (1355a20–24, 29–33) about the usefulness of the art of rhetoric indicate that, at least in judicial and deliberative oratory, where there are speakers on both sides, the joint function of the artistic orators who speak on any question is to help the hearers to reach the best, most truthful decision possible on the matter at hand. By listening to excellently prepared speeches on all sides of the question, a mass of people are placed in the best position such a mass can be in to decide correctly: they have before them all the relevant truth-indicators, each as favorably presented as possible.

[2] See 2.1.1378a23–28, where Aristotle gives this threefold division of the material to be treated in preparing the orator for his task—except, of course, that there he says he will investigate how people *are* when they are angry, etc., not how any audience will think they are.

and is responsible to, the very *endoxa* that dialectic and rhetoric are specially directed to acquire effective control over. So, if in learning about the various passions—their surrounding psychology, their objects and occasions—the "artistic" orator turns to the recognized and reputable opinions about these matters, and not somehow directly to the phenomena themselves, he is at least behaving no differently from the way Aristotle's full-fledged moral and political philosopher behaves, in beginning his own investigations of these matters.[3] If what results is less than what Aristotle thinks a fully independent philosophical theory might ideally be able to achieve, he himself thinks there is good reason to accept the accounts he will provide as approximately true. As we proceed we will see for ourselves that what Aristotle offers his aspiring orators, and us modern readers too, is well grounded in an appropriately thoughtful study of the emotions themselves, and not merely what people say about them.

II

As I have said, Aristotle distinguishes and devotes at least some direct attention to the defining characteristics of fifteen emotions. He gives separate, formal treatment to twelve, in the following order: feeling angry (*orgē*), feeling mildly (*praotēs*), feeling friendly (*philia*, i.e., *to philein*), feeling hatred (*misos*), feeling afraid (*phobos*), feeling confident in the face of danger (*tharrein*), feeling disgraced (*aischunē*), feeling kindly (*charin echein*), pity (*eleos*), righteous indignation (*nemesan*), envy (*phthonos*), and feeling eagerness to match the accomplishments of others (*zēlos*). Actually, it is not perfectly clear whether Aristotle means to say that *praotēs* (feeling mildly) is a state of feeling on its own, or only the absence of angry feelings when they would be expected or justified; his definition of *praünsis*, becoming calm or mild, explicitly makes it simply a settling down and quieting of anger (1380a8).[4] But I take this to be a lapse, and suppose he does mean to treat feeling mildly as a separate emotion. Two further feelings are named more or less incidentally and accorded briefer, but still not insubstantial treatment: schadenfreude (an accompaniment of envy [1386b34–1387a3 and 1388a23–25]), and feeling disdainful, an accompaniment of eagerness

---

[3] On this see Chapter 12 above, pp. 288–89; and Chapter 18, pp. 398–99.

[4] By contrast, in his treatments of the other two "negation" feelings on his list, hatred and confidence, it seems fairly clear that he regards them as positive states of feeling on their own, not merely the absence of the feelings with which they are contrasted—friendly feelings and fear, respectively. But he gives no formal definition of *misos* at all, and the closest he comes to a definition for *tharsos* (1383a17–18) is partial at best, so we are left to draw this inference from his descriptions of the circumstances, etc., for these feelings. One should note, however, that at one place Aristotle equates those experiencing confidence simply with those who are *apatheis* under certain circumstances (1383a28): he means, of course, free of the *pathos* of fear, but this is certainly a careless remark at best if he thinks of confidence as one *among* the *pathē*, as it seems clear that, officially, he does.

to match others' accomplishments (1388b22–28). A third, unnamed feeling, which stands to righteous indignation as schadenfreude does to envy—it is pleasurable feeling at the punishment or other come-down of those who deserve it—also comes in for brief treatment (1386b25–33 and 1387b14–20).

In studying these chapters it is important to bear in mind that Aristotle means to discuss throughout states of *feeling*—passions or emotions, conditions in which one's mind or consciousness is affected, moved, or stirred up. This applies equally to *philia* and *charis* (feeling friendly and kindly) despite some awkwardness of expression, as it does to anger, fear, and the other more obvious cases of such feelings. I begin, then, with some remarks on Aristotle's discussions in 2.4 and 2.7 of these two feelings.

Awkwardly, Aristotle defines *charis* (what I am translating as "kindly feelings") in 2.7 in terms of action not feeling: it is "helping someone in need, not in return for anything[5] nor for the good of the one helping, but for that of the one helped." Formally, then, the person who "has *charis*" is the one who acts in this helping way; the definition apparently makes no reference to the emotion that might lead to such action. Or does it? Perhaps one should take Aristotle's reference to helping actions as indicating, elliptically, the emotion that leads to them (akin to friendly feelings, I suppose: a warm feeling of attachment to someone, with a desire to do that person good for her or his own sake). But of course what Aristotle should primarily be telling aspiring orators about is a feeling that they need either to engender in or remove from their audience's mind. And in what follows in 2.7 (1385a30–1385b11) he seems to limit himself to discussing the means of showing an audience that someone has shown *them charis* or failed to do so. Nevertheless, the connection to an emotion of the audience's is perhaps implicit even here, as is suggested at two places (1380a27 and 1380b32) in 2.3, where Aristotle says we don't (can't) get angry at people who are apparently mistreating us, if they have treated us excessively kindly in the past. His point is that, just as fear of someone conflicts with and prevents simultaneous anger at them (1380a31–33), so the emotion of kindly feeling (that results from one's recognizing kind treatment from a person in the past) conflicts with and prevents simultaneous anger against them for a present apparent insult or unjustified belittlement. So his point in talking in 2.7 about who has and who has not behaved kindly to the audience in the past is to provide the orator with a means of engendering, out of naturally arising gratitude, or preventing, feelings of kindness in the audience—for example, toward persons in court or toward the people of other cities whose petitions might be before an assembly or council for decision.

I turn now to 2.4, on friendly feelings and hatred. This chapter is

---

[5] That is, not so as to get anything in return: acting to return a favor already received is not being ruled out here, as Cope, *The Rhetoric of Aristotle*, wrongly feared the language might suggest.

anomalous in several ways. In every chapter except this one Aristotle overtly organizes his discussion in accordance with a tripartite pattern for discussing the emotions that he lays down at the end of 2.1 (1378a23–30). After giving his definition of the specific state of feeling, he goes on to discuss (not always in the same order) (a) what personal conditions or circumstances, especially what psychological conditions (what other feelings or beliefs, in general what frames of mind), make people apt to experience the feeling (pōs echontes or diakeimenoi), (b) what sorts of people they do or do not feel the feeling toward (tisin or pros tinas), and (c) what the occasions are of their having, or not having, the feeling for that kind of person (epi poiois or dia poia). His allegiance to this program is quite striking in each chapter, even where he understandably lumps together the discussion of the second and third points. We get this tripartite structure presented in every chapter, in virtually the same language each time.[6]

This language and this structure for the discussion are totally absent from the chapter on friendly feeling and hatred. It is true that the chapter begins with a promise first to define friendly feelings[7] and then to say who people feel that way (tinas) toward and why (dia ti). But there is no separate mention anywhere in the chapter of the very important first point, the frames of mind that tend to promote our feeling that way. And the language here (and subsequently in the chapter where he addresses the third point, the occasions of friendly feeling) is not paralleled in any of the other chapters (see poiētika philias, 1381b35, poiētika echthras, 1382a1–2). Finally, the whole discussion, although genuinely illuminating and insightful, has fewer signposts and is more of a miscellany than any other discussion in this part of the treatise.

As a consequence, we face special difficulties in interpreting what Aristotle says about these emotions in this chapter. I mentioned just now that he begins by giving a definition of friendly feelings, to philein. This is exactly as we should expect: in the Nicomachean Ethics (8.5.1157b28–29) he ranks friendly feeling (philēsis) as an emotion or feeling, in contrast to friendship

---

[6] See 2.2.1379a9–10, 1379b27–28; 2.3.1380a5–7; 2.5.1382b27–29, 1383a14–15; 2.6. 1383b12–13; 2.7.1385a16–17, 30–31; 2.8.1385b11–12, 1386a3–4, 16–17; 2.9.1387a5–8; 2.10.1387b21–24, 1388a23–24; 2.11.1388a29–30, 1388b24–27.

[7] He writes: τὴν φιλίαν καὶ τὸ φιλεῖν ὁρισάμενοι λέγωμεν, 1380b34. I believe the kai here is likely to be epexegetic; that is, I think it likely that philian has the sense here that Aristotle gives to it at Nic. Eth. 2.5.1105b22 and Topics 4.5.126a12, where the contexts put it beyond doubt that it means not "friendship" (an established personal relationship, or a settled state of character of some sort) but an occurrent feeling, or type of feeling. In effect, philia substitutes in these contexts for philēsis as the noun for to philein. Hence in the first sentence of Rhetoric 2.4 Aristotle is not promising to give us two definitions, one of friendship and one of friendly feeling, but only the one definition, of friendly feeling, that he immediately provides. (This is the only formal definition, with the usual estō, anywhere in the chapter.) When he adds (1381a1–2) a statement about what makes someone a friend of someone else, this is not a backward way of fulfilling a promise to define friendship, but the needed introduction of the notion of a friend—the sort of person who regularly experiences friendly feeling—on which so much of what follows is going to be based.

(*philia*), which he says is a settled state involving decision. The definition itself in the *Rhetoric* is very close to the account given in the *Nicomachean Ethics* of goodwill (8.2.1155b31–32), which helps to make the connection that Aristotle promised at the beginning of Book 2 (*Rhet.* 2.1.1378a19–20) between the discussion of the emotions and instruction in how to present yourself in speaking as having the interests of your audience at heart (i.e., as he says, having goodwill for them).[8] The definition of *to philein* runs as follows: "Let us suppose having friendly feelings to be wishing someone what you think are good things, for his sake and not for your own, and being ready, as far as you can, to act accordingly."[9]

However, he goes on immediately[10] to speak instead of friendship, or rather what it is to be friends with someone—the established relationship in which two persons are disposed to feel friendly toward one another at appropriate times. This shift of focus continues virtually throughout the chapter, to such an extent that people sometimes take the chapter to be about not mere friendly feelings, but friendship itself. But that is a mistake. Aristotle's introduction into a discussion of friendly feelings of talk about friends and friendship is quite understandable, from two points of view. First of all, one purpose of the discussion is to provide an orator with material from which to represent himself in speaking as moved by genuine concern for his audience's interests, and he will succeed especially well in this endeavor if he can get them to think of him as actually a friend of theirs—someone who is habitually moved by such feelings in relation to

---

[8] I take it that Aristotle's language at 1378a19–20 (περὶ δ' εὐνοίας καὶ φιλίας ἐν τοῖς περὶ τὰ πάθη λεκτέον), linking the two terms together in this way, indicates that we are to go to the chapter on friendly feeling to find out how to represent this aspect of our own characters. Alternatively, one might think he is directing us to the entire subsequent discussion—so that, for example, one might pick up pointers from 2.7 on kindly feelings and 2.8 on pity to use in presenting oneself as "well-disposed" to the audience by making oneself appear to feel pity or kindness for them or theirs. In view of the special linkage at 1378a19–20 between *eunoia* and *philia*, however, I think this alternative interpretation is not likely to be correct.

[9] The Greek for "wish" here is *boulesthai*. In Aristotle's technical philosophy of mind, a "wish" is a rational kind of desire, one deriving from our capacity to reason about what is good or bad for us, whereas what he is talking about here is supposed to be a *pathos*, a nonrational feeling. (*Boulēsis* never appears in any of Aristotle's lists of *pathē*, in the *Rhetoric* or elsewhere—as both of the other two sorts of *orexis* do, at one place or another.) It is worth noting, also, that earlier in the *Rhetoric* (1.10.1369a1–4) Aristotle presents his division of desires into rational and nonrational, with "wish" serving as the name for the former kind, as grounded in *endoxa*. How can Aristotle think that friendly feeling is based in wishing and yet that it is a *pathos*, something essentially nonrational? Perhaps we should take his use of the word *wish* in some broader way in 2.4, one that permits it to cover at least some nonrational desirings; see 2.11.1389a8 where he seems to use "wishes" to refer in a general way to the desires of young people, which he characterizes before and afterward as appetitive, sharp but not persistent.

[10] I do not believe Kassel is right to put 1381a1–2, *philos . . . antiphiloumenos* in brackets as a later addition, possibly by Aristotle himself, to the text. The *d'* after *philos* is perfectly in order, as marking the additional remark about friends that this sentence introduces, and the sequence of thought runs a lot better with the sentence than without it.

them. Moreover, knowing who is ordinarily taken to be someone's friend could give an orator excellent means of getting an audience to feel friendly feelings toward himself or those for whom he may be a spokesman: describing someone as their friend is a likely way to induce the audience to respond with friendly feelings. We must, then, guard carefully against the mistake of thinking that Aristotle's advice to the orator is aimed at helping him to make his audience actually become his own or his client's friends, rather than merely to make them have friendly and well-disposed feelings. The latter task is difficult enough: if taken seriously the former would actually be impossible in the time available!

III

In introducing the topic of the emotions at the beginning of Book 2, Aristotle characterizes emotions generally as follows (1378a20–23): they are things "that change people so as to alter their judgments and are accompanied by *lupē* (conventionally translated "pain") and *hēdonē* (conventionally translated "pleasure")—for example anger, pity, fear, and the like, and their opposites." The association of the emotions with *lupē* and *hēdonē* occurs so standardly in Aristotle[11] that one is apt to accept it here, too, without much thought—as if he meant nothing more than that when we experience these things we always have a mild like or dislike for the way we are then feeling, and/or that we tend to experience some pleasures or pains in consequence of feeling an emotion. I think it will repay us, however, to stop and ask carefully what Aristotle can or does mean by this. To begin with, we should notice that six of the ten emotions for which he gives formal definitions are defined as instances of *lupē* (*lupē tis*): fear, the feeling of being disgraced, pity, righteous indignation, envy, and eagerness to match others' accomplishments are all defined this way. A seventh (anger) is defined as a certain desire accompanied by *lupē* (*meta lupēs*). So he makes *lupē* a central, essential feature of many of the emotions: it is even the genus of six of them. Curiously, he does not mention either *lupē* or *hēdonē* in his formal definitions of kindly and friendly feelings (which I quoted earlier); one would think the parallel with these other emotions would have led him to define them in terms of *hēdonē*. Nor does he explicitly mention pleasure in his definition of confidence in the face of danger (*to tharrein*)—although when he says that confidence essentially involves "the impression (*phantasia*) of what keeps us safe as being near, of what is fearsome as being non-existent or far off" (1383a17–18),[12] one might think that indicates that

---

[11] See *Nic. Eth.* 2.5.1105b23; *Eudemian Ethics* 2.2.1220b13–14 (with the potentially significant addition of *aisthētikē* before *hēdonē*); *Magna Moralia* 1.7.1186a13–14. It appears that in some way Aristotle is following Plato in this: see *Philebus* 47e1–48a2, and what follows there (to 50e4).

[12] Aristotle does not offer a formal definition of *to tharrein*. He only says that what it is can be gathered easily from the definition already provided of fear, of which it is the opposite

pleasure *is* essential to it. "The pleasant" is counted by him as one sort of apparent good, namely what impresses one as good quite independently of what one *thinks* is good,[13] and safety here would count as such an apparent good. And in discussing schadenfreude and the unnamed accompaniment of righteous indignation (to neither of which does he give a formal definition), he mentions pleasure (*chairein, hēdesthai*) in such a way as to suggest that he thinks it is their genus, just as the genus of envy and righteous indignation is said to be *lupē*.[14]

There is, then, ample evidence that Aristotle actually defines those emotions that he thinks involve *lupē* in terms of it, and weaker evidence that he is correspondingly inclined toward defining the emotions that involve pleasure in terms of *hēdonē*.[15] What does he intend here by *lupē* and *hēdonē*? Let us take *lupē* first. Elsewhere Aristotle uses the term (together with its verb) quite variously, to cover both bodily pain and all kinds and degrees of negative mental response and attitude, ranging from mild dislike to deep distress.[16] In nonphilosophical Greek *lupē* usually indicates a pretty strong state of feeling, some real distress, and it has a special application to people when they are grieving.[17] It is in something close to this ordinary usage that Aristotle uses the word in this context in the *Rhetoric*. He speaks of pity, righteous indignation, and envy each as being a pain characterized by turmoil (*lupē tarachōdēs*, 1386b18–19; and see 1386b22–25), although he mentions only pain and not turmoil in their formal definitions (1385b13–16, 1386b10–12, 1387b22–24). And he actually defines both fear and the feeling of being disgraced as "pain and turmoil" (*lupē tis kai tarachē*, 1382a21,

---

(1383a14–15), and then adds this remark about the impression of what keeps us safe. Perhaps one is licensed to infer from this (mimicking the definition of fear) that confidence actually is ἡδονή τις ἐκ φαντασίας τῶν σωτηρίων ὡς ἐγγὺς ὄντων, τῶν δὲ φοβερῶν ὡς ἢ μὴ ὄντων ἢ πόρρω ὄντων. But Aristotle does not explicitly say this.

[13] See *EE* 2.10.1227b3–4, 7.2.1235b25–29.

[14] See *Rhet.* 1386b26–32, 1387a1–3.

[15] I have been led in examining this evidence to suppose that the general association of the *pathē* with *lupē* and *hēdonē* announced at 1378a21–22 anticipates these definitions in terms of these two opposites. This does not preclude, as Aristotle makes explicit in the case of anger (see 1378b1–9), that in an emotion that was based in *lupē* there should be involved (*hepesthai*) also some pleasure; but these pleasures will be, as they are for anger, secondary ones, ones that depend upon special further features of the state of mind of the person feeling the emotion. These secondary pleasures are not part of the definition of the emotion. On anger, see further below.

[16] For bodily pain, see for example *De Anima* 2.2.413b23 (the pain of worms), *EE* 3.1.1229a34–41 (the pains that can kill you), and *EE* 7.8.1241b9 (the pains of childbirth); for bodily pain plus physical disgust, *Nic. Eth.* 7.7.1150a9–10 (the pains of touch, and of taste); the dislike of doing sums or writing, *Nic. Eth.* 10.5.1175b17–20; the distress caused a proud man if he is not given some honor or if he is put under the rule of some unworthy person, *EE* 3.5.1232b12.

[17] At *MM* 1.7.1186a16 we find *lupēthēnai* given alongside *orgisthēnai* and *eleēsai* as examples of emotions: there *lupēthēnai* presumably has the sense of "grieving," rather than generic "distress," so as to be coordinate with these other two emotions, which are of course quite specific ones.

1383b14) about something.[18] If, as I just did, one translates *lupē* here as "pain," one must understand this as meaning "distress," "feeling upset," something that in these more extreme instances can be accompanied and qualified by psychic turmoil. Aristotle's words for pleasure have a similarly various usage elsewhere, covering everything from some bodily sensations to mental attitudes varying from simple liking and gladness to elation and vivid enjoyment.[19] Given the contrast with feelings of distress about something brought about by the pairing of *hēdonē* and *lupē* in this context, it would seem reasonable, perhaps mandatory, to take *hēdonē* here as connoting some sort of positive mental excitement—the active relishing of something, and not merely being pleased or glad about it, or just liking it in some way or other.

So the terms *lupē* and *hēdonē* in Aristotle's definitions of the emotions, explicit or implied, serve much the same function that is covered in Stoic accounts by such picturesque terms as throbbing (*ptoia*), contraction and expansion (*sustolē* and *diachusis*), being uplifted and cast down (*eparsis* and *ptōsis*), depression (*tapeinōsis*), and gnawing (*dēxis*). *Lupē* and *hēdonē* indicate, with less descriptive ingenuity than the Stoics' terms do, the character of the emotions as psychic disturbances in which we are set psychically in movement, made to experience some strong affect.

Accordingly, the emotions as Aristotle represents them in *Rhetoric* Book 2 are feelings either of being distressed and upset about something, or of being excited about and relishing something. In both cases they are taken to be intrusive feelings, ones that occupy the mind and direct the attention (so that, as Aristotle says, they can "change people so as to alter their judgments"). Anger, fear, the feeling of being disgraced, pity, righteous indignation, envy, and the eagerness to match other people's accomplishments are feelings of distress at one or another apparent circumstance currently within one's attention that one takes to be a bad thing. Confidence in the face of danger, schadenfreude, and the unnamed accompaniment of indignation that gives a person pleasure at the punishment or other comedown of those meriting it, are all instances of relishing what impresses one as being a good thing.

It is worth emphasizing that in his discussion of each of these ten emotions, with the exception of the last two, Aristotle is quite firm and explicit that the emotion arises from one's having the impression or appearance (*phantasia*) that something good or bad has happened, is happening, or is about to happen. Indeed, for seven of them—anger, fear, the feeling of disgrace,

---

[18] Thus of the emotions based in *lupē* Aristotle omits to associate *tarachē* only with anger and eagerness to match the accomplishments of others (*zēlos*).

[19] For bodily pleasures, i.e., pleasurable sensations, see *Nic. Eth.* 2.3.1104b5–6, 7.13.1153b 33–34, and *EE* 1.4.1215b5; the pleasure of eating sweets in the theater, indulged especially when the play is bad, *Nic. Eth.* 10.5.1175b10–16; the refined pleasure in well-turned and becoming jokes taken and given by the tactful person, *Nic. Eth.* 4.8.1128a25–28; the wondrous pleasures philosophy is said to give, *Nic. Eth.* 10.7.1177a25.

pity, envy, righteous indignation, and the eagerness to match another's accomplishments—he includes this impression in the formal definition; and for confidence it is included in the nearest thing to a definition that he provides (1383a17–18, discussed earlier). Similarly, one finds references to such appearances also in his account of feeling mildly (1380a10 and 35), as one would expect if that is the emotion opposed to anger. The omission in the case of schadenfreude and the unnamed accompaniment of righteous indignation should not cause surprise, given the extreme brevity of his treatment of them; but we are entitled to infer a role for such impressions in the generation of these emotions from their relationship to envy and indignation, respectively (as we also can for disdain from its relationship to "eagerness"): all these latter emotions are said to depend upon one's impressions of things. It seems likely that Aristotle is using *phantasia* here to indicate the sort of nonepistemic appearance to which he draws attention once in *De Anima* 3.3 (428b2–4), according to which something may appear to, or strike one, in some way (say, as being insulting or belittling) even if one knows there is no good reason for one to take it so. If so, Aristotle is alert to the crucial fact about the emotions, that one can experience them simply on the basis of how, despite what one knows or believes to be the case, things strike one—how things look to one when, for one reason or another, one is disposed to feel the emotion. It is not merely when you know or think that someone has mistreated you that you may become angry. Being unable to control an emotion is, partly, taking as a ground of it something that you know was not one at all.

Thus it is fairly clear that, for a majority of the emotions he deals with, Aristotle regards them as involving essentially a feeling of distress or pleasure caused by the way things currently in his or her attention strike the person in question. About hatred, and, as we have seen, friendly and kindly feelings, Aristotle is less forthcoming in identifying precisely what the feeling is, whether one of distress or of relishment. But on Aristotle's emerging general view one would expect friendly and kindly feelings, at least, to be cases of pleasurable excitement, just as confidence, schadenfreude, and the unnamed accompaniment of indignation are. Nor with hatred and friendly and kindly feelings does he make a point of including in his account a reference to things appearing in some particular way. That is partly because for these emotions he makes no allusion at all in the definition itself to the emotion's objects and occasions.[20] For it is because he does that in the other cases that he finds the opportunity to insert the reference to such appearances.

On Aristotle's view, what, however, is the nature of the affect involved in hatred? Here I confess myself puzzled. He does not say anything to link hatred positively to either pleasure or distress, and it does not seem plausible

---

[20] At 1381b12 one reads that "we hate people if we merely think (*hupolambanōmen*)" they are thoroughly wicked. This might be taken to assign a role in hatred for full belief where in the other emotions an impression is said to be sufficient. But that would probably be to place too much weight on a somewhat incidental remark.

to identify it as essentially a feeling of pleasurable excitement of any kind (however much, like anger, it might involve pleasurable thoughts about what you will do to the one you feel that way toward if you get the chance). On the other hand, Aristotle denies that it involves being distressed at all (2.4.1382a13). So it is quite unclear how he envisages hatred as based in the one or the other sort of feeling, as his general conception of the emotions seems to require. He is led to say that it does not involve a feeling of distress as a consequence of his correct, and very interesting, observation (1382a8–12) that anger makes you want to subject the person you are angry at to pain (physical or mental), in return for the distress he or she has caused you in belittling or insulting you and so making you angry, whereas hatred makes you want the person hated to be badly off, even to cease existing (1382a15). He seems to think that because in hatred there is no special desire to inflict pain (to affect how the hated one feels), but only to ruin him (to affect how he is), hatred ought not to involve any underlying feeling of distress either. That does not, however, seem a good reason: Aristotle recognizes that the feelings of disgrace and eagerness to match others' accomplishments both involve a distressed state of mind, but neither aims at causing distress in another; nor, it seems, does either of these feelings (seem to Aristotle to) derive in any way from imagining distress as felt by another person, as perhaps pity does. And, of course, there is no danger of failing to keep anger and hatred distinct if both are based in feelings of distress; the same is true of envy and pity, for example, on Aristotle's account, and they are nonetheless kept perfectly distinct by other features of the two definitions. But perhaps in saying that hatred does not involve a distressed state of mind, as anger does, Aristotle is thinking of the impersonality of hatred: you can hate whole classes of people, not merely individuals, as he points out (1382a4–7), and you need not have been personally affected in any way by a person you nonetheless hate (1382a2–3). It might seem to Aristotle that distress must have some local or immediate external cause of a kind that would therefore be lacking in hatred. Hatred is, in any event, an especially complex emotion: it seems much more a settled state, although subject to increased or lessened intensity, than many of the other emotions are, and it seems that unlike many of them there is no plausible ground for thinking that other animals experience it. In fact, one might make the case that hatred rests upon a fully reasoned judgment, and not the mere appearance or impression, that the hated person is bad and detestable—so that it could seem to be an emotion of the reason itself, and not of the other parts of the soul as Aristotle conceives them.[21] So it may be to Aristotle's credit

---

[21] To make this case one would want to take seriously Aristotle's reference (see n. 20) to belief in (not an appearance of) the wickedness of the hated person. Even if hatred is an "emotional" state of reason, however, that would provide no good grounds on which to deny that it involves distress or pleasure: on Aristotle's understanding of these latter phenomena, they can be experienced in the thinking of reasoned thoughts, as readily as in nonrational sorts of activity.

that he shows himself not comfortable imposing upon hatred his general account, according to which each emotion involves essentially either pleasurable excitement or a distressed state of mind.[22] Still, one remains puzzled.

IV

I come now to some special features of Aristotle's treatment of anger. Aristotle defines anger as "a desire (*orexis*), accompanied by distress, for what appears to one to be punishment for what appears to one to be belittlement by people for whom it was not proper to belittle oneself or someone close to one."[23] Of the several definitions, or partial definitions, of anger that one finds elsewhere in his works, this is closest to that which, with slight variations, occurs several times in the *Topics*[24]—as suits the dialectical character

[22] In any event, the opinion that hatred does not involve a distressed state of mind appears a well-entrenched one with Aristotle. He repeats it, again by contrast with anger, in a very different context in *Politics* 5.10.1312b33–34 (anger and hatred are, together with contempt, the leading causes of the overthrow of tyrannies). His description of hatred there makes one almost think he is talking about no emotion or passion at all, but a fully reasoned, dispassionate rejection and dislike. (I have benefited from discussion with Myles Burnyeat about the issues raised in this paragraph.)

[23] 2.4.1378a31–33: I translate the text of Kassel taking *tōn ... mē prosēkontōn*, as he suggests (following the construction at 1379b12), to refer to the perpetrators of the insult. It is odd that Aristotle only specifies within this appended explanatory phrase that the objects of the insult are the person himself or someone close to him, but there seems no reasonable alternative to so taking the text, as transmitted.

It is surely evident that the two occurrences of forms of *phainesthai* here are to be taken as references to how the angry person takes things (how they strike him, how they appear to him to be), if only because of the parallel here to the similar, and unmistakable, references to such appearings that occur regularly also in the case of other emotions analyzed in this part of the *Rhet.* (fear, 1382a21, etc.; confidence, 1383a17; *aischunē*, 1384a23, etc.; pity, 1385b13, etc.; righteous indignation, 1387a9; envy, 1387b11; *zēlos*, 1388a30; and see also 1380a10, on feeling mildly, the feeling opposed to anger). And note the free variation between *hupolēpsis oligōrias* and *phainomenē oligōria* in the texts of the *Topics* cited in note 24 of this essay. The badly mistaken tradition of translating the forms of *phainesthai* in the *Rhetoric*'s definition of anger by "conspicuous" or the like (one finds this both in Roberts's Oxford translation and in Dufour's in the Budé) seems to go back to Cope-Sandys (ad loc.). I doubt if it would even have occurred to anyone to take the Greek so, if it were not for the (odd-looking) first occurrence of *phainomenēs* here with *timōrias*: it certainly does seem attractive to suppose that anger involves a desire for *conspicuous* punishment for the insult, and that rendering seems more appropriate to the facts about anger than "apparent" or "what one takes to be." But it does not do well for the belittlement itself: anger does not require a conspicuous lack of regard, just one that one notices or takes to be there. One may suspect the text, as Spengel, followed by W. D. Ross in the OCT, did in overboldly bracketing *phainomenēs*; but in any event there seems no doubt at all that, if Aristotle did write it, he meant by it not "conspicuous" but "apparent," "what impresses one as being."

[24] See *Top.* 4.6.127b30–31, καὶ ἡ λύπη καὶ ἡ ὑπόληψις τοῦ ὀλιγωρίας ἐν τῷ τί ἐστι; 6.13.151a15–16, λύπη μεθ' ὑπολήψεως τοῦ ὀλιγωρεῖσθαι; 8.1.156a32–33, ἡ ὀργὴ ὄρεξις εἶναι τιμωρίας διὰ φαινομένην ὀλιγωρίαν. It is worth noting that in the first two of these definitions, but not the third, the angry person's view that he has been belittled is cast in terms

of the definitions in the *Rhetoric*. Interestingly, anger is the only emotion he examines in these chapters that he defines formally as an instance of desire, that is *orexis* (which is Aristotle's usual word for desire in general)— although it is worth noting that, in contrasting hatred and anger, he says that hatred is a desire (*ephesis*) for what is bad (for the person hated) (1382a8). That friendly feeling is also an instance of desire is perhaps implicit in his definition of it as "wishing someone what you think are good things . . ." (1380b35–1381a1), since "wishing" is regularly treated by Aristotle as one of the three basic forms of desire. Presumably kindly feeling, too, involves a similar wish.[25] Both before beginning his detailed survey (at 2.1.1378a4) and immediately afterward (at 2.12.1388b33), Aristotle does indeed mention appetitive desire (*epithumia*) as itself being one of the emotions, but he does not devote a chapter or part of a chapter to it.[26] Appetite comes in for prominent and highly interesting discussion at two places in the treatment of other emotions, anger (1379a10–22)—we will have a look at this passage shortly—and kindly feelings (1385a22–30), but it is not subjected there or anywhere in this part of the work to analysis as an emotion all on its own. So anger really does stand out from the other emotions as Aristotle treats them here: only it is defined in part as an *orexis* (desire) for anything.

From what we have already seen, it is clear enough what makes anger not only a desire but an emotion, according to Aristotle. Because it is accompanied by *lupē,* anger is a distressful, agitated desire for revenge; the angry person is upset about having been treated with apparent disregard and belittlement. In other words, it is not a cool and "rational" desire, a desire judiciously considered, to inflict pain or other punishment. In *Rhetoric* 1.10.1369a1–4, Aristotle uses "anger" (*orgē*) itself as the name of one of the three types of desire that he there distinguishes (the other two being wish and appetite). That would imply that the type of desire to which anger belongs, according to the *Rhetoric* definition, was by its nature agitated

---

of belief, as opinion rationally arrived at (*hupolēpsis*), rather than merely an impression or appearance. The *Rhetoric* seems more self-consciously decisive in favor of the latter type of definition, not only in the case of anger but in that of other emotions as well.

[25] But, as we have seen, Aristotle's formal definition of friendly feeling speaks rather of what the person with this feeling is moved to do (to help someone in need) than the feeling itself and its characteristics. I have already mentioned (n. 9) the difficulties Aristotle causes himself by defining friendly feeling, supposedly an emotion and so something nonrational, as based in a "wish."

[26] In taking up anger and appetite as causes of potentially condemnable actions at 1.10.1369b14–16, he refers the reader forward to his discussion of the emotions in Book 2 to find out about anger, but goes on right there to speak about appetite (at the end of 1.10 and in 1.11). The omission of a discussion in Book 2 of appetite therefore seems to have been well planned. The fact that in Book 1.10–11 he explains what *epithumia* is, by way of telling us what pleasure is and what gives pleasure to different people, may explain why he omits to discuss *epithumia* as a *pathos* in 2.2–11; in effect, he had already said in 1.10–11 what he thought needed to be said about it, and saw no need to go further. However, he nowhere gives or openly implies this explanation, so I put it forward only as a conjecture.

and distressful. In other writings, however, Aristotle regularly distinguishes between anger and "spirited" desire (*thumos*), using the latter as the name for his second type of desire and treating anger as a special case of it, the case where the desire is extremely agitated and distressed.[27] It is perhaps understandable that in such a dialectical discussion as that provided by the *Rhetoric* such refinements are neglected. But when they are taken into account, anger on Aristotle's view turns out to be (*a*) an especially agitated and distressful instance of "spirited" desire, (*b*) aroused by and directed specifically at what strikes the angry person to have been inappropriate and unjustified belittlement of himself or someone close to him, (*c*) aiming at inflicting a compensating pain on the belittler—as a means of demonstrating that he is not an inferior and trivial person, but a person whose power to inflict pain in return shows that he must be respected and paid heed to. Thus, in his account of anger, Aristotle combines three distinct elements that are indeed found elsewhere in his discussion but are nowhere else so clearly integrated: the angry person is in an agitated state of mind, caused by the way certain events or circumstances have struck him (whether or not he also believes that that is how they are), which is also a desire to respond in a well-motivated way to those events or circumstances as they appear to him.

As I mentioned above, anger has a special relationship, according to Aristotle, to the other type of nonrational desires, the appetites. The passage where he brings this out is worth quoting in full (1379a10–22):

> As for our own frame of mind: we become angry when we are distressed. For a person who is feeling distressed is bent on something. So if anyone blocks him directly or indirectly in whatever it may be, for example a thirsty man in his drink, or if anyone acts contrary to him or does not act to support him, or makes trouble for him when he is in this state of mind, he becomes angry at them all. Hence people who are ill, or poor, or in love, or thirsty—in general, experiencing some appetitive desire and not getting what they want—are prone to anger and easily stirred up, especially against those who belittle their present condition. Thus a sick man is made angry when belittled in regard to his illness, a poor man in regard to his poverty, a man fighting a war in regard to the war, a man in love in regard to his love, and so with the others. Each of these people is carried along to his own anger by the emotion he is already feeling.[28]

The upset feeling that belongs to anger in all these cases is an offshoot of the upset feeling the person has been experiencing in having some aroused, but unsatisfied, appetite. It is as if a preexistent energy, the appetite, gets

---

[27] On *thumos* see, for example, *De an.* 2.3.414b2 and *MM* 1.12.1187b37; for *orgē* as a special case of *thumos*-desire, see *De an.* 1.1.403a30 and *Top.* 8.1.156a32, with *Top.* 4.5. 126a8–10 and 2.7.113b1.

[28] I translate the text of Kassel, omitting the bracketed words in 1379a13 but disregarding the brackets in 1379a15–18.

redirected when blocked or obstructed, and becomes or gives rise to this new feeling of distress, the anger.

It is only in connection with anger, and only in this passage, that Aristotle devotes full attention to the ways in which different emotions interact so as to cause or prepare the ground for one another. As I have mentioned in passing, he does allude two or three times elsewhere to the opposite effect, the prevention of one emotion by the presence of another: for example, he says that people do not have friendly feelings for those of whom they are afraid (1381b33), that fear for oneself prevents feeling pity for another (1385b32–34), and that people feel disgraced when something apparently dishonorable about themselves comes to light before persons whom they esteem or admire (1384a26–29). But it is only here that he points toward any general theory of the underlying psychology of the emotions through which one might attempt to explain such phenomena as these, and work out other interactions among the different emotional states.

In other respects, too, the discussion of the emotions in the *Rhetoric* offers a less than fully comprehensive theory. Aristotle limits himself to just fifteen states of mind, ones selected so as to cover the range of emotions that the orator needs to know about in order to compose his public addresses with full effectiveness—whether by representing himself as motivated by them, or by finding means to arouse them in his audience and direct them suitably for the purposes of his discourse. So Aristotle neglects, as not relevant for this purpose, a number of emotions that a more general, independently conceived treatment of the emotions would presumably give prominence to. Thus grief, pride (of family, ownership, accomplishment), (erotic) love, joy, and yearning for an absent or lost loved one (Greek *pothos*) hardly come in for mention in the *Rhetoric* and are nowhere accorded independent treatment.[29] The same is true even of regret, which one would think would be of special importance for an ancient orator to know about, especially in judicial contexts. Furthermore, as we saw especially clearly in the case of anger, Aristotle seems to recognize three central elements as constituting the emotions—they are agitated, *affected* states of mind, arising from the ways events or conditions *strike* the one affected, which are at the same time *desires* for a specific range of reactive behaviors or other changes in the situation as it appears to her or him to be. However, he does not draw special attention to this common structure, and he does not accord equal attention to each of the three elements in the case of every emotion he discusses. Thus he may seem to neglect unduly the element of desire in his accounts of fear, confidence, pity, and the feeling of disgrace, and the second element, that of being struck by an impression that things are a certain way, is barely indicated in his accounts of friendly and kindly feelings and hatred. Similarly, we have seen that he denies that hatred involves feelings of distress, and that seems to imply that the first element, an affected state of mind, is

---

[29] The last two emotions are among the ones Aristotle lists in *Nic. Eth.* 2.5.1105b21–23.

absent from this emotion; and the corresponding pleasurable affect is no part of his definition of friendly and kindly feelings. So one cannot say more than that there seems to underlie Aristotle's discussions of the emotions in *Rhetoric* Book 2 an emerging general theory along these lines. Having done the dialectical work of assembling the data about these fifteen emotions in the *Rhetoric,* he might have gone on to address similarly the remaining major emotions, and advanced to the construction of a general, independent theory that would surely have held great interest. I hope I have been able to show that, nonetheless, his accounts of the emotions in the *Rhetoric* are richly suggestive, and rewarding from the point of view of the history of philosophy and of philosophy of mind and moral psychology too.

SELECTED FURTHER READINGS

Frede, Dorothea. "Mixed Feelings in Aristotle's *Rhetoric.*" In *Essays on Aristotle's "Rhetoric,"* edited by A. Rorty, 258–85.

Rorty, Amélie Oksenberg. "The Psychology of Aristotle's *Rhetoric.*" *Proceedings of the Boston Area Colloquium in Ancient Philosophy* 8 (1992): 39–79.

Sherman, Nancy. "The Role of Emotions in Aristotelian Virtues." *Proceedings of the Boston Area Colloquium in Ancient Philosophy* 9 (1993): 1–33.

Sihvola, Juha. "Emotional Animals: Do Aristotelian Emotions Require Beliefs?" *Apeiron* 21 (1996): 106–44.

Striker, Gisela. "Emotions in Context: Aristotle's Treatment of the Passions in the *Rhetoric* and His Moral Psychology." In Rorty, *Essays on Aristotle's "Rhetoric,"* 286–302.

PART THREE

Hellenistic Philosophy

CHAPTER TWENTY

Eudaimonism, the Appeal to Nature, and "Moral Duty" in Stoicism

ALL THE MAJOR SYSTEMS[1] of moral philosophy in antiquity, including that of the early Stoics, are eudaimonist in their structure. In giving their accounts of the right way to lead a human life in general and of the reasons that there are for wanting, feeling, and doing anything in particular, they all refer ultimately to the individual agent's *eudaimonia* (happiness). Apparently following Aristotle, the Stoics speak of an "end" (*telos*)[2] of our lives, such that "everything is appropriately (*kathēkontōs*) done for the sake of it, while it is done not for the sake of anything," or again such that "everything done in life appropriately has its reference to it, while it has reference to nothing."[3] And they explain this end as "gaining happiness, which is the same as being happy."[4] They also explain it in other terms, including those of "living in agreement with nature" and "living virtuously," which they say are or come

This essay was first prepared for the NEH-sponsored conference at the University of Pittsburgh entitled "Duty, Interest, and Practical Reason." I thank the organizers, Stephen Engstrom and Jennifer Whiting, for giving me this opportunity, and the other participants for a very stimulating and valuable three days of discussion. My co-panelist, J. B. Schneewind, made helpful comments on the next to final version of the conference paper, and I benefited in preparing this printed version from comments by and discussion with Michael Frede, Brad Inwood, and Stephen Menn. Parts of this essay appeared in somewhat altered form in a symposium on Julia Annas's *The Morality of Happiness*, with a response by the author, in *Philosophy and Phenomenological Research* 55 (1995).

[1] As Julia Annas has reminded us in several recent writings, there was one exception, that of the Cyrenaics. See, e.g., *The Morality of Happiness*, pp. 230, 235–36.

[2] See *Nicomachean Ethics* I 2, 1094a 18–19; at I 7, 1097a 34-b 6 Aristotle identifies this end with "happiness."

[3] Arius Didymus's *Epitome* of ethical theory as it occurs in Stobaeus, *Excerpts* (hereafter referred to as Arius at Stobaeus) II 7 (p. 46, lines 5–10 Wachsmuth). The passage quoted comes not in his exposition of Stoic views "in the ethical division of philosophy" but in Arius's general introduction, where he explains the use of the word *telos* and gives these definitions as Stoic ones. Arius's work, which unfortunately has not yet been translated into English (except for the portion on Stoic ethics; see Chapter 3, n. 30 above, p. 96), is one of the only three continuous, more or less comprehensive presentations of Stoic ethics to have survived from antiquity. (The other two are in Cicero, *On Ends*, Bk. III, and Diogenes Laertius, *Lives of Eminent Philosophers*, VII 84–131.)

[4] Arius at Stobaeus (77, 26–27 W), within his exposition of the Stoic theories. Just above (77, 16–17 W), Arius repeats the characterization of the end, identified now as "being happy," as "that for the sake of which everything is done, while it is done but not for the sake of anything." This time he leaves off the qualification "appropriately," but that may be because he has already been speaking at length of virtue and the virtuous person, who does of course do everything in this way.

to the same thing.[5] Thus, on the Stoic theory there is for each of us some single end to which it is appropriate for us to refer everything we do in life, and this end is identical, first, with our own "happiness" (or rather, with our gaining happiness and so living happily),[6] second, with our living in agreement with nature, and third, with our living virtuously. Now according to the Stoics the virtues, taken together with the actions that express them, are chosen, and choiceworthy, for their own sakes;[7] they are both "productive" goods, as being what generates or brings about happiness, and "final" goods, or goods of the nature of ends, since together they "fill happiness up" and so are its parts.[8] Furthermore, insofar as living virtuously is the same as living in agreement with nature, it is—at any rate according to Chrysippus, the most important early theoretician of the Stoic school—living "without acting in any of the ways usually forbidden by the universal law,[9] that is to say by the right reasoning that goes through all things and is the same as Zeus, he being the ruler of the administration of existing things." And Diogenes Laertius, from whom I cite this, immediately adds that that amounts to "doing everything in accordance with the harmony (*sumphōnia*) of the individual's *daimōn* [guardian spirit: i.e., here, his mind] with the will of the administrator of the universe."[10] So on the Stoic theory virtuous persons act always, first, for the sake of their own happiness (referring all

---

[5] Diogenes Laertius VII 87 *ab init.*, attributed to Zeno; see also Arius at Stobaeus 78, 1–6 W.

[6] They distinguish, quite reasonably, between "living happily" as the predicate that we want to be true of us (our *telos* is that it shall be the case that we are living happily) and the condition of happiness as the "target" (*skopos*) that we aim at in order to bring that about: Arius at Stobaeus 77, 25–27 W. In what follows I will not take care to observe this distinction.

[7] Diogenes Laertius VII 89, 127.

[8] "Productive" here translates *poiētika*, "final" *telika*. See Diogenes Laertius VII 97 *ab init.* and Arius at Stobaeus 72, 3–6 W: the two passages use identical language.

[9] The Greek here is *ho nomos ho koinos,* normally translated as "the law that is common (to everyone or everything)." "Universal law" (i.e., the law of the universe as a whole) seems to me to express the intended idea better; in any event we find the same adjective, *koinos,* used just below in Diogenes' text, to qualify "nature" so as to mark off the nature of the universe as a whole as opposed to human nature in particular (*phusin . . . koinēn* in 89 is a variant for *tēn tōn holōn* [*phusin*] in 88), and there translators quite rightly render it with "universal."

[10] Despite the very clear and explicit evidence of Diogenes Laertius, who mentions Chrysippus by name and describes his view at some length, as a view *within* ethical theory, Julia Annas boldly seeks, in *Morality,* chap. 5, to deny that any such thought belonged to ethical theory as it was constructed and taught by the early Stoics—as against a metaphysical or theological addendum, within physics or metaphysics itself, showing how the ethical views already reached fit together with the conception of the cosmos as a whole; according to her, it was a later addition to the foundations of ethical theory made by Stoics of the Imperial period, such as Epictetus and Marcus Aurelius. Her chief arguments are philosophical, not textual: she does not see how the early Stoic ethical theory could be a eudaimonist theory, as it plainly claimed to be, while also relying in its account of the virtues on such an "external" standard of right action. Once one discards her too limited account of what eudaimonism is and entails (see later in this essay), one can see that early Stoic eudaimonism does not in the least speak against the appeal within Stoic ethical theory to such a conception of Zeus's will as a universal law, conscious obedience to which is essential to virtuous action.

their actions to happiness as their single comprehensive "end"); second, choosing virtuous acts for their own sake, as parts of their happiness; and third, choosing them as conforming to the universal law, that is, to the will of Zeus.

In what follows I want to defend the philosophical respectability of each of these three elements in the Stoic theory of the virtuous life, and of their coherence when combined within a single theory. I will be especially concerned to explain the third element, the aspect of the virtuous life that introduces something that might be compared with Kant's theory of virtuous action, and that must indeed in some indirect way be an important historical antecedent for it. (I am not competent to, and so won't, pursue such historical connections.) Kant's conception of virtue covers, in comparison with that of the Stoics and other ancient philosophers, a sharply reduced area of our lives: it deals only with what one could call the morality of right and wrong[11]—the treatment of other persons, and also the treatment of oneself insofar as it makes sense to think of having moral duties to oneself—but not with whether one is unseemly in one's liking for sex or food, or knows how to deal in a balanced and intelligent way with the stresses and strains of daily life, rather than falling into furies or depressions, or even with whether one knows and honors the value of true friendship.[12] There are deep, even deep theoretical, reasons for this limitation, to which I will allude later on. But Kant holds that virtue or morality, understood in his reduced way, involves obedience to a law, which as rational beings we each lay down to ourselves, and which consists essentially in subjecting our proposed actions to judgment from the point of view of all other rational beings, and to doing and omitting only what passes that judgment. The universal law of the Stoics is imposed by Zeus, not formally by ourselves, but it is a *rational* law—it rests on good reasons; and the Stoics hold that it is up to each of us, in the use of our own rational powers, to recognize this law's application to us and to determine its content by working out its rationale, sufficiently anyhow for our own needs in deciding what to do. The Stoics, like other Greek philosophers of their time and before, equate honoring and following Zeus with honoring and following reason. In that sense, as with Kant, this universal law is our law qua rational beings for ourselves, and not only Zeus's for us. How far is it legitimate to think that the Stoics

---

[11] I have picked up this useful terminology from Thomas Scanlon.

[12] In the *Doctrine of Virtue*, Part II of the *Metaphysics of Morals*, Kant shows how the "duties to oneself as a moral being with an animal nature" and the duties of respect for and benevolence to others may ground virtues covering some aspects of the parts of our lives here referred to. But the scope of these Kantian virtues is quite limited in comparison with the corresponding virtues of the Greek theorists, just because of their grounding in and control by these duties. For the Greeks there are many more nuanced ways of showing defects—in relation to sexuality, to the consumption of food and drink, to social occasions, to friendship—than the ones that Kant's theory permits him to take notice of. (I thank J. B. Schneewind for discussion on this point.)

incorporate into their ethical theory, through their notion of virtuous action as obedience to the universal law, a deontological element of a Kantian kind? In the last section of this essay I try to answer this question.

I. EUDAIMONISM

I said that the major Greek ethical theories, the Stoics' included, are eudaimonist in their structure. What does this mean? In *The Morality of Happiness,* Julia Annas brings much-needed illumination to this subject, though as I shall explain I think she seriously underestimates the intellectual resources available to an ethical thinker working in this tradition. I can best introduce and explain my own understanding of the structure and substance of Stoic ethical theory by referring first to her discussion. In Annas's felicitous phrase, the "point of entry for ethical reflection" in the ancient philosophical tradition is the discomfort one experiences when, as a mature or nearly mature person already having a whole set of evaluative views and fairly settled motivations in line with them, one begins to do what Socrates had famously urged we ought to do, and looks to one's life as a whole. From where one stands already, within one's life as it has developed so far, one seeks a way of bringing unity to one's life, so that one can be said to be *leading* a life, a single one, and not just living—going on from one thing to the next until one dies. Here is where the notion of a single final end for one's life comes in: as Annas suggests, it was felt that "a single final end is what is required to make sense of a single life as a whole" (p. 33). It is also where one's own happiness enters, as a way of giving some preliminary substance to the sought-for single end. The point of entry for ethics is the concern to improve your life by ordering and unifying it: ultimately, it is the concern to make your life as good as possible. One's antecedent commitments and the end that is finally settled upon may take one outside oneself, to affirm the value of objectives lying outside the confines of one's own experiences and activities. Nonetheless, the value, to the one leading the life, of leading it *with* those commitments is inevitably the focus of attention. When the Greek philosophers identify the final end with the agent's happiness, they are simply making this point explicit. As Annas rightly emphasizes, the eudaimonist orientation does not prevent an ethical theorist from developing a conception of happiness under which happy people will lead their lives on the basis of quite extensive commitments to the intrinsic value of moral action, or even to providing other people with what they need simply because they need it. If such actions make for happiness *by* being done according to those commitments, the fact that one is acting also for one's own happiness need do nothing to undermine the integrity of one's commitments and one's actions in furtherance of them. This is particularly so if one identifies happiness directly with a life made up of actions done on the basis of such commitments as those, with no determinate further conception of happiness as a value, beyond the value of such commitments themselves, together perhaps with the value of having them integrated into some unified structure along with other similarly basic values.

Given these "entry" assumptions about Greek ethical theory, how can one expect it to proceed? At the very least the search for such a unifying end and for an adequate conception of happiness will require reflection leading to some considerable integration of what antecedently will have been a disparate set of concerns, commitments, and practical attitudes. It may also lead to reordering one's existing priorities and rethinking certain of one's commitments, as the difficulty or even impossibility of fitting them together with others into a unified scheme of living, comes to light. Furthermore such reflection could conceivably lead you to drop some earlier ideas about what was valuable in life. And it could lead you to add some new values, discovered as you explore previously unnoticed implications of what you had already valued, and as you remove obstacles that earlier ideas, now rejected, posed to recognizing them as deserving such a rank. But Annas thinks that that is pretty much it—not that I wish to suggest that to get as far as that would not be to accomplish something potentially of some significance. She thinks this follows from facts about the "entry" point that I have explained: because the process of ethical reflection begins from the basis of an antecedent set of evaluational beliefs and associated motivations, aiming to bring unity to a life already begun on that basis, she thinks it is limited to arguing within and from the set of such beliefs and motivations,[13] with only such extensions or revisions as that might accomplish. At any rate she legislates, as part of what eudaimonism means or implies, that no appeal can be permitted to anything "outside" the "ethical" as constituted by this set so reflected upon, so as to justify or ground and confirm something already there, or lead to something new to be added.[14] Hence, contrary to what has usually been thought, the "appeal to nature" in an ancient ethical theory cannot—consistent with its eudaimonist character—amount to going outside ethics, so construed, in order to find reason for believing anything of ethical significance.

But *does* it follow from the nature of the "entry point" for Greek ethical theory that its processes and results should be limited in this way? Does its

---

[13] Subjected to such pressures as may arise from (1) the acceptance of the agreed-upon formal conditions that any candidate for a "final end" must aim to satisfy—those of finality and comprehensiveness and, perhaps less explicitly, "self-sufficiency" adopted from Aristotle (*Nic. Eth.* I 7) (see Annas, *Morality*, pp. 39–42)—and in some way also (2) the most general, agreed understandings of what "happiness" entails: it is tied closely with activity, not passivity, and yields a positive view of one's life, satisfaction with the way it is going, i.e., with the bases on which it rests and with their consequences in the conduct of one's life.

[14] See Annas, *Morality*, pp. 161–62, in discussing the role of the appeal to "cosmic nature" in Stoic ethics.

commitments to eudaimonism in ethics mean that it must? I see no reason
to think so. Why should a person entering upon ethical reflection in the
position I have described be denied the freedom, in their reflections about
their life and how to unify it, to draw on general views, established or
anyhow accepted independently of their antecedent "ethical" outlook? Why
should they not use these in order to see their situation in a new light and
thereby find valuable confirmation of some element in that outlook, or
grounds for believing some of the prior priorities misguided, or even grounds
for believing of no importance some things previously so thought of and
for believing of serious importance things not previously thought important?
If one assumes that reasons for action must always be, in Bernard Williams's
sense, "internal reasons," one may think that this is in fact excluded, given
that these reflections are intended to give the agent reasons on which then
to act in structuring and living their life, simply because of what reasons
are.[15] But that only shows that any eudaimonist theory that permitted such
an appeal was deeply confused and in error, not of course that none might,
consistent with its being eudaimonist in character, have attempted such a
thing. And on an "external" conception of reasons for action (or of some
such reasons)—which there is certainly no doubt that some philosophers,
like other people, have sometimes accepted—such an appeal would not by
any means be precluded. Did these eudaimonist philosophers, or some of
them, perhaps accept an "externalist" conception of (at least some) reasons
for action?

I think both Aristotle and the Stoics did think of reasons for action in
the externalist way. But without having to go into that more fundamental
question, I think one can see that Aristotle, surely the paradigm of a eudaimonist ethical philosopher, did engage in the sort of "outside" appeal that
Annas wishes to legislate away. As Annas rightly emphasizes, it is accepted
by all the ancient theorists, as part of the set of evaluational views that one
brings in entering upon the philosophical enterprise, that the virtues and
virtuous living are not only very good things, but things of such importance
for any human being that no acceptable candidate for either the final end
or happiness can fail to include them in one way or another as central,
essential goods. This is impossible to miss in the ethics of Aristotle. He
indicates firmly that those who have not reached the point in their upbringing
where they have had experience of the essential quality of morally virtuous
action, that it is "fine" or "noble" (*kalon*), and moreover prize such actions
because they have it, are not capable of engaging in and learning from
philosophical inquiry about ethical matters. Thus, Aristotle's listeners or
readers are assumed to know in their own experience, and know in that
way the value in, moral action. So it is out of the question that Aristotle
should construct and present an argument, addressed to any degree to a
reader who does not have this knowledge (or, more noncommittally, does

---

[15] See B. Williams, "Internal and External Reasons," in his *Moral Luck*, pp. 101–13.

not see things this way), to establish that the moral virtues and morally good living do have a special value, one that is fundamentally important for a human life.

However, even people who know all this about virtue and are quite deeply committed to the truth of what they have come to experience about the value in virtuous action, can very well look to philosophical theory to confirm, on some basis that doesn't just say over again what they already know or merely expand on it a little bit, the truth of what they know through their upbringing. And it is quite clear that Aristotle offers them precisely this. The argument in *Nicomachean Ethics* I 7 leading to his first formulation of his own candidate specification of happiness or the human good contains the following thought: all animals (the same goes for plants) have a natural good, consisting in the particular kind of flourishing life that their specific natures fit them for, and this life is the life of a thing that is an excellent specimen of its kind—our common and obvious practice of speaking of some things as being good and others bad for specific kinds of living thing rests upon this fact, and brings it to light. The application of this general scheme to human beings produces the result that our good consists in a life directed by the use of our rational powers, when they are structured by their excellences, that is, by the virtues; that is what, in our case, an excellent specimen of our kind leading a flourishing life amounts to. Seeing this connection between, on the one hand, the virtuous living we have already had some experience of and already, as it were from the inside, know to value, and, on the other hand, the patterns of thought to which we are committed in dealing with and studying plants and animals—and these are of course not *ethical* patterns of thought—gives powerful confirmation, from outside ethical thought itself, of the truth of something we are committed to within it. We come to see virtuous living in a new way, one that we did not come to in our upbringing and that we need nonethical philosophical thought to reach.[16] And it enables us to say of our own ideal of virtuous living exactly what we say about the life of a fine hydrangea bush, that in it the good of the creature is achieved, and in both cases we can say this neutrally and objectively, without judging the question on the basis of needs, desires, or motivational commitments of our own, of any kind.[17] Here the appeal to human nature[18] is no self-congratulatory mere rhetorical flourish (at any rate, it is not intended by Aristotle that way—whatever a postmodern

[16] See further Chapter 11 above, "Reason, Moral Virtue and Moral Value."

[17] It also does not involve application of any "universal" teleology, of plants and animals having been made as part of some unified grand plan, each contributing in its way to the overall good of the whole. The good of each species is judged merely on the basis of its single nature, and without assuming it was made for any further purpose.

[18] Annas (*Morality*, p. 144) dismisses this argument from her discussion of the "appeal to nature" in Aristotle on the inadequate ground that Aristotle "does not prominently present [it] as involving nature." She apparently has in mind that the word for "nature" does not prominently appear in his argument, but that obviously does not matter.

philosopher might have to say about it); it is doing real and valuable work.[19] It is a further question, of course, on which this argument is silent, whether the specific content, the specific forms of action and specific concerns, of the virtues that we already accept when we enter philosophical ethics can be given some confirmation similarly from the outside. I believe it does not occur to Aristotle to think so.

II. The Appeal to Nature

I think that does occur to the Stoics, however. And here I mean the so-called old Stoics, including in particular Chrysippus—and not merely the later Stoics of Imperial times, such people as Seneca, Epictetus, and Marcus Aurelius. Cicero in *On Ends* III 16 has his spokesman Cato begin his exposition of the Stoic view on the final end by discussing the initial instincts with which an animal, including of course a human being, is born. To understand fully the content and the ethical significance of this theory of what is called in Greek *oikeiōsis*, we need also to take into account the exposition of Stoic ethics in Diogenes Laertius's *Lives of Eminent Philosophers* VII, 84–131, which starts similarly with an account of the initial instincts of animals according to the Stoics. We are to understand these initial, innate instincts as goal-directed states; the Stoics assume (or think one can observe) that newborn animals have certain attachments and desires innately that show themselves immediately upon birth—these are not mere reflexes called forth for example in a human baby by pressure against its cheek that leads it to find the breast and start sucking, but an impulse *for* the food that sucking will in fact bring it. Cicero explains that these initial instincts are all directed at the preservation of the "constitution" (Lat. *status* = Gk. *sustasis*) of the animal or else at things that in fact do serve to preserve its constitution. These are desires, based upon a liking for what it actually is—how it is in

---

[19] I said that Aristotle does not address his argument to any person who does not already know and value virtuous action highly. Would his argument nonetheless reasonably give such people pause, give them some reason to think they are wrong not to value it, to regret that they have not learned to appreciate the things virtuous people appreciate and to see things their way? Obviously, the argument does not attempt to convey to anyone a knowledge *of* what is so valuable about this sort of action; so no one is being brought, through accepting the argument, thereby to know virtue and value it the way the virtuous person does. Equally obviously, the argument does not attempt to show completely nonvirtuous people that something that they already know from their own experience and find to be good and desirable is achieved especially well by the virtuous, so that they are missing out by not being virtuous on something they are already motivated to get. However, the argument operates with a conception of the good of a creature with which anyone is familiar and is not likely to feel comfortable simply dismissing, and it gives a certainly very plausible basis for saying that the good of a creature like us, corresponding to the good (= the flourishing life) of a plant, essentially involves the virtuous use of our powers of reasoning. That is enough to give even immoralists pause, if they pay attention to reason at all, and in any event it does give such people reason to think they ought to take the steps necessary (whatever those might be) to acquire virtue—whether they pay attention or not.

fact constituted—to preserve that into the future, for itself, and also to get such things as milk and warmth and so on that its constitution in fact needs if it is to be preserved. (Much later on, but equally as a matter of natural endowment, the Stoics say that animals experience a goal-directed impulse to care for their offspring;[20] human beings also experience in the same way an instinctual and so innate liking for knowing the truth and in general for the exercise of their rational powers in learning things, simply for its own sake, once they have developed enough to make that possible [Cicero III 17–18].)

Cicero represents the Stoics as inferring from this description of their initial natural endowment—by this time they are speaking specifically of human beings—that what newborn animals do automatically from their instincts are things they *ought* to do. He continues his exposition, after a brief digression, with the claim (¶ 20) that the things that are in accordance with nature (i.e., the things that are the objects of these initial instincts, such as milk and warmth) are things *to be taken* for their own sakes (*propter se sumenda*): they not only *are* taken—automatically, on impulse—but are such that they ought to be. Hence, they are "worth selecting" and have some positive value. Why? Not because the animal wants them or feels attracted to them—*that* doesn't constitute any reason why it ought to take them, nor does it give them any value—but because in being so motivated it is in fact motivated, as follows from the assertions about the character of nature's initial endowment of an animal at birth, in ways that are (as we could loosely say) *good* for it. Suppose instead that an animal was born with instincts (goal-directed desires, remember) that were either deleterious to it, or were neither for things it needed for self-preservation nor for things that would harm it, but for some bunch of harmless frivolities (e.g., perhaps as the Stoics would think, merely with an instinctive liking for certain pleasurable sensations). In that case the Stoics would not say that it *ought* to do what it nonetheless did do, automatically and on impulse: there would be no *reason* for it to do it, even if it felt very much like doing it, as of course it would.

We can see this because Diogenes Laertius (VII 85) adds something that Cicero leaves out: an argument to show that the instincts with which nature is assumed to endow newborn animals really are ones, as Cicero also says that they are, for its good (again, I use the word *good* loosely here). This is an argument by elimination. Assuming, presumably from observation, as I have said, that nature does endow animals with instincts, these instincts must either be for its good, or for its harm, or for neither,[21] but it is not plausible (*eikos*) that nature would either endow an animal with an

---

[20] Cicero III 62–63. This is said to be the origin of all the instincts of natural sociability, which are in turn the natural psychological basis for the duties of justice and humanity. Its effects are seen already in small children, even though it is present in its primal form only when one has become a parent.

[21] The assumption seems to be that on each option all the instincts are of the one character indicated: a mixed natural endowment is either not considered or thought to be ruled out on the same grounds as the third option is ruled out.

instinctive disliking for itself and a liking for things that would harm or destroy it, or endow it with desires that had nothing to do with its actual needs as the organism that it is. Why is this not plausible? Plainly because, as the Stoics are assuming from the outset that we will all agree, nature is a benevolent agency. It brings animals into existence each with a particular natural constitution and a particular pattern of development into a flourishing thing of its kind, and gives it the instincts that it normally needs to further that development. The corresponding point holds for plants, too, as Diogenes Laertius (¶ 86) but not Cicero adds: these are "regulated" by nature not by instincts, but nonetheless by physical processes that are aimed at their development into a particular kind of flourishing thing.

Although it begins life acting entirely on instinct, as the other animals do (and continue to do throughout their lives), a human being gradually— during the course of a natural (and inevitable) development—comes into possession of the power of reason, that is, the power of acting *on* reasons, and no longer on instinctive impulse. Cicero continues his exposition by telling us something about the course of this development (Cicero III 20–21). He begins by remarking that the very things he has just said are things that are "to be taken" are the objects of the first *officia* or (in Greek) *kathēkonta*— the first things that it is right to do. These are "appropriate acts," as they are often translated, following one common use of the Greek participle in nonphilosophical contexts, or else "duties," following the connotations of the Latin noun. It is worthwhile noticing that Diogenes Laertius tells us later on (VII 108 *ab init.*) that Zeno, who is said to have introduced this terminology into Stoic theory, explained it etymologically along the following lines, yielding a quite different sense from that of what is simply "appropriate" to do: he derived it from the phrase *kata tinas hēkein;* that is, it is what "comes down on a particular person" to do, what it is your turn or your place to do.[22] So an "appropriate act" is not simply one that fits well with the circumstances in some unspecified way or because it gets you what you want; it is one that it is incumbent upon the one doing it to do, because in those circumstances it is assigned to it by its nature and by the nature of

---

[22] In explaining the intended etymology, Liddell-Scott-Jones (LSJ), helpfully cite s.v. *kathēkein* 2 the use of *kata* (s.v. B. 1. 3), in which Epictetus speaks (*Enchiridion* 15) of a guest at a feast who must wait quietly until the wine or whatever "gets down to you" (*gignesthai kata se*), until it is your turn. This seems the best way of understanding what Zeno intended, in part precisely because it does not attempt to derive the participle in such a way as to make it mean directly what everyone would automatically take it to mean anyhow ("appropriate"): such a derivation is intended to reveal something that is hidden. Alternatively (but to much the same effect) we could understand, with Inwood and Gerson, *Introductory Readings,* p. 140 "extending [or applying] to certain people." Long and Sedley, *The Hellenistic Philosophers,* 59C, seem to be trying to produce the obvious derivation (not very intelligibly, either) when they give the etymology as from "to have arrived in accordance with certain persons." (I don't know why they say the etymology has not yet been satisfactorily interpreted: the proposal I have accepted was not only already in LSJ, but it or the not very different Inwood-Gerson version was in essence already well argued for by Dyroff, *Die Ethik der Alten Stoa,* p. 134. Certainly, the idea that *kata* in the etymology is to be understood as "in accordance with" was shown to be wrong by Dyroff.)

things in general, which made it the way it is.[23] If an act is "appropriate" to do and fits the circumstances, as indeed it does, that is because not only is it assigned to you by nature to do in those circumstances, but since nature acts to further the life of its creatures, doing whatever it is is "suitable" from the creature's own point of view.

With the terminology of "appropriate" or (as we can now also call them) "incumbent" acts in hand, then, Cicero can now describe the automatic, instinctive behavior already discussed, as consisting of acts of this kind. The further course of development consists in several steps by which, in effect, reason in a human being gathers its strength so as to do its natural job of "crafting the impulses" as Diogenes Laertius describes it (see below). Young persons first do what they used to do automatically and on instinct but now not in that way, but rather *because* it is "appropriate" to do it—that is, for the reason that it preserves their constitution and advances their life. It then becomes not an intermittent but a constant and fixed way of behaving to act on reasons of that kind, aiming at one's constitution and its needs as things of ultimate concern. The final stage is reached when, reflecting on what one has been doing while acting for these earlier reasons, one comes to realize that merely acting that way has tremendous appeal, that it is a mistake to think, as one has been doing, of the value of so acting in any given instance as derivative from, needed because of its presumed efficacy in achieving, the assumed value to oneself of the continuance of one's consti- tution or of getting whatever it was one was then acting appropriately so as to get. Such action is then seen as having an intrinsic value of its own, consisting in the fact that it is reason-directed action, where what is done is "appropriate" because it fits in with one's natural needs. In fact, this intrinsic value is seen as being of so great and unique a kind that one now withdraws, in one's thinking about the value to oneself of the objects for which one was acting previously, all qualification of them as being *good* for you to have. You now see the value of this reason-directed acting as the sole good that you can get, while the objects that it is from time to time "appropriate" for you to direct your actions toward (or away from) are now seen as having a value (or disvalue) of a totally different rank, such that having or not having them makes no difference as to the totality of good or bad in your life. The objects pursued or avoided in such appropriate or incumbent action have, as one might put it, "pursuit" or "avoidance" value *within* reason-directed acting, but nothing more: they have *no value at all* outside it.[24]

---

[23] Cicero does not mention that "appropriate acts" are done by plants as well as by animals: see Diogenes Laertius VII 107. When a plant, e.g., grows and then unfolds its flower in the way that is normal for the kind of plant that it is, those are "appropriate acts" on its part. Presumably if, due to some abnormality, it grew in altogether the wrong way, those acts would not be "appropriate."

[24] The Stoics present this final "development" as equally as "natural" as the previous ones, despite the fact that it is of course not an inevitable part of the maturation process that all but agreed cases of defective people undergo. Obviously we are not in a position to discover

We can understand that this is so and see what it means if we attend for a moment to the comparisons and contrasts that Cicero (III 24–25, 32) draws between wise or fully reason-directed action, and the acts of other arts. First, "wisdom" is not to be compared to "stochastic" arts like navigation and medicine (or for that matter archery—despite his own use of it in ¶ 22).[25] Fully accomplished navigators or doctors may have it as their "work" simply to do the best that can be done in the existing circumstances to get safely to port or to restore the patient to health, but since the latter are their *goals* they are regretful if for reasons beyond the control of their art that is not achieved: their idea was not merely to do their best (and the devil take the hindmost), but to succeed by that means, so that in such a case in some way *the art* has failed, even if the individual artist has in every way lived up to the highest professional standards. ("For wisdom involves . . . a sense of superiority to all the accidents of man's estate, but this is not the case with the other arts"; III 25.)[26] Rather, the right comparison (though itself only partial) is with the arts of dancing or of acting on the stage.[27] Just as the artistic acts of navigator or physician are given direction by the goals of their arts, so too those of dancers and actors are given direction—not, however, from some goal lying outside the actions themselves which the performer aims to effect, but from the script and the interpretations of the director, or correspondingly from the choreographer. The goals here are simply to act or dance, so directed, in a fully artistic way. Similarly, "wise," fully rational agents, according to the Stoics, take their direction in their actions from whatever may be the natural objective to pursue at the moment, but their goal is to act "artistically" in a thus-directed way, not actually to

---

a "defect" in anyone who does not reach this final stage by the sort of methods we use to assign the failure of some plant to produce a fruit to a congenital defect or developmental anomaly. It seems best to interpret the Stoics' account of human development as intending to show how, *if* (i.e., given that) their theory of the good is correct, we could see human beings coming to grasp it by a series of steps of gradual illumination about what human life involves, each of which can seem fairly natural given its predecessors (and some of which are in fact inevitable): it is by this development that nature or Zeus has intended that we shall develop, whether or not we actually all do complete it.

[25] A stochastic craft is one in which the correct performance by the craftsman does not guarantee the achievement of the craft's aim. The contrast here is with, e.g., the "crafts" of geometry and arithmetic: correct performance in these latter guarantees getting the right result, the one sought after by the art and by the artisan as such. See Gisela Striker, "Antipater, or the Art of Living."

[26] Trans. by H. Rackham in the Loeb edition (Cambridge, Mass.: Harvard University Press, 1914).

[27] It seems very likely that Cicero's preference for these arts as (partial) analogues for wisdom, rather than a stochastic craft such as archery, reflects debates among the Stoics and between them and the academic skeptic Carneades in the middle and end of the second century B.C.— rather than presenting comparisons drawn by anyone of Chrysippus's generation, much less Zeno's (see Striker, "Antipater," pp. 201, 203). However, whatever its provenance, it seems clear to me that the analogy of acting and dancing is very apt for bringing out the true relationship between acting virtuously and pursuing the "natural objective" of the moment, as this was understood by the early Stoics.

get anything, as the navigator or physician as such wants to do, by acting on those directions. So there is no room for any regret or for a sense of failure of any kind in case the objectives acted for do not materialize. And, Cicero concludes, seeing one's actions and oneself as an agent in that way is the essential prior condition of learning to lead a life of consistently and fully virtuous action.

There is much in this developmental story that needs discussion, and it has been much puzzled over in the scholarly literature.[28] But the crucial point for my purposes here, and the only one I will pursue, is that because again all this happens (allegedly) by nature, and nature is a benevolent agency, we can infer immediately that not only do we live (perforce) by reasons rather than automatically implanted impulses, but this is *good* for us, and that not only do we if unperverted or not defective in some way come to *find* that reason-directed acting of the kind indicated is good for us, and indeed the *sole* good[29]—but this is *true*. In Cicero's exposition this is left implicit, but again in that of Diogenes Laertius the point is made explicitly. Continuing his account, cited earlier, of how benevolent nature endows and directs plants and animals (normally) to a life that is a flourishing one for creatures with their natural constitutions, Diogenes Laertius says (VII 86 *sub fin.*): "And since reason has been bestowed upon the rational animals by way of a more perfect kind of management [than that merely through impulses implanted directly by nature], living in accordance with reason rightly turns out to be natural for them.[30] For [in their case] reason is added as a craftsman of impulse." And he goes on immediately (VII 87) to say, "That is why in his book *On the nature of humans* Zeno said (he was the first to say this) that the end is living in agreement with nature." Because nature gives human beings reason as a craftsman of their impulses, the end for human beings, that is, their overall and final good—what corresponds for them to the flourishing of a plant or an animal—becomes living in agreement with nature, living on the basis not of impulses implanted in them by nature but rather of ones created by themselves through the use of their own reasoning powers, and, further, as Cicero explains, but Diogenes does not (or anyhow not here), ones created by themselves in a quite particular way—the way I described in the preceding paragraph in explaining Cicero's comparison of "wise" action with artistic dancing or acting. Cicero

[28] Among the more recent contributions, see part 1 of G. Striker, "Following Nature: A Study in Stoic Ethics," and Troels Engberg-Pedersen, *The Stoic Theory of Oikeiosis*.

[29] Because for the Stoics nothing can be good, strictly speaking, except rational processes carried out to perfection, I have in the preceding occasionally qualified my talk of a person's or an animal's "good" as "loose." No nonrational animal or plant has a good strictly speaking, and our good does not include our comfort, health, etc. In what follows I continue occasionally to speak in this loose way of a thing's good, but without encumbering the exposition with an explicit qualification to that effect.

[30] The Greek is ambiguous as to the placement of the adverb translated by "rightly": it might, as my translation also would permit, go with the main verb or with the participle. The distinction does not matter for present purposes.

says, and Diogenes Laertius agrees, that for the Stoics that is the same as living virtuously.[31]

To assess Cicero's proposed natural progression from instinctual behavior to living "in agreement with nature" and the role of nature in fixing its terms, we need especially to ask how and why it should be thought "natural" (part of being in agreement with nature) to adopt the very peculiar and certainly quite counterintuitive policy of regarding everything else besides fully rational and virtuous action as having no value except what I have called "pursuit" or "avoidance" value. I argue that one cannot even begin to understand the reasons for this unless one takes into account, in conceiving the nature we are to live in agreement with, what Chrysippus says about the relation that holds between our natures as human beings and the single nature of the whole world.

Cicero omits all mention of this point in his exposition.[32] Cicero speaks of the developing rational agent as taking over from its instincts the rational pursuit of the objects at which they were aimed, and we must bear in mind

[31] Diogenes Laertius continues the sentence last quoted, in which he cites Zeno's specification of the end as living in agreement with nature: "and that is living virtuously; for nature leads us to virtue." Cicero, who as we saw concludes his exposition in ¶21 with the claim that at the final stage of development, human beings come to see their final good as consisting in virtuous action, also refers back to this result in ¶26 by citing this same Zenonian specification of the end and saying that it was that which the developmental argument had established. Thus, Cicero and Diogenes come as it were each from a different direction to the same identification of virtuous living with living in agreement with nature. (Cicero had alluded already in ¶21, but indistinctly, to "agreement" as what virtuous action amounts to.)

[32] But since he recognizes that the end we are to come to accept as the true one is "living in agreement with nature," and that, in fact, means for the Stoics primarily living in agreement with *universal nature* (see in my text below), he is silently relying on presuppositions about what that would entail. Despite this and the clear and explicit evidence from Diogenes Laertius about Chrysippus, Annas (*Morality*, chap. 5) wishes to exclude all reference to universal nature from an account of the foundations of Stoic ethical theory. Partly this is because she thinks that to include it would go against the order Chrysippus and the other older Stoics followed in expounding their philosophy: ethics preceded physics, and since physics is required in order to establish anything about universal nature and its manner of working, it follows, she thinks, that ethics must forgo any reference to claims about those matters. She also draws on Jacques Brunschwig's article "On a Book-title by Chrysippus" to show that Chrysippus prominently used "dialectical" styles of argument in his ethical writings, and that such quotations from Chrysippus by Plutarch in *On Stoic Self-Contradictions,* chap. 9 as that "there is no other or more suitable approach to the theory of good and bad or to the virtues or to happiness than from universal nature and from the management of the cosmos" (1035c) come not from ethical writings but from physical ones. She infers that no such approach was made in ethics proper but came only when at the end of the day the already-established ethical conclusions were permitted to be seen in the light of physics and theology. She neglects to consider that reliance in ethics on dialectical premises need not be restricted to premises about "ethical" matters but could well include some premises indicating (in the rough and undetailed way that suits dialectical argument) the unity and the rational nature of the whole cosmos and its unitary functioning. To include such ideas in the foundations of the ethical theory does not require a premature preview of the whole panoply of Stoic physics and theology, as expounded in physical treatises, and there is plenty of enrichment and deepening of one's ethical insights still to be achieved when in studying physics one learns more about these ideas and the

that the instincts in question include not only physical self-preservation but also the instinct to love one's offspring, which is the origin (from a very young age) of the instincts of sociability. We must understand developing rational agents as also seeing that they have reasons, given the benevolence of nature's initial endowments, to care about other people as such and for their own sakes, to treat them fairly, and considerately, and humanely.

Let us consider the Stoic theory, as so far presented, from the point of view of those coming to the study of ethics through the "point of entry" specified by Aristotle. How, and how successfully, have the Stoics engaged such people's desire to improve their lives by listening to philosophy? As with Aristotle, they offer valuable confirmation to an agent of the rightness of his or her own commitment to the value of living virtuously: acting virtuously is the same as acting with a fully developed power of practical reason, and considerations about our human nature and the foundation within it of our true good are offered to show that acting in the latter way is at least an essential requirement for achieving our good. But in their conception of how facts about nature ground this result, the Stoics go well beyond Aristotle's very limited appeal to the good life of a member of a natural species, and therefore much farther outside the "ethical" than does Aristotle. For them nature is a benevolent, *reasoning* agent: it plans and constitutes each kind of living thing with an eye to a specific sort of development to maturity and a particular sort of integration of life functions thereafter as its good. Nature is something *to be* followed for that reason, and it comes in as such in two places in the Stoic account of the human good. On the one hand, the material objectives for which the agent living well will act on each occasion are those that are "in accordance with nature" (*kata phusin*): they are the objects of the initial natural instincts, plus—no doubt we are to understand—obvious extensions that we can see for ourselves as we learn our way around the world and as our constitution itself expands and unfolds over the years we are growing to maturity. On the other hand, as we have seen, a particular (and quite counterintuitive) sort of rational attention to these objects is also said to be natural: this is what is referred to in the phrase "in agreement with nature" (*homologoumenōs tē(i) phusei*) in the Stoics' most usual formulation of the *telos*.

Now the first of these two appeals to nature allows the Stoics to derive at least the rudiments of a theory of what one ought to do. In the theory

---

scientific basis for them. As for sources for dialectical arguments (apart from such arguments as Chrysippus gave starting from the premise that "nothing is better than the world," see, e.g., Diogenes Laertius VII 142 *sub fin.*–143), one need only think of the arguments of Plato's *Timaeus*—appeal to these would of course count as "dialectical." Thus, when Chrysippus claims (according to Plutarch, *On Stoic Self-Contradictions* 1041e) that his theory of goods and bads is "most in harmony with life and most in contact with the preconcepts we naturally have," these preconcepts don't at all have to be only specifically *ethical* ones: preconcepts about the unity and rationality of the world-animal and so on can perfectly well be included. So the evidence that Annas cites to support her effort to exclude reference to the nature of the world as a whole from Stoic ethical theory does not in fact support it.

of "appropriate" or incumbent acts—derived from a knowledge of how nature usually works, in the case of human and other animals, and not at all from inside the "ethical"—the Stoics offer both a confirmation of what we may have already thought at the "entry point" about what we ought to concern ourselves with, and a means of revising and extending it. (I think here especially of the famous Stoic insistence that we have duties of justice and humanity to all human beings merely as such: observation of nature gives us many bases, they think, for supposing that we were "made" for that sort of thing.) This is something, I said, that seems quite lacking in Aristotle. But it is the second appeal to nature that I want to concentrate on. What does it mean to be "living in agreement with nature"? Diogenes Laertius tells us that Cleanthes, Zeno's successor as head of the Stoic school, interpreted the nature here in question simply as that of the universe as a whole—not as the nature of a human being. Chrysippus, too, understood it as the universal nature but corrected Cleanthes on the ground that to live in agreement with human nature actually *was* to live in agreement with universal nature: "living in agreement with nature," he said, is living in agreement with the universal nature and also, in particular, with human nature (Diogenes Laertius VII 89). It is important to observe that in this sequence the reference to universal nature came first, not just chronologically but even (at least in Diogenes Laertius's formulation) within Chrysippus's own explication: the end, he thought, is living in agreement with our own nature as well as with that of the universe as a whole, because it *belongs* to our human nature to be in agreement with the nature of the whole. That is why he can say also that the end is "living in accordance with experience of what happens in the course of nature."[33] And Diogenes Laertius in reporting this immediately adds, "for our natures are parts of the nature of the whole." Thus, the experience in question is experience of what happens in the course of nature at large.

But what does happen in the course of nature that we have to have experience of if we are to live in agreement with nature? Part of this we have already seen: universal nature, through its processes of forming the world's plant and animal life, is benevolent, in the sense that for each of its creatures, universal nature establishes a coherently structured constitution and a life pattern that corresponds, which makes possible for each of them, under normal and usual conditions, a flourishing and good life. But, of course, still in the course of nature, it also frequently happens that plants or animals, or whole systems of them, are deprived of the conditions in which they *can* flourish, according to the norms laid down by nature itself for things of their different kinds. To consider only the human case, although good health is something for which the nature of our bodies normally works

---

[33] Diogenes Laertius VII 87, *kat' empeirian tōn phusei sumbainontōn zēn*; Cicero III 31: "vivere scientiam adhibentem earum rerum quae natura eveniant, seligentem quae secundum naturam et quae contra naturam sint reicientem, id est convenienter congruenterque naturae vivere."

automatically as part of what benevolent nature wants for us, that same nature, working from outside, infects us with diseases, or causes famines and avalanches and in other such ways destroys or maims the lives that, working from inside, it is striving to advance. What do we learn from knowing this sort of thing? One could say, of course, that it must be that though nature continues to *want* things to go well for its creatures even while doing these things to them, it is just not always possible: to keep the whole thing going, which makes possible the continuance of all these marvelous life forms, sometimes some of the individuals have to be sacrificed. But that does not go far enough—not far enough, I mean, to get us to the conclusion Chrysippus wants us to reach.

If that were what one should think, one might well, in now living "in agreement with nature," realize that it could not rationally be helped that one's child got cancer and died a horrible death at the age of 15: nature couldn't rationally have done otherwise than to cause all that. And so one would accept the loss, as one accepts in one's own calculations the necessity to give up something one wanted—indeed, wanted very much—in order to get what overall one thinks is best. But the Stoics want us to do more than accept such things as inevitable *losses*—and this is the very core of what "living in agreement with nature" means for them. We are to think of them as no losses at all; we are not just to accept but to welcome them, and welcome them not just, I take it, as what the universe needed, but as what *we* as parts of that universe needed too. As Chrysippus said, according to Epictetus: "So long as the events coming in sequence are unclear to me I always hold to the things that are better adapted for getting things that are in accordance with nature. God himself [i.e., Zeus] has made me such as to select these. But if I knew that I was fated to get sick now I would also have an impulse toward that. After all, the foot, if it had a mind, would have an impulse toward getting muddied."[34] As we have seen, Chrysippus emphasized in this connection that our natures are parts of the nature of the whole, from which the inference apparently to be drawn is that even our "local" advantage—what advances our individual lives—is to be measured by reference to the needs of the life of the world as a whole, just as the "local advantage" of the foot is rightly measured by what it needs to do *as* a foot in the life of the whole person. Even the cancer and horrible death of a child is not to be seen, once it happens, as a loss, a sacrifice that nature has called on the child's parent to accept in the interest of the whole; if the life of the whole has been advanced by that means, so has the parent's own life, since it is nothing but a part of the life of the whole.[35] So far as I can see, it is only if we think of ourselves and our lives in this way that we can see the point of the demand that living in agreement with nature (i.e.,

[34] Epictetus, *Discourses* II 6, 9.

[35] Thus, I think that accounts such as that of F. H. Sandbach, *The Stoics*, pp. 35–37, approved by Long and Sedley, *The Hellenistic Philosophers,* vol. II, p. 354, do not go far enough. Striker, "Following Nature" (see esp. pp. 10–12) is along the right lines.

universal nature) should lead us to regard all that happens to us on a par—
all the failures or successes we may have in relation to the "material"
objectives of our virtuous actions—and not to think of anything that happens
to us as any better or worse than anything else that we might imagine as
having happened instead. I do not see at all how one could reasonably be
invited to reach that conclusion simply from within the "ethical," that is,
from within our practical attitudes and our motivational set as we come to
the study of philosophical ethics, plus our commitment to finding a conception of a single overall good to direct our lives by. That "ethical" starting
point would include the idea that virtuous action is a crucial and indispensable value for a good human life. But I can find no pressure from within
the "ethical" view we would have been brought up with that would, or that
the Stoics might reasonably have thought would, lead us all by itself to this
totally new way of conceiving the value of all things other than virtuous
action itself.[36] The Stoics' appeal to nature as I have explained it, however
much supplemented by such "ethical" considerations, is an indispensable
part—indeed, the core—of their argument.

III. "Moral Duty"

With the structure of their theory now before us, what can we say about
the Stoics' concept of "moral duty"? How significantly, if at all, do their
eudaimonism, with its strong teleological commitments, or other features
of their view, distinguish their conception of duties from that of Kant? First,
as I said at the beginning of this essay, following Julia Annas, the Stoics'
eudaimonism poses no obstacle at all to the moral integrity of virtuous
agents. When such agents identify living virtuously with living happily, they
do not have some determinate further conception of their happiness as a
value, beyond that of living according to the commitments constitutive of
virtuous attitudes themselves; they do not subordinate virtuous action to
some other thing they know and value independently, as a means of achieving
that value. On the contrary, it is the value of living virtuously itself, that
is, living in agreement with nature, that they see as the basic value. Logically
speaking, the identification of this with living happily is a subsequent move.
    But does not this simple identification of virtuous with happy living intro-
duce, from the opposite direction as it were, at least as great a distortion
of what virtue and duty are, according to our modern conception, as would
the effort to subordinate virtuous action to the pursuit of one's own happiness conceived as Kant conceives happiness? If you abolish altogether all
even potential conflict between virtue and happiness, don't you remove a

---

[36] T. H. Irwin's arguments in "Stoic and Aristotelian Conceptions of Happiness," constructed
on this basis, to support the Stoic views as against those of Aristotle, are mostly very weak and
tortured, and the whole effort leads, by his admission, to an entirely predictable, uneasy standoff.

contrast that is essential to giving sense to what virtue and duty are? For us a dutiful life is *essentially* one requiring frequent self-denial and sacrifice of our own good to that of others. One can respond to this challenge at two levels. First, someone who accepted the Stoic outlook, and recognized in their calmer and more reflective moments that their highest good really does consist entirely in virtuous living, understood in the Stoics' way, might very well, when it came to practice, find it quite difficult to act in accordance with that vision. They might find that what that required of them was by no means what, at the moment, they most wanted to do, or most cared about. If nonetheless they found the strength of mind to do what their own happiness (= virtue) would require, this would be experienced by them as, and would in fact be, an act of self-denial, and if not precisely a sacrifice of their own good (as they saw that in doing the action), at any rate a sacrifice of what they had antecedently most wanted, most cared about, and most felt like doing. If happiness is placed on the side of virtue, there is still plenty of room for a sharp contrast between both of those things and one's perceived interests and advantage, one's material needs and welfare, one's pleasure, one's deep (non-moral) life projects (if one puffs oneself up by thinking of one's life in such terms at all), and so on. On the Stoic view, of course, the act of such a conflicted agent, however commendable, would not be a fully virtuous one: it derived not from a permanent and deeply reasoned commitment to living in agreement with nature, but at best from a temporary and wavering acceptance of the value of doing that. On the other hand, it is also the case on the Stoic view that that sort of "virtuous" action is in fact the best that almost any human being actually manages to produce. So one is entitled to say, for the Stoics just as much as for Kant or for us, that virtue (or rather, "virtue"—the closest any of us actually comes to true virtue) is essentially bound up with self-denial and self-sacrifice.[37]

Second, even fully virtuous persons (so-called sages) experience virtuous action as something imposed on them by Zeus and by themselves qua rational, something that requires vigilance and discipline so that they do not follow the tendency usual for human beings to identify their perceived interests and advantage, material needs and welfare, pleasure, and nonmoral life projects as being of independent value, separate from what I have called their "pursuit" value.[38] Even if their conviction otherwise is so deeply imbedded in their minds that there is no chance at all that they will ever adopt

[37] Of course, for Kant virtue requires *real* self-sacrifice that only moral faith can allow us to think may be made up for in the end. I thank J B. Schneewind for reminding me of this.

[38] According to Galen, Chrysippus mentioned two causes to explain the fact that people generally are corrupted as they grow up and do not follow the natural development that leads to being virtuous: they learn the wrong values from what others around them say about the values of things, or else they acquire them from "the nature of things itself" (*ex autēs tōn pragmatōn tēs phuseōs*; Galen, *On the Doctrines of Hippocrates and Plato,* trans. DeLacy, V 5, 15, p. 320), glossed by Galen as "the persuasiveness of appearances" (*dia tēn pithanotēta tōn phantasiōn,* 5, 19). (This passage supports the variant reading of *pragmatōn* in place of the editors' *pragmateiōn* at Diogenes Laertius VII 89.)

such a mistaken view even temporarily, and they do not actively have to fight off any tendency to do that, what guarantees this success is precisely the active, forceful, and constant use of their minds in understanding things rightly. They know that in the interest of acting virtuously they often deny themselves things that can with plausibility be thought good for them: most people do think them good, and anyone, the fully virtuous person included, can readily see why, given the character of our experience of them. Moreover, even if the virtuous are so strong minded that it is certain that they will never give in to such appearances, it seems reasonable to think that they, like all other human beings, will continue to be affected by the plausible appearance of these things as if they were good. Even virtuous persons, therefore, experience their virtuous actions and outlook as requiring that they sacrifice things that they continue to be *able* to see as if they were good. They have not ceased being human beings and become gods; they experience "duty" as going against something within them, even if not against what amounts to a Kantian "inclination."

"Living in agreement with nature" as the Stoics understand it involves modeling one's thoughts in deciding on and doing one's actions, on nature's own thought in designing the world (i.e., itself), establishing the physical laws, and causing the events that happen within it. To be sure, not even a perfectly virtuous person can know the particular reasons why nature causes the events that it does—why, for example, one person falls ill when another does not. Even if a virtuous person enjoys happiness just as great as Zeus's, as Chrysippus scandalously maintained,[39] nonetheless Zeus understands what he is doing vastly more completely. So one has to accept as reasonable, and benevolent, what one often cannot know the reasons for—though, one knows, there *are* reasons, and Zeus or nature does know them. This gives emphasis to the idea that in living virtuously one lives in obedience, as Chrysippus puts it in the striking passage from Diogenes Laertius we began from, to the *koinos nomos* or the law of the universe, or universal and right reason, or the will of Zeus. This obedience involves two fundamental things: (1) acting so as to pursue or avoid the things that can be seen *normally* to accord with or go against our physical constitution and the social circumstances that naturally suit beings with that constitution, and (2) pursuing or avoiding them always with the idea that it may turn out that achieving those objectives on that occasion was not after all what we or anyone else truly needed, because it does not fit in with the needs of the whole universe of which we are organic parts.

In considering this aspect of the Stoic theory of duty, one should note two points. First, the thought that in doing a virtuous act one is doing it because it is commanded by the universal law and by universal reason applies just as much, and in exactly the same way, to what one does in maintaining an appropriate diet or tending to one's daily hygiene or working hard at

---

[39] See Arius at Stobaeus 98, 18–99, 2 W.

one's profession or behaving charmingly at a dinner party, as it does to what, according to one contemporary usage and the dominant one nowadays anyhow among philosophers, we would call *moral* decisions and actions— treating other people fairly and considerately, standing up for moral principle when that is inconvenient and one's associates or more generally one's fellow citizens would gladly override it, refusing to disobey the law even if no one will find out, or accepting financial sacrifice and personal hardship in order to serve the public good. The notion of "duty" among the Stoics covers a vastly wider range than it does, for example, for Kant: it covers, in fact, crucial aspects of the whole of one's life and virtually everything one does, if one is truly virtuous. So if we should choose to call all the Stoic duties *moral* duties, we should frankly admit that we are employing so widened a conception of morality as to risk losing contact with what we nowadays understand by that term.[40] Moreover, because in this theory the more private and personal side of life is lumped together with the morally right and morally wrong, without any fundamental discrimination between them, the latter, though certainly present and accounted for in the theory, do not receive the priority that moralists nowadays typically think they are entitled to. We have a deontology, perhaps, but it is not a deontology that tells us first to tend to the morally right and wrong, and only then to our private and more personal concerns. It simply tells us to follow reason and not to act ever on what we might otherwise like to do, or on how the appearances of things to us might make us think it would be a good idea to act.

Second, the notion of universal reason here at work has further special features that mark it sharply off from the Kantian conception, however much it may be an important ancestor of the latter. For the Stoics, universal reason is the reason common to all human beings. But it is also, and more fundamentally, the single reason that governs the unified world as a whole. When I consult universal reason in deciding what to do—say, to do an act of justice or humanity—I do of course consult the very same ideas that any other rational human being in my situation would consult, and the very same ones that the recipient of my action, qua rational, will have in mind in considering and assessing what I am doing. But more fundamentally what I am consulting are the ideas to be found in reasoned experience of nature at large as to what that nature *intends* for me to do. There is no appeal, and no room for any appeal, to individual rational beings, such as myself, as having the power to set their own ends, or to any requirement to respect, just because it came from a free exercise of that power, any other person's preferences and decisions about what to care about in their lives. So there is no basis for attributing to the Stoics any idea of the "rights of man" where that has at its core the idea that adult persons have an inviolable

---

[40] For this reason I feel very uncomfortable with Annas's uncompromising insistence that in the Stoics' and other ancient discussions of the primacy of virtue over all other values, we are getting, quite simply, theories of *morality*. See *Morality*, e.g., pp. 14, 452–55, and J. Annas, "Ancient Ethics and Modern Morality."

right to live as they please, so long as they don't interfere with the same right of others, and a similar right to take part equally in the establishment or authorization of public policy in their countries and communities. Since Kant's conception of universal reason as the source of moral duties has its place in a political and religious world that made human freedom and equality in precisely this sense the central moral idea, one should not fail to see that the Stoic idea of universal reason, together with its consequences for ethical theory, constitute what amounts to a different moral universe.

CHAPTER TWENTY-ONE

Posidonius on Emotions

I Introductory

Repeatedly in books IV and V of *On the Doctrines of Hippocrates and Plato (PHP)*, Galen asserts that Posidonius abandoned certain views on the psychology of human action that at least since Chrysippus had generally been regarded as central and indispensable to the Stoic philosophy.[1] Specifically, Galen says he rejected Chrysippus's theory of the *pathē*. As a term of ordinary Greek, *pathē* are conditions, especially noxious or otherwise objectionable ones, including bodily diseases, that someone undergoes or suffers. But the word is used in a somewhat special way by philosophers to refer generally to anger, grief, fear, sadness, elation, and so on—what *we* call emotions—as well as excited, agitated desires and aversions, notably agitated desires for food, drink, and sex, and agitated aversions to bodily pain, physical harm, financial loss, and death. For convenience I use the English word *emotions* to refer to the phenomena here in question (though, as we shall see, substantial philosophical issues are raised by any effort to give a clear specification of the phenomena that are to be covered by this term). Here at the outset, the important point to bear in mind is the agitation and excitement involved in all the *pathē*.

Chrysippus held "emotions," so understood, to be functions of the reasoning power, the ability adult human beings have to think out and decide what to do. Instead, according to Galen, Posidonius adopted the rival, tripartite psychology of reason, spirit, and appetite that is most familiar to us from Plato's *Republic* but was accepted also, as Galen correctly notes, by Aristotle:[2] he regarded each emotion as a function not of reason, but of one or the other of the other two parts of the soul recognized by Plato and Aristotle. Galen supports these assertions with a rich series of verbatim quotations and paraphrases from Posidonius's treatise *On Emotions (Peri pathōn)*. These make it clear that Posidonius did indeed disagree openly, seriously, and explicitly with Chrysippus on these matters, and that he cited and praised Plato precisely for having recognized that human nature

---

[1] See especially *PHP* IV 3. 3, IV 4. 38, V 1. 5–6, V 6. 42. (Throughout I cite this work from the edition of Phillip DeLacy; I use, as here, his chapters and sections, often with the addition of the page and line in his edition.) See also VII 1. 9 and VII 1. 14. Galen was writing in the A.D. 160s, more than two centuries after Posidonius's death (see DeLacy, p. 46, referring to Galen's report in *De libris propriis*, his account of his own authorship).

[2] See above, Chapter 10, "Some Remarks on Aristotle's Moral Psychology," sect. II and Chapter 11, "Reason, Moral Virtue, and Moral Value."

encompasses two other psychic powers besides that of reasoning and decision that also play a role in the generation of human actions. But is Galen right to say simply that Posidonius abandoned the standard Stoic view (Chrysippus's) about the psychic source and nature of the emotions, in favor of a reversion to the psychology of action defended by Plato (and Aristotle)?

Galen quotes Posidonius as maintaining that virtually the whole of an adequate moral theory depends upon the correct understanding of the emotions—in particular, that the theory of the virtues and the theory of the ultimate end of human life itself do so (see pp. 477–78, below). So this was no isolated or minor matter on which he disagreed with Chrysippus. One would expect that on a fundamental point of moral theory, defection to Plato and Aristotle, the Stoics' traditional opponents in this realm, would be perceived as the abandonment of Stoicism altogether—as happened in the case of Posidonius's contemporary Antiochus.[3] But Posidonius appears consistently in all our sources as one leading Stoic among the others, and, indeed, with almost the sole exception of Galen,[4] he seems to have been universally regarded as a leading authority for orthodox Stoic moral theory

---

[3] Cicero expounds the Stoic theory of the good and happiness in bk. III of *On Ends*, but that of Antiochus in bk. V, where Piso (Antiochus's spokesman) describes it as the doctrine of the Old Academy and of the Peripatetics (V 8, cf. V 14), tricked out later in new and misleading language, but without differing in content, by innovation-seeking Stoics (V 74, 88–89). Despite Piso's claim that Antiochus's "Old Academic" view is also the Stoic one, Cicero himself refuses to accept this (V 79–85): The "assimilation" of the Stoics to the old Academics and Aristotle really means the abandonment of essential points of their theory. (Antiochus—though he is said to have studied with the Stoic Mnesarchus—was an Academic, indeed head of the school for a time; unlike Posidonius, he was not counted as a Stoic philosopher at all, whether orthodox or not.)

[4] Diogenes Laertius attributes to Posidonius, without further explanation, the very unorthodox views (VII 103) that health and wealth are good things (*agatha*), and (VII 128) that (in consequence?) virtue is not sufficient by itself for a good and happy life, as orthodox Stoicism maintained it was. There is a trace of the same interpretation of Posidonius in a remark of Epiphanius (*De fide* 9.46). Neither report reveals anything about any textual basis on which it may rest, and they are roundly contradicted by Seneca. In an elaborate discussion (*Letters*, 87) of Stoic syllogisms aimed at showing wealth not to be a good thing Seneca provides convincing evidence that Posidonius not only adhered to the orthodox Stoic view that wealth and health and the like are neither good nor bad things but "preferred indifferents," but employed elegant and original arguments to defend it. Seneca quotes the following syllogism from Posidonius (87. 35): "Things that give neither greatness of soul nor self-confidence nor freedom from care are not goods. But riches and good health and the like do not bring about any of these conditions. Therefore they are not goods." And Seneca shows that in developing this view he made excellent use of the Stoic distinction between antecedent and efficient (or "principal" or "containing") causes. He argued that wealth harms us, not by its own nature and force, but as an antecedent cause, by encouraging its possessors to become arrogant and feel false delight with their circumstances (87. 31–32). Plainly, Posidonius's acceptance of the orthodox view on these matters was a settled, fully considered commitment. Given the state of our evidence, we can only speculate what Posidonius may somewhere have written that permitted Diogenes Laertius and Epiphanius (or their sources) to misunderstand him so grossly. For some suggestions about this, see Kidd, *Posidonius*, II, pp. 639–41.

in particular.[5] How can Galen's testimony, and the rest of his evidence, be squared with these facts? Did our other sources for Posidonius simply not know, or even know of, Posidonius's views in *On Emotions*? (Of our authorities for Posidonius, only Galen ever refers to a work of Posidonius by that name.) Or were his ethical views in other writings significantly different from those attributed to him by Galen, so that *On Emotions* was for the most part silently discounted by later writers?

A third possibility, which I wish to argue for here, is that when carefully examined Galen's own evidence, despite the terms in which he reports and comments on what he found in *On Emotions*, does not support the extreme claims of unorthodoxy that he himself bases on it.[6] The philosophical issues dividing Plato and Chrysippus on the nature of the emotions are extremely difficult ones, more difficult than scholars have recognized. As recent investigations have confirmed,[7] both Plato's and Chrysippus's views on these matters are so complex and intricate that it would be surprising if there were *no* interesting and plausible alternative positions lying somewhere between the two—positions, to be sure, rejecting important elements in each, but arguably preserving some of the central insights distinctive of the two views and ordinarily thought of as mutually exclusive. I believe Posidonius's theory of the emotions was one such intermediate view.

In sum, according to the interpretation I advance in what follows, Posidonius accepted the traditional Stoic commitment to the thesis that all human motivational states, including, in particular, the *pathē*, are ultimately functions of the rational faculty, and of it alone: they depend upon and express the agent's decisive opinion, at the time they are experienced, about what is worth reacting to and acting for. But the *pathē* are a very special case. In them, some of the force of the impulse toward action that one experiences derives from an independent, nonrational power (something comparable, but no more, to Plato's appetite or spirit), which is the source of certain feelings, not themselves full-fledged *pathē*, that reason takes up into the impulse (the *pathos*) that it creates. In effect, Posidonius attempts, within the traditional Stoic psychology of action, to recognize and assign an appropriate role to the *sort* of nonrational power of which the Platonists and Peripatetics made so much. His intention was to improve on Chrysippus's analysis, in such a way as to protect the Stoic position from one powerful

---

[5] See, e.g., Cicero, *Tusculan Disputations* II 61, *On Ends* I 6, *Hortensius* frg. 18; Seneca, *Letters* 33. 4, 108. 38. J. Fillion-Lahille (*Le "De ira" de Sénèque*, pp. 122–23) points out that neither in Seneca's *On Anger* nor in Cicero's *Tusc. Disp.* III and IV, nor in any other ancient discussion of the emotions, where one would certainly expect to catch wind of it, does one hear any indication of the abandonment of Stoic psychological principles that Galen attributes to Posidonius.

[6] In this general opinion I am in agreement with J. Fillion-Lahille: see *Le "De ira,"* Part 3, chs. 1–3.

[7] See above, Chapter 4, "Plato's Theory of Human Motivation," and Michael Frede, "The Stoic Doctrine of the Affections of the Soul."

and frequent line of attack against it. He did not abandon the fundamental
Stoic contention that all motivational states of adult human beings depend
upon and express judgments reached through the use of the rational faculty,
and he did not accept instead the rival Platonist view that some motivating
states of mind (the "emotional" ones) are independent of reason.[8]

If nonetheless Galen describes Posidonius simply as rejecting Chrysippus's
view in favor of Plato's, that can be understood easily enough. Galen's
purpose in *PHP* is to argue, primarily against Chrysippus, that Plato and
Hippocrates were right to recognize three distinct psychological forces in
human beings (called appropriately by Plato *to logistikon, to thumoeides,*
and *to epithumētikon*), located respectively in three distinct bodily organs—
the brain, the heart, and the liver. Given this agenda there are obvious
rhetorical advantages in being able to say, as Galen repeatedly does, that
even a Stoic, the Stoic most renowned for his careful attention to scientific
and philosophical methodology (and possessed of the intellectual honesty
that Galen insinuates any true scientist must have),[9] was ashamed to follow
Chrysippus in his account of the emotions and felt constrained to follow
the "ancients" instead. To follow Chrysippus would require rejecting the
"obvious" facts that point to a plurality of independent psychological powers
at work in producing human motivational states, in favor of adherence to
alleged principles of reason: but correct methodology requires selecting first
principles in accord with the "obvious" facts and forbids denying the facts
because they are inconsistent with one's "principles." Moreover, the Stoic
dogmas were themselves the product of nothing but contentiousness and
the desire to glorify oneself at the expense of such eminent ancient authorities
as Plato and Aristotle (see *PHP* V 1. 10–11, p. 294, 15–25). This, too,
Posidonius refused to do. At the same time, given the complexity of the
philosophical issues as stake, there is room for Galen (however mistakenly) to
have thought that his own interpretation of Posidonius as a straightforward
adherent to the Platonic psychology was a fair and reasonable one, fully
responsible to Posidonius's views as he expressed and argued for them in
On Emotions. One need not accuse Galen of dishonesty—only of inattention
to important details of Plato's, Chrysippus's, and Posidonius's views.

So much, then, for a summary of what I try to show.

---

[8] Fillion-Lahille also attempts an interpretation of Posidonius along these general lines. Her
discussion of Galen's evidence is the best, and by far the most complete, in the scholarly
literature, and I have learned a good deal from it. She fails, however, to give a clear, philosophically convincing account of exactly how, according to Posidonius, the nonrational powers
function in relation to reason in causing emotions, nor does she adequately distinguish Posidonius's conception of the nonrational powers from Plato's. In section III below I attempt to make
up for these deficiencies in her account.

[9] Posidonius the most scientifically trained of the Stoics: Galen *PHP* IV 4. 38, p. 258, 19–22;
VIII 1. 14, pp. 482. 32–484. 4 (= F32 Edelstein-Kidd); *De sequela*, Kühn 819 (*Scripta minora,*
vol. II, pp. 77.17–78.2) (= T58 Edelstein-Kidd).

II Chrysippus

Galen implies that Posidonius expounded his own theory of the emotions through criticism of Chrysippus, whose work *On Emotions* may possibly have been the formal target for Posidonius's treatise, similarly named in order to bring out that relationship.[10] The best way to understand Posidonius's views is therefore through seeing their relationship to Chrysippus's.

Chrysippus held that *pathē* are instances of what he, in common with other Stoics, called *hormai*, "impulses": psychic movements of the kind that directly cause voluntary bodily movements.[11] Thus anger and fear, for example, are to be thought of as themselves directly causing the behavior that expresses them, in just the same way as an agitated desire (an "appetite," *epithumia*) for food or sex causes the voluntary behavior in which it is indulged; and the more reactive emotions, such as sadness and depression, or delight, are similarly to be thought of as directly causing the grimaces and groans, grins and whoops, and other more articulate and demonstrative behaviors that express them. In the terminology of contemporary philosophy, Chrysippus would class the *pathē* as a type of occurrent desires, fully completed psychic movements toward action. This much of the Stoic understanding of the *pathē* was generally shared in Hellenistic and later times by philosophers of all schools. And it does not appear that Aristotle or Plato would find anything in it to disagree with—except that for them not every *pathos* directly causes voluntary bodily movements. For them, as we saw, *pathē* belong to further parts of the soul alongside reason; and though they *can* effect voluntary bodily movement on their own, they can also be overruled and held in check by reason (while continuing to be felt).

So *pathē* must—and this goes equally for the Stoics and for Plato—be carefully distinguished from feelings that, as we would say, merely *incline* one toward acting in some way: hunger or thirst, for example, understood simply as the bodily feelings of discomfort usually caused (as we know) by the need for food or drink. If those bodily feelings are at all a cause of subsequent action, it is only by giving rise in some way to an intervening desire to eat or drink; it is that intervening desire, if anything, that will be

---

[10] That Posidonius's book was formally directed against Chrysippus's is only a guess, but it is encouraged by the very wide range of topics connected to the emotions on which Galen cites extended criticisms of Chrysippus by Posidonius; and see *PHP* V 6. 45, p. 336, 10–11, where Galen speaks summarily of all these criticisms as having been directed by Posidonius against Chrysippus's *treatise*.

[11] See Stobaeus, *Eclogae* II, p. 86, 17–87, 6 Wachsmuth (= *SVF* III 169); Origen, *De principiis* 3. 1. 2–3 (= *SVF* II 988, beginning); Philo, *Legum allegoriae* 1. 30 (= *SVF* II 844). It should be noted that such impulses need not cause action immediately: one may experience one while waiting for the moment for action, as indicated in the impulse itself. Also, though one is already "set" on action through experiencing an impulse to act in some particular way, it is possible to revoke the impulse before doing so (by deciding not to act after all, and so ridding oneself of it).

counted by Chrysippus (or by Plato or Aristotle, for that matter) as an
epithumia or appetite, i.e., a *pathos*.[12] These discomforts, like actual bodily
pains, are objects of awareness belonging to psychic states of a very different
category from the one ("impulses") into which Chrysippus places the emotions. Likewise, pleasure consisting simply in the experience of pleasant
sensations must be sharply distinguished from enjoyment of or delight in
anything (even the enjoyment of such sensations). Only pleasure of this
second kind (enjoyment or delight) counts as an emotion for the Stoics; the
other kind of pleasure, the experience of pleasant sensations, belongs to a
psychic state of a very different kind.[13]

Now Chrysippus also held that in adult human beings, simply as a fact
of human nature, any "impulse" (any completed psychic movement toward
action) has a certain specific structure or constitution, different from that
of the corresponding impulses of other animals and even of biologically
immature human beings. His fundamental idea, put simply and as uncontroversially as possible, is this. Whenever we adults experience a psychic movement that is an immediate cause of voluntary bodily movement[14]—one that
does not require an intervening psychic event or process for the movement

---

[12] When any of the Greek philosophers use as names of types of appetite (*epithumia*) words
that we must translate as "hunger" or "thirst" (or the equivalents in other modern languages),
one must take care to realize that it is not the bodily feeling that is in question: the appetite
is a certain *desire to eat or drink* that has the bodily feeling as some kind of cause, but is not
identical with it. See, for example, Plato, *Philebus* 34d10–35d7 (the *epithumia*, thirst, requires
in addition to the perceptual experience of a bodily depletion the memory of a replenishment
perceived in the past, which makes it possible to conceive a desire for another replenishment
in the immediate future).

[13] Pleasure of the first kind, and the pain that stands in opposition to it, are counted by the
Stoics as neither good nor bad. These are caused by our physical constitution and what impinges
on it. Given our constitutions and what happens to us, it is not up to us whether we experience
pleasure or pain of this first kind. Pleasure of the second kind and the pain opposed to it (being
distressed or upset about something), being emotions, are counted as thoroughly bad things,
to be avoided in all circumstances: they rest, allegedly, upon erroneous evaluation of the things
being so responded to. The Stoics appear to have used the same Greek word (*hēdonē*) to refer
to pleasure in both these senses (contrast Diog. L., VII 102 with VII 110–11, 114); the distinction
between the two senses is marked by the fact that it is given *ponos* (i.e., physical pain) as its
opposite in the first passage, but *lupē* (distress) in the second pair of passages. (The Arius
Didymus summary of Stoic ethical theory agrees with Diog. L. in reporting this double usage
of the word *hēdonē*, again distinguishing the two uses through the two opposites *ponos* and
lupē: Stob. II 81. 13–15 vs. 88. 18–21 Wachsmuth.) On this see A. A. Long and D. N. Sedley,
The Hellenistic Philosophers, vol. I, p. 421, vol. II, p. 405. J.C.B. Gosling and C.C.W. Taylor
seem to overlook these decisive passages when they reject as mistaken the attribution by modern
writers of this distinction to the Stoics (*The Greeks on Pleasure*, 426–27).

[14] I mean to exclude here, as not voluntary bodily movements, not just (1) automatic movements that are not psychologically caused at all, though we are at least sometimes aware of
them and they can be affected by our psychological states (e.g., the beating of the heart), and
(2) reflexes like being startled by a loud nearby sound, but also (3) automatic doings (blinking,
breathing) that we can nonetheless inhibit at will (up to a point), and (4) the involuntary bodily
signs of emotional states (blushing, elevated pulse, hot skin, etc.)—even if, as Chrysippus
thinks, those states are at bottom themselves voluntary.

in question to occur—that psychic movement always expresses a practical view (involving both an asserted evaluative thought and what we would call an intention to act accordingly) that we are actually holding at the time. Whenever I do anything voluntarily, that is because I think something to the effect that *that is the thing to do*; the immediate psychological cause of my action, the "impulse," is or represents that thought and (as it were) carries it into the action. This means that when, for example, I act from anger (and so am moved by an impulse that is also an emotion), the anger that I feel includes somehow both the thought that this act of vengeance (or whatever sort of act it is) is the thing to do in the circumstances, and the intention to do it. In some cases quite an elaborate and well-articulated view may lie behind that summary thought, but in others there may be very little indeed beyond the bare summary thought itself, plus the intention. Chrysippus's claim is only that, however much or little there may be by way of grounds on which the person feeling the anger is basing that judgment and intention, the anger involves essentially (whatever else it may involve) precisely such a summary practical thought.

I believe this fundamental idea provides the grounds for the theory of Chrysippus and the other Stoics that human emotions, and indeed all other species of "impulse" in mature human beings, are functions of our mind, of our power to reason about and decide for ourselves what to do. It seems difficult to deny that in judging that something or other is *the thing to do* we are employing our rational power (how fully, and how adequately, are further questions); and if such a judgment lies at the center of each of our "impulses," then our "impulses" must be functions of the rational power— the power to think out and decide what to do. At any rate, it certainly seems fair to say that anyone (for instance Plato or Aristotle) who thinks some impulses, emotions for example, are functions of some psychic power other than reason must give some account of how a *non*rational power acquires its ability to issue such rational-seeming judgments on things. Or else they have to show us that *some* "impulses" do not, after all, represent a "summary practical thought" at all, that they are intentions to act but contain no summary evaluation of the action as *to be done*. Aristotle, of course, holds that reason acquires control over appetite and spirit (when it does) by "persuading" them to yield to its own judgments and directives (see *Nicomachean Ethics* 1 13, 1102b30–35), and Plato's account of the virtue of "temperance" in *Republic* IV as involving a friendly agreement among the soul-parts as to which of them should rule has a similar effect. So on the Platonic-Aristotelian view, appetite and spirit do, at any rate, have substantial conceptual resources in common with reason: but those are not enough, by themselves, to support summary practical judgments, saying (in effect) that *this is the thing to do*. (See further below, sect. IV.)

It should now be clear why Chrysippus thought that nonhuman animals have *hormai* of a fundamentally different kind from human beings. If it is granted that only human beings among the animals can formulate judgments, it follows at once that whatever psychic states produce the other animals' "voluntary" bodily movements—I mean the ones that we ordinarily attribute to their desires or instincts—cannot have the propositional content ("This is the thing to do") essential to the impulses of adult human beings. The same consideration does not suffice, however, to show that the impulses of immature human beings differ fundamentally from those of grown-ups. For on any reasonable view of when maturity is attained, and certainly long before the age of 14, favored among the Stoics for this event, children acquire enough mastery of language to formulate to themselves and assert the propositions needed for adult impulses: they too in wanting to do something are capable of thinking, and presumably often do think, that just that is the thing to do.

If nonetheless Chrysippus insists that children's impulses are just as different from ours as those of lower animals, that is apparently because he thinks the role of such thoughts in the constitution of their impulses is different. With us, he thinks, we are moved toward doing an action essentially because we hold that it is the thing to do; if we did not think that, then no matter what else might be going on in our souls (no matter what other sorts of movements there might be in it), we would not be actually *moved* at all *to do* it. (Feeling tempted, or inclined, to do it, or to decide to do it, is something else again.) But children are on each occasion, in advance of having any such thought, already moved quasi-instinctually to their actions, just like the lower animals; they would continue to be moved to do them (and would actually do them) whether or not they had these particular thoughts—that it is the thing to do, for these or those reasons. They are learning to be, but are not yet, rational creatures, because their ability to think does not yet control how they are moved to act. In them, instinct or other forms of nonrational desire are in control instead. To be sure, in ordinary language we speak equally of young people and adults as being affected on occasion by anger or grief or delight or sadness or agitated desires (appetites). But careful attention to fundamental facts about the psychological processes by which human beings at different stages of maturity are governed in their actions shows clearly, Chrysippus thinks, that the phenomena in the two cases are radically distinct. It should be no surprise that ordinary language, based as it largely is on the surface appearance of things, should fail to reflect underlying differences in similar phenomena. And in any event, these features of our language certainly do not disprove Chrysippus's analysis, which attempts to base itself on careful and thoughtful attention directly to the psychological facts themselves. Only a better account of those facts could effectively undermine it.

These, then, are the background principles (the "elements" or *stoicheia*, cf. Galen *PHP* V 6. 39, p. 334, 10–11) on which Chrysippus attempts to develop his account of the emotions: what they are; how they arise and subside; how they can be assuaged, or avoided, on particular occasions; how they can be prevented altogether from arising; and so on. So far I have simply wished to explain Chrysippus's view about adult human "impulses" and his reasons for holding it; critical examination is best reserved until we consider Posidonius's and Galen's objections. It should already be clear, however, that his is a serious and well-motivated philosophical view that deserves careful and thoughtful attention. It is much more than the impertinent effort of a contentious self-glorifier to contradict Plato and Aristotle, which is Galen's view of it.

Given, then, that all adult human "impulses" are functions of the rational power, what is one to say about this special case, the human emotions? To begin with, everyone agrees that many instances of emotional arousal and response are inappropriate (even as judged by the one experiencing them) and often enough blameworthy as well: it can be a blameworthy defect of character, for example, even to become angry at *some* things. Moreover, it is common ground among the Greek philosophers, even those who like Plato and Aristotle think there are other sources of motivation as well, that reason is a source of motivations (*hormai*, in technical Stoic terminology) all on its own.[15] Now Plato and Aristotle, holding that emotions are functions of our souls' nonrational powers, are free to maintain that some emotions are appropriate (rational in the sense of being the right way to feel in the existing circumstances) and not in the least blameworthy. On the Platonic-Aristotelian theory, such motivations can exist simply alongside the motivations of reason itself, as additional "impulses" directed at the actions to which reason's motivations are also directed. But this course is not open to Chrysippus. If reason is functioning as it ought to, it will produce all on its own appropriate and totally blame-free impulses perfectly sufficient to produce all the right actions—and these impulses would be counted even by Plato and Aristotle as reasoned and not emotional motivations. On Chrysippus's view there is simply no room for additional appropriate and blame-free motivations, motivations of an emotional character. Any motivation must, for him, derive from reason itself, and one cannot see why or how a well-functioning reason would sometimes produce two impulses to act—one a calm reason-based decision to act, the other an additional emotional one, also entirely appropriate and correct. From Chrysippus's perspective, the presence of emotional motivation can only betray some sort of defectiveness in reason's own functions. For him, the Platonic-Aristotelian idea that a well-functioning reason might sometimes or always need, or even accept, the help of the emotions in the production of actions must look like the very confused thought that there is an essentially defective way of thinking and feeling that is nonetheless sometimes appropriate and blame-free! Accordingly, Chrysippus condemns as a thorough-going chimera the idea, accepted by Platonic and Aristotelian philosophical theory (but also by common sense), that only some emotions are inappropriate and blameworthy. The allegedly innocent ones are simply less obviously and openly

---

[15] See Chapters 4 and 10 above and Frede, "The Stoic Doctrine," p. 100f.

products of a defective reason than the others; they may impel us toward the very actions reason's own motivations are directed to (or would be if reason were functioning correctly), but, being products of a defective reason, they must impel us with an incorrect conception of why the actions are worth doing.[16]

What incorrect conception is that? Like other Stoics, Chrysippus identifies the defect as taking the object of the emotional impulse—the event or circumstance or thing reacted to—as actually good or bad (depending on whether the affect itself is a positive or a negative one). To be moved with an appetitive impulse—for example, an agitated desire to get some sexual gratification with some particular person—is on Chrysippus's view to be taking that gratification as something truly good to have, something such that if one does not get it one will miss out on, and if one does get it one will achieve, something important in one's life. Similarly, fear is a response to some threat as something that, if it happens, will seriously harm one— affect one's life for the worse. On the Stoic theory of what is in fact good or bad for a person, however, none of the things feared or appetitively pursued, or otherwise responded to with emotional impulses, is in fact good or bad at all. The quality of a human life, for better or for worse, is never affected by any of these events or circumstances; only the person's own inner state, of virtue or vice, makes any difference to that. To be moved emotionally or passionately is therefore to be reacting to circumstances and events in a way that a correct, reasonable outlook on life cannot approve but must indeed strenuously reject. It betrays one's own inner state as unreasonable and incorrect—indeed vicious. Having sex with some particular person on some occasion, or carefully avoiding some bodily harm may well be the right and appropriate thing to do, but one ought not to do it with *that* kind of (in the first case) inflated feeling or (in the second case) tight, constricted, narrowly defensive feeling, of its importance.

As a class, then, emotions can only be described as incorrect and vicious *hormai*. For this reason Chrysippus defines them, on the one hand, as movements of the soul that are "irrational and unnatural" (irrational in the sense that they are unreasonable—never rationally justified or appropriate; unnatural in that our permanent, adult nature does not include either our *inevitably* experiencing them, or our being inclined as a natural norm to experience them). On the other hand, he defines them as impulses that are "excessive"—greater or more intense and agitated than reason, if correctly employed, would judge appropriate and accordingly bring into existence.[17] In connection with this "excess" (*pleonasmos*), he speaks of emotions as involving "runaway" movement:[18] these are impulses that rush out toward

---

[16] On this see Frede, "The Stoic Doctrine," p. 94f.

[17] For these two "definitions" see Galen, *PHP* IV 2, p. 240, 12–13, and the following discussion. (See *SVF* III 462.)

[18] Galen speaks (*PHP* IV 5, p. 262, 4–5) of *ekphoros kinēsis* as a customary term of Chrysippus's and goes on to quote from him an explanation of the "excess" of an emotion as consisting

action on their own, beyond reason's ability subsequently to control and direct the action once it is underway.[19] They are thus comparable to running, as opposed to walking in a measured way: if you run you cannot immediately stop once you decide to do that, but will, by the force of the body, have to take a few extra steps while slowing down, whereas you can interrupt a walk immediately, before the next step, or even in mid-step. Similarly, in acting passionately the force of the impulse itself, though a function of reason, is such that a sudden change of mind will leave it in place and it will continue (briefly) to affect your action; with proper use of reason, by contrast, this does not happen, but the impulse is firmly under reason's *immediate* control. Thinking especially of the conflicts of reason and desire appealed to by Plato and Aristotle in order to establish the existence of a nonrational part of the soul, Chrysippus also describes emotions as movements in the soul that are disobedient to, and indeed dismiss and reject, reason. He has in mind the fact that people in the grip of a passionate desire refuse to listen to reason, refuse to attend to the arguments by which reason

in *ekpheromenai kinēseis*, lines 6–12 (= *SVF* III 479) (cf. IV 2, p. 240, 33ff.). Clement of Alexandria gives *hormē ekpheromenē kai apeithēs logōi* as one definition of *pathos* (*SVF* III 377), obviously drawing on these passages of Chrysippus. Plutarch uses the same language at *On Moral Virtue* 3, 441c-d, in describing the Stoic view of the passions. Arius Didymus (Stob. *Ecl.* II, p. 89. 8 Wachsmuth) uses the same term in describing people in emotional states as "carried away" as if by a disobedient horse—a very striking borrowing, this last, from Plato's *Phaedrus* (perhaps it owes something to Posidonius; see *PHP* V 5. 34–35, p. 324, 11–23). Chrysippus's metaphor of a "runaway" motion clearly became part of the standard Stoic doctrine of the emotions.

[19] Presumably Chrysippus thought that any impulse that counts external objects, events, or circumstances as either good or bad would in a sense be "excessive": it ranks their value more highly than can be rationally justified, since they are in fact at best "preferred" or "dispreferred" "indifferents" (see Diog. L. VII 105, Cic. *On Ends* III 52–53). But not all such impulses would have to involve anything that the person feeling them would describe as agitation (excitement or distress and upset feelings), and so be "excessive" in felt intensity—however much they might be theoretically described as "excessive." Almost everyone regards nice-tasting food as good and desires it as such when they are wanting to eat, but they might nonetheless sometimes feel quite unconcerned at the prospect of possibly having to settle for something relatively unappetizing, or even having to abandon for the time being the idea of eating altogether. One's attitude to something as a good (or bad) thing might include the idea that it is nonetheless quite readily dispensable (or tolerable not to have it), that nothing much hangs on one's getting (or avoiding) it. Our sources do not make it entirely clear whether Chrysippus and other Stoic philosophers counted as *pathē* all impulses directed at "indifferents" as if they were good or bad, even these undemanding, unintense feelings, or only the (overtly) agitated—excited or upset—ones. When, for example, Arius Didymus tells us (Stob. *Ecl.* II 38. 18–24 and 39. 4–7 Wachsmuth) that Aristotle defined *pathē* as movements of the soul *liable* to excess, but Zeno as movements already actually in excess, one supposes he means that Zeno also counted as instances of *pathos* all the mild feelings that Aristotle had counted as such—but insisted that those too really were excessive. But in speaking of emotions quite generally as "runaway" impulses, it seems that Chrysippus would not be counting mild, undemanding impulses as emotions at all. (Of course, the latter would still be objectionable and morally reprehensible, from the Stoic point of view, on other grounds.) I concentrate, as Chrysippus and Posidonius themselves do, on instances of overtly agitated states of mind, without attempting to resolve this larger issue.

(their own or someone else's) could establish that what they are, and are bent on, feeling and doing is an inappropriate thing to do or way to feel; they shut the door on reason's essential critical function, that of finding *good* reasons for believing and acting, and they defiantly accept the course of action on which they are bent, whether there are good enough reasons in favor of it or not.

In these definitions and descriptions of the phenomena, Chrysippus professes to be describing a quite particular defect of a person's reasoning power, distinct (as he is careful to point out explicitly) from a merely intellectual incapacity.[20] The person experiencing an emotion is not simply misunderstanding what the right thing to do and the right way to feel is in the circumstances: people being led by emotion to act against their better judgment are proof enough of that. This is not a case of error or oversight, comparable in any way to miscalculation in arithmetic. On Chrysippus's account, it is in fact a perversity of reason itself, a state of mind in which reason resolutely sticks to erroneous views, refusing to concern itself seriously, or at all, with the truth, and as a result gets carried away into an excited state in which (often enough) precipitate and ill-considered action is the outcome.[21] Sometimes the victim of an emotion stubbornly sticks to a practical view despite having himself seen clearly just moments before (or intermittently even while acting) that according to him it is false: this is the case, as Chrysippus understands it, of one "acting against his better judgment as a result of passion."[22] But even in more humdrum cases, where the anger or delight or agitated desire is perfectly in accord with what the agent thinks the situation calls for, Chrysippus insists that really the same basic perversity is at work: the victim only thinks and feels the way she does because she is

---

[20] See *PHP* IV 2. 12, p. 240, 23–29; IV 4. 17, p. 254, 17–19 and 4. 23, p. 256, 1–2. Galen's inability to understand how this can be so is the source of most of the charges of self-contradiction he levies against Chrysippus. In particular, he takes the claims by Chrysippus that emotions are disobedient to reason and that they exceed the measures on feeling about things that reason itself imposes (or would impose) as directly and flatly in contradiction to his central claim that emotions are functions of the reasoning power. That he cannot understand what Chrysippus has in mind here is a very serious philosophical failure on Galen's part. He thinks so little of Chrysippus's own philosophical ability (see his extraordinary dismissal of Chrysippus at *PHP* V 1. 11, p. 294, 23, as simply "untrained in argument") that he is unwilling to try seriously to follow his line of thought. These deficiencies in his treatment of Chrysippus are sufficient ground for great caution in accepting any of Galen's statements about the relationships among the various views in this area that he discusses—those of Plato himself, of Aristotle, and of Posidonius, as well, of course, as Chrysippus's own. It is very surprising to me that scholars who are well aware of how unreasonable and unfair Galen's interpretations of Chrysippus are nonetheless so willingly and uncritically accept his interpretations of Posidonius.

[21] *PHP* IV 6, p. 274, 35–39 and p. 276, 6–10, 11–17, 19–22; Plut. *On Moral Virtue* 10, 450c-d.

[22] See Plutarch, 446f–447a. On the Stoic analysis the oscillation in a person's view about what to do can sometimes be so rapid and continuous even while he is acting that both ordinary people and philosophers have got the erroneous impression that it is a "fact of experience" that people are sometimes subject to *simultaneous* conflicting impulses, one stronger than and "outweighing" the other.

refusing to raise or take seriously the question whether it is *true* that the situation does call for that reaction. There is, apparently, something appealing about the false practical view contained in the emotion, because of which a perverted reason insists on asserting it as true, but without serious regard to whether it really is true or not. In indicating this perversity Chrysippus frequently uses (as in the quotations in the Galen and Plutarch passages cited in n. 21) the striking notion of a "rejection" or "turning aside" (*apostrophē, apostrephesthai*) of reason by itself: reason itself refuses to follow its own reason-giving calling.[23]

I hope I have said enough about Chrysippus's analysis to make it clear that his account of emotional states as functions of the rational power is perfectly coherent. The sort of perversity of reason that he describes seems perfectly intelligible, even fairly familiar—though one might wonder how purely mental processes, which is all that Chrysippus's view of emotions can recognize, can lead someone's reason to behave thus pervertedly. And his novel contention that the agitated feeling involved in the experience of emotional states simply derives from that perversity and is no evidence of a nonrational origin for the emotions, seems not at all impossible (however shocking it may be to Galen and other late Platonists, and even to ordinary ways of thinking). Whether such a hypothesis is capable of providing a satisfactory framework into which to fit all the relevant facts, or apparent facts, is a further question. I turn now to Posidonius's arguments for saying that, as it stands, it does not provide this framework.

III POSIDONIUS: WHAT THE EMOTIONS ARE

The fundamental cause of Posidonius's dissatisfaction appears to be the difficulty of explaining how reason gives rise to the "excessive impulse" that, as he and Chrysippus agree, is an essential mark of any emotion—the feeling of agitation. As we have just seen, Chrysippus says that it is when one's reason is perverted, disobedient to itself (to its own capacity to discover or recognize good reasons), that it generates such impulses. But why is it that stubborn and irrational clinging to falsehood has just this effect—agitation, excitement, a sense of psychic expansion or (as the case may be) contraction and shock? Why does reason do precisely this when it is in this perverted condition? In his very first reference to Posidonius in book IV of *PHP* (IV 3. 4, p. 248, 6–8), Galen reports that in his *On Emotions* Posidonius repeatedly pressed upon Chrysippus this question: what is the cause of an excessive impulse? And in his subsequent discussion Galen gives much solid

---

[23] So there is not merely a "recognition, but deliberate rejection, of what a reasonable human being would do in these circumstances" (so C. Gill, "Did Chrysippus Understand Medea?" p. 141); one might think (whether rightly or wrongly) that one had good reasons for rejecting the idea of acting as a "reasonable human being" would, but that is not what Chrysippus has in mind. This is a rejection by reason itself of the very idea of acting on (good) reasons.

evidence of Posidonius's persistence in searching out acceptable causes for various agreed-upon phenomena concerning the emotions—not just the "excessive" feelings they bring, but also such facts as that they tend to dissipate over time, of themselves, and that our overall mental state can sometimes favor or exacerbate emotional arousal, sometimes effectively prevent it in us. It seemed to Posidonius that Chrysippus had no satisfactory explanations for these phenomena and (I suggest) it was in order to shore up the Stoic position in the debate with his contemporary Platonists and Peripatetics that Posidonius offered his criticism of Chrysippus and his revisions in the Stoic theory as he had inherited it.

One way of taking Posidonius's challenge is this: "What is the cause of this 'excessive impulse' that Chrysippus says is produced under certain conditions by a person's *reason*?" Put this way, with the emphasis on the word *reason*, it invites the answer: Obviously it can't be produced by reason at all, as Chrysippus thinks. (How could something produced simply by reason exceed reason's dictates?) No: the whole cause of the excessive emotional impulse must lie elsewhere, in an independent, nonrational power of the soul capable all on its own of producing such excesses. This is how Galen himself takes the question when he first introduces it; he goes on at once to answer it himself in the way I have just indicated (p. 248, 9–13). But Galen's own evidence shows that that was not how Posidonius meant it.[24] Posidonius meant it this way: "What is the cause of this 'excessive

---

[24] (1) At IV 3. 8, p. 248, 25–27, Galen, now granting (correctly) that Chrysippus's view is that *pathē* are *kriseis* (judgments) and that he understands these *kriseis* as themselves *hormai* and *sunkatatheseis* (assents), but ones reached precipitately, not by thinking the matter out, puts Posidonius's question this way: in that case an emotion will be an excessive assent, so what is the cause of the assent's being excessive? This way of putting the question grants that reason, through its assent, plays the essential role in the generation of emotions—that emotions are activities of the reasoning power itself. (2) In IV 5. 8 Galen first restates the question as follows: "This paradoxical movement, that is not generated by reason yet is generated by something as its cause—what, we ask you, brought it into being?" And he gives as "our" (the Platonists') answer that the cause is "sometimes the spirited power, sometimes the appetitive" (p. 260, 23–26). But shortly afterward (5. 12), developing Chrysippus's analogy with people running, he points out that people running downhill proceed with an impetus that is the joint result of their will and the force of their body's weight, and complains that Chrysippus "should have explained what that other thing is in the case of the emotions of the soul that is added to the reasoning power and becomes the cause of the immoderate and, as he himself habitually called it, runaway movement" (p. 262, 3–5). Again, this grants that reason is involved in some way in the generation of emotions: reason generates the impulse, something else generates (or contributes to) the excessive, rushing movement in it. Though Galen is speaking for himself here, this seems to reflect his reading of Posidonius's critique of Chrysippus. (3) At V 5. 28–29, p. 322, 17–26, Galen explains how one may achieve the "cure" (*iasis*) of the emotions, in a context that is clearly marked (see 5. 22, p. 320, 39–30) as deriving from Posidonius. In neither of the two sorts of case he considers does the cure consist simply of moderating allegedly irrational feelings proceeding from a nonrational power of the soul; in order to get rid of emotions, either the reasoning power and the nonrational power must both be trained, in the way appropriate to each, or else (in the case of those whose *pathētikai kinēseis*, "affective movements," are already weak) only the reasoning power needs attention. This makes it clear

impulse' that, as Chrysippus correctly says, is produced under certain conditions by a person's reason?" That is, given that reason does turn and transform itself under certain conditions so as to generate excessive impulses, what is responsible for its so transforming itself then? Chrysippus has said that it is due to perversity that sometimes a person's reason stubbornly holds to a false practical view, and that the result of its doing this is an excessive impulse. But surely nothing we can point to in the nature of reason itself explains why just this is what that perversity causes. Something else must be involved in the generation of these impulses, in addition to (not, as Galen would have it, instead of) reason.[25] What does (or can) Chrysippus think this extra factor is? What is it in fact?

It is clear how Chrysippus should attempt to meet this challenge. He should argue that, on the contrary, something in the nature of reason itself *does* explain the agitation in emotional impulses. The practical views held by those undergoing emotional states of all the different kinds have this much in common: They all involve asserting that some event or circumstance (a) believed to obtain in the present or past or expected in the future, and (b) not securely in one's own power to bring about or prevent (or cause to cease, or not to have happened), is (c) a serious and important good or bad thing for oneself. The Stoics hold, of course, that no such event or circumstance is or can be a good or bad thing for anyone, let alone an important one. The question, then, is why those stubbornly holding a false practical view of this kind turn out to feel impulses having the special features we recognize as belonging to emotional states: anxiety, excitement, a sense of being uplifted or depressed, etc. It seems open to Chrysippus to appeal here to natural, in the sense of reasonably expectable, consequences of holding precisely these beliefs. For example, suppose someone believes an important

that according to Posidonius an emotion is always somehow a joint product of erroneous thinking and decision (in the reasoning part) and some movements of a nonrational part. (On this last passage see below, pp. 470–72; see also IV 7. 28, p. 286, 23–26 and 7. 33, p. 288, 10–12.) All these passages make A. W. Price's suggestion impossible to sustain (*Mental Conflict*, pp. 175–78), that for Posidonius, unlike orthodox Stoics, *pathē* are not *hormai* and do not involve "assents" of reason. That idea also conflicts with the evidence of Plutarch cited in n. 25 below.

[25] Only on this understanding of Posidonius's theory can one reconcile Galen's quotations from and discussion of his *Peri pathōn* with Plutarch's report of Posidonius's classification of *pathē* in *De libidine et aegritudine* ch. 6: according to Plutarch, Posidonius held that *epithumiai*, *phoboi*, and *orgai* (i.e., the *pathē* of the soul) involve and depend upon rational judgments and suppositions (they are *en krisesi kai hupolēpsesin*). Kidd's comment on this passage (*Commentary*, p. 562) is unsatisfactory. He fails to see that a view like the one I argue Posidonius held makes *pathē* depend upon reason's judgments and assents without however either identifying them with any such judgments (as Chrysippus did) or making them supervene necessarily upon them (as on Galen's—presumably mistaken—interpretation Zeno had done). Hence he is driven into the hopeless position of having first to take *en krisesi* etc. here loosely, as meaning "in the field or area of" judgments of reason, and then to interpret its meaning in light of his own very unsatisfactory interpretation of *PHP* V 5. 21, p. 320, 23–28. On this latter passage see below, pp. 470–71.

good has come his way that he has not brought about—he sees it as in some significant measure a matter of luck, or some sort of special favor granted to him personally by someone else, or by nature or god. Then it might be thought reasonable of him to feel delight and elation. The delight and elation might seem appropriate—and so rationally generated—responses to good luck, or to being in a position of special favor, when the result is some important good for oneself: after all, he has not only got (as he thinks) an important good, but one that was unexpected, or such that his getting it showed special interest on the part of the universe or some other person in his good. This extra element deserves a special response, going beyond the welcoming response owed simply to the good thing itself. And similarly mutatis mutandis for the other emotions: the "excess" in the impulse can be treated in each case as an appropriate, reason-generated response (of unpleasant "contraction" or pleasurable "expansion") to these special circumstances of good or bad luck, favor or disfavor, in which (as he thinks) he has received something importantly good or bad for him. Thus one can argue that people holding a practical view of this specific type will reasonably judge that this "excessive impulse" is the right way to feel in the circumstances in which they think they find themselves. Here we must bear in mind that on the Stoic analysis the emotions of pleasure and distress include the judgment that the supposed good or bad thing is of such a sort that it is appropriate to feel "expansion" or "contraction" in relation to it.[26] Accordingly, their feeling that way can, after all, be due to something in the nature of reason itself, and no cause beyond reason is needed to explain it. A person's reason, in holding the practical views in question, also holds that this kind of feeling is appropriate, and accordingly reason itself brings it into existence.

It is a claim of this general type that Chrysippus seems to have made—that the emotionally affected person feels the way he does because his reason judges the feeling appropriate. Surprisingly, however, there appears to be no evidence that he argued as I have just done, from special consequences of the thought that some important good or bad that one has received, or expects to receive, was or is outside one's own control, or results from special favor or disfavor on the part of some outside agency. If he had, Posidonius would have to have argued differently to defend his view that the nature of reason itself cannot explain the excess in emotions. Chrysippus seems instead, without giving any such detailed account, to have emphasized alleged natural consequences simply of representing some external thing to oneself as good or bad, or an important good or bad, though he also took note that only when such a thought is fresh or vivid (*prosphatos*)[27] does it

---

[26] See [pseudo-]Andronicus *Peri pathōn* 1 [*SVF* III 391], Stob. *Ecl.* II 90. 14–18 Wachsmuth, Cic. *Tusc. Disp.* III 74 and IV 14.

[27] Scholars are right to emphasize that (as Galen himself points out, V 7. 4, p. 280. 25–26) *prosphatos* means, and was understood in this context by Chrysippus as meaning, simply "recent." But it is important to notice that Cicero, who so translates it, also explains it (*Tusc.*

produce these emotional effects.[28] But all such explanations run up against a formidable obstacle. For it seems undeniable that different people holding the same practical view may be and often are differently affected; and the same person without apparently changing his state of opinion on a certain matter will at one time experience an emotion in relation to it and at another time not. And if it is only vivid thoughts that produce emotional effects, one would have to explain how and why vividness always makes this difference. Again, there is the matter of the strength of the emotional feeling. That seems to vary greatly from person to person and with the same person from one time to another, and yet it is extremely difficult to see how these variations could always be explained by differences in the state of opinion, or the stubborn attachment to it, of different persons or the same person at different times. Posidonius appealed to all these considerations in his effort to undermine Chrysippus's claim that the explanation of the "excess" and agitation in emotional impulses is wholly to be sought in a perfectly natural behavior of a perverted reason.[29] Something more than erroneous practical

---

Disp. III 75) in such a way as to make it clear that it was the typical vividness of recent events in a person's mind that Chrysippus and other Stoics meant to convey by their use of this word in this context.

[28] In citing Posidonius's criticisms of Chrysippus, Galen gives the impression that Posidonius found Chrysippus unclear or undecided on this last point: at IV 7. 5 he suggests that usually Chrysippus sought to explain emotions as due simply to the thought (whether a recently acquired or vivid one or not) of oneself as possessing (or going to possess) some great and important good or bad thing—something intolerable and unbearable, or transcendently wonderful. Accordingly, in IV 5. 26 ff. Posidonius is quoted objecting to the idea that what causes a *pathos* is the opinion that one is, was, or will be in the presence of some great or important good or bad (external) things. But at IV 7. 6 ff. Posidonius objects to Chrysippus's appeal to the notion of vividness, on the ground that though the vividness of an opinion does in fact play a causal role in generating emotions Chrysippus' rationalist presuppositions prevent him from being able to accommodate this fact within his theory. (Posidonius seems to be wrong about this: see n. 29 below.)

[29] In the foregoing I have spoken of Chrysippus's view of emotions as involving assent, and stubborn adherence to, a (false) practical view or opinion, to the effect that some event or circumstance is good or bad for one. That is how, on Galen's evidence, Posidonius conceived (and objected to) it. In "Affections of the Soul," pp. 103–7, Frede has argued (and cf. Sextus Empiricus *Adversus mathematicos* VII 154) that in fact for Chrysippus the assents in emotions (and indeed in impulses generally) are not strictly to propositions but rather to those *as* contained in *phantasiai* (impressions): one assents to a richly detailed representation of the object or circumstance as possessing the features in virtue of which it strikes one as good or bad. I am strongly inclined to think Frede is right on this interpretative point. If he is, then Chrysippus's view is rendered much more plausible, and Posidonius's criticisms would need some refinement: for example, pointing to mere identity of *opinion* when an emotional state is and is not present does not suffice in order to discomfit Chrysippus; identity of the complex overall assented-to impression is required. I think however that Posidonius's basic points arguably still apply (whether they are decisive against Chrysippus is another matter, not easy to determine with any assurance). For even if what is assented to in a case of intense sexual attraction, say, is a complex representation—a representation of someone as having all the various bodily and mental properties that form the basis for carnal infatuation and for wanting to have sex with them as an important good—it still seems arguable that the one *now* emotionally moved in assenting to that thought will *not* at another time be moved that way at all in

views stubbornly adhered to, he argued, must be responsible for the occurrence of emotions.[30]

What more did Posidonius think is involved? Reflection on the sorts of variation just mentioned in the character of the "impulses" experienced by different people, or the same people at different times, naturally leads to two ideas. These constitute Posidonius's central innovation in the Stoic theory of the emotions. (1) There must exist another sort of psychic energy, besides that which reason itself produces through the holding of practical views, that is capable of being joined to the "impulse" from reason so as to increase its force in the ways required to generate emotions. Every "excessive impulse" is the result of reason's drawing on such preexistent and reason-independent energies, accepting that they are appropriate to feel in the given circumstances, and thereby joining them to its own "impulse" toward action. (2) Because these other psychic energies are reason-independent, we do not voluntarily control how much of them we feel, or when and for how long. These energies are due to other parts of our individual physical and psychological make-up. Different individuals tend to experience differing amounts and degrees of them, and in different circumstances; and because they arise and subside independently of variations (or constancies) in our states of mind, the same individual may experience more or less of them on different

assenting to it (or possibly moved rather to disgust or exasperation that *that* is how one has to get one's good—by having sex with someone having those properties). Likewise, it seems arguable that *some* people would always be either altogether unmoved emotionally by assenting to such a representation or moved emotionally in a different way and direction (perhaps to disappointed distress at what one has to do to get what is good). Still, it is noteworthy that on Galen's account Posidonius seems not to have taken note of these interesting complexities in Chrysippus's theory (if indeed Frede's interpretation is correct). Perhaps Chrysippus himself did not make much of them or emphasize their significance. Or perhaps Posidonius did take due note of them in his objections, but Galen left no sign of this, thinking them needless or even incorrect complications in a basically simple and silly account.

[30] Less successfully, he also attacked Chrysippus's explanations head-on. If holding the opinion that you possess or are going to receive some great good entails that you are moved emotionally in relation to it, why do not sages feel an emotion of elation at their own possession of virtue, and why, conversely, do not those who are making progress toward virtue feel very downcast at their continued possession of the vice in their souls they now know to be such a bad thing for them (*PHP* IV 5. 26–28, p. 264, 18–30)? Chrysippus can reply easily to these objections. The mental state of one holding true practical views, for all the right reasons well and completely understood (as the sage does) or partially understood (as the *prokoptōn* or "improving" person does), is necessarily a very different one, and one different even subjectively, from that of a person holding the extremely false views that according to Chrysippus give rise to emotion. If you know the full truth about what is good for a human being, and what makes it such a good thing, this knowledge will be sufficient to prevent you from having the sort of impression (*phantasia*) of it that will lead you to think it a good idea to feel elated (with an expanded sense of your own accomplishment) for having it, or (in the case of the "improving" person) depressed and deflated for not yet having achieved it. Your knowledge will tell you that elation and depression are bad, and prevent you from thinking them, even for a brief moment, appropriate things to feel. If, by contrast, you think that having external things is the good (or part of it), at least nothing prevents your holding the opposite opinions. It is surprising that Posidonius did not see this.

occasions in relation to the same or exactly similar circumstances; indeed one may sometimes not feel them at all when this might have been expected (and even desired by the person herself). Hence the "impulses" reason produces by drawing on these energies also vary in intensity, and in these other ways, in accordance with variations in the underlying nonrational psychic energies. Sometimes a person feels no emotion, because the relevant energies are not available to be drawn upon; some people are more given to emotion than others, because of the frequency with which they experience these energies and because of their typical magnitudes; the same person feels a greater or a lesser degree of emotion at different times in relation to the same or a similar state of affairs, similarly conceived, because it so happens that he is experiencing more or less of these energies at the times in question.

This explanation of the excessiveness of emotional impulses involves a sharp distinction between the emotion itself (the anger, or delight, or sadness, etc.) and the nonrational psychic energy that underlies it. The emotion is an impulse, and as we have seen all adult human impulses are produced, according to Stoic psychological theory, by the agent's holding a practical view; no psychological phenomenon (including whatever movements or feelings there may be in the soul) can be an impulse or *hormē*, i.e., a direct psychic cause of voluntary bodily movement, unless it involves and depends upon that crucial activity of the reasoning power. But the underlying energy is, in itself, not a *hormē* at all; apart from an act of reason in which it is accepted as appropriate and combined with the impulse that reason creates by adopting a practical view, to experience this energy is not at all to be actively moved toward action. It is, at most, to feel inclined (to decide) to act in some way. Posidonius marks this distinction by introducing a new quasi-technical term, alongside the established word *pathos,* used, as we have seen, by the Stoics to refer to fully completed emotional impulses: *pathētikai kinēseis,* affective movements of the soul.[31] These derive directly from the further psychic powers, the appetitive and spirited, that Posidonius took over from Plato.[32] Posidonius holds that it is fundamental to human

[31] At *PHP* V 5. 26, p. 322, 13–14, Galen says Posidonius "customarily" used this expression, but instead of noting the special significance of such special terminology Galen treats it simply as an alternative equivalent for *pathē*: see, e.g., V 1. 5, p. 292, 20–25, where in summarizing his own account in book IV of Posidonius's views, he says that Posidonius showed that "emotions are neither judgments nor things that supervene on judgments, but certain movements of other nonrational powers which Plato called appetitive and spirited." Nonetheless, in the passages Galen quotes, both in book IV and book V, and in his paraphrases of other passages, it is easy to see that Posidonius reserved the term *pathos* to denote the completed *hormē* to which the nonrational powers contribute, and employed *pathētikai kinēseis* for the sub-"impulsive" movements through which they make this contribution. See e.g., V 5. 21, p. 320, 27–28, where the *hormē* is clearly distinguished from the *pathētikē kinēsis*; similarly IV 7. 28, p. 286, 23–26 and 7. 33, p. 288, 10–12.

[32] There is evidence in Galen that Posidonius sometimes used the Platonic term *to logistikon* as one way of referring to the reasoning power (see the quotation from Posidonius in V 5. 33, translated and discussed below, p. 475); the evidence for his having taken over the standard Academic terminology (*to thumoeides* and *to epithumētikon*) for referring to the other two

nature that we experience such "affective movements," just as on the related Platonic-Aristotelian view it is a fixed and ineradicable fact about human beings that they experience some appetitive and spirited desires or other. On Posidonius's view, however, unlike the related view of Plato and Aristotle, these natural affective movements are not (according to Stoic technical terminology) *hormai*. Accordingly, when he insists that fully virtuous persons never do experience *pathē* (anger, appetitive desires, and the like), this does not mean (as the corresponding statement from Plato or Aristotle would) that in the virtuous person the *epithumētikon* or appetitive aspect and *thumoeides* or spirited aspect are totally inactive.[33] It only means that, whatever "affective movements" virtuous persons do experience, these are never taken up into a decision of reason in favor of acting and thereby elevated into full-fledged emotional impulses.

In order to appreciate the significance of Posidonius's analysis, it may help to situate these affective movements in relation to other forms of awareness recognized in the Stoic psychological theory that were also distinguished from impulses but were regarded as in some way causes of them. Earlier (sect. II above) I pointed out that being in bodily pain, or experiencing

---

powers is less decisive. Passages like VIII 1. 14, p. 482, 33–484, 3; V 6. 38, p 334, 4–8; and IV 3. 3, p. 248, 4–6 seem strongly to imply that he did; but when one reads V 1. 5, in which Galen paraphrases the same passage of Posidonius as in IV 3. 3 but says merely that the nonrational powers recognized by Posidonius were called by these names by *Plato*, one hesitates. Nonetheless, in light of Galen's repeated assertions that he admitted exactly two nonrational powers of the soul, of exactly the same natures as Plato's, it seems likely that he did use this terminology. It seems unlikely, given that he used the rather archaic Platonic term *to logistikon*, that he would not also have used the standard Platonic terms for the other two powers.

[33] See V 2. 2, where Galen remarkably says that not only Stoics like Chrysippus held that only the vicious (*phauloi*) experience *pathē*, but this was the view also of "the ancients." Here Galen incautiously accepts Stoic usage, according to which anything entitled to the name *pathos* is "unnatural and irrational," and offers to interpret Plato's and Aristotle's theories in accordance with it. If this were done systematically, the anger, grief, fear, appetitive desire, etc., that on these theories are experienced by a virtuous person (or are such that a virtuous person would experience them in the given circumstances) would have to be treated as psychologically of a very different nature and origin from all other cases of such nonrational feelings; the latter will be without exception *pathē*, the former quite a different kind of phenomenon— in effect, a Platonic-Aristotelian version of the Stoic *eupatheiai* or "good feelings" of joy, caution, and the rest restricted to morally perfect persons. Plainly, by taking for granted the Stoic usage, as Galen does, he assigns to two different psychological categories phenomena that it was a central concern of Plato and Aristotle to characterize as essentially the same sort of thing. This is not the only place where Galen falsifies Platonic doctrine by imposing on it distinctions and terminology originally introduced through Stoic psychological theory. He presents the evidence for the role of the nerves (originating in the brain) in all voluntary movement as supporting the "Platonic" vs. the Stoic theory of human psychology—this shows that the "command center" or *hēgemonikon* is in the brain, where the *logistikon* is located, not the heart, where in fact only "spirit" is found (see *PHP* p. 110, 1–3; p. 156, 13–19; p. 162, 2–6; p. 206, 24–36; p. 210, 16–25; p. 480, 4–11). But it would follow that "spirit" and "appetite" do not, of themselves, give rise to voluntary action or any "impulse" toward it; only reason does that, perhaps under influence from spirited or appetitive attachments. Here Galen's grasp of Plato's own theory is lax at best, or even quite confused.

the pleasant gustatory sensations obtained from eating while in need of food, are psychological phenomena of a different type from *hormai*. They are not active movements of any sort toward or away from action. Nonetheless it seems natural to think, and Chrysippus did think, that they play an important causal role in relation to such movements. When for example someone is experiencing excruciating physical pain, that experience is a powerful incentive to hold, anyhow so long as the experience lasts, that the pain is a bad thing and that one's well-being depends crucially upon getting rid of it. Or again, when one remembers the pleasant taste of cake and sees some cake available nearby, that memory is a powerful incentive to think that eating a piece of cake would be a good thing and very much worth doing. On Chrysippus's analysis, in such cases the experience of the pain and the memory of the pleasant sensations give rise to a certain kind of representation of the objects of the envisaged actions, a representation he calls a *hormētikē phantasia*, an "impulsive impression,"[34] which represents them as having the character of a bad or a good thing, respectively. But it is only when an agent, with an act of his reasoning power, accepts such an impression as representing things truly that the impulse itself is generated; merely to have the impression is not yet to yield to it, to assert as true the way it represents things as being.

Now it seems that Posidonius intended his affective movements as an additional and, as he thought, needed link in this two-step chain of explanation. For one must ask, as Galen reports Posidonius doing in a slightly different context,[35] why anyone has the tendency to accept such *phantasiai*, or even to experience them in the first place. What is it in the experience of bodily pain, for example, or of pleasant sensations, that makes people in such very large numbers view them in this light, as bad and good things,

---

[34] See Stob. *Ecl.* II, p. 86, 17–19 Wachsmuth, and the discussion in Frede, "Affections of the Soul," pp. 103–7.

[35] At V 5. 16–17, p. 320, 10–14, Galen presses this question in propria persona, in the course of discussing how it is that children who on the standard Stoic story have no natural inclination to wrongdoing nonetheless grow up to be malefactors. He is evidently following Posidonius (see V 5. 9, p. 318, 22–23) in raising this challenge. In interpreting this whole passage (V 5. 9–21), one must however be careful not to attribute to Posidonius the details of Galen's way of developing his point. It is Galen himself who introduces (V 5. 1–8) the idea of multiple *oikeiōseis* (natural feelings of "kinship")—one coming from each of the Platonic soul-parts: for pleasure, for victory in competitions, and for noble action—that he subsequently uses as his central analytical device in attacking Chrysippus. He formulates this idea in his introductory remarks at the beginning of the chapter, before bringing Posidonius into his discussion; indeed, he concludes this introduction by saying that the ancients (i.e., Plato and Aristotle) were the only philosophers who saw that human beings have all three natural kinships: so, if he is to be taken strictly, no Stoic philosopher, not even Posidonius, saw this. He also says, in a gross misrepresentation of Chrysippus's view that it would be very hard to believe Posidonius capable of, that Chrysippus held our only natural *oikeiōsis* is to that which is morally good! It is a serious error to attribute Galen's own idea of the three natural feelings of kinship to Posidonius (as Kidd does, *Commentary*, pp. 616–18, making it a central element in his reconstruction of Posidonian ethics).

respectively, on which one's well-being crucially depends? Sages do not so view them (but then no actual sage is certified ever to have existed).[36] The reason, according to Chrysippus, is that sages have strong minds and understand the truth so deeply that even if they should experience such misleading impressions they would not for a moment consider accepting them as true representations. But why is it that ordinary people, with their admittedly weak ability to grasp and hold on to the truth, so very uniformly receive and accept just *these* false impressions? Why not the equally false impressions that pain is good and pleasure bad? Again, why is it that all sorts of other false impressions arise and prove so persuasive to people—e.g., the impression, when they think someone has insulted them, that striking back is such a good thing? Posidonius's answer is that because we are all constructed by nature in such a way that we experience (right from birth) the "affective movements" that he has postulated—movements of excitement and so on, in relation to bodily pain, pleasant sensations, insults and so on—we find ourselves already attracted toward or repelled, more or less strongly, by various experiences and events, and it is these excited feelings of attraction and repulsion that give rise to the false "impulsive impressions" and make them so persuasive to us, i.e., to our reasoning faculties. Chrysippus thought that this kind of excitement in the full-fledged emotions was a natural response to a certain sort of belief that external things are (important) goods or bads—one based upon a vivid, detailed representation of them in our minds as such. Posidonius postulates that we already, by nature, experience the excitement in advance of holding the belief: it is the excitement that gives rise to the impression and thence to the belief. According to Posidonius the belief takes up a pre-existing excitement into the full-fledged emotion to which it gives rise. Feeling in this nonrational way attracted toward or repelled from various things, we have already within ourselves something that causes us to represent them as good or bad, as the case may be, and provides the incentive to accept those representations as true: this is, after all, a way *we* are already feeling.

That this is Posidonius's view comes out in a passage of *PHP* V 5 where Galen cites Posidonius for his view on the causes of the erroneous assumption people make that pleasure and victory are good, pain and defeat bad. Galen writes: "In fact, Posidonius criticizes Chrysippus on these points and

---

[36] It is not perfectly clear from our sources whether sages according to Chrysippus (or the Stoics generally) never have such impressions, or only never accept them as representing things truly. I presume that on Chrysippus's view the perfection of the sage's understanding brings with it a change in his tendency to experience *phantasiai*, so that he certainly does not regularly or often get the strong impression, always experienced by most people when experiencing it, that pain is a bad thing or bodily pleasure a good thing; the impression he gets of pleasure and pain corresponds somehow, at least most of the time, to how he thinks of these things, even although the character of his impressions is no more a voluntary matter with him than it is with any other human being. If he does still sometimes receive erroneous "impulsive impressions," the strength of his mind is such that these are rejected at once by him and never assented to. See further, sect. V below.

tries to show that the causes of all the false suppositions [in question] lie indeed in their theoretical views, due to the force of affect, but this force is preceded by the false beliefs of a rational power that is weak in judgment. For impulse in animals is generated sometimes on the basis of the judgment of the rational power but often on the basis of the movement of the affective power."[37] Here Galen indicates particularly clearly that according to Posidonius emotions or *pathē* always depend upon an assent of the rational power. Galen is discussing how moral vice (and with it *pathē*) arise, arguing that on Chrysippus's assumptions you cannot give an adequate explanation. Chrysippus tries to explain vice and emotions as arising through "the persuasiveness of impressions"—the impression, e.g., that pleasure is good being so persuasive that most people give in to it, come to believe that pleasure is good and therefore to desire it with an emotional desire. It is in this connection that Galen cites Posidonius's criticism, in the passage just translated. Posidonius accepts, with Chrysippus, that for emotions an opinion (*hupolēpsis*), and so an act of the rational power, is necessary; he only disputes over how a person is induced to make the vicious suppositions in question. To judge from this brief paraphrase-cum-quotation, he gave a

---

[37] V 5. 21, p. 320, 23–28; accepting the ms. reading and finding no indication of a lacuna, I have translated the following text: καὶ γὰρ ταῦθ' ὁ Ποσειδώνιος μέμφεται καὶ δεικνύναι πειρᾶται πασῶν τῶν ψευδῶν ὑπολήψεων τὰς αἰτίας ἐν μὲν τῷ θεωρητικῷ διὰ τῆς παθητικῆς ὁλκῆς, προηγεῖσθαι δ' αὐτῆς τὰς ψευδεῖς δόξας ἀσθενήσαντος περὶ τὴν κρίσιν τοῦ λογιστικοῦ· γεννᾶσθαι γὰρ τῷ ζῴῳ τὴν ὁρμὴν ἐνίοτε μὲν ἐπὶ τῇ τοῦ λογιστικοῦ κρίσει, πολλάκις δ' ἐπὶ τῇ κινήσει τοῦ παθητικοῦ. (The text would read more easily if, with Müller, one adds γίνεσθαι after ὁλκῆς, but I believe it can be construed in the same sense without even that addition; γίνεσθαι or εἶναι is to be understood.) Kidd, DeLacy, and others, following a trend begun by Pohlenz ("De Posidonii libris Περὶ παθῶν," pp. 560 ff.), find a lacuna after ἐν μὲν τῷ θεωρητικῷ. Any inclination to find a lacuna disappears once one sees that in Galen's context πασῶν τῶν ψευδῶν ὑπολήψεων clearly does not mean *all* false suppositions on all subjects, but only all false suppositions of the sort he illustrated with examples immediately previously (5. 16–20). These false suppositions bad people make to the effect that pleasure, or victory, or honor and praise are good things and that pain, defeat, dishonor, and blame are bad. I should add that there is no reason to expect some completion for the μέν here, such as DeLacy provides with his supplement <γίγνεσθαι δι' ἀμαθίας, ἐν δὲ τῷ πρακτικῷ> (so that that does not give any basis for finding and filling a lacuna here): this μέν is satisfactorily matched by the δέ already in the text after προηγεῖσθαι. As for the expression ἐν τῷ θεωρητικῷ in line 24, which I like DeLacy take to mean "in the theoretical realm," two points should be noted: First, we must not in any event assume that this was a term Posidonius himself used in the passage being reported; Galen may do no more than paraphrase something he wrote. Second, as noted above, it is extremely likely that πασῶν τῶν ψευδῶν ὑπολήψεων, whether or not it is taken verbatim from the passage of Posidonius, is being made by Galen to refer not to all beliefs generally but only to all the particular beliefs in question in this context. Hence there is no reason to suppose (as Kidd and DeLacy do) that in the passage Galen paraphrases or quotes from, Posidonius was talking about the causes of error in general (including "intellectual" error as one sort of error, to be contrasted then with "practical" error, a reference to which needs to be supplied in a "lacuna"). There is no reason at all not to accept the fundamental soundness of the text here as transmitted. (On this passage I have profited from reading Fillion-Lahille's sensible discussion, Le "De ira," pp. 156–59; I am in broad agreement with her understanding of the passage and of the issues involved in interpreting it.)

complex answer, involving acts of the rational power at two stages. When an emotion arises on some particular occasion, the person supposes falsely that some particular thing thought to be present or available is good or bad for him, and he is induced to suppose this by the force of the affect (i.e., of the "affective movement") he happens to be feeling in relation to it at that time. This supposition is something he infers to; it is a conclusion, and so the error is aptly describable as a sort of theoretical one—it lies *en tōi theōrētikōi*, in the theoretical sphere. But the affect has force sufficient to drive him to that conclusion only because, having a generally weak mind, he made prior mistakes of judgment: Galen unfortunately does not indicate which prior false beliefs Posidonius had in mind here—perhaps erroneous general judgments about the goodness or badness of the relevant types of external things. If so, Posidonius is saying that emotions are false suppositions caused by the force of affect working on a weak intellect, which has made itself susceptible to that force by having come to believe that those sorts of things are good or bad and worth getting excited or upset about, as the case may be. But in any event, his view is that emotions are caused, not by mere attractive but false appearances, but rather by the force of some affect in the agent, which leads him to form the belief "on the basis of the movement of the affective power" that something is good or bad, and so generates the emotional state on that basis. This brief quotation does not make it clear that this force influences the judgment by itself causing Chrysippus's attractive appearance, but Posidonius is being cited here as pressing the question "why pleasure projects the persuasive impression that it is good" (p. 320, 18–19), so that is presumably what he thought.

Thus, on Posidonius's view, we are all, because of our natures as human beings, inevitably subject to some extent to these "affective movements" and their ill effects; but some of us feel them more insistently and in greater intensity or have greater difficulty in reducing them to levels that do not seriously threaten our ability to form practical views having a sounder basis in the facts than do the emotional ones to which the "affective movements" incline us. In this way Posidonius is able to give a plausible account of the full range of phenomena familiar to us in the psychological lives of adult human beings which he challenged Chrysippus to explain.[38] By postulating the natural existence in the adult human soul of two nonrational sources of psychic energies, in addition to and completely independent of reason, he can explain: (1) why most people, perhaps all human beings, regularly have the impression that external things are good or bad for them, matter greatly to their well-being; (2) why, having this impression, they are so apt not just to accept it, but in doing so to experience full-fledged emotional states of mind in relation to them; (3) why even among those who accept these impressions some are more apt than others to fall into emotions, and why some typically experience more extreme emotions than do others;

[38] See *PHP* V 6. 13–39, p. 329, 23 ff.

(4) why the same person at different times experiences different intensities of emotion, and sometimes, apparently, no emotion at all, even though she holds the same opinion about the same or essentially similar states of affairs; (5) why, in particular, the vividness with which one conceives something as good or bad makes such a difference in this respect;[39] (6) why sometimes one is, as we say, emotionally so drained that one cannot again or any longer feel an emotion one might wish and think it appropriate to feel. It is an essential condition of any emotion that one experience some relevant affective movement; but it is the specific condition of a person's nonrational capacities that determines when, how intensely, and for how long that person experiences these movements. Given plausible assumptions about the functioning of such nonrational capacities, and about individual differences in respect to them, all these phenomena can be seen as natural effects of them.

In addition to offering a plausible explanation of these aspects of the agreed-upon phenomena that Chrysippus arguably could not explain satisfactorily, Posidonius's postulation of these natural "affective movements" allows him to offer a more attractive account of the relationship between the psychic processes that produce the voluntary behavior of immature human beings and the psychology of the adults into whom they naturally develop. On the standard Stoic theory (accepted by Posidonius: *PHP* V 5. 34), it is at age 14 than we become full adults, capable of directing our behavior by assents and decisions of our reasoning power; before that we have been governed by nonrational desires. But this common Stoic doctrine takes on new significance in Posidonius's theory. For Chrysippus must simply say, as I noted above (sect. II), that at age 14 we cease altogether to experience the sort of impulses that we experienced, and experienced exclusively, before that. The discontinuity is total. But Posidonius can say that as adults we

---

[39] At V 6. 24–26, p. 330, 24–31 Posidonius argues that, being nonrational, the affective movements are not aroused by argument nor simply by beliefs about what is good or bad for you. It is by picturing things (*anazōgraphēsis tis*, p. 330, 28), not by describing them, that you arouse nonrational movements in yourself: a vivid image of a ferocious lion poised to leap upon you (whether produced by perception or in imagination) is sufficient to arouse these movements, and so to help generate the emotion of terror, whereas with the belief alone, unsupplemented by such an image, one might indeed run to safety but would do so without feeling terror. Chrysippus, too, I am inclined to think (see n. 29 above), believed that it was *phantasiai* ("impressions"—a sort of picturings), not mere beliefs, that are assented to when any impulse to action is brought into being; as we have seen, Posidonius proposed that, in the case where the result is an emotional impulse, those impressions are caused by "affective movements" of excited expansion of alarmed constriction. Here he is explaining how (in typical cases) the "affective movements" are themselves aroused: by picturing, not describing, terrible alleged evils or great goods. Thus Chrysippus was right to emphasize the importance of vividness in the causation of emotion, but it is not vividness of belief that matters (*doxa prosphatos*), as he had said, p. 280, 26 (see above, p. 464), but vividness in the way one pictures the phenomena to oneself; and vividness matters here because emotions involve movements of nonrational elements in our psychological make-up, which, as nonrational, respond to pictures in ways they would not respond to argument and merely linguistic descriptions.

continue to experience the same things that, as children, we experienced as *hormai*—namely, the *pathētikai kinēseis*. Now that we are in possession of the power to reason, these very same feelings no longer are full-fledged impulses at all. Once we come into full possession of our power to think out and decide for ourselves what we shall do, we disengage ourselves as voluntary agents from the previously impulsive force of the affective movements. Henceforth they only influence our behavior by inducing us to adopt erroneous practical views and so to sink into full-fledged emotion— something that, of course, in the nature of things as children we could not experience. As children the impulses we experienced were not emotions (those require assent by reason, something not yet possible for children); they were, however, the same sort of affective movement that as adults we experience but are no longer ruled by.[40] In this way the Posidonian theory can offer a less extreme account, and one less offensive to common sense, of what it is to be born a nonrational animal but grow up to be a rational one, than standard Stoicism was condemned to do.

IV Posidonius: Prevention and Cure of the Emotions

As we have seen, Posidonius's theory of what precisely the functions are of the nonrational powers of the soul differs substantially from Plato's and Aristotle's. For Plato and Aristotle the nonrational powers are the direct source of full-fledged *hormai* of their own, appetitive and spirited desires that not only express a practical view (the desirability of doing what they are desires for) but do so with what the Stoics call an "assent." Just in experiencing anger or an appetite for good, a person is holding the view that retaliation (say) or eating something that will satisfy his hunger would be a good thing, something intensely worth doing. In his anger or his appetite, he has (as it were) decided to do these things, and is actively moving toward acting on this decision of his spirited or appetitive nature. Of course he may

---

[40] In three passages (V 6. 37–38, p. 332, 31–334, 8; IV 7. 35, p. 288, 14–19; V 1. 9–10, p. 294, 8–20), Galen distances Posidonius from the standard Stoic doctrine that neither children nor nonhuman animals experience emotions, *pathē*, and does so (no doubt knowingly) in such a way as to give the impression that Posidonius maintained, on the contrary, that children and the other animals experience emotions of basically the same sort as adults do. (That is the view he himself holds about children and animals.) If my interpretation of Galen's evidence as a whole is correct, this must be a misinterpretation or misrepresentation: what Posidonius insisted on was, not that other animals and children experience full-fledged emotions, but only that the very same affective motions that adults experience, and that in adults often give rise to emotions, are experienced also by other animals and children. Galen's references in these passages to Posidonius's views are loose enough not to rule out this alternative interpretation of his views; and if Posidonius, once he had worked out and presented his full view, did occasionally speak of the "emotions" of children and animals, that would presumably have been, in the context of his own writings, an understandable assimilation of the *basis* for emotion to emotion itself, without implying what Galen takes it to imply.

simultaneously experience an opposed impulse, for example one coming from his rational evaluation of what is the best thing to do, everything considered; in that case, in different parts or aspects of himself, he will in effect have decided to do two different and incompatible things.[41] In Stoic terms, this amounts to saying that the functions of the nonrational powers of the soul are, or include, full-fledged *pathē*. For Posidonius, however, in accordance with fundamental Stoic principles, all assent is reserved to the reasoning power alone. Hence on his view the actual functions of the nonrational powers (in adults) are limited to the more inchoate movements that he calls *pathētikai kinēseis*: full-fledged *pathē* (actual anger, appetitive desires, etc.) are not functions of the nonrational powers, but complex functions requiring an activity of one of these powers combined with an activity of reason.

Despite these important differences between Posidonius's and Plato's conceptions of spirit and appetite, Posidonius can adopt major portions of Plato's analyses in *Republic* and *Laws* of how the education of children should proceed, if they are to grow up to be free of disturbing bad desires, and how therapy and training should be conducted for adults who already experience them. Galen says (*PHP* V 5. 32, p. 324, 2–9) that Posidonius expressed special admiration for what Plato wrote about the rearing and training of children, and in the first book of *On Emotions* gave a kind of epitome of Plato's views on this topic. It could well be that it is Posidonius's acceptance early on in his treatise of Plato's views on the training of spirited and appetitive feelings in children that led Galen (precipitously and wrongly, as we have seen) to gloss over the significant differences between the two philosophers on narrower technical questions about the nature of the emotions, and to classify Posidonius simply as a "Platonist" on the whole topic. Following Plato, Posidonius declared (5. 33, p. 324, 9–11) the best education for children to be "the preparation of the affective aspect (*tou pathētikou*) of the soul so as to be most serviceable to the rule of reason (*pros tēn archēn tou logistikou*)," and Galen implies (V 6. 20–22) that he intended this to be achieved in the Platonic fashion, through making them listen to appropriate types of music—music, Galen says, that would arouse, sharpen and strengthen the affective movements of those who are sluggish by nature, and calm and weaken the movements in those who are too high-spirited (see also V 5. 34, p. 324, 15–16). And, in general, he stresses (pp. 324, 22;

---

[41] At *Nicomachean Ethics* VII 3, 1147a35 Aristotle says that *epithumia* or appetite can move the limbs, and the same thing is implied by his description of *akrasia* at I 13, 1102b16–21 as involving a *hormē* that moves the limbs in a way that goes against the agent's reasoned decision. He holds that such an impulse succeeds in producing action only when, so to speak, the impulse of reason disengages itself and so no longer actively opposes it, but, nonetheless, it is the appetite itself that produces the action—not a co-opted impulse of reason. In the *Republic* Plato makes appetite itself draw inferences from experience, have thoughts about what it wants, and in effect make (something very like) decisions to have it. (Again, as with Aristotle, it is possible that Plato assumes that such "decisions" can have effect only if not opposed by reason.) On the *Republic* see Chapter 4 above, sect. III.

330, 17–20) that because these movements derive from a nonrational psychic power it is habituation, not argument and instruction, that is effective in their training.

It is easy to see how Posidonius could have thought proper preparation of the nonrational powers would involve musical training aimed at reducing and weakening their movements; if in childhood and youth these movements are allowed to grow powerful or flare up at the least provocation, one will have as an adult an ingrained tendency to feel strong affective movements, which will draw one to give in to them, with the result that one experiences full-fledged emotions. But it is not clear exactly what value Posidonius could have seen in musical training in the opposite direction—aimed, e.g., at arousing the tendency to have angry feelings in those who are not naturally given to them, or great pleasure at successful endeavors. His declared goal is to eliminate emotions altogether, not to produce the "moderate" emotions that Plato and Aristotle aimed at, and even moderate affective movements, felt in support of the same courses of action as reason decides on taking, will if assented to lead to the experience of emotions (even if relatively weak ones). Perhaps he envisaged an intermediate stage in moral development, at which, as he supposed, reason needs the help of (moderate) affective movements in order to recognize, and generate effective impulses toward, correct actions, or even to learn to value properly the objects of pursuit and avoidance in correct action. Only later, once reason's independent grasp of the true grounds for selecting a course of action becomes secure, would it cease altogether to be influenced and aided by affective movements—and so, gradually, cease to feel them, at least in significant degrees. Galen, however, tells us nothing to this effect, and we are left to our own speculation.[42]

As for the proper methods of treatment for emotions, once one is already adult, Posidonius again held that Plato had developed the correct view (*PHP* V 4. 15, p. 316, 12–14). Galen gives few interesting details, but the essential point is clear. Emotions involve reason's assenting, under pressure from the affective movements in the soul, to erroneous practical views about the value (or disvalue) and importance of bodily pleasure and pain, and of external events and circumstances of all kinds. Therefore, to get rid of the emotions will usually require that one reduce the affective feelings that are an essential cause and component of them, so that they are no longer severe enough to have these bad effects. In particular, to prevent an emotion to which one is prone from arising under the stimulus of circumstances suitable to it, Posidonius recommended advance preparation, through dwelling in advance (*proendēmein*) on the event that would trigger the emotion—imagining the event vividly and so gradually becoming used to it, at a time when, since it has not actually happened, the imagination has a much smaller

---

[42] In his comments elaborating on Posidonius's use of Plato's account of proper child-rearing, Galen, in accordance with his own Platonic predilections, adopts Plato's goal of "duly measured" levels of appetitive desire and spirited impulse. We do not have to assume that Posidonius did the same in the texts on which Galen is commenting.

emotional effect, so that when it actually does happen it will seem like something that has already happened to you that you have learned to bear unemotionally (*PHP* IV 7. 7–8, p. 283, 10–14). To cure an emotion already being felt on some particular occasion, one may only be able to let the affective movements run their course (meanwhile delaying action): they will die down in time, and with that the emotion will disappear as well. For a permanent cure, he seems to have relied on recommending redoubled efforts to educate the affective movements through music, as with children.

At V 5. 22–29 Galen reports that Posidonius drew on physiognomy and the study of the effects of the environment on animals to buttress his account of the emotions and their cure. According to Galen he adopted the position that in different persons "the affective movements of the soul always follow on the condition of the body" (p. 322, 3–4), which is itself determined partly by natural constitution, partly by environment. Indeed, Galen reports Posidonius's view with the language of necessity (p. 322, 21–23), saying that in some persons "the emotional movements (*kinēseis hai kata pathos*— I take this to be a variant on *pathētikai kinēseis* just above, 322, 18), which occur by necessity (*anankaiōs*) because of the constitution of the body, are great and intense." Movements that occur by physical necessity, of course, are ones we are plainly not to be blamed for feeling; whereas, for Posidonius as for all other Stoics, we are very much to blame for any *pathē* we may experience—they depend upon an assent of reason, which it is up to us to render or refuse. From this one sees the crucial importance if one is to understand Posidonius correctly of not confusing affective movements with emotions: even if some one, by natural constitution, cannot rid himself entirely of "affective movements" or even reduce their intensity as greatly as would be ideally desirable, he can come to know the truth that being emotionally moved is bad and undesirable, and accordingly not assent to the impressions his affective movements may cause him to experience and so not take up the energy of those movements into any impulse to action that his reason itself issues. In general, as Galen puts it, Posidonius maintained that two things must be done "if one is to point to an improvement in a man's character": his reason must "acquire knowledge of the truth, and the emotional movements must be blunted by habituation to good practices" (p. 322, 24–26).

V Posidonius: Consequences for Ethical Theory

At *PHP* V 6. 2, p. 326, 14–16, Galen quotes Posidonius from near the beginning of his *On Emotions* as saying that a correct investigation of the nature of the emotions is the necessary foundation on which to develop a correct account of what is good and bad for human beings, the ends of life, and the virtues. In effect, as Galen put the matter earlier on (IV 7. 23–24), apparently in reference to the passage from which this quotation is taken,

Posidonius maintained that all the matters that traditionally define the subject of moral philosophy are bound together "as by a single cord" by the knowledge of the three different powers of the soul. We have already seen how Posidonius was able to build on this foundation in order to deal with the training of the young and the cure of the emotions, and to reveal the psychological source of the very common error of treating external things, and indeed anything other than virtuous states of mind and virtuous actions themselves, as being either good or bad for us. In order to complete our account of Posidonius's theories, and show where its principal weakness lay from the point of view of Stoic moral philosophy generally, we need to consider briefly what Posidonius had to say about the "end" and about the nature of virtue.

In a lengthy and difficult passage in book V of *PHP* (V 6. 3–16), near the end of his refutation of Chrysippus, Galen discusses Posidonius's views on the correct way of formulating and explaining the *telos*. From the beginning the Stoics had always seen a close connection between "living in agreement with nature" (their official formula for the "end") and living in agreement with oneself, i.e., without internal conflict and disharmony, at peace with oneself as well as with the world—in fact, happily.[43] And, of course, it was traditional with the Stoics to identify the psychological disturbances, the conflicts and disharmonies, that are to be avoided with the *pathē*. So it is obviously justifiable for Posidonius to think that until the nature and causes of the *pathē* are discovered one cannot correctly grasp the "end." If, as he has argued, emotions are caused by the force of affective movements of the nonrational powers influencing reason to cling to false practical views, then, in order to attain happiness and our natural end, we must rigorously and constantly refuse to be led by these nonrational powers—and so, not experience the disturbances that reflect internal conflict and disharmony. Hence Posidonius (as quoted by Galen V 6. 5, p. 326, 26–27) proposes the following way of explicating the correct end at which to aim our lives: "the principal thing in happiness is being led in nothing by the nonrational and unhappy and godless power in the soul,"[44] but instead following one's reason, "the divinity in oneself, which is akin and similar in nature to the divinity that rules the whole cosmos" (6. 4, p. 326, 21–23).

[43] This is how Arius Didymus (Stob. *Ecl.* II, p. 75, 11–76. 1 Wachsmuth) explains Zeno's original formulation of the end simply as *to homologoumenōs zēn*. For the connection between the *telos* so formulated and *eudaimonia*, see further ibid., II, p. 77. 16–21.

[44] In a survey of various leading Stoics' ways of formulating or explicating the *telos*, Clement of Alexandria gives Posidonius's view as follows: τὸ ζῆν θεωροῦντα τὴν τῶν ὅλων ἀλήθειαν καὶ τάξιν καὶ συγκατασκευάσαντα αὐτὴν κατὰ τὸ δυνατόν, κατὰ μηδὲν ἀγόμενον ὑπὸ τοῦ ἀλόγου μέρους τῆς ψυχῆς (*Stromateis* II 21. 129. 4–5). This is translated by Kidd, *Commentary*, pp. 671–72, as follows: "to live contemplating the truth and order of all things together and helping in promoting [or establishing, or organising] it, in no way being led by the irrational part of the soul." The last clause in Clement's formulation is virtually identical to this quotation in Galen from *On Emotions*, which suggests that Galen may have reported only part of a

But would this in fact be enough for happiness? Would it eliminate all stress and internal disharmony? On Posidonius's theory people have no direct voluntary control over the affective movements they experience. Indeed, as we have just seen, he insisted (if Galen is to be trusted) that it is by a physical necessity, deriving from their natural bodily constitution, that some people experience extreme and violent affective movements and others milder, more tractable ones (*PHP* V 5. 23 and 26, p. 322, 3–5 and 12–13, discussed above). To be sure, the sort of necessity he has in mind is such that by altering our physical and psychological state we can change at least to some extent our "natural constitution" and so alter the necessities here at work. And he considers that with proper training it is open to all of us, despite these natural differences, to reduce or control our tendencies to feel affective movements so that they will never lead us to hold false practical views about external things and so to feel emotional desires in relation to them. As we have seen, this will partly be a matter of training ourselves not to feel affective movements very strongly and acutely, partly a matter of deepening and solidifying our understanding of the reasons why it makes no sense to judge the objects of these feelings as either good or bad, and accordingly why it is unreasonable to feel "impulses" to which these movements make any contribution. But it is part of Posidonius's theory that experiencing affective movements is a permanent aspect of our nature as human beings. There is no question of ceasing to feel affective movements altogether (ceasing the experience of full-fledged *pathē* is of course another matter). This means that even the perfected, fully virtuous person will be beset by feelings (however mild and tractable) of excited attraction to and repulsion from objects and courses of action that he does not and cannot accept or approve of; these movements are constantly inclining him to adopt practical views that he knows are false and must not be agreed to. Would that not mean that the fully perfect person would live constantly subject to inner conflict and disharmony, as he would regularly feel inclined (even if not actually ever *pulled*) toward objects, experiences, and actions that, and in ways that, he nonetheless firmly rejected as inappropriate?

Of course, even for Chrysippus the perfected human being can and will suffer bodily pain, and he will undergo many other psychological experiences that, antecedently, he would have preferred not to experience at all; but it seems to me right to concede to Chrysippus that these do not amount to,

---

longer and more complete statement in Posidonius. Clement's more elaborated formulation is of special interest, in that it shows that Posidonius (presumably consciously following Plato and Aristotle) introduced into the Stoic conception of *eudaimonia* special reference to the value in itself of theoretical knowledge of nature, which had been conspicuously absent from earlier Stoic conceptions. That Galen is silent on this point is no good evidence that Posidonius himself omitted it from his discussion of the end in *On Emotions*, since Galen may simply have thought it irrelevant to the understanding of the *pathē*, his own chief concern in this work.

or otherwise introduce into his life, any feelings of disharmony or conflict, and so they do not reduce his happiness or affect it in any adverse way at all.[45] He controls his own evaluative attitudes, and it is only through these, if at all, that he could suffer any disturbance on their account: in themselves, bodily pain and these other counter-preferred experiences cannot affect one's happiness. What, however, about "impulsive impressions" of pleasure as something good or pain as an evil, and so on—the cause, according to Chrysippus, of emotions, when they are assented to (but not otherwise)? On Chrysippus's theory these are involuntary: would not the virtuous person, on Chrysippus's theory, continue to experience these impressions at least some of the time? It is admittedly unclear from our evidence (and so Chrysippus may himself have left it unclear) whether we should think the virtuous person does experience such impressions. Seneca reports (*On Anger* I 16. 7) that Zeno (and so, perhaps, Chrysippus too) recognized that the "wise man" would retain a "scar" of his previously vicious state of mind, resulting in an occasional, brief "hint or shadow" of emotion—small feelings of inappropriate excitement or irritation, for example, in circumstances in which he used to feel full-fledged emotion. Presumably these are themselves either "impulsive impressions" or direct consequences of them—in either case, this would be a sign that the wise man retains some susceptibility to inappropriate "impulsive impressions." On the other hand, according to Chrysippus the impressions (*phantasiai*) of an adult are always "rational" in the sense that they are states (albeit receptive ones) of his reason (see Diog. L. VII 51 *sub fin.*), and the acquisition of virtue means a total transformation of one's reason. So it would seem in order for Chrysippus to say that once that transformation has taken place even the "impulsive impressions" themselves that one receives about external things will be permanently different from the ones one received previously, and that ordinary people habitually receive. In any event, even if the wise person does occasionally give evidence of a remaining "scar," any inappropriate impression he may receive is at once set aside or disposed of, so it seems fair to say that that susceptibility would not count as a source of conflict and disharmony in the virtuous person's life. Such fleeting normative impressions, immediately revoked, do not betray any split or conflict within the sources of the wise person's agency.

But Posidonius's affective movements cannot so easily be kept at such a distance from what constitutes oneself as an agent. For, though just as involuntary as bodily pain and as impulsive impressions themselves, they also constitute at least inchoate evaluative attitudes: if you are feeling even fairly mildly inclined to depression over the death of a child or a friend, it is you who are therein feeling that you have lost something of real value to you. To be sure, the practical view that you adopt and retain throughout may very well proclaim it as no loss—and that is the view with which, as rational, you principally identify yourself. But the other attitude is there

---

[45] See J. M. Cooper and J. F. Procopé, *Seneca: Moral and Political Essays*, pp. xxii–xxiv.

too, and it cannot be denied to be yours as well. Moreover, since the affective movement does not belong to reason itself, the transformation of reason that virtue brings would not enable the virtuous person simply to set it aside or get rid of it once he began to feel it, as we saw Chrysippus and Zeno could say about the inappropriate impulsive impression. Indeed, given that for Posidonius the affective movement gives rise to the impulsive impression, one can assume that for him the virtuous agent could not in fact simply set aside or get rid of that impression either—so long as he continued to experience the movement. It would seem, then, that the virtuous agent would be in conflict with himself, after all, and in a state of disharmony that should be counted as detracting from his happiness.

Essentially the same difficulty can be approached by considering the consequences for Posidonius's account of the human virtues of his analysis of the nature and causes of emotions. In book V Galen gives only a brief and, as he himself admits, incomplete account of Posidonius's treatment of the virtues: for his purposes in refuting Chrysippus's theory of the emotions this is a side-issue.[46] However, it is clear that, consistently with his account of the emotions as arising from the effects of nonrational movements on our capacities for practical judgment, Posidonius must have maintained that human virtue overall consists of two separate components.[47] First, there is the perfection of the rational part through the acquisition of knowledge, and then there is the perfection of the nonrational parts through habituation to feel in certain ways and not feel in others, depending on the circumstances. Now there are immediate dangers for any Stoic in recognizing among the human virtues any conditions at all belonging to nonrational powers (however exactly these virtues are conceived). For since according to Stoic first principles all and only virtues are a good (and all and only vices a bad), it follows that one part of our overall good and bad is not directly under our own control. We do not directly control, even in principle, whether the condition of any of our nonrational powers is virtuous or not: that much follows immediately from the fact that they are *non*rational powers. In the case of the capacity for affective movements, conceived as Posidonius conceives these, we have to depend upon the chancy effects of our own and

---

[46] Cf. V 6. 1–2, p. 326, 9–16; and V 7. 10, p. 338, 14–18. Despite what one might infer from these passages, when Galen does return to the topic of the virtues (in VII 1–2) he does not offer any substantial account of Posidonius's theory. At VII 3. 1 he abandons the subject, with the promise (not kept) to write a separate work on the differences among the virtues. At VII 1. 9 he may imply that Posidonius followed Plato (as interpreted by Galen himself, cf. VII 1. 25–26) in making courage the virtue of the spirited part and temperance that of the appetitive; but since Galen also admits (V 7. 10) that there are differences of opinion between Posidonius and Plato on the natures of the different virtues, it is best not to attach much weight to what Galen says there.

[47] At V 5. 34–36, p. 324, 11–23, where he professes to be paraphrasing Posidonius, Galen clearly attributes to him a distinction between the virtue of the rational faculty (knowledge of some sort) and the virtues of the nonrational parts, achievable by some processes of nonrational habituation and training.

others' efforts to train them by some processes or other of habituation. But what if someone's nonrational powers were by his or her individual nature simply such that they *could not* be brought into whatever condition might be thought required? One cannot just dismiss this possibility; but facing it threatens to force the admission that full human virtue is not after all under our own control to achieve, even in principle. Yet the insistence that we are all fully responsible for our own moral condition is fundamental to Stoicism.

In order to meet this objection, Posidonius might insist that in order to possess the nonrational virtues you are only required to reduce your tendencies to feel affective movements to a level that would not cause anyone to adopt false practical views *if* he possessed the full knowledge of what is good, bad, and indifferent that comes with the perfection of human reason. And he might plausibly claim that the required level is such that equally virtuous persons might nonetheless vary fairly widely in the intensity, frequency, etc., with which they experience the affective movements, both in general and with reference to the different specific types of such feelings. In this way he might attempt to accommodate such natural variations as may exist among individual persons' capacities for achieving control of these feelings through habituation, by maintaining that everyone's individual nature makes it possible to control them at some level within the range required for virtue.

But in that case he seems forced to admit that *some* virtuous persons will experience rather more insistent affective movements than others (movements, of course, whose effects they successfully resist, through the strength of their correct understanding of what is truly good and bad for them). But surely at least *those* virtuous persons experience the sort of tension and lack of internal peace and tranquility that must be regarded as incompatible with a full measure of happiness. Virtue may in principle be achievable by all, and by nothing but their own voluntary efforts, including those involved in the discipline of their nonrational powers, no matter what their individual natures may be. But then it seems that virtue can no longer be held sufficient for happiness—where happiness is understood as consisting in part of internal peace and freedom from tension—or at any rate not for a full and perfect measure of it.

It would seem, then, that as a Stoic Posidonius is in a very uncomfortable position. Once one admits, as he does, that some powers in the human soul need to be trained by more than rational argument and reflection, it appears that one cannot clearly guarantee even in theory, as the Stoics standardly insisted on doing, that it is entirely up to us whether we lead both virtuous and happy lives or not. I conjecture that it was the recognition of this fact that led most Stoics after Posidonius (as Galen reports)[48] to reject his analysis

---

[48] See *De sequela* Kühn 819–20, pp. 77. 17–78. 2 Müller: this passage is noteworthy for its emphasis on later Stoic adherence to Chrysippus's theory of the virtues, with perhaps the

of the nature and causes of the emotions, and to cling to Chrysippean orthodoxy—however much an improvement on Chrysippus Posidonius's theory might have seemed if one restricted one's attention simply to the phenomenology of the emotions themselves. Posidonius made much of his insistence that a correct account of the human virtues depends upon the correct account of the emotions. But, as these considerations show, that logical connection itself provides any Stoic good grounds for doubt whether Posidonius's account of the emotions can after all be correct. One person's *modus ponens* is another's *modus tollens*.

Despite these difficulties there is evidence that several later Stoics followed Posidonius in accepting the existence of nonrational affective movements, while (again like Posidonius) insisting as strongly as Chrysippus himself on the necessity for an assent by reason in order to cause voluntary action (and so, in order to generate an emotion). Most noteworthy is Seneca's carefully articulated account in *On Anger* II 2–4 of certain agitated movements of the mind that are nonetheless not emotions, for example, anger (since they do not involve assent to angry thoughts of vengeance), but at worst "the preliminaries, the prelude" to emotions (*principia proludentia adfectibus*, 2. 5), caused involuntarily—for example, by the perception of someone's objectionable or insulting behavior.[49] Elsewhere (*Letters* 113. 17–18) Seneca similarly explains the genesis of human voluntary action in general in three stages that are strikingly reminiscent of Posidonius's account of emotional action (as I have interpreted it). In another letter (57) he describes a personal experience in terms that clearly draw upon this theory, while adding the significant detail that such an involuntary response is a *naturalis adfectio* (57. 4), a "natural feeling" that all of us (even sages) experience, simply because of our common human nature. Cicero's passing reference in *Tusc. Disp.* 3. 83 to *morsus et contractiunculae quaedam animi* ("bites and minor contractions in the soul") that may remain after one no longer assents to the idea of grieving, may similarly reflect Posidonius's analysis. Likewise Aulus Gellius (*Noctes Atticae* 19. 1) tells a story about a Stoic philosopher who in justification of the fearlike disturbance he felt during a storm at sea cites from Epictetus what seems to be the Posidonian and Senecan distinction between involuntary affect and assent-involving emotion.[50] Only scholars'

---

suggestion that this was for them the crucial point. Accordingly, when Galen implies elsewhere (e.g., *PHP* IV 4. 38) that other Stoics held fast to Chrysippus's theory of the emotions, we can perhaps infer that they did so because they recognized that they could not otherwise clearly sustain cardinal points of the Stoic theory of the virtues and happiness.

[49] See Fillion-Lahille's discussion, *Le "De ira,"* part III, ch. 4.

[50] On the other hand, the sage's *suspiciones quaedam et umbrae affectuum* of Seneca *On Anger* I 16. 7 (mentioned above, p. 480), which Inwood, *Ethics and Human Action*, p. 177, cites in this connection, are clearly a different phenomenon: they are described as being a consequence of the vicious state of mind the sage was afflicted with before attaining perfection (*etiam cum vulnus sanatum est, cicatrix manet*), not as a natural and unavoidable mental stirring, of a sort experienced by all human beings simply in consequence of their human nature.

failure to understand Posidonius's own theory has prevented wide recognition of its influence on later Stoics.[51]

[51] The first version of this chapter was presented at Cornell University in 1990, with Phillip Mitsis as commentator, and again the same year as a philosophy department colloquium at Princeton. It circulated in typescript (also under the title "Stoic Theories of the Emotions") and was referred to and discussed in Annas, *Hellenistic Philosophy of Mind*, 118–20, and A. W. Price, *Mental Conflict*, 175–78. In preparing the paper for publication, I have taken account of comments of Mitsis and Michael Frede on the 1990 version, and Daniel Devereux on a somewhat revised version read at the University of Virginia in the fall of 1995. I also wish to thank Christopher Gill, Juha Sihvola, and Troels Engberg-Pedersen for a series of very helpful questions and comments, of which I tried to take account in my final revisions of July 1996.

CHAPTER TWENTY-TWO

Pleasure and Desire in Epicurus

EPICURUS WAS A HEDONIST. The remains of his writings, meager though they are, leave no doubt that he advanced the thesis that obtaining pleasure and avoiding pain are the sole ultimate grounds on which anything is rationally pursued and desired, or rationally rejected. He is, in other words, a hedonist in ethical and more generally normative theory. Pleasure and pain are in fact, he claims, the sole ultimate values for a human being (or any other animal, for that matter); they are the only correct norms for evaluating options and for deciding on action rationally. But is he also a hedonist in the further sense of claiming that whenever any human being decides and acts he or she always, as a matter of fact, does so ultimately with the idea of obtaining pleasure and/or avoiding pain for himself or herself? Epicurus has often been so interpreted.[1] That is, he has often been interpreted as a hedonist as to the psychology of human motivation, choice, and action, as well as in the theory of *rational* choice and decision. I think this is a mistake. There is very little evidence in favor of the idea that Epicurus was a psychological hedonist; such evidence as there is, is readily and better interpreted in another way; and there is considerable positive evidence from Epicurus's own writings that he believed a person could perfectly well learn to be motivated by other considerations than the pleasure or pain of an action or of its consequences. I begin by reviewing this evidence so as to establish, I hope, that Epicurus was no psychological hedonist. Then I turn to his theories of desire, rational and irrational, and of pleasure itself—theories that lie at the center of his true hedonism, hedonism in normative ethical theory.

I NORMATIVE VS. PSYCHOLOGICAL HEDONISM

The principal evidence suggesting that Epicurus was a psychological hedonist comes in his *Letter to Menoeceus*, the only remaining exposition by Epicurus's own hand of Epicurean ethical theory as a whole. Before I present that evidence, let me first provide the context. At the end of section 127[2] of this

---

[1] See, among many examples, Bailey, *Epicurus: The Extant Remains*, p. 334 (note on *Letter to Menoeceus* 127–29); D. Glidden, "Aristotle and the Pleasure Principle," pp. 192–93; Guyau, *La Morale d'Epicure*, pp. 25–26; Long, *Hellenistic Philosophy*, pp. 63, 73; Long and Sedley, vol. I, p. 122. Many of the passages cited come in their authors' discussions of *Letter to Menoeceus* 127–29, so it seems reasonable to suppose that they think that that is where Epicurus makes this commitment clearest.

[2] That is, section 127 of Diogenes Laertius, *Lives of Eminent Philosophers*, book X, where this *Letter* is preserved, along with Epicurus's other summaries of philosophical doctrine in epistolary form. (In what follows I abbreviate *Letter to Menoeceus* as *LM*.)

Letter, Epicurus sets out briefly his theory of the three basic types of desires, to which I return below for detailed comment—desires that are natural and necessary, desires that are indeed natural but not necessary, and groundless desires. Then in section 128 he proceeds as follows:[3]

> The unwavering contemplation of these [distinctions among human desires] enables one to refer every choice and avoidance to the health of the body and the freedom of the soul from disturbance, since this is the goal of a blessed life.

That is, once one has a completely clear and firm understanding of the different types of desires that there are, one can see clearly which kinds of desires to have and which ones to avoid. As a result, one can then "refer every choice and avoidance" to the true goal of a blessed life (since choice and avoidance are the immediate effects of one's desires, and, Epicurus is assuming, we can rationally control which desires we will experience). Epicurus is referring here, of course, to what *he* proposes as the goal, the steady pursuit of which will achieve for anyone a happy and blessed life: namely, the constant and uninterrupted enjoyment of a certain specific form or circumstance of pleasure—pleasure given by bodily health and freedom from disturbance in the soul. This is not an uncontroversial view about the "goal of a blessed life"; it is not one that everyone will accept. Among well-known Greek philosophers at least Plato, Aristotle, and the Stoics clearly do not accept it. It is the exclusively Epicurean conception of the correct organizing goal for leading a life that will be blessed and happy.

Now we come to the apparent evidence of psychological hedonism. For Epicurus then adds:

> For we do everything for the sake of being neither in pain nor in terror. As soon as we achieve this state, every storm in the soul is dispelled, since the animal is not in a position to go after some need nor to seek something else to complete the good of the body and the soul.

A little later, at the end of the section and the beginning of the next (129), he continues:

> And this is why we say that pleasure is the starting-point and goal of living blessedly. For we recognized [pleasure] as our first and congenital good, and this is the starting-point for every choice and avoidance and we come to this by judging every good by the criterion of feeling.

It might seem natural to take the "we" in these two passages to refer to all us human beings. In that case Epicurus would be saying that the starting point for all of us in all our choices and avoidances is pleasure—all human beings, presumably as a natural fact about their mental and affective constitution, always act with pleasure as the "starting-point," that is, the goal,

---

[3] In quoting Epicurus here and in what follows, I use the translation of Inwood and Gerson in *Epicurus Reader*, often silently altered (sometimes considerably).

of their action. But notice that "we" are being said in the first passage to "do everything for the sake of being neither in pain nor in terror." So whoever "we" are here, what he claims as the basis of all these people's actions is, in the first instance, the avoidance of bodily pain and terror: pleasure as the ultimate object of pursuit is added only afterward. Epicurus's Greek for "terror" here is *tarbos*, a distinctly poetical word for "alarm" or "fear," and Epicurus seems to be using it instead of a more general term for mental upset or distress—fear, to be sure, but also anxiety and turmoil of any and every kind. So presumably what Epicurus means is that "we" base all our actions on avoidance of bodily pain and mental distress.

Notice, then, that in Epicurus's first statement about "us," there is no explicit mention of any positive pursuit of pleasure at all. However, it is a special, Epicurean doctrine (about which I will have more to say below) that as a matter of fact the highest attainable level of pleasure is given by the absence of bodily pain and mental distress. Epicurus has in fact alluded to this doctrine in the first sentence from section 128 quoted earlier: The "goal of a blessed life," according to him, is "the health of the body and the freedom of the soul from disturbance." That is, the goal of a blessed life is simply to attain and stay constantly in this highest level of pleasure. So we can easily reconcile everything that Epicurus says about "us" and what "we" do everything for if we suppose he means that everything an *Epicurean* does, he or she does to avoid pain or distress, that is to say, in the pursuit of the highest pleasure—since the two in some way coincide, on Epicurean theory. But these two things—pleasure and the absence of pain—would certainly not coincide for ordinary, non-Epicurean persons, who surely do make a distinction in their desires and motivations (mistakenly or not) between absence of pain or distress and presence of pleasure: all their actions surely are not motivated solely by avoiding expected bodily pain or mental distress—at least, that is not how they themselves think about their desires and about what motivates their actions in having those desires and doing their actions, and so, presumably, it is not in fact true of them. Nor can one see how Epicurus could have thought otherwise. (I come back to this point below.) So on examination it does seem very likely that in these passages the reference to what "we" do everything for is to us Epicureans—not to human beings generally. It is not a remark about human psychology at all, but one about the behavior of a person persuaded of and committed to Epicurean doctrines, who moreover always acts only in the light of them.

That it is we Epicureans that Epicurus is referring to is in fact confirmed already in the last of the sentences I quoted above. Here we get "we" again, and this time there is no possibility of doubt this is we Epicureans. It is not everybody, but only Epicureans, who have "recognized" (note the past tense) pleasure as our "first and congenital good"; it is Epicureans who "have come to this" as their "starting point for every choice and avoidance" by appealing to the criterion of feeling as the means of judging what is the ultimate good. With this "criterion of feeling," Epicurus is referring to his own theory that there are three, and only three, "criteria of truth"—that is, infallible bases for determining what is true. One of these is the criterion of feeling (in Greek, *pathos*), and—consistently with what Epicurus says here—Cicero appeals to this criterion in his *On Ends* (or *De finibus*) I 30 when he reports the Epicurean argument to establish that pleasure is indeed our "first and congenital good." The argument[4] claims that newborn animals all feel an impulse to seek pleasure and an impulse to avoid or get rid of pain, right from birth, that is to say, at a time when they have had no chance to form opinions of their own about what to go for or pull away from, a time when they are therefore necessarily not yet "perverted" in their attitudes, as Cicero puts it. And these are the only impulses of pursuit and avoidance that they feel right from birth. Any other impulses any one might experience, later on, may possibly be due to arbitrary and perverted ways of thinking or feeling—ones induced, perhaps, by processes of socialization or faulty individual inferences from the character of their experience. Only these initial, congenital impulses that are simply and directly for pleasure and against pain are necessarily trustworthy, as guides to the truth about what is to *be* pursued and to *be* avoided. Hence we adults, who do of course continue to feel impulses toward pleasure and away from pain—whatever additional impulses we may also have come to experience through later development—can be sure that those impulses are correct ones, at least in the sense that what they go for and push away from truly are respectively good and bad in themselves. Such necessarily unperverted impulses or feelings of attraction and dissatisfaction are, then, what Epicurus means to refer to in *Letter to Menoeceus* 129 when he speaks of feelings as constituting a "criterion" of what is good (i.e., desirable) and bad; and it is only Epicureans who accept this account of these initial impulsive feelings as a "criterion" of the truth about what is to be desired. Accordingly, in saying that "we" recognized pleasure as our first and congenital good by applying this criterion, Epicurus without doubt means to refer only to himself and his Epicurean followers.

The same is true in the next two sections (129–31), where Epicurus repeatedly says things about what "we" do in pursuing pleasure and what "we" believe about self-sufficiency as a great good, or what pleasures "we" have in mind by making pleasure the goal, and so on. All the way through these sections, the "we" is very clearly "we Epicureans."

The whole *Letter to Menoeceus* is, in fact, written as an exhortation to a fellow Epicurean, in the form of a brief summary of Epicurean doctrine

---

[4] In addition to Cicero, *On Ends* I 30, see also briefer references to and summaries of this argument in Diog. L., X 137 (*sub fin.*) and Sextus Empiricus, *Outlines of Pyrrhonism* III 194. As Sextus makes plain, the appeal is not to the fact (if it is a fact) that newborn animals like pleasure when they get some and dislike pain when they experience that, but to naturally arising impulses toward getting and continuing to experience the one and avoiding or getting rid of the other. See Jacques Brunschwig, "The Cradle Argument."

on ethics and rational decision-making. This summary will serve as a reminder of the doctrine as he faces situations where otherwise he might do the wrong thing, resulting in the loss of pleasure. The *Letter to Herodotus*, which summarizes Epicurean physical theory, recommends that its reader actually memorize the general, leading doctrines that it outlines.[5] It seems that that is what Menoeceus is supposed to do, too, though Epicurus does not make this explicit. After a brief introduction on the great importance for everyone, young or old, of the continuous study of philosophy, since that is what produces happiness, he says to Menoeceus (123): "Do and practice what I constantly told you to do, believing those things to be the elements of living well." What then follows in the body of the *Letter* is a fairly systematically structured statement of the main ethical doctrines of the school, which Menoeceus has already been taught and has already, so to speak, signed on to. So it is no surprise that in setting out this statement Epicurus often refers in the first person plural, as we have seen he does, to "us" adherents of the school.

The evidence of Epicurus's text itself, therefore, indicates that when he says in the *Letter to Menoeceus* that "we" do everything we do for the sake of pleasure, he means only that Epicureans who live consistently with their principles act this way—not that every human being, by a natural necessity, does so. So he is not expressing a commitment there to psychological hedonism. He is only appealing to the normative hedonism that is the special contribution of the Epicureans to Hellenistic ethical theory. Another passage, however, this time one from Cicero, might indicate that, nonetheless, Epicurus was in fact a psychological hedonist. At any rate in the Loeb translation by H. Rackham, Cicero quotes him as saying quite precisely that "pleasure and pain" "lie at the root of every act of choice and avoidance" (*On Ends* I 23). But in fact the Latin verbs for acts of choice and avoidance are put into the subjunctive here, not the indicative, and what Cicero actually says is that *ad haec* [sc. *voluptatem et dolorem*] *et quae sequamur et quae fugiamus* [*Epicurus*] *refert omnia*: "to pleasure and pain Epicurus refers everything both that we are to pursue and that we are to flee."[6] Thus, in fact, what Cicero says is that Epicurus told us that we ought to pursue and flee, ultimately, only pleasure and pain, respectively; he is expressing, again, his normative hedonism, not psychological hedonism. The passage just quoted occurs in the introductory part of the dialogue, where Cicero is stating in his own person the doctrines of Epicurus that he finds impossible to accept.

---

[5] See sects. 35 and 36 at the beginning of the *Letter*, and 83 at the end.

[6] This is what grammarians call a "deliberative" subjunctive, a kind of jussive use of the mood. It is true that, in principle, one might take the relative clause here as a "relative clause of characteristic" (see *Allen and Greenough's New Latin Grammar*, paragraph 534), thus simply putting into the subjunctive what might equally well have been put in the indicative. But there seems no doubt that translators into other modern languages, such as Gigon, are correct to take it the way I suggest we ought to, because only then is the subjunctive really functional here.

Later, after the Epicurean Torquatus agrees to present Epicurus's ethical theory in the hope of persuading Cicero of its truth, we find again that in stating Epicurus's fundamental view Cicero writes (I 29) that, for Epicurus, pleasure is the end "to which all other things ought (*oporteat*) to be referred, while it is not to be referred to anything else,"[7] and repeatedly after that (already in the very next paragraph, I 30) pleasure is spoken of as *expetenda* (to be pursued), pain as *fugiendus* (to be fled or avoided). There is no place in Torquatus's exposition where psychological hedonism is attributed to Epicurus. Indeed, it is always as a hedonist in the theory of *rational* decision, desire, and action that Cicero presents Epicurus, whether in his own voice or that of another, if his Latin is everywhere correctly translated.

So far my argument has been negative: Epicurus constantly says things that commit him to hedonism in the theory of rational decision, and (despite what might be initial appearances) he does not say things that commit him to hedonism as a thesis about human psychology in general. Passages in the *Letter to Menoeceus* and in Cicero's *On Ends* that might at first glance be taken to refer to general psychology turn out on examination to express only normative, not psychological, hedonism. But there is positive evidence as well, some direct and some indirect, that I would like now to draw attention to. First, in *Principal Doctrine* XXV we read:

> If you do not, on every occasion, refer each of your actions to the goal of nature, but instead turn prematurely to some other [goal] in avoiding or pursuing [something], your actions will not be consistent with your principles (*logoi*).

This appears to be an excerpt from some writing of Epicurus's, apparently a letter of admonition to some Epicurean struggling to hold fast to the school's doctrine. Notice the specific way it pictures his possible retrogression: not by misunderstanding the correct implications in some circumstances of the Epicurean conception of the goal of a blessed life—this is not a case of opting for an inviting near-term pleasure that is in fact incompatible with maintaining the pain- and distress-free condition that gives the highest level of pleasure, while fooling oneself into thinking that it *is* compatible. No, the case envisaged is one of actually adopting, in some action, a goal quite other than the Epicurean one.

To be sure, one possible way to shift to a non-Epicurean goal would be continuing the pursuit of pleasure, or some pleasure, as one's goal in an action, but now on a different understanding from the Epicurean one of what the rational pursuit of pleasure demands that one set up as one's goal. For example, one might pursue as one's goal the maximal excess of intense pleasurable feeling over pain in one's life as a whole—something, as we will see more fully below, that Epicurus argues is a terrible error, however "hedonistically" motivated. But this is not the only or the most obvious

---

[7] Again, Rackham mistranslates into the indicative: it is "the End to which all other things are means, while it is not itself a means to anything else."

possibility. If there is to be some special bite to this remark in its original context which could have led early Epicureans to include it among the master's *Principal Doctrines*, it is more likely that we should think, for example, of someone who has been reading Aristotle, or Chrysippus or another Stoic, or even the Socratic dialogues of Plato. He or she has become inspired by the thought of nobility of action itself as a beautiful and wonderful thing, and backslides by doing some act of courage or justice for its own sake, for the inherent nobility of acting that way—instead of with the Epicurean idea that acts of courage and justice should be done only for the pleasure inherent in them plus the effects they have in sustaining conditions for the future in which you will be best able to continue in the highest level of pleasure, as that is defined by Epicurean theory. If this is right, then this *Principal Doctrine* is warning Epicureans to beware of drifting off in their day-by-day practical thinking into the snares of these other—rationalist— philosophers' ethical doctrines. Epicurus is insisting strongly that the whole range of ideas about nobility of action and about the supreme value of simply having a mind constituted in a certain way which produces actions in accord with itself, which lie at the center of this philosophical tradition in ethics, is totally at odds with the "empiricist" approach to human life for which Epicureanism stands. And of course, in insisting on this, he is presupposing that it is psychologically possible for a human being, even an educated and committed Epicurean, to act in pursuit of other goals than pleasure as the ultimate object of their action—goals other than any pleasure, goals other than pleasure according to any construal of the form or circumstance of pleasure that is the right one to take as one's ultimate guide in life. This shows that Epicurus cannot, consistently with this *Doctrine*, at any rate, have been a hedonist in the psychological theory of human decision and action.[8]

This way of reading *Principal Doctrine* XXV connects it with a theme that we know of from other fragments of Epicurus and from Cicero's *On Ends*, which provides indirect evidence in support of the same conclusion. In his *Learned Banquet* Athenaeus, writing about A.D. 200, quotes the following two passages of Epicurus, the first from his principal work on

---

[8] It is worth pointing out that Diogenes Laertius in his life of Aristippus (II 89) attributes the same view to the Cyrenaics: "And they say that it is possible for some people not to choose pleasure, because they are perverted." This report comes just after Diogenes has recorded one major point on which the Cyrenaics differed from Epicurus and just before two further such points are added, but I do not believe we should take Diogenes or his source to be including this one among the points of difference. In fact the construction of the Greek, in connecting this report with what follows, rather suggests that the author means to be saying that the possibility of nonpursuit of pleasure was held in common by the two schools. The whole sentence reads: δύνασθαι δέ φασι καὶ τὴν ἡδονήν τινας μὴ αἱρεῖσθαι κατὰ διαστροφήν· οὐ πάσας μέντοι τὰς ψυχικὰς ἡδονὰς καὶ ἀλγηδόνας ἐπὶ σωματικαῖς ἡδοναῖς καὶ ἀλγηδόσι γίνεσθαι. The μέντοι clause denies to the Cyrenaics something that is well known to have been a central doctrine of Epicurus. So the strong contrast marked by this particle indicates that what immediately precedes was something that they held in common.

ethics, *On the Goal*: "One must honor the noble (*to kalon*), and the virtues and things like that, *if* they produce pleasure. But if they do not, one must bid them goodbye." And: "I spit upon the noble and on those who vainly admire it, whenever it causes no pleasure." At least included among those who admire the noble are certainly Socrates, Plato, Aristotle, and the Stoics (as well as Cicero in a later time). So Epicurus is saying that he spits upon such philosophers and upon the noble conceived the way they conceive it, that is, as something supremely good just in itself. Torquatus in Cicero's *On Ends* I frames his extended discussion of the virtues (I 42–54) with two dismissals of the view on the "final end" or "chief good" of philosophers who maintain that virtuous action, done for its own sake alone, constitutes the true happiness of a happy life. He is obviously thinking of the Stoics, historically the Epicureans' most formidable opponents in the battle for adherents. In the first of these dismissals (I 42), he accuses the Stoics of being "beguiled by the glamor of a name," of carrying on emptily about "the transcendent beauty of the virtues"—in fact, as Epicurus has argued, nature demands of us no such actions, but only the orderly and intelligent pursuit of pleasure. He returns to this point at the end of his exposition of Epicurean virtues, saying this time (I 54) that he has now shown that "the praise of the virtues, in which all other philosophers love most of all to exult so eloquently, has no point unless it is directed to pleasure—the only thing that is intrinsically attractive and alluring." He returns to the point a third time a little later (I 61), this time naming the Stoics as his target and saying, "They maintain that nothing is good save that vague phantom (*umbram*) which they entitle Moral Worth [*honestum*, Cicero's translation for Greek *kalon*—nobility or fineness or beauty of action], a title more splendid than substantial."[9] Torquatus is not maintaining that these philosophers and those who have been taken in by them do not in fact act as they say they do—performing acts of virtue for their own sake, as constituting the goodness in a happy life—but instead are self-deceived and always act for pleasure of some sort or other. That would be a great dialectical mistake: all they (or Cicero) would need to do to refute him then would be to claim, reasonably, that it is they who are in a position to declare their own motivations, not he. No: Torquatus is insisting simply that it is a gross error to set up any such conception of the good and any such goal of living as these competing philosophical schools set up. These philosophers and their followers should stop living the way they are in fact living. They should accept the Epicurean arguments that establish pleasure as the only ultimate good and they should adopt as the goal of their life the Epicurean goal of maintaining in all their actions a constant, steady state of that highest pleasure which is given by absence of bodily pain and mental distress.

Before concluding, however, that Epicurus definitely did not espouse hedo-

---

[9] The translations from Cicero in this paragraph, and elsewhere in this chapter, are adapted from the Loeb translation of H. Rackham, often altered considerably.

nism as a general theory about the ultimate objects of human desire and action, one objection remains:[10] We are familiar nowadays with psychoanalytical accounts of human motivation, according to which people can be very wrong about the character of their own desires, and quite mistaken about what they are really pursuing as the goal in some of their actions: they say and even think that what they want and are trying to achieve is one thing, whereas (according to these theorists) it is really something quite else—something that, after psychotherapy, they may come to discover for themselves is or was actually motivating them all along, though they did not know it. In fact, the Epicurean poet Lucretius engages quite markedly in a similar sort of analysis in discussing the fear of death. He envisages a man (III 870–93) who professes to agree fully with the Epicurean view that at death a person permanently ceases to have any sort of consciousness, but who nonetheless continues to shudder and be upset at the prospect of his burial and the decomposition of his body, or its cremation, and thinks it is perfectly reasonable to feel that way—indeed, unreasonable not to. But, Lucretius insists, if he thinks this, this man cannot really be granting that no one has any consciousness of anything after death: subconsciously he is picturing himself witnessing the burial and decomposition or cremation and being pained by it, and it is only because he anticipates that pain that he can now shudder and be upset at the prospect. If he did really understand that at death we cease altogether to be conscious, and why that must be so, he could not continue to repine in this way at the thought of his own death. Thus, according to Lucretius, we have good grounds for denying that what the man *says* he believes, and no doubt believes he believes, about what will happen to him at death is what he really does believe. But if people are not necessarily authorities on what they believe, then perhaps they are not necessarily authorities on what they desire, nor on the goals of their actions. In short, if Lucretius's psychoanalyzing analysis of the fear of death represents a style of analysis that goes back to Epicurus himself, then perhaps Epicurus, employing the same sort of analysis, claimed that everyone desires pleasure and the avoidance of pain as their sole ultimate motivations—even if many people do not recognize this fact about themselves but delude themselves into thinking, as the Stoics and Cicero did, that they often or always perform acts of virtue simply for their own sakes, as possessing an inherent goodness that is not reducible to or comparable with any other sort of good. I do not find any evidence at all, however, that Epicurus did argue in this way. As we have seen, he does not argue so in the *Letter of Menoeceus*, where all his assertions about what "we" always aim at and ultimately desire are claims about Epicureans, not people in general; and *Principal Doctrine* XXV seems clearly to envisage that a person might actually desire as ultimate something other than pleasure, however irrationally. Furthermore, if Cicero had thought it was any part of basic Epicurean

---

[10] Both Alexander Nehamas and T. H. Irwin raised this objection in discussion.

doctrine to hold that everyone always acts for pleasure, whatever they may say to the contrary, he would surely have been outraged and could not have lost the opportunity in book II of *On Ends* to berate Epicurus, as he does for so much else, for having the gall to tell *him* about the character of his own desires—to make upstanding Romans like himself or Torquatus's distinguished ancestors nothing but pleasure-seekers!

II THE HIGHEST PLEASURE AS A STATE OF CONSCIOUSNESS CAUSED BY ABSENCE OF PAIN

Epicurus, then, was no hedonist in the psychology of human action. Rather, he advocated a hedonist theory of rational decision and action. Let me turn now to some details of this theory.

To begin with, it is very important to keep two questions distinct. First there is the question what our (sole) "natural and congenital" good is—in effect, what is the only thing good in itself. Epicurus's answer here is "pleasure," and we have seen him confirm this from considerations about babe-in-the-cradle impulses and behavior. Then there is the further and distinct question what the proper and true goal is for a whole human life, in the sense of the single, comprehensive goal that properly organizes and relates to one another all the activities of a lifetime. This second question, too, Epicurus is sometimes reported by Cicero to answer verbally in the same way: the right goal is pleasure.[11] But that now means "*living* pleasantly" and this is carefully explained in a quite specific way (and justifying arguments are offered).[12] It means living constantly, securely, and uninterruptedly in a

---

[11] See *On Ends* I 29: *hoc* [i.e., the final good, the ultimate end to which everything else is to be referred, but it to nothing beyond itself] *Epicurus in voluptate ponit*. See also *LM* 131: "when we say that pleasure is the goal . . ." (for the continuation, see the following note).

[12] See Cic. *On Ends* I 40 where Torquatus puts the Epicurean position this way: *extremum esse bonorum voluptatem* (pleasure is the goal, the highest good); but then he goes on in I 42 to explain that *ut cum voluptate vivatur* (to live with pleasure) is that at which all right and praiseworthy actions are ultimately aimed; what the Greeks term the *telos*, or the highest, ultimate and final good is *iucunde vivere*, "to live pleasantly." (There is similar language already in I 41; see also I 54.) See also *LM* 131: the continuation of the sentence I began to quote in the preceding footnote follows: " . . . we do not mean the pleasures of the profligate . . . but rather the lack of pain in the body and disturbance in the soul." This shift in the meaning of "pleasure" when it is used to refer to the goal of the happy life, and not merely to the only thing that is good in itself, is clearly signaled by Torquatus in I 43. Here, just after he has established that the true goal for a human life is "living pleasantly," that is, in a constant state of enjoyment of a painless bodily and distress-free mental state, he begins to explain how the pursuit of *this* pleasure, this goal, can ground the virtues. Cicero has him interrupt his exposition of how this works with the first virtue he takes up, wisdom, by pointing out that when he says that it is the "artificer that procures and produces pleasure" his hearers must now understand "the meaning that I attach to pleasure . . . , you must not be biased against my argument owing to the discreditable associations of the term." That same meaning, he implies, is to be understood in all that follows when he speaks of pleasure as the object of pursuit.

condition of the highest pleasure, which itself is explained as the pleasure that one experiences when one is completely without pain in the body (or, equivalently sometimes, when one is in a state of bodily health)[13] and without suffering any mental disturbance.[14] Thus it is one thing to say that pleasure is the only thing that is good in itself (and pain the only thing bad in itself), and quite another to say that living pleasantly (that is, in the constant and secure enjoyment of the highest pleasure) is the correct goal for the blessed and happy life. The first only implies that any and every pleasure is good in itself: Epicurus is careful to affirm this quite clearly in the *Letter*, and one of the *Principal Doctrines* elaborates on the point.[15] But it says nothing at all, yet, about precisely what goal for living is the correct one—what goal to set up as the basis for organizing one's whole life, by referring all one's choices and actions ultimately to attaining and then preserving it.[16]

The central thesis of Epicurus's hedonism, then, is the claim that all our

---

[13] See, e.g., *LM* 128, quoted above, sect. I.

[14] One might wonder how it could even be possible for a human being to sustain for any length of time the complete lack of bodily pain. By some mental gymnastics one might, I suppose, keep one's mind clear from all disturbance caused by anything that happens or that threatens to, but bodily pain is something else again. Epicurus has, I believe, a not uninteresting response to this challenge; see below.

[15] See *LM* 129: "So every pleasure is a good thing, since it has a nature congenial to us"; *Principal Doctrine* VIII: "No pleasure is a bad thing in itself. But the things that produce certain pleasures bring troubles many times greater than the pleasures." (Hereafter I abbreviate "*Principal Doctrine*" by "*PD*.")

[16] Cicero blurs the distinction between pleasure as the only thing good in itself and pleasure as the correct goal of life when he gives his version of the "cradle" argument. He sets this argument out at the beginning of Torquatus's exposition of how Epicurus establishes what the correct goal for life or the true final good is (I 30). There he writes that "every animal, as soon as it is born, desires pleasure and delights in it as the Highest Good (*ut summo bono*) and recoils from pain as the Highest Bad and so far as possible avoids it." As seems certain *summum bonum* here is intended as a reference to the final good or goal of life (see, e.g., I 42, where he gives indifferently as Latin equivalents for the Greek philosophers' notion of the *telos: vel summum vel ultimum vel extremum bonorum*), this certainly cannot be a correct account of how Epicurus began his "cradle" argument; newborns cannot reasonably be assigned even implicit ideas on how best to organize a whole life! Notably, when Cicero reverts to this argument in II 31 in order to give his criticism of it, he only says (correctly) that according to Epicurus newborn animals desire pleasure as good (*ut bonum*) and recoil from pain as bad (*ut malum*)—not as the highest good and highest bad respectively. In fact in I 30 Torquatus is only beginning his exposition of the Epicurean argument to the conclusion that living pleasantly is the goal. Notice the first words of the section, followed immediately by the "cradle argument": *idque* [sc., that pleasure is the highest or final good, the goal of life] *instituit docere sic*, "he set to work in demonstrating this as follows." This conclusion itself is finally, and formally, reached only in I 42, where Torquatus announces it with some emphasis: "It must therefore be admitted that the Highest Good or goal of life (*summum bonum*) is to live pleasantly (*iucunde vivere*)." Before that conclusion can be claimed as established, much more than simple reference to the character of newborn animals' impulses of pursuit and avoidance is needed—and provided: see the account of the distinction between pleasure in the "movement" of the senses and pleasure in the removal of all pain and distress (¶37–39), and the two formal arguments beginning at *quod si vita* . . . in ¶41 and continuing on in ¶42 (note the initial *praeterea*), from which Torquatus then urges us to conclude that living pleasantly (in the sense

choices and actions ought to be aimed at attaining and then preserving in our lives a secure, constant, uninterrupted enjoyment of the pleasure that is given by the absence of pain from our bodies and of distress, anxiety, agitation, and disturbance of any kind from our minds. I do not inquire here into Epicurus's reasons for supposing that, if indeed pleasure is the only thing good in itself and pain the only such bad thing, this particular pleasure is the goal we ought to aim at in organizing and conducting our lives. Taking that as given, I want rather to examine this doctrine itself more closely, and to explore its connections with Epicurus's theory of the three kinds of desires referred to above. To begin with, I take Epicurus to have thought, not that life characterized by absence of pain *as such* together with absence of distress *as such* constitutes the highest pleasure. Rather, I take him to have proposed that it is a natural, inevitable fact about our physical constitution that when anyone is in that condition he or she experiences some pleasurable feeling, and that it is the prolongation of that pleasurable feeling over a lifetime that he means to identify as the highest or final good. Cicero and other ancient critics criticized Epicurus severely for the paradoxical, even outrageous, conflation of absence of pain, as such, with pleasure. But in fact when Torquatus formally presents this aspect of the Epicurean doctrine, Cicero has him say (I 37):

> The pleasure we pursue is not that alone which sets in motion our physical being itself in some agreeable way and is perceived by the senses with a certain delight, but rather we hold that the greatest pleasure is that which is perceived when all pain has been taken away.[17]

In other words, as his language of "perception" shows, he is claiming that just as when, let us suppose, we have a sexual orgasm, our physical being is set in motion in an agreeable way, such that we have a delightful perception of the senses, so also when we find ourselves with all pain removed we have another delightful perception, another pleasure. Indeed, this latter delightful perception is the greatest pleasure and most delightful perception that nature permits us. A little later in the same section Torquatus makes the same point: "the very taking away of annoyance brings pleasure in its train as a result."[18]

Given the persistence of the criticisms just referred to, it seems possible, or even likely, that in his own writings Epicurus was not always careful to make it clear that what he intended as the goal of life was, as we could put

---

established in §37) is the Highest Good. On the structure and organization of *On Ends* I 29–42, see Striker, "Epicurean Hedonism," pp. 5–6.

[17] *Non enim hanc solam sequimur quae suavitate aliqua naturam ipsam movet et cum iucunditate quadam percipitur sensibus, sed maximam voluptatem illam habemus quae percipitur omni dolore detracto.* Note the double occurrence of *percipitur*, once with each instance of (alleged) pleasure.

[18] *. . . ipsa detractio molestiae consecutionem affert voluptatis.* See to the same effect Plutarch *That Epicurus Actually Makes a Pleasant Life Impossible* 7, 1091b (frag. 423 Usener).

it, a certain state of consciousness caused or occasioned by the complete absence of pain and distress. Certainly, he must often have spoken, as he does in the passage from *Letter to Menoeceus* 128 quoted above (sect. I), of the goal simply as the continued and secure absence of pain and distress—without carefully underlining that by this he intends, in a way that is quite common in the philosophical practice of his time, to refer to a result (pleasurable consciousness) that follows immediately and necessarily upon this condition as its cause. We have a well-known example of this practice in Chrysippus's frequent declaration that emotions are just a certain class of judgments of a person's reason. In fact Chrysippus is counting as not to be distinguished from those judgments the characteristic ways of feeling that are their immediate consequences—the mental affects, the ways those judgments impress themselves on the mind of the one judging. These affects (the feeling of psychic uplift, or the constricted, stunned feeling of a disappointed hope, say) are what alone another philosopher, or an ordinary person, might want to count as the emotions; Chrysippus insists that the proper way to identify an emotion is by reference to the essential cause of the whole complex phenomenon in question, namely the underlying judgment. So Epicurus: when he says that the highest pleasure is living in the absence of pain and distress, he means that the highest pleasure is the one given by—the one immediately and necessarily perceived as a result of—this bodily and mental condition. He is referring to that pleasurable consciousness by means of the most natural, and arguably the essential, means of identifying it, its necessary cause. Conceivably at least at some stages of his career, Epicurus may really have regarded simply that absence, as such, as the highest good—and so he may at some stage of his developing doctrine have been subject to Cicero's and others' complaints. But passages like those just cited from *On Ends* I 37 support the attribution to him of the more interesting and plausible interpretation I am adopting, as at least his central or final view.

The pleasure that Epicurus is proposing as the correct goal for a whole life is therefore a certain state of consciousness or perception. So the objections of ancient Cyrenaic hedonists, that the alleged highest good of Epicurus is really the condition of a dead person or of one asleep, rests on a gross and merely polemical misrepresentation of the doctrine.[19] But I think there is good evidence that so far was Epicurus from thinking of absence of pain or the highest good as like the condition of one dead or asleep, he actually understood the pleasurable consciousness with which he identified the highest good not even as something basically passive. It did not entail sinking into a state of quiescence, into a feeling of relief at not having anything to do and at not having to do anything—no pain to get rid of or worry about for the future, no needs to be seen to (whether of one's own or one's family and friends), no desires to prepare to satisfy in the future, no active

---

[19] See Diogenes Laertius II 89 (in his *Life of Aristippus*) and Clement of Alexandria *Stromateis* II 21 (Epicurus frg. 451 Usener).

engagement with specific enjoyable ways of passing the time. Instead, I believe, what Epicurus is pointing to is the enjoyably active experience at once of the pain-free, healthy capacities of one's body and the undisturbed, unstressed, unconstricted, free play of one's mental faculties. When Epicurus speaks of the highest good as a life of the constant, secure, uninterrupted pleasure given by the absence of pain and distress, this is to be understood as a pleasure maintained on a constant and secure basis by actively engaging the pain-free body and the distress-free mind in activities that make possible in the first place and sustain the pleasurable consciousness of the condition of the body and mind at this highest level.

In order to see that this really is what Epicurus taught, we need to take account of three specific further doctrines of his. We need to bear in mind, first, the crucial and overwhelming importance he assigned to friendship in the best, most pleasant life. Second, we need to pay heed to his doctrine that although, when the condition of highest pleasure is once attained one cannot go beyond it to achieve any level of pleasure greater than that, one certainly can vary this pleasure. And, third, we need to take account of the distinction between what he calls "groundless" desires, which are strictly to be avoided, without exception, and what he calls natural but not necessary desires. I want to suggest that Epicurus emphasized the development by each person of a wide variety of such natural and not-necessary desires for the enjoyment of a large number of different ways of actively engaging one's pain-free bodily state and distress-free mind—most particularly, ways that involve essentially the sort of shared activities that are most characteristic of friendship. He thought, I believe, that, as a matter of fact, only so will the person leading the life that he holds out as the highest good be able constantly and without interruption to enjoy the pleasure that body and mind under those conditions can yield. In developing this interpretation, let me begin in reverse order with Epicurus's distinction of desires into three classes.

III THREE TYPES OF DESIRES

Epicurus summarizes this doctrine, as I mentioned above (sect. I), immediately before the passage of the *Letter to Menoeceus* with which I began this chapter. There he says that

> of desires, some are natural, some groundless. And of the natural desires some are necessary and some merely natural; of the necessary, some are necessary for happiness and some for keeping the body free from disturbance and some for life itself.

The same three types of desire are distinguished also in *Principal Doctrine* XXIX though in a different order and arrangement, according to which the ones simply called "groundless" in the *Letter* are called "neither natural nor necessary but occurring as a result of groundless opinion"; and in this *Principal Doctrine* we do not get any indication, as we do in the *Letter*, of different types of necessary desire.[20] With *Principal Doctrine* XXIX we also have the benefit of a note added to an ancient manuscript of Diogenes Laertius (where the *Principal Doctrines* are preserved) which explains a bit and gives examples of the three categories:

> Epicurus thinks that natural and necessary are those that rid us of pains, for example drinking when thirsty; natural and not necessary are those that only provide variations of pleasure and do not remove the feeling of pain, for example luxurious foods; neither natural nor necessary are, for example, crowns and dedications of statues.[21]

[20] *PD* XXIX: "Of desires, some are natural and necessary, some natural and not necessary, and some neither natural nor necessary but occurring as a result of groundless opinion." It is the order given in *PD* XXIX that Cicero follows in *On Ends* I 45 (and criticizes in II 26 as illogically presented). Cicero complains at length that this doctrine, so presented, identifies as three coordinate types of desire what on its own showing are in fact two basic sorts of desire (the natural and the groundless), of which the first, the natural desires, are then subdivided into necessary and not necessary. This alternative presentation, he says, is how thinkers trained in logical theory—something Epicurus dismisses as of no value—state the division. It is a mark of the lengths Cicero was willing to go in captious criticism of Epicurus that he suppresses the fact that Epicurus presents the doctrine in *LM* with precisely what he himself counts as the logically correct division.

[21] Cicero explains the basis for Epicurus's distinctions quite differently. At I 45, after setting out the three classes of desires, he writes: "The principle of this classification is that necessary desires are gratified with little trouble or expense; the natural desires also require but little, since nature's own riches, which suffice to content her, are both easily procured and limited in amount; but for the groundless desires no bound or limit can be discovered." What Cicero says here about the three different sorts of desires may very well reflect things that Epicurus did say about them, but it seems evident that this cannot be the basis for the classification. How can "necessary" get explained, or necessary desires get marked off, in terms of the little trouble and expense it takes to satisfy them? And to what do the remarks about natural desires apply? All natural desires (the necessary as well as the not necessary)? Or merely the natural and not necessary? They are presumably meant to apply only to the latter: the necessary desires have already been explicated in the previous clause, and the clause following is devoted to the groundless ones, so this clause must be intended to characterize the third group, that of natural and not necessary desires. But in fact Cicero's remark about the easy procurement and limited quantities of nature's riches required to satisfy these "natural" desires sounds as if it ought to apply especially, or even only, to the natural and *necessary* ones: if the Scholiast to *PD* XXIX is right, the *not necessary* natural desires include ones for luxuries, and those are surely not of easy procurement. Finally, Cicero is surely not giving any real clarification of the idea of groundlessness as that is attributed to the third kind of desires, when he tells us that there is no "bound or limit" to them: what has the lack of bound or limit to do with being groundless? In fact, Cicero's attention in proposing this "principle" of Epicurus's classification seems drawn exclusively to the ease or difficulty of satisfying these different kinds of desire: his main point seems to be that the groundless desires are actually impossible to fulfill, whereas the other two are easily satisfied. But while the ease or impossibility of fulfilling these desires might be important to Epicurus in working out his views on the use and value (or lack of any) to a human being of these desires, it can hardly constitute the basis on which the classification itself is introduced.

The classification is illustrated differently in a scholium to Aristotle's *Nicomachean Ethics*

Let me first make a few comments on these presentations of the theory, after which I will offer an overall interpretation of its significance.[22] I begin with the necessary desires (all of which are, of course, natural as well), go on to the groundless ones, and conclude with the natural but not necessary desires. Clearly, for Epicurus a paradigmatic necessary desire is naturally arising thirst or hunger or sexual arousal, or the natural discomfort that all normally endowed humans have in extreme cold or heat which motivates them to escape it. In all these cases, as the Scholiast says, by satisfying the desire we get rid of the pain or discomfort that is bound up with the desire itself, because it is based in some bodily need. Here one might naturally think of the "necessity" Epicurus has in mind in calling these desires necessary as betokening the inevitability for human beings of these desires: we do not have the option of not getting thirsty if we are without appropriate liquid refreshment for long, and so on for the other cases. However, this seems

---

III 11, 1118b8, printed as part of Epicurus frg. 456 by Usener, from the way it is in the scholium to *PD* XXIX. After naming the three classes of desire, the scholiast continues: "the desire for nourishment and clothing is necessary; that for sex is natural but not necessary; that for such and such foods or such and such clothing or such and such sex is neither natural nor necessary [i.e., groundless]." This note, coming in a text of Aristotle, naturally has less authority than the scholium to *PD* XXIX. Furthermore it hardly makes sense. How can we understand desires for particular foods as altogether groundless? And apparently, on this explication, no desire that was not for clothing, food, drink, or sex could ever count as anything but groundless.

[22] The best exposition and discussion of this crucial Epicurean doctrine that I know of is that of Annas in *Morality*, ch. 7. I disagree with Annas, however, on two crucial points. First, not all Epicurean natural desires can be either for the satisfaction of basic needs (understood generically), the ones she proposes to count as necessary—or for specifications of these needs in terms of particular ways of satisfying them, the ones she counts as natural and unnecessary. At any rate, it is very hard to see how some desires that are very important for Epicurus, such as the desire for philosophical discussion, or even the desire to play or listen to music, or paint a picture or read a book, could be construed as a specification of some generic desire aimed at satisfying a basic need. (Or if you do construe them that way, you trivialize and render useless the notion of a need in this context.) Second, as I explain below in my main text, I believe it is a serious mistake to say, as Annas does, that natural and *un*necessary desires are all of them such that they do not involve caring at all about having their objects; on her account a natural and unnecessary desire for lobster (as opposed to a groundless one) has to be merely for lobster "as a kind of food, a way of stilling my hunger" (p. 193). On the contrary, I believe such a desire is for the pleasure of eating lobster, that is, it involves regarding the lobster as *lobster* and not merely as food, and so not merely as a way of stilling hunger but a particularly pleasant way of doing that. Annas's mistake here is shared by Mitsis (*Epicurus*, pp. 45–50): the different kinetic pleasures of eating fish and meat, he says, "are mere variants that give us no rational grounds for preference" between them (p. 47). Both Annas and Mitsis disregard the important possibility that one might desire such a food as lobster, both as a standing and as an occurrent desire, in such a way as to take particular pleasure in it when one can easily enough have it, but without desiring it in such a way that one feels set back or deprived if one does not get what one wants (that is, prefers to have), or so that one becomes obsessively occupied with searching out and storing up the means to satisfy this desire—as if disaster would befall you if you had to settle for some other foodstuff. The fact that a natural desire for lobster is one that is ready to give way when the person decides to still his hunger with something else more readily available does not in the least mean that it is not a desire to eat lobster as such but only as a way of filling one's stomach.

not to be how Epicurus himself means the term, as we can see from his comments (above) in *Letter to Menoeceus* 127 on the different ways desires can be necessary. He explains that some of the necessary desires are necessary for life itself, some others necessary if we are to avoid bodily disturbance, and a third group are necessary for happiness. I take it he means that, for example, if we did not all have naturally occurring desires for food and drink, for example, and did not satisfy them on an ongoing basis, then we would not even stay alive. The same would hold for the instinctive desire to withdraw from what is causing us acute bodily pain. We have to have, and to satisfy, these desires or else we will die. If, on the other hand, we did not have naturally arising desires to get out of the heat and cold (or the wet), and did not satisfy them promptly enough, we might very well not die, but we would surely suffer illness or some damage to our bodies that would bring discomforts and debilitations later on. So these are examples of the second way a desire can be necessary: necessary if we are to avoid bodily troubles. What then are the third sort of necessary desires, the ones "necessary for happiness"? Perhaps the bare desire for pleasure and the desire to avoid pain would count. Certainly, if we did not have these desires— as we have seen, Epicurus thinks we all have them by automatic natural endowment, as with the other necessary desires I have mentioned—we would not be able to live happily at all, if to live happily *is* to live pleasantly. Or we might think here of that very refined desire for the pleasant life, defined Epicurus's way—as a life without bodily pain and mental disturbance—that would largely motivate any good Epicurean. That is certainly, on Epicurus's views, absolutely necessary if anyone is to attain true happiness. No one just falls into that condition; given its nature, it requires care and attention on the part of any agent if it is to be achieved. So that might be an instance of a "desire necessary for happiness."

Thus, in general, the necessary desires are ones that we all need to have and need to satisfy—whether to stay alive, or to live without bodily disturbance, or to achieve happiness. There is a further important feature of the necessary desires that Epicurus may have in mind in so denominating them. It is clear straight off that if necessary desires of the first two sorts are completely frustrated for any considerable period of time we inevitably experience pain, even considerable pain (and, perhaps partly in a different way, the same holds good for the desires necessary for happiness). Hunger approaching starvation is extremely, and unavoidably, painful, as is thirst unquenched for long enough, or extended exposure to heat and cold. And if we do not satisfy our desire for Epicurean happiness, or our simple desire for pleasure and to avoid pain, then in those cases as well, we inevitably experience pain. In all these cases, we can do nothing. We do not have the option of somehow learning not to experience the pain of deprivation, if any of the physically necessary desires goes completely frustrated for long enough, and likewise for the desires necessary for happiness. Of course, it might still be possible not to get upset if by chance one does fall into bodily pain, and perhaps even of distracting oneself from noticing it much, or of "counterbalancing" it with memories of pleasant bodily or other experiences in the past. These are among the means that Epicurus cites of remaining completely free of bodily pain, so far as one's overall bodily state goes, even while some pain of that sort may be experienced.[23] In one of the maxims preserved in the collection of *Vatican Sayings* (no. 71), Epicurus says, "One should bring this question to all desires: what will happen to me if what is desired and sought is achieved, and what will happen if it is not?" With necessary desires, the answer to the second question is always (in principle): I will suffer pain, and there is nothing I can do about that. This will not be an optional, self-inflicted pain, but one that the nature of things imposes on me. And in *Principal Doctrine* XXVI (first part) Epicurus by implication characterizes the necessary desires in just those terms: "The desires which do not bring a feeling of pain when not fulfilled are not necessary. . . ." (I will return to the continuation of this maxim below.) At any rate, that is what he is doing if we interpret this as saying that any desire that does not *in the nature of things* have to lead to pain if not fulfilled is not a necessary one; thus the necessary desires as those that do meet this condition: they do bring a feeling of pain when not fulfilled. The reason for adding the qualification "in the nature of things" is that groundless desires, of course, are not necessary, though they do lead to a feeling of pain if not fulfilled. However, as we shall see, in their case it is not the nature of things that leads to this pain, but our own stupidity and obstinacy in forming and retaining such desires in the first place.

Let us, then, turn to the so-called groundless desires. These are described as both unnecessary and unnatural. If we accept the Scholiast's examples, then one can easily see why they are unnecessary. No one has to desire to have a crown awarded him by his fellow-citizens for outstanding service if he is not to die or suffer physical deprivation or if he is to achieve happiness (at least not on Epicurus's theory of happiness). Furthermore, if he should happen to have that desire, he does not have to satisfy it, at the price of inevitably dying or suffering serious bodily harm or being literally barred from all possibility of happiness if he does not. And one can understand

---

[23] See Epicurus's famous deathbed letters in which he claims that that day, despite the awful pain caused by his terminal bladder and intestinal disorders, was his happiest (actually, if he is speaking as an accomplished Epicurean sage, it was his co-happiest: in that case, all his days had been equally happy since he first achieved happiness): these sufferings are "counterbalanced" (*compensabatur*, Cic. *On Ends* II 96) by his memories of philosophical discussions in earlier years—with the effect, I take it, that overall he can say that his bodily state is not one of pain, but one of pleasant painlessness. He experiences the bodily pains from the disease (no one has an option as to that), but in remembering the pleasures of past philosophical discussions or other bodily pleasures (for even the pleasure of philosophical discussion is a pleasure of the exercise of his physical as well as his intellectual capacities) he creates for himself significant bodily pleasures that "counterbalance" them so as to render his overall bodily condition not one of pain, but of pleasure. (See also Diog. L. X 22; Cic. *On Ends* I 57.)

readily enough at least part of why this desire and the other desire the Scholiast mentions, for a memorial statue to be dedicated to you by your city after your death, could be called "groundless" by Epicurus. Once you are dead, he argues, nothing can be either good or bad for you, so it is really and deeply irrational to care about and try to achieve such posthumous recognition: you will not be there to receive the alleged good when it is awarded to you. (Here, and elsewhere in what follows, I restrict myself to explaining Epicurus's reasons for calling his "groundless" desires groundless; I do not mean to suggest that there may not be other reasons—legitimate ones—for having some of these desires than the ones that Epicurus considers and discounts.) And likewise Epicurus thinks it can easily be shown that there simply cannot be good enough reason to live the sort of public life that you would have to live if you were to have any chance of achieving a civic crown: to aim at that is necessarily to give up on your own happiness, and that too is deeply irrational. Thus at least these specific examples of desires of this third class are groundless in the sense that (according to Epicurus's theory) there is never any good reason to desire these particular objects at all. But are all the objects of any and every groundless desire similarly such that Epicurus thinks there is never any good reason at all to desire them? And why are these and other groundless desires also called "unnatural"—in addition to "groundless" and "unnecessary"?

We can hope to answer these questions if we shift for a moment to the remaining class of desires, the natural but not necessary ones. The Scholiast's example here is desire for luxuries of the table. I take it that when he says that these provide variations in pleasure but do not remove the pain (viz., the pain that satisfying the *mere* desire for food removes) he is not meaning to count as luxurious food only food that has no nutritional value and so does not satisfy one's hunger at all. I take him to mean that a natural, nonnecessary desire specifically for eating luxurious foods, or some particular luxurious food, is a desire for variation in one's diet, and not, or not just, for getting rid of hunger. Satisfying such a desire does indeed get rid of hunger, but that is not really what it is a desire for. It is a desire for the particular pleasures of that particular luxurious food, as a specific variation in one's diet. It seems clear that it is to such desires only—natural, but not necessary ones—that Epicurus is referring in *Principal Doctrine* XXVI, the first part of which I quoted above. There he speaks of desires that do not bring a feeling of pain when not fulfilled as not necessary ones. He goes on to say that "the desire for them is easy to dispel when they seem to be hard to achieve or to produce harm." Now this last seems clearly false of the unnatural and *un*necessary desires—the ones that are groundless. The groundless desire for a civic crown or a memorial statue is obviously a persistent, even perhaps an obsessive one; it is not going to be dispelled when the person subject to it sees that it is hard to achieve or even will produce harm if acted upon. If you have such a desire, it rankles and disturbs you to have to forgo or delay acting to satisfy it. But a desire for some particular luxurious food that is a desire simply for the specific pleasures that food brings as a variation of one's diet could very well be easy to dispel if under given circumstances it is seen as hard to achieve or likely to produce harm if indulged. If such circumstances should obtain, there are plenty of other enjoyable foods to eat, and one could sensibly just shift one's attention to some other prandial satisfaction: even, if necessary, to simple bread and water, if that were the only thing securely available at all.

This suggests that there might in fact be two quite different ways of desiring luxurious food, or some particular such food that one had a particular predilection for. One such desire—a desire, for example, for steak, as one of one's favorite foods—would lead one to eat steak in preference to other things if they were all on offer. If, however, steak were not available, well then, no matter, this desire could be easily set aside—dispelled—and some other would take its place: perhaps a desire for lasagna, if that were the thing one most felt like having from among the menu choices offered. Or, if none of one's preferred foods were available, then one would set aside the interest in—desire for—luxurious foods altogether and settle happily for whatever was available that would satisfy one's hunger. One would continue to prefer one or another of one's favored variations of the pleasure of eating, but one would nonetheless readily settle for whatever was available, if it came to that. This sort of desire for steak, as one of one's favorite foods, would be counted by Epicurus as a natural, but of course not necessary, one—it is an instance of the sort of desire for luxurious food that the Scholiast to *Principal Doctrine* XXIX cites to illustrate Epicurus's category of "natural and not necessary" desires. Another way of desiring some particular luxurious food would not be so accommodating as the one just described. We are all familiar with occasions when people throw a fit and fall into a sulk if they were planning on and expecting to have the famous steak dinner at a restaurant only to discover that the kitchen is all out by the time they order. Such a person was desiring the same thing, the same object, as the first person would be desiring, but in a different way. In the latter case, the desire was *not* easy to dispel; the person felt great frustration and disappointment and had a very hard time accepting any of the substitutes. They felt that the meal was ruined, they were stressed out and grumpy and unpleasant the rest of the evening; they remained dissatisfied with the meal they actually had to eat, they continued to feel the effects of a dissatisfied desire for steak for quite some time, even after their hunger had been stilled. They were not desiring steak as a preferred variation on the pleasure of eating but were desiring it in some absolute way, which brooked no substitution.

I think Epicurus is describing this other kind of desire in *Principal Doctrine* XXX; and there he describes it as one due to "groundless opinion"—that is, as a groundless desire. According to what I believe is the best interpretation of some difficult Greek, this maxim says:

Whenever intense effort is present in natural desires which do not lead to pain if they are unfulfilled, these have their origin in groundless opinion; and the reason for their not being dispelled is not their own nature but the groundless opinion of the person in question.[24]

Natural desires that "do not lead to pain if they are unfulfilled" are, as we have seen, the unnecessary ones: the necessary desires inevitably *do* lead to pain if unfulfilled. Given, then, Epicurus's sharp separation of "groundless" from "natural" desires (including natural and unnecessary ones), it seems that the right way to construe this maxim is as follows: Epicurus is saying that what would otherwise have been a natural and unnecessary desire becomes instead a groundless one—one with its origin in groundless opinion—if it is infected with intense effort, that is, with the sort of insistent effort toward its own satisfaction that leads to its not being dispelled if it cannot be fulfilled; and in that case the nature simply of that desire—that is, a desire *for the object in question*—is not responsible for its not being dispelled when it cannot be satisfied (as would indeed be true of a necessary desire simply for food or drink). No, the groundless opinion on the basis of which the person who had the desire formed it bears the responsibility for its not being dispelled if it cannot, or cannot safely, be satisfied.[25] What groundless opinion is this? Clearly not the groundless opinion that the object of the desire—some luxurious food or drink, some particular way of having sex or some particular person to have it with—is something worth having. As we have seen, Epicurus thinks that it is possible to desire luxurious food with a natural, and not a groundless, desire; in setting value on it through having such a natural desire, one must be right that it is of some value. So it is not that there is no good reason for anyone ever to want the object of such desires (as we saw was the basis for the groundlessness of the desire for civic crowns). Here the groundlessness must consist in the fact that the person, in wanting the object, makes the mistake of not wanting it merely as a variation on some acceptable pleasure, but wants it instead in some

---

[24] Translation adapted from Long and Sedley, *The Hellenistic Philosophers*, vol. 1, p. 115 (passage 21E). The Greek reads ἐν αἷς τῶν φυσικῶν ἐπιθυμιῶν, μὴ ἐπ' ἀλγοῦν δὲ ἐπαναγουσῶν ἐὰν μὴ συντελεσθῶσιν, ὑπάρχει ἡ σπουδὴ σύντονος, παρὰ κενὴν δόξαν αὗται γίνονται, καὶ οὐ παρὰ τὴν ἑαυτῶν φύσιν οὐ διαχέονται ἀλλὰ παρὰ τὴν τοῦ ἀνθρώπου κενοδοξίαν. Inwood-Gerson, *The Epicurus Reader*, translate differently.

[25] Long and Sedley's comment on this *Principal Doctrine* offers a different interpretation (*The Hellenistic Philosophers*, vol. II p. 119): In *LM* 127 Epicurus "divided desires initially into natural and empty [i.e., groundless]. We now learn that this division does not exclude a combination of natural and empty: a desire (e.g., for sex) can be natural, yet derive its intensity entirely from empty opinion." Yet the passage does not say that the desires in question derive merely their intensity from empty opinion; it says that the desires themselves derive from that source. I think that clearly means that they are not natural, but rather groundless desires; when in the first part of the passage Epicurus describes a class of desires that are natural but are characterized by intense effort, he means to be describing the transformation of a natural desire for a given object *into* a groundless one for that object.

absolute way. In fact, in the nature of things, Epicurus is saying, these objects *are* desirable, but they are *only* desirable as variations. The mistaken way of desiring them that focuses on them as absolutely to be had, and not to be substituted for if circumstances prevent their satisfaction, makes them groundless desires.

Thus the groundlessness of some groundless desires is simply the result of the groundless belief, on the basis of which they are formed, that the object of the desire is desirable in an absolute way, and not just as a variation on some general type of pleasure, such that one can happily shift to some other variation on that pleasure in case one cannot satisfy it in particular, or for some reason it becomes advisable not to. In these cases it is no part of the basis for claiming them to be groundless that the desired object itself is never, for anyone, something in fact desirable—as presumably is the case for the Scholiast's examples of a civic crown and a memorial statue. In fact, one can assume that there is to be found in those cases, too, this additional sort of groundlessness: the one whose heart is set on a civic crown doubtless is committed to getting it in some absolute way, and not as some easily substitutable-for variation of his pleasure. So it seems that Epicurus's central basis for counting a desire as groundless is its irrational, absolute commitment to obtaining its object, with the consequence that it brings upon the person unnecessary pain when, as must necessarily often happen with such desires, it is not satisfiable. This pain is unnecessary because it was open to the person to desire that same object in a way that would not have involved any such pain; he could have enjoyed it without exposing himself to the risk of painful frustration. Thus the groundlessness of these desires in the end consists in the pointlessness of this self-exposure to the pain of frustration which the nature of these desires itself entails when they go unsatisfied.[26] You can always desire these same things, and get the pleasure of them, altogether without this exposure. And even if on some occasion satisfaction for such a groundless desire does turn out obtainable, anyone who knows the absolute nature of his commitment and is aware of the things that can go wrong and force non-satisfaction, must look forward with anxious uncertainty whenever he sets out to seek to satisfy it. Presumably, then, this unnecessary and irrational opening of oneself to anxiety and the pain of frustration is also Epicurus's basis for calling the groundless desires "unnatural," in addition to groundless and unnecessary. By forming such desires a person is going flatly against the natural order, which establishes the pursuit of pleasure and the *avoidance* of pain as our natural ends—it is totally

---

[26] This seems a better interpretation of the force of *kenai* here than the one Annas gives (*Morality*, p. 190). She thinks that in these contexts "groundless" (or "empty," "futile," "vain," "pointless"—all possible translations for the Greek) means simply false and *harmful* (based on false and harmful opinions—ones that undermine one's happiness); for her the pointlessness consists in the fact that following such desires leads one away from happiness. It is odd to say (merely) that a desire that ruins your happiness is pointless. To me it sounds much worse than that.

unnatural to court the pains of anxiety and frustration in this way. By contrast, the corresponding natural, but not necessary, desire for the same object will count as natural because it is fully in conformity with the natural order in this respect. If one desires it in this other way, one conforms to the natural order, since under favorable conditions one can have the pleasure that the satisfaction of the desire brings, but with absolutely no liability to anxiety, or to frustration in case it cannot be satisfied. If one cannot satisfy it, one just drops it, and since that is what one intends all along to do in such circumstances, there is no basis for anxiety as one looks to the future in pursuit of its satisfaction.

It is sometimes rashly assumed that Epicurus taught, as part of the pursuit of the Epicurean goal of life, that we should limit ourselves only to the necessary desires—that not only are all groundless ones to be eliminated from our lives, but also all the other unnecessary desires, that is, all the desires for variations in our continuing pleasure in the enjoyment of our pain- and distress-free state of mind and body.[27] On this view, Epicurus holds that we should limit ourselves exclusively to bare desires for food and drink, for example, and remain perfectly indifferent as to what we might eat to satisfy naturally arising hunger. This is a bad mistake; once we understand correctly the character of the natural but unnecessary desires and their vast difference from the groundless ones, it is obvious that Epicurus could have no objection whatsoever to anyone's having lots of those (since they cost absolutely nothing in terms of pain, either bodily or mental), and it is also clear how great their value in an Epicurean life might be, by adding some needed spice to the life of pleasure and providing the basis for avoiding the boredom that might otherwise infect it. An Epicurean with varied innocent interests and tastes supported by natural desires for their objects is perfectly willing to forego indulging them and to settle, if circumstances require or favor this, for some less preferred variation—in the knowledge that even the less preferred are sufficient to sustain the continued enjoyment of his pain- and distress-free condition, that is, the highest level of pleasure. Having a more preferred variation does not increase this pleasure. But this does not in the least mean that an Epicurean cannot have any favorite foods and drinks, or favorite ways of experiencing other bodily pleasures, nor that he would not opt to indulge in them, as such, in preference to lower-ranked ones when occasion offers, or try to arrange his life, so far as he reasonably could, so that he will regularly have them on hand when the fancy strikes him. Indeed, it seems that precisely this is what Epicurus says

[27] This is the view of Mitsis; see *Epicurus*, p. 48: "Since some goods may be hard to secure and dependent on chance features of the world, my preferences for the kinetic pleasures associated with such goods would make me more vulnerable" (and so, if I reason correctly according to Epicurean principles, I will not have any such preferences). Mitsis fails to realize that not every type of preference for such goods *does* make me more vulnerable. It is only a groundless type of desire for such a thing, not a natural desire for it, that adds to any vulnerability to distress or disappointment or anxiety on my part.

in *Letter to Menoeceus*, 130–31 when he explains the Epicurean commitment to self-sufficiency:

> We believe that self-sufficiency is a great good, not in order to live off little in all circumstances but so that if we do not have much we can content ourselves with little, being genuinely convinced that those enjoy luxuries with the greatest pleasure who need them least.

This clearly expresses a preference for good things to eat over mere bread and rude cheese, but the sort of conditional preference that goes along with the ability and willingness smoothly and happily to eat the bread and cheese if that is all that is readily available. It certainly does not express indifference over what one eats, the total absence of any preferences in this regard—as if, faced with finer foods farther down the table requiring that one get up to serve oneself, but bread, rude cheese, and water set immediately before you, you would, if an Epicurean, always content yourself with the latter.

IV VARIETIES OF PLEASURE AND THE HIGHEST PLEASURE

Accordingly, when Epicurus says, in *Principal Doctrine* XVIII that "As soon as the feeling of pain produced by want is removed, pleasure in the flesh will not increase but is only varied," this should not be taken as dismissive or deprecatory of such variation. Variation has a crucial and central, positive role to play in the articulation of Epicurean hedonism. So far I have been speaking mostly of the "bodily pleasures" and the ways in which Epicurus valued variation in those pleasures and the associated development of a rich schedule of "natural" desires for differently interesting, "luxurious" foods and drinks and and, in general, for the varied sights, tastes, smells, touches, and sounds that can give sensory pleasures in the satisfaction of natural bodily appetites. But Epicurus's distinction between "unnecessary" desires that are natural and groundless ones, and the possibilities for enriching an Epicurean life through the variations that the optional natural desires can bring, have a much wider application. We should recall that according to Epicurus the correct goal of life is to enjoy without interruption a pain-free bodily condition and a distress-free mental one. This, according to him, is the highest pleasure, a condition of pleasurable consciousness that cannot be hedonically heightened, though it can be varied.[28] So far I have concentrated on only a narrow range of ways in which, according to Epicurus, the pleasure in this condition can be varied by the gratification, when circumstances permit, of

---

[28] As mentioned above, I am leaving aside for present purposes Epicurus's reasons for so regarding the pleasure given by this pain-free condition. Note, however, that in saying that pleasure cannot be increased beyond the point reached when one is in this condition he does not at all mean that no more intense pleasure can be felt. Intensity is not the only, or, Epicurus would insist, the correct way of measuring comparative quantity of pleasure at a moment or a time. See *PD* III, Cic., *On Ends* I 38.

optional natural desires. But we should notice that Epicurus's theory provides for a much wider, indeed essentially open-ended, range of similar variations. (I postpone for the moment certain difficulties that our ancient sources cause us in understanding how Epicurus can have thought that the pleasure one is experiencing in, for example, gratifying a liking for lobster might simply be the pleasure that one would anyhow have experienced simply from being in the pain- and distress-free condition—but "varied" now in some particular ways due to the special tastes and so forth of the meal.)

If the approved pleasures of eating and drinking "luxuriously" can be regarded as variations on the pain- and distress-free condition of mind and body, then so can similar pleasures in almost any other activity or object. Epicurus, as we have seen, emphasized particularly the pleasures of philosophical discussion, but equally pleasures in all sorts of pastimes, intellectual and nonintellectual alike, would count, provided that the interest in them was of the correct—optional and substitutable—sort. Thus the pleasures of bridge, playing or listening to music, athletic exercises, reading novels, doing crossword puzzles, cooking gourmet meals, gossiping with one's friends, growing and tending a garden, throwing darts in contests at the pub, spending a day at the beach—and millions of other such ways of investing one's energies and spending one's time—could have a focal place in some Epicurean's life, depending on his or her own personal experience and natural affinities. On Epicurus's view a person needs lots of things that he or she takes an interest in and enjoys for their particular pleasurable qualities, so that if you cannot occupy your time pleasurably in one of them, there will always be another to take its place. He seems to think, and quite reasonably so, that only in this way will a person be able constantly to enjoy the pleasure of the pain- and distress-free condition of mind and body. Otherwise, boredom (a distressing mental state) might set in, depriving one of that condition.

Here we should recall the special emphasis Epicurus places on the value of personal friendships.[29] Presumably one important ground for this evaluation is the fact that friendships are an especially fruitful context for developing and sharing interests, and engaging one's developed capacities for such enjoyments with others who value them equally, and in the same way as such an Epicurean would value his favored pursuits. No doubt one way to arrange one's life so as to find frequent and regular opportunities to meet with other like-minded friends and indulge one's fancies would be by moving into an Epicurean compound, and of course that is precisely what so many ancient Epicureans actually did. It may be worth adding that Epicurus's approval of the natural but unnecessary desires and his theory about the importance of having developed capacities for varied pleasures also allow him to support the constituent activities of friendship themselves—the ones in which the friends' caring for one another and wanting to spend time

---

[29] See *PD* XXVII, XXVIII; *Vatican Sayings* 52, 78.

together "for one another's own sake" find their expression. Furthermore, it seems plausible to say, these mutual attitudes of mutual regard and interest in one another "for one another's own sake" open up to a person forms of active engagement with another person (in sharing in leisure-time activities, discussions on daily events, mutual trust, and so forth) which have specially complex and interesting features that would not be available in the absence of these attitudes. In that case Epicurus can say that the enjoyment of the resulting special pleasures gives a sufficient motive for developing and maintaining true friendships of that sort. If so, it would be a plain mistake to object that Epicureans who form friendships "for the sake of pleasure" are really no true friends because they subordinate their interest in their friend's good to their interest in pleasure: on the contrary, the specific pleasure they pursue in their friendships and the activities of friendship, as such, is the pleasure *of* taking an interest in the friend's good for his or her own sake, as that is combined with the pleasure of the specific activities that the friends engage in together in maintaining their friendship.[30]

I have spoken of the fulfillments of all these specialized natural desires (the ones for "luxurious" sensory pleasures as well as the others) as variations of and on the basic pleasure that constitutes the goal of life on Epicurus's theory. There is, however, a difficulty here that we must address before we can rest content with this interpretation. It is well known that Epicurus drew a distinction between what he called pleasure "in movement" or "(depending) on movement" and "katastematic" pleasure (for the moment I leave the Greek untranslated, only slightly anglicized).[31] We have the evidence of Cicero as well as Plutarch that the highest good, according to Epicurus, is the constant enjoyment over one's life of katastematic pleasure—the pleasure given by a distress- and pain-free condition; pleasure "in movement" is illustrated by sensory bodily pleasures when the senses are titillated in one

---

[30] It is possible that this explanation and defense of friendship lies behind the first of the three Epicurean accounts that Cicero provides (*On Ends* I 66–68). Unfortunately, as the existence of the two other accounts (I 69–70) seems to show, later Epicureans did not always understand or appreciate its viability within Epicurean hedonism. Neither, of course, did Cicero.

[31] This terminology does not occur in any of Epicurus's surviving *Letters* or the *Principal Doctrines* or *Vatican Sayings*, and the distinction itself is at best presupposed, in texts of Epicurus where some of its consequences are noted. However, Diogenes Laertius quotes him as using this terminology in *On Choices* to distinguish two classes of pleasure: "Freedom from mental turmoil and freedom from bodily pain are *katastematic* pleasures; while joy and delight are seen in activity depending on movement." (I translate the text of the mss. at the end of the sentence; Long is possibly right to emend so that we get this sense: " . . . are regarded as activities depending on movement." See Long and Sedley, 21R.) In the same paragraph, Diogenes quotes Epicurus's close associate Metrodorus as speaking together of "the pleasure depending on movement and that which is *katastematic*." So there seems no doubt that both this terminology and the distinction itself go back to Epicurus. In the passages just cited we find "on movement" (*kata kinēsin*) rather than "in movement" (*en kinēsei*) for the first class of pleasures (and see Athenaeus XII, 546e-f, frg. 413 U). So that, rather than "in movement" (so Diogenes Laertius himself at the beginning of X 136), may have been the standard Epicurean terminology.

way or another.[32] Now, for purposes of criticism, Cicero makes Epicurus's distinction one between two *genera* of (alleged) pleasure—in fact he is talking about two totally different things which, Cicero argues, he arbitrarily and unjustifiably decides to treat as two species of the same broader kind, pleasure.[33] In fact, according to Cicero, we have on the one hand a "sweet and exhilarating movement of the sense" (*On Ends* II 8)—this is what everyone knows is in fact the only thing referred to by the words for "pleasure" in the different languages[34]—and on the other hand, some totally different thing, the absence from the mind and body of pain and distress. We are entitled, as I have already argued, to set aside Cicero's insistence that Epicurus's second class of "pleasures" is just a fraudulent way of referring to the pain-free state, as such; it is instead a positive state of consciousness. If, however, we continue to use Cicero's two-genus interpretation of Epicurus's distinction—introduced in the first place for its polemical effects, and therefore quite legitimately open to suspicion—then we (and Epicurus) face difficulties. Cicero tells us, quite believably, that it is by pleasures "in movement" that a happy man is to vary his "katastematic" pleasure. This has to be understood as the actual variation *of* that pleasure itself, not as the addition of some pleasures of one kind by bringing them into the presence of pleasure of another kind. On the latter view, Epicurus could speak of a person's overall state of mind as being varied by the presence of the pleasures "in movement," but that is not in fact what he does say: he says that the pleasure in the pain-free condition, itself, gets varied.[35] But this obviously makes no sense if he regarded pleasure "in movement" and katastematic pleasure as two distinct species of phenomenon belonging to a common genus. In fact,

---

[32] See Plutarch, *A Pleasant Life Impossible*, chs. 4–5, 1089d, 1090a-b.

[33] Perhaps cunningly, he has his Epicurean spokesman, Torquatus, himself adopt this way of viewing the distinction (*On Ends* II 9), when pressed by Cicero himself to say how freedom from bodily pain can *be* pleasure: it is a "different kind" (*aliud genus*) of pleasure from the kind we experience when we enjoy drinking while thirsty, says Torquatus. Notably, in book I (37, 39), when Torquatus is made to expound this part of the Epicurean ethical theory, he never uses any such terminology and never says anything other than that each is a pleasure, while the second is the highest pleasure. In book I, as well, as we have seen, he identifies the highest pleasure, not flatly with absence of pain and absence of all mental distress, but with a state of consciousness that that absence produces; yet in book II, immediately before the passage just cited, Torquatus in effect obliges Cicero in setting up his target for criticism by now flatly insisting that "freedom from pain" has the same force (*vis*) or means the same as "pleasure."

[34] It is of course not at all clear that this is true of either Greek or English; it may, however, come close to the truth for Latin *voluptas*.

[35] See the last sentence of *On Ends* I 38, and II 10 (also II 75). In I 38 it seems particularly clear (note the singular noun *voluptas* in referring to what gets varied—by contrast with II 10) that the doctrine as Cicero understands it is that the pleasure that results when we are completely free from pain and distress is the very pleasure that gets varied in the experience of the pleasures of movement. This is confirmed by what Epicurus himself says in *PD* XVIII, where it is *the* pleasure in the flesh that increases as far as the removal of pain but thereafter can only be varied; see also the scholiast to XXIX, quoted above.

it seems clear, Epicurus's distinction between pleasure in movement and katastematic pleasure was not a distinction of pleasures into two kinds at all. Instead, Epicurus thought there is a single state of consciousness—pleasure—which, however, comes in connection with importantly distinct, different conditions of the body and mind.[36] This pleasure can be greater and less, better and worse of its kind, but it is the same phenomenon, and the distinction between pleasure "in movement" and katastematic pleasure is a distinction based on the objects or causes of that phenomenon under different conditions, not a distinction of kind at all within the phenomenon in question, itself. Once we see this, we can find in Epicurus's theory an account of the variation of katastematic pleasure, and the connection between the two classes of pleasure, that makes a great deal of sense.

Before proceeding, we need to correct some bad effects of Cicero's translation of Epicurus's term *katastematic*, in which he has been followed by modern translators. Cicero translates (or paraphrases) this by *"stabilis"* or *"in stabilitate"* or *"stans"* and he also sometimes uses the noun *"status"* in connection with the condition of no pain or distress.[37] So Rackham in the Loeb edition often translates Cicero's Latin by "static": Epicurus's katastematic pleasure becomes thus a "static" pleasure, or one (so Hicks in the Loeb edition of Diogenes Laertius, now translating the Greek term itself at X 136) "which is in a state of rest." Long and Sedley in their important collection of ancient materials on the Hellenistic philosophers follow suit (as do most other twentieth-century translators and commentators): katastematic pleasure for them is "static" pleasure, by neat contrast with the pleasure "in" or "depending on" movement, which is "kinetic." In fact, it appears that Epicurus probably intended to indicate by this term that this was the pleasure given simply by the settled condition or constitution (*katastēma*) of the organism (mind and body) when it is in a state of natural and healthy, self-maintaining equilibrium—that is, when it is not suffering any disturbing and potentially destructive departure from that naturally self-maintaining equilibrium state. Epicurus thought this would be a tranquil and stable condition, but his term *katastēmatikos* meant "of or belonging to the natural constitution"—not "static" or "inactive" or "quiet."[38] If we notice this and keep it in mind, we should have no difficulty understanding that the pleasure we get from the experience of our organism when it is in

---

[36] See *PD* XVIII, cited in the previous note, among other places.

[37] For these terms see *On Ends* II 9, 16, 28, 31, 32, 75.

[38] One should note that Plutarch, *A Pleasant Life Impossible*, end of ch. 4, 1089d, mostly describes the condition of the flesh that according to Epicurus gives rise to the highest pleasure using the Greek term *eustatheia* and cognates—Greek that could very properly be translated by Cicero's *stabilitas* and *stabilis*. But he refers there once (and a second time in ch. 5, at 1090a), more fully, to a *katastēma eustathes sarkos* (stable constitution of the flesh). Here we see precisely the distinction I insist on preserving. In a discussion of an Aulus Gellius passage whose language is similar to Plutarch's, Jeffrey Purinton rightly also insists on preserving this distinction ("Epicurus on the *telos*," 296–97).

this tip-top condition might not necessarily be a static, inactive, so to speak drugged and passive one at all. In fact, the terms of "katastematic" and "in movement" or "on movement" refer to the source of the respective pleasures, not to the pleasures' own inherent characteristics. As we should now see, Epicurus might very well have thought that in order to experience our organism (including in that, of course, our minds) as it is when in this tip-top condition we need to exercise some or other of our various capacities of mind and body: it is only in such activity that we can experience it at all, or at least experience it fully.

The pleasures in movement, then, with which we vary our constitutional pleasure when in the pain- and distress-free state, will be any of the pleasant activities—sensory ones like eating, drinking, or even sex, or activities based in the body in a more complex way, such as engaging in philosophical discussions, or playing bridge, or taking care of an ill friend—which, in themselves, involve movement and active employment of one's bodily and mental faculties.[39] But these activities give rise to and color in their particular ways the same state of consciousness that Epicurus can describe as "steady" and "stable" since it comes ultimately from the healthy constitution being activated in them. At the same time, other pleasures of movement can be experienced even when the constitution is in a debilitated condition, for example when in extreme thirst or hunger we throw down food or drink, or when we have self-tormenting desires that lead to great discharges of energy in their fulfillment. These are pleasures in bodily movements of a somewhat different sort from those of eating and drinking or any of the other pleasures of the stably constituted natural condition, and they do not, of course, vary any constitutional pleasure, since the person experiencing

[39] Notice that on his own theories Epicurus is entitled to claim, as he does, that all pleasures except the pleasures of memory and anticipation are to be counted as bodily, in a broad sense, and that there *are* no other specifically mental pleasures. See Cic., *On Ends* I 55, *Tusculan Disputations* III 41–42; and notice that the remembered pleasures that Cicero reports Epicurus delighted himself with on his last day—all allegedly bodily pleasures, since the pleasures of memory are declared to be all recollections of previous bodily ones—were pleasures in philosophical discussion (see *On Ends* II 96). Epicurus does not mean to say that all bodily pleasures are pleasures of the senses in the limited way that eating when hungry or sex are; any pleasure whose real source is the exercise of our bodily powers, including the ordinary powers of mind that are involved in reading, following an argument, listening to music, playing bridge and so on, is a bodily pleasure. We must bear in mind that Epicurus was a thoroughgoing materialist, who denied firmly that there is any special, nonmaterial mental substance. When he denied that there are any specifically mental pleasures (other than those from the memory or anticipation of the pleasures of the body, construed thus broadly), he meant that there could be no pleasures coming from some exercise of any such mental substance. Plato and Aristotle would be among the opponents whom Epicurus would have in view here. Thus for Epicurus any actual mental pleasures one might get, for example, from working on an arithmetical problem or appreciating a good philosophical argument or contemplating a philosophical truth, would really be pleasures in the use of our body-based mind—they would not result from some specially wonderful access to some higher realm through some "divine spark" of a higher mind that we happen to be endowed with.

them has lost or never attained that stable constitution in the first place.[40] In both cases, however, the pleasure experienced is the same mental phenomenon (even if mixed with pain in the one case but not in the other), and the same phenomenon that is given in its highest form simply and directly by the pain- and distress-free constitution of our organism.

I have argued that Epicurus was a hedonist in the theory of rational choice and decision only, and that he did not also adopt a hedonist theory about all human beings' actual desires, decisions, and actions. I have also explained his theory of the three sorts of desires that human beings actually can have, and I have shown how it combines with his theory that the uninterrupted awareness over a lifetime of a pain- and distress-free constitution is the highest good so as to give an extremely, and perhaps unexpectedly, interesting overall theory of the best human life. One begins to see, perhaps, how Epicurus's moral philosophy could have appealed as widely as it apparently did in antiquity, at least for a certain period.[41]

[40] Thus I agree with Long and Sedley, *Hellenistic Philosophers*, I, 123, that we have no good reason to think Cicero's testimony is mistaken when he says (*On Ends* II 9) that the pleasure of quenching one's thirst (and so getting a pleasure while removing a pain) is a pleasure in movement.

[41] The first version of this chapter was prepared for a Werkmeister Conference at Florida State University, March 1997. I benefited from the discussion at the conference in preparing the final version, as I also did from discussion in subsequent departmental colloquia at McGill and Stanford Universities and the City University of New York Graduate Center.

CHAPTER TWENTY-THREE

Greek Philosophers on Euthanasia and Suicide

THE WORD *euthanasia* is not always used and understood in the same way. Nor, for that matter, is *suicide*. The first thing to do in approaching the Greek philosophers' views about euthanasia and suicide is, therefore, to be clear about the senses of these words in which there existed for the philosophers of Greece corresponding moral categories. Which of the different kinds of action that might be called, or have by someone or other in modern discussions been called, euthanasia or suicide seemed to the Greek philosophers sufficiently interesting or problematic, from the moral point of view, so that they developed lines of argument and analysis in order to accommodate them? And which of these did they group together sufficiently closely for it to make sense to speak of Greek views on the morality of euthanasia or suicide? The answers to these questions will not just help us to avoid misunderstanding, by making it clear in what senses of these words it is acceptable to speak of Greek philosophers' views on euthanasia and suicide. They will also constitute an important first step in the substantial characterization of the Greek tradition in moral theory: one learns a lot about the character of any moral theory by seeing how, given that theory and its intellectual resources, the different kinds of human actions are arranged in significant groupings and which ones of these groupings are seen to call for philosophical comment.

I

Neither Greek nor Latin has a word that could be translated either "euthanasia" or "suicide." To be sure, our word *euthanasia* is borrowed from the Greek, but the Greek word (a coinage of the Hellenistic period) means simply a good death—an easy, painless, happy one or (possibly—so Cicero in *ad Atticum* 16, 7, 3) a fine and noble one. In fact, it was with the meaning of an easy, painless, happy death that the word *euthanasia* first entered English: the O.E.D. cites it in this sense as early as 1646 (1633 for the variant *euthanasy*), and it apparently continued to be used exclusively in that sense (with metaphorical extensions) until the 1860s. The earliest citation the O.E.D. gives for "euthanasia" in the current (and now-dominant) sense of the action of inducing a gentle and easy death, especially as an act of mercy to those suffering from incurable and extremely painful diseases, is taken from W.E.H. Lecky, *A History of European Morals from Augustus to Charlemagne*, published in 1869.

Our word *suicide* is apparently a 17th-century formation on Latin roots, but classical Latin knows no such word. Classical authors have to resort to one or another of a set of noun- and verb-phrases that were in fairly standard use to refer to the act of intentionally killing oneself (likewise for the person who does it).[1] So does classical Greek, though there existed in later usage an adjective *autothanatos* (dying by one's own hand), and another, *biaiothanatos* (dying a violent death), applied especially to suicides. Both in nonphilosophical usage in Greek and Latin and (as we shall see) in philosophers' discussions of suicide, what gets counted as a suicide is always a death that a person both intended and brought about by some action of his own that was aimed, at least proximately, at bringing that death about. Cases, including some that might be described as "self-sacrificial," in which the agent knowingly risks death, even where the subjective probability of death amounts to virtual certainty, because he finds his own death, if that should in fact eventuate, an acceptable price to pay for the attainment of the goal being pursued, are not in Greek or Latin usage, or in the philosophers' discussions, grouped together with these intentional self-killings. So for our purposes these should not be described as suicides. This may seem (and is, in my opinion) natural enough not to call for special notice; but since in current discussions one sometimes finds the word *suicide* used, presumably under the influence, direct or indirect, of Durkheim, in such a way as to cover these willing self-sacrifices, as well as the cases where one's own death was itself actually intended, it is worthwhile making note explicitly of the restricted scope it is appropriate to give the word *suicide* in discussion of the classical philosophers' views. Hereafter, by *suicide* I mean a person's death both intended by him and brought about by some action of his own that was aimed, at least proximately, at bringing it about (or, of course, the person who brings about his death in this way).

II

There existed in Latin and Greek, then, standard ways of referring to suicide, so understood, and philosophers of all periods, beginning with fifth-century Pythagoreans, had things to say about it. For euthanasia the case is different. Not only is there no single word in Greek or Latin that means (roughly) causing someone else's death in order to free him from an incurable, extremely painful, or permanently debilitating disease or irreversible such

---

[1] For the action, Cicero writes *mors voluntaria*, e.g., at *Ad familiares* (*Letters to His Friends*) 7, 3, 3, and *De finibus* III 61, and *mortem* (or *necem*) *sibi consciscere*, at *Brutus* 43; in discussing philosophical, especially Stoic, views about suicide he usually writes "*e vita excedere*" (or similar), translating the Greek circumlocution *heauton exagein ek tou biou* favored by Stoic writers in this context. Standard classical Latin phrases like "*vim* (or *manus*) *sibi* (or *suae vitae*) *adferre* (or *inferre*)" lay special emphasis on suicides involving a violent attack on one's own life, by stabbing or by poison. Similar terminology is used in Greek.

condition; there is not even a standard phrase in general use, comparable to our "mercy-killing," having this meaning. Nor do any of the Greek systems of philosophical ethics seem to have selected precisely *this* kind of action for special consideration or comment. Probably this is partly to be explained by the fact that in antiquity people must have been fairly acutely aware of the uncertainty, given their current medical knowledge, of any judgment of incurability or imminent death, so that the conditions in which one might have found euthanasia a reasonable or even a mandatory course of action might have been so relatively rare that such actions either did not occur very often or, when they did, might have seemed aberrations that invited no special philosophical attention. No doubt religious prohibitions against the killing of human beings by private persons, backed by the threat of pollution and its ill effects on the killer, played a role, too.

But more needs to be said. For although there is, so far as I am aware, no discussion in an ancient philosophical text of the morality of killing, or allowing to die, persons who are incurably ill and wish (or may be presumed to wish) to die, Plato, in a well-known passage of the *Republic*, emphatically defends rules for the practice of medicine that would require some who are incurably ill not to be medically treated but instead allowed to die—without regard to their wishes (explicit or presumed) in the matter. In defending these rules Plato in effect applies a broader principle of social policy which selects as relevant features of the sick person's predicament not the pain caused by the disease, or the unpleasantness of the available medical treatment, or his own reflective assessment of the acceptability or supportability of continued life under the circumstances—the considerations we would look for in a case of euthanasia—but his inability, if treated and so kept alive, to continue to live the sort of full, active life devoted to socially useful employment that his nature and talents have previously suited him for. In so conceiving the issue, Plato places these persons and the question how they are to be dealt with in a broader category—one which includes, for example, defective new-borns, about whom parallel questions can be raised, and for whom, on fundamentally the same ground, Aristotle in the *Politics* defends similar treatment.[2] Thus, where Plato does approach most closely what for us would be potential candidates for euthanasia, his discussion makes it plain that he is not conceiving them so. This point is important enough to make it worthwhile to look closely at what Plato says about these cases.

In the part of the *Republic* in question (III, 405a–410a), Socrates is

---

[2] At *Politics* VII, 1335b19–26, adopting the Spartan practice of having new-borns examined by magistrates to determine whether they are well-formed and fit enough to be allowed to live, Aristotle says that in the ideal city there should be a law that no deformed child (*pepērō-menon*) will be brought up. He gives no detailed justification for this law, but presumably it rests on basically the same ground as Plato's rules for the practice of medicine: allegedly, the congenitally deformed are (known to be) permanently debarred from developing the sort of full, active life in living which a human being's good consists.

discussing what the practice of medicine will be like in the ideal city he is constructing together with Glaucon and Adeimantus. He insists that originally, with the first sons of Asclepius, who learned the practice of medicine directly from their father, the aim of medical treatment was limited to repairing damage due to wounds and ridding patients of "annual" diseases, i.e., maladies (especially, no doubt, infectious ones) that people are especially subject to at particular times of the year (405c8–9). Systemic disorders which if untreated would eventually lead to death but which 4th-century doctors could control so as to prolong the patient's life, but only by elaborate regimens involving special diets, special forms of exercise, prescribed periods of rest, etc., were not treated by the original Asclepiads. Socrates approves of this ancient scheme and adopts it for the practice of medicine in his ideal city.[3] His objection to such treatment of the systemic disorders is that it requires the patient to give himself over substantially and permanently to the management of his disease and so, in large measure, to give up the normal productive pursuits that characterized his prior life.[4] Such a person, he says (407e2, 408b2–3), would benefit (*lusitelein*) neither himself nor other people by his mode of life; the treatment would lengthen his life, but also make it a very bad one (cf. 407d6–7), and it is an abuse of the art of medicine to use it for that end. He should be allowed to die a natural death untreated.

Plato's policy here invites several comments. First, it clearly rests on the central contention of the *Republic*, that the sort of life that is in actual fact best for each individual person is one so organized that the good of other people in his community is significantly advanced by it. Being just, or, failing that, living justly, is a paramount good for any human being, and living

---

[3] There seems no reason to doubt Socrates' seriousness in his prescriptions here; they follow quite clearly and directly from the overall theory of human good to which Socrates is committed in the *Republic*. Shorey's talk of "exaggeration" and "satire" (*What Plato Said*, p. 220) and his claim of the "humor" of the whole passage (*Republic*, vol. I, pp. 272, 276, n. *ad* 405d, 406e) should not mislead us, as they perhaps misled Shorey himself, into thinking that Socrates is only adopting a salutary pose here: there is (*pace Republic*, vol. I, p. 273 *ad* 406a) no discrepancy between Socrates' rejection of dietary regimens here and Plato's acceptance of them in *Timaeus* 89c, since the *Tim.* approves diet as the most effective means of *ridding* oneself of disease (cf. 89a5–6: diet is to be preferred to drugs as a means of purifying and restoring the constitution of the body), not as an acceptable way of prolonging a diseased existence.

[4] Socrates does not seem to recognize systemic disorders that could be managed effectively by less disruptive and intrusive regimens than those he objects to. But since his grounds for objecting to the disruptive and intrusive ones would not extend to prolonging the lives of sufferers from disorders that could be managed without forcing them to devote substantial amounts of their time and energy to the management of their diseases, Shorey is wrong to say that here Socrates austerely rejects "whatever goes beyond the training and care that will preserve the health of a normal body" (*ad* 407b). On the contrary, it is right to infer that he would have no objection to medical treatment for people whose diseases could be managed by not very intrusive and disruptive regimens: one thinks perhaps of insulin-and-diet treatment of diabetics.

justly requires living in such a way as to advance the good of others in the community. The patient Socrates describes has to abandon permanently those activities in which at once his own good in large part consists and the good of others is advanced, and that is what Socrates thinks justifies saying that such a person's life is of no benefit either to himself or to others. From the point of view of his own theory of the human good, Plato is not guilty of heartlessly requiring the death of people who are no longer, through no fault of their own, useful to society: the requirement is imposed equally, in fact primarily, for the good of the sick person himself.

But second, in accord with his conviction that what is good or bad for a person is an objective matter, to be determined by studying the facts of his case, the patient's wishes need not be consulted, and Socrates nowhere in the passage so much as mentions them. One who understands in what his good consists and has proper control over his desires will not want to have his life prolonged; for others, persuasion and, in any event, gentleness will be appropriate, but continued protestation will be unavailing. People who have fallen incurably ill in this sort of way will be allowed to die for their own good, whether they recognize their death as a good or not.

Third, it is important to notice that the treatments Socrates objects to immediately and necessarily deprive the patient not just of continued application to his previous productive life-pursuits but pretty well of *any* productive life at all. That is because, as Socrates describes these cases, the patient, in order to prolong his life, has to devote most of his time that might have been available for productive activity of one sort or another to staying alive: his time is simply preempted by the management of his disorder. The remedies are in this way immediately and necessarily self-defeating, if the purpose of a remedy is to restore to someone a life that he will be free to make some or other use of. This means that Socrates' policy would not have as a natural extension a rule that persons who have life-threatening accidents that one knows will result, even if treated, in their inability to return to their former work and other usual pursuits should not be ministered to.[5] In such a case the medical treatment would have a limited duration, after which the patient would be free, though with diminished capacities, to find something productive to do with his life, and even if it might seem quite certain, for one reason or another, that a given patient would not in fact succeed in finding anything useful to do, nothing in Socrates' remarks suggests that a doctor, or anyone else, should be qualified to opt for "euthanasia" in such a case.[6]

[5] Note that at 405c8–9, in characterizing the ancient Asclepiads' practice of medicine, Socrates cites the treatment of wounds as one of the legitimate aims of medicine; there is no suggestion that a doctor would refuse to treat a treatable wound just because, in his judgment or in actual fact, the patient, though recovered, would not be able to lead a socially useful life.

[6] I use the word "euthanasia," in quotation marks, here advisedly. In standard contemporary usage the word is, I take it, applied only when the agent acts upon the wishes, express or presumed, of the patient to die, and for the sake of the patient's own good—not, as in the

Fourth, it is perhaps worth adding that throughout his discussion Socrates seems to be considering only the treatment of persons in youth or mid-life. Elderly people who have lived past the time when active pursuits in the community's interest are in any event expected of them would not come under the provisions of Socrates' rule. For all he says here, doctors might be permitted to prolong the lives of elderly, retired persons, even by intrusive regimens that would not be permitted under the rule for people at other times of life. In Plato's republic, such persons, of whatever class, are due honor and respect, and retain their place in the community as members of the household (or its equivalent for guardians and rulers) valued for their past services and for their experience. The intrusive regimes that would undermine the lives of persons of other ages and social roles would not necessarily do so for these members of the community. Accordingly, the rationale Socrates uses to justify withholding medical treatment in the case of younger people would not apply to the very aged.

In this, as in other aspects of his social and political theory, Plato's concern is to arrange things so that people are really made better off, that is, are enabled and required to live so that they achieve what are in *fact* the best possible lives, the ones that are the best possible for them personally. Since what is good and what is bad for a person are objective questions, there is in general no reason to be guided by people's wishes in the application of social policies to them; a person's wishes are no reliable indication of what is in fact best for him overall. Hence in his prescriptions for the practice of medicine Plato makes no reference to consulting the wishes of the patient, but only to the actual, objective quality of his subsequent life if it should be prolonged. This means that what his rules provide for is euthanasia only in an extended, even somewhat Pickwickian, sense. Neither he nor any other Greek philosopher ever discusses euthanasia in our contemporary sense of the word.

III

With suicide things are quite different. From very early times Greek philosophers found occasion to discuss the rightness or wrongness, the appropriateness and rational acceptability, of suicide. In the *Phaedo*, that most

---

case envisaged (but rejected) here, partly because the patient has ceased to engage in any employment useful to the community. It is worth noting however that H. J. Rose (a classical scholar) actually defines euthanasia in such a way that the future usefulness of a person's life would be a prominent consideration in acts of euthanasia: "Euthanasia may be defined as the doctrine or theory that in certain circumstances, when, owing to disease, senility, or the like, a person's life has permanently ceased to be either agreeable or useful, the sufferer should be painlessly killed, either by himself or by another" ("Euthanasia"). Was Rose, self-consciously or not, showing the influence of this discussion in Plato, or of (what he took to be) Greek attitudes? (It was, perhaps, knowledge of Greek that led him here also to classify at least some suicides as special cases of euthanasia.)

Pythagorean of his dialogues, Plato has Socrates sympathetically report the views on suicide of Philolaus, an important fifth-century member of the Pythagorean brotherhood, about whom much was written in later antiquity but, unfortunately, not much was known (*Phdo.* 61b–62c). Diogenes Laertius VIII 85, reports that Philolaus wrote a single "book," and other evidence strongly implies that this was the earliest published writing by a Pythagorean; Pythagoras and Pythagoreans before Philolaus relied exclusively on secret, oral communication. However, Socrates' way of reporting Philolaus's views on suicide indicates that his knowledge of them was based on reports of what Philolaus had said in lectures or discussions (cf. 61d9), and not on anything in his book; and that the book contained nothing about suicide is confirmed by the fact that later Greek commentators on the *Phaedo* are unable to cite anything from what they knew as Philolaus's book to confirm or elaborate Socrates' report.

Interpreted narrowly, all Socrates says is that Philolaus maintained that it was not right to kill oneself (61c10, d6–7). He does not clearly attribute to Philolaus any reason for this prohibition; he goes on to suggest a reason that might actually support it, but this seems rather to be his own suggestion, presumably based on Pythagorean ideas but not reporting Philolaus's actual argument. It is noteworthy that Cebes, who admits to having heard Philolaus speak on this subject, is fairly emphatic that he has not heard from Philolaus or anyone else anything very clear about these matters (61d8, e8–9). But the rationale Socrates provides does cohere well with other Pythagorean ideas,[7] and it makes good sense of Socrates' reference to Philolaus to suppose that he means to be giving Philolaus's, or anyhow a Pythagorean, justification of the prohibition. But whether the justification of the prohibition on suicide that Socrates proposes in the *Phaedo* is a pre-Platonic Pythagorean one, or merely Plato's own suggestion, its importance for later discussions of suicide can hardly be exaggerated. Socrates first (62b2–6) reports a theory (*logos*) he says is passed around in secret, as was typically reported of Pythagorean doctrines, that human beings live in a kind of "guard-post" (*phroura*), so

---

[7] See especially Iamblichus, *Vita Pythagorae* 86 (Diels-Kranz 58C, vol. I, p. 465.5–6): one ought to beget children, for it is our duty to leave behind us other people to worship the gods—a piece of Pythagorean oral teaching apparently adopted and adapted by Plato in *Laws* VI, 773e. On this see Burkert, *Lore and Science*, p. 171. Reference is also sometimes made (e.g., by Rose, "Euthanasia") to the Pythagorean idea that a soul's embodiment is a punishment by God for sins it committed in a past life, so that suicide would be an offense against justice (as well, of course, as perfectly futile, since it would be an additional sin for which an extension of the period of embodiment would be the expected penalty). It is true that Philolaus is quoted (by Clement of Alexandria *Stromateis* III 17 = Diels-Kranz 44 frag. 14) as having written that souls are buried in bodies as punishment, and that Athenaeus attributes to one "Euxitheos the Pythagorean" the thought that because that is so suicide is wrong and will call down further punishment on the offender; but this reasoning is not attested for Philolaus. Whether one finds some such line of thought in or lying behind the *Phaedo* passage will depend on how one interprets Socrates' reference at 62b to the "guard-post" in which human beings are supposedly placed: is this a post in which we are *under* guard (in effect, therefore, in a kind of prison), or one where we are *serving* as guards (so Cicero interpreted it, cf. *De senectute* 73)?

that one must not (by committing suicide) "release oneself from (*heauton luein ek*) it and run away." It is not perfectly clear whether this guard-post is supposed to be a place where human beings serve as guards, keeping some kind of watch on behalf of the gods and under their direction, so that suicide is assimilated to desertion from one's battle-station, or a place, something like a prison, where we are kept under guard by the gods or their agents, in which case suicide would be compared to avoidance of some kind of judicial or quasi-judicial sentence. But Socrates' reference to the suicide's *releasing himself* from the guard-post strongly suggests that he is a captive there (Socrates might have spoken instead of abandoning one's post, if he had intended the other interpretation). And this seems confirmed when, just below, he says that, even if one does not accept this whole story, at least this much contained in it is reasonable, that the gods have charge of us (*einai hēmōn tous epimeloumenous* 62b7): this seems a natural enough generalization from the idea of gods as the ones who are keeping us in prison, but much less natural if the idea was that they are our superior officers who command us in some further enterprise of their own. If so, the secret, presumably Pythagorean, theory has it that suicide is forbidden because it entails evading the full execution of a just sentence and so is itself something unjust.

Socrates, as just noted, is not willing to commit himself to this theory, apparently because of reservations he has about the idea that life is a punishment for something, but he does approve of the thought, which he finds expressed in it, that the gods are our keepers, who tend us and take care of us as possessions of theirs. As their possessions, we have no right to decide to cease to be tended and used by them as they see fit, any more than anything that belongs to us as a possession of ours has any right to decide to be our possession no longer. Suicide, then, would be an injustice, a violation of the rights of ownership possessed by the gods in us. There is also the suggestion, to judge from Cebes' immediate response (62c-e), that suicide would be stupid, too, and wrong on that ground, because being under the charge and tendance of the gods, who are wise and good, we must expect to be exceedingly well cared for in whatever way, as their possessions, we are treated, so that we can hardly do better for ourselves by committing suicide than the gods are doing for us in keeping us alive: when it *is* better for us to die, we can be sure the gods themselves, in their concern and tendance for us, will bring our deaths about.

In this whole passage, then, Socrates is offering to explain the Pythagorean prohibition on suicide, as put forward by Philolaus. The suggestion is that Philolaus did defend, or might plausibly, given other Pythagorean beliefs, have defended, this ban by arguing that human souls are placed in bodies by god as some kind of punishment, so that to commit suicide is to do the injustice of attempting to avoid serving the full term of a just sentence. Socrates himself sees in this theory, once questionable eschatological assumptions are pared away, the good idea that we are possessions of the gods and under their care and tendance. Hence suicide would be both an injustice (violating an owner's rights in his property) and the height of foolishness, since we should know that the gods, in tending us, will always act for our own good. If we do not die from causes the gods control, that can only be because it is better for us personally to continue to live than to die. Nonetheless, it deserves emphasis that this, though Socrates' own contribution to the discussion, is put forward simply as an explication and defense of the specifically Pythagorean ban on suicide, based on ideas Socrates finds plausible and attractive. He does not definitely commit himself to accepting the ban, even when defended in this plausible and attractive way. For he stresses in advance the tentativeness with which he entertains the idea, whether on these grounds or on others, that suicide is never justified. He prefaces his account of these reasons for the ban by saying (62a) that it would be strange that, when virtually everything else one can think of would sometimes, for someone, under some circumstances, be the proper thing to do, suicide alone should be plainly and simply *wrong*; surely, for some people it is better that they should die, and if so it is impossible to see why it should not be permitted to them to bring about their own deaths, rather than having to linger on until someone or something else does them the favor.

IV

The Socrates, then, of the *Phaedo* sees a good argument on each side of the question about suicide; he is no dogmatist on this question. It is true that in his account of the philosopher's attitude to death he seems to give more weight to the argument against it: he says (61c) that the philosopher will welcome his own death when it comes, as freeing him from dependence on the body and putting him finally into full contact with the ultimate truth of things, but will presumably not do himself violence since, as people say, that is not right (*ou themiton*). But this is stated fairly perfunctorily, and the argument, which I have just cited, that suicide must surely be sometimes permitted, is left standing, without any suggestion of rebuttal. This is significant because in the *Laws* Plato is quite explicit about the permissibility, and indeed the moral advisability, of suicide under certain circumstances. One does not find Plato elsewhere than in this passage of the *Phaedo* even seriously entertaining an absolute ban on suicide on general moral grounds.

In *Laws* IX, in discussing the criminal law, Plato twice has occasion to refer to suicide. The first comes at the very beginning of the book, in a kind of general preamble (854a3–5)[8] to what are presented as the most awful capital crimes (temple robbery, treason, political subversion, and others unspecified—it is not clear to me what the intended scope is of "similar

---

[8] In citing the *Laws* I use Trevor J. Saunders' translation, now in Cooper, ed. *Plato: Complete Works*.

crimes which are difficult or even impossible to cure," 854a12, and "all these impious deeds that bring about the ruin of the state," c6–7, which are the only indications Plato gives as to which crimes the preamble is meant to cover). The preamble is addressed to those who might be tempted to contemplate robbing a temple or committing some other such horrendous offense. First they are advised that anyone who feels any such temptation is subject to an evil impulse (an *epithumia kakē*, 854a6) that arises in human beings from no normal human or any divine origin, but as a result of unexpiated crimes done by other human beings (presumably their ancestors) in the distant past. One must do everything possible to rid oneself of, or at least control, such desires, destructive as they are both of the inner life of the person who experiences them and of the social order. When any such thought enters your head, the lawgiver advises, you should seek relief by rites of purification and by supplicating the gods, and try to strengthen your own belief that everyone has reason to honor what is fine and just (*ta kala kai ta dikaia*) by seeking the company of good people, listening to and trying to say, as your own conviction, what they say about this. If by this means the "disease" abates, well and good; but if not, "you should look upon death as the preferable alternative, and rid yourself of life" (854c4–5).

I have quoted from and summarized this passage so fully because it strikingly expresses a view about suicide—the view that suicide is justified when one's own moral character has proved irreparably to be very bad— that the Stoics later on strenuously denied. According to the Stoic theory, for reasons I explain below, the moral goodness or badness of oneself and one's life are not only not important reasons against or for suicide, they do not count in the balance *at all*. Plato apparently thinks, to the contrary, that if one is subject to *extremely* immoral desires, which after serious efforts one can neither get rid of nor diminish so that they are fairly easily controlled, then one ought to end one's life. His thought, I take it, is not so much that suicide will preempt the possibility that at some future time one will yield to the desire and actually do something really horrendous, but that it will end a life that is so thoroughly bad, whether or not one does any of the horrendous things one is constantly wanting to do, that it is better for oneself not to live it at all.[9] Plato is thus, in this passage of the *Laws*, the most prominent opponent among their predecessors of the Stoics' doctrine that

---

[9] It is perhaps worth reminding oneself at this point that in the *Republic*, for example, Socrates is emphatic that what really matters for a person, and so the ultimate source of all one's real reasons for acting, is the good internal condition of one's own soul (see, e.g., 443c9–444a2). Doing bad things is wrong because it brings about or reinforces or simply expresses a bad internal condition of the soul. So, too, here in the *Laws*, Plato is not saying that the potential criminal's suicide is ultimately desirable so as to prevent him or her from doing harm to society: doing that harm is itself to be avoided, on Plato's view, only because it is the expression or cause of a bad internal psychical condition, and it is the avoidance or the riddance of that that must provide the fundamental reason for the suicide.

the moral quality of one's own life is in principle irrelevant to the question whether to go on living it.

Later in *Laws* IX (873c-d) the Athenian Visitor proposes a criminal law against (certain) suicides, and here too considerations having to do with one's own moral failings are mentioned as justifying suicide. What Plato says is this. With the exception of three special cases, suicides are to be punished with burial in unmarked, solitary graves in deserted, outlying districts. The special cases, for which neither this nor any other punitive action is to be taken are these: when the agent acted (1) (as Socrates did) under judicial order, or (2) being forced (*anankastheis*, 873c6) by some excruciating and unavoidable misfortune, or (3) having come to participate in some irremediable disgrace that he cannot live with. Plato's language here, though it appears to be carefully chosen, is not completely clear to me,[10] but there seems to be a clear difference between the first two of these exceptions, on the one hand, and the third. The first and second, being cases where the agent is represented as acting under compulsion (*anankē*), legal or emotional—a typical case of the second kind might be suicide due to understandable grief or depression, caused perhaps by the loss of one's whole family in a fire—are apparently being conceived of as excused homicides. The third, however, appears to cover justified suicides (there is no reference in this case to compulsion), where the justification lies in the fact that the person has (perhaps intentionally, perhaps not—think of Oedipus!) done something *morally* very disgraceful: in the excellent city of Magnesia, for which these laws are being promulgated, one would not expect anything not involving moral failure to count as a disgrace, or at any event as a great enough disgrace to justify such drastic action. So, whereas earlier in book IX Plato had said that a person whose moral character was irremediably extremely bad should kill himself, here he counts suicide as justified as a way of extricating oneself from extreme moral disgrace brought on by one's actions.[11]

All other suicides than the three classes just indicated the law of Magnesia will punish in the way specified above, on the ground that anyone who commits suicide in other circumstances "imposes [an] unjust judgment [of death] on himself in a spirit of slothful and abject cowardice" (*argiāi kai*

[10] It is not clear, for example, why it matters that the misfortune under (2) should have been *unavoidable*.

[11] Thus it seems correct to say that in 873c-d Plato exempts from punishment suicides on moral grounds (viz., as responses to extreme moral disgrace) that are closely connected to those he earlier recommended (854c4–5)—the suicides of those incurably afflicted with morally awful desires. But it is an exaggeration to say (with Apelt, nn. to 854c and 873c in his translation, *Die Gesetze*; and see *Platonische Aufsätze*, p. 163) that the exemption *explicitly* covers these recommended cases. There is no mention at all in the earlier context of overt criminal acts, giving rise to disgrace, which is clearly what the *aischunē* in 873c refers to. So the suicides recommended earlier would have to be understood as covered by the exemption here granted, if at all, only by a natural extension of the provisions of the law as explicitly formulated.

anandrias deiliāi, 873c7). Apparently, then, anyone who commits suicide when his judgment is unclouded by grief, depression, or other severely distorting emotions, because he considers that morally neutral bad things, such as pain, disease, the absence of interesting work to do, or the inability to do it, etc., so outweigh any good that his life can bring him that it is better not to go on living it, will be judged to have shown cowardice and a reprehensible unwillingness to take action against these evils and their effects on his life. That is to say, Plato here denies that the sorts of consideration that the Stoics later held *did* justify committing suicide ever actually do so, just as we have seen that he maintains that the moral considerations that they denied were ever even relevant to the decision sometimes in fact justified it. Plato's position in the *Laws*, therefore, appears to be, on both its positive and its negative sides, diametrically opposed to the Stoics'. As in other parts of their moral philosophy it seems reasonable to think of opposition to Plato's views as a principal component of the early Stoics' theories about suicide.[12]

V

But before turning to discuss the Stoics' views, I want to consider what Aristotle says about suicide in a short and difficult passage of the book on justice (*Nicomachean Ethics* V = *Eudemian Ethics* IV), 1138a5–14. The topic of suicide, which does not come up elsewhere in Aristotle's political and ethical writings, arises here in a discussion of the question whether it is possible for a person to treat himself unjustly, i.e., knowingly and willingly to do something to himself that is unjust. Suicide is knowingly and willingly killing oneself, and if to kill someone knowingly and willingly is to do an injustice, then it seems to follow that, because one is oneself the victim of one's suicidal act, to commit suicide is to do *oneself* an injustice. Yet, as

---

[12] In my discussion of Plato's views on euthanasia and suicide, I have limited myself to discussing views that are put forward and discussed in the context of a philosophical argument, i.e., in the context of what Plato himself describes as *logos* in contradistinction to *muthos* (e.g., *Protagoras* 320c3–4, 324d5–6). As is well known, Plato appends eschatological myths to illustrate and extend the philosophical content developed in the *logos* of certain of his dialogues. Especially in the cases of *Gorgias, Phaedo*, and *Republic*, these myths have much to say that is relevant to the topic of suicide. However, as Socrates' discussion of his own rhetorical displays in the myths of the *Phaedrus* makes abundantly clear, myths convey truth in a derivative and secondary way and are not to be confused with properly philosophical exposition. (Nor is it in the least a straightforward matter to decide how they are to be interpreted—as Socrates also makes clear). Accordingly, in discussing Plato's philosophical views one must begin from the philosophical argument, taken on its own terms, and if one goes on to consider the myths, one must always control their interpretation by reference to the philosophical argument they are intended to illustrate. Where the myths go beyond anything established by argument, their contents cannot be attributed to the character Socrates, much less to the author Plato, as items of philosophical opinion.

Aristotle sees, there is something paradoxical in the idea that it is possible to treat *oneself* unjustly. His aim in the passage is to address and attempt to remove this apparently paradoxical consequence of the existence of suicide, when this is juxtaposed with the fact of Athenian and Greek law generally, that suicide is legally forbidden.

In order not to misunderstand what Aristotle says here, it is important to bear in mind that on his theory of justice *just* and *unjust* can refer to either of two distinct sets of behaviors. On the one hand, they can refer to behavior characteristic of a person having a specific virtue or vice of character, one that has to do with the way he treats other people with respect to bodily harm and the distribution or assignment of external goods like money, property, etc. This specific virtue and vice are coordinate with the other virtues and vices Aristotle discusses in the central books of the *Ethics*— courage, temperance, good temper, etc. and their opposites, each with its own distinctive specific area of control over a person's behavior. On the other hand, *just* and *unjust* can also refer to behavior characteristic of someone who is simply law-abiding or lawless, who pays, or does not pay, heed to the law as such, who does or does not regard the fact that the law requires or forbids something as constituting some reason for or against doing it. In this broader usage what will count as just or unjust will depend directly on what the laws in fact do require or forbid. There is, antecedent to the institution of the law, no kind of action that counts as just or unjust in this broader sense, as of course there is for justice and injustice in the other, narrower sense, just as there is for courage and cowardice, temperance, self-indulgence, unreasonable self-denial, and so on.

Now this double usage of the terms *just* and *unjust* means that the question whether a person can treat himself unjustly can mean either of two things. First, can one knowingly and willingly treat oneself unjustly in the matter of bodily harm, assignment of external goods like money, and so on? Second, can one knowingly and willingly do something to oneself in violation of the law and so (in *that* sense) treat oneself unjustly? Since Aristotle thinks that, in general, the purpose of laws is to make people act in accordance with the whole range of the specific moral virtues he discusses, and so to help them to become morally good people, a well-framed legal system will include laws requiring the citizen to act justly (in the narrower sense), courageously, temperately, etc., and not to act unjustly, in cowardly fashion, and so on. Hence, under such a system of law, an act of injustice in the broader sense will also be an act of some specific vice as well—*perhaps* an act of injustice, forbidden by the law for the reason that that is what it is, but perhaps instead an act of cowardice, or one done from excessive or inappropriate anger, and so on.

Now Aristotle is careful to take note of the two types of injustice in answering his question about the possibility of a person knowingly and willingly doing something unjust to himself. It is in connection with injustice in the broader sense (and only in that sense) that he considers the case of suicide. The suicide does what the law forbids,[13] and, on Aristotle's theory, this means that in addition to doing something unjust (in the broad sense, i.e., illegal) he also does something contrary to one of the specific virtues. But which one? Aristotle does not indicate the full range of possibilities here; the (only) example he cites is one where the person acted in anger (a9–10), presumably a case where out of anger at himself for some real or imagined fault he kills himself, thinking that people with that fault don't deserve to live. So the case of suicide Aristotle considers is a case where the agent acted out of excessive anger; his was an act of the vice of irascibility, and it was as such that the law forbade it.[14] The question, then, whether in killing himself he has done anyone an injustice, and in particular whether he has done *himself* an injustice, ought to be simply the question who, if anyone, suffers the injustice that consists in his disobeying the law. Since, as described, the suicide is not an act of injustice in the narrow sense, but an act of the vice of irascibility, there should be no question of the suicide's doing an injustice to himself in the narrow sense. Understood that way the answer seems obvious, and it is the one that Aristotle himself goes on to give (a11–14); it is the city itself that has been unjustly treated by the law-breaker, viz., the suicide, and this is evidenced by the fact that what he suffers in punishment is some *atimia*, some loss of civic status (in the form, presumably, of an undignified burial: recall Plato's penalty in the *Laws*).

In reaching this conclusion, however, Aristotle confusingly refers (a7–9) to the conditions in which, where someone harms someone else, he acts

---

[13] The manuscript reading at 1138a6–7 (translated by Ross) makes Aristotle adopt the very peculiar view (not elsewhere reported) that what the law does not require of us it forbids us to do, so that since no law requires (nonjudicial) suicide the law forbids it. Stewart, *Notes on the "Ethics,"* p. 533 attempts to defend this line of thought, by emphasizing that "law" (*nomos*) really means customary at least as much as statute-law (it is more plausible to say that what custom does not require, it forbids), but not very successfully: there are plenty of matters about which custom is silent, not requiring but also not forbidding specific ways of acting (e.g., drinking iced water with meals). Aristotle himself seems to speak of the law as directly forbidding suicide just one sentence below (*ouk eāi*, a10), and goes on to speak of an established penalty for breaking the law against suicide (a13), which seems to imply that he is thinking of a statute expressly prohibiting it (as in Plato's *Laws* IX), so he does not need to rely on this dubious line of thought to reach a legal prohibition of suicide. There is much to recommend Joachim's emendation of the text at 1138a6–7 (translated by Irwin), which makes Aristotle say simply that the law forbids anyone to kill himself.

[14] Presumably, like Plato in *Laws* IX, Aristotle thinks that other suicides will be motivated by excessive fear and so will be acts of cowardice rather than irascibility. The crucial point is that, if he thinks the law will contain a blanket prohibition of suicide, he must think that *every* suicide will be brought about by some excess or deficiency that makes the act an act of some or other specific vice. So he thinks that anyone who *thinks* he has adequate reason to kill himself only thinks that because of the distorting influence on his process of reasoning of some desire he either ought not to have had, or ought to have been able to resist.

unjustly in doing so—conditions, that is to say, in which an act of injustice in the *narrow* sense takes place. This gives the, perhaps mistaken, impression that he considers the suicide done in anger also an act of injustice in the narrow sense (and so doubly, as it were, an act of broad injustice—a violation of the law against excessively angry behavior, and simultaneously a violation of the law against unjust behavior). And this may give his reader the impression that Aristotle holds that the suicide does an injustice in the narrow sense to his city—as if by depriving the city of his productive capacity or other services he takes away from his fellow-citizens a good that they, as a matter of justice, had a right to.

Now it is in fact easy enough to see how it might seem that the suicide-in-anger also does an injustice in the narrow sense to somebody. For to do an injustice in the narrow sense is simply to injure someone wrongfully with respect to bodily goods (health, life, etc.) or the distribution or assignment of external goods like money, etc. And of course the suicide clearly does at least do someone (viz., himself) an injury of one of these types. However, in order to be an act of injustice, his act must not merely do such an injury to someone. It must be a wrongful act of such injury, and wrongful in the sense that it is something forbidden by the particular virtue of justice. (That it is wrongful in the general sense of being forbidden by the law is, of course, not enough to make it wrongful in this particular way). And it is certainly not obvious that an act of suicide is a wrongful act in this sense; nor does Aristotle elsewhere say or imply that it is. I think Aristotle becomes confused at this point in his argument. Assuming, on the basis of existing law, that suicide is always unjust in the broad sense—i.e., always violates some particular virtue—and seeing that, of course, it always involves bodily injury, he unwisely and unnecessarily grants that suicide always involves *narrow* injustice (perhaps simultaneously with violations of other virtues as well). Pressed, then, with the question who is the victim of the injustice—who is the one who is unjustly treated by the suicide—he has to confront the common-sense intuition, an intuition he has himself defended less than two pages previously (1136b3–12), that one cannot do oneself an injustice in the narrow sense: injustice in the narrow sense requires two distinct persons as agent and victim. And so he concludes, confusedly, that not only is the city the victim of the suicide's illegal act—this makes good sense—but that the city, and not the suicide himself, is also the victim of a supposed injustice in the narrow sense that, in acting illegally, the suicide perpetrates.

Aristotle argues in the following way that the suicide-in-anger does his city an injustice (my comments are contained in parentheses):

1. When someone knowingly and willingly injures someone, contrary to the law and not in retaliation, he acts unjustly (—i.e., unjustly in the *narrow* sense).

2. But the suicide-in-anger slaughters himself knowingly and willingly, contrary to the law.

3. So he acts unjustly (—but with which kind of injustice? Injustice in the narrow sense, or in the broad sense? or in both?)

4. But he cannot be acting unjustly to *himself*, because he suffers knowingly and willingly, and we have already argued (1136b3–12—but there the discussion concerned *narrow*-sense injustice only) that no one can knowingly and willingly be treated unjustly.

5. So the suicide-in-anger acts unjustly to his city, not to himself.

The problem with this line of argument is that at the beginning of the chapter Aristotle specifically introduces suicide as an action that naturally invites the question whether it is possible for a person to do himself an injustice in the *broad* sense. Aristotle has already completed his discussion of whether anyone can do himself an injustice in the narrow sense, giving an unequivocal answer of "No." Hence he ought to be discussing only the question whether it is possible for a person knowingly and willingly to do something illegal, and so unjust in the broad sense, of which he is himself the victim. So his conclusion at (3) ought to be that the suicide acts unjustly in the broad sense, and that the victim of this injustice—this illegality—is the city, his fellow-citizens in general. And it does follow from premise (2) that the suicide-in-anger acts unjustly in this sense; to establish that, it is sufficient to point out that he knowingly and willingly acts contrary to the law. By confusingly, and confusedly, adding premise (1) as well, Aristotle gives the impression that he means to say that the suicide acts unjustly in the narrow sense in addition. Furthermore, when he goes on in (4) to argue that the injustice done cannot be to himself, he *has* to have narrow-sense injustice in mind. For previously he has only argued that no one can knowingly and willingly be treated, or treat himself, unjustly in the narrow sense. So in this argument Aristotle does rely essentially on the highly questionable idea that in killing himself the suicide does a narrow-injustice.[15] Nonetheless, the conclusion he uses this erroneous idea to reach is, plainly, just that the suicide does his city, not himself, a *broad* injustice in killing himself, and that does not in the least entail that in doing so he violates the *rights* of his fellow-citizens (justice in the narrow sense), say rights they have to economic

---

[15] What is worse, Aristotle's own account of narrow-injustice appears to imply that this idea is actually erroneous. If the claim in steps (1)–(3) is that the suicide does a narrow-injustice *simply* in that he knowingly and willingly injures someone (viz. himself), then this conflicts with Aristotle's theory. According to this account of when someone does a narrow-injustice (1136a31–b5), there must be someone who is injured (the one who is treated unjustly) and this injury must be something his *boulēsis* (his rational desire) is actively opposing at the time. But the suicide does not have a rational desire *not* to die, at least not when he acts, so *he* is not unjustly treated. And it certainly does not seem that the city's *boulēsis* (that of the fellow citizens in general) can be actively opposing the suicide, since there is no reason to suppose anyone at all even knows it is taking place. That means that simply *in* killing himself he does not do an act of narrow-injustice at all. At 1138a7–9 Aristotle misstates his own account of when a person acts unjustly, by omitting the requirement that what is done is contrary to the rational desire of the victim.

or other services from him. When Aristotle momentarily argues himself into suggesting this further point, it is in confusion and is no part of the main line of argument he is pursuing.

VI

It is of some significance that Aristotle's and Plato's most extensive discussions of the morality of suicide come in the context of their treatments of the law. The Greek city-states generally had laws against suicide. At Athens, for example, suicides were buried with their right hands amputated—presumably in origin a measure designed to placate or render innocuous the ghost, as victim of a violent death, even though one at his own hands. And the thrust of both Plato's and Aristotle's remarks on suicide is to interpret in the light of their own general theories of justice and morality, and thereby to defend, at least the central provisions of the traditional legal codes in this matter. This reflects the conservative stance that both philosophers adopt toward the free city-state and its institutions (though this is perhaps nowadays more widely recognized in Aristotle's than Plato's case):[16] a major motive of their moral and political theories is to provide philosophically acceptable rationales for, if not the actual practices of any Greek city, at least a refined and purified version of the kind of social and political life that was led within Greek cities during classical times. No such motive was at work among the early Stoics. On the contrary, as the scanty reports about Zeno's *Republic* (cf. Plutarch *De Alexandri Magni fortuna aut virtute* I 6, printed in von Arnim, *Stoicorum Veterum Fragmenta*, vol. I, as fragment 262; Clement and Plutarch in *SVF* I, 264), as well as the traditional associations of Zeno and the Cynic Crates, show, early Stoicism was sceptical, even iconoclastic, in its attitude to the provisions of traditional social and personal morality in the Greek city-states. And so one finds in the Stoic tradition, perhaps reaching as far back as Zeno himself,[17] a strong and very well-articulated defense of the appropriateness and correctness of suicide in many circumstances: whenever, for example, one can judge that, because of incurable illness, or extreme pain, or the absence of the necessary means to support oneself, a "natural" life, in the sense of a biologically smoothly functioning, unhindered one, is no longer possible. As I mentioned above,

[16] But Hegel in the *Philosophy of Right* is rather emphatic in saying that Plato's *Republic*, at any rate, is not at all a mere philosopher's ideal, unconnected except negatively with Greek political and social reality at Plato's time: it is actually nothing but "an interpretation of the nature of Greek ethical life" (p. 10; see also paragraph 185, p. 124). For Plato, no less than for Hegel himself, the owl of Minerva spreads its wings only with the falling of dusk.

[17] Seneca reports (but without citation, and in a form that may suggest that "Zeno" here just means "the Stoics") that whereas Socrates will teach you to die if it is necessary, Zeno will teach you to die before it is necessary (*Moral Letters* 104, 21).

the Stoic position is the precise opposite of Plato's in the *Laws*: according to the Stoics, consideration of one's life prospects with respect to such external and bodily (so-called) goods does sometimes provide an adequate ground to put an end to one's life, but furthermore the fact that one is (and can expect to continue to be) a morally good person in itself gives no reason whatsoever in favor of continuing one's life, nor does the fact that one is a moral monster (and can expect to continue to be one), just in itself, give one any reason, however slight, in favor of putting an end to one's life.[18]

In holding this view the Stoics are simply applying to the special case of suicide their general theory of what a correct and appropriate action is in any given circumstances, and what the correct basis is for deciding what that is. To explain their general theory fully and make it comprehensible would be a major undertaking in itself; I hope the following brief summary will be sufficient for present purposes. The Stoics, following up hints contained in arguments developed by Socrates in Plato's *Euthydemus* (278e–282d) and *Meno* (87d–89a), recognize two radically distinct kinds of value. First, there is the value (which they call goodness and badness) of that in which a person's good or ill (happiness or unhappiness, well-being or ill-being, etc.) actually consists. This they identify with a virtuous character and its exercise, and certain normal mental accompaniments of it, such as the joy, gladness, confidence, etc., that "supervene" upon virtue, and their vicious opposites. Anything other than your inner state and its expression in your decisions and actions is neither a good nor at all a bad thing for you; all else is indifferent, so far as being good or bad for you is concerned. But, second, there is the kind of value, subsidiary to this first kind, possessed by anything that, given its nature and the circumstances of human life, human beings generally have reason either to prefer to have or to avoid. It is right to prefer health to illness, for example; so a healthy life, though not better for you than a sickly one, is to be preferred: it has positive value of the second kind. The Stoics connected these two kinds of value to one another in the following way. A person's good (his being virtuous and acting virtuously) is the perfection of his nature as a rational being, that is, the condition in which his rational capacity is fully developed and properly employed, employed as nature intended reason to be employed in human beings. Now nature, as we can observe, sees to the growth, reproduction, maintenance, etc., and takes care, of the rest of the earth's animal life by means of the instincts and other nonrational impulses that such animals regularly experience and on which they act, in the light of the way things appear to them at the time. For human beings, however, "reason has been bestowed . . . for a more perfect way of leading their lives" (Diogenes Laertius VII 86) than nature provides in the case of the other animals. Reason

---

[18] Consideration of what, being a good person or a moral monster, one will *do* for or to other people if one remains alive is of course another matter; as we shall see, on Stoic principles that counts as relevant to the decision whether to kill oneself or not.

is added in human beings, as Diogenes Laertius in reporting the Stoic theory puts it, as the "craftsman of impulse": the adult human being, like other animals, leads his life in response to his impulses, but in his case the impulses in question are themselves the product of his rational reflection upon and judgment about what is worth having and doing. The "more perfect way of leading their lives" that reason makes possible for human beings consists in the production by reason of the impulses on which we go on to act, and reason exists in us for the purpose of producing those impulses. This is where the second kind of value comes in. Our own reason, in taking on the direction of our lives, has to determine what sorts of impulses we ought to have, and directed to what ends. The things we ought to have impulses toward are just all the things that are (correctly) "preferred," and the things we ought to have aversions from are those that are (correctly) "avoided," i.e., the things that in fact have positive and negative value of the second kind.

But which are these? We can tell from observation of the course of nature that for all the other animal (and plant) species (leaving aside for the moment the human beings) there are certain norms for the members of those species that are in the general case (though obviously not in every individual case) attained in the life-span of its members. So we can see that it is part of nature's plan for the members of each species, in the general case even if not in every individual one, to grow to maturity in a certain way, perform certain sorts of activities including reproductive ones, and so flourish in a particular way that depends on the natural capacities that belong to members of that species. Plainly, then, for human beings, too, whose own reasoned impulses (and not *natural* impulses) direct their lives, those impulses will be correct that aim at the naturally flourishing life that corresponds for human beings to the flourishing life of a plant or a beast. In the human case this will involve, the Stoics think, being and remaining physically healthy; having sharp and unimpaired sensory and other organs; having certain sorts of family and other human relationships, including ones built upon mutual cooperation and help involving political and social ties giving rise to obligations to respect one another's independence and integrity; and having and using money and other material resources in furtherance of the objectives implied in all these natural human attachments and interests. These, then, are the norms that nature itself establishes for the conduct of a successful and flourishing human life, corresponding to that of a successful member of a plant or (brute) animal kind. They are "natural advantages" for a human being, and so are things that we have reason to take an interest in and try to obtain and maintain in our lives. Because reason is given to us by nature for a more perfect way of leading our lives than the other animals have got, we must conclude that we ought to shape our impulses so that we want to have and try to get, preserve and appropriately use, these things that contribute to the naturally flourishing life for a member of our species.

Thus, according to the Stoics moral virtue, the sole good for human beings, is, as it were, a purely formal condition: it consists in one's reason's being correctly informed about what things other than virtue itself are, by nature's plan for human beings, such as to promote the full and fully developed functioning of the natural capacities belonging to human beings as such, and shaping one's impulses to action in accordance with that knowledge. All the specific, substantive content of this state of mind—everything that determines what the virtuous person wants, cares about, makes an object of pursuit or avoidance in his actions, etc.—is drawn from the list of "preferred" and "avoided" (or "rejected") things, the things having value, positive or negative, of the second kind. Thus, Plutarch and Cicero both report the Stoics as maintaining that things of this kind constitute the "underlying material" for virtue, that which virtue judges about and chooses (or rejects) whenever it gets exercised in the virtuous person's life.[19] Thus, to pursue the good in which virtuous action consists is to pursue a purely formal end; one pursues it in pursuing some other, concrete goal, which is not and is not thought of as *good* at all (but only "preferred"), and in pursuing which, for that agent in those circumstances, virtue itself consists.

How does this general theory apply to the special case of suicide? Cicero states the Stoic view as follows (*De finibus* III 60–61, trans. Rackham):

> When a man's circumstances contain a preponderance of things in accordance with nature, it is appropriate for him to remain alive; when he possesses or sees in prospect a majority of the contrary things, it is appropriate for him to depart from life . . . . [T]he primary things of nature, whether favorable or the reverse, fall under the judgment and choice of the Wise Man, and form so to speak the subject-matter, the given material with which wisdom deals. Therefore the reasons both for remaining in life and for departing from it are to be measured entirely by the primary things of nature aforesaid. For the virtuous man is not necessarily retained in life by virtue, and also those who are devoid of virtue need not necessarily seek death. . . . Even for the foolish, who are also miserable, it is appropriate to remain alive if they possess a predominance of those things which we pronounce to be in accordance with nature.[20]

It is easy to caricature the Stoic view: What's this? A person is *not* to take into account at all in deciding whether to continue his life or end it the only

---

[19] Plutarch, *De communibus notitiis* 1071b; Cicero, *De finibus* III 61. See also Arius Didymus in Stobaeus, *Eclogae* II 47.12–48.5 Wachsmuth, on *hypotelis* v. *telos* in virtuous action.

[20] In this passage Cicero is thinking exclusively of the potential suicide's private good—his health, his ability to carry on an active life. Other sources make it clear that other concerns, e.g., concern for his friends or for his country (Diogenes Laertius VII 130), could appropriately motivate suicide: the good of one's friends and one's country are also among the things that are naturally "preferred" by human beings. Olympiodorus, the 6th century A.D. Neo-platonist commentator, reports (*Comm. on Plato's "Phaedo"* I, 8, 19–39, ed. Westerink) that the Stoics recognized five cases where suicide is appropriate (so also Elias, *Eisagoge* in *CAG* XVIII I, 14.15–15.22, cited in *SVF* III 768): (1) in discharge of some duty, e.g., to defend one's country; (2) to avoid doing something disgraceful, e.g., betraying an important secret when pressed by a tyrant to do so; (3) when beset by mental deterioration in old age or (4) incurable, debilitating disease; (5) when extreme poverty prevents one from supplying one's basic needs.

things that really matter for him, namely, what is for his own good and what is bad and harmful to him? Instead he is to decide this momentous question on the basis of how things stand for him that are literally neither good nor bad—things like his own continued health, the needs of his friends and family, and so on, things which the Stoics count as relatively to be preferred, but, strictly speaking, absolutely indifferent so far as his own good or bad is concerned? Understandably enough, philosophers like Plutarch and Alexander of Aphrodisias, writing in the late first and second centuries A.D., when most philosophers were preoccupied with Plato and Aristotle, convinced of the superiority of their philosophies, and Stoicism had ceased to have able and original exponents, freely indulge in such caricatures and succeed in making the Stoic view seem ridiculous.[21]

But in fact their view is both coherent and not obviously implausible. First of all, it is not true that a fully virtuous person (a Wise Man) in deciding whether or not to commit suicide is not considering his own good (the continuance of his own virtuous inner state and its expression in action). He knows he will continue to be virtuous and will act virtuously (and so achieve good for himself) only if he does the appropriate thing, and in the right way, in the circumstances. Provided he does that, he will preserve and achieve his own good. So in deciding what *is* the appropriate thing to do, appeal to the continuance of his own good inner state and to continued good action on his part necessarily drops out: he will achieve those if, but only if, he does what he decides on other grounds, grounds having to do with non-moral values, is the correct and appropriate thing to do. And correspondingly, a morally bad person, concerned (as no doubt few such persons would in fact be) to avoid for himself the continuance of his morally bad inner state and its expression in action, must want to do the thing that is appropriate to his circumstances, and in the right way: that is the only way to avoid the harm that comes to oneself by being morally bad. Paradoxically, if the vicious person aims to rid himself of this burden by putting an end to his life, in circumstances where consideration of non-moral values alone would not support such an action, he only does one more vicious thing and so simply extends and confirms his possession of the bad. But, one might object, surely it is better for a bad person to do just this one more bad act, rather than to continue a life of repeated bad actions? Is not a shorter time in possession and use of the bad better, or anyhow less bad for him? And does not that give him a reason to commit suicide? The answer to these questions is: no, not in the least. Where a person's good and bad are at issue, only his moral state and its expression in action make any contribution. So it is no improvement in the goodness, or diminishment of the badness, of an agent's life to shorten the time he is morally bad; the only improvement in its goodness or diminishment in its badness there can

[21] See Plutarch, *De Stoicorum repugnantiis* ch. 18, *De communibus notitiis* ch. 11, Alexander of Aphrodisias *De anima* II, pp. 159.16–22, 160.20–31, 168.1–20 Bruns.

be is for him to take steps to make a better person of himself. And the necessary first step in that direction is to start doing the appropriate things, as these are determined by the balance of non-moral reasons. But if these, taken by themselves, do not indicate that suicide is right and appropriate, then an agent who *is* truly concerned to improve his life or diminish its badness will refuse to commit suicide. Thus, as Cicero says, the bad person has *no* ground for appealing, in deciding whether to commit suicide, to anything other than the balance of reasons provided by the non-moral values that go to make up the class of things that are preferable and not preferable from his own point of view. It is not that a bad person has no reason to be concerned with his own moral state and with the fact that it is bad for himself to be like that; rather, a proper concern for that will lead him precisely to do whatever on these other grounds is rationally indicated.[22] And so, he will rationally commit suicide or not only because of how the prospects stand for him of a continued life in possession of a preponderance of "natural advantages."

VII

As one might expect, Epicurus, too, like the Stoics, did not hesitate to say that each of us is free to end his own life, if we encounter unendurable pain: at any rate, Cicero attributes to him the thought (*De fin.* I 49) that we may "serenely quit life's theatre, when the play has ceased to please us," i.e., when it is causing us extreme pain that we cannot endure by recollecting previous pleasures and that we know will not be brief and intermittent. But, to judge from his extant remains, Epicurus was much more insistent on the *un*reasonableness of suicide than on its permissibility under such circumstances. He remarks in *Vatican Saying* 38 that "he is of little account who finds many good reasons for departing from life," and Seneca (*Letter* 24, 22–23) quotes three very interesting passages (frgs. 496, 497, 498 Usener)

---

[22] The Stoic view as expounded in Cicero and discussed above is that of the original Stoics of the 3rd century B.C. Later Stoic writers, such as Seneca and Epictetus, have a good deal to say about suicide, and maintain the old Stoic position that suicide is sometimes appropriate (see Seneca, *Letters* 14, 70, 77; Epictetus, *Discourses*, I, 9, 10–17; I, 24, 20; I, 25, 18; II, I, 19–20; etc.). But Seneca tends to forget that according to Stoic doctrine virtue *requires* a full commitment to life, so long as it continues, as well as permitting (even requiring) departure from it under certain circumstances. He writes as if, really, life itself is a burden and a bore, so that one is free to leave it *whenever one pleases* (see the last lines of *Letter* 77: "stop living whenever you *want*"!) Epictetus, too, though he goes out of his way to deny that one should return promptly to God (*Disc.* I, 9, 10–17), is responsible for encouraging that view in the negative and world-weary way he describes our lives in "this" world. The most he can say on the other side is that God has stationed us in our bodies, so we should wait for a signal from him to leave them (a reflection, of course, of Socrates' discussion in Plato's *Phaedo*)—a far cry from the carefully articulated, anything but pessimistic and world-weary, theory of the old Stoics.

in which Epicurus analyzes as pathological the motives that lead many people to kill themselves. "It is absurd," he says, "to run towards death because you are tired of life, when it is by the manner of your life that you have brought it about that you ought to run towards death"—what you should do instead is to revise the way you live so that you no longer feel so tired of living that death is a reasonable option for you. Again: "What is so absurd as to seek death, when it is by the fear of death that you have unsettled and disturbed your life?" and, "So great is men's foolishness, indeed madness, that some are driven to death through the fear of death."[23] Epicurus diagnoses various deranged states of mind—especially, perhaps deep depression and acute anxiety—that cause some people to kill themselves as ultimately due to the irrational fear of death. Again, the right thing to do is to rid oneself of the fear of death, and so the state of mind that causes one to think of death as a reasonable option, rather than actually to commit suicide. So, although Epicurus did think suicide the right and appropriate thing under certain circumstances, namely, ones where the prospects for an acceptably pleasant subsequent life are irretrievably slight, he is insistent that many people find these prospects slight only because of the state of mind they have themselves fallen into and could get themselves out of if only they would listen to Epicurean reason.

VIII

The revival of Platonism as a system of dogmatic philosophy, beginning in earnest in the first century A.D., naturally carried with it a heightened interest in and appreciation for the views on the morality of suicide expressed in Plato's dialogues, and especially for those found in the *Phaedo*. Already by the time of Albinus, the leading Platonist teacher of the second century, the *Phaedo* occupied a central place, along with the *Alcibiades*, *Republic*, and *Timaeus*, in the exposition of the Platonic system (see *Eisagoge* 5). Over the following several centuries a large number of commentaries on the *Phaedo* were written, in which the passage on suicide was a major focus of attention. Of the three surviving commentaries, the comments of Olympiodorus (sixth century A.D.) on the philosophical argument of this passage are particularly full and interesting.[24] In reviewing the Platonists' contribution to the debate about suicide, we must also take into account the ennead (I 9) that Plotinus (third century) devoted to the topic, together with some relevant comments in the treatise on happiness (I 4), and a passage in the Neoplatonist

---

[23] Compare the remarkable passage of Lucretius III 79–84, in which he recounts how fear of death drives people to all kinds of foul deeds, in an effort to accumulate wealth and other resources as a bulwark against death—including finally the foul deed of their own suicide.

[24] Olympiodorus's commentary is printed with English translation and notes in Westerink, *In Platonis Gorgiam Commentaria*.

Elias (sixth century) professedly reporting views of Plotinus apparently expressed in a passage that has not survived.[25]

For a Platonist like Plotinus the central question about suicide is whether it is ever recommended by, or even compatible with, the rational pursuit of the purification of one's soul, a purification that consists in the soul's finally realizing its inherent capacity to be completely engaged in thinking and understanding the system of first principles of reality (the Platonic Forms): it is in that final self-realization that happiness for a human being consists (see *Enneads* I, 4, 3, 24–40; I, 4, 4, 4–15). He seems to assume that Plato's view was that suicide never is justified in the pursuit of happiness,[26] and so sets himself to argue, especially of course against the Stoics, that when properly understood the true system of reality supports this opinion. Thus (the same is true, *mutatis mutandis*, of other parts of his work), Plotinus does not so much begin from an independent consideration of the question whether suicide is ever rationally justified in pursuit of one's own happiness, and the various arguments that might be developed on either side. He takes it for granted that the view of Plato, the wisest philosopher, who somehow infallibly knows the truth about all such fundamental matters, is the soundest and truest, though not always as fully and clearly argued for as one might wish. His own task in I 9 is simply to explain and defend the Platonic view, by supplying the arguments that are needed to reveal its truth fully to other philosophers.

One can distinguish five arguments in this very brief treatise (I 9, totaling 19 lines), but the initial and central one (lines 1–8) is both highly original and specially interesting to us because it contains the basis of Plotinus's response to the Stoics. As I interpret it, this argument combines two lines of thought. First, it is a bad mistake to think that what one's soul needs, in order to exercise fully its capacity to think and understand the ultimate principles of reality, is to dissociate itself from the body in the sense of actually cutting itself free from it and going elsewhere. What is required is, rather, an internal transformation of the soul itself; the "return" to the first principle is not anything at all like a movement from one place to another (though that is a natural and useful metaphor for what is involved). In fact, the soul is always already separate from the body (I 9, line 5), i.e., a separate substance, and separation in the sense of a spatial removal is not in any event something that can happen to an immaterial entity like a soul. And in order for the needed transformation to take place, the attachment of the soul to the body is not in any way, or in any circumstance, a hindrance:

---

[25] This passage is printed, for example, as an appendix to I 9 in Armstrong's translation. For the different scholarly views about its relation to I 9, see Armstrong's introduction thereto, pp. 320–21.

[26] I take it he bases this opinion on the *Phaedo*; what he made of the *Laws* passages he nowhere makes clear, but perhaps he believed the *Laws* meant to recommend suicide only for the sake of the good of others, and not as a step towards one's own fuller achievement of happiness.

that transformation depends entirely on the free exercise of a power of intellect that is in any case always entirely separate from the body. Just as God is always fully present to the material world, and the passing away of things within it depends entirely on their own unfitness to receive being from him (not upon any withdrawal on his part), so our soul should remain fully present to our body until our body itself through its own unfitness is no longer able to hold fast to it (I, 9, lines 4–7, together with Elias, *Prolegomena* 6.15.23–16.2, which may be only a particularly full, expanded paraphrase of these lines).[27]

What enables Plotinus to argue in this way is his clear recognition that although as he and the Stoics agree, human good consists in rational activity in accordance with the dictates of reason itself, there is a kind of rational activity that lies beyond and above the rational tendance of the body and living a correct social life. The Stoics think suicide is sometimes rational because they see as the only function of reason the maintenance of these lower life-activities; when they can no longer *be* maintained adequately, reason tells us to cease living altogether. But because, according to Plotinus, reason has a separate and prior task, a purely intellectual one (and one not at all aimed at tendance of the body or governing one's social relations), and this task is performed entirely without dependence on or reference to the body and its needs, or events that befall it,[28] one has no basis at all for arguing that reason itself (i.e., as it is in its own self) will ever dictate the termination of one's own life.[29] So, although the Stoics are right to insist

[27] Combined with this first line of thought is the idea that if one does commit suicide, instead of waiting for a natural demise (or some other death, by accident or the action of another soul), the involvement of one's own soul in actively separating the body from its hold on the soul will leave the soul itself still somehow bound up with the body—the separation will only in any case be complete if it is the *body* that loosens its grip on the soul, not the other way about.

[28] On this see *Enneads* I 4, 2, 38–55; 4, 18–32.

[29] As my exposition of Plotinus's argument in I 9 and I 4 makes clear, I do not accept A. H. Armstrong's view (footnotes to pp. 192 and 324–25) that Plotinus, in either treatise, regards suicide as reasonable under any circumstances. Plotinus is explicit at I 9, lines 11–14 (and compare I 4, 9) that incipient madness is no reason to commit suicide—and what could Plotinus, with his views about the value of rational activity, think *would* give us reason to commit suicide, if going mad did not? And in I 4, 8, 1–2 and 8–12 he makes it clear that if pains become unbearable without ceasing of their own accord they (not oneself) will bring one's life to an end. Though he pointedly says (lines 8–9) that under such circumstances one retains one's power of choosing what action to take in the face of such torments, he plainly excludes the choice of suicide: as he goes on to say (lines 24–30) the good and wise man will set his virtue against these and all other adversities, thus keeping his soul unperturbed by them. Armstrong, in holding that despite all this, Plotinus admitted suicide as legitimate in "absolutely desperate circumstances" (similarly R. Harder, *Plotins Schriften*, p. 546), apparently has in mind (or could have in mind) three passages (I 9, lines 15–17; I, 4, 4, 31–32 and 43–45), but I do not think any of them need be so interpreted. The reference to some necessity's leading to one's death in advance of the destined time (I 9, 15–17) need not envisage anything more than a death caused not by natural events but by another person's action (or, perhaps, the reference maybe to the sort of judicial and forced suicide Socrates underwent—Plotinus's *anankaion* may recall Socrates' *prin anankēn tina theos epipempsēi*, *Phaedo* 62c6, as the

that it is up to us whether to continue living or not, and "the door remains open," this choice will never be made by the wise and good person.[30]

To Plotinus's argument in defense of the Platonic thesis, Olympiodorus (Lecture I, section 2) adds two others. The first of these usefully expands upon Plotinus's claim that the pure rational activity of the intellect is independent of and not hindered by the soul's active tendance of the body.

> If God has two kinds of powers, elevative and providential, and if those by which he extends his providential care to secondary beings do not impede his powers of elevation and conversion upon himself, but he exercises both simultaneously, then there is no reason why the philosopher as God's imitator . . . should not be active creatively and providentially, while at the same time leading a life of purification. . . . (trans. Westerink)

The second, apparently expanding upon a remark at the end of the paraphrase in Elias, adds to the reasons why it is right to await our body's disengagement with our soul to bring about our death.

> The voluntary shackle should be unfastened voluntarily, the involuntary shackle involuntarily, and not conversely. That is to say, from natural life, which is involuntary, we should be released in the involuntary way, by natural death, while from a life in dependence upon passions, which we have chosen of our own free will, we should release ourselves in the voluntary way by purification (trans. Westerink, with one change).[31]

IX

With the Neoplatonists Plotinus and Olympiodorus we come full circle, with a return to the Pythagorean view explored by Socrates in the *Phaedo*, that suicide is never permitted. I hope my exposition and discussion of the

---

phamen at I 9, 17 perhaps indicates). The two passages of I 4, 7 say no more than that it is up to oneself what to do in response to being taken into slavery, and that one is free to depart, by committing suicide, *if* under those circumstances it is not possible to be happy (*eudaimonein*)—and, as we have seen, *his* view is that under those circumstances that definitely is *not* impossible. It is important to emphasize that none of the interpreters who, on the basis of these passages, take Plotinus to have thought suicide rationally justified under certain circumstances has yet explained how this opinion is to be derived from, or even squared with, his theory of human *eudaimonia*.

[30] I think J. M. Rist is probably right (*Plotinus*, pp. 174–77) to point to Plotinus's acceptance of the Stoic thesis of our freedom to commit suicide at I 4, 7, 44–45 (and see lines 31–32 and I 4, 8, 8–9), while combining it with the claim that it is never right to *use* this freedom that way, as a pointed rejection of the Stoic view about the reasonableness of suicide under some conditions.

[31] Oddly, Olympiodorus cites (without explanation) Plotinus's treatise I 9 (under the title "On Reasonable Suicide") as providing reason to think suicide is sometimes permitted (I 8, 17–18). I have no explanation for how he can think this. And, when he gets round to drawing his own conclusions about suicide (9) he surprisingly says that suicide *is* sometimes permitted, whenever it is beneficial to the soul—but he does not say when that would be, or respond to Plotinus's arguments to show it never could be beneficial to the soul.

Greek philosophers' views on suicide have brought out the philosophical richness and interest of the treatment of the morality and rationality of suicide in this tradition. Practically all the recurrent theses in the subsequent centuries-long debate about suicide were not just adumbrated but developed with such ingenuity and insight that one may with some justification feel that the Greek philosophers, taken collectively, already said everything of value on this topic.

SELECTED FURTHER READINGS

Amundsen, Darrel W. *Medicine, Society, and Faith in the Ancient and Medieval Worlds.* Baltimore: Johns Hopkins Press, 1996.

Battin, Margaret P. *Ethical Issues in Suicide.* Englewood Cliffs, N. J.: Prentice-Hall, 1994.

Englert, Walter. "Stoics and Epicureans on the Nature of Suicide." *Proceedings of the Boston Area Colloquium in Ancient Philosophy* 10 (1994): 67–98.

van Hooff, Anton J. L. *From Autothanasìa to Suicide: Self-killing in Classical Antiquity.* London and New York: Routledge, 1990.

Included here is bibliographical information for all the texts, translations, and secondary literature cited in the footnotes. Excluded are additional titles in the Selected Further Readings appended to certain chapters. Editions and translations of ancient works are normally listed under the ancient author's name, but sometimes, where discussion in the text focuses on the editor or translator, the listing appears instead under the editor or translator's name.

Ackrill, John L. "Aristotle on Eudaimonia." In *Essays on Aristotle's Ethics*, edited by Amélie Rorty, 15–33.

Alexander of Aphrodisias. *De anima. Commentaria in Aristotelem Graeca (CAG). Supplementum Aristotelicum* vol. 2, pt. 1, edited by Ivo Bruns. Berlin: Reimer, 1887.

———. *Quaestiones Ethicae. Commentaria in Aristotelem Graeca (CAG). Supplementum Aristotelicum*, vol. 2, pt. 2, edited by Ivo Bruns. Berlin: Reimer, 1892. Translated by Robert W. Sharples as *Ethical Problems*. Ithaca: Cornell University Press, 1990.

Allan, Donald J. "Aristotle's Criticism of Platonic Doctrine concerning Goodness and the Good." *Proceedings of the Aristotelian Society* 64 (1963–64): 273–86.

———. "The Fine and the Good in the *Eudemian Ethics*." In *Untersuchungen zur "Eudemischen Ethik,"* edited by Paul Moraux and Dieter Harlfinger, 63–71. Berlin: De Gruyter, 1971.

———. "*Magna Moralia* and *Nicomachean Ethics*." *Journal of Hellenic Studies* 77, pt. 1 (1957): 7–11.

———. "Quasi-Mathematical Method in the *Eudemian Ethics*." In *Aristote et les problèmes de méthode*, edited by S. Mansion, 303–18. Reprinted in Müller-Goldingen.

———. Review of Dirlmeier, *Aristoteles: "Eudemische Ethik."* *Gnomon* 38 (1966): 138–49. Reprinted in Müller-Goldingen.

Allen, Joseph II., and James B. Greenough. *Allen and Greenough's New Latin Grammar*. New Rochelle, N.Y.: College Classical Series, 1983.

Annas, Julia. "Ancient Ethics and Modern Morality." *Philosophical Perspectives* 6 (1992): 119–36.

———. *Hellenistic Philosophy of Mind*. Berkeley: University of California Press, 1992.

———. *The Morality of Happiness*. New York and Oxford: Oxford University Press, 1993.

———. "Plato and Aristotle on Friendship and Altruism." *Mind* 86 (1977): 532–54.

Apelt, Otto. *Platonische Aufsätze*. Leipzig: Teubner, 1912.

———, ed. and trans. *Platon: Die Gesetze*. Leipzig: Meiner, 1916.

Aristotle. *Historia animalium*. Translated by A. L. Peck. Loeb Classical Library. Cambridge, Mass.: Harvard University Press, 1965.

Armstrong, Arthur Hilary, ed. and trans. *Plotinus*. Vol. 1. Loeb Classical Library. Cambridge, Mass.: Harvard University Press, 1965.

Armstrong, G. Cyril, trans. *Magna Moralia*. Loeb Classical Library. Cambridge, Mass.: Harvard University Press, 1935.

Arnim, Hans von. *Die drei aristotelischen Ethiken.* In *Akademie der Wissenschaften in Wien, Philosophisch-historische Klasse, Sitzungsberichte* vol. 202, pt. 2, 1924.

————. "Die Echtheit der Großen Ethik des Aristoteles." *Rheinisches Museum* 76 (1927): 113–37, 225–53.

————. "Xenophons *Memorabilien* und *Apologie des Sokrates.*" *Det Kongelige Danske Videnskabernes Selskab*, Historisk-Filosofiske Meddelelser, 8, 1, 1923.

————, ed. *Stoicorum Veterum Fragmenta (SVF).* Leipzig: Teubner, 1903–5.

Aspasius. In *"Ethica Nicomachea" Commentaria. Commentaria in Aristotelem Graeca (CAG)*, vol. 19, pt. 1, edited by G. Heylbut. Berlin: Reimer, 1889.

Baier, Annette C. "Intention, Practical Knowledge, and Representation." In her *Postures of the Mind*, 34–50. Minneapolis: University of Minnesota Press, 1985.

Bailey, Cyril, ed. and trans. *Epicurus: The Extant Remains.* Oxford: Clarendon Press, 1926.

Barker, Ernest, ed. and trans. *The "Politics" of Aristotle.* Oxford: Clarendon Press, 1946.

Barnes, Jonathan. "Aristotle and the Methods of Ethics." *Revue Internationale de Philosophie* 34 (1980): 490–511. Reprinted in Müller-Goldingen.

————, ed. *The Complete Works of Aristotle.* Princeton: Princeton University Press, 1984.

Bärthlein, Karl. "Ὀρθὸς λόγος in den *Magna Moralia.*" *Archiv für die Geschichte der Philosophie* 45 (1963): 213–58.

Bodéüs, Richard. "L'Animal politique et l'animal économique." In *Aristotelica: Mélanges offerts à Marcel De Corte*, 65–81. *Cahiers de philosophie ancienne* 3. Brussels: Ousia; Lièges: Presses Universitaires, 1985.

Bonitz, Hermann. *Index Aristotelicus.* Prussian Academy Edition of the Works of Aristotle, vol. 5. Berlin, 1870.

Bruns, Ivo. "Attische Liebestheorien und die zeitliche Folge des platonischen Phaedros sowie der beiden Symposien." *Neue Jahrbücher für das klassische Altertum* 3 (1900): 17–37.

Brunschwig, Jacques. "The Cradle Argument in Epicureanism and Stoicism." In *The Norms of Nature*, edited by M. Schofield and G. Striker, 113–44.

————. "On a Book-title by Chrysippus." *Oxford Studies in Ancient Philosophy*, supp. vol. (1991): 81–95.

Burkert, Walter. *Lore and Science in Ancient Pythagoreanism.* Cambridge, Mass.: Harvard University Press, 1972.

Burnet, John, ed. *The Ethics of Aristotle.* London: Methuen, 1900.

Burnyeat, Myles F. "Aristotle on Learning to Be Good." In *Essays on Aristotle's Ethics*, edited by Amélie Rorty, 69–92.

Bury, R. G., ed. *The "Symposium" of Plato.* Cambridge: Heffer, 1909.

Bywater, Ingram, ed. *Aristotelis "Ethica Nicomachea."* Oxford: Clarendon Press, 1894.

Cicero. *De finibus bonorum et malorum (On Ends).* Text with English translation by Harris Rackham. Loeb Classical Library. Cambridge, Mass.: Harvard University Press, 1914.

————. *De senectute, De amicitia, De divinatione.* Text with English translation by W. A. Falconer. Loeb Classical Library. Cambridge, Mass.: Harvard University Press, 1923.

————. *Letters to His Friends.* Text with English translation by W. Glynn Williams et al., 4 vols. Loeb Classical Library. Cambridge, Mass.: Harvard University Press, 1927–29.

———. *Tusculanae disputationes (Tusculan Disputations).* Text with English translation by J. E. King. Loeb Classical Library. Cambridge, Mass.: Harvard University Press, 1927.

Claus, David B. *Toward the Soul.* New Haven: Yale University Press, 1981.

Clay, Diskin. "The Origins of the Socratic Dialogue." In *The Socratic Movement,* edited by Paul Vander Waerdt, 23–47. Ithaca: Cornell University Press, 1994.

Cooper, John M. Critical Review, "Anthony Kenny, *The Aristotelian Ethics.*" *Nous* 15 (1981): 381–92.

———. "Eudaimonism and the Appeal to Nature in the Morality of Happiness." *Philosophy and Phenomenological Research* 55 (1995): 587–98.

———. "Plato, Isocrates and Cicero on the Independence of Oratory from Philosophy." *Proceedings of the Boston Area Colloquium in Ancient Philosophy* 1 (1985): 77–96. Lanham, Md.: University Press of America, 1986.

———. *Reason and Human Good in Aristotle.* Cambridge, Mass.: Harvard University Press, 1975; reprint, Indianapolis and Cambridge, Mass.: Hackett, 1986.

———. "Rhetoric, Dialectic, and the Passions." *Oxford Studies in Ancient Philosophy* 11 (1993): 175–98.

Cooper, John M., and J. F. Procopé, eds. *Seneca: Moral and Political Essays.* Cambridge: Cambridge University Press, 1995.

Cope, Edward M. *An Introduction to Aristotle's "Rhetoric."* London: Macmillan, 1867.

———, ed. *The "Rhetoric" of Aristotle.* Revised and edited by John E. Sandys. Cambridge: Cambridge University Press, 1877.

Cornford, F. M. "Psychology and Social Structure in the *Republic.*" *Classical Quarterly* 6 (1912): 246–65.

Cross, Rupert C., and Anthony D. Woozley. *Plato's "Republic": A Philosophical Commentary.* London: Macmillan, 1964.

Décarie, Vianney, trans. *Aristote: "Ethique à Eudème."* Paris: Vrin, 1978.

Diels, Hermann, and Walther Kranz, eds. and trans. *Die Fragmente der Vorsokratiker.* 7th edition. Berlin: Weidmann, 1952.

Diogenes Laertius. *Lives of Eminent Philosophers.* Text with English translation by R. D. Hicks. Loeb Classical Library. Cambridge, Mass.: Harvard University Press, 1925.

———. *Vitae philosophorum.* Edited by H. S. Long. Oxford: Clarendon Press, 1964.

Dirlmeier, Franz. ed. and trans. *Aristoteles, "Eudemische Ethik."* 1962; 2d edition, Berlin: Akademie-Verlag, 1969.

———, ed. and trans. *Aristoteles, "Magna Moralia."* Berlin: Akademie-Verlag, 1958.

———, ed. and trans. *Aristoteles, "Nikomachische Ethik."* 1956; 5th edition, Berlin: Akademie-Verlag, 1969.

———. *Die Oikeiosis-Lehre Theophrasts.* Philologus, suppl. vol. 30, 1 (1937).

Dodds, E. R, ed. *Plato: "Gorgias."* Oxford: Clarendon Press, 1959.

Donini, Pier Luigi. *L'Etica dei "Magna Moralia."* Torino: Giappichelli, 1965.

Dreizehnter, Alois, ed. *Aristoteles' "Politik."* Munich: W. Fink, 1970.

Dufour, Médéric, ed. and trans. *Aristote: "Rhétorique."* Paris: Les Belles Lettres, 1932.

Düring, Ingemar. *Aristoteles*. Heidelberg: Carl Winter, 1966.

——. *Aristotle's "Protrepticus."* Göteborg: Acta Universitatis Gothoburgensis, 1961.

——. Review of Dirlmeier, *Aristoteles: "Magna Moralia." Gnomon* 33 (1961): 547–57. Reprinted in Müller-Goldingen.

Durkheim, Emil. *Suicide: A Study in Sociology.* 1897; translated by J. A. Spaulding and G. Simpson. Glencoe, Ill.: The Free Press, 1951.

Dyroff, Adolf. *Die Ethik der Alten Stoa.* Berlin: S. Calvary, 1897.

Edelstein, Ludwig, and Ian G. Kidd, eds. *Posidonius Volume I. The Fragments.* Cambridge: Cambridge University Press, 1972.

Elias. *In Porphyrii "Isagogen" et "Categorias." Commentaria in Aristotelem Graeca (CAG)*, vol. 18, pt. 1, edited by A. Busse. Berlin: Reimer, 1900.

——. *Prolegomena.* In *David: "Prolegomena" et In Porphyrii "Isagogen." Commentaria in Aristotelem Graeca (CAG)*, vol. 18, pt. 2, edited by A. Busse. Berlin: Reimer, 1904.

Engberg-Pedersen, Troels. *The Stoic Theory of Oikeiosis.* Aarhus: Aarhus University Press, 1990.

Epictetus. *Discourses.* Text with English translation by W. A. Oldfather, 2 vols. Loeb Classical Library. Cambridge, Mass.: Harvard University Press, 1925, 1928.

Eustratius. *In "Ethica Nicomachea" Commentaria. Commentaria in Aristotelem Graeca (CAG)*, vol. 20, edited by G. Heylbut. Berlin: Reimer, 1892.

Fabro, C. Review of Dirlmeier, *Aristoteles: "Magna Moralia." Paideia* 16 (1961): 206.

Fillion-Lahille, Janine. *Le "De ira" de Sénèque et la philosophie stoicienne des passions.* Paris: Klincksieck, 1984.

Fortenbaugh, William. "Aristotle's Analysis of Friendship: Function and Analogy, Resemblance, and Focal Meaning." *Phronesis* 20 (1975): 51–62.

Frede, Michael. Introduction to *Protagoras.* Translated by Stanley Lombardo and Karen Bell. Indianapolis and Cambridge, Mass.: Hackett, 1992.

——. "The Stoic Doctrine of the Affections of the Soul." In *The Norms of Nature*, edited by M. Schofield and G. Striker, 93–110.

Freese, John Henry, trans. *Aristotle: The "Art" of Rhetoric.* Loeb Classical Library. Cambridge, Mass.: Harvard University Press, 1926.

Galen. *On the Doctrines of Hippocrates and Plato.* 3 vols. Text with English translation and commentary by Phillip H. DeLacy. Corpus Medicorum Graecorum. Berlin: Akademie Verlag, 1978–84. Text with Latin translation by I. Von Müller. Leipzig: Teubner, 1874.

——. *De sequela (That the Faculties of the Soul Follow the Mixtures of the Body).* In *Galen: Scripta minora,* edited by I. Von Müller, vol. 2, 32–79. Leipzig: Teubner, 1891. Translation in P. N. Singer, *Galen: Selected Works,* 150–76. Oxford: Oxford University Press, 1997.

Gauthier, René Antoine, and Jean Yves Jolif, eds. and trans. *Aristote: L'Ethique à Nicomaque.* Louvain: Publications Universitaires, 1958–59.

Gert, Bernard. Introduction to *Man and Citizen* by Thomas Hobbes. Garden City: Doubleday, 1972.

Gigon, Olof, ed. and trans. Cicero, *"Über die Ziele des menschlichen Handelns."* Munich and Zurich: Artemis, 1988.

——. Review of Dirlmeier, *Aristoteles: "Magna Moralia." Deutsche Literatur-Zeitung* 83 (1961): 14–19.

————. "Die Sokratesdoxographie bei Aristoteles." *Museum Helveticum* 16 (1959): 174–212.

Gill, Christopher J. "Did Chrysippus Understand Medea?" *Phronesis* 28 (1983): 136–49.

Glidden, David. "Epicurus and the Pleasure Principle." In *The Greeks and the Good Life*, edited by David DePew, 177–97. Indianapolis and Cambridge, Mass.: Hackett, 1980.

Gosling, Justin C. B. *Plato*. London: Routledge, 1973.

————. "*Republic* Book V: τὰ πολλὰ καλὰ etc." *Phronesis* 5 (1960): 116–28.

Gosling, Justin C. B., and Christopher C. W. Taylor. *The Greeks on Pleasure*. Oxford: Clarendon Press, 1982.

Grant, Sir Alexander, ed. *The Ethics of Aristotle*. London: Longmans, Green, 1866.

Grube, George M. A., trans. *Plato's "Republic."* Indianapolis and Cambridge, Mass.: Hackett, 1974.

Guthrie, W.K.C. *A History of Greek Philosophy*. Vol. 3. Cambridge: Cambridge University Press, 1969.

Guyau, Jean Marie. *La Morale d'Epicure*. 1886; 6th edition, Paris: Alcan, 1917.

Haldane, E. S., and Frances H. Simpson, eds. and trans. *Hegel's Lectures on the History of Philosophy*. London: Routledge, 1894.

Hamilton, Edith, and Huntington Cairns, eds. *The Collected Dialogues of Plato*. Princeton: Princeton University Press, 1961.

Hansen, Mogens Herman. "The Athenian 'Politicians,' 403–322 B.C." *Greek, Roman and Byzantine Studies* 24 (1983): 33–55.

————. "The Trial of Socrates—from the Athenian Point of View." Copenhagen: *Det Kongelige Danske Videnskabernes Selskab*, Historisk-Filosofiske Meddelelser 71, 1995.

Harder, Richard, ed. and trans. *Plotins Schriften*. Hamburg: Meiner, 1956.

Hardie, W.F.R. "Aristotle on the Best Life for a Man." *Philosophy* 54 (1979): 35–50.

————. *Aristotle's Ethical Theory*. Oxford: Clarendon Press, 1968.

————. "The Final Good in Aristotle's *Ethics*." *Philosophy* 40 (1965): 277–95. Reprinted in *Aristotle: Critical Essays*, edited by J.M.E. Moravcsik. Garden City, N.Y.: Doubleday, 1967.

————. *A Study in Plato*. Oxford: Clarendon Press, 1936.

Hegel, G.W.F. *Hegel's Philosophy of Right*. Translated by T. M. Knox. Oxford: Clarendon Press, 1952.

Heliodorus. In "*Ethica Nicomachea*" *Paraphrasis*. *Commentaria in Aristotelem Graeca (CAG)*, vol. 19, pt. 2., edited by G. Heylbut. Berlin: Reimer, 1889.

Heylbut, Gustav. "Zur Ethik des Theophrast von Eresos." *Archiv für Geschichte der Philosophie* 1 (1888): 194–99.

Hoffman, Ernst. "Aristoteles' Philosophie der Freundschaft." In *Festgabe für H. Rickert*, edited by A. Faust, 8–36. Bühl-Baden: Konkordia, 1933. Reprinted in *Ethik und Politik des Aristoteles*, edited by Fritz-Peter Hager, Darmstadt: Wissenschaftliche Buchgesellschaft, 1972.

Hohfeld, Wesley N. *Fundamental Legal Conceptions as Applied in Judicial Reasoning*. New Haven: Yale University Press, 1923.

Inwood, Brad. *Ethics and Human Action in Early Stoicism*. Oxford: Clarendon Press, 1985.

Inwood, Brad, and Lloyd P. Gerson, eds. *The Epicurus Reader*. Indianapolis and Cambridge, Mass.: Hackett, 1994.

————. *Hellenistic Philosophy: Introductory Readings*. 1988; 2nd edition Indianapolis and Cambridge, Mass.: Hackett, 1998.

Irwin, Terence H., trans. *Aristotle: "Nicomachean Ethics."* Indianapolis and Cambridge, Mass.: Hackett, 1985.

————. "Aristotle's Conception of Morality." *Proceedings of the Boston Area Colloquium in Ancient Philosophy* 1 (1985): 115–43. Lanham, Md.: University Press of America, 1986.

————. "Coercion and Objectivity in Plato's Dialectic." *Revue Internationale de Philosophie* 40 (1986): 49–74.

————. "Disunity in the Aristotelian Virtues." *Oxford Studies in Ancient Philosophy*, suppl. vol. (1988): 61–78.

————. "The Good of Political Activity." In *Aristoteles' "Politik,"* edited by Günther Patzig, 73–98. Göttingen: Vandenhoeck and Ruprecht, 1990.

————. "Permanent Happiness: Aristotle and Solon." *Oxford Studies in Ancient Philosophy* 3 (1985): 89–124.

————, ed. and trans. *Plato: Gorgias*. Oxford: Clarendon Press, 1979.

————. *Plato's Ethics*. New York: Oxford University Press, 1995.

————. *Plato's Moral Theory*. Oxford: Clarendon Press, 1977.

————. "Stoic and Aristotelian Conceptions of Happiness." In *The Norms of Nature*, edited by M. Schofield and G. Striker, 205–44.

Jaeger, Werner. "Ein Theophrastzitat in der *Großen Ethik*." *Hermes* 64 (1929): 274–78.

Joël, Karl. *Der echte und der xenophontische Sokrates*. 2 vols. in 3. Berlin: R. Gaertner, 1893 and 1901.

Kahn, Charles. "Drama and Dialectic in Plato's *Gorgias*." *Oxford Studies in Ancient Philosophy* 1 (1983): 75–121.

————. *Plato and the Socratic Dialogue*. Cambridge: Cambridge University Press, 1996.

Kant, Immanuel. *Lectures on Ethics*. Translated by Louis Infeld. London: Methuen, 1930; New York: Harper and Row, 1963; Indianapolis and Cambridge, Mass.: Hackett, 1980.

Kassel, Rudolf, ed. *Aristotelis "Ars Rhetorica."* Berlin: De Gruyter, 1976.

Kenny, Anthony. *The Aristotelian Ethics*. Oxford: Clarendon Press, 1978.

Keyt, David. "Intellectualism in Aristotle." In *Essays in Ancient Greek Philosophy*, vol. 2, edited by J. P. Anton, and A. Preus, 346–87. Albany: SUNY Press, 1983.

Kidd, Ian G. *Posidonius Volume II. The Commentary*. Cambridge: Cambridge University Press, 1988.

Kraut, Richard. "A Dominant-End Reading of the *Nicomachean Ethics*." Unpublished, 1985.

————. "The Importance of Love in Aristotle's Ethics." *Philosophy Research Archives* 1 (1975).

————. "Reason and Justice in Plato's *Republic*." In *Exegesis and Argument*, edited by Edward N. Lee et al., 207–24. New York: Humanities Press, 1973.

Kullmann, Wolfgang. "Der Mensch als Politisches Lebewesen bei Aristoteles." *Hermes* 108 (1980): 419–43.

Labarrière, Jean Louis. "De la phronèsis animale." In *Biologie, logique et métaphysique chez Aristote*, edited by Daniel Devereux and Pierre Pellegrin, 405–28. Paris: CNRS, 1990.

Lecky, William E. H. *A History of European Morals from Augustus to Charlemagne.* London: Longmans, Green. 1869.

Liddell, H. G., R. S. Scott, and S. H. Jones. *A Greek-English Lexicon* (LSJ). 9th edition. Oxford: Clarendon Press, 1940; new edition with Supplement, 1968.

Long, Anthony A. *Hellenistic Philosophy.* London: Duckworth, 1974.

Long, Anthony A., and David N. Sedley, eds. and trans. *The Hellenistic Philosophers.* 2 vols. Cambridge: Cambridge University Press, 1987.

Lord, Carnes, trans. *Aristotle: "The Politics."* Chicago: University of Chicago Press, 1984.

———. *Education and Culture in the Political Thought of Aristotle.* Ithaca: Cornell University Press, 1982.

MacDowell, Douglas M. *The Law in Classical Athens.* Ithaca: Cornell University Press, 1978.

Maier, Heinrich. *Sokrates.* Tübingen: Mohr, 1913.

Mansion, S., ed. *Aristote et les problèmes de méthode.* Louvain: Publications Universitaires, 1961.

Merlan, Philip. *Studies in Epicurus and Aristotle.* Wiesbaden: Harrassowitz, 1960.

Miller, Fred D. *Nature, Justice, and Rights in Aristotle's "Politics."* Oxford: Clarendon Press, 1995.

Mitsis, Phillip. *Epicurus' Ethical Theory.* Ithaca: Cornell University Press, 1988.

Moraux, Paul. *Der Aristotelismus bei den Griechen.* Berlin: De Gruyter, 1973.

Morrison, Donald. *Bibliography of Editions, Translations and Commentary on Xenophon's Socratic Writings.* Pittsburgh: Mathesis, 1988.

———. "On Professor Vlastos' Xenophon." *Ancient Philosophy* 7 (1987): 9–22.

———. "Xenophon's Socrates on the Just and the Lawful." *Ancient Philosophy* 15 (1995): 329–47.

———. "Xenophon's Socrates as Teacher." In *The Socratic Movement,* edited by Paul Vander Waerdt, 181–208. Ithaca: Cornell University Press, 1994.

Mulgan, R. G. "Aristotle's Doctrine that Man is a Political Animal." *Hermes* 102 (1974): 438–45.

Müller-Goldingen, Christian. *Schriften zur aristotelischen Ethik.* Hildesheim: Olms, 1988.

Murphy, N. R. *The Interpretation of Plato's "Republic."* Oxford: Clarendon Press, 1951.

Nagel, Thomas. "Moral Luck." *Proceedings of the Aristotelian Society,* suppl. vol. 50 (1976): 137–51. Reprinted in his *Mortal Questions.* New York: Cambridge University Press, 1979.

Nehamas, Alexander. *The Art of Living: Socratic Reflections from Plato to Foucault.* Berkeley: University of California Press, 1998.

———. "Plato on the Imperfection of the Sensible World." *American Philosophical Quarterly* 12 (1975): 105–17.

Newman, William L. *The "Politics" of Aristotle.* Oxford: Clarendon Press, 1887.

Nussbaum, Martha C. *The Fragility of Goodness: Luck and Ethics in Greek Tragedy and Philosophy.* New York: Cambridge University Press, 1986.

Owen, Gwilym E. L. "Logic and Metaphysics in Some Earlier Works of Aristotle." In *Aristotle and Plato at the Mid-Fourth Century,* edited by Owen and I. Düring, 163–90. Göteborg: Elander, 1960. Reprinted in Owen, *Logic, Science and Dialectic,* 180–99.

Owen, Gwilym E. L. *Logic, Science, and Dialectic*. London: Duckworth, and Ithaca: Cornell University Press, 1986.

———. *"Tithenai ta phainomena."* In *Aristote et les problèmes de méthode*, edited by S. Mansion. Reprinted in Owen, *Logic, Science and Dialectic*, 239–51.

Patzer, Andreas. *Bibliographica Socratica*. Munich: Alber, 1985.

———. *Der Historische Sokrates*. Darmstadt: Wissenschaftliche Buchgesellschaft, 1987.

Pédech, P. Review of Dirlmeier, *Aristoteles: "Magna Moralia." Erasmus* (1961): 358–59.

Penner, Terrence M. I. "Socrates on the Impossibility of Belief-Relative Sciences." *Proceedings of the Boston Area Colloquium in Ancient Philosophy*, vol. 3 (1987): 263–325. Lanham, Md.: University Press of America, 1988.

———. "Thought and Desire in Plato." In *Plato II*, edited by G. Vlastos, 96–118.

Plato. *Complete Works*. Edited by John M. Cooper, associate editor D. S. Hutchinson. Indianapolis and Cambridge, Mass.: Hackett, 1997.

———. *Platonis Opera*. Edited by John Burnet. 5 vols. Oxford: Clarendon Press, 1900–1907.

———. *Platonis Opera*. Vol. 1. Edited by E. A. Duke et al. Oxford: Clarendon Press, 1995.

———. *Plato: "The Republic."* Edited and translated by Paul Shorey. Loeb Classical Library. Cambridge, Mass.: Harvard University Press, 1935–37.

Plutarch. *De libidine et aegritudine. (Desire and Grief: Psychical or Bodily Phenomena?)*. Text with English translation by F. H. Sandbach. Plutarch's *"Moralia,"* vol. 15. Loeb Classical Library. Cambridge, Mass.: Harvard University Press, 1969.

———. *On Moral Virtue*. Text with English translation by W. C. Helmbold. *Plutarch's Moralia*, vol. 6. Loeb Classical Library. Cambridge, Mass.: Harvard University Press, 1939.

———. *On Stoic Self-Contradictions* and *On Common Conceptions*. Text with English translation by Harold Cherniss. *Plutarch's Moralia*, vol. 13, pt. 2. Loeb Classical Library. Cambridge, Mass.: Harvard University Press, 1976.

Pohlenz, Max. "De Posidonii libris Περὶ παθῶν." *Fleckeisens Jahrbücher für Klassische Philologie*, supp. vol. 24 (1898): 535–634.

Praechter, Karl. ed. *Die Philosophie des Altertums*, by Friedrich Überweg. 12th edition. Berlin: E. S. Mittler, 1926; Basel/Stuttgart: Schwabe, 1960.

Price, Anthony W. *Mental Conflict*. London: Routledge, 1995.

Purinton, Jeffrey S. "Epicurus on the *telos*." *Phronesis* 38 (1993): 281–320.

Putnam, Hilary. *Reason, Truth and History*. Cambridge: Cambridge University Press, 1981.

Ramsauer, Georg, ed. *Aristotelis "Ethica Nicomachea."* Leipzig: Teubner, 1878.

Rawls, John. *A Theory of Justice*. Cambridge, Mass.: Harvard University Press, 1971.

Rist, John M. *Plotinus: The Road to Reality*. Cambridge: Cambridge University Press, 1967.

Roberts, W. Rhys, trans. Aristotle's *"Rhetoric."* In *The Complete Works of Aristotle*, edited by J. Barnes.

Robin, Léon. "Les *Mémorables* de Xenophon et notre connaissance de la philosophie de Socrate." *L'Année Philosophique* 21 (1910): 1–47.

Roche, Timothy. "*Ergon* and *Eudaimonia* in 'Nicomachean Ethics' I: Reconsidering the Intellectualist Interpretation." *Journal of the History of Philosophy* 26 (1988): 175–94.

Rorty, Amélie Oksenberg, ed. *Essays on Aristotle's Ethics*. Berkeley: University of California Press, 1980.

Rose, Herbert J. "Euthanasia." In *Encyclopedia of Religion*, vol. 5, edited by J. Hastings, 598–601. Edinburgh: Clarke, 1914.

Ross, William David. *Aristotle*. London: Methuen, 1949; New York: Meridian, 1959.

———, trans. *Aristotle, "Nicomachean Ethics."* In *The Works of Aristotle Translated into English*, edited by Ross, vol. 9. Oxford: Clarendon Press, 1915. Altered version, with footnotes omitted, in J. Barnes, *The Complete Works of Aristotle*.

———, ed. *Aristotelis "Politica."* Oxford: Clarendon Press, 1957.

Rowe, Christopher J. *Plato: "Statesman."* Translated with introduction and commentary. Warminster, England: Aris and Phillips, 1995.

Sandbach, Francis H. *The Stoics*. London: Chatto and Windus, 1975.

Schleiermacher, Friedrich E. D. "Sokrates' Werth als Philosoph." *Abhandlungen der Königlich-Preussischen Akademie der Wissenschaften zu Berlin*, Philos. Kl. 1814–15, 50–68. Berlin, 1818. Reprinted in his *Sämtliche Werke*, vol. 3, pt. 2, 297–98. Berlin, 1838. Reprinted also in Andreas Patzer, *Der Historische Sokrates*, 41–58.

Schofield, Malcolm, and Gisela Striker, eds. *The Norms of Nature*. Cambridge: Cambridge University Press; Paris: Maison des Sciences de l'Homme, 1986.

Seneca. *Ad Lucilium "Epistulae Morales" (Letters)*. Text with English translation by Richard H. Gummere, 3 vols. Loeb Classical Library. Cambridge, Mass.: Harvard University Press, 1917–25.

———. *De ira (On Anger)*. Text with English translation by John W. Basore. *Moral Essays*, vol. 1. Loeb Classical Library. Cambridge, Mass.: Harvard University Press, 1928.

Shorey, Paul. *What Plato Said*. Chicago: University of Chicago Press, 1933.

Solmsen, Friedrich. *Die Entwicklung der Aristotelischen Logik und Rhetorik*. Berlin: Weidmann, 1929.

Spengel, Leonhard von. *Über die unter dem Namen des Aristoteles erhaltenen ethischen Schriften*. Abhandlungen der Bayerischen Akademie, vol. 3, pt. 2, 437–96, and vol. 3, pt. 3, 497–551. Munich, 1841 and 1843.

———, ed. *Aristotelis "Ars Rhetorica."* Leipzig: Teubner, 1867.

Stewart, J. A. *Notes on the "Nicomachean Ethics" of Aristotle*. Oxford: Clarendon Press, 1892.

Stobaeus. *Eclogae*. Edited by C. Wachsmuth. Berlin: Weidmann, 1884.

Stock, St. George, trans. *Magna Moralia*. In *The Works of Aristotle*, edited by W. D. Ross, vol. 9. Altered version, with footnotes omitted, in J. Barnes, *The Complete Works of Aristotle*.

Strauss, Leo. *Natural Right and History*. Chicago: University of Chicago Press, 1953.

Striker, Gisela. "Antipater, or the Art of Living." In *The Norms of Nature*, edited by M. Schofield and G. Striker, 185–204.

———. "Epicurean Hedonism." In *Passions and Perceptions*, edited by J. Brunschwig and M. Nussbaum, 3–17. Cambridge: Cambridge University Press, 1993.

———. "Following Nature: A Study in Stoic Ethics." *Oxford Studies in Ancient Philosophy* 9 (1991): 1–73.

Süss, Wilhelm. *Ethos, Studien zur Älteren Griechischen Rhetorik*. Leipzig: Teubner, 1910.

Taylor, A. E. *Plato: The Man and His Work*. London: Methuen, 1926.

Theiler, Willy. "Die Großen Ethik und die Ethiken des Aristoteles." *Hermes* 69 (1934): 353–79.

Trude, Peter. *Der Begriff der Gerechtigkeit in der aristotelischen Rechts- und Staatsphilosophie.* Berlin: de Gruyter, 1955.

Usener, Hermann, ed. *Epicurea.* Leipzig: Teubner, 1887.

Vlastos, Gregory. "An Ambiguity in the *Sophist.*" In his *Platonic Studies,* 270–322.

———. "The Argument in the *Republic* that Justice Pays." *The Journal of Philosophy* 65 (1968): 665–74.

———. "Justice and Happiness in the *Republic.*" In *Plato II,* edited by G. Vlastos, 66–95.

———. "The Paradox of Socrates." In *The Philosophy of Socrates,* edited by G. Vlastos, 1–21. Garden City, N. Y.: Doubleday, 1971.

———. *Plato II.* Garden City, N.Y.: Doubleday, 1971.

———. *Platonic Studies.* Princeton: Princeton University Press, 1973.

———. *Socrates, Ironist and Moral Philosopher.* Ithaca: Cornell University Press, 1991.

———. "Socratic Irony." *Classical Quarterly* 37 (1987): 79–96.

———. "The Unity of the Virtues in the *Protagoras.*" In his *Platonic Studies,* 221–65.

Westerink, Leendert Gerrit. *The Greek Commentaries on Plato's "Phaedo."* Vol. 1. Amsterdam: North Holland, 1976.

———. ed. *Olympiodorus, In Platonis "Gorgiam" Commentaria.* Leipzig: Teubner, 1970.

White, Nicholas P. "Rational Prudence in Plato's *Gorgias.*" In *Platonic Investigations,* edited by Dominic J. O'Meara, 139–62. Washington: Catholic University of America Press, 1986.

Whiting, Jennifer. "Human Nature and Intellectualism in Aristotle." *Archiv für Geschichte der Philosophie* 68 (1986): 70–95.

Wilamowitz, Ulrich von. "Neleus von Skepsis." *Hermes* 62 (1927): 371.

Williams, Bernard. "Internal and External Reasons." In his *Moral Luck,* 101–13. Cambridge: Cambridge University Press, 1981.

———. "Moral Luck." *Proceedings of the Aristotelian Society,* suppl. vol. 50 (1976): 115–36. Reprinted in his *Moral Luck,* 20–39.

Wilson, John Cook. *Aristotelian Studies.* Vol. 1: *On the Structure of the Seventh Book of the "Nicomachean Ethics," Chapters I–X.* 1879; Oxford: Clarendon Press, 1912.

Woodhead, W. D., trans. *Socratic Dialogues.* Edinburgh: Nelson, 1953.

Woods, Michael, trans. *Aristotle's "Eudemian Ethics" Books I, II, and VIII.* Oxford: Clarendon Press, 1982.

Xenophon. *Memorabilia.* Translated by E. C. Marchant. Loeb Classical Library. Cambridge, Mass.: Harvard University Press, 1923.

———. *"Symposium" and "Apology."* Translated by O. J. Todd. Loeb Classical Library. Cambridge, Mass.: Harvard University Press, 1922.

Zuntz, Günther. *The Political Plays of Euripides.* Manchester: Manchester University Press, 1955.

NOTE: All **boldface** numbers indicate primary source citations; all others refer to pages in this volume.

virtue(s) *(continued)*
  Menedemus on, 90–96; Aristotle on,
  108–9, 251, 253–55; Chrysippus on,
  96ff., 100–102, 433–39, 444–48, 532–
  36; of city (Plato, *Rep.*), 141n.7; and
  civic friendship, 334–35; "complete" (in
  Aristotle), 214 and n.1, 222; courage and
  moderation, 114–16, 181–83 and n.29;
  excludes *pathē* (Stoics vs. Aristotle), 248–
  49; happiness, as activity of (Aristotle,
  Stoics), 219, 225, 444–45, 482;—, as activity of complete (Aristotle), 221–22,
  226; human good through constant exercise of all, 235–36; as identical with
  knowledge, 106–7; Menedemus on, 90–
  96, 105; moral, defined in terms of intermediate (Aristotle), 275; —, as giving
  "2nd best" happiness, 214–15, 218, 231–
  33 and n.17, 235; —, practical wisdom
  necessary for, 255n.3; —, as sole good
  (Stoics), 533–34; —, and *thumos*-desires,
  278–79; natural vs. full, in Aristotle and
  Plato, 109, 182 and n.26, 196n.6; optimal exercise of (Aristotle), 300, 303–4,
  385; Plato on, 107–8, 109–13, 118, 181–
  85; practical reason in, 111–12, 112–13,
  122; rational vs. nonrational (Posidonius), 481–82 and n.47; of reason, 246,
  253–55; Socrates on, x–xi, 22–26, 83–90,
  118–19 and n.1; subordinate "swarm" of
  (Chrysippus), 97–98; suicide as violation
  of, 529; and temperance, 88, 100–101;
  wisdom as, 108, 270–71. *See also* courage; good, the; Stoics; virtue, unity of
virtue, unity of: ch. 3 *passim*; Aristotle on,
  108–9, 114; Chrysippus on, 96–104; doctrine, 68n.59; Menedemus and Ariston
  on, 83–90; nature of, 81–83, 90; origin
  of idea, 78; Plato on (*Rep.*), 107–8, 109–
  13, (*Statesman*) 114–15; Plato and Aristotle on, 77–78, 107–16, 116–17; Socrates on, 23–26, 78–79, 81–82, 89–90;
  Stoics on, 80, 91, 95–107; Zeno on, 105–
  7. *See also* virtue
Vlastos, G., 30, 82n.8, 83n.10, 91n.18,
  134n.10; on just city, 141n.7; on Xenophon on Socrates, 9n.13, 24n.43

Wachsmuth, C., 96–97n.30
Wallach, J. R., 377n.24
waterbearers, myth of (in *Gorgias*), 60–
  61n.49, 68n.59

weaving, model for statesmanship, 172–76
  and n.15
Westerink, L. G., 537n.24
White, Nicholas, 56n.41, 72n.66, 75n.68,
  309n.25
White, Stephen A., 96–97n.30
whiteness, degrees of, 157–58
Whiting, J., 215n.2, 427
Wilamowitz, Ulrich v., 198n.15
Wildberg, C., 169n.6
Williams, B., on internal/external reasons
  for action, 432
Wilson, J. Cook, 258–59n.12
wisdom/practical wisdom (*sophia/phronē-
  sis*), 55–57, 62 and n.51, 63–64 and
  n.54, 95–96 and n.26; 216–17; in Ariston, 92; in Chrysippus, 95n.26, 102; as
  component of *ēthos*, in rhetoric, 396 and
  n.13; as component of virtue, 108; in controlling nonrational desires (Aristotle),
  254–55; defined, 255n.3, 271n.27; as directive virtue in Plato, 111; necessary for
  moral virtue, 255n.3; and the "orderly"
  life, 62 and n.51, 55–57, 63–64 and
  n.54; philosophical, 223; training in,
  111–12n.49; virtue of, 108, 270–71; in
  Zeno, 95–96 and n.26. *See also boulēsis*;
  intelligence; knowledge; *sophia*
Woodhead, W. D., 33n.5
Woods, M., 214n.1, 256n.5

Xenophon, 64n.54; *Anabasis,* 4, 6n.9; *Apology,* 10, 13, 14; credibility of, ch. 1 *passim*; *Cyropaedia,* 27n.38; as historian,
  4ff.; *Hellenica,* 4; *Memorabilia,* 3, 4–5, 6
  and n.10, 10, 21–28; *Oeconomicus,* 5,
  10; refutes *Accusation of Socrates,* 5; *Symposium,* 3, 12n.17, 15–20. *See also Index
  of Passages*

Young, C. M., 335n.28, 354n.30

Zeno of Citium: Chrysippus on, 95n.26; on
  kathēkonta, 436–37 and n.22; on living
  in accordance with nature (*apud* Diog.
  L.), 439; on suicide, 531 and n.17; on
  telos (Arius), 478n.43; unclear information on, 26; on unity of virtue, 105–7; on
  wisdom, 95–96 and n.26; as writer of dialogues, 3n.3
Zeus, will of (in Stoicism), 443, 446. *See
  also* god(s)
Zeyl, D. J., 62n.52
Zuntz, G., 169n.6

John M. Cooper is Stuart Professor of Philosophy at Princeton University. He is the author of *Reason and Human Good in Aristotle* and *Plato's "Theaetetus."* He is the general editor of *Plato: Complete Works* and also coedited *Seneca: Moral and Political Essays* with J. F. Procopé.